# The Social Organization
# of Early Industrial
# Capitalism

# The Social Organization of Early Industrial Capitalism

Michael B. Katz
Michael J. Doucet
Mark J. Stern

Harvard University Press
Cambridge, Massachusetts
and London, England   1982

**Library of Congress Cataloging in Publication Data**

Katz, Michael B.
  The social organization of early industrial capitalism.

  Includes bibliographical references and index.
  1.  Hamilton  (Ont.) — Social  conditions.    2.  Social  classes — Ontario—Hamilton.      3.  Family—Ontario—Hamilton.      4.  Urbanization—North America—Case studies.    I.  Doucet, Michael J.
II.  Stern, Mark J.      III.  Title.
HN110.H28K38      305.5'09713'52      81-7044
ISBN 0-674-81445-2                    AACR2

For Edda, Susan, and Natalie

# Contents

# Preface

For over a decade I have worked on the reconstruction of population and social structure in the Canadian city of Hamilton, Ontario. The first major result of that study was my book *The People of Hamilton, Canada West*. The book's first purpose was to lay out the major empirical relationships between occupation, economic rank, property ownership, ethnicity, religion, the components of the life cycle, and the organization of families in a commercial city. It was primarily a work of social description. It also attempted to engage the literature in the field and to examine the adequacy of the leading formulations in some areas, most notably Stephan Thernstrom's on social mobility and Peter Laslett's on the structure of the family and household.

In both of those objectives the book was reasonably successful. It has three weaknesses, however. First, it lacks a coherent social theory that would tie together its disparate observations. Second, and partly as a consequence, it dodges the issue of class. At the time of writing the book I found it extremely difficult to formulate a satisfactory conception of class. Consequently the book is mostly about stratification. Third, the analysis uses only descriptive statistics when it is clear that some of the topics with which it deals would be analyzed more elegantly and effectively with multivariate techniques.

In the work done since that time I have carried the analysis forward into the early industrial period and added to parts of the study a comparison with Buffalo, New York. The result is this book, written with Michael Doucet and Mark Stern.

Many people have read portions of this manuscript in various stages. From their reactions I feel confident about only one point: this should be a controversial book. Once again, as in *The People of Hamilton*, the object has been to combine reliable empirical evidence with rash speculation; only here in places the speculation, although more theoretically disciplined, is even more bold. I do hope, however, that we have provided enough detailed; solid material to make this book useful even to those scholars who will disagree with its theoretical direction.

I suspect that most of the controversy about the book will center on its attempt to portray early industrial society as dominated by two great classes. Some readers will feel that the complexity of social patterns—of which most of this book provides abundant evidence—makes the use of class either pointless or reductionist. We hope that Chapter 1 will help dispel those objections to some extent. Almost by definition a more complex explanation of social phenomena is more complete. Anyone who attempts to analyze large bodies of social data must be impressed by the intricacy and subtlety of the patterns within them. Simply unraveling those patterns often becomes an overwhelming task. Indeed that certainly was my problem in *The People of Hamilton*. And yet the tired cliché about the forest and the trees remains important. The intricate, complex patterns of social structure can obscure the principles on which the social order itself rests, for it is my assumption that social orders are not accidental arrangements, tangled skeins of yarn wound around a hollow shell, but rather that they arise out of particular historical circumstances, that they are generated by powerful, identifiable forces. For this reason they have a shape, a distinct morphology, a series of basic relationships that underlie and indeed generate the complex patterns that preoccupy social analysts. It is the attempt to balance these two aspects of social structure—its underlying dynamic properties and its complex patterns—that provides the essential tension in this book.

I cannot pretend that this book achieves the balance it seeks in a wholly successful fashion or that it solves all the problems it raises. In writing it we faced a choice: provide a tight and almost unassailable account of empirical relations, or venture a broader, ultimately incomplete explanation that tries to set those relations in a context that illuminates broad questions in history and social theory. We chose the latter. At the very least we hope that the book poses questions about the social order of nineteenth-century North America in a reasonably fresh way and makes it abundantly clear not only that certain questions can and should be pursued but that some hypotheses are more likely to be valid than others. Because we have sought to go beyond the empirical patterns in the data, the book concludes with a broad chapter about the institutional legacy of early industrial capitalism, an account that goes beyond the limits of Hamilton and Buffalo to attempt to assess some of the interrelationships between social structure, domestic organization, and the shape of public life. In this way the book attempts a synthesis between the three major concerns of American social history: social structure and social mobility, the family, and social institutions.

We faced another choice, although of a greatly different order, in deciding how to present the material in this book: namely how much of the vast quantitative evidence to provide. The data in the book represent only a fraction of the data that we assembled. We hope, however, that enough data are offered to permit readers to follow the logic of the arguments and to assess the general character of the evidence. More data can be found in the working papers and interim reports produced by the project.

Although we tried to confront the issue of class directly in this book, we did not pay similar theoretical attention to ethnicity as a concept. We have not taken a position on the issues surrounding the meaning of ethnicity as a concept. We use the term, rather, to indicate a combination of birthplace and religion and to assess the relationship of those factors to the various topics with which we are concerned. We felt it preferable to use *ethnicity* rather than the more cumbersome, but perhaps more exact, designation *birthplace and religious group.*

As extensive as the discussion is, it does not fully exploit the data base or explore all aspects of the topics raised. The major omission in the data analysis is a section on social geography. Since the data are geocoded, this is especially unfortunate. The reason for the absence of geographical analysis is that we ran out of time; the project ended. The major topic that we do not discuss more than tangentially is class culture. This, of course, is a lively and controversial historical issue. To some extent our data enable us to make some observations relevant to contemporary debates, and we have done so at appropriate places. But we simply did not undertake a full exploration of the issues.

The discussions of individual privacy in recent years have forced us to rethink our obligations to the people about whom we write and to their heirs. Individuals offered anonymity during their lifetimes on censuses or related documents deserve, we believe, to have their privacy protected after their death to avoid, as the Hamilton *Spectator* put it, being "dragged to light by some curious enquirer of resurrectionary proclivities." Therefore in case histories based on census records we have used pseudonyms. Real names are used only to refer to people listed in public sources, such as newspapers.

The research on which this book rests began in a desultory way in 1967 at the Ontario Institute for Studies in Education, and during the next few years grew into a more coherent project. The people who contributed to that effort have been mentioned in *The People of Hamilton, Canada West*, which issued from the project's first phase.

The second phase was supported by the Canada Council (Grants S75-1536), the National Institute of Mental Health Center for Studies of Metropolitan Problems (R01MH-27850-02), and York University. Most of the work was done at York University, where my coauthors and I enjoyed a few years of intensive collaboration. We are particularly indebted to the Institute for Behavioural Research at York, which provided technical assistance. In particular we should like to thank Mirka Ondracek, who did most of the programing represented in this book, Elena Peskova, Jim Wirt, John Tibert, and Michael Ornstein. A great deal of the coding and key-punching was performed by Marie Hand and Cindy Ashmead. In many ways our greatest debt at York is to Rosemarie Schueler, our administrative assistant, who typed, comforted, organized, and encouraged. Our work on Buffalo was facilitated greatly by Shonnie Finnegan of the University Archives at the State University of New York at Buffalo. We are also indebted to Brenda Torpy, who was largely responsible for gathering the evidence on the Police Court presented in Chapter 6 and for the preliminary statistical analysis of the jail registers.

The first revisions of this manuscript were undertaken at the University of Pennsylvania. We are particularly grateful to Theodore Hershberg and the staff of the Philadelphia Social History Project for their encouragement and assistance in a variety of ways. I want to express too my own thanks to Dell Hymes, dean of the Graduate School of Education, for his encouragement, support, and friendship.

The final revisions were made in the serenity of Clioquossia. They were prompted by an unusually detailed and thoughtful reading of the manuscript by an anonymous reader for Harvard University Press. His comments have saved us from considerable embarrassment.

Chapter 7 is a revised version of an essay written with Ian E. Davey, "Youth and Early Industrialization in a Canadian City," which appears in John Demos and Sarane Spence Boocock, eds., *Turning Points: Historical and Sociological Essays on the Family* (Chicago, 1978). We are grateful to Ian Davey for his research on youth and schooling in Hamilton. Versions of other parts of our book have appeared in the following sources: *Journal of Interdisciplinary History* (Spring 1978 and Spring 1981); *Social Science History* (Winter 1978); *History of Education Quarterly* (Winter 1977 and Fall 1978); *Marxist Perspectives* 4; and David J. Rothman and Stanton Wheeler, eds., *Social History and Social Policy* (New York, 1981). The 1978 essay in the *History of Education Quarterly* was also written with Ian Davey.

All previously published work has been substantially revised or reorganized for this book.

The manuscript was edited with great care and intelligence by Amanda Heller. She improved it very much, and we are grateful. We would also like to thank Aida Donald of Harvard University Press for her encouragement and assistance.

Many people have made substantive criticisms and suggestions, and we cannot at this point even remember all of them. But the collective scrutiny that the ideas in this book have received over several years has been very important. We would like to mention, especially but not exclusively, Michael Frisch, Daniel Calhoun, Michael Ornstein, Susan Houston, Charles Rosenberg, Daniel Scott Smith, Gordon Darroch, Glen Elder, Theodore Hershberg, Ian Davey, Harvey Graff, John Weaver, and the members of the discussion group that met in my living room on and off for two years in Toronto.

I have two special debts. One is to the Guggenheim Foundation whose fellowship made it possible for me to write most of this book. The other, as always, is to Edda.

Michael Katz

Oquossoc, Maine
July 1981

The Social Organization
of Early Industrial
Capitalism

# Introduction

## The Problem

Throughout Europe the development of capitalism undid the bonds that tied ordinary people to communities. In the vast surge of migration those who crossed the Atlantic were only one of many streams of people—displaced, uprooted, starving, restless, or ambitious. Some moved short distances, from farms to local villages or to regional centers. In fact for many the move to North America was the culmination of a journey that took place in stages. The voyage, however, did not end the wandering of migrant peoples. Even in the New World their restless movement continued as they passed in and out of towns and cities, sometimes settling, sometimes returning to the lands from which they had come.

Thus, the population flow through nineteenth-century North America was not merely a continental phenomenon; it must be understood as part of the international movement of people during the development of industrial capitalism. Capital-intensive, high-technology North American industries depended on the importation of cheap, unskilled labor to sustain economic growth. The migrants were a reserve labor army lured across the Atlantic, a surplus population attracted to industrial opportunity, responsive to local labor-market conditions, drifting from place to place in search of work.[1]

The population of American industry until at least the 1920s was as transient as the population of American towns and cities. One observer proposed 100 percent as a conservative estimate of the annual turnover in American factories.[2] Popular images of early industrial capitalism—great gray factories, orderly hordes of workers massed in their concrete yards for company photographs or filing quietly in and out of massive gates—portray a false sense of permanence. The physical structure of industrial capitalism and its social and economic relations remained entrenched, but the identity of the work force in any one place continually altered.

In fact the American labor force presented a curious paradox. Continual complaints about the shortage of skilled labor coexisted with a great surplus of industrial workers. Employers had no difficulty replacing the unskilled workers who drifted in and out of their factories. Hundreds of men usually answered each advertisement for factory hands.[3] According to a student of the labor market in the early 1920s the American system of factory organization depended on this casual reserve army of industrial workers. Employers had become accustomed to pools of ready labor waiting at factory gates. They recruited easily and informally, taking on or laying off hands as their needs required. The irregularly employed, impoverished workers at their gates served obviously useful functions with respect to wages and discipline. Only in the years following the First World War did progressive employers and social scientists begin to point out the disadvantages of a highly transient labor force. At that time labor turnover became a widely discussed issue, and ways of decreasing it were for the first time seriously proposed and considered.[4]

Transiency formed one key component of capitalism in both Europe and North America. Another was a rigid structure of inequality reproduced with startling similarity from decade to decade. "The great beauty of capitalist production consists in this," wrote Marx, "that it not only constantly reproduces the wage-worker as wage-worker, but produces always, in proportion to the accumulation of capital, a relative surplus-population of wage-workers. Thus the law of supply and demand of labor is kept in the right rut, the oscillation of wages is penned within limits satisfactory to capitalist exploitation, and lastly, the social dependence of the labourer on the capitalist, that indispensable requisite, is secured."[5]

The coexistence of transiency and a rigid structure of inequality appears at first paradoxical, but it is not. They both were defining attributes of the social structure of industrializing capitalism. Capitalism is a mode of production that gives rise to a distinctive class structure. That structure is the basis of the system of inequality; and just as the essential attributes of capitalism remain fixed, its structural inequality continues to define social and economic relations. The similarity of the structure of inequality between places and across time provides compelling evidence of the hegemony of capitalism in North America and of the interconnection between the social and economic organization of material life.

Capitalism did not develop by accident; its expansion was not left to chance. The drive to accumulate capital and to create the political and institutional framework necessary for its security, expansion, and perpetuation form a dominant theme in North American history. Nonetheless the hegemony of capitalism remains a problem of great importance. It has required the largely willing acquiescence of most people in a system of inequality in which they are the losers. How most people came to accept the legitimacy of a social and economic order that systematically perpetuates privilege and poverty is a puzzle that historians must seek to solve, and one on which we hope to shed some light.

This book attempts to set forth the evidence to sustain an interpretation of nineteenth-century North American urban social structure as marked by population transiency and a rigid structure of inequality. Both of these characteristics were consequences of a capitalist order whose basic properties emerged prior to the development of industry. The features we describe characterized both the commercial and the early industrial city, both of which may be portrayed in terms of a model organized into two great classes that reproduced themselves with startling regularity from one generation to another.

Our case rests on the presence in nineteenth-century urban social structure of four defining characteristics: a high rate of population turnover; a clear class structure rooted in capitalist economic and social relations; a sharply etched and relatively rigid structure of inequality; and a pattern of social mobility that resulted in the transmission of class position from one generation to another.

Mass transiency and a rigid structure of inequality characterized early capitalist social structure. Their coexistence was neither accidental nor paradoxical. Both were needed to sustain and reproduce capitalist social relations. A similar apparent dichotomy marked the history of institutions, but the demarcation of the boundaries between public and private life was integral to early capitalist development as was the division of society into two great classes. Social welfare and education became increasingly public tasks carried out by special, clearly defined agencies. By contrast, as the family shed its role in production, welfare, and education, it became a more superficially private institution. As with transiency and inequality the divergence of public and private institutions emerged from the dynamic forces shaping social life.

## Context

It is important to point out the particular features of Hamilton, Ontario, and Buffalo and Erie County, New York, that are of immediate significance to the interpretation offered throughout this book.

An instant city that grew from a few thousand in the mid 1840s to 14,000 by 1851, Hamilton, Ontario, served as the center of a prosperous agricultural region. Hamilton's supporters hoped that their city, with a fine harbor whose exploitation had spurred its growth, would rival and even surpass Toronto, forty miles to the east, as the leading port in Canada West (Ontario). In its heyday as a commercial city little industry existed in Hamilton. Most manufacturing took place in small shops, while land speculation and trade made up the dynamic aspects of the city's economy. Within twenty years the economic base of the city had changed. Hamilton had been transformed from a commercial into an industrial city. The major question that this study attempts to answer is: What consequences for social structure and domestic organization did this shift from commercial to industrial capitalism entail?

During the course of this critical development in its history the population of Hamilton grew from about 14,000 in 1851 to 19,000 in 1861 to 26,000 ten years later. Most of the immigrants who swelled the size of the city came from Great Britain. In 1851 and 1861 fewer than one in ten adult male heads of household had been born in Canada West. In 1871 the proportion was still only slightly higher. Most of the rest came from Ireland, Scotland, and England, with a smattering from the United States and, beginning especially in the 1860s, from Germany as well as a few from other countries. Until the depression of the 1850s immigrants continued to pour into commercial Hamilton.

During the years between 1851 and 1871 the city fathers undertook to modernize the city's transport system, public services, and educational facilities. The city council invested heavily in a railroad, which started operation in the early 1850s; lighted the streets with gas lamps; authorized the construction of an elaborate waterworks; and radically reconstructed the institutions of formal education, creating in the process a school system remarkably progressive for the times.[6]

The efforts of the city fathers did not reflect disinterested benevolence, for they had invested their own funds heavily in the railroad, waterworks, and gas company. Thus their decision to overcommit the city's funds is understandable if not condonable. When the depression of the late 1850s struck the city its effect was severe, decimating the population and driving the city to bankruptcy as its investments proved shaky. By 1861 the crisis had passed, and a period of recovery, interrupted briefly in the mid-1860s, turned into a boom that lasted into the early 1870s.

However Hamilton did not recover as a commercial city. Toronto's entrepreneurs strung out the Grand Trunk Railway straight through

Hamilton's hinterland, ruining the city's prospects of overtaking its rival as the major center of trade for the region. In these circumstances the city's promoters realized that the future required industrialization, which they began to promote actively as an economic policy. They were remarkably successful. By 1871, when an industrial census was taken, Hamilton had emerged as a modest but unmistakable industrial center.

Why did the city begin to industrialize in only two decades? The main outlines of the answer appear reasonably clear. First, the city's leading citizens wanted to industrialize quickly; thus the motivation existed. Second, entrepreneurs had access to capital markets in both Britain and the United States, which made it relatively easy to raise money. Third, the technology of industrialization already existed in other countries and could be imported without much difficulty. Fourth, the railroad had created an adequate transportation system linking together a solid domestic market dependent at the time on imported manufactured goods. Fifth, the infrastructure of industrialization already existed in the extensive workshops of the Great Western Railway, located in Hamilton since the 1850s. Sixth, there existed in the city a supply of cheap, mobile labor. This labor supply came in part from immigration, but large numbers of local men and women as well were ready and eager for industrial employment.

Industrialization increased the size of the setting in which most people worked. In 1851 only about 24 percent of the labor force worked in establishments that employed ten or more people; by 1871 that proportion had increased to 83 percent. By the latter year 53 percent of the workers in manufacturing were employed by firms with fifty or more employees. (To put the rapid development of Hamilton in perspective, the proportion in Philadelphia in 1870 was about 57 percent.) The new firms varied greatly in their organization and technology, but a significant fraction of the largest employed steam-driven machinery.[7]

The most modern and consistently mechanized sector was the metal industry, which included several foundries, three sewing machine factories, a metal rolling mill, one large agricultural implement firm, and the yards of the Great Western Railway. Within the other large sector of the economy, the apparel industry (clothing, hats, shoes), firms of a variety of sizes coexisted. The largest of these used sewing machines rather than steam power and employed women much more frequently than other industries. Throughout the city small firms and sweated labor in homes continued to flourish. Indeed the pace of industrialization remained uneven. Industrial growth did not destroy the city's commercial role; rather, it added to Hamilton's economic functions, and the city remained an important center of commerce.

In many accounts the development of textile mills is synonymous with early industrialization.[8] This was emphatically not the case in Hamilton. No substantial textiles manufacture took place in the city during this period. Moreover the absence of textiles manufacture created crucial differences between the economy of Hamilton and that of other early industrial cities, for the textile industry utilized considerable numbers of young children and women, including married women. In Hamilton though women exchanged domestic service for industrial work, they did not remain employed after marriage, and there is no evidence that large numbers of young children toiled in factories.

The years 1851 to 1871 encompassed two dramatic events in Canadian history: the origins of industrial capitalism and Confederation. This book is about the consequences of the former in one city. However the process was not unique to Hamilton, as most notably Steven Langdon and Leo Johnson have pointed out.[9] Confederation, the focus of most historical accounts of this period in Canadian history, is not our subject here. We have not attempted to trace the connections between economic and social change and the political creation of Canada. Surely, though, important connections do exist, and we hope that other Canadian historians will begin to explore more explicitly the way in which the development of industrial capitalism and nation building intertwined in this country. Indeed here too important parallels with American history exist. The great event in American history in the same period, the Civil War, also reflected some of the forces at work in Confederation. In both instances an alliance of industrial capitalism with nationalism forged a powerful political movement, though each worked itself out in a radically different way appropriate to its context.

Irregularity and insecurity were the two dominant features of the industrial work experience in Hamilton and in most other cities as well. Neither was new, though some men in Hamilton argued that these problems had become increasingly acute during early industrialization. It is hard, of course, to evaluate the testimony of elderly men trying to make a case, in this instance before the Royal Commission on Capital and Labour.[10] Nonetheless evidence from a variety of sources does support their claim that whether or not they had increased over time, irregularity and insecurity scarred the lives of workers. In both the commercial and early industrial city work took place in a system of structured inequality buffeted by the vagaries of seasonal demand and the business cycle. Almost as serious as the problem of low wages were the workers' inability to predict the number of days on which work would be available and the vulnerability of workers to arbitrary firing, falling profits, and business failure. Mechanization added the anxiety that younger, relatively untrained workers would flood the labor market, dilute wages, and weaken the precarious hold of established artisans on their jobs.

Insecurity and irregular employment marked working-class life in mid-nineteenth-century Buffalo, New York, as much as in Hamilton. A commercial city only about fifty miles away Buffalo forms an interesting and appropriate comparison. Despite the similarity of geographical location, commercial function, and lack of large-scale industry, important differences existed between the two cities. For one thing Buffalo was much larger and grew much more dramatically. Indeed in 1855 Buffalo was one of the fastest-growing cities in the United States: in the previous ten years its population had increased from approximately 35,000 to 72,000. As the western terminus of the Erie Canal Buffalo was a great center for the transshipment of goods between West and East. In the mid-nineteenth century several railroads also provided an extensive transportation network that sustained the city's economic life. The commercial character of the city's economy is an important point: although the rudiments of an industrial infrastructure were already present and indeed in considerably more developed form than in Hamilton during the same years, Buffalo had not yet become a manufacturing center.

Although Buffalo was primarily a commercial city in 1855, its transition from commerce to manufacture differed in one important respect from that of the Canadian city. Hamilton turned to industry in the wake of the debacle of the late 1850s, when the depression led the city into bankruptcy. As Toronto smashed Hamilton's hopes of becoming central Canada's commercial capital, the business class of Hamilton deliberately turned to manufacture. No such break exists in the economic history of Buffalo. Its industry in the 1850s derived from its commerce, just as it would half a century later. The products that dominated the Great Lakes and Canal trade—lumber, wheat, and livestock—formed the basis of the city's industrial growth.

The leading industry in Buffalo on the eve of the Civil War was leather, which in 1860 produced over $750,000 in value added. The grain-related industries—flour milling and brewing—each with a value added in excess of $200,000 followed, and the lumber industry produced $175,000. These industries and related products—malting, slaughtering and meat packing, and soap and furniture making— formed the nucleus of Buffalo's industrial growth throughout the rest of the century. As the Chamber of Commerce observed accurately in 1855: "All the natural advantages make this city one of the most important commercial points in the United States . . . As the West becomes more largely populated, the demand for manufactured articles increases, as our locality obliges us to receive from the West the great bulk of her produce, so it enables us to send forth to her with the greatest facility and at the least expense the articles which she requires in return."[11]

The rapid growth of Buffalo posed serious problems, especially for public health. Despite its obvious bias the following comment by the editor of the *Buffalo Medical Journal* in 1849 evokes some of the essential characteristics of the city during its initial expansion. The editor was explaining why the poorer areas of Buffalo had been affected severely by the cholera epidemic of the previous year:

> The position of Buffalo is such, that it contains a large floating population, consisting of immigrants from all countries, in transition to places farther westward, and newcomers of all kinds, seeking for occupation and new homes, in addition to the usual population of the laboring class, the destitute, and the devotees of vice. The class of laborers were greater than usual the present year, in consequence of the public works occupying a large body of men, mostly Irish and Germans. The various kinds of population just designated are peculiarly exposed to causes of disease. They are crowded together, many have recently endured the confinement, and privations, and sickness of a voyage across the Atlantic, not a few are impoverished, and the majority are desirous of consulting the strictest economy in their mode of living, they are strangers without homes, and often depressed by disappointments and anxieties incident to their position. Adding to these circumstances ignorance, recklessness, intemperance, and other vices, which will apply to a considerable number of the persons referred to, and we have sufficient reasons for regarding them as favorable subjects for any Epidemic disease like that under consideration.[12]

These observations demonstrate that Buffalo, like most American cities of the period, experienced a flow of population in and out of the city that created problems for public health and order. Yet the editors of the journal missed the fact that Buffalo had a relatively low rate of transiency. Despite the sickness, squalor, and suffering that accompanied the Irish migration of the late 1840s, Buffalo enjoyed a steady, orderly growth that allowed it to provide a level of public services far above the average for American cities. Buffalo always ranked among the nation's leading cities in housing, roads, water lines, and public transportation.

The social elite of Buffalo, particularly the transplanted New Englanders who dominated its economic life, brought the civic spirit of the Eastern seaboard to their midwestern city. Like Boston and New York, Buffalo had a park system designed by Frederick Law Olmsted. A student of Pierre L'Enfant, the designer of Washington, D.C., Joseph Ellicot gave the city a system of radial streets reminiscent of the nation's capital.

Civic mindedness extended beyond the physical layout of the city, for Buffalo's elite remained loyal to the tradition of social reform. In 1854 the nation's first YMCA was founded in the city; in 1878 the city became the home of the first Charity Organization Society. William Letchworth, a long-time activist on the State Board of Charities and in other statewide social reform, was a successful businessman in the city before moving into public service.[13]

Thus on the eve of the Civil War Buffalo was a hybrid. It ranked with Chicago, Cleveland, Pittsburgh, and St. Louis as one of the emerging industrial giants of the nation's heartland. At the same time its physical form, public services, and elite consciousness were similar to those of the cities of the Eastern seaboard. It was this mixture of western expansion and eastern sensibility that set Buffalo's course during the remainder of the nineteenth century.

In sharp contrast to the city the region surrounding Buffalo consisted of rural areas and some sixteen villages of varying size that acted as service centers in the city's agricultural hinterland. Settlement began in most parts of Erie County during the first decade of the nineteenth century, and by 1855 considerable progress had been made in establishing a successful agricultural area. Two distinct types of farmland characterized this region: the flat, grain-growing area of the north and the hilly, grazing, livestock-raising area to the south of the city. Thus at midcentury, prior to industrialization, the county represented a varied, dynamic region.[14]

The spectacular growth of Buffalo should not obscure the fact that the population of rural Erie County was also growing, if at a slower rate. In the same years that Buffalo expanded from 35,000 to 72,000 people the population of the rest of the county increased from about 44,000 to 60,000. As should be expected given these different rates of growth, the average head of household had lived in the county about six years longer than his counterpart in Buffalo. Though the proportion of houshold heads who had lived in Buffalo less than five years (44 percent) was greater than in the county (36 percent), the share there one year or less was quite close (16 percent in Buffalo and 14 percent in the county). The point of these comparisons is that despite the pull of the dynamic city, rural Erie County remained an attractive, expanding place. Indeed it should have had extraordinary appeal for farmers, because Buffalo provided both a huge, expanding market and excellent transportation facilities for the shipping of produce elsewhere.

Of course it would be a mistake to think of the county solely as a region of farms. Though most heads of household were farmers (64 percent), a considerable degree of occupational diversity existed as well: 12 percent of household heads were laborers, about 13 percent skilled artisans, 6 percent in various kinds of nonmanual work, and 5 percent unclassifiable, mainly "gentlemen" (apparently well-to-do land-owners). Given the absence of a transport industry, semiskilled workers were almost nonexistent—1 percent in the rural area (Table I.1).[15]

By contrast the importance of transportation and the key place held by the transshipment of goods in the local economy created a large

Table I.1 Occupational and demographic characteristics of household heads: Hamilton, 1851, and Buffalo and rural Erie County, 1855.

| Variable | Hamilton (N = 2,314) | Buffalo (N = 14,040) | Erie County (N = 1,158) |
|---|---|---|---|
| *Birthplace* | | | |
| Native[a] | 8.3 | 21.5 | 58.0 |
| England | 27.4 | 7.0 | 3.8 |
| Ireland | 39.1 | 17.0 | 3.5 |
| Germany | 0.8 | 39.2 | 28.5 |
| Other | 24.4 | 15.3 | 6.2 |
| *Occupational rank* | | | |
| Professional/proprietor | 9.9 | 4.2 | 2.9 |
| Other white collar | 15.3 | 11.7 | 2.6 |
| Skilled | 38.0 | 36.5 | 13.1 |
| Semiskilled | 7.2 | 4.6 | 1.1 |
| Unskilled | 18.6 | 14.3 | 11.5 |
| Unclassified | 11.0 | 28.6 | 4.9 |
| Farmers | — | — | 63.8 |

SOURCE: Census of New York State, 1855; Census of Canada, 1851.
a. For Hamiltonians native birthplaces include Canada, Nova Scotia, New Brunswick, and Prince Edward Island. For residents of Buffalo and Erie County natives are considered to be those born in the United States.

number of semi- and unskilled jobs in Buffalo. Indeed with its grain mills, canal traffic, and railroads Buffalo offered opportunity to unskilled workers that few cities could rival. It is this presence of economic opportunity for ordinary workers in a dynamic, expanding city that made mid-nineteenth-century Buffalo better able than Hamilton to retain its population.

Important demographic differences existed between the city of Buffalo and its surrounding countryside. In the county the largest proportion of household heads (37 percent) had been born in New York State, though only 14 percent in Erie County itself. In Buffalo the corresponding proportions were 13 percent and 2 percent. As in Buffalo the next largest American-born contingent came from New England, though in the city only 6 percent of household heads had been born there. Thus Buffalo had a substantially higher proportion of native-born adults than Hamilton. It differed too in the size of its German community. In rural Erie County 29 percent of household heads had been born in Germany and only a sprinkling (4 percent) in Ireland, contrasted to 39 percent and 17 percent, respectively, in Buffalo. It is clear that Irish immigrants clustered disproportionately in the city, while Germans often moved to the country. At the same time the English born (4 percent) were a smaller proportion than the 7 percent in the city, and a significant cluster of household heads born in France lived in the country as well.

The population of country and city varied in more than national origin, for emigrants also came from different sections of New York State. The leading areas in terms of sending people to Buffalo were among the largest and most heavily urbanized of New York's sixty counties. For the most part the agricultural counties contiguous to Erie County were not the source of significant numbers of the city's residents. On the contrary one major component in the circulation of people throughout New York State involved movement from city to city.

## Sources

We have reconstructed the population of Hamilton during its period of early industrialization and of Buffalo and rural Erie County in 1855. Our research effort centered for some years solely on Hamilton, but we were fortunate to be given a copy of the manuscript census of 1855 for Buffalo, put into machine-readable form under the direction of Laurence Glasco. To this we added two samples from rural Erie County, a 10 percent sample of household heads for immediate use in a comparison of patterns of population persistence, and a 20 percent sample of the entire population, upon which we drew in our analysis of the family.

In order to study Hamilton we put the following sources into machine-readable form: the entire manuscript censuses for 1851, 1861, and 1871; the assessment rolls of 1852 (actually closest in time to the taking of the 1851 census), 1861, and 1881; the tax roll of 1871; the city directory for 1853; marriage records for 1849-1869; selected school attendance records; jail records from 1851-1881; and a few other sources as well. All of the census and tax rolls for the years 1851-1871 have been linked together, making it possible to trace the histories of the people who remained in the city. The directory of 1853 was also linked to the other sources for that year, as were the names of local people listed in the newspaper. The business directory and industrial census of 1871 were used to identify master artisans and manufacturers not otherwise identified on the census. Demographic trends were also calculated from parish records.

The censuses of 1851 to 1871 were coded because they were the only ones open and relevant to this study; 1851 was the first year in which each person, as opposed to each household, was separately enumerated, and 1871 is the last Canadian census that could be consulted at the time of our research.

The methods through which people were traced from one source to another ranged from hand searching to computer linkage. One aspect of classification needs to be mentioned here. For the most part the research suffered from our inability to distinguish master artisans from those they employed. On the census and tax rolls men were listed simply as shoemakers, tailors, or carpenters. After most of the analysis for this project had been completed, we discovered how to identify the masters through the business directories and industrial census.[16] In some cases we repeated analyses in which the distinction was critical. In other instances we made separate comparisons of masters and their employees in order to understand the effect that the introduction of the distinction would have had on larger analyses. However in a number of instances the cost of redoing an analysis was prohibitive, especially because the gains would be quite small. Thus throughout this book different occupational classifications are used. In some places we simply divide the employed males into five vertically ordered ranks. The advantage of a scale of this sort is its simplicity, and for some purposes it provides an adequate, if rough, differentiation. At other times we use a more elaborate scheme based on the sector of the economy (primary, secondary, tertiary) and the type of work and rank within sectors. The third scheme is based on a notion of class and employs the distinction between masters and workers. In some places we use representative individual occupations. Throughout we have tried to group occupations in the way most appropriate to the problem under discussion.[17]

The reader should note that the tables are based on different populations in various places. That is, at some times we use the entire population from a census and at others only those people linked between census and assessment or between census and census. Each source has its biases, and we have tried to make these clear. The unavoidable differences in base populations create inconsistencies in the numbers in various tables. The context should make this evident. Most other methodological points are understood best in the course of the discussion of particular problems.

# 1  A Two-Class Model

"Thirty years ago," wrote Charles Loring Brace in 1854 in the first annual report of the New York Children's Aid Society, "the proposal of an important organization, which should devote itself entirely to the class of vagrant, homeless, and criminal children in New York, would have seemed absurd." Although poverty existed, "the city was young and thriving," and "the scum of poverty . . . would soon be floated off through the thousand channels of livelihood over the whole country." It was inconceivable that in only fifty years an American city would acquire a "London St. Giles or Spitalfields." It had seemed contrary to "human probability" that in such a short time "those hideous and unnatural conditions of the European cities—the result of ages of ignorance and inequality and over-crowded population—could be realized here."[1]

Those calculations about America's future had overlooked one important factor: immigration. "During the last twenty years, a tide of population has been setting towards these shores, to which there is no movement parallel in history." Although many of the immigrants —"sober, hard-working people, who have spread over the country and mingled with our population"—were welcome, others posed ominous problems. For they were "the offscouring of the poorest districts and the most degraded cities of the Old World. The pauperism and poverty of England and Ireland has been drained into New York."[2]

Too poor to move west, where they could have been absorbed into America's vast open territory, the immigrants crowded into cities. "Our poorest streets began to be filled up with a thriftless, beggared, dissolute population. As is always the case in such circumstances, vice and laziness stimulated each other." As the "poor and idle" herded into certain quarters of the city, the "respectable and industrious moved out," creating slum districts such as the notorious Five Points.[3]

To Brace the emergence of a dissolute and dangerous lower class had two primary causes. One was the immigration of desperately poor and degraded people from the slums of Ireland and England. The other was their congregation within cities. Something about cities themselves, especially their population density, eroded character. "The very *condensing* of their number within a small space, seems to stimulate their bad tendencies."[4]

Thus Brace's argument was both demographic and ecological. Immigrants trapped in cities degenerated into a dangerous lower class. Indeed Brace made plain the danger to American social structure posed by the emergence of this new social class: "The greatest danger that can threaten a country like ours, is from the existence of an ignorant, debased, and permanently poor class, in the great cities. It is still more threatening if this class be of foreign-birth, and of different habits from those of our own people. The members of it come at length to form a separate population. They embody the lowest passions and most thriftless habits of the community. They corrupt the lowest class of working-poor who are around them. The expenses of police, of prisoners, of charities and means of relief, arise mainly from them."[5] Given this view of the threat to American character and social institutions, it is understandable that Brace adopted the emigration of city urchins to the West as a strategy designed to promote their reformation and to break up the malignant tumors gnawing at urban life.

Brace was representative of antebellum social critics who believed that relatively simple, direct solutions could cure the problems of American urban life. Brace was an exceptionally perceptive social commentator with an acute sense of the interrelationship of the demographic, economic, and ecological factors reshaping cities, but he still believed that their social problems were temporary. Like others of his time he did not view the emergence of a degraded urban lower class as an inevitable and permanent consequence of American capitalism. Rather he believed that it was an unfortunate aberration threatening to corrupt a fundamentally healthy social structure where inequalities of rank did not translate into hard divisions of class, where a self-perpetuating pauper class was unknown. Thus for Brace and other social reformers the problem was finding a strategy to prevent American cities from replicating the European experience.[6]

Within twenty years the antebellum optimism had faded. America had not escaped the European experience, and commentators routinely described American social structure as dominated by two great, permanent, and antagonistic classes: Capital and Labor. The fear of a degraded lower class which had alarmed Brace had been transformed into the concern with the "development of a permanent working class" that seemed the most serious problem to the first American practitioners of social science.[7]

For example, in 1875 Edward Young, chief of the United States Bureau of Statistics, published his massive survey of the wages and living conditions of workers in Europe, America, and Canada. Young's discussion stressed the altered class relations that had developed in the "era of machinery." Unlike Brace's his account stressed the way in which goods were produced, not demography or ecology. Consequently he portrayed two great and permanent classes as dominating modern social structure.[8] Young emphasized the impact of the stream engine on methods of production, especially the great increase in the "aggregate wealth of the community." That wealth, however, had not been distributed equally: "In this increase the working class have undoubtedly shared to a considerable extent, though in a degree not at all comparable to that in which the wealthiest classes have benefitted. Indeed, each new application of machinery was a source of temporary inconvenience, or even of severe distress, to the particular class of workmen whose manual labor it superceded."[9]

The new methods of production, Young emphasized, made necessary "associated industry and . . . large establishments carried on by accumulated capital." It was the effect of capital accumulation in particular that Young wished to highlight, by which he meant "masses of capital vastly in excess of the average possession of individuals, even in the most prosperous communities—masses so large that the possession of one such mass implies, as its necessary counterpart, the comparative poverty of scores or even hundreds of others and their dependence upon the one for employment."[10] According to Young, capital accumulation and the increase in wage labor had profoundly altered the nature of social structure. First it cut off traditional patterns of social mobility. "When industry was carried on in small separate establishments," he pointed out, "a steady and industrious workman might reasonably hope to accumulate the means of setting up in business for himself, and thus the workman of this year might next year be numbered among the employers." It was in fact "a common boast" of Americans that precisely this process often took place. Reality, however, was quite different from national myth. "It is quite evident that the number of industries which may be started with such an amount of capital as a workingman can save out of his wages, is not only comparatively small," but that "it is steadily diminishing as the sphere of machinery extends."[11] Except temporarily at the moment of its introduction, machinery had not driven men out of work. Rather the machine had changed "the conditions under which they work." It had reshaped class structure by "dividing all that large portion of society employed in connection with it into two distinct, and in respect to their circumstances, widely separated classes": employers and employees.[12]

This great difference in condition partially accounted for the "discontent of the working classes." Even more than absolute inequality, however, their "aggressive attitude toward capital" arose from the "fact that to the great mass these conditions appear to be practically permanent." Earlier, when mobility had seemed possible, when a "journeyman mechanic . . . could see a prospect that within ten years he might become the owner of a shop he was not disposed to feel or act unkindly toward a class of which he hoped soon to become a member." In this way "machine labor" had infused the mass of working people with "the cohesion and the common sentiments of a permanent class apart from the class of their employers." Moreover, through its "gregarious industry" and extension of "the sphere of urban life," it had given to the working classes increased opportunities for "mutual intercourse."[13] To Young therefore class consciousness had two roots: the emergence of a rigid and permanent structure of inequality with little opportunity for social mobility and the creation of large work settings. Both of these developments arose from the process with which industrial capitalism divided society into two great classes.

The chief difficulty with Young's analysis is that it missed the distinction between capitalism and industrialization.[14] The two, though closely related, are not identical. Capitalism, defined as a system of market-directed production for profit based on wage labor, preceded the creation of factories and the application of machinery to production, themselves two separable processes. Capitalism implies a social not a technical organization of production. By contrast, as Anthony Giddens observes, the "most essential feature" of industrialism is "the transformation of human labour via the application of inanimate sources of energy to productive activity." Joined to this are other factors, notably the "physical proximity of workers, together with machinery, in a clearly circumscribed workplace: i.e., the factory." Industrialism, therefore, is defined as *the transfer of inanimate energy sources to production through the agency of factory organization.* Before the advent of industry two distinct and relatively permanently separated classes characterized urban social structure. Industrialization may have increased the barriers between them and decreased what chances for mobility did exist. Most certainly, and for the reasons Young gives, industrialization increased the working class's awareness of its circumstances and promoted the militancy of the labor movement, especially in the 1870s.[15]

It must be remembered that industrialization in North America took place within an already capitalist society, a point of fundamental significance to the history of social structure. It was in fact this point that Brace and other social commentators of the mid-nineteenth century missed. The emergence of the new class that they lamented did have its immediate origins in the immigration of impoverished people into American cities. However that immigration itself was one of the first visible consequences of a change in the social relations of production, the massive upsurge in transiency unleashed by the spread of capitalism in Europe. The immigrants, to use Gabriel Kolko's phrase, represented the "internationalization of the Western world's labor supply."[16]

Had Brace probed more deeply he would have discovered that the denizens of Five Points were among the most unfortunate members of a wage-labor class that already existed in American and Canadian cities. By the mid-nineteenth century most urban dwellers were already dependent on wages, and few could have a realistic expectation of independence. The journeyman mechanic had little prospect of acquiring a shop within ten years unless he was the son of a master craftsman, because journeyman often was a permanent status, not a phase in the life cycle.[17]

Nor, had Brace looked a bit more closely, would he have contrasted a group of stable Americans with rootless immigrants, for the population of American and Canadian cities was continually in motion. In fact mass transiency was one of the defining characteristics of urban social structure, as people wandered from place to place in search of work and a relatively secure livelihood. Nor did industrialization, as Young implied, fundamentally transform this social structure. Rather it heightened its visibility, solidified its shape, and by amassing people in large settings brought to public consciousness the nature and magnitude of the change that had taken place during the previous century.[18]

By the late nineteenth century the existence of a social structure dominated by two great classes based on capital and labor was recognized widely by both employers and working people. Later generations of social commentators would attempt to blur or complicate the stark social imagery of early industrial capitalism. Indeed it was a signal achievement of twentieth-century sociology to transform class into social stratification. But the strength of the early industrial view was its contact with the real world.[19]

## Capitalism and Class

The history of nineteenth-century social structure has three major phases. The first is the commercially-based capitalism that spread after about the mid-eighteenth century. The second is early industrial capitalism, which emerged between 1840 and 1860. The third is the corporate capitalism increasingly dominant after 1880. This book is concerned with the first two phases: commercially-based and early industrial capitalism. We argue that social structure during this period may best be thought of as increasingly dominated by two great classes: the working class and the business class.

In Hamilton even people with opposing interests routinely accepted the bifurcation of social structure into the two great classes Capital and Labor. Of course the relationship between the awareness of class and the objective features of social structure is enormously complex. The mere fact that any fundamental group within the social structure possesses all the objective attributes of a class does not mean that its members share a sense of collective identity or a militant desire either to defend or change their condition. Structural factors such as the distribution of workers into small groups may retard the development of either class awareness or class consciousness, to use a distinction developed by Anthony Giddens to separate a sense of class membership from a desire to undertake militant collective action. So may ideological influences, which establish the hegemony of one class by legitimating inequality, for instance through the notion that society is classless. A variant of this idea, called nonegalitarian classlessness, according to the late Stanislaw Ossowski characterizes official images of social structure in both the Soviet Union and the United States.[20]

Indeed the link between objective circumstance and the recognition of class remains elusive, imperfectly understood, a source of constant reflection for leaders of social democratic movements perplexed by their inability to persuade the working class to vote in terms of its own interests. In fact the awareness of class may have varied throughout North American history. It cannot be described by a smooth curve reaching progressively higher levels of intensity or insight. Its peak may instead have been reached in the late nineteenth century.

The situation in Hamilton reinforces the need for caution in making assumptions about the connection between the conditions of class and individual consciousness. In 1851 capitalism had already become the dominant mode of production in Hamilton; the ratio of masters and manufacturers to skilled workers was about 1 to 10 or 11, and for each proprietor a large number of semi- and unskilled workers existed as well. The ratio of wage workers to proprietors did not change very much during the next twenty years, despite the early industrialization of the city. However the consciousness of class did alter.

Historians have pointed to the frequent opposition between *working* and *nonproducing* classes popular in the early and mid-nineteenth century.[21] However the earlier use of *working class* embraced both masters and artisans. It was meant to divide society not into wage workers and their employers but into all those who actively produced goods or wealth and a nebulous, ill-defined group of *drones* —rentiers, speculators, or financiers—who skimmed the profit from their labor. This conception partially reflected a precapitalist social order in which independent commodity producers formed a distinct unit in the class structure and in which issues of credit were paramount.[22] It served too to retain the description appropriate to an earlier period during the early years of capitalist ascendancy, thereby eliminating the distinction between capital and labor and diverting attention from the major source of conflict and exploitation developing at the time.[23]

When threatened the business class, whatever its rhetoric, revealed a clear understanding of its interests and a capacity for collective action. The working class by contrast remained largely unorganized, and strikes were sporadic. This had been the situation in Hamilton in the early 1850s, when the city's business class acted quickly and effectively to put down the striking laborers on the Great Western Railway. By the early 1870s all of this had changed. The nine-hour movement, which culminated in a widespread if largely unsuccessful strike across many industries in 1872, demonstrated unambiguously that a collective sense of class had developed among the city's working men.

The story of the nine-hour movement and the strike that signaled the emergence of the organized labor movement in Canada has been told elsewhere, and there is no need to repeat it here.[24] For our purposes what matters are some of the ideas about the shape of the social order articulated by both opponents and sponsors of the strike, for the issues raised by the conflict forced people to comment on class with a directness unusual in more placid times. The business class's point of view was put forward by the *Hamilton Spectator*, which opposed the strike and the nine-hour movement; the working-class case was argued by the *Ontario Workman*, which began publication in Toronto in 1872 in order to support the nine-hour cause.

Articles and editorials in the *Spectator* assumed that two great classes divided modern society and routinely referred to relations between capital and labor. Those relations, according to the voice of the city's business interests, should be marked by harmony and cooperation, not conflict. Indeed at the start of the agitation in January 1872 the editor commented, "We have been hitherto free, in Canada, from the unfortunate collisions between capital and labor which have taken place in other countries . . . " and hoped that the nine-hour issue could be handled with "such wisdom as to form no exception to the rule which has hitherto prevailed."[25]

The *Spectator* put its case most clearly in an argument for a theory of value. Labor, the editor acknowledged, had become a commodity. "Viewing a workingman's day's labor as the commodity which he has for sale, while admitting the sentimental question of his *right* to sell it to the highest bidder, the more matter-of-fact question of the *value* he is to receive in return for it cannot be ignored." That value was determined very simply by the law of supply and demand. "If the supply be greater than the demand, the value is reduced by just the same proportion that the supply exceeds the demand." Although both labor and cash were types of capital, it was the interplay of supply and demand that determined their relative value. Thus the issue was "which class of capital—that called money, or that called labor—is in excess in the market, and then what is the value of each as compared to the other." The editor of the *Spectator* did not doubt which class of capital was in excess supply, and he proposed a straightforward test. The employees of the Wilson, Bowman and Company sewing machine factory had struck. If a sufficient number of men could be found to fill their places, then an oversupply of labor would have been demonstrated conclusively. Events appeared to support the *Spectator*. According to the paper two hundred workmen applied for the vacant positions, and the plant resumed operation with a new work force. Poor, underemployed workers thus formed a reserve army of labor that may have consituted a greater barrier to working-class organization than the resistance of employers.[26]

The issue, however, was not as straightforward as the *Spectator* maintained. When the labor disturbance subsided, Wilson, Bowman hired back a number of their former employees, including two of the three foremen who had been fired for sympathy with the workers. Though the company could easily find unskilled hands, it obviously had not been able to replace its skilled work force. In fact the owners had been forced to compromise with the strikers by rehiring an employee whose support of the nine-hour movement had been the occasion of his dismissal and the immediate cause of the strike. Their action demonstrated the situation confronting North American industrialists: a shortage of highly skilled workers amidst a relative abundance of labor.[27]

To the *Spectator* the transformation of labor into a commodity for sale constituted a progressive step in human history by emancipating the workers from dependency. Before, under the "old theory," the laborer had been "a humble dependent upon the capitalist . . . That notion has, as we have said, given place to the more enlightened notion of bargain and sale between the seller and the purchaser of labor." The *Spectator* made no attempt to disguise its argument by denying the existence of class. Class formed an integral aspect of capitalism, which in the long run benefited everyone if its basic law— the interplay of supply and demand—was left unchecked by forces that arbitrarily and artificially altered the true value of commodities, especially of labor.[28]

Although the editors of the *Ontario Workman* also saw two great classes in modern society, they agreed with the *Spectator* about few other economic issues. The paper's motto was "The Equalization of All Elements of Society in the Social Scale Should Be the True Aim of Civilization," and its first issue carried an excerpt from Marx's *Capital.* The editor of the paper proclaimed, "We shall endeavor to lay plainly before our working brethren the true cause of all the evils that labour complains of (and we believe justly), and shall endeavor, with equal plainness and fearlessness, to show that a simple and effectual remedy can be applied."[29]

Though labor and capital were also commodities to the *Workman,* they did not reflect the working of an unfettered law of supply and demand. The great imbalance in the share of production flowing to each arose "from the selfishness of our natures . . . we have created artificial means whereby wealth can be centralized in the hands of the few . . . Production drawn from its natural channel, the few pocket and control, the masses toil on, and remain poor." According to the editor the production of the country increased annually about 7 percent, of which labor received 3 percent. "It does not require a great amount of knowledge," he wrote, "to comprehend why wealth centralizes. It not only absorbs all surplus production, but robs the labourer of 4 percent, that naturally is his subsistence money."[30]

As a consequence of the industrial transformation of the modern era, argued the paper, relations between classes had to change. The "steam engine, and the marvellous improvement in the labour-saving machinery which have followed in its wake, have introduced a new order of things, and it should not surprise us to find the new system of work in factories, with its closely defined division of employments, calls for new industrial arrangements and for a revision of those laws which have hitherto regulated the mutual relations between labor and capital."[31] Thus, far from adopting a backward-looking position, the *Workman* argued that the increased production made possible by machinery should improve the lives of working people and not simply enrich their employers.

In fact, according to the paper, the prevailing organization of industrial life not only returned to working men an inadequate share of their production but stunted their human development. Hard at work for ten hours a day, went one complaint repeated time and again, working men could not improve their minds through reading or other forms of education. Improvement would have to be won through struggle. The paper consistently encouraged collective action and urged the abolition of legal restraints on union activity. Neither charity nor abstract theory, one contributor perceptively noted, would substitute for struggle: "Extremes of poverty and wealth are not the normal conditions of man. The instincts at present moving the masses of man will ere long prove more potent to ameliorate the condition of society than all the class philanthropy of the age, and more wise to properly adjust the systems of society than all the philosophy possessed by the savants of our time."[32]

The most pointed comment on social relations came from a Montreal paper quoted in the *Workman*. "Heretofore the working-man's share," wrote the author, succinctly stating the fundamental issues, "has been just as little as he could live on, and the non-producers and the so-called employers mean that it shall be so still." Workers, however, no longer would acquiesce, and "the contest, which can end only in a reconstruction of society, is already entered upon." Neither party was sufficiently aware of the "true nature of the conflict," which was not "simply a question of hours of labor or wages" but rather "of social organization, of the true idea of property and what gives a just title to it, of personal estimation and of the relative rank of men." The confict, then, was about class in the most comprehensive sense of that term, about the relationship of people to one another and the basis of human esteem. It was a question, said the author, of "whether a working-man shall be looked upon as a man, or as an economical producing machine; in a word it is a social revolution."

The author dismissed the notion that the two great classes shared common interests that would permit a peaceful and satisfactory reso-lution of their differences. As "long as there is a class who buy labor and another class who sell labor," he wrote, "these two classes will have hostile interests and be at war, the one class seeking to buy the greatest amount of labor at the cheapest price, the other seeking to get the highest price possible, and to give the least possible labor for the pay he gets." The only way to eliminate class conflict, he concluded, was "to do away with this distinction of classes."[33]

Despite its economic radicalism the *Workman* reflected cultural values that would have been shared by the editors of the *Spectator*. Consider, for instance, the article entitled "The Accurate Boy," which offered a case history of a young man who had earned a very desirable position as a clerk for a railway. How did he obtain his job? "Not by having a rich father, for he was the son of a laborer. The secret was his beautiful accuracy. He began as an errand boy, and did his work accurately. His leisure time he spent perfecting his arithmetic."[34] Or ponder the advice to "young employees": "There is no greater mistake a young man can commit than that of being indifferent to the interests of his employers . . . The wages may be small—too small; but if you have contracted to work for one dollar a week, when your work is worth ten, stick to your bargain like a man until your term of service has expired. It may seem very hard, but it will instill the great principle of being true to your word."[35] What more could an employer ask?

The *Workman* not only advocated accuracy, diligence, and reliability but also supported temperance and contemporary notions of domestic life. Indeed popular sentimental stereotypes of home, mother, and woman appeared frequently in the fiction in its columns. In its adoption of bourgeois Victorian cultural standards the *Workman* was hardly unique in the labor movement in Canada, Britain, or the United States. Throughout the nineteenth century labor leaders revealed the same curious juxtaposition of economic radicalism and cultural conservatism. It is the interpretation, not the fact, of that cultural stance that is debatable. At least two explanations are possible. One holds that the acceptance of temperance, diligence, and reliability revealed the successful exertion of ideological hegemony by the business class. The intellectual emancipation even of working-class leaders was only partial, and their inability to transcend the cultural categories through which social issues were presented to them limited their capacity to mount an effective challenge to capitalism. A quite different interpretation assigns to working-class leaders a much more active and self-conscious role. In this view cultural spokesmen manipulated bourgeois standards in the interests of their class. An appearance of respectability disarmed critics of working-class behavior, but those same standards could be put to purposes quite different from those their promoters had intended. Temperance, for instance, underlay the discipline necessary for both individual survival within the capitalist order and successful collective action.[36]

In a sense both arguments may be correct. Some working-class leaders may have manipulated cultural values; others may have accepted them at face value, and many by and large undoubtedly ignored them. While the *Workman* defended collective action, hundreds of workers applied to Wilson, Bowman and Company to take the jobs of the strikers. The structural conditions of early industrial capitalism created contradictory pressures on the working class and fostered the internal divisions that undercut sustained collective action. The development of large work settings provided conditions essential to the development of a common consciousness, but the internal divisions within the work place and the mass of underemployed worked in precisely the opposite direction. In these circumstances cultural standards scarcely could have a consistent meaning or float free of the contradictions at the basis of working-class life.

Did the workers who hurried to replace the strikers at Wilson, Bowman or at other factories accept the capitalist theory of value, or were they simply desperate people whose activity contradicted their beliefs? The question is important, but there is little evidence on which to base an answer. At any rate the question leads away from the more straightforward issue of primary concern here: the perception of class structure. On that the evidence appears unequivocal. A two-class model describes not only the objective relations of early industrial cities but the perception of their principal interpreters as well.

## The Business Class

Hamilton's economic and political life was dominated by its business class: the capitalists of the commercial and early industrial city and their associates, primarily the professionals and business employees who shared their outlook, aspirations, and interests. Three questions of fundamental importance must be asked about the business class: Was there any distinctive pattern of activity common to its members? Did industrialization involve a change in class leadership? Were there important differences between commercial and industrial capitalists?

Evidence for the first question has been presented in detail in *The People of Hamilton, Canada West.* Here we summarize the main features of that argument, though we now prefer to use *business class* to designate what in that book was labeled the *entrepreneurial class.*[37] Members of the business class shared a point of view about the development of the city, the role of local government, and the behavior of labor. Though they often sued each other and squabbled over particular issues, they were capable of fast, effective action when they perceived their class interests to be threatened.

For instance when the laborers building the Great Western Railway struck in 1852, twenty-five property owners signed a petition requesting the Governor-General to send in troops to quell riots and force the men back to work. The men who signed the petition were leaders of their class, the most prominent men in a variety of trades and businesses; they represented twenty-one distinct occupations. Except for three men—a one minister, a gentleman, and the local Member of Parliament (himself a wealthy speculator)—all were businessmen despite the fact that nine had artisans' titles, for those artisans owned their own businesses and were the leaders of their trades in the city. The composition of the group of signers had obviously been orchestrated with care. That it included both masters and merchants suggests the essential similarity in class position of men in manufacturing and commerce. What counted was ownership of the means of production and of private property.

These signers were part of a larger segment of the business class we isolated for analysis. In all the sample comprises 161 men, probably over half the city's proprietors in 1851. These men may have found collective action relatively easy because they knew each other well. Hamilton remained small enough to be intimate at the upper reaches of its commercial and productive life. More than that, all nine signers of the petition about whom detailed information exists had lived in the city since the 1840s, when the city had begun its meteoric transformation from an overgrown village into a commercial center. They were for Hamilton the founding fathers. These were also relatively affluent men. Of the twenty-one signers for whom economic rank can be inferred, nineteen were in the top ten percentiles. Of the 161 men as a whole 62 percent were in the top ten percentiles and 83 percent in the top twenty.

The signers of the petition had a deep personal involvement in the economic development of the city. At least thirteen had interests in railroads, and at least seven were concerned with the introduction of public utilities (gas and water), building societies, and the board of trade. Among the larger group of men at least 40 percent participated in the greatest developmental activity of the century—the railroad. At least 44 percent sponsored other types of activities associated with urban development.

Significantly, these men were general entrepreneurs, not just specialized businessmen or tradesmen. Besides conducting their own businesses and promoting railroads and utilities, most speculated in real estate, several lent money, and a number were officers of insurance companies. Their particular businesses served as a base and as a source of capital accumulation from which they branched out into a variety of speculative and promotional activities, especially real estate.

The signers of the petition were the political as well as the commercial leaders of the city. They included the Member of Parliament and six men who served on the city council in either 1851 or 1852. Of the larger group 19 percent served on the city council in 1851 or 1852 and

14 percent on juries. These men promoted education as well as railroads. Four of the signers were on local school boards, one was an officer of the Mechanics Institute, and one an officer of the Mercantile Library Association. They supplied the leadership in the modernization of the schools that took place in the 1850s, symbolized by the founding of the Central School. Twenty-two percent of the 161 entrepreneurs volunteered their time to promote education.

They were the core not only of commercial, educational, and political leadership but of social life as well. They were prominent in every important voluntary organization. Fewer participated in philanthropic than in fraternal, honorific, and public activities. This however did not represent an indifference to philanthropic activity but a division of labor: charity in Hamilton remained mostly an activity for women. The wives of at least twelve of the signers were visitors for the Ladies' Benevolent Society. Among the 161 men as a whole 35 percent in 1851 and 1852 participated in benevolent and philanthropic activity, mostly through one of the benevolent societies or through raising funds to help victims of disasters. Few spent time in the actual operation of philanthropic societies or institutions, probably leaving this work for the most part to their wives. At least 60 percent were members, generally officers, of one of the city's leading voluntary societies, and that figure probably understates their actual participation.

None of the men who signed the petition, it is critical to note, was a Catholic. Although about a quarter of Hamilton's population was Catholic, including two-thirds of its laborers, all the members of the business class who called for troops to quell the striking laborers were Protestant. In the group of 161 business-class members there were far fewer Irish- and far more Scottish- and Canadian-born men than in the population as a whole, and almost all of them (129 out of 135) whose religion is known were Protestant.

Hamilton's business class governed all the major activities of the city, whose economic prosperity they had made identical with their own through their investments. They invested the city's money in the railroad and utilities in which they were stockholders. They bought land that the coming of the railroad would make more valuable. They made the public interests of Hamilton and their private economic prospects the same. Nowhere was this more evident than in the public debates that preceded the purchase of a large block of railway stock by the city, an act that required the already hard-pressed city to go even more deeply into debt. Arguing the case at the public meeting that overwhelmingly urged the eager city council to buy the stock, S. B. Freeman predicted, "The property in the City would be greatly enhanced in value, and in this manner we would be paid; and again, if profits resulted from the road, we would possess them." The *we*, of course, was partly the city in its corporate capacity; it was also its business class, who owned most of its land. Pushing the case from another direction, again blending public and private interest in a fortunate harmony, Freeman continued, "Every person acquainted with the position of Hamilton, must be aware, that without this road it would remain an inland town, with little commerce and manufacture; but if this railroad were once constructed, Hamilton would be the great mart for the business of the West, as well as for a large portion of the United States."[38] Freeman conveniently forgot that the Burlington Bay Canal, opened in 1826, had ensured that Hamilton would no longer be an inland town. And he was gloriously overoptimistic about the impact of the railroad on the city's immediate future. Nonetheless many of his fellow citizens shared his hope. Eager for the success that the railroad would bring to their speculations, they saw nothing amiss in using the credit of the city to promote the value of their own investment.

The men who governed the city did not always agree with one another. Indeed as Eric Ricker has shown, squabbling and dissent marked city council meetings, and some local elections were fiercely fought. Although Reformers and Tories often nominated candidates for city council elections and waged highly partisan compaigns, there is no evidence whatsoever that the members of the two parties differed from each other socially or economically or that they had divergent views of the future of the city; virtually all came from the business class. Indeed this characteristic of the city's leadership certainly did not change with early industrialization: only two of the city councilors for 1851, 1861, or 1871 (one in each of the latter two years) might be considered working class. The only notable trend in fact was the increase in the proportion of lawyers on the council from 5 percent to 27 percent between 1851 and 1871. In the former year one-fourth and in the latter one-third were associated with the building trades— sizable minorities that reflected the interests of builders in city policy.

In 1851 the only relationship discovered between actions in city council and some other characteristic was the association of voting on particular issues with the ward a councilor represented. Extremely localized issues apparently divided councilors coming from different parts of the city. But this did not detract from what Eric Ricker, in his detailed analysis of city politics, called "the mutuality of interests, of shared concerns and values, of the city's leadership cadre, and of Reformer and Tory alike."[39]

Young, aggressive Protestant entrepreneurs worked to propel

Hamilton into the mainstream of nineteenth-century social and economic development. Unfortunately their zeal, their confusion of
public and private interests exemplified by their overcommitment of
city resources to the railroad in which they were investors, and their
lack of restraint plunged the city into economic disaster during the depression of the late 1850s. Nor were these men as a group much more
successful with their own than with the city's affairs. The calm, solid
facade of power conveyed by a static group portrait masks the tur-
moil, striving, and disaster that frequently characterized the experience of the individual members of the business class during the 1850s
and early 1860s. Of fifty-one of the 161 whose careers could be traced
through the credit records of R. G. Dun, 40 percent failed in business.
There were a few—but very few—cases of dramatic upward mobility.
Neither staying wealthy nor failing, many men struggled from year to
year, their economic state marginal and fluctuating.[40]

Despite their confusion of the public and the private in their actions
as civic officials, most businessmen were relatively honest. Credit
raters reported questionable moral character in only seven instances
and shady business practices in only seven, and some of these were
duplicates. Mortality among entrepreneurs, honest or not, was
relatively high. Eight of the 51, or nearly 16 percent, died during the
period for which records exist, and they were by no means elderly:
three were in their thirties, two in their forties, and three in their
fifties.

Credit records certainly convey an image of men scrambling an-
xiously for success. Almost a quarter of the men changed partners at
least once during the period of record, some several times. Indeed only
one or two partnerships not based on kinship survived during the
years for which credit ledgers exist. In many instances it is clear that
partnership changes represented attempts to reorganize businesses in a
way that would ease the burden of credit, present a new face to those
from whom credit was sought, or take advantage of new
opportunities. Changing the form of partnership was often a form of
artful dodge.

Kinship was a fact of extraordinary importance in business life.
Some form of kin ties was present in about 40 percent of the enterprises run by Hamilton's business class during its early history. Most
kin ties operated through the male line. In seventeen firms the partners
were brothers, sometimes working together in Hamilton or running
branches of the family firm in various places, with the Hamilton
branch not infrequently dependent on the capital and good name
supplied by the headquarters of the family operation in Scotland or
Montreal. In three cases the tie was between father and son; in only

two was it between a man and his son-in-law, and in only one was a brother-in-law involved. Kinship connections may have been expected to serve as a buffer against the insecurity of commercial life, providing men with a hedge against the failure that happened all around them. However, kinship connections appear to have had little actual impact on business success: eight of the twenty-one firms operated or supported by kin failed, a percentage comparable to that of the group as a whole. In fact in some cases kinship ties may have promoted failure by protecting incompetent or irresponsible family members.

One other factor concerning the business class must be stressed: namely, their speculation in real estate during the commercial phase of the city's history. No matter what the nature of a man's business he was expected to play the land market. Sometimes speculation spurred success; in other instances it was a cause of failure. But no more than stock speculation today, whose equivalent in some ways it was, did speculation in land hurt the reputation of a businessman with those who assured his creditworthiness.

Speculation posed some real problems for the society in which it took place. One of these was a shortage of cash and the fragility of an economy based on the credit of overextended investors. Indeed speculation and business practices knit together the business class. Wholesalers in Hamilton depended on the fortune of the family business in Montreal or abroad or on capital and credit from New York, London, or Glasgow. Wholesalers and importers in turn supplied local retailers with both goods and credit. City merchants extended supplies on credit to their counterparts in the country. Thus when a firm in the country failed, it could shake a commercial house in the city. The entire commercial structure resembled a house of cards, fragile and insecure.[41] That structure could collapse quite easily, as the depression of the late 1850s clearly showed. It was in fact their experience with the fragility of an economy based upon commerce and lacking large-scale commodity production that was an important part of the motivation of Hamilton's business class as they sponsored the industrialization of their city.

Their expectations proved realistic, for industrialization brought a measure of stability to the city's economic life. Contrasting the condition of the city in the "delightful but delusive days of '57" with its solidity in 1871, one observer pointed out: "Then we traded; now we manufacture. Then we over-traded and over-speculated, and sunk into debt and we became bankrupt: now our industry is steady and calculating, and we are getting out of debt. Our prosperity rests not on the money we may make as agents in the transmission of goods from the manufacturer to the consumer which may not be paid for if disaster overtake the latter, but upon manufactures which cannot fail of a market unless disaster should simultaneously overtake every part of the world."[42] The "period of early industrialization," writes J. A. Bryce, "was attended by pressures which exerted . . . a steadying and calming influence on the businesses of the city. Both in their individual capacity and as members of a common class, their position was stabilized and strengthened as that of the urban economy itself."[43]

Bryce selected a sample of early industrialists whom he traced to census, tax, credit, political, and associational records. The product, a collective portrait of the business class in the early industrial city, serves as an important contrast to the picture of the city's commercial leadership. Nonetheless, despite important differences between the experience of commercial and industrial capitalists, the distinction often made between mercantile and industrial leadership is inaccurate; no conflict between the two characterized Canadian development.[44] Bryce traced 122 of the 329 entries in the 1871 industrial census of Hamilton to the records of R. G. Dun and Company, a credit-rating service. Using these records as a base, he was able to link 110 firms and 136 individuals to the population census and/or tax rolls for either 1861 or 1871 or both. These firms constituted a reasonable sample of the larger manufacturing establishments in the city, though the sample did contain relatively small companies too.[45] Especially important is that many of the men listed in the industrial census were "manufacturers or industrialists only in a subordinate capacity, their major concerns and principal pursuits lay in other directions." In fact the primary activity of a third of them was finance, commerce, or "service." Indeed significant overlap marked individual careers. During the 1860s and 1870s over 70 percent were involved in both manufacture and either commerce or finance. The "confusion and fluidity of economic activity," writes Bryce, "belied either a rigid compartmentalization or a specialized 'division of labor.' The distinction often made between a commercial or financial and an industrial class lacks meaning for Hamilton." To the contrary the structure there supports L. R. MacDonald's forceful criticism of the "industrial-mercantile conflict model" of Canadian economic development. "If mercantile capital and industrial capital were separate domains," wrote MacDonald, "the capitalists themselves were unaware of it."[46]

Nonetheless some differences did distinguish the business class of the commercial city from the industrial capitalists studied by Bryce. One of these was age. The leaders of the commercial city were young: 62 percent were less than 40 years old, compared to only 41 percent of the 1871 industrialists. The lower figure for the commercial group probably reflects the relative youthfulness of the city itself. More consistent, with minor exceptions, were statistics for birthplace. With the exception of Germans, who emerged as important during the period, the same nationalities remained over- and underrepresented. The relative representation of the English remained about proportional; that of the Scottish continued disproportionately high and of the Irish Catholics quite low. The native Canadians slipped from a particularly favored to a more or less representative position. The relative advantage of men born in the United States also declined during the period.

Credit raters for the most part found the industrialists, as they had the commercial leaders, to be a sober, industrious group of men. They also noted kin connections in a substantial proportion (38 percent) of cases. Indeed family members provided capital in 60 percent of all cases identified as requiring outside financial assistance. The firms with kin connections, however, were more often medium sized rather than large, a situation very similar to that found by Clyde and Sally Griffen in their study of Poughkeepsie, New York.[47]

Partnerships, in contrast, were common among the larger firms. In fact partnerships were twice as likely as kin-based firms to report large resources and, undoubtedly as a consequence, to be judged good credit risks. Though partnership was common in both the commercial and early industrial city, it was a less stable type of organization in the former; almost a quarter of the firms studied in the commerical period experienced a change of partnership, compared to a much lower proportion of those traced in the industrial period.

The decline in the incidence of partnership change reflected the generally increased stability of the firms in early industrial Hamilton. The "objective evidence" for the 1860s and 1870s, observes Bryce, points to "a substantial mitigation of the insecurity, anxiety, and stress which had earlier informed the daily quest for the rewards and profits of the marketplace." Accompanying that new stability was a general decline in family capitalism, measured by the decreasing proportion of firms with kin ties, a drop from 41 percent in the first sample years to 39 percent, 33 percent, and 26 percent of those linked to the credit registers in 1860-1863, 1868-1873, and 1875-1877.

Kin connections, according to Clyde and Sally Griffen, had proved "a rational adaptation to the insecurity of a highly competitive business environment." Given the greater security of the industrial period, they became less necessary. Besides, as Bryce points out, Bernard Farber has argued that though kin ties helped to "foster the development of enterprise and the process of economic modernization," they proved simultaneously "inherently unstable . . . prey to internal ten-

emphasized the stability of the structure of inequality. The basic relationships between the key components of a capitalist social order that existed in commercial Hamilton persisted relatively unaltered into the early industrial city. The changes that did occur strengthened the distinctions between groups differentially situated on the economic and occupational rank orders. The extent of inequality became if anything more pronounced; but overall stability rather than change emerges as the defining characteristic.

Multivariate analysis is especially useful because it shows clear and direct relationships between occupation and economic standing and reveals their strong, independent effect on other measures, notably the employment of servants. The influence of ethnicity on economic standing or the employment of servants, apparent in descriptive statistics, simply reflects its association with other factors. By itself ethnicity had little independent impact on the structure of inequality. Age had somewhat more, especially in the bifurcation of career lines according to class. However the most important determinant of wealth was occupation.

## Inequality in Buffalo and Hamilton

It is now time to ask whether the structural characteristics of inequality common to Hamilton were peculiar to that city or if patterns there reflected a more general structure of inequality in nineteenth-century urban capitalism. To shed at least some light on that key issue it is useful to examine the situation in Buffalo in 1855.

With only one census it is not possible to study the stability in Buffalo's structure of inequality across time, though given its similarities to Hamilton there is no reason to doubt that the American city's social structure was equally enduring. However it is possible to study one issue in Buffalo about which we can learn relatively little in Hamilton. That is the impact of length of residence on economic rank, employment of servants, and property ownership, for the 1855 New York census records how long each individual had lived in the place where he or she was enumerated. Most historical analyses of social mobility study individuals who remained in the same place between the dates of at least two censuses.[17] The limitations of this approach are clear. It is not possible to know what happened to people who left, who were in this case the majority. Perhaps their experience differed radically from those who remained behind. Using the information on length of residence in the Buffalo census we were able to explore this question and discover if, with other factors controlled, the length of time a person had lived in the city affected his prospects. That information helped make our guesses about the biases in linked populations at least a bit more educated.

First we considered economic rank, defined here as dwelling value per capita, divided into octiles and utilized as a dependent variable.[18] In this analysis occupation and birthplace were combined into one variable in order to reduce interaction between them. The other factor variables were property ownership, length of residence in the city, and age (Table 2.8). Taken together the variables account for a substantial 39 percent of the variation in economic rank, quite close to the amount in Hamilton in 1871. The influence of the most important factor, occupation and birthplace (beta = .52), far exceeded that of any of the others. Land ownership and years in the city ranked next, and the importance of age was negligible.

In general economic rank and occupational rank increased together in a linear fashion. However clear distinctions separated the native born from the Germans and Irish, the two largest immigrant groups. In each occupational rank except the lowest, men born in New York or New England had a higher economic rank than Irish or Germans. In fact birthplace counted so heavily that native-born artisans had a higher economic rank than Irish- and German-born men in clerical or proprietary occupations.

To look more closely at the distinctions between birthplace and occupation we divided the men in each of the four major birthplace groups into separate files and performed analyses using a more elaborate set of occupational categories. This analysis confirms the economic advantage of native-born men in specific occupational categories. The predicted economic rank of a New York-born household head in a middle-ranking nonmanual occupation was 6.8, that of a New Englander 7.2, a German 4.8, and an Irishman 5.5. In the construction trades, to take another example, the comparative predicted ranks were 5.9, 6.2, 3.7, and 4.1. In the same occupations New Englanders usually ranked slightly higher than New Yorkers, and with the exception of laborers Irish ranked higher than Germans. However it was the distinction between native and foreign birth that most effectively distinguished between the economic rank of men in the same occupations.

Birthplace exerted a much stronger influence on economic rank in Buffalo than in Hamilton, though the relationships between occupation and economic rank were quite similar. The reason for the difference lies in the demography of the two cities. Hamilton, like most Ontario cities, not only lacked a large native-born contingent but was dominated by immigrants from Great Britain, who, with the important exception of the Irish, were reasonably heterogeneous in

Table 2.8   Predicted rank (octiles), dwelling value per capita, by birthplace and occupation, property ownership, length of residence, and age, multiple classification analysis: Buffalo, 1855.

*Birthplace/occupational rank*

| Rank | New York | Born in — New England | Germany | Ireland |
|------|----------|-----------------------|---------|---------|
| 1 | 7.2 | 7.0 | 5.8 | 5.7 |
| 2 | 6.7 | 6.8 | 4.9 | 5.6 |
| 3 | 5.8 | 6.2 | 3.9 | 4.3 |
| 4 | 5.4 | 4.9 | 4.4 | 4.4 |
| 5 | 4.4 | 5.0 | 3.3 | 3.1 |

*Property status*
| | |
|---|---|
| Renter | 4.2 |
| Owner | 4.9 |

*Length of residence*
| | |
|---|---|
| 0–1 year | 4.0 |
| 2–5 years | 4.3 |
| 6–9 years | 4.6 |
| 10–14 years | 4.7 |
| 15–19 years | 4.8 |
| 20 or more years | 5.0 |

*Age*
| | |
|---|---|
| Under 25 | 3.9 |
| 25–34 | 4.4 |
| 35–44 | 4.6 |
| 45–54 | 4.6 |
| 55 and over | 4.2 |

*Summary statistics (eta)*
| | |
|---|---|
| Birthplace/occupation | .52 |
| Property | .14 |
| Length of residence | .14 |
| Age | .08 |
| $R^2 = .390$ | |

economic standing. Thus the presence of economically mixed and often very successful Scottish and English immigrants diminished the distinction between native and foreign born that characterized Buffalo. (Indeed another analysis shows that in Buffalo English and Scottish birth had a modest positive effect on economic standing.)[19] Nonetheless it is important to recall that native-born men in Hamilton did very well just as they did in Buffalo, and in both cities the Irish fared quite poorly. Hamilton did not yet have a sizable German population.

Property ownership had a much weaker relationship to economic rank than occupation and birthplace, even though as in Hamilton the economic rank of owners was consistently higher than that of renters. Length of residence in the city also had a clear if not especially strong relationship to economic rank. The major difference separated those who had lived in the city for two to five years from those there six to nine years. However the difference between men who had lived in Buffalo for one year or less and those there twenty years or more was only 1.4 economic ranks.

Age and economic rank had a curvilinear relationship, important because it signified an association between the life cycle and economic welfare. The predicted rank of the youngest and eldest men was lower than that of those at the peak of their earning capacity—men 35 to 44 and 45 to 54. Older men had more difficulty retaining jobs that paid relatively well.

The influence of major social and demographic characteristics on economic rank in Buffalo closely resembled their effect in Hamilton. The greater independent weight of birthplace in Buffalo, the only striking difference, reflected not structural discontinuity between the two cities but rather the origins of their populations.

Parallels in the nature of relationships within the two cities appear also in patterns of servant employment in Buffalo. There 17 percent of households employed a resident domestic servant in 1855, a proportion about midway between that in Hamilton in 1861 and in 1871. The amount of variation in servant employment accounted for by a multivariate analysis (38 percent) is somewhat higher in Buffalo but still roughly similar. In Buffalo economic rank affected the employment of servants more than occupation. Indeed the influence of economic rank was strikingly similar to that in Hamilton in 1861. Though the overall influence of occupation on servant employment was low in Buffalo, the probability that professionals and men in high-ranking commercial occupations would employ a resident domestic resembled the odds for men with similar occupations in Hamilton in 1861 and 1871. As in Hamilton in 1871 a sharp distinction separated the men at the very top of the occupational rank order from those below them. No other group of men was at all likely to employ a resident domestic. Similarly below the seventh octile on the economic rank order wealth added little to the likelihood of servant employment. In fact the largest increment, 30 percentage points, occurred between the seventh and highest octiles. The odds were 54 percent at the top, compared to 24 percent at the seventh and 10 percent in the lowest octile, again a situation resembling that in Hamilton in 1871. In both places keeping servants distinguished a small and wealthy sector of the business class.

Length of residence in Buffalo exerted no influence on the employment of servants and very little on economic rank. However it did have some impact on occupation.[20] First, however, consider the impact of birthplace on occupation. Native birth clearly promoted membership in the highest occupational ranks (Table 2.9). The likelihood that a man born in New England would be in rank 1 was 22 percent and for one born in New York 17 percent, compared to 2 percent for men born in Ireland or Germany. Though the differences were less extreme, similar patterns existed for rank 2. Birthplace mattered less, however, in the skilled trades, and chances of membership in rank 3 were high for Germans (58 percent), compared to 39 percent for New Englanders, 40 percent for New Yorkers, and 36 percent for the Irish. Highest of all were the English, with odds of 61 percent. Birthplace had no influence at all on membership in rank 4 but a very strong impact on rank 5. The likelihood that a man born in Ireland would work as a laborer (rank 5) was 36 percent, compared to 24 percent for one born in Germany, 2 percent for New Englanders, and 6 percent for New Yorkers.

The number of years that a man had lived in Buffalo affected primarily the chances that he would be a laborer. Men who had been in the city twenty years or more were only half as likely to be laborers as those who had lived there two to five years. Length of residence obviously served as one way in which men could rise out of the ranks of laborers.

Literacy had little effect on occupational rank except, as should be expected, that illiterates and semiliterates were more often laborers and less often skilled workers. Age influenced occupational rank selectively, acting only among artisans and laborers. The probability that a man would work as an artisan declined steadily with age from 56 percent of men 18 to 24 to 39 percent of those aged 55 or more. Conversely the likelihood that a man would toil as a laborer increased with age from 14 percent to 35 percent during the same years. These patterns confirm the relationship between the life cycle and earning power also evident in the analysis of economic rank. As they aged working-class men found increasing difficulty competing with younger workers, and a substantial fraction of them drifted from a craft to unskilled labor.[21]

In order to study the important relationships between occupation, age, and length of residence more carefully, we divided the adult male population into groups according to their birthplace (New England,

Table 2.9   Probability of membership in occupational ranks for males ages 18 and over, by selected birthplaces, years in city, literacy, and age: Buffalo, 1855.

| | Occupational rank | | | | | |
| --- | --- | --- | --- | --- | --- | --- |
| | 1 | 2 | 3 | 4 | 5 | N |
| Total population | 6% | 17% | 50% | 7% | 19% | 13,308 |
| *Birthplace* | | | | | | |
| New England | 22 | 31 | 39 | 5 | 2 | 735 |
| New York | 17 | 29 | 40 | 7 | 6 | 1,916 |
| Middle states | 8 | 27 | 49 | 10 | 6 | 194 |
| Canada | 6 | 19 | 55 | 12 | 8 | 326 |
| England | 5 | 17 | 61 | 11 | 9 | 914 |
| Ireland | 2 | 12 | 36 | 12 | 36 | 1,830 |
| Scotland | 5 | 16 | 55 | 10 | 12 | 226 |
| Germany | 2 | 11 | 58 | 7 | 24 | 5,439 |
| Scandinavia | 4 | 15 | 48 | 11 | 18 | 29 |
| West Europe | 4 | 20 | 52 | 6 | 18 | 939 |
| *Years in city* | | | | | | |
| 0–1 | 5 | 14 | 51 | 6 | 25 | 2,774 |
| 2–5 | 0 | 15 | 50 | 7 | 22 | 3,881 |
| 6–9 | 7 | 19 | 51 | 7 | 17 | 2,616 |
| 10–14 | 0 | 19 | 50 | 8 | 15 | 1,396 |
| 15–19 | 7 | 20 | 50 | 8 | 14 | 1,043 |
| 20+ | 0 | 20 | 53 | 8 | 11 | 1,598 |
| *Literacy* | | | | | | |
| Literate | 6 | 17 | 51 | 7 | 18 | 12,549 |
| Semiliterate | 4 | 8 | 31 | 10 | 47 | 241 |
| Illiterate | 5 | 13 | 36 | 10 | 35 | 518 |
| *Age* | | | | | | |
| 18–24 | 3 | 17 | 56 | 9 | 14 | 2,263 |
| 25–34 | 0 | 17 | 53 | 7 | 17 | 4,956 |
| 35–44 | 8 | 17 | 48 | 7 | 20 | 3,478 |
| 45–54 | 8 | 17 | 43 | 6 | 25 | 1,767 |
| 55 and over | 7 | 19 | 39 | 5 | 35 | 844 |

New York, Ireland, Germany) and repeated the analysis of each occupational rank separately for each group.[22] Did number of years resident in Buffalo alter the job prospects of men born in different countries? Did age have a different impact on the work histories of natives and immigrants? Insofar as it is possible to tease life cycle inferences out of cross-sectional data, the answer to both questions is yes, though the complex patterns varied between occupational ranks.

The advantage of New Englanders and New Yorkers was not offset either by years of residence in the city or by age. However, length of residence, though not age, did affect the chances that men born in Germany or Ireland would enter occupational rank 2. The likelihood that a German immigrant resident in Buffalo for two to five years would be in occupational rank 2 was 9 percent, compared to 14 percent for one who had lived there ten to fourteen years. For the Irish the chances improved from 9 percent to 12 percent during the same span of time. Similarly length of residence affected the probability that Irish and Germans, but not New Englanders and New Yorkers, would work in rank 3. For the immigrants the likelihood of skilled work increased with the number of years they lived in the city. Conversely the likelihood that a German- or Irish-born man would work as a laborer decreased with the duration of his residence in Buffalo.

These figures taken by themselves are misleading. The impact of age largely offset the increasingly favorable occupational prospects of Irish and German immigrants who remained in Buffalo. Older German- and Irish-born men were less likely to be artisans and more likely to be laborers. The probability that a man born in Germany would be an artisan decreased from 71 percent among 18- to-24-year-olds to 41 percent among those aged 55 and over. In the same period the odds for a man born in Ireland dropped from 38 percent to 24 percent. Conversely for the same ages the odds that a German- or Irish-born man would work as a laborer increased from 14 percent to 38 percent and from 33 percent to 53 percent, respectively.

For men born in Germany and Ireland length of residence and age acted as two independent and offsetting forces. The increased chances that length of residence would boost occupational rank were counteracted by the handicaps imposed by age. Only relatively young immigrants who had lived in Buffalo for a long time could expect to improve their occupational position, and in 1855 there were not very many of them. Length of residence, however, did have an independent effect on economic rank in certain instances, and one not wholly offset by age. Neither length of residence nor age made any difference to the economic rank of men born in New York or New England. However, among the Irish- and German-born, economic rank increased steadily with the number of years a man had lived in the city. For example the predicted economic rank of a German immigrant who had lived in Buffalo two to five years was 3.7, compared to 4.1 for one there ten to fourteen years. For a man born in Ireland economic rank rose from 3.8 to 4.0 for the same residency periods.

Age did not offset the effect of length of residence on economic rank. The predicted economic rank of Irish and German immigrants did peak and then decline. However the peak occurred at 35 to 44 among Germans and 25 to 34 among the Irish, and in both cases the decline was slight. Indeed age affected economic rank much less than did length of residence. Therefore the effect of age among Irish and German immigrants did not completely wipe out the modest economic gains that prolonged residence in Buffalo probably brought. An immigrant German or Irishman who remained for a decade or more in Buffalo could look forward to a modest improvement in economic well-being, including a more realistic anticipation of property ownership. In fact among long-term residents of the city distinctions in property ownership between men born in different places had virtually disappeared. Property ownership does not fit easily, however, into the general discussion of stratification, because its significance differed for men at various points in the economic and social hierarchies of Buffalo and Hamilton.

What can we conclude about the issues with which we began the discussion of inequality in Buffalo? First, a distinct, identifiable structure of inequality characterized Buffalo. Marked divisions existed between the economic standing of men in different occupations, and within occupations native- and foreign-born men fared differently. Second, the shape of Buffalo's stratification system resembled Hamilton's. Birthplace appeared a more significant factor in Buffalo, but its importance reflected demographic differences between the two cities. Third, the length of time a person had resided in Buffalo definitely influenced his occupation, economic standing, and property status. However the nature of the influence was complex. Length of residence dramatically increased property ownership among all groups, while it made no difference to the employment of servants. It promoted the economic standing of men born in Ireland and Germany but not those from New England or New York. Finally, the handicaps of age offset the otherwise helpful influence of length of residence on the occupational standing of immigrants.

A sharp, solid, relatively fixed structure of inequality counterbalanced the transiency of the people of Hamilton and Buffalo. The social structure of commerical capitalism obviously suited industrial capitalism, for it remained intact during the critical transition in Hamilton's history and, there is every reason to believe, in Buffalo's as well.

This stability underlines the importance of the relationships generated by a system of wage labor in a market economy, as distinct from technology, as the source of social structural patterns. Indeed the social structure of commercial capitalism facilitated the emergence of industry through the coexistence of a mobile wage-labor class easily shifted between various sorts of work and a class in relatively secure control of commerce and production. Capitalists had the power to organize work and to accumulate capital. Workers had little choice but to accept the work that was offered. In this sense it would have been surprising if the structure of inequality had altered. It served its purpose far too well.[23]

## Women, Class, and Industrialization

Not everyone in Hamilton, or in any nineteenth-century city, had an unambiguous place in the two great classes or in a conventional occupational hierarchy. Certainly the largest group that is difficult to place consists of women. Women most often took their class positions from their fathers or husbands. Relatively few of them worked after marriage. Yet though the contours of women's experience remained similar throughout the period, important changes accompanied early industrialization, and these must be explored in their own right.

Between 1851 and 1871 the number of female domestic servants declined from 827 to 807, while the total number of employed women rose from 1154 to 1724. This shift out of domestic service was the most striking aspect of the initial impact of industrialization on the work experience of women. Early industrialization did not increase the proportion of women working but brought about their redeployment into jobs that still could be associated with traditional women's work.[24]

The proportion of women aged 15 or over at work declined slightly from 25 percent to 22 percent between 1851 to 1871. These proportions account only for those women reporting an occupation on the census and undoubtedly exclude a large number who worked casually at home, either assisting husbands or taking in work under the putting-out system. Despite the small decline in the proportion employed, the number of different occupations at which women worked increased throughout the two decades from 41 to 54 to 79. This represents a real increase in variety, since the number of different occupations per each thousand employed women rose from 36 to 39 to 46.

In 1871 industrial employment accounted for about 33 percent of female employment, domestic service for about 47 percent, and various other respectable or genteel jobs for about 15 percent. The remaining 5 percent are difficult to classify. The so-called respectable or genteel jobs were mainly some form of storekeeping or teaching. The proportion of employed females who were servants dropped from 72 percent to 59 percent to 47 percent during the period. Those women who worked in industry generally made clothing of some sort: in 1871 about 25 percent of employed women were dressmakers or tailors or worked in related occupations compared to about 14 percent in both 1851 and 1861.

Thus the work of women during early industrialization remained compatible with traditional female roles. Women made clothing and taught children (the number of female teachers rose from 22 to 83 during the two decades), work as customary as domestic service. As Joan Scott and Louise Tilly have argued a continuity existed between the work of women in pre- and early-industrial society.[25] In fact early industrialization presented young women with a welcome opportunity. They did not leave domestic service because jobs became less available. Instead all the evidence points to a shortage of servants in the late nineteenth century. Norman Macdonald asserts:

> The domestic servant question was a major headache to many a housewife in nineteenth-century Canada—there was in fact a veritable famine in this department of human affairs . . . So desperate was the situation in the 1870s and 1880s, and so persistent the pressure on the emigration officials that the Dominion Government was practically forced to subsidize the immigration of domestic servants . . . Goldwin Smith traced the servant difficulty in part to the "pervading domestic democratic sentiment," in part "to the treatment of the domestic by the mistress, to the dullness of the small households, and to the low rates of wages as compared with other kinds of work."[26]

Young women consciously sought work other than service, for almost anything appeared preferable to the confinement of a domestic. Though their opportunities remained limited and though they continued to be exploited, the job prospects of women widened notably during the first years of industrialization.

The preference of young women for industrial rather than domestic work emerges clearly from a survey conducted by the Minnesota Bureau of Labor Statistics in 1887-1888. The results show that women did not choose the factory primarily for economic reasons; other factors influenced them to leave domestic service whenever alternate opportunities became available.[27] When asked their objections to domestic work only 5 percent of young working women listed "small pay." The severity of the work, the length of the hours, and the assault on their dignity were much more serious objections. Indeed the pay received by domestics in Minnesota did not compare unfavorably with that of most other working women. They received on the average $2.50 to $3 per week plus board and room. The latter cost between $5 and $8 per week, which made the total pay equal to at least

$7.50. By comparison women working in boot and shoe factories earned an average of $6.02, in cigar factories $6.87, and at dressmaking $6.72. Only those in nonmanual work appeared to earn substantially more: clerks $7.04, copyists $9.27, stenographers $13.11, and bookkeepers $13.07. Thus reasons other than the pay undoubtedly did encourage young women to choose the factory over domestic service.[28]

The reluctance of young women to enter service was a puzzle to people at the time. The secretary of the Minnesota Bureau of Labor Statistics claimed; "The question is frequently asked: 'Why do not girls who are paid so poorly in factories apply themselves to housework; there is always a good demand, at fair wages, for capable house girls.' This is . . . the question upon which the public mind is most centered, and one which demands a complete, thorough and comprehensive answer." The answer emerged clearly enough from a comparison of the comments of working girls themselves with those of women who had employed domestics. Employees in a bag factory said, "The hours are too long for the wages paid, and a girl is treated as an inferior." "I do not like to do housework because people look down upon you. Girls who work in factories are more respected." A women in a book bindery asserted, "I would not do housework under any consideration. In the first place, I would not be any one's servant. In the second place, I am not obliged to. In the third place, girls as a rule, are not treated properly. I know a woman who compels her girls to eat in the back shed." An employee in a cigar factory stated succinctly, "Don't like to serve anybody. No Sundays or evenings." With rather more class consciousness a clerk objected, "Consider it degrading the way in which servant girls are generally treated. I object to doing housework for others. Have no objection to doing it at home." Finally, from a shirt maker, "My objection to housework is that in many places a hired girl is much less than a dog; all hours are working hours; never any extra pay for any kind of extra work. Have had many years of personal experience at housework."[29] These objections were not frivolous. They reflected a clear reluctance to be exploited through long hours and a striking concern with personal dignity. It was the combination of drudgery and degradation that caused young women to prefer the factory to domestic service.

By and large, women who employed domestics did not appear to appreciate the complaints of their servants. To them the girls were a shiftless, hedonistic, irresponsible lot. The lack of shared perceptions must certainly have aggravated the unhappiness of domestic servants and often made a bad situation intolerable. Consider the following comments from women who employed servants: "Help quite incompetent; they do not know their proper place. Foreigners come here, having been accustomed to the peculiar methods of living in their native country, and possessing no special training, they are not fitted to do work in American households. Many are not conscientious." "Girls too independent; if they know anything about work it is impossible to govern them." "Do not think it necessary to give a hired girl as good a room as that used by members of the family. She should sleep near the kitchen and not go up the front stairs or through the front hall way to reach her room." "Do not think a girl ought to be allowed to use the front door." "I think I will close my house and board at a family hotel rather than be annoyed any more by the average servant girl." "Servants are too independent, want to receive their company in their parlor and eat at the same table with the family. Don't think it is proper to allow them to do so." "Many servants don't care for steady employment—had rather float around and see different places." "Girls forget they are hired expressly for servants. They want to be the equal of their employers."[30] Is it any wonder that young women preferred the fixed hours, companionship, and relatively impersonal authority of the factory?

Throughout the early industrial period work for a wage remained confined by and large to unmarried, hence young, women. In Hamilton almost no women with husbands at home reported an occupation after marriage in either 1851, 1861, or 1871. However the situation of women who headed their own households differed sharply. In each year about 45 percent of these women were employed, an indication of economic hardship. Indeed young women who headed households worked most often, probably to support their young children. Older women usually had a child of working age at home who could help support the family, and a substantial number took in boarders. With the exception of wealthy widows most adult women who had to support themselves were poor. The index of wealth for women household heads listed on the assessment roll who were not domestics was 46 in 1851 and 40 twenty years later. Almost no women who headed households were domestics, because servants nearly always had to live at their place of employment.

The proportion of widows increased during the depression of the late 1850s but dropped by 1871 to a point lower than it had been twenty years earlier. Still the extent of widowhood should not be minimized. In 1871, 32 percent of all women in their fifties and 61 percent of those aged 60 or over were widows. Most widows and other female household heads had children at home. In 1871 the proportion of the total was 71 percent and 78 percent for those aged 50 to 59. In fact 37 percent of the latter had at least three children living with them, as did more than half of the female household heads in their forties. By and large these women formed a permanently impoverished class, for most widows did not remarry. Widows, however, increasingly headed their own households. The proportion of household heads among widows aged 20 to 24 climbed from 33 percent in 1851 to 56 percent twenty years later; among those 40 to 44 years old the proportion rose from 50 percent to 76 percent. With the expansion of employment opportunity close to home for themselves and their children, widows increasingly were able to make ends meet on their own.

As might be expected some ethnic variation existed in the patterns of female employment. Generally Irish-born Catholic women worked most often. However the largest differences occurred in the proportion of women employed as servants. Age was extremely important: older women were much more likely to have found employment in a capacity other than as a domestic. Among the Irish-born Catholics for instance the proportion employed in service in 1871 ranged from 100 percent of women 15 to 17 to 75 percent of those 18 to 20, 70 percent 21 to 23, and 57 percent 24 to 26. Among Canadian Protestant women of Scottish origin the proportion decreased from 61 percent to 31 percent between the ages of 15 to 17 and 24 to 26. Age aside Irish-born Catholics were by far the most likely to be servants—roughly twice as likely as Canadian-born women of Irish Catholic origin. Interestingly among women over the age of 18 the English-born Anglicans were much more likely to be servants than the Methodists, perhaps reflecting the greater prosperity of the latter. Overall, foreign-born women were rather more likely than the Canadian-born to be domestics.

Despite the increased ability of women to avoid domestic service the relationship between women, work, and wealth remained essentially unchanged during the early industrialization of Hamilton. Job opportunities were still restricted; marriage effectively excluded women from the wage-earning work force during the lifetime of their husbands; and women had virtually no opportunities to accumulate wealth through their own work unless they turned to the one major available form of entrepreneurship, the acquisition of a bawdy house. Indeed if it could be undertaken the study of the nineteenth-century madam—her method of accumulating the capital with which to enter business, her recruitment and management of labor, her relationship with her clientele and community, the trajectory of her career—might more effectively illuminate the relationship between women and capitalism than another shelf of books about the ideal of domesticity and its reflection in the life and writing of genteel authors.[31]

# 3 Transiency

"There is," asserted the New York Board of State Charities in 1881, "a large class of persons that have no fixed habitation, nor follow any steady employment. These engage upon public works, corporation improvements, and the canals when open, and they change from locality to locality, as opportunities for labor of this kind offer." The board did not view migratory workers as innocent casualties of irregular employment opportunity. To the contrary they portrayed them as irresponsible, as burdens on public benevolence. "As a class they are careless of their earnings, and unmindful of their obligations to themselves and to society. When in health, and the kind of employment they seek is abundant, they are independent, but when in sickness and without such employment, they are dependent."[1] That is they turned to charity and the poorhouse.

The migrants seeking temporary employment composed only one class of the dependent poor who streamed into New York State "from influences over which the Board has no control." Indeed the board saw New York as a magnet for the wandering poor. "The pressure of want in other states and countries . . . induces large numbers of these classes to leave their homes and come to this state, while many others are influenced by a desire to obtain the relief offered by our numerous public and private charities. The geographical position of the State, with its extended and exposed borders, and the varied lines of communication leading to it, give them easy access."[2] The "Canadian Dominion," the board pointed out, "has no organized [network] of public charities, and the poor-houses of many of the adjoining States are small and imperfect." Therefore the indigent eagerly availed "themselves during the inclement season, of the generous provision of the county poor-houses and almshouses of this State."[3]

Within ten years the problem of migratory poor achieved national recognition. "Hardly less important than immigration itself, and likely to be more important as time passes," reported a committee of the National Conference on Charities and Correction, "is the passage by myriads, even by millions in the aggregate, of newly arrived or long resident persons from one State to another."[4] Administrators of public charities worried about the consequences of this mass transiency, which they believed had a distinctive class character. As the New York State Board of Charities asserted, "The migration or passage of residents of one State to another State, especially the infirm, feeble and thriftless classes, liable to fall upon the public for support in communities distant from their homes or places of legal settlement, has become an evil of great magnitude in this country, and is everywhere attracting attention."[5]

Public officials were right about the large scale of internal migration. They were less accurate, however, about its class character and about the morals of migrants. Although a disproportionate share of transients were poor, migration was common among every sector of the population, and most people moved not from capricious motives but rather to the rhythms of a capitalist labor market—its periodic dislocations and its shifting demands for wage labor.

The life of Dr. Amariah Brigham shows that mobility characterized the experience of professionals as well as paupers. Brigham was born in New Marlborough, Berkshire County, Masschusetts, on December 26, 1798. His father, a farmer born in the same town, moved to Chatham, in Columbia County, New York, in 1805 and died there in 1809. Brigham, then 11 years old, went to live with his uncle, Dr. O. Brigham, in Schoharie, New York. He hoped to remain there and "follow the profession of his uncle." But his uncle died within a few years, and left with little money Brigham had to "seek a new home and employment."[6]

He lived a short time with his mother in Chatham, but, disliking farm life, went to Albany, where he found work in a book and stationery store and lived with the proprietor. During the three years he worked in Albany Brigham retained his desire to study medicine, and at the age of 18 he returned to live with his mother who had moved back to New Marlborough. There he began to study medicine with Dr. Edmund G. Peet. Brigham spent four years with Dr. Peet, taking time out to teach school during the winter and one year to attend lectures in New York City.

When his professional studies with Dr. Peet ended in 1820, Brigham practiced medicine for a year in Canaan, Connecticut, with a Dr. Plumb. The next year he began to practice by himself in Enfield, Massachusetts, remaining there for two years, until a more attractive opportunity opened in Greenfield, Massachusetts. Brigham spent two years in Greenfield and then traveled for a year in Europe. He returned to Greenfield but stayed only a short time, moving in April 1831 to Hartford, Connecticut, where "he had a large and successful practice, most of it in the line of surgery." Brigham practiced in Hartford until 1837, when he went to New York City and lectured at the Crosby Medical College. However his health was poor, "and not liking the confinement, to which he was so unused, he returned, in October, 1838, to Hartford."

Despite problems with his health Brigham accepted an appointment as the first superintendent of the New York State Lunatic Asylum, which opened in Utica on January 16, 1843. There he remained until his death on September 8, 1849. Brigham was survived by his wife, the former Susan C. Root of Greenfield, Massachusetts, whom he had married in 1833, and by three of their four children.

In fifty-one years Dr. Amariah Brigham had moved between different towns or cities thirteen times. In part his mobility reflected the common accidents of life, the death of a parent or guardian. In part it was related to his life cycle, as he sought first work and then education. And the last moves were primarily professional, as he advanced his career by moving from one place to another until he settled in the eminent position in which he remained for the relatively brief duration of his life.

Brigham's story is not unusual. Indeed it is reinforced strongly by recent historiography. Mass transiency remains the most striking and consistent finding to emerge from quantitative studies of nineteenth-century North America. In almost every place that historians have looked at least half, often two-thirds, of the adults present at the end of one decade were gone ten years later, and rates based on shorter periods reveal a stream of people constantly flowing through cities. Although 363,000 people lived in Boston in 1880 and 448,000 in 1890, during the decade about 1.5 million people in all had actually lived there.[7] When Victorians sought a symbol of progress they often chose the steam engine; had they wanted a metaphor for their cities they could have found none more apt than the railroad station.

## Rates of Persistence

The rate of population persistence in the nineteenth century, Stephan Thernstrom has observed, varied little from place to place or with economic conditions.[8] He finds most striking not the differences in the rates of persistence reported by historians but their general similarity. Given the impossibility of making precise comparisons between the studies on whose findings he comments, Thernstrom has drawn the most reasonable conclusion. All the historical studies rest on the

sions and divisiveness whose active agency was family itself." Perhaps the capitalists of the early industrial era shed kin ties in business with relief.[48]

The increased stability of firms in the early industrial city is also evident in the decline in rates of failure. Recall that the failure rate of capitalists in the commercial city had been at least 37 percent. This proportion was halved among those whose careers were traced from 1860 onward. Among the latter 83 percent of credit ratings reported the firm doing reasonably well or improving. Increased stability undoubtedly had a variety of causes. One of them may have been the greater security offered by manufacturing as opposed to commerce. Capital, moreover, probably accumulated more rapidly in manufacturing enterprises. Indeed the proportion of firms in Bryce's sample listing their means as "ample" more than doubled during the period of study, while those assessed as "small," "limited," or "none" shrank by almost 40 percent. Perhaps too the decline of family capitalism encouraged a more efficient and adventuresome use of resources.

A decreased emphasis on capital accumulation through real estate speculation probably contributed as well to the greater stability of the business class. Early credit raters had commented approvingly on real estate speculation as a form of economic activity. However over time their comments became more guarded. Indeed the credit raters now viewed "playing the land market" with "a novel and decided disapproval." For they feared "overextension and reduced liquidity." In their judgment, "prudent investment, preferably in some industrial venture, or in quality securities, was invariably pronounced an auspicious decision; speculation, even among the largest and richest of the city's businessmen, was just as regularly condemned."[49]

Land speculation apparently did decline during the city's early industrialization, for ownership of vacant land became less concentrated, and building lots were more widely diffused among people less likely than earlier owners to speculate. In 1852 the 6 percent of owners of vacant lots with more than ten properties controlled 64 percent of all vacant land in Hamilton. By 1881 the proportion of vacant lot owners with more than ten lots had dropped to 3 percent, and they now controlled a far smaller share (39 percent) of the city's undeveloped property. From a different perspective the characteristics of the original owners of the city's lots points to the presence of speculators among them: 26 percent were in the development industry, 27 percent were rentiers, and 25 percent lived outside Hamilton. Only 5 percent were skilled artisans. By contrast in 1881 the share of the final owners of the same properties in the development industry had dropped to 19 percent, the proportion of rentiers had fallen to 10 percent, and the share of owners who lived outside Hamilton had dipped to 8 percent. Simultaneously the proportion of skilled artisans among the owners had more than tripled, climbing to 16 percent.[50]

Despite their greater stability and their shift away from real estate speculation the industrialists shared many of the characteristics of the city's leadership in its commerical era. Both groups of course were wealthy. Moreover the industrialists retained the commercial leaders' intense involvement in the political and associational life of the city. During the 1860s and 1870s almost one-quarter of the group held elected municipal office, and the sample also included a member of Parliament and future Dominion senator. At least 82, or 63 percent, "filled executive or highly visible participatory positions in one and generally more of the city's voluntary organizations." In all about 70 percent of the sample occupied leadership positions in either political or associational life.[51]

The businessmen of the commercial and early industrial city composed an overlapping core of leadership controlling all its major activities. Similar in background and outlook they formed a stable group that guided the city through the transition from commercial to industrial capitalism. Throughout this momentous development, the "general patterns of dominance and authority" within the city scarcely changed.[52]

Still, writes Bryce, "if the fundamental structure was not significantly changed during the period, the 'experience of power' decidedly was." Reflecting the growth in the size of their operations and their increased stability, businessmen revealed "a new confidence" in interclass relations, especially as they confronted labor. Compare the anxiety with which the city's leaders confronted the striking laborers of 1851, their fear of riot and call for troops, with the behavior of the sewing machine manufacturer Tarbox during the strike that accompanied the nine-hour movement in 1872. On June 3 a group of workers gathered outside the Wanzer sewing machine company in order, so it was said, to intimidate employees who had returned to work under the old ten hour system. "Presently, Mr. Tarbox, one of the first offenders in the eyes of the nine hour league men, lit a cigar and sauntered out of his office into the street and cooly walked through the crowd, apparently perfectly unconcerned, 'puffing his Havana,' as he walked along entirely unmolested, although one would have imagined in the first instance that broken bones would have been his portion. After reconnoitering for a time he walked back into his office to await events and abide the consequences." As Bryce comments, "A caricature of the class struggle . . . the episode did not exaggerate the underlying 'sense of power' the behaviour and posture

of the business class exuded throughout the affair . . . the early industrial period witnessed the city's business community, in its relations
with the working class, in firm and settled command."[53]

## The Working Class

The self-confident if internally stratified business class confronted a
working class pulled by the same forces toward both increased
diversity and cohesion. Although the most prosperous members of the
working class—foremen in large plants and engineers—earned more
than young clerks, by and large sharp distinctions in economic rank
also separated members of each class. Within the working class itself
the fundamental economic distinction differentiated unskilled from
skilled workers. This difference remained as sharp in the early industrial as in the commercial city. In Hamilton in 1851 the proportion of
skilled workers in the lowest 40 economic percentiles had been 36 percent and 44 percent in 1871, compared to 70 percent and 77 percent
of the laborers. Similarly in 1873 wages for skilled workers in Hamilton ranged generally from $1.75 to $2.50 per day. Laborers earned
only about $1.00 or $1.25. Likewise in Buffalo very many more unskilled than skilled workers clustered in the lower economic ranks,
and in New York State as a whole in 1874 wages for skilled workers
generally ranged from $2.12 to $3.50 per day, while laborers earned
around $2.00.[54]

Even though early industrialization did not erase the distinction in
pay between skilled and unskilled labor, it did reshape the work
setting. The "increase in manufacturing's scale and specialization progressively undermined the previously sharp distinction between artisan and laborer for men who remained in manual work."[55] In Hamilton, insofar as we can estimate, the size of the average establishment
increased from about five to seventeen employees during the twenty
years between 1851 and 1871, and the proportion of the work force in
establishments with ten or more employees grew from about 24 percent to 83 percent. Some plants had already grown quite large: the
Wanzer sewing machine factory employed about 275 hands; S. D.
Sawyer's agricultural implement factory about ninety; and the Great
Western Railway 984. Indeed, by 1871, 53 percent of the manufacturing work force labored in plants with fifty or more employees.[56]

Large manufacturing establishments not only brought wage workers together in large groups on a daily basis; they also confronted
workers with an altered structure of authority. Foremen had been
interposed between proprietors and workers. Ultimately authority
emanated from a more distant and impersonal source. To what extent

skilled wage workers in different industries still retained control of the process of production—whether they determined how and at what pace work would be done—remains largely unknown. Nonetheless even if the final process in the alienation of the worker from the control of his labor had not yet been completed, two fundamental aspects of the work setting—its size and authority relations—had been altered in ways that touched the daily lives of most working people.[57] These developments provided the structural underpinning for the development of a collective consciousness on the part of working people, for they facilitated the interaction of working people with each other and detached them from the paternalism that might at one time have fostered an identification of workers with their employers. Yet simultaneously the same increased size and altered authority relations promoted the diversification of the work force in ways that worked against the development of class consciousness.

Theodore Hershberg and his associates found striking differences in the pay of skilled and unskilled workers in industries of different size. Throughout the industries of Philadelphia in 1880 skilled workers generally earned more than unskilled. However within the same industries both skilled and unskilled men earned more in larger factories. For example in the iron and steel industry in 1880 skilled mechanics working in firms with one to five employees earned $1.97 per day; those in the firms with six to fifty employees were paid an average of $2.30, and those in the largest firms $2.48. Among unskilled workers in the same industry average daily wages increased across the three categories of firm size from $1.25 to $1.35 to $1.42. Note here not only the discrepancy between firms of different sizes but also that the unskilled workers in the largest factories earned less than the skilled in the smallest. Also observe that the variation in pay by firm size was much greater in the case of the skilled than the unskilled workers.[58]

Within firms distinctions existed not only between skilled and unskilled work but between the different grades of skilled workers as well. By the 1870s all over North America fine distinctions in job titles and identifiable job hierarchies had emerged within industry. Consider, for instance the situation in some Canadian factories reported by Edward Young.[59] In a locomotive factory in Kingston twenty-five different job titles existed. Men in these various categories were paid at at least thirteen different rates. In an agricultural implement factory in Whitby there were sixteen different job titles and seven different rates of pay. In January 1863 in just the inside locomotive department of the Great Western Railway 264 employees had thirty-nine different job titles. (Aside from this department, the mechanical pay rolls of the

Great Western in Hamilton alone also include two hundred employees in the outside locomotive department, 265 in the car locomotive department, seven in the mechanical office, which supervised the works, and one draftsman. The superintendent was paid a handsome $92.60 fortnightly.)

The differences in pay were substantial. In the Kingston locomotive factory they stretched from $.50 to $1.25 per week for apprentices to $15 a week for foremen. The three grades of machinists (best, ordinary, inferior) earned $9.60, $8, and $7 per week, respectively. Blacksmiths were paid $10.50, their helpers $6.50. Pattern makers, a well-paid group everywhere, earned $12 per week. In the agricultural implement factory in Whitby they earned $15 a week, compared to $10 for machinists, $7 for laborers, and $2.50 for "apprentices or boys."

Rates varied at the Great Western too. One person in each major skilled category (fitter, turner, smith, boilermaker) was paid $3 per day. The other workers in the same categories earned considerably less. One fitter was paid $2.25 per day; seven more earned $2, and the remaining forty-eight were paid less—$1.60 to $1.70 was typical, though a number earned only $1.25. As a group machinists were paid much less, earning between $.875 and $1.50 per day. The fifteen laborers were paid even more poorly on the average—generally $1 or $1.10—as were the thirty-two handymen. Not surprisingly the worst paid were the thirty-nine "lads," whose daily wage ranged between $.25 and $1.10, with most well under $1.

Not only actual salary but number of days worked affected the income of wage workers. Thus at the Great Western some men with a lower rate of pay actually earned more than others with a higher rate who were employed for fewer days. Between January 4 and January 17, 1863, for instance, the fitter who worked 13.5 days at $2 per day earned $27, compared to $23.63 for the one who worked 10.5 days at $2.25. Indeed the number of days worked during this fortnight varied considerably within each category of employment, and it is likely that few men could count on working as often as they wished. Among the smiths, to take one case, one man worked 13 days, one 12, one 11, four 10.25, nine 10, two 9.5, two 9.75, and one 5.5.

Differences in pay were thus substantial. The difference between $7 and $12 per week, for instance, represented half the rent of a six-room house in Hamilton, 50 pounds of beef, or over 8 bushels of potatoes. It would buy over half a ton of coal, perhaps two pairs of men's boots, or over thirty-one yards of medium quality flannel cloth. Thus there existed within the working class substantial differences in purchasing power and by implication in standard of living. The latter of course varied with family size and the addition of extra income provided by working children. Nonetheless it is reasonable to assume that very sharp distinctions in economic well-being existed among working-class families with similar composition.

It is difficult to estimate the economic standing of individual working men on the basis of job title alone. Certainly anyone called a laborer would very likely earn less than someone with a title indicating a skill, though figures for different types of factories in New York State make it clear that substantial variation characterized the income of laborers too. Also men with certain jobs—foremen, engineers, first-class machinists, pattern makers—very likely earned wages that were above the average. But for most the particular industry and the size of the firm made a substantial difference in the wages received by men with the same occupational title.

Specific variations aside, the fact is that an economic hierarchy did exist within the working class. The elaboration of occupational specializations associated with distinctions in pay created what John Foster has called "limited ladders of success," which restricted working-class militancy. "The most important instrument of mass control" exercised by ruling-class authority, claims Foster, "seems to have been provided by the sub-grouping process itself. Sub-grouping was, in essence, the way people accomodated social 'unfairness'—by creating small-scale success systems of their own." The leaders of the sub-groups (the "labor aristocracy"—foremen or union leaders) held their authority "fairly directly from the ruling class" and "acted, then, as link-men in the overall political system . . . the sub-grouping process, besides allowing people to accomodate deprivation, functioned as an authority system by which labour could be tied politically to the ruling-class."[60]

The situation of the working class in the late nineteenth century was thus marked by contradictions. Industrialization gathered working people into factories and established the structural preconditions for the emergence of class consciousness. At the same time within industries sharp differences in income separated working people from each other and created "limited ladders" that they could aspire to climb and whose uppermost rungs brought within reach if not the affluence of an industrialist or professional at least the satisfaction of an income on which a man and his family could live with modest comfort.

Is the image of internal stratification within the business and working classes consistent with the notion of a two-class society? The answer is yes, for three reasons. First, despite the elements that complicate the portrait, the image of an urban social order dominated by two ascendant classes coincides with the way in which representatives of both capital and labor described the world in which they lived. Second, empirical evidence proves class to be a powerfully discriminating variable on a number of key features of social structure. When objective circumstances and perception coincide, they provide powerful evidence about the character of social organization. Third, class is also a theoretical question. It is not to be confused with stratification. To grasp this point it is necessary to dwell briefly on the definition of class and the underpinnings of the two-class model.

## Defining Class

The two-class model is not reductionist, nor does it strip the notion of social structure of its complexity. Rather a sharp distinction is made between class and stratification. Class is an analytic category with which the social structure is defined. Stratification describes the divisions within the class structure, the complex rank ordering of people in each class such as by wealth, ethnicity, and property. Certainly all societies dominated by two classes are not identical, for social formations manifest different expressions of class. In North America, for instance, the intersection of class and ethnicity is a key problem for social historians.

The question of class has rarely been tackled by American historians. That is because American historiography has for the most part reflected American sociology. Class has been confused with stratification and classes defined more or less arbitrarily as bumps along a rank order. The distinction most often used to differentiate classes has been that between white and blue collar, a characteristic that may be appropriate for describing social distinctions (though not a theoretical criterion of class) in the twentieth century but that cannot be used indiscriminately to describe stratification in an earlier period.[61]

It is this failure to come to grips with the underlying properties of the social structure that has undercut most of the recent American historiography on social mobility. Aside from the field of labor history, which is shedding its preoccupation with the history of unions and exploring broader topics, the historiography of American social structure in the last ten or twelve years has been dominated by the question of social mobility: Was the rags-to-riches theme a reflection of experience or a myth? Did men commonly move from manual to nonmanual occupations? Did unskilled laborers often manage to improve their occupational position? Have there been important distinctions between the mobility experience of men from different ethnic groups?

Those questions were prompted by a major concern: the issue of whether American society has become more or less open, whether industrialization closed or broadened opportunity. Although at the moment that issue does not seem very urgent or even particularly well phrased, it was an important concern of social science in the early 1960s, when the mobility studies received their initial impetus. Underlying the question, however, is an important assumption: that the good society is to be defined in terms of individual opportunity and judged by the extent to which individuals are able to rise as far as their talents may take them. This assumption presupposes a highly unequal social structure in which able individuals climb. The good society is the one that removes artificial barriers to their achievement.[62]

In America mobility has rarely been evaluated as a group rather than an individual process. The reduction in the disparities between groups by and large has not been used as the yardstick with which to measure the quality of social experience. Indeed the extent to which individual rather than collective mobility has held scholars' attention is revealed by the way it shaped the questions about social structure asked even by historians of the left. Parenthetically its pervasive hold on national values is revealed at present in the hostility toward affirmative action, which is the first sustained attempt in American history to foster the mobility of particular groups, if necessary at the expense of individuals.

American historical writing about social structure has been hampered by the uncritical acceptance of individualistic assumptions about social justice and by the adoption of contemporary social-scientific categories such as the distinction between manual and non-manual labor. It has been hindered as well by two other factors. One has been the avoidance of a serious theoretical encounter with class. Because of their lack of theory mobility studies are increasingly criticized as unilluminating compilations of statistics of occupational change in local communities. In part those criticisms are justified, because most studies do not attempt to analyze the social structure in which movement takes place, to discern its underlying properties and dynamic principles. Yet there is a danger that valuable data and a useful technique will be rejected, ignored, or undervalued because their theoretical potential has not been demonstrated adequately. This would be unfortunate because the quantitative analyses of social mobility done in the last decade or so have provided a rich body of data whose interpretation should reorient the study of American history. Unfortunately there is a problem with the data themselves, which is the second factor that has hampered progress in the field. Most of the data have been collected in ways not strictly comparable.

Historians have employed different classifications and different methods of tracing people over time. These differences, it has been shown, can result in very large discrepancies between the results of different studies. The conclusions of existing studies of different communities can thus be compared only roughly and with great caution.[63]

In one sense we are issuing the familiar plea for more research with better methods grounded in theory, and few practitioners of social history would disagree. To some extent most historians at work in the field during the last several years are critical of their own earlier research and eager to use what they have learned in new and better studies. Indeed the work of the last decade or so is best regarded as pioneering and preliminary—the opening of a new field. Nonetheless it must be admitted that much of the work in the field has been imitative rather than cumulative. Stephan Thernstrom in his marvellous book *Poverty and Progress* showed how a quantitative approach to the history of social mobility can help uncover the experience of common people, address questions of social justice, and correct the ahistorical bias of much social science. Much of the work that followed his lead did not build on his initial achievement by exploring its theoretical and methodological limitations as well as its strengths. Rather it was often repetitive. As the initial reproductions have appeared in recent years, the field has seemed stalled and a reaction has set in. It has become commonplace to attack mobility studies and the use of quantification in social history.

The backlash is not constructive. What it threatens is a return to descriptive and narrative history justified by the perceived failure of quantification. The consequences of such a development would extend beyond the understanding of social history in and of itself. Whatever its faults quantification encourages movement toward an analytic, structural view of social experience. That type of view reflects the belief that the dimensions of social and human experience are not random, the result of luck or genetic superiority. To the contrary, the relations between inequality, exploitation, bureaucracy, and the pain and contradictions of private life are neither accidental nor ephemeral. They are integral to our contemporary social formation and only properly understood historically. A view of history that separates these developments from each other and relegates them to chance, individual volition, temporary coalitions, or some nebulous force such as social complexity supports a contemporary orientation toward social and political issues that rejects the reality and permanence of class, the structured inequality of social experience, and that ultimately leaves every person responsible for his own failure. It must be made plain to those who consider themselves politically on the left but who are skeptical about analytic and quantitative approaches to the past that this is what the politics of historiography are all about.

It is easiest to state what class is not. As Anthony Giddens stresses, class is not an entity. It has no physical dimensions, boundaries, or legal status. Thus it differs from a school, a hospital, or a club. Nor is it a stratum or even a system of stratification. "Stratification, comprising what Ossowski terms a gradation scheme, involves a criterion or set of criteria in terms of which individuals may be ranked descriptively along a scale . . . The divisions between strata, for analytical purposes, may be drawn very precisely, since they may be set upon a measurement scale—as with 'income strata.' The divisions between classes are *never* of this sort."[64] Classes are the fundamental groups within a social structure; their identity is determined by the underlying properties of a mode of production, defined by David Harvey as "those elements, activities and social relationships which are necessary to produce and reproduce real [material] life." In each society, in other words, social, economic, and technological relationships cluster together in distinctive ways. Though distinctive, modes of production are not exclusive. One mode usually dominates a given time and place, but others—either lingering, older formations or new, ascendant ones—often will be found at the same time. As Harvey writes, "one historical epoch is not the exclusive domain of one mode of production, even though a particular mode may be clearly dominant. Society always contains within itself potentially conflicting modes of production." In fact different historical eras derive much of their distinct identity from "the conflict between different modes of production."[65]

Within a mode of production the cluster of social relations that unites people into classes has certain common properties in various theories. Stanislaw Ossowski listed four of them: (1) They are ordered vertically. (2) The interests of the classes are permanent. (3) People within them share a sense of class identity, which may take several forms. At one extreme it may simply be what Giddens terms *class awareness*, a realization "and acceptance of similar attitudes and beliefs, linked to a common style of life, among the members of the class." At the other pole it may become a shared and militant sense of exploitation. (4) Classes are relatively isolated from each other. Individuals from different classes have minimal social contacts, and membership within them is relatively permanent. This, asserts Ossowski, "is the behavioral criterion of class divisions."[66]

Despite these common properties the class structure of any given society varies with the mode of production that generates it. Indeed the class structure in any given place is often extremely complex because it must be conceived in terms of parallel structures generated by the coexistence of different modes of production.[67] The analytic problem and the potential for conflict vary, of course, with the size and strength of the alternative modes. In Europe, for instance, the competition between feudal and capitalist modes of production is a classic example. In British North America the absence of a feudal tradition eliminated for all practical purposes the conflict played out in Europe. Here the struggle waged in the late eighteenth and early nineteenth century took on a different form, one not yet adequately analyzed by historians. It consisted of the competition between capitalism and a mode of production dominated by independent yeomen farmers creating primarily their own subsistence and independent artisans producing goods for local consumption. These people did exist, of course, in the context of a metropolitan market economy dominated by merchants, but the emergence of the essential features of capitalism were for a time checked by the abundance of land, the shortage of labor, and the ease with which men could establish themselves on the land or in a trade.[68]

Two characteristics distinguish capitalism, according to Giddens: "(1) Production is primarily oriented to the realization, or search for the realization, of profit accruing to privately owned capital. (2) This process is organized in terms of a market upon which commodities, including labor itself, are bought and sold according to standards of monetary exchange." Capitalism, in Maurice Dobb's words, was "not simply a system of production for the market . . . but a system under which labour-power had 'itself become a commodity' and was bought and sold on the market like any other object of exchange." These are the two basic components from which the class structure of capitalism derives.[69]

Capitalist society possesses two classes because most people share a common relationship to both of its key aspects: the private ownership of capital and the sale of their labor as a commodity. Most people who sell their labor do not own capital, and those who own capital are the purchasers of labor. Immense complications accompany any attempt to use this theoretical distinction to describe actual societies. The situation is perhaps most difficult today, given the rise of a nonowning managerial group and the expansion of white-collar work.[70] In the mid-nineteenth century however neither managers nor bureaucrats yet existed in large enough numbers to create a serious difficulty for class analysis, and a good case may be made for their inclusion in the business class. The more difficult problem concerns artisans, independent proprietors who produced goods but did not employ labor. Usually these are treated as a transitional class, remnants of a social order replaced by the hegemony of capitalism. They are understood as part of the class sturcture of a mode of production that capitalism replaced.[71]

The problem for the historian of nineteenth-century cities is only partially simplified by the use of theory. Mid-nineteenth-century cities may have had three classes: a business class and a working class, reflecting ascendant forces, and an artisan class belonging to an older social order. Or it could be the case that by the mid-nineteenth century capitalism had estalished its hegemony so thoroughly that craftsmen by and large worked for wages even prior to the mechanization of production. This is the case that we argue here.

The nature of occupational designations on censuses makes difficult the resolution of the artisan question. Men were listed simply with an artisan's title: shoemaker, tailor, or carpenter. Rarely is it possible to determine if they were masters or employees. Fortunately the problem is not insurmountable, and we have overcome the limitation of census designations and identified master artisans and manufacturers, a step essential to the construction of our model. The distinction between masters and employees became the pivotal division in a new system of occupational classification. First we divided occupations into two classes: the business class and the working class. Within each class we identified a number of groupings of individuals engaged in different sorts of work. The business class consists of those individuals who owned the means of production or those whose interests and aspirations identified them with the owners. The groups are professionals and rentiers; agents and merchants (vendors of commodities); proprietors of service establishments and semiprofessionals (vendors of services); business employees (largely clerks, whose identification with the business class is clear from their social origins, career prospects, and from an abundant literature from the period); government employees (a miscellaneous and not entirely satisfactory grouping); and masters and manufacturers. The working class consists of four groups: skilled workers (people with an artisan's title); transport workers; "other" working class (a miscellaneous group assumed to be part of the working-class social universe—peddlers, waiters, hucksters, and so on); and laborers.

In view of late-nineteenth-century and twentieth-century connotations of clerical work, it appears ludicrous to include clerical workers in the business class. However here we are dealing with the mid-nineteenth century, prior to the feminization of office work, the elaboration of very many organizational bureaucracies, or the widespread existence of department stores and supermarkets. In that period clerical work had a different meaning. Sons of men in the business class often began their working lives in clerical occupations, and the mobility of men out of clerical work and into proprietorship was quite high. For many men clerical work was the initial phase of a career in commerce. Clerks were paid a salary, not a wage; this was a crucial distinction at the time. It indicated that they could expect to work throughout an entire year and did not experience the seasonal fluctuations to which men paid daily wages were subjected. Indeed the distinction between the two types of work was the basis on which Carroll Wright divided the subjects of his extensive survey of standards of living in Massachusetts in 1875. To Wright the employed working population consisted primarily of two groups: those paid wages and those paid salaries. The latter, his investigation revealed, earned substantially more than the former. The distinction, that is, was not merely between method of payment and security of employment; it translated itself into standards of living that quite clearly separated the families of salaried business employees from those of manual wage workers.[72]

The case for including nineteenth-century clerks in the business class has been put especially well by the late Harry Braverman. "The place of the handful of clerks in the early industrial enterprise—and there were generally fewer than a half-dozen in even the largest firms—was semi-managerial," wrote Braverman. In various studies clerks emerge as "assistant manager, retainer, confidant, management trainee, and prospective son-in-law." Of course, Braverman notes, the condition and prospects in life" of many clerks hardly exceeded "those of dock workers." Overall, however, "in terms of function, authority, pay, tenure of employment (a clerical position was usually a lifetime post) prospects, not to mention status and even dress, the clerks stood much closer to the employer than to factory labor."[73] For example, between January 4 and 14, 1863, 793 men were included on the Great Western Railway mechanical payrolls. Of these only seven were clerks, of whom six worked with one superintendent in the mechanical office separate from the various other departments they supervised. The seventh worked in the inside locomotive department in Windsor, undoubtedly to handle the paper work at that branch of the company's operations.[74]

Additionally we identified groups that did not fit easily or properly into the class structure as defined here. One was women, whom we have divided into female domestics and women with other occupations. Economically and socially they might have been placed with the working class, but it is important to study women's experience separately.[75] Two other groups have agricultural occupations: agricultural proprietors and nonproprietors. The class position of agriculturalists is not clear. By separating them out we retain the possibility of studying the distinct social structure of rural areas.[76] In the cities of course there were few agriculturalists, but this classification should be applicable in rural as well as urban areas. Finally a small group of people with occupational designations that did not fit into any category we called simply *other*.

## Class: Empirical Evidence

In the remainder of this chapter we offer evidence that supports our contention that Hamilton and Buffalo—and, we suppose, most other North American cities of this period—may be described as dominated by two classes. Let us begin with summary relationships. In the case of Hamilton: Did significant differences exist between members of the work force grouped in various ways? Were the differences in economic measures between classes significant? Were there greater differences between masters and skilled wage workers than between trades? To answer these questions we utilized four groupings: the occupational classification based on class and described above; the work force divided into business and working classes with others omitted; masters and skilled wage workers only; trades—masters and skilled wage workers divided into twenty-one major trade groupings. In the latter the distinction is between the trades; no distinction is made between owners and employers. It is not possible to give approximate ratios of masters to workers within trades. Not all the non-proprietor blacksmiths, for instance, worked for master blacksmiths. Many worked for the railroad or foundries. The same is true in a variety of other trades as well. Thus any attempt to use these figures to establish ratios within trades would be inaccurate. Overall the ratio of masters and manufacturers to male skilled wage workers in Hamilton in each year and in Buffalo hovered at around 1 to 10.

It is not yet possible to state when urban social structure came to be dominated by two classes—when, that is, most men became wage workers. From the scattered evidence available it appears likely that the transition occurred between the mid-eighteenth and the mid-nineteenth century. Carl Kaestle showed that the proportion of laborers in the assessed population of New York City increased from 6 percent in 1796 to 27 percent in 1855. And as late as 1819, also in New York, there was only about one master artisan for every 3 journeyman wage workers.[77]

Our question must be phrased in this way: Was the distinction between groups greater than the distinctions within them? Was there for instance more difference in wealth between masters and skilled wage workers than within each of the two categories? A simple average or any other measure of central tendency does not answer that question reliably. Two groups might have different averages, but those averages might result from a few extreme cases and mask an overall similarity in the distribution within each category. The statistical test that does give a precise answer is called an analysis of variance. It produces a statistic, the F-ratio, which is derived from comparing the distributions within and between categories. If the F-ratio is significant (that is if the odds are very low—in the standard employed here no more than 1 to 1000—that the results could have happened by chance), then the difference between the groups is greater than the difference within them.

If our contention that Hamilton was a two-class society is correct, then the distinction between classes on critical measures should be greater than the differences within them. Similarly the distinctions between masters and skilled wage workers should be significant; the distinctions between trades with no separation of masters and workers should not. Consider, first, assessed wealth (Table 1.1). In general the relationships between assessed wealth and various groupings were quite stable throughout the twenty-year period, though more variation did exist in the depression year 1861. For 1871 the F-ratio is significant in three out of the four groupings. It was not significant at the .001 level for individual trades, which shows that little variation in assessed wealth divided trades when masters and employees were not separated from each other. This provides critical evidence for our contention that the two groups should be distinguished from each other. That is, it was relationship to the ownership of productive enterprises rather than membership in a specific trade that counted in the determination of economic rank.

In both Hamilton and Buffalo the majority of the variation in economic rank attributable to occupation was in fact accounted for by class. In Hamilton in 1871 the sixteen occupational categories accounted for 24 percent of the variation in economic rank between individuals. Class, however, as measured by the two-class model, accounted for 18 percent, or 75 percent of the variation seemingly attributable to occupation. In Buffalo in 1855 the sixteen occupational categories accounted for 11 percent, while class accounted for 9 percent of the variance in dwelling value per capita. This means that in both cities most of the individual variation that seemed to stem from occupational position was in fact the product of class. Although significant differences in wealth separated the sixteen occupational groups, most of those differences stemmed from the position of those occupational groups within the class structure.

Table 1.1  Measures of association of occupational variables and economic standing, age, property ownership, servant employment, and persistence: Hamilton, 1851–1871, and Buffalo, 1855.[a]

| Dependent variable | Independent variable | Eta | Eta$^2$ | F | Significance |
|---|---|---|---|---|---|
| *Hamilton, 1851* | | | | | |
| Assessed wealth[b] | Occupation | .474 | .225 | 40.158 | .001 |
| | Social class | .361 | .130 | 145.761 | .001 |
| Age | Occupation | .265 | .070 | 10.453 | .001 |
| | Social class | .136 | .018 | 18.245 | .001 |
| Property[c] | Occupation | .171 | .029 | 4.182 | .001 |
| | Social class | .033 | .001 | 1.085 | NS[e] |
| Servants[d] | Occupation | .404 | .163 | 26.953 | .001 |
| | Social class | .372 | .138 | 156.136 | .001 |
| *Hamilton, 1861* | | | | | |
| Assessed wealth | Occupation | .295 | .087 | 18.642 | .001 |
| | Social class | .168 | .028 | 40.039 | .001 |
| Age | Occupation | .294 | .086 | 18.394 | .001 |
| | Social class | .227 | .052 | 74.458 | .001 |
| Property | Occupation | .148 | .022 | 4.351 | .001 |
| | Social class | .023 | .000 | 0.749 | NS[e] |
| Servants | Occupation | .405 | .164 | 38.221 | .001 |
| | Social class | .354 | .126 | 196.779 | .001 |
| *Hamilton, 1871* | | | | | |
| Assessed wealth | Occupation | .493 | .243 | 98.327 | .001 |
| | Social class | .425 | .181 | 473.734 | .001 |
| | Sector | .102 | .010 | 2.125 | .002 |
| | Rank | .442 | .196 | 208.880 | .001 |
| Age | Occupation | .313 | .098 | 33.333 | .001 |
| | Social class | .217 | .047 | 106.059 | .001 |
| | Sector | .195 | .038 | 8.052 | .001 |
| | Rank | .174 | .030 | 26.755 | .001 |
| Property | Occupation | .175 | .031 | 9.622 | .001 |
| | Social class | .079 | .006 | 13.079 | .001 |
| | Sector | .164 | .027 | 5.586 | .001 |
| | Rank | .099 | .010 | 8.474 | .001 |
| Servants | Occupation | .413 | .171 | 63.008 | .001 |
| | Social class | .348 | .121 | 296.815 | .001 |
| | Sector | .164 | .027 | 5.617 | .001 |
| | Rank | .412 | .170 | 175.390 | .001 |

Table 1.1, *continued*

| Dependent variable | Independent variable | Eta | Eta² | F | Significance |
|---|---|---|---|---|---|
| Persistence, 1861ᶠ | Occupation | .155 | .024 | 7.479 | .001 |
| | Social class | .130 | .017 | 36.815 | .001 |
| | Sector | .113 | .013 | 2.614 | .001 |
| | Rank | .126 | .016 | 13.844 | .001 |
| Persistence, 1851ᶠ | Occupation | .133 | .018 | 5.539 | .001 |
| | Social class | .102 | .010 | 22.541 | .001 |
| | Sector | .102 | .010 | 2.128 | .002 |
| | Rank | .094 | .009 | 7.685 | .001 |
| *Buffalo, 1855* | | | | | |
| Dwelling valueᵍ | Occupation | .320 | .109 | 147.471 | .001 |
| | Social class | .302 | .091 | 605.396 | .001 |
| Age | Occupation | .175 | .031 | 37.99 | .001 |
| | Social class | .146 | .021 | 132.114 | .001 |
| Property | Occupation | .197 | .039 | 48.631 | .001 |
| | Social class | .147 | .022 | 133.667 | .001 |
| Servants | Occupation | .395 | .156 | 223.512 | .001 |
| | Social class | .369 | .136 | 950.238 | .001 |

a. Occupation (sixteen categories): (1) professionals and rentiers, (2) agents and merchants, (3) service and semiprofessionals, (4) business employees, (5) government employees, (6) masters and manufacturers, (7) skilled workers, (8) transport workers, (9) other working class, (10) laborers, (11) women (domestics), (12) other women, (13) agricultural (proprietors), (14) agricultural (nonproprietors), (15) other, (16) none.

Social class (three categories): business class (occupation categories 1 through 6), working class (categories 7 through 10), other (categories 11 through 16).

Rank (six categories): (1) professional and high commercial, (2) low commercial, (3) skilled workers, (4) semiskilled workers, (5) unskilled workers, (6) unclassified.

Sector (twenty-one categories): (1) bakers, (2) butchers, (3) blacksmiths, (4) coopers, (5) builders and carpenters, (6) other construction, (7) metal trades, (8) cabinetmakers, (9) printers, (10) coachmakers, (11) broom makers, (12) shoemakers, (13) tailors, (14) tobacco workers, (15) marble workers (16) saddle and harness makers, (17) jewelry makers, (18) marine workers, (19) musical instruments makers, (20) machinists, (21) other.

b. Log of assessed value of real and personal property, taken from Hamilton city assessment rolls (the 1871 figures are taken from the tax rolls). See Chapter 2.

c. Two categories: owners, nonowners.

d. Two categories: employers, nonemployers.

e. NS: not significant at .5 percent level.

f. Individuals linked to the year's census.

g. Log of dwelling value per capita. See Chapter 2.

The same point can be made about servant employment, although not about property ownership. This is because the ownership of property only partially reflected the class structure. Indeed figures for property ownership mask the two meanings of property at the time: its use value and exchange value. (These two meanings will be discussed in Chapter 4. Here our concern is simply to show that the dynamics of property ownership were clearly separate from those of wealth.) Significant differences did separate occupational categories on property ownership, but they were much smaller than the distinctions by economic rank. Moreover differences between masters and skilled wage workers and between classes were significant only in 1871, but differences between trades, in direct contrast to economic rank, were significant in each year. Different factors were obviously at work in the ownership of property.

At least one important question remains: Were the class groupings relatively permanent, or did they reflect the life course? It could be that the working class was composed primarily of young men who later left it. If this were the case it would destroy the argument that relationship to the means of production most meaningfully divided people into fundamental groups within the social order. A careful examination of the question of age shows that with a few exceptions class was not a life-course phenomenon. Consider first the significance of the variation of age between the various groups. There were significant distinctions between classes in age; however these differences were smaller by far than distinctions between groups according to assessed wealth, servant employment, or persistence. They do not point to a wholesale movement of men out of working-class jobs as they aged. Indeed the mean age of the men in various sorts of work was similar, with the exception of clerks, who were quite young.

In fact the differences in age between groups traced from census to assessment were much smaller than those on the census alone. The reason is that the traced population contains almost entirely household heads, and the census lists all working people, including young, unmarried men and women. The traced group clearly shows the presence of large numbers of adult, skilled wage workers who headed households and did not become masters. Younger men usually did not start their working lives as masters or manufacturers; some became proprietors later in life, but only a small proportion. (In Hamilton between 1851 and 1861 13 percent and in the next decade 15 percent of skilled workers became masters or manufacturers.) However the movement of younger skilled workers into the ranks of proprietors was not random, for they were no doubt frequently the sons of masters and manufacturers. Indeed 28 percent of the sons of masters and manufacturers living at home had the same occuaptional rank as their fathers, a higher proportion owning productive enterprises than among the sons of any other group. Even more of them (38 percent) were skilled workers, and 3 percent were laborers. Compare these figures to those for the sons of skilled workers: only 10 percent of them were masters and manufacturers, 58 percent were also skilled workers, and 8 percent were laborers. Similarly 16 percent of the sons of masters and manufacturers compared to 9 percent of those of skilled workers were business employees.

At the same time sons of the business class dominated the ranks of business employees: 25 percent of the sons of professionals and rentiers, 55 percent of agents' and merchants' sons, 46 percent of service proprietors' and semi-professionals', 72 percent of business employees', and 46 percent of government employees' sons were themselves employed in commerce. Obviously that is the rank at which many of the sons of the business class began their careers. A solid minority, nonetheless, were in skilled wage work: 13 percent of the sons of professionals and rentiers, 15 percent of those of agents and merchants, 22 percent of business employees. Only a sprinkling, significantly, were laborers.

Our discussion of social mobility will show that relatively few young men began their working lives in the upper ranks of the business class. Professionals and merchants were recruited heavily from business employees, masters and manufacturers from young skilled workers. Most probably these young people who moved upward were disproportionately sons of men already in the business class. The skilled trades served the masters and manufacturers much as clerical jobs served agents and merchants: as entering points and training grounds for their sons. In this way the process of occupational mobility was partially a product of the life course. But the life course itself reflected and did not contradict the class relationships of this nineteenth-century city.

If we are right about the life course—if class was primarily a result of social origin—then we should be able to explain relatively little of the variation in class membership with solely demographic measures. Age, ethnicity, and marital status should exert a minimal effect on the likelihood of an individual's being found in the business or working class. This was in fact the case, as two multivariate analyses showed (Table 1.2). The analysis shows quite clearly that demographic factors had little influence on class membership. In each case it accounted for only 6 percent of the variation. The highest betas (general measures of association, with other factors held constant) were not striking: only .20 for ethnicity and .13 for age.[78]

Table 1.2   Probability of membership in business or working class, multiple classification analysis: Hamilton, 1871.

A. PROBABILITIES (ALL FACTORS CONSTANT)

| | Business class (%) | Working class (%) | N |
|---|---|---|---|
| *Age* | | | |
| Under 20 | 18 | 82 | 736 |
| 20–29 | 26 | 74 | 1,981 |
| 30–39 | 35 | 65 | 1,603 |
| 40–49 | 36 | 64 | 1,296 |
| 50–59 | 36 | 64 | 648 |
| 60 and over | 36 | 64 | 419 |
| *Ethnicity* | | | |
| Irish Catholic | 8 | 92 | 766 |
| Irish Protestant | 30 | 70 | 590 |
| Scottish Presbyterian | 34 | 66 | 866 |
| English Anglican | 29 | 71 | 1,074 |
| English Methodist | 26 | 74 | 505 |
| Canadian Protestant | 41 | 59 | 1,278 |
| U.S. white | 36 | 64 | 277 |
| Other | 36 | 64 | 1,327 |
| *Marital status* | | | |
| Single | 33 | 67 | 2,453 |
| Married | 30 | 70 | 3,997 |
| Widowed | 28 | 72 | 233 |
| *Persistence since 1851* | | | |
| No | 30 | 70 | 5,881 |
| Yes | 37 | 63 | 802 |
| *Persistence since 1861* | | | |
| No | 28 | 72 | 4,527 |
| Yes | 37 | 63 | 2,156 |

B. SUMMARY STATISTICS

| | Business class | | Working class | |
|---|---|---|---|---|
| Variable | Eta/beta | Significance | Eta/beta | Significance |
| Age | .07/.13 | .001 | .07/.13 | .001 |
| Ethnicity | .18/.20 | .001 | .18/.20 | .001 |
| Marital status | .03/.03 | .142 | .03/.03 | .142 |
| Persistence since 1851 | .11/.05 | .001 | .11/.05 | .001 |
| Persistence since 1861 | .12/.09 | .001 | .12/.09 | .001 |
| Main effects | — | .001 | — | .001 |
| Grand mean | 31 | — | 69 | — |
| $R^2$ | 6.0 | — | 6.0 | — |

The probability of membership in the business class actually doubled from 18 percent for men under the age of 20 to 36 percent for those at least 40 years old. However the rise first occurred among men in their twenties and evened out after the age of 30. Thus an initial resorting of young men took place as a number who entered working-class positions joined the business class. These, the data lead us to believe, were disproportionately sons of men already in the business class. By and large, then, age made little difference.

Irish Catholic birth did promote working-class membership. However Irish Catholicism was almost synonymous with poverty and low occupational rank. Thus with no other indicator of parental social standing it serves almost as a surrogate for a disadvantaged family background. No other religion or birthplace was so clearly associated with any economic or occupational rank. The likelihood that an Irish Catholic would be in the working class was 92 percent. Next came English Methodists (74 percent), a substantial difference. The distinctions among other ethnic groups were quite minor.

Marital status made almost no difference in class membership, but persisters, or people who had lived in the city for a certain period of time, had a slight advantage. The probability that a twenty-year persister would be in the business class was 37 percent, compared to 30 percent for someone who had lived in the city for less than twenty years; for ten-year persisters the probability was 37 percent, compared to 28 percent for newcomers.

Youth, Irish Catholic birth, and a recent arrival promoted working-class membership. The odds that a 45-year-old Canadian Protestant resident in Hamilton since 1861 would be in the business class in 1871 were about 53 percent.[79] The chances for a 19-year-old unmarried Irish Catholic who had arrived between 1861 and 1871 were nil; for an Irish Protestant with otherwise identical characteristics the chances were 16 percent. Thus within limits demographic factors had a cumulative impact on class membeship. However among non-Irish Catholics their influence was small, and the greatest force on class membership—social origin—is not measured directly by this analysis.

Some demographic differences between classes and their constituent occupational groups are worth noting. These distinctions are concomitants rather than causes of class relations. They reflected important aspects of social organization, and they had tangible consequences for the character of social structure and the experience of people at the time. One of these distinctions concerns the age structure of particular trades. The relative youth (mean age 33) of masters in the rapidly expanding metal trades and the low mean age (28) of machinists, an occupation that had grown very swiftly, show in what sectors of the economy opportunities for younger men were particularly widespread. The most dynamic, most mechanized, and largest industries obviously offered the most attractive and abundant work. Both masters and skilled wage workers in the relatively stagnant traditional crafts—shoemaking, tailoring, butchering—were older, on the average about 37 in 1871. In fact their average age had increased seven years between 1851 and 1871, which shows that relatively few young men were entering these trades.[80]

On the whole, as we should expect, the youngest average ages occurred among business employees and domestic servants. The former were in their late and the latter in their early twenties. The relative stability in the average age of people in these occupations points to the continued entry of young people into them and the movement of older people out. Business employees frequently became proprietors; domestic servants married and left the wage-labor force.

By and large, differences in the proportion of persisters among occupational categories exceeded those attributable to age. In 1871 40 percent of the business class and 29 percent of the working class had been in Hamilton for ten years. Within the business class the exception to this pattern occurred among business employees, whose proportion of persisters was low, a result of their youth and marital status, for 65 percent were unmarried. The proportion of persisters among the different occupational categories in the business class was generally about 40 percent and between 26 percent and 30 percent for the different working-class groups. Even the lowest proportion of persisters in the business class exceeded that of any working-class group. Not surprisingly the groups with the highest proportion of ten-year residents (47 percent and 46 percent) were, respectively, professionals and rentiers and masters and manufacturers.

Nonetheless the city's economic life was run by newcomers: about 60 percent of its commercial, 53 percent of its professional, and 54 percent of its manufacturing proprietors had arrived between 1861 and 1871. Over a twenty-year period the comparable proportions were 84 percent, 74 percent, and 80 percent. The working class had entered the city even more recently: 90 percent of skilled workers and 93 percent of laborers had arrived since 1851 and 70 percent and 74 percent, respectively, since 1861. (See Chapter 3 for detailed tables on persistence.)

It is clear that sharp differences in assessed wealth separated classes and to some extent the occupational groups within them. However the magnitude of those differences has not yet been specified. On an index of representativeness no working-class group in Hamilton had a score as large as any business-class group in any of the three years studied (Table 1.3).[81]

For the business-class group the index of representativeness for total assessed wealth shifted from 248 to 362 for professionals and rentiers; from 341 to 310 for agents and merchants; and from 161 to 171 for masters and manufacturers. Business employees scored considerably lower: 70 and 79 at the two ends of the study period. From another viewpoint the proportion of each of the three main business-class groups in the top 20 economic percentiles in 1871 was 60 percent, 45 percent, and 37 percent, compared to 22 percent for business employees (Table 1.4).

The skilled workers ranked distinctly below the business groups. Their index score varied from 51 to 57, and only 10 percent of them were in the top 20 economic percentiles. Conversely in 1871 44 percent of the skilled workers, compared to 11 percent of the masters, were in the bottom 40 economic percentiles. Other working-class groups also had low scores: the index for laborers shifted from 26 to 36, and the proportion of them in the lowest 40 economic percentiles rose from 70 percent to 77 percent. Transport workers occupied an intermediate

Table 1.3  Index of representativeness, wealth by occupation: Hamilton, 1851–1871, and Buffalo, 1855 (base = 100).[a]

| Occupational group | Hamilton | | | Buffalo, 1855 |
|---|---|---|---|---|
| | 1851 | 1861 | 1871 | |
| Professionals/rentiers | 248 | 456 | 362 | 321 |
| Agents/merchants | 341 | 254 | 310 | 223 |
| Service/ semiprofessionals | 178 | 115 | 127 | 296 |
| Business employees | 70 | 92 | 79 | 157 |
| Goverment employees | 89 | 81 | 146 | 148 |
| Masters/manufacturers | 161 | 125 | 171 | 203 |
| Skilled workers | 51 | 53 | 57 | 69 |
| Transport workers | 38 | 55 | 42 | 97 |
| Other working class | 33 | 72 | 78 | 99 |
| Laborers | 26 | 18 | 36 | 34 |
| Female domestics | 100 | 33 | 25 | 38 |
| Other females | 46 | 45 | 40 | 110 |
| Agricultural proprietors | 165 | 50 | 22 | 202 |
| Other | 38 | 130 | 100 | 143 |
| None | 50 | 57 | 105 | — |

a. See note 81.

Table 1.4   Occupation and assessed wealth: Hamilton, 1851–1871.

| Occupational group | Year | Proportion in economic rank | | | N |
| | | 0-39% | 40-79% | 80-99% | |
|---|---|---|---|---|---|
| Professionals/rentiers | 1851 | 14.7% | 24.7% | 60.5% | 179 |
| | 1861 | 5.3 | 32.2 | 62.5 | 225 |
| | 1871 | 7.2 | 38.0 | 60.1 | 195 |
| Agents/merchants | 1851 | 7.0 | 37.3 | 55.7 | 239 |
| | 1861 | 8.4 | 39.5 | 52.1 | 371 |
| | 1871 | 8.4 | 46.9 | 44.5 | 475 |
| Service/semiprofessionals | 1851 | 5.3 | 34.7 | 59.7 | 97 |
| | 1861 | 14.9 | 43.9 | 41.2 | 158 |
| | 1871 | 7.0 | 48.0 | 44.9 | 188 |
| Business employees | 1851 | 42.9 | 35.4 | 11.8 | 270 |
| | 1861 | 17.6 | 64.8 | 17.6 | 402 |
| | 1871 | 23.0 | 55.1 | 22.0 | 772 |
| Government employees | 1851 | 11.5 | 63.4 | 25.0 | 86 |
| | 1861 | 24.4 | 50.0 | 25.6 | 110 |
| | 1871 | 25.9 | 48.2 | 25.9 | 183 |
| Masters/manufacturers | 1851 | 7.4 | 46.5 | 46.0 | 225 |
| | 1861 | 14.4 | 50.0 | 35.6 | 306 |
| | 1871 | 11.1 | 51.4 | 37.4 | 441 |
| Skilled workers | 1851 | 36.0 | 54.7 | 9.3 | 1,653 |
| | 1861 | 42.5 | 47.5 | 10.0 | 1,632 |
| | 1871 | 43.7 | 46.7 | 9.6 | 3,256 |
| Transport workers | 1851 | 50.0 | 42.1 | 7.9 | 198 |
| | 1861 | 46.3 | 48.7 | 5.0 | 233 |
| | 1871 | 48.2 | 44.7 | 7.1 | 358 |
| Other working class | 1851 | 56.5 | 37.0 | 6.5 | 175 |
| | 1861 | 36.7 | 49.1 | 14.2 | 224 |
| | 1871 | 41.4 | 46.5 | 12.1 | 285 |
| Laborers | 1851 | 70.4 | 26.7 | 2.8 | 725 |
| | 1861 | 80.1 | 17.9 | 2.0 | 899 |
| | 1871 | 76.8 | 19.8 | 3.8 | 1,148 |
| Female domestics | 1851 | 100.0 | 0.0 | 0.0 | 983 |
| | 1861 | 42.9 | 42.8 | 14.3 | 981 |
| | 1871 | 93.8 | 6.3 | 0.0 | 804 |
| Other females | 1851 | 38.4 | 53.8 | 7.6 | 210 |
| | 1861 | 47.5 | 41.0 | 11.5 | 300 |
| | 1871 | 41.0 | 50.0 | 9.1 | 580 |
| Agricultural proprietors | 1851 | 26.4 | 38.2 | 35.2 | 67 |
| | 1861 | 42.3 | 46.2 | 11.5 | 74 |
| | 1871 | 40.8 | 46.9 | 12.2 | 82 |
| Other | 1851 | 36.0 | 56.0 | 8.0 | 56 |
| | 1861 | 39.2 | 42.9 | 17.9 | 118 |
| | 1871 | 19.1 | 67.1 | 23.8 | 79 |

position between laborers and skilled workers, while the "other" working class, an unstable group, shifted its position. Those few female domestics on the tax rolls were all poor; women with other jobs fared slightly better. (The situation of women is discussed in detail in Chapter 2.)

When the occupational categories are combined into classes, differences remain very sharp. The ratio of the mean business- to the mean working-class assessed wealth shifted from 4.5 to 4.6 to 3.7 during the twenty-year period. The proportion of business-class members in the bottom 40 economic percentiles decreased slightly from 15 percent to 14 percent, and the proportion of working-class men in the same position rose from 46 percent to 53 percent. Conversely the proportion of the business class in the top 20 economic percentiles dropped slightly from 44 percent to 37 percent, while the share of the working class in those percentiles remained steady at 8 percent.

Classes differed too in types of housing as well as in economic rank. The material of which housing was constructed provided a visible measure of distinctions in wealth. In 1851 the proportion of household heads living in brick or stone dwellings was highest among groups in the business class: professionals and rentiers 52 percent, agents and merchants 67 percent, proprietors of services and semiprofessionals 41 percent, business employees 56 percent, government employees 44 percent, and masters and manufacturers 36 percent. Compare these to the 14 percent for skilled wage workers and 8 percent for laborers. Conversely the proportion of households dwelling in log, shanty, or other improvised structures was highest among laborers at 9 percent.

In Buffalo a direct association also existed between occupation and type of housing, measured in this instance by the proportion of families living in single- or multiple-family dwellings. Household heads in occupational groups in the business class lived more often in single family dwellings than did men in the working class or female household heads. The proportion of household heads in single-family dwellings varied within the business class from a high of 91 among professionals and rentiers to between about 75 to 80 percent of each of the other occupational groups. Compare this to 50 percent for skilled wage workers and 44 percent for laborers, the two major groups within the working class. Lowest of all were the few female domestics who headed households (33 percent), though also low was the proportion (48 percent) for other female household heads. Looked at another way, nearly a third of the laborers' and skilled wage workers' families lived in dwellings with three or more families.

Economic distinctions between classes and between occupational groups in Buffalo generally paralleled the situation in Hamilton. In

Buffalo too all the business-class occupations scored higher on the index of representativeness than any of the working-class ones (see Table 1.3). There too within the business class the index for business employees was substantially lower than for other business-class groups. However its score in Buffalo (157) was about double its score in Hamilton. The index for the other major business-class groups was: professionals and rentiers 321; agents and merchants 223; proprietors of services and semiprofessionals 296; masters and manufacturers 203. Within the working class scores were much lower: 69 for skilled wage workers, 97 for transport workers, 99 for other working-class members, and 34 for laborers. The ratio of business- to working-class wealth as approximated by dwelling value per capita was 3.7, identical to that in Hamilton in 1871.

In Buffalo 75 percent of the professionals and rentiers, 66 percent of agents and merchants, and about 65 percent of masters and manufacturers were in the top 25 economic percentiles. Even business employees who headed households did quite well: about 60 percent were in the top quarter. By contrast only 17 percent of skilled wage workers and 4 percent of laborers ranked as high on our measure of economic standing. They were much more often at the bottom: about 40 percent of laborers and 22 percent of skilled wage workers were in the lowest quarter of the economic rank order, compared to 3 percent of professionals and rentiers, 6 percent of agents and merchants, 5 percent of business employees, and 7 percent of masters and manufacturers. As a whole 26 percent of the working class was in the bottom quarter of the economic rank order, compared to 7 percent of the business class, and 67 percent of the latter and 15 percent of the former were in the upper quarter.

Classes, it must be underlined, were not homogeneous groups. Substantial variations in wealth, ethnicity, property ownership, and persistence existed within them. These will be discussed in greater detail in the next chapter. However one very important distinction within the business class should be noted now. That is the division of the masters and manufacturers into two fairly distinct groups. For Hamilton the clue that there is something distinct about these men comes from their extraordinary rate of downward mobility, which far exceeded that of any other group in the business class. Between 1851 and 1861 27 percent and in the next decade 43 percent moved downward into the ranks of skilled wage workers. Did downward mobility occur randomly, or did some characteristics distinguish those masters who retained from those who lost their position? We consulted a file of men linked between the assessment and census of 1861 and the census and tax roll of 1871. We separated out all the men listed in each of these four sources as skilled artisans in either year and divided them into four groups: those who moved from skilled wage worker to master; those who dropped from master to skilled wage worker; those who remained skilled wage workers; and those who remained masters. There were no significant differences in age between any of these groups.

However there were differences in wealth (Table 1.5). First the mean wealth of the groups differed within each year. Those who moved either into or out of the ranks of masters were less well-to-do than those who remained masters throughout the decade but more well off than those who remained wage workers. (These differences were statistically significant.) The mobile masters formed a distinct stratum of marginal, petty producers. In this way the situation in Hamilton paralleled that in Edinburgh in the same period, where R. Q. Gray also identified a group of men who shifted back and forth across the line that separated masters from wage workers.[82] Note, however, that the mobile masters were themselves substantially more well-to-do than those who remained artisans; they were clearly an unstable intermediate group. Indeed their distinction from those who

Table 1.5  Economic ranking of artisans and masters traced from 1861 to 1871: Hamilton.

| Occupational category[a] | | Mean wealth ($) | | Index of relative wealth | | |
|---|---|---|---|---|---|---|
| | | Total assessed value, 1861 | Tax paid, 1871 | | | |
| 1861 | 1871 | | | 1861 | 1871 | N |
| Artisan | Artisan | 78.8 | 37.4 | 63 | 73 | 190 |
| Artisan | Master | 119.3 | 48.9 | 95 | 96 | 42 |
| Master | Artisan | 181.6 | 59.7 | 145 | 118 | 40 |
| Master | Master | 289.1 | 105.7 | 230 | 207 | 42 |

| | | Economic rank (percent) | | | |
|---|---|---|---|---|---|
| | | 0–40 | | 80–100 | |
| 1861 | 1871 | 1861 | 1871 | 1861 | 1871 |
| Artisan | Artisan | 43.2 | 27.4 | 9.5 | 17.9 |
| Artisan | Master | 35.7 | 9.5 | 19.0 | 33.4 |
| Master | Artisan | 7.5 | 7.5 | 25.0 | 37.5 |
| Master | Master | 7.1 | 7.1 | 40.5 | 47.6 |

a. Analyses of variance with occupational category as an independent variable and total assessed value and tax paid as dependent variables are significant at .01.

were wage workers in each year becomes even clearer when we recall that those wage workers traced to the four sources were disproportionately well-to-do and not economically representative of all artisans.[83] Thus the mobile masters appeared more economically comfortable than even the most stable and prosperous skilled wage workers.

An index of relative wealth for the four groups makes the same point.[84] Clear distinctions separated each group, and their index score was quite similar for each year. However the gap between them had decreased somewhat by 1871. The reasons for this become clearer from the distribution of the groups by economic rank. At the lowest economic rank, the bottom 40 percentiles, a large gap separated those who were wage workers in each year from those who were masters in at least one. However among those who remained wage workers and those who were upwardly mobile into the ranks of masters the proportion in the lowest economic percentiles dropped notably—for the former from 43 percent to 27 percent and for the latter from 36 percent to 10 percent. Among those who slipped from master to wage worker the proportion in the bottom ranks remained stable (8 percent), as it did among those who were masters in each year (7 percent).

A substantial difference separated the proportion of each group who were in the top twenty percentiles as well. In 1861 the share of the stable wage workers was 10 percent, compared to 41 percent for stable masters. During the decade the proportion of each of the four groups in the top twenty percentiles increased, and the lead of the stable masters decreased somewhat. Thus the slight reduction in the distinction between groups came about from the improvement in economic standing within each of them, an improvement relatively greater among those least well-to-do at the start of the decade.

The four groups of masters and wage workers did not differ in age; they did differ in economic rank. The other major dimension on which they were compared was specific occupation. Were some types of work more unstable or more promising than others? First, in answer to the question, the members of each group followed a wide variety of trades. Indeed so great was the variety that only a few patterns existed. There were no carpenters among those who were masters in each year. Carpenters were represented most heavily among those who were wage workers at each end of the decade. Obviously those men who had secured positions of stable proprietorship in the building trades called themselves something other than carpenter. Likewise none of the stable wage workers were painters, and painters dropped from master to wage worker more often than they rose. In this period, as Gray has shown, painters were in a precarious position, their ranks easily diluted by relatively untrained and unskilled workers. Indeed they usually earned less than men in other trades.

Somewhat surprisingly in light of technological developments in these years no important differences separated the proportion of shoemakers or tailors in each group. However the Griffens in their study of Poughkeepsie, New York, observed that as trades declined, their work forces became older and more stable. This paradoxical stability does not indicate prosperity among these groups.[85] A somewhat disproportionate amount of movement into the trade of machinist took place among those who remained wage workers, a reflection of more general structural trends in the economy. Generally also few molders and masons were masters. However a substantial fraction (10 percent) of masters were plumbers, and only one person in the other three groups (an employed plumber who became a master painter but remained in the same economic rank) was a plumber. Builders were notable among those men who became masters during the decade. In sum, most masters and wage workers remained in the same line of work. Shifts of status from employer to worker or the reverse by and large did not signify movement into a different trade. Men in some trades were more likely than others to be masters or workers, but it was the distinction in their wealth, and by implication in the size of their operation, rather than in the sort of work they did that separated the men who remained masters from those whose experience was more fluid or who remained in the working class.

Why, it might be asked at this point, do we continue to make a case for a two-class model of the mid-nineteenth-century North American city? Given the fluidity of the masters and the distinctly lower economic position of business employees, would it not make more sense to introject a middle class?[86] We believe the answer is no, on various grounds. Our reasoning is in part theoretical. Class is not simply an empirical phenomenon. It expresses an analytical relationship. Whatever their wealth masters and manufacturers in Hamilton and Buffalo had a relationship to the means of production shared by other proprietors. They owned private enterprises and employed wage labor. However the patterns of mobility do show that while the boundary between classes was relatively distinct, the experience of a small segment of the population led them to cross that boundary at relatively frequent intervals. As the Griffens have demonstrated the degree of mobility between artisans and proprietors was in constant decline between 1850 and 1880 in Poughkeepsie. Thus in one important respect the class structure of the city became more clearly defined by the late-nineteenth century.[87] Whether the declining group of small proprietors who drifted occasionally into the ranks of wage workers saw themselves as business or working class remains an elusive and important question that we cannot answer.

The other group that causes problems for the two-class argument is the business employees, and we already have given reasons why they should be included in the business class for this era. Thus theory, contemporary perception, patterns of activity, and empirical features of social structure all can be brought together to make a case that early industrial society was dominated by two great classes.

There is an irony in this chapter. It has taken a corps of research assistants, the most modern electronic data-processing equipment, and powerful statistical techniques to make a case for what most late-nineteenth-century social commentators would have accepted without argument. They knew that a great change in social organization had taken place and that two great classes, Capital and Labor, were increasingly dominating social, economic, and political life. Moreover straightforward action often followed from the frank recognition of class. Capitalists, for instance, did not hesitate to ask the government to use the national guard or the army to repress strikes. Indeed no one witnessing the violent confrontations between Capital and Labor in the years between the late 1870s and the turn of the century could deny that class had become a major aspect of social life.

Nor did the most observant commentators confuse class with industrialization. Rather they realized that a profound and painful alteration in social relations had taken place. They watched, often with dread, as the defining feature of capitalism—wage labor—permeated North American life. Daniel Rodgers writes, "Nothing more clearly distinguishes the years in which the factory system was built from the modern age, inured to its ranks of wage and salary earners, than that the simple fact of employment should have deeply disturbed so many Americans. But labor at the beck and call of another was not among the ideals even of work-obsessed, mid-nineteenth-century America."[88]

By the early twentieth century, class had begun to fall from favor as a category in social analysis. Tainted by its association with Marxism, the idea of class was increasingly portrayed as determinist, reductionist, alien to American experience, an inappropriate category for serious social science unless redefined as stratification. Because stratification is a descriptive rather than an analytic concept, it has focused attention on the complex connections between the features of social life but diverted attention from their explanation. It has provided descriptions of the relationships between occupation and income but said very little about the origins of inequality and exploitation or the principles that underlie the social system. In the same way progressive industrialists in the early twentieth century tried to obscure the issue of class by shifting their strategy of control from repression to welfare capitalism, which offered material improvements to workers without any corresponding increase in power or control. Perhaps too, as Rodgers implies, its ubiquitous quality gave wage labor an air of inevitability, even of ordinariness, which has made it seem nonproblematic.

But in fact wage labor is only one form that human relations may assume. It is, as nineteenth-century people knew, a historical product the emergence and spread of which defined a new society dominated by two great new classes. Although the wage-labor relation does not account for all aspects of human relations or behavior, it cannot be ignored by an inquiry into any of them, as we hope not only this chapter but the rest of this book makes clear. Indeed the wage-labor relation is critical not only because of its impact on the distribution of power and resources but because it embodies the principles on which the social system rests. As the defining feature of capitalist social organization, wage labor has become the template of human and social relations outside as well as within the marketplace, and the extent to which we transform ourselves and others into commodities is a measure of the extent to which class, whether we admit it or not, retains its grip on social life.

# 2 Social Stratification

The strength of a two-class model can also be its weakness. It can reduce the complexity of social structure by cutting through surface divisions and exposing the dynamic properties of a social formation; but in the process the model can foster a false simplicity, obscuring very real differences between social structures, ignoring the effect of time and place, and bypassing the intricate task of unraveling the relationships between the components of actual situations. This last task is best conceived as the analysis of stratification, which it must be remembered is distinct from the discussion of class. In a two-class society it is by no means self-evident how the major components of stratification—wealth, occupation, ethnicity, age, and sex—will be related and how their relationships will change under the impact of major social and economic events.

Our analysis of stratification is not divorced from the conception of class advanced in the preceding chapter. Here, however, our focus is on the division of resources among the population, especially on what we term the *structure of inequality*. The analysis is framed by a central problem: Did the structure of inequality represent a rigid and fixed characteristic of nineteenth-century urban life, or did it alter with major social and economic changes, particularly with the onset of industrialization?

We begin with an expectation of rigidity. Hamilton, as we have shown, was a capitalist city. Though the economic base shifted from commerce to industry, the primacy of capitalist labor and property relations remained unchanged. Given the drive of capitalism toward greater accumulation, the degree of inequality should increase over time. Since occupation primarily identified class position, close and stable connections should exist between occupation and economic rank, for sharp differences in economic rank separated the city's classes.

We have already outlined some of the major economic differences between occupations. To consider the stability of those relationships it is necessary to look at some basic distributions across time and to use multivariate techniques to examine the simultaneous impact of various factors on the major components of stratification. Using these techniques we shall show: a general persistence in the pattern of stratification in Hamilton during its early industrialization; a stability in the processes underlying the structure of inequality; a parallel between the structure of inequality in Hamilton and Buffalo.

Our discussion of stratification, like our treatment of class, centers on males. This is because most of the wage earners, professionals, and proprietors as well as most household heads were men, and their earnings by and large determined the economic rank of most families. However sex also forms a key component of stratification, related in complex ways to the social structure. Hence it is necessary to discuss separately the relationship between the position of women and early industrialization in Hamilton.

The distribution of people between different sorts of occupations and along an economic scale does not reflect only abstract principles of stratification. This distribution is also a product of the demographic composition of the population and of the nature of the work force. The patterns of stratification were bound intricately to the age, ethnic, and sexual composition of the population and to the way in which industrialization reordered the labor force.

## A Note on Hamilton's Demography

During the years between 1851 and 1871 Hamilton's ethnic composition altered as a result of shifting patterns of immigration. Between 1851, 1861, and 1871 the Irish Catholic share of the city's population declined from about 21 percent to 14 percent to 8 percent, indicating a sharp drop in their in-migration. The Irish Protestant proportion revealed a similar trend. The Scottish share hovered between about 9 percent and 11 percent, while the proportion of English Anglicans and of native-born people rose, the latter from 31 percent to 42 percent to 51 percent.

The children of immigrants, of course, swelled the proportion of native born. In fact when children living at home are assigned the same birthplace as their fathers, the composition of the city appears rather different and more constant (Table 2.1). In 1851 the population was about 42 percent Irish (25 percent Catholic and 18 percent Protestant); the Scots made up another 14 percent, the English 23 percent, the natives 11 percent, and the rest scattered. By 1871 the Irish share had dropped to about 26 percent (15 percent Catholic and 11 percent

Table 2.1 Ethnic structure of entire population: Hamilton, 1851–1871.

| Ethnic group[a] | 1851 | 1861 | 1871 |
|---|---|---|---|
| Irish Catholics | 24.5 | 20.0 | 14.9 |
| Irish Protestants | 17.7 | 13.5 | 10.9 |
| Scottish Presbyterians | 9.7 | 15.0 | 5.3 |
| Other Scottish | 4.6 | 3.2 | 11.6 |
| English Anglicans | 10.6 | 13.0 | 15.0 |
| English Methodists | 4.6 | 5.4 | 6.8 |
| Other English | 8.2 | 4.4 | 6.3 |
| Canadian Protestants | 9.6 | 11.6 | 15.8 |
| Canadian Catholics | 1.6 | 2.4 | 2.8 |
| U.S. nonwhite | 1.2 | 1.5 | 0.9 |
| Other U.S. | 4.9 | 4.2 | 3.6 |
| Other | 2.8 | 5.6 | 6.1 |
| Total | 100.0 | 100.0 | 100.0 |
| N | 13,807 | 19,030 | 26,021 |

a. Children living at home were assigned the ethnicity of their fathers.

Protestant), the Scots held generally steady at 17 percent, and the English and natives increased their share to 28 percent and 19 percent, respectively.

As the population became increasingly native born, its dependency rate (defined as the percentage of people under 14 and over 60) also rose. In 1851 the rate (40 percent) was rather low, reflecting the youthfulness of a city of immigrants. Throughout the next two decades the proportion of people aged 60 and over rose from 2 percent to 3 percent to 4 percent, while the share under 14 years of age increased too. Consequently by 1871 the dependency rate had reached 44 percent, and the city's age distribution had become less distinctive.

Although sex ratios for the entire population were not far from unity (100, 93, 97), these overall figures mask age-specific variation. In general the number of women substantially exceeded the number of men in the age groups 15 to 19, 20 to 24, and 25 to 29. For example among the 20- to 24-year-olds in each of the three years the sex ratios were 87, 65, and 86. These ratios, of course, imply severe problems for women who wished to find a spouse. Over the age of 30, however, the ratios were more similar.

Striking variations in age-sex ratios differentiated ethnic groups. These reflected primarily variations in the timing and age-sex structure of immigration. Most notable were the very low sex ratios among Irish Catholic young people, which varied for 20- to 24-year-olds from 78 to 52 to 78. For the most part variations reflected in-migration rather than out-migration. Young women between 15 and 20 or 25 often came by themselves, perhaps intending to work as servants. By contrast young men who migrated alone usually were older, often in their late twenties. Thus in some cases the sex ratios were reversed between people aged 15 to 24 and 30 to 34.

Although a substantial proportion of the population remained foreign born, the fraction that had lived in Canada for ten or twenty years rose dramatically. This fraction has been estimated using the number of children of specific ages born in Canada to immigrant men and women. Using only birthplace as a criterion, the proportion of women born outside Canada decreased only from 83 percent to 70 percent between 1851 and 1871 (Table 2.2). However the proportion who had lived in Canada for less than a decade dropped from 77 percent to 25 percent during the same period. If adjustment to new circumstances increased with length of residence, then the 1871 population was far more stable and far better adapted to Canada than the adults of 1851.[1]

This method of estimation also shows major patterns in the timing of migration. During the two decades Irish Catholic migration dropped most notably. In 1851 only 18 percent of adult females and 17 percent of males had lived in Canada for a decade, compared to 93 percent of both men and women twenty years later. Irish Catholic migration had clearly slowed to a trickle.[2]

More Irish Protestants than Catholics had lived in Canada in the 1840s. About 41 percent of the adult women and 45 percent of the men there in 1851 had been in the country at least a decade, though as in the case of the Irish Catholics immigration slowed markedly, and 92 percent of the adults present in 1871 had been in Canada ten years earlier as well. Of all ethnic groups in 1851 the Scottish had the highest proportion of ten-year residents—about 62 percent of women and 56 percent of men. Scottish migration remained fairly steady so that by 1871 the proportion in the country for the decade (87 percent of adults) was a bit lower than that of the Irish.

The English continued to migrate in the greatest numbers. In 1871 only about 60 percent of English Anglicans had been in Canada a decade earlier and 29 percent had been there twenty years, compared to roughly half of the other major groups. Thus in 1871 the English Anglicans were the newest immigrants, not the Irish, a fact that helps explain the drop in the group's relative economic position. Finally the English Methodist pattern resembled that of the Anglicans, especially during the 1850s. However their migration during the 1860s was not as heavy: 76 percent of those present in Hamilton in 1871 had been in the country for at least a decade.

Table 2.2   Percentage of ethnic group estimated to have arrived in Canada by selected dates: Hamilton, 1851–1871.

| Ethnic group | Year | Women, 20–49 | | | Men, 20–49 | | |
|---|---|---|---|---|---|---|---|
| | | 1851 | 1861 | 1871 | 1851 | 1861 | 1871 |
| Irish Catholic | 1871 | | | 100 | | | 100 |
| | 1866 | | | 95 | | | 95 |
| | 1861 | | 100 | 93 | | 100 | 93 |
| | 1856 | | 70 | 65 | | 91 | 85 |
| | 1852 | 100 | 52 | 48 | 100 | 52 | 48 |
| | 1847 | 69 | 36 | 33 | 69 | 36 | 33 |
| | 1842 | 18 | 9 | 9 | 17 | 6 | 8 |
| Irish Protestant | 1871 | | | 100 | | | 100 |
| | 1866 | | | 97 | | | 97 |
| | 1861 | | 100 | 92 | | 100 | 92 |
| | 1856 | | 93 | 86 | | 94 | 86 |
| | 1852 | 100 | 76 | 70 | 100 | 75 | 69 |
| | 1847 | 72 | 55 | 50 | 83 | 62 | 57 |
| | 1842 | 41 | 31 | 29 | 45 | 34 | 31 |
| Scottish | 1871 | | | 100 | | | 100 |
| | 1866 | | | 90 | | | 90 |
| | 1861 | | 100 | 87 | | 100 | 87 |
| | 1856 | | 94 | 82 | | 94 | 82 |
| | 1852 | 100 | 58 | 50 | 100 | 57 | 50 |
| | 1847 | 81 | 47 | 41 | 82 | 47 | 41 |
| | 1842 | 62 | 36 | 31 | 56 | 32 | 28 |
| English Anglican | 1871 | | | 100 | | | 100 |
| | 1866 | | | 68 | | | 72 |
| | 1861 | | 100 | 60 | | 100 | 61 |
| | 1856 | | 90 | 54 | | 91 | 56 |
| | 1852 | 100 | 49 | 29 | 100 | 49 | 30 |
| | 1847 | 88 | 43 | 26 | 88 | 43 | 26 |
| | 1842 | 48 | 24 | 14 | 42 | 21 | 13 |
| English Methodist | 1871 | | | 100 | | | 100 |
| | 1866 | | | 84 | | | 84 |
| | 1861 | | 100 | 76 | | 100 | 76 |
| | 1856 | | 93 | 71 | | 93 | 71 |
| | 1852 | 100 | 51 | 39 | 100 | 51 | 39 |
| | 1847 | 91 | 46 | 35 | 92 | 47 | 36 |
| | 1842 | 50 | 26 | 20 | 51 | 26 | 20 |
| All foreign | 1871 | | | 100 | | | 100 |
| | 1866 | | | 82 | | | 82 |
| | 1861 | | 100 | 75 | | 100 | 74 |
| | 1856 | | 50 | 38 | | 50 | 37 |
| | 1852 | 100 | 47 | 35 | 100 | 46 | 34 |
| | 1847 | 71 | 36 | 25 | 70 | 35 | 24 |
| | 1842 | 33 | 17 | 12 | 24 | 12 | 8 |
| Total population All foreign | | 83 | 82 | 70 | 92 | 90 | 84 |
| In Canada 10 years or less | | 77 | 52 | 25 | 76 | 54 | 26 |

Thus in 1851 the population of the city was very new to Canada. Only 33 percent of foreign-born women and 24 percent of men had been in Canada for at least a decade. These immigrants composed, respectively, 83 percent and 92 percent of the adult population. By 1871 the proportion who had been in the country for at least ten years had risen dramatically to about 75 percent, a development that should have enhanced the stability of the community and even affected the achievements of its residents.

Industrialization had less impact than immigration on the demography of the work force, for industrialization did not spark the incorporation of previously unemployed people in the work force. The share of the population listing an occupation on the census actually dropped from 39 percent to 34 percent between 1851 and 1871. In fact the effect of industrialization on the labor force was primarily redistributive, for there were some marked shifts in the type of work that people did.

Both before and after industrialization one outstanding characteristic of the labor force was its youth. In 1851, 55 percent of the work force was under the age of 30, a proportion that decreased to 49 percent twenty years later. During the same twenty years the proportion of the youngest workers—those under the age of 15—to the total dropped from 5 percent to 3 percent, and the proportion of employed 15- to 19-year-olds declined as well from 17 percent to 15 percent. At the same time, as should be expected, the share of the work force over the age of 50 rose from 9 percent to 14 percent, a reflection of the age structure of the city. These proportions show clearly that early industrialization in Hamilton did not require the labor of large numbers of young children.

The shifts in the type of work people did reflect both the depression of the late 1850s and the influence of industrialization (Table 2.3). For instance, the proportion of skilled workers declined between 1851 and 1861, though the absolute number remained almost constant. This points to the out-migration of skilled workers from the city during its economic crisis. Indeed the numerical decline took place among young men, not among married household heads. In the next decade the exodus was reversed, and the number of skilled workers, attracted by opportunities in the industrializing city, increased at a rate that more than compensated for the decline in the previous decade: their numbers rose 100 percent at a time when the population as a whole increased 47 percent. The other very substantial increase took place among business employees, whose proportion nearly doubled from 5 percent to 9 percent of the work force between 1851 and 1871. Obviously an expansion of clerical as well as of skilled manual work accompanied early industrialization.

Table 2.3 Demographic characteristics of occupational groups: Hamilton, 1851–1871.

A. TOTAL WORK FORCE

| Occupational group | Number | | | % change | | % of work force | | |
|---|---|---|---|---|---|---|---|---|
| | 1851 | 1861 | 1871 | 1851–1861 | 1861–1871 | 1851 | 1861 | 1871 |
| Professionals/rentiers | 179 | 225 | 195 | 25.7 | −13.3 | 3.5 | 3.7 | 2.2 |
| Agents/merchants | 239 | 371 | 475 | 55.2 | 28.0 | 4.6 | 6.1 | 5.4 |
| Service/semiprofessionals | 97 | 158 | 188 | 62.9 | 19.0 | 1.9 | 2.6 | 2.1 |
| Business employees | 270 | 402 | 772 | 48.9 | 92.0 | 5.2 | 6.7 | 8.7 |
| Government employees | 86 | 110 | 183 | 27.9 | 66.4 | 1.7 | 1.8 | 2.1 |
| Masters/manufacturers | 225 | 306 | 441 | 36.0 | 44.1 | 4.4 | 5.1 | 5.0 |
| Skilled workers | 1,653 | 1,632 | 3,256 | −1.3 | 99.5 | 32.0 | 27.1 | 36.8 |
| Transport workers | 198 | 233 | 358 | 17.7 | 53.6 | 3.8 | 3.9 | 4.0 |
| Other working class | 175 | 224 | 285 | 28.0 | 27.2 | 3.4 | 3.7 | 3.2 |
| Laborers | 725 | 899 | 1,148 | 24.0 | 27.7 | 14.0 | 14.9 | 13.0 |
| Female domestics | 983 | 981 | 804 | −0.2 | −18.0 | 19.0 | 16.3 | 9.1 |
| Other females | 210 | 300 | 580 | 29.0 | 93.3 | 4.1 | 5.0 | 6.6 |
| Agricultural proprietors | 67 | 74 | 82 | 10.4 | 10.8 | 1.3 | 1.2 | 0.9 |
| Agricultural non-proprietors | – | – | 2 | 110.7 | – | – | – | 0.0 |
| Other | 56 | 118 | 79 | 16.9 | −33.1 | 1.1 | 2.0 | 0.9 |
| Total population | 5,163 | 6,033 | 8,848 | 16.9 | 46.7 | | | |

B. TRADE GROUPS

| Trade | Number | | | | | | | | | % change 1851–1871 |
|---|---|---|---|---|---|---|---|---|---|---|
| | 1851 | | | 1861 | | | 1871 | | | |
| | M[a] | W[a] | T[a] | M | W | T | M | W | T | |
| Bakers | 4 | 61 | 65 | 16 | 62 | 68 | 25 | 72 | 97 | 49.2 |
| Butchers | 1 | 35 | 36 | 9 | 25 | 34 | 14 | 16 | 80 | 122.2 |
| Blacksmiths | 10 | 113 | 123 | 12 | 81 | 93 | 14 | 147 | 161 | 30.9 |
| Coopers | 1 | 14 | 15 | 3 | 10 | 13 | 3 | 42 | 45 | 200.0 |
| Builders/carpenters | 26 | 292 | 318 | 25 | 337 | 362 | 39 | 504 | 543 | 70.7 |
| Other construction workers | 14 | 162 | 176 | 23 | 222 | 245 | 36 | 292 | 328 | 86.4 |
| Metal workers | 26 | 135 | 161 | 33 | 136 | 169 | 29 | 286 | 315 | 95.7 |
| Cabinet makers | 14 | 80 | 94 | 11 | 75 | 86 | 12 | 138 | 150 | 59.6 |
| Printers | 6 | 59 | 65 | 15 | 74 | 89 | 13 | 109 | 122 | 87.7 |
| Coach makers | 7 | 65 | 72 | 8 | 35 | 43 | 8 | 44 | 52 | 27.8 |
| Broom makers | 2 | 8 | 10 | 3 | 13 | 16 | 6 | 43 | 49 | 390.0 |
| Shoemakers | 17 | 204 | 221 | 28 | 143 | 171 | 30 | 209 | 239 | 8.1 |
| Tailors | 14 | 155 | 169 | 26 | 115 | 141 | 38 | 183 | 221 | 30.8 |
| Tobacconists | 1 | 13 | 14 | 5 | 16 | 21 | 9 | 75 | 84 | 500.0 |
| Marble workers | — | 40 | 40 | 1 | 20 | 21 | 1 | 42 | 43 | 7.5 |
| Saddle and harness workers | 5 | 29 | 34 | 5 | 24 | 29 | 8 | 55 | 63 | 85.3 |
| Jewelers | 8 | 19 | 27 | 5 | 23 | 28 | 6 | 28 | 34 | 25.9 |
| Marine workers | 1 | 2 | 3 | 3 | 3 | 6 | 9 | 12 | 21 | 600.0 |
| Musical instrument makers | 3 | 1 | 4 | 9 | 1 | 10 | 9 | 11 | 20 | 400.0 |
| Machinists | 3 | 50 | 53 | 7 | 123 | 130 | 13 | 455 | 468 | 783.0 |
| Other | 18 | 63 | 86 | 37 | 73 | 110 | 52 | 242 | 292 | 242.0 |

a. M = master; W = worker; T = total.

The proportion of master artisans and manufacturers increased in about the same proportion as skilled wage workers. Agents and merchants remained about 5 percent of the work force—about the same share as the masters and manufacturers. Professionals and rentiers dropped from 4 percent to 2 percent, largely as a result of the increasing abandonment of the title *gentleman*, a group included in this category.[3] The vendors of services and semiprofessionals remained at about 2 percent, and government employees increased their small share somewhat. Within the working class transport workers remained at about 4 percent, miscellaneous nonskilled workers at about 3 percent, and unskilled laborers dropped slightly from 14 percent to 13 percent. Agricultural proprietors remained about 1 percent of the work force. Most notable was the absolute drop in the number of female domestics from 983 to 804, or from 19 percent to 9 percent of the work force. At the same time the number of women employed in other sorts of occupations increased 176 percent—from 210 to 580, or from 4 percent to 7 percent of the work force.

The fastest-growing trade not surprisingly was machinist, whose numbers increased almost 800 percent from 53 to 468 during the two decades. Combined with other members of the metal trades the machinist group was second in size in 1871 only to the 871-member building trades, which had grown 92 percent during the two decades. At the other extreme the number of shoemakers remained practically unchanged, rising only 8 percent, a development to be expected given the technological revolution in shoemaking.[4] Other traditional trades also grew very little in comparison to the 71 percent overall rise in the work force: bakers (49 percent), blacksmiths (31 percent), coach makers and related crafts (28 percent), tailors (31 percent), and marble workers (8 percent).

In some cases the unattractiveness of an occupation was revealed by the decreasing proportion of young men recruited. The proportion of men 15 to 24 among shoemakers dipped most dramatically from 35 percent to 3 percent during the twenty years. Less steep but still substantial was the decrease in the number of men the same age among grocers—27 percent to 13 percent. At the same time the proportion of men the same age among two more attractive occupations, chemist and clerk, rose from 29 percent to 42 percent for the former and from 50 percent to 61 percent for the latter.

Attorneys, as a group, aged. The proportion under 30 years old decreased from 46 percent to 24 percent, while the proportion aged 40 or more rose from 14 percent to 38 percent. By contrast the age of physicians did not increase, probably because they were older (more than half were over the age of 40) at the start of the period and thus many died during the two decades. Like attorneys, the merchants aged as a group: the share under 30 dropped from 28 percent to 22 percent, while the proportion over 40 rose from 21 percent to 46 percent. In their case and that of the attorneys, the rise in age probably reflects the development of the city. Some of the eager young entrepreneurs and lawyers who arrived early in its history managed to succeed and solidify their position during the following decades. By 1871 it may have become more difficult for a young man to break into a position of power and influence.[5] However even if this was so the constriction of opportunity had little to do with industrialization but rather reflected the timing of the city's development and the demography of its work force.

The only fragmentary data on cost of living that we have located highlight the difference in economic climate between Hamilton and New York State. In 1873 and 1874 Edward Young, chief of the United States Bureau of Statistics, attempted to compare wages and living costs in Europe, the United States, and British North America.[6] His book is a massive compendium of tables arranged by country with little analysis. Unfortunately it also contains little information about how the data were gathered or on the number of cases on which observations about wages were based. Thus the data must be utilized with extreme care. Nonetheless some gross differences relevant to our purposes do emerge.

Young presented the average wages paid (in terms of U.S. dollars) to "mechanical labor" in a number of categories by state for the United States and by selected Canadian cities and towns, one of which was Hamilton. It is striking that in every single category the average wage paid in New York State exceeded that in Hamilton. Blacksmiths earned on the average $2 per day in Hamilton and $2.64 in New York State, carpenters $1.75 and $2.75, painters $1.60 and $3.63, shoemakers $2 and $2.36. The difference extended to unskilled workers as well. Ordinary laborers with board earned $13 per month in Hamilton, compared to $25 in New York State; domestic servants with board were paid $7 per month in the Canadian city and $10.60 in New York State.[7]

Wages of course are relative to living costs. Young did present budgets for working men's families in both Hamilton and Buffalo. He did not specify whether they were based on one case or on an average. It is most likely that they represent only one instance, probably a workman referred to him for steadiness and sobriety. In each instance the man's earnings were based on fifty-two weeks of work per year. The budget for the Hamilton worker included no expenses for alcohol or tobacco; the Buffalo budget included only $.30 per week. The men interviewed not only were steady but were paid well above the average. The Buffalo working man earned $25 per week, the one in Hamilton $15. To make the comparison even more difficult, the Buffalo worker had three children and the one in Hamilton five. The total earnings of the Hamilton worker did not meet his expenses: the difference was nearly 10 percent. The wages of the Buffalo worker on the other hand exceeded his expenses by 16 percent. Obviously many factors could affect the balance in either case. A few weeks without work, a lower rate of pay, or a serious illness (no money was budgeted for medical care or insurance) could easily have put the Buffalo worker in the red or worsened the position of his counterpart in Hamilton. Certainly, though, the Buffalo worker appeared to have more room to maneuver. Despite his smaller family he spent $220 on clothes, compared to $100.24 for the worker with the larger family in Hamilton. The Buffalo worker also spent substantially more on food. Moreover the Buffalo worker owned his own home and the Hamilton worker rented. The cost of housing for the two men was nonetheless quite similar. The Hamilton man paid $3.38 per week in rent and $24 per year in taxes, giving him a weekly housing cost of $3.79. The Buffalo workman's interest on his mortgage and taxes yielded a weekly housing cost of $3.65, quite a similar figure. A slightly higher cost for the Buffalo worker resulted from his expenses for fuel and light—$106.60 annually, compared to $72.80 for the worker in Hamilton.

In Hamilton four-room tenements rented for $8 per week and six-room ones for $10, compared to $6.76 and $10.85 in New York State as a whole. Food, however, was a little cheaper in Hamilton than in New York State. Flour in the Canadian city cost $7 a bushel, compared to $7.50 in New York State; a pound of beef cost $.10, compared to about $.16; and a bushel of potatoes cost $.60 as opposed to $.77. Milk, eggs, tea, coffee, and sugar were almost identical in price. On the other hand fuel was more expensive in Hamilton. Coal there cost $8 per ton, compared to $7.88 in New York State, and hardwood cost $8 a cord, compared to $5.27. Though figures for Hamilton are not available, coal oil was considerably more expensive in Kingston, Cornwall, and Goderich than in New York State. The cost of boots and dry goods appeared comparable in the Canadian city and New York State.

If these figures are even approximately correct, they show that wages were higher in New York State and living costs about the same. That is certainly one reason why Buffalo not only grew more rapidly than Hamilton but also retained a higher proportion of its population.

## Patterns of Inequality

Despite the redistribution of its work force the relative size of Hamilton's two major classes remained quite constant throughout the shift from commercial to industrial capitalism. Between 1851 and 1871 the proportion of the male work force in the business class shifted only from 35 percent to 33 percent and the proportion in the working class from 62 percent to 65 percent. Given the imperfections in nineteenth-century data, the small shifts in proportion should not be stressed. The important point is the relative stability in the size of each class.

Within each class shifts took place in the distribution of men among various sorts of work. The number of clerks and men in associated types of work grew especially rapidly, while the number of professionals and merchants increased more slowly. In the working class the number of skilled workers increased at about the same rate as clerks, and the number of unskilled laborers grew much less. Individual trades increased at different rates: the number of machinists and other workers in the metal trades rose meteorically; the number of shoemakers increased very little. These shifts, however, did not alter the distribution of the work force by class; they represented shifts within class into the types of work appropriate to industrial capitalism.

The distribution of wealth did not alter very much either. Consider the index of representativeness between 1851 and 1881 (Table 2.4).[8] A score of 100 shows that the proportion of the assessed wealth in the

Table 2.4   Index of representativeness, distribution of wealth: Hamilton, 1851–1881.[a]

| Economic rank (percentile) | Year | | | |
|---|---|---|---|---|
| | 1851 | 1861 | 1871 | 1881 |
| 0–19 | 8 | 8 | 10 | 5 |
| 20–39 | 21 | 17 | 19 | 19 |
| 40–59 | 36 | 29 | 30 | 30 |
| 60–79 | 66 | 57 | 58 | 62 |
| 80–89 | 136 | 131 | 115 | 136 |
| 90–94 | 263 | 268 | 223 | 270 |
| 95–98 | 625 | 638 | 576 | 607 |
| 99 | 2,220 | 2,255 | 2,627 | 2,145 |
| N | 2,554 | 4,040 | 6,029 | 8,870 |

a. Index = (% of total wealth held by economic rank / % of assessed population in economic rank) × 100.

city held by members of an economic rank was exactly proportional to its share of the population. It is clear that the distribution of wealth remained generally stable and highly unequal. A slight decline took place in the index for people in the lower economic ranks, from 8 to 5 for those in the bottom twenty percentiles and from 21 to 19 for those between the twentieth and fortieth. Similarly a small decline occurred from 625 to 607 at the ninety-fifth to ninety-ninth and from 2,220 to 2,145 among the top one percent. But it is the similarities in the magnitudes of the differences that stand out. Indeed the index figures for each rank were at least two and often three times larger than the ones for the rank beneath them. Looked at another way the proportion of assessed wealth held by people in the poorest forty economic percentiles shifted between 1852 and 1881 only from 6 percent to 4 percent, a difference that could easily be accounted for by errors of measurement. The only possible trend, again small but in the expected direction, took place among the wealthiest ten economic percentiles, whose share of assessed wealth rose from 60 percent to 66 percent.

Relationships between class and wealth remained steady. The proportion of the working class in the bottom 40 economic percentiles shifted from 46 percent to 53 percent between 1851 and 1871. In the same years the ratio of the mean assessed wealth of the business to that of the working class changed from 4.5 to 3.7.

A similar stability characterized the relationships between occupational groups and wealth. Consider a simple grouping of occupations into five categories with an index score calculated for each (Table 2.5). At the top of the rank order, primarily merchants and professionals, the index for each of the four years hovered around 350, while at the

Table 2.5   Index of representativeness, distribution of wealth by occupation: Hamilton, 1851–1881.[a]

| Occupational rank | Year | | | |
|---|---|---|---|---|
| | 1851 | 1861 | 1871 | 1881 |
| 1 | 367 | 399 | 327 | 374 |
| 2 | 129 | 119 | 125 | 145 |
| 3 | 59 | 63 | 63 | 59 |
| 4 | 45 | 40 | 38 | 50 |
| 5 | 22 | 18 | 21 | 21 |
| Other | 50 | 68 | 121 | 87 |

a. Index for selected occupations = ( % of total wealth held by occupational rank / % of assessed population in occupational rank) × 100.

second rank, mainly clerks and related workers, it remained near 120. The index scores for ranks 3 (skilled workers) and 4 (primarily semi-skilled workers) were close, with the former a bit higher, about 60, compared to 40 to 50 for the latter. (The score for the skilled workers in this case would be lowered by the removal of the master artisans.) At the bottom of course came the laborers with a score that stayed close to 20. Thus four levels of wealth clearly persisted across time. Those levels, it is important to stress, did not represent four distinct classes. Rather they point to the existence of two fairly stable economic strata within each of the city's two major classes.

One other measure shows the stability in the relationship between occupation and wealth over time. That is the coefficient of variation, which permits the comparison of the degree of economic heterogeneity within occupational categories.[9] This measure is calculated by dividing the standard deviation by the mean. The lower it is, the less the variation within a category. On the grossest level, using five occupational ranks, the internal variation within each did not alter very much between 1851 and 1881. In rank 2 the coefficient shifted only from 1.67 to 1.65 in the course of thirty years and in rank 5 from 1.18 to 1.09 during the same period. The most notable shift happened in rank 3, where the variation increased from 1.52 to 2.37, a reflection of the growing diversity of a rank that contained industrial wage workers and some of the proprietors of new manufacturing establishments. At a more specific level the coefficient of variation for each of fifteen representative occupations in 1851 did not differ very much from the same measure thirty years later.

## Class and Ethnicity

Simply through population growth many jobs of all sorts opened in Hamilton between 1851 and 1871. However they did not go in equal proportions to people of varying ethnic backgrounds. The Irish Catholic share of the work force decreased from 25 percent to 12 percent during the twenty years. Nonetheless the Irish Catholics continued to occupy the bottom of the occupational hierarchy. We have expressed the occupational composition of ethnic groups by an index of representativeness. A representation within a trade matching an ethnic group's representation within the work force would give a score of 100. Some improvement in the position of Irish Catholics did take place: their index score among professionals and rentiers had risen from 11 to 26, among agents and merchants from 22 to 51, among vendors of services and semiprofessionals from 37 to 103. This last is a testimony to the entrance of Irish Catholics into hotel and tavern keeping. The improvement among masters and manufacturers (20 to 29) and skilled workers (61 to 63) was less notable. Importantly, the index for laborers rose from 233 to 281. Thus, though they improved slightly within the business class, Irish Catholics were concentrated even more disproportionately in unskilled labor at the end of twenty years.

Irish Protestants, whose share of the work force dropped from 17 percent to 8 percent, were overrepresented among vendors of services and semiprofessionals (for reasons similar to those affecting the Irish Catholics) and made substantial gains among professionals and rentiers. Their representation among business employees remained rather low and among government employees quite high, mainly on account of Irish constables. Otherwise, unlike the Catholics, they were a generally representative group.

Scottish Presbyterians, who made up 10 percent of the work force in 1851 and 12 percent in 1871, continued their overrepresentation throughout the business class, though their score declined in some specific categories. They composed a representative share of skilled workers and a low proportion of laborers. The non-Presbyterian Scots were a small group growing in strength among occupational categories in the business class and also among female domestics.

English Anglicans lost their distinctively high position between 1851 and 1871, though they retained a modest overrepresentation in the business class. Their share of the total work force, swelled by the immigration of poor wage workers, had risen from 9 percent to 14 percent between 1851 and 1871. Particularly notable was the sharp rise in their index score for laborers (from 54 to 121) and for servants (from 36 to 67). English Methodists, whose share of the population rose from 4 percent to 7 percent, also had an increased index score for laborers, though their score for female domestics dropped. However their index for professionals and proprietors and agents and merchants declined as well. Though their score for masters and manufacturers decreased, it still remained very high (264 in 1851 and 200 in 1871), and they were overrepresented as well among skilled workers (125). Apparently the English Methodists arrived with more experience and interest in industrial work than either English Anglicans or Scottish Presbyterians.

The Canadian Protestants lost some of their distinctiveness as the native-born children of immigrants entered the work force. As the proportion of Canadian Protestants doubled from 11 percent to 22 percent, the composition of the group became more heterogeneous. Nonetheless they still remained disproportionately successful: the index score for professionals and rentiers dropped from 171 to 129; the score for agents and merchants remained at 93; for business employees and masters and manufacturers it dropped from 212 to 143 and from 132 to 94, respectively. Interestingly the Canadian Protestants had the highest index score in 1871 among women with occupations other than domestic service (132), an indication of the ability of native-born young women to take more attractive job openings.

The size of the Canadian Catholic group also increased with the coming of age of immigrants' children. By 1871 the index score for laborers was only 26, compared to 281 among Catholics who had been born in Ireland. Similarly the native-born Catholic index among skilled workers was 92, compared to 63 among the Irish, and among business employees 218 compared to 15. Young men born in Canada clearly had much greater access to the world of commerce than those born in Ireland and entered the least rewarding sector of the working class much less frequently.

American-born blacks were a small group with very uneven representation in different occupational categories. They concentrated in services and had a fairly high index score among masters and manufacturers (probably on account of barbers who were self-employed). Interestingly their score among laborers was very low (perhaps they had been excluded from laboring jobs) and among agriculturalists the highest of any group in 1871.

Throughout the period American-born whites continued to be very successful. They scored high in all business-class occupations except business employees, and their index score among masters and manufacturers (221) was especially notable. They scored high too among skilled workers, (171), and quite low among laborers (50) and domestic servants (66).

Birthplace, occupation, and class intersected in a similar way in Buffalo. There the major places of birth were New England, New York, Ireland, Germany, other United States, and other foreign, with 6 percent, 12 percent, 17 percent, 40 percent, 3 percent, and 22 percent of household heads, respectively. The natives much more often found more rewarding occupations. Using the index of representativeness, the New England score on professionals and rentiers was 366, the New York one 360, and the other United States 336, compared to 14 for Ireland, 27 for Germany, and 54 for other foreign. The New Englanders clustered even more disproportionately among agents and merchants (292), compared to 173 for New Yorkers, 62 for men born in Ireland, and 61 for Germans. The natives concentrated not only within commerce but within the ownership of manufacturing enterprises. Among masters and manufacturers the New England index was 269, the New York one 172, the Irish 32, and the German 60. Nor did the foreign representation improve among the lower ranks of the business class. The index for the Irish among business employees was 56 and for Germans 29, compared to 258 for New Englanders and 267 for New Yorkers.

Within the working class, obviously, the situation was reversed. New Englanders and New Yorkers were underrepresented among skilled workers at 59 and 69. However so were the Irish at 47, compared to an index score of 136 among Germans. Though Germans clustered more often in skilled work than the Irish, they were no less disproportionately represented among laborers. For both Irish and Germans the index scores (144 and 142, respectively) were quite high and those for people born in New England and New York (5 and 11) exceptionally low.

Looked at another way, 41 percent of the Irish household heads, 27 percent of the German, 1 percent of the New Englanders, and 3 percent of the New Yorkers were laborers. By contrast quite similar proportions of New Englanders, New Yorkers, and Irish-born men (31 percent, 36 percent, and 31 percent) were in skilled work compared to a striking 61 percent of Germans. However very few Germans were masters and manufacturers (3 percent), a figure only insignificantly higher than the 2 percent for the Irish and much lower than the 14 percent for New Englanders and 9 percent for New Yorkers. Indeed the New Englanders fared best: a third of them were either professionals and rentiers or agents and merchants. In fact 62 percent of them, compared to 31 percent of New Yorkers, were in the business class. For the Irish the proportion was much lower (14 percent), though the group with the least was the Germans (under 10 percent).

Thus each of the major groups had a distinctive profile. New England-born men clustered heavily in business-class occupations with disproportionately large numbers among professionals, merchants, and masters. New York-born men also did well, though their representation among the higher branches of commerce and among masters was lower than that of the New England born. About a third of each group were skilled wage workers, and very few were lower on the occupational rank order. About a third of the Irish were skilled wage workers as well, but only a few were in the business class and two-fifths were laborers. Germans, though also infrequently proprietors, professionals, or clerks, clustered in skilled work and were laborers much less often than the Irish.

It is clear that ethnic and class distinctions—and within classes distinctions between particular occupational groups—overlapped. Particular positions in the social and occupational structure had distinctive ethnic identities. Most notable was the concentration of Irish

Catholics and blacks at the bottom of every scale and the advantages of natives. Less immediately apparent but also quite real was the affinity of the Scottish for commerce, the clustering of groups of English immigrants in metal trades, the connection between Germans and cigar-making. For the most part the differences reflected the position, skill, and capital of the immigrants who entered North American cities. The Irish came impoverished; many British metal workers migrated; Scottish men often had connections to mercantile families. However, over time ethnicity decreasingly exerted an independent influence on economic characteristics such as wealth or the employment of servants or behavioral ones such as age at marriage or school attendance. For the most part ethnicity affected social structure through the characteristics with which immigrants arrived.

There were of course exceptions. The racism that confronted blacks denied them and their children the advantages of native urban birth. Irish Catholics too faced discrimination, which made it especially difficult for them to escape poverty. However, by itself native birth had a positive impact on the opportunities of most men.

Two points must be stressed: the first, already stated, is the extent to which the experience of immigrants in their native countries influenced their position in the social and occupational structure of North America. The second is the long-term impact of the overlap between class and ethnicity in North America. Membership in the working class, especially its lowest ranks, has consistently been identified with racial or cultural difference. At various points blacks, Irish Catholics, and southern or eastern Europeans have clustered disproportionately in the worst jobs that this continent has had to offer. The result of poverty, discrimination, and a capitalist labor market, that clustering has continued to feed the association of culture and race with class. To the animus with which the prosperous always view the poor in capitalist societies it has added a nasty edge of racism.

## The Process of Inequality

Ethnicity has also had clear and persistent connections with occupation and wealth. Indeed wealth, occupation, and ethnicity formed stable, interconnecting patterns. Individual economic standing apparently reflected both characteristics. However the relative influence of occupation and ethnicity remains unclear. Was their influence independent, or did they overlap? Was the apparent weight of ethnicity due to the occupations customarily followed by people of different backgrounds? To sort out the answers to these questions, multivariate analysis is essential.

In addressing these questions we considered the factors associated with economic rank and attempted to identify precisely the unique contribution of each measurable independent variable. In this analysis the dependent variable was assessed wealth, divided into five levels, hereafter called economic rank.

The first statistics of importance provide summaries of the general strength of the relationships between each factor or independent variable and economic rank, with all other factors held constant. These measures—the betas—show that a set of stable relationships underlay the structure of inequality during the transition from commercial to industrial capitalism in Hamilton. Not only the surface characteristics of the social structure but a complex set of relationships remained intact despite alterations in the city's economic base and in the very identity of its population.

The most influential factor was the combined variable occupation and age, with a beta of .37, .41, and .39 in each of the three census years, respectively (Table 2.6). The influence of this factor can be attributed for the most part to occupation. Next in influence came ethni-

Table 2.6   Predicted economic rank of household heads, multiple classification analysis: Hamilton, 1851–1871.

A. Selected predictions (all factors constant)

1. Ethnicity and property

| Ethnicity | Renters in — | | | Owners in — | | |
|---|---|---|---|---|---|---|
| | 1851 | 1861 | 1871 | 1851 | 1861 | 1871 |
| Irish Catholic | 2.7 | 2.7 | 2.5 | 3.5 | 3.6 | 3.2 |
| Irish Protestant | 3.0 | 2.8 | 2.8 | 4.0 | 3.7 | 3.6 |
| Scottish Presbyterian | 3.0 | 3.0 | 3.0 | 3.7 | 3.6 | 3.6 |
| English Anglican | 3.2 | 3.1 | 2.8 | 3.7 | 3.7 | 3.7 |
| English Methodist | 3.4 | 3.3 | 2.9 | 4.0 | 3.9 | 3.8 |
| Canadian Protestant | 3.0 | 3.2 | 3.0 | 4.1 | 3.9 | 3.9 |
| U.S. white | 3.2 | 3.4 | — | 4.5 | 4.1 | — |
| Other | 3.0 | 2.8 | 2.9 | 3.9 | 3.6 | 3.7 |

2. Relatives and boarders (categories with 100 or more cases)

| No. of relatives | No. of boarders | 1851 | 1861 | 1871 |
|---|---|---|---|---|
| 0 | 0 | 3.1 | 3.0 | 3.1 |
| 1 | 0 | 3.6 | 3.4 | 3.2 |
| 0 | 1 | 3.7 | 3.4 | 3.3 |
| 0 | 2+ | 3.7 | 3.7 | 3.6 |

Table 2.6, *continued*

### 3. Servants

| No. of servants | 1851 | 1861 | 1871 |
|---|---|---|---|
| 0 | 2.9 | 3.1 | 3.0 |
| 1 | 3.7 | 3.5 | 3.8 |
| 2 or more | 4.3 | 4.3 | 3.9 |

### 4. Occupation and age

| Age | Occupational rank[a] | | | | | |
|---|---|---|---|---|---|---|
| | 1 | 2 | 3 | 4 | 5 | Unclassified |
| *Under 25* | | | | | | |
| 1851 | 4.4 | 2.6 | 2.7 | 2.4 | 2.6 | 2.7 |
| 1861 | — | 3.2 | 3.3 | 3.2 | 2.6 | — |
| 1871 | — | 3.1 | 2.7 | 1.9 | 2.3 | 2.1 |
| *25–34* | | | | | | |
| 1851 | 4.5 | 3.5 | 3.2 | 2.9 | 2.5 | 2.4 |
| 1861 | 4.1 | 3.6 | 3.0 | 2.6 | 2.3 | 3.1 |
| 1871 | 4.0 | 3.6 | 2.6 | 2.4 | 2.2 | 3.0 |
| *35–44* | | | | | | |
| 1851 | 4.2 | 4.1 | 3.3 | 3.0 | 2.5 | 2.6 |
| 1861 | 4.0 | 4.1 | 3.3 | 3.5 | 2.2 | 3.1 |
| 1871 | 4.1 | 3.8 | 3.1 | 2.7 | 2.2 | 2.9 |
| *45–54* | | | | | | |
| 1851 | 3.7 | 4.1 | 3.2 | 3.1 | 2.6 | 3.3 |
| 1861 | 4.0 | 4.1 | 3.3 | 3.5 | 2.2 | 3.1 |
| 1871 | 4.3 | 4.0 | 3.4 | 2.9 | 2.3 | 2.4 |
| *55–64* | | | | | | |
| 1851 | 4.3 | 4.2 | 3.3 | 3.7 | 2.4 | 1.2 |
| 1861 | 4.8 | 3.8 | 3.2 | 3.2 | 2.4 | 4.0 |
| 1871 | 4.2 | 3.7 | 3.2 | 2.9 | 2.3 | 3.9 |
| *65 and over* | | | | | | |
| 1851 | 4.1 | 3.7 | 2.4 | —[b] | — | — |
| 1861 | — | 4.2 | 3.1 | — | 2.7 | — |
| 1871 | 4.2 | 3.7 | 3.2 | 3.0 | 2.2 | — |

### B. BETAS

| Variable | 1851 | 1861 | 1871 |
|---|---|---|---|
| Occupation and age | .37 | .41 | .39 |
| Ethnicity and property | .27 | .26 | .27 |
| Sex and number of children | .11 | .09 | .10 |
| Relatives and boarders | .21 | .13 | .10 |
| Servants | .22 | .28 | .18 |
| $R^2$ | .50 | .52 | .42 |

a. Occupational rank: (1) professional, high commercial; (2) lower commercial; (3) skilled workers; (4) semiskilled workers; (5) unskilled workers.

b. —, cell frequency five or less.

city and property. Sex of the household head and number of children remained constant but negligible in influence. The effect of servants, also quite similar across the decades, was weaker than that of ethnicity and property. The only change of any note occurred in the case of the variable relatives and boarders, whose beta dropped from .21 to .10, a reflection of the general elimination of extensions to the household (see Chapter 8). As a whole the factor variables accounted for a substantial 50 percent, 52 percent, and 42 percent of the variation in economic rank in each decade, respectively, very high proportions for data of the sort used here.

Within each ethnic group, property owners had a higher economic rank than renters, and the distinctions remained quite stable throughout the decades. In fact the differences between ethnic groups within each category of property status (owner or renter) were quite small. Between the highest- and lowest-scoring ethnic groups (rank 1 is lowest and 5 highest) among owners in 1871 the predicted rank varied only from 3.2 to 3.9; among renters in the same year the scores spread only from 2.5 (Irish Catholics) at the bottom to 3 (Canadian Protestants) at the top. Note that the highest score among renters still remained below the lowest score among owners. Thus the relationship of ethnicity to wealth largely evaporates with occupation and property kept constant.

Occupation and age affected economic rank through their relationship with each other. The predicted economic rank of people within each age group varied sharply with their occupation. For instance it dropped among the 35- to 44-year-olds in 1871 from 4.1 for men in rank 1 to 2.2 for those in rank 5. The predicted rank of men in rank 2 generally remained closer to that of men in rank 1 than in rank 3, which reflects the greater variation between than within classes. The relationships between occupation, age, and economic rank remained relatively constant.

The relationship of age to economic rank is particularly significant because it points to class differences in life cyle.[11] The economic rank of men in occupational rank 2 rose until they reached their mid-fifties. By contrast the economic rank of laborers did not alter very much with age. The economic rank of artisans, which rose until their mid-thirties, reveals still a third pattern. If we can make inferences from cross-sectional data, the assessed wealth of young laborers did not differ sharply from that of young clerks or artisans. Over time, however, the gap between the groups increased when the wages of the laborers failed to rise. Clerks, on the other hand, often found themselves in a career that brought continually increased rewards as they aged. This difference in the relationship between income and the life cycle probably underlay the emerging distinction in marriage age between laborers and clerks (see Chapter 8).

Working men realized the relationship between their life cycle and their earning power. A survey conducted by the Wisconsin Bureau of Industrial Statistics in the late 1880s asked over five hundred workmen in a variety of trades, "At what age do persons begin to decline physically so as to affect their work and wages?" The assumption in the question that skill and wages would decline was not challenged by the men.[12] Of those surveyed 64 percent answered the question; roughly 8 percent put the age at 30 to 39, 19 percent at 40 to 44, 22 percent at 45 to 49, 41 percent at 50 to 59, and 12 percent at 60 or over. In other words nearly half expected a man's earning power to decline before the age of 50, and 88 percent expected the drop to start before the age of 60. These expectations, which did not vary with specific trades, confirm the pattern indicated by the statistics showing the relationship between age and economic rank in both Hamilton and Buffalo. Earning hardly enough to support his family, frequently unable to save, subject to periodic unemployment, facing a decline in his wages starting at around the age of 50, and holding no private or public pension, the nineteenth-century skilled wage worker entered old age with bleak prospects. The lucky ones might have a small house or a married child to look after them; the rest could expect only charity or the poorhouse.

In Hamilton larger households (those with two or more relatives or boarders) were associated with higher economic ranks. Given the relationship between household complexity and wealth, any other finding would have been startling. Naturally the employment of servants also had a direct relationship with economic rank, though not nearly as strong as that of occupation. The employment of servants provides an important index of social standing in nineteenth-century cities. More than one observer has argued that the employment of a resident domestic servant separated the social classes in Victorian cities.[13] Of course servants provide an indication of class membership; they are not a cause. The source of class membership, as we have argued, lay in the social relationships of the productive process. Thus the division of household heads into two groups—those likely to employ resident domestics and those unlikely to do so—offers a rough way of ordering the population into two relatively distinct groups whose characteristics expose important aspects of the interrelationship between the structural characteristics of Hamilton's social order. In particular it sheds light on the sharpness of distinctions between and within classes and permits an evaluation of the utility of keeping servants as an indicator of class in nineteenth-century cities.

The proportion of households employing servants dropped sharply from 28 percent to 25 percent to 12 percent by 1871. It is therefore unlikely that measures of association will be as similar to each other as they were in the case of economic rank. We should expect instead a decline in the strength of the relationship during the period.

As Table 2.7 shows, occupation and age (again used as a combined factor variable) and economic rank had the strongest relationship to the employment of servants (used as the dependent variable in this analysis). In 1861, perhaps on account of the depression, economic

Table 2.7   Percent of households employing a servant, multiple classification analysis, Hamilton, 1851–1871.

A. SELECTED PROBABILITIES (PERCENT)

1. Occupation and age

| Age | Occupational Rank[a] | | | | | Unclassified |
|---|---|---|---|---|---|---|
|  | 1 | 2 | 3 | 4 | 5 |  |
| *Under 25* |  |  |  |  |  |  |
| 1851 | 10 | 23 | 18 | 36 | 24 | 35 |
| 1861 | —[b] | 40 | 24 | 35 | 10 | — |
| 1871 | 25 | 19 | 5 | 5 | 2 | 3 |
| *25–34* |  |  |  |  |  |  |
| 1851 | 52 | 44 | 25 | 27 | 27 | 27 |
| 1861 | 50 | 39 | 20 | 29 | 20 | 28 |
| 1871 | 36 | 27 | 7 | 4 | 4 | 10 |
| *35–44* |  |  |  |  |  |  |
| 1851 | 44 | 47 | 22 | 22 | 13 | 31 |
| 1861 | 46 | 41 | 20 | 17 | 19 | 30 |
| 1871 | 38 | 25 | 17 | 13 | 17 | 35 |
| *45–54* |  |  |  |  |  |  |
| 1851 | 42 | 43 | 18 | 18 | 16 | 32 |
| 1861 | 38 | 25 | 17 | 13 | 17 | 35 |
| 1871 | 40 | 20 | 3 | 7 | 5 | 13 |
| *55–64* |  |  |  |  |  |  |
| 1851 | 34 | 31 | 14 | 12 | 10 | 43 |
| 1861 | 32 | 15 | 18 | 19 | 14 | 17 |
| 1871 | 40 | 24 | 5 | 1 | 6 | 10 |
| *65 and over* |  |  |  |  |  |  |
| 1851 | 37 | 47 | 13 | —[b] | — | — |
| 1861 | 41 | 31 | 10 | 10 | 25 | — |
| 1871 | 26 | 24 | 9 | 2 | 5 | — |

Table 2.7, *continued*

2. Economic rank[c]

| Rank (percentile) | 1851 | 1861 | 1871 |
|---|---|---|---|
| 0–19 | 15 | 9 | 7 |
| 20–39 | 19 | 12 | 6 |
| 40–59 | 21 | 15 | 7 |
| 60–79 | 35 | 30 | 15 |
| 80–89 | 46 | 50 | 19 |
| 90–99 | 44 | 64 | 34 |

B. BETAS

| Variable | 1851 | 1861 | 1871 |
|---|---|---|---|
| Occupation and age | .26 | .24 | .34 |
| Ethnicity and property | .07 | .11 | .08 |
| Economic rank | .25 | .41 | .25 |
| Sex of household head and number of children | .19 | .07 | .09 |
| Relatives and boarders | .12 | .05 | .04 |
| Mean | 28 | 25 | 12 |
| $R^2$ | .28 | .32 | .28 |

a. Occupational rank: (1) professional, high commercial; (2) lower commercial; (3) skilled workers; (4) semiskilled workers; (5) unskilled workers.

b. —, cell frequency under five.

c. Economic rank = assessed wealth.

rank had a stronger association, whereas by 1871 occupation and age had emerged as the most influential factor. None of the other factors—composition of the household, number of children, sex of household head, ethnicity, and property ownership—had very much effect on the employment of servants. The probability that a person with any set of characteristics would employ a servant generally decreased over time, as the proportion of households with domestics dropped steeply. Even among men in the highest occupational rank the decline was notable, though it occurred much more sharply among younger men.[14] The probability that a man 25 to 34 years old in the highest occupational rank would have a servant dipped from 52 percent to 36 percent between 1851 and 1871, compared to a shift from 44 percent to 38 percent among 35-to-44-year-olds. Though the odds that a middle-aged man in the top occupational rank would employ a servant remained substantial, they lessened considerably for men at the next rank. Thus, despite their relatively solid economic standing the ability of men in rank 2 to employ a servant declined drastically. In 1851 servant employment distinguished by and large between the business and working class. Twenty years later it separated the strata within the business class itself. In 1851 an artisan aged 45 to 54 years old was less than half as likely to employ a servant than a man in rank 1. By 1871 the gap had widened to one in thirteeen. Thus the general decrease in servant employment widened the differences between occupational groups.

As with occupation men in all economic ranks became less likely to employ servants. The most important distinction separated those people in the top ten percentiles from the group just beneath them, those in percentiles 80 to 89. In 1851 the odds that each group would employ a servant were quite similar: 46 percent for the latter and 44 percent for the former. Twenty years later they were 19 percent and 34 percent, respectively. In fact by 1871 there was only about a 7 percent chance that anyone beneath the sixtieth economic rank would employ a servant. The employment of servants thus became increasingly restricted to wealthy middle-aged professionals and proprietors. Whether the situation in Hamilton had parallels elsewhere cannot be determined from the historical work that currently exists.[15] However comparisons are important, for the significance of keeping servants altered markedly in nineteenth-century Hamilton. The result was that the servant-employing group of the early industrial city differed markedly from its predecessor in the commerical era. In 1851 a reasonable probability existed that anyone in the business class would employ a servant; it was highly unlikely that anyone in the working class would do so. Twenty years later only the most privileged sector of the business class could expect to have resident domestic help. Thus the utility of keeping servants as an indication of class depends on the time and place to which it is applied.

The reasons why servant employment declined relate as much to supply as demand. Young women were attracted to industrial employment and left domestic service as jobs in manufacturing became available. The relative scarcity their exodus created may have raised the wages of servants and priced them out of the reach of all but the most well-to-do families. Certainly the attempt to import large numbers of young servant girls from England to Canada in the late nineteenth century suggests the existence of an unfilled demand. And the one bit of wage information from the 1870s, which is that servants in Hamilton were paid $7 per month plus board, shows that they were expensive.[16] The total income of a well-paid skilled wage worker was unlikely to exceed $40 per month, and a clerk was unlikely to earn very much more. Thus a servant's wages would consume a large portion of a family's income.

This discussion of economic rank and employment of servants has

attempt to trace individuals from one source to another. Record linkage, as this process is called, is an intricate, hazardous undertaking, and different methods can alter radically the number of people located through two different sources. For example the historian must establish the conditions under which a name listed on two censuses should be accepted as identifying the same individual. The proportion of individuals claimed to be listed on two different sources will vary directly with the nature and stringency of the conditions. The problem is particularly acute since people did not generally record their identifying characteristics in an identical way on each source. Indeed even the spelling of the same individual's name often varied.[9]

The problems of record linkage must enter into any evaluation or comparison of rates of population persistence, because with very few exceptions historians have used different rules to establish the identity between people listed on two or more sources and, even more troubling, have not specified precisely the conditions they employed. It is thus impossible to compare or replicate their results in any precise way. That is why Thernstrom is correct to emphasize the rough similarity in the rates reported by other historians rather than to stress the differences between them.

However one source does permit the study of population persistence without recourse to record linkage: the remarkable New York State census of 1855, which reported the length of time each person had lived in the town or city in which he or she had been enumerated. This information makes possible three types of measures: average length of residence, rates of population persistence, and the social and demographic determinants of length of residence.

Through the calculation of these measures we have been able to provide the first systematic account of variations in length of residence between a city and the rural area that surrounded it. In order to test the representativeness of patterns in Buffalo and Erie County we compared them to those in Hamilton. The Hamilton figures rest on record linkage, which is a weakness, but we have done the linkage ourselves in a systematic and rigorous fashion.[10]

The rate of persistence in Buffalo was significantly higher than the rate in Hamilton and indeed in most cities that historians have studied in recent years. This difference reflected economic environment: the booming growth of Buffalo compared to the slower pace in Hamilton.

Nonetheless most people in Buffalo were newcomers. It is to be expected that a population that had doubled in ten years would have consisted mainly of immigrants. In 1855 the average resident had lived in Buffalo 6.2 years. More meaningfully, the average household head had been there only 8.8 years, and the difference between the length of time the average member of the youngest cohort of employed males (18 to 24) and the oldest (over 55) had lived in the city was only 7 (6 versus 13) years. By contrast the household heads had lived in rural Erie County an average of 13.8 years, about 5 years longer than in the city.

However the recent date of arrival of most people reveals little about the proportion of those present ten years earlier who had remained. To estimate this figure, the rate of persistence, it was necessary to calculate the proportion of the 1845 population formed by 1855 residents who claimed to have lived in the city for at least ten years. It also was necessary to introduce corrections for mortality.[11]

The rate of persistence in Buffalo was high compared to that found in other large cities in roughly the same period. Just over half (51 percent) of all survivors—53 percent of women and 49 percent of men—had remained in the city for ten years. The relationship between persistence and age assumed a predictable U-shaped curve among men: 52 percent of residents under 9 years old in 1845 persisted, a figure that dropped to a low of 37 percent among 20- to 29-year-olds, rose rapidly to 52 percent among men in their thirties, and became nearly universal among men 60 years old and over. Thus as all studies of migration have shown, men moved most freely in their twenties, prior to settling down, and only infrequently during old age (Table 3.1).

For women the relationship between age and persistence was similar, with two significant differences. The persistence of women under 9 and 20 to 29 was higher than that of men: 59 percent compared to 52 percent and 44 percent compared to 37 percent. Young women probably left the city in search of job opportunities much less frequently than men, and they married on the average four years earlier. After the age of 30, persistence rates among surviving men and women became virtually identical.

Household heads migrated less often than other individuals of the same age, though it was the number of children rather than the fact of heading a household that affected their propensity to remain in the city. Here the figures are most reliable for those household heads aged 30 or over in 1845, for it is difficult to estimate what proportion of the men 30 to 39 in Buffalo in 1855 actually had been household heads ten years earlier. Persistence was lowest, though still high (58 percent), among 30- to 39-year-olds; it increased about 5 percent among 40- to 49- and 50- to 59-year-olds and jumped to 79 percent among those over 60. About 60 percent of household heads aged 30 to 69 in 1845 stayed in Buffalo for a decade.

In rural Erie County surviving households heads persisted at a rate

Table 3.1 Persistence figures, corrected for mortality: Buffalo, 1845–1855.[a]

| Age in 1845 | N | $N_s$ | | $N_p$ | Percent |
|---|---|---|---|---|---|
| *All males, Buffalo* | | | | | |
| 0–4 | 2,807 | 2,408 | | | |
| | | | 4,337 | 2,269 | 52.3 |
| 5–9 | 2,011 | 1,929 | | | |
| 10–19 | 3,120 | 2,939 | | 1,402 | 47.7 |
| 20–29 | 4,749 | 4,369 | | 1,629 | 37.3 |
| 30–39 | 2,981 | 2,647 | | 1,372 | 51.8 |
| 40–49 | 1,456 | 1,025 | | 709 | 69.2 |
| 50–59 | 624 | 441 | | 286 | 64.9 |
| 60–69 | 208 | 101 | | | |
| | | | 121 | 120 | 99.2 |
| 70 and over | 104 | 20 | | | |
| Total males | | 15,879 | | 7,787 | 49.0 |
| *All females, Buffalo* | | | | | |
| 0–4 | 2,739 | 2,375 | | | |
| | | | 4,233 | 2,516 | 59.4 |
| 5–9 | 1,941 | 1,858 | | | |
| 10–19 | 3,536 | 3,334 | | 1,649 | 49.5 |
| 20–29 | 3,952 | 3,652 | | 1,590 | 43.5 |
| 30–39 | 2,288 | 2,071 | | 1,085 | 52.4 |
| 40–49 | 1,213 | 1,054 | | 600 | 56.9 |
| 50–59 | 589 | 449 | | 294 | 65.5 |
| 60–69 | 243 | 134 | | | |
| | | | 158 | 144 | 91.1 |
| 70 and over | 104 | 24 | | | |
| Total females | | 14,951 | | 7,878 | 52.7 |
| Total population | | 30,830 | | 15,665 | 50.8 |

a. $N$ = number present, 1845; $N_s$ = number surviving, 1855; $N_p$ = number present, 1855; Percent = decennial persistence ($N_p/N_s$).

about 10 percent higher than in the city. Roughly 70 percent of the surviving 25- to 54-year-olds in 1845 remained in the same township, town, or village during the next decade. Differences between country and city existed within age groups as well as between the populations as a whole: for instance 67 percent of the rural 30- to 39-year-olds persisted, compared to 58 percent of those in the city. Thus, rural household heads formed a stable group: only about 30 percent left during the decade.

The 60 percent rate of household head persistence in Buffalo is high —between 50 percent and 100 percent higher than most scholars in the field would have predicted on the basis of work published to date. From a different perspective a very substantial fraction (40 percent) of household heads were on the move.

To put patterns in Buffalo in perspective, compare them to those in Hamilton. Our calculation of persistence in Hamilton utilized records of individuals traced from 1851 to 1861 and from 1861 to 1871.[12] (Hereafter all rates, unless otherwise noted, have been corrected for mortality). Stability is the most striking characteristic of the rates of population persistence between decades: 35 percent and 30 percent of males in each decade, respectively, remained in Hamilton. Many females could not be linked because they married and changed their names. Thus the number located was adjusted upward to make the sex ratio among persisters identical to that among the entire population. Adjusted according to sex ratio the proportion of persisting females remained identical at 37 percent. Among household heads persistence shifted only from 44 percent to 46 percent, and an estimated 44 percent and 42 percent of households continued in the city throughout each decade. (A continuing or surviving household was one headed by the same individual or by his widow.) These rates are substantially lower than in Buffalo.

The striking similarities between decennial rates of persistence in Hamilton point to the existence of a stable process of population turnover that did not alter during the city's early industrialization. Why? Perhaps a depression in each decade and a consequent decline and rise in population played a role. Perhaps more important was the general stability in the proportion of the population in the work force. Thus the number of jobs relative to the population remained quite steady. If migration were tied to the labor market, this stability might account for the similarity in the amount of out-migration in each decade.

The relationship between the age of males and persistence assumed the same U shape during each decade and was also very similar to the pattern in Buffalo (Table 3.2). In each decade the bottom of the curve occurred at the same age group, whose rate of persistence was identical: only 26 percent of those young men aged 15 to 24 in 1851 and 1861 remained in the city during the next ten years. Similarly the curve reached its highest point in each decade among the oldest: 69 percent of them persisted in the first decade and 52 percent during the second. Here the relatively small numbers might account for the differences between the two decades.

Men in the two youngest age groups increased their rate of persistence. Among those less than 5 years old at the beginning of either decade the rate of persistence increased during the decade from 35 percent to 45 percent and among those 5 to 14 it rose from 34 percent

Table 3.2   Male persistence by age, corrected for mortality: Hamilton, 1851–1861, 1861–1871.[a]

| Age | 1851–1861 | | | | 1861–1871 | | | |
|---|---|---|---|---|---|---|---|---|
| | N | $N_s$ | $N_p$ | Percent | N | $N_s$ | $N_p$ | Percent |
| 0–4 | 976 | 866 | 304 | 35.1 | 1,398 | 1,240 | 555 | 44.8 |
| 5–14 | 1,636 | 1,564 | 530 | 33.9 | 2,247 | 2,148 | 881 | 41.0 |
| 15–24 | 1,449 | 1,339 | 350 | 26.1 | 1,638 | 1,514 | 395 | 26.1 |
| 25–34 | 1,305 | 1,176 | 412 | 35.0 | 1,531 | 1,379 | 498 | 36.1 |
| 35–44 | 843 | 722 | 290 | 40.2 | 1,181 | 1,011 | 416 | 41.1 |
| 45–54 | 444 | 341 | 153 | 44.9 | 668 | 514 | 236 | 45.9 |
| 55 and over | 243 | 124 | 85 | 68.5 | 512 | 257 | 134 | 52.1 |
| Total | | 6,132 | 2,124 | 34.6 | | 10,383 | 3,115 | 30.0 |

a. N = number of men present in first year; $N_s$ = number surviving to second year; $N_p$ = number present in second year; Percent = decennial persistence ($N_p/N_s$).

to 41 percent. Among young men in their teens or early twenties at the end of each decade the propensity to remain in the city reflected an important development (discussed in Chapter 7): the prolonged length of time that young people spent in the homes of their parents. During these years of early industrialization the average age at which young people left home increased by about four years. In 1851 young men characteristically left home soon after they had found work. Twenty years later they were living with their parents during their first years of employment. The rapid drop in the rate of persistence among men in the next oldest group (15 to 24) shows that when men left their parents' home, they also very often left the city as well.

Among men of other ages rates of persistence remained very similar during each decade—for example 35 percent and 36 percent for those 25 to 34, 40 percent and 41 percent for 35- to 44-year-olds, and 45 percent and 46 percent for men 45 to 54. Thus the relationship of age to persistence among men remained remarkably stable across the decades, modified only by the prolonged residence of children in the homes of their parents.

Other characteristics of the linked population remained quite similar in each decade. Those more likely to persist were household heads, wives, and children. Those less likely were other relatives, boarders, and servants, the people one should expect to be most mobile. The proportion of children among the linked population increased from 44 percent to 52 percent, again a reflection of the prolonged residence of children at home. Conversely the proportion of boarders dropped from 9 percent to 4 percent, and the proportion of servants decreased from 2 percent to 1 percent. In each decade those who persisted were more likely to be married, though not widowed, than those who did not and, if household heads, disproportionately male. Finally persistent households were slightly more likely to contain children and servants than ones that were transient.

Relationships between birthplace, religion, and persistence did not change very much. In Table 3.3 they are expressed as an index of representativeness. If the proportion of a group among persisters were identical to its proportion among the entire population, its index score would be 100. Here we consider as disproportionate only those scores more than 25 percent above or below 100. Using birthplace as a characteristic no groups were found to be disproportionately represented in the period 1851-1861, and only the U.S. born (65 percent) and the Scots (135 percent) were so during the next ten years. The index for religion points to a similarly stable situation. Catholics had a low score in each decade, while members of the Church of Scotland

Table 3.3   Index of representativeness[a] for demographic characteristics of linked population: Hamilton, 1851-1861, 1861-1871.

| | Population linked census to census[b] | | Four way link[c] | |
|---|---|---|---|---|
| Demographic characteristics | 1851–1861 | 1861–1871 | 1851–1861 | 1861–1871 |
| *Birthplace* | | | | |
| England | 113 | 106 | 115 | 114 |
| Scotland | 113 | 105 | 113 | 135 |
| Ireland | 82 | 85 | 101 | 93 |
| Canada | 117 | 117 | 112 | 89 |
| United States | 86 | 65 | 114 | 86 |
| *Religion* | | | | |
| Anglican | 116 | 98 | 119 | 101 |
| Church of Scotland | 141 | 106 | 138 | 105 |
| Catholic | 75 | 87 | 53 | 71 |
| Free Church Presbyterian | 170 | 115 | 178 | 103 |
| Presbyterian | 118 | 121 | 116 | 148 |
| Wesleyan Methodist | 116 | 113 | 119 | 113 |
| Methodist | 107 | 96 | 131 | 85 |
| Baptist | 121 | 97 | 155 | 121 |

a. Index = (% in category / % in base population) × 100.
b. Base population = total population 1851 / total population 1861.
c. Base population = population linked from census to assessment 1851–1861, 1861–1871.

and Free Church Presbyterians were overrepresented among the persistent population.

Table 3.4 presents a more refined analysis of the relationship between ethnicity and religion. It shows the rates of persistence among ethnic groups in each decade. In each the Irish Catholics had the lowest rate (27 percent and 30 percent) and the English Methodists the highest (58 percent and 46 percent). The group ranking next highest remained the Scottish Presbyterians (39 percent and 41 percent). The rates for English Anglicans (39 percent and 37 percent) and for Canadian Protestants (37 percent and 41 percent) stayed quite similar. The low rate for Irish Catholics was probably a reflection of their poverty. However the important points to emphasize are, first, the ubiquity of a high rate of out-migration among all ethnic groups and, second, the relative similarity of the rates in each decade.

Striking continuities existed in the socioeconomic characteristics of persistence as well. First, consider occupation. Though the extremely small numbers make the comparisons somewhat tenuous, some patterns do emerge. No clear relationship existed between persistence and occupational status. Laborers did not persist notably less than other groups. The rate for merchants was not markedly higher: 41 percent of laborers and 40 percent of merchants persisted between 1851 and 1861, compared to 34 percent and 40 percent during the next decade.

Young women who were domestic servants persisted the least frequently of any group between 1861 and 1871. Although the rate (7 percent) would be substantially higher if we could trace them after marriage, it is still extremely low; the rates for other occupations con-

Table 3.4  Persistence of major ethnic groups, corrected for mortality: Hamilton, 1851–1861, 1861–1871.[a]

|  | 1851–1861 | | | 1861–1871 | | |
| Religion | $N_s$ | $N_p$ | Percent | $N_s$ | $N_p$ | Percent |
| --- | --- | --- | --- | --- | --- | --- |
| Irish Catholic | 2,500 | 682 | 27.2 | 2,175 | 662 | 30.4 |
| Irish Protestant | 1,565 | 495 | 31.6 | 1,315 | 453 | 34.4 |
| Scottish Presbyterian | 756 | 294 | 38.9 | 1,533 | 630 | 41.1 |
| English Anglican | 842 | 328 | 39.0 | 1,399 | 523 | 37.4 |
| English Methodist | 387 | 223 | 57.6 | 560 | 256 | 45.7 |
| Canadian Protestant | 3,285 | 1,229 | 37.4 | 5,650 | 2,299 | 40.7 |

a. $N_s$ = number surviving to second year; $N_p$ = number present in second year; Percent = decennial persistence ($N_p/N_s$).

sisting almost entirely of young women of the same age were considerably higher (34 percent for seamstresses and 20 percent for dressmakers). Those servants who had married would have had to leave domestic service. Thus at most 7 percent of the servants remained in domestic service in the city for a decade. Mostly young, they worked in service for a period of only a few years before marriage. Service represented not a career but rather a phase in their life cycle.

As to other occupational groups, although the rate of persistence for lawyers dropped from 92 percent to 50 percent and for plasterers from 91 percent to 36 percent, these shifts probably resulted from the interplay of accidental factors and very small numbers. In general occupation had only a slight relationship to persistence.

Economic rank had a more direct relationship with persistence. Again using an index of representativeness the relationship between economic rank and persistence remained quite similar in each decade.[13] Both of the top ranks scored highest; the poor had a notably low score; and those in the middle of the economic ranks had a score midway between top and bottom (Table 3.5). The same relationship holds for rates of persistence, corrected for mortality, between 1861 and 1871. They were, in order of increasing economic rank, 35 percent, 43 percent, 54 percent, and 50 percent. Thus the poorest were the least likely to remain, while the situation at the top of the rank order remained a bit ambiguous. However the important points to draw from these figures are that the differences between rank order, though notable, were not exceptionally large; moreover at least half of the wealthiest people left the city.

As in most analyses, property ownership distinguished persisters more than any other characteristic. Fifty percent of home owners and

Table 3.5 Index of representativeness and persistence of households heads, by wealth: Hamilton, 1851–1861, 1861–1871.

| Economic rank (percentile) | Index[a] | | Persistence | | |
|---|---|---|---|---|---|
| | 1851–1861 | 1861–1871 | 1851–1861[b] | 1861–1871[b] | 1861–1871[c] |
| 0–39 | 82 | 85 | 34.8 | 28.5 | 35.3 |
| 40–79 | 101 | 102 | 42.8 | 34.6 | 43.0 |
| 80–89 | 112 | 130 | 47.9 | 43.8 | 54.3 |
| 90–100 | 123 | 118 | 52.7 | 39.6 | 50.4 |

a. Index = (% in category / % in base population) × 100. Base population = all household heads linked from census to assessment, 1852 and 1861.
b. Uncorrected for mortality.
c. Corrected for mortality.

34 percent of renters in 1851 persisted in the city for at least ten years; for the 1861-1871 period the rates were 44 percent and 30 percent. Moreover among those who remained from 1851 to 1861 the proportion of property owners increased from 43 percent to 45 percent, and in the second decade it increased from 36 percent to 52 percent. Thus people who owned homes at the end of each decade were much more likely than renters to have remained in the city: 43 percent of the homeowners in 1861 and 30 percent in 1871 had stayed in the city at least ten years, compared to 12 percent and 15 percent of the renters. Property ownership among the 403 household heads who remained in Hamilton for two decades was even higher. It increased from 45 percent to 61 percent between 1851 and 1871. By 1871 these men, who constituted only 8 percent of the city's population, controlled 24 percent of all houses and building lots in Hamilton.

These patterns point to a number of conclusions about persistence:

1. Population turnover, even corrected for mortality, was very high: about two-thirds of the entire population and over one-half of the household heads left Hamilton during each of the two decades studied.

2. Population movement was ubiquitous: out-migration was high among people in all occupations, ethnic groups, and economic ranks.

3. Within the pattern of overall high out-migration some trends did exist: those young men aged 15 to 24 moved most often; the wealthy moved somewhat less frequently than the poor; homeowners were especially persistent.

4. The only real change in the structure of persistence between decades was the increased rate of persistence among people under the age of 15, a reflection of their prolonged residence in the home of their parents.

5. Persistence was a continuous, stable process. Despite the changing identity of the population the rate at which people left the city remained remarkably unaltered throughout its early industrialization.

## Buffalo and Rural Erie County

Similar factors affected length of residence in both Buffalo and Hamilton and even in rural Erie County. Despite the variations in rates of persistence the forces affecting residential mobility revealed striking parallels. Here the relative influence of various factors on mobility in Buffalo and rural Erie County is assessed through the use of a series of multiple classification analyses. The factors that affect length of residence are grouped into three broad categories: ascribed qualities, position in the life cycle, and achieved characteristics.

Table 3.6   Average number of years in city for selected categories of people, multiple classification analysis: Buffalo, 1855.[a]

A. TOTAL POPULATION

| Variable | Mean years in city |
|---|---|
| *Age* | |
| 10–17 | 6.1 |
| 18–24 | 7.5 |
| 25–34 | 7.7 |
| 35–44 | 9.6 |
| 45–54 | 11.2 |
| 55 and over | 12.9 |
| *Sex* | |
| Male | 6.1 |
| Female | 6.3 |

B. MALES AND FEMALES, BY AGE COHORTS

| | Males | | | Females | | |
|---|---|---|---|---|---|---|
| Variable | 18–24 | 25–54 | 55 and over | 18–24 | 25–54 | 55 and over |
| Mean years in city | 6.0 | 8.0 | 13.0 | 6.6 | 8.2 | 11.0 |
| *Birthplace* | | | | | | |
| New England | 6.4 | 10.0 | 17.2 | 6.5 | 10.6 | 16.2 |
| New York | 10.4 | 11.2 | 17.0 | 10.8 | 11.8 | 15.7 |
| Ireland | 4.6 | 8.0 | 8.9 | 4.8 | 6.6 | 8.0 |
| Germany | 4.4 | 6.5 | 10.6 | 5.1 | 6.5 | 9.1 |
| *Household and marital status* | | | | | | |
| Single child | 10.0 | 13.7 | — | | | |
| Single boarder | 4.6 | 6.0 | 9.3 | | | |
| Single relative | 6.3 | 7.9 | 9.9 | | | |
| Married child | 9.3 | 13.1 | 15.4 | | | |
| Married boarder | 2.3 | 4.7 | 1.0 | | | |
| Married relative | 7.7 | 7.0 | 10.1 | | | |
| Married household head | 6.2 | 8.2 | 13.4 | | | |
| Widowed boarder | — | 4.9 | 15.3 | | | |
| Widowed relative | — | 5.1 | 14.5 | | | |
| Widowed household head | — | 8.7 | 12.5 | | | |
| *Household Status* | | | | | | |
| Head | | | | 5.0 | 9.3 | 15.6 |
| Spouse | | | | 6.4 | 8.3 | 13.8 |
| Child | | | | 8.5 | 11.5 | 6.8 |
| Relative | | | | 5.3 | 6.4 | 9.1 |
| Boarder | | | | 4.5 | 6.6 | 7.0 |
| Servant | | | | 5.7 | 6.9 | 14.9 |
| Inmate of institution | | | | 3.2 | 2.9 | 0 |

Table 3.6, *continued*

## C. HOUSEHOLD HEADS

*Occupational rank, by birthplace*

| Birthplace | Occupational rank | | | | |
|---|---|---|---|---|---|
| | 1 | 2 | 3 | 4 | 5 |
| New England | 9.1 | 10.1 | 11.6 | 10.1 | 10.3 |
| New York | 9.1 | 11.0 | 12.4 | 11.6 | 12.0 |
| Ireland | 8.1 | 7.2 | 8.6 | 9.1 | 8.4 |
| Germany | 7.1 | 8.9 | 7.8 | 8.0 | 6.8 |

*Age and number of children*

| Age | Number of Children | | | |
|---|---|---|---|---|
| | 0 | 1–2 | 3–4 | 5+ |
| Under 25 | 6.6 | 8.2 | 9.1 | 13.0 |
| 25–34 | 6.4 | 7.2 | 8.5 | 9.7 |
| 35–44 | 7.8 | 7.9 | 9.0 | 10.9 |
| 45–54 | 9.9 | 11.0 | 11.1 | 11.9 |
| 55 and over | 13.5 | 12.7 | 12.4 | 11.3 |

*Dwelling value per capita and property ownership*

| Dwelling value per capita (octile) | Property status | |
|---|---|---|
| | Owner | Renter |
| 1 (lowest) | 10.2 | 6.2 |
| 2 | 10.1 | 6.2 |
| 3 | 10.1 | 6.3 |
| 4 | 10.5 | 6.4 |
| 5 | 10.7 | 6.7 |
| 6 | 12.8 | 6.7 |
| 7 | 13.4 | 7.5 |
| 8 (highest) | 27.6 | 8.8 |

## D. SUMMARY STATISTICS

| | N | $R^2$ |
|---|---|---|
| Total population | 69,323 | .270 |
| Males | | |
| 18–24 | 2,208 | .335 |
| 25–54 | 10,151 | .272 |
| 55 and over | 840 | .298 |
| Females | | |
| 18–24 | 6,884 | .230 |
| 25–54 | 12,249 | .138 |
| 55 and over | 1,440 | .165 |
| Household heads | 10,022 | .280 |

a. All results derived from multiple classification analysis. All factors significant at the .001 level.

First, ascribed qualities: age, birthplace, and sex. Among the entire population of the city length of residence increased in a linear fashion with age (Table 3.6). However the differences between groups were relatively small, which reveals that other factors lessened the impact of age.[14] For instance a person 25 to 34 years old had been in the city only .2 year longer than an 18- to 24-year-old and a 45- to 54-year-old 1.6 years longer than a 35- to 44-year-old. If age alone had been operative, we should expect these differences to have been closer to 10 years. Similar differences existed among male household heads: a 45- to 54-year-old had lived in Buffalo 1.6 years longer than a man aged 35 to 44.

With one exception patterns in rural areas paralleled those in the city (Table 3.7). The exception occurred among household heads less than 25 years old, who actually had lived in the same town or village longer than either those 25 to 34 or 35 to 44. These young men probably had been given land by their fathers. Otherwise 25- to 34-year-old household heads had lived in the same town or village 6 years less than those over the age of 55 and 5 years less than those 45 to 54. Thus though age was important, other factors obviously diluted its effect.

Younger people born in New York State, as one could predict, had lived longer in the city (Table 3.6). The average residence of 18- to 24-year-old males born in New York, for example, exceeded the average by 4.4 years and that of women 16 to 24 exceeded their average by 4.2 years. Those born in New England had lived in Buffalo for the second longest period but lagged behind New Yorkers, except among men and women at least 55 years old, at which point the averages for the two groups become very nearly equal. These averages mean that a man 55 years old or more born in New England had lived in Buffalo about 17 years, or since 1838. Those 25 to 54 had been there about 10 years, or since 1845. These figures point to a heavy migration into Buffalo from the mid-1830s through the mid-1840s of adults born in New England.

The average length of residence of the two major foreign-born groups, Irish and Germans, reflected the recency of their migration to America. Among all 25- to 54-year-old employed males, for instance, the Irish born had been in Buffalo 2 and the Germans 3.5 years less than the New Englanders. For women of the same age the discrepancy between New Englanders and the Irish and Germans was 4 and 4.1 years, respectively.

The interaction between birthplace and occupation does not alter these conclusions. Within each occupational rank New Englanders and New Yorkers had lived in Buffalo substantially longer than Irish and Germans. With the exception of clerks and lower-level white-

Table 3.7    Average number of years resident in same township or
village, household heads, all factors constant, multiple classification
analysis: rural Erie County, 1855.[a]

| Variable | Years resident | N |
|---|---|---|
| Total population | 13.6 | 1,158 |
| *Sex* | | |
| Male | 13.7 | 1,119 |
| Female | 10.2 | 39 |
| *Selected birthplace* | | |
| New England | 17.2 | 184 |
| New York | 17.2 | 430 |
| Middle states | 20.0 | 49 |
| England | 9.6 | 44 |
| Ireland | 9.7 | 40 |
| Germany | 8.4 | 330 |
| West Europe | 12.0 | 54 |
| *Land* | | |
| Non-land owning | 9.9 | 329 |
| Land owning | 12.3 | 829 |
| *Age* | | |
| Under 25 | 12.6 | 45 |
| 25–34 | 11.4 | 326 |
| 35–44 | 12.5 | 322 |
| 45–54 | 15.9 | 233 |
| 55 and over | 17.2 | 232 |
| *Occupation* | | |
| Professional/proprietor | 10.3 | 34 |
| White collar | 9.4 | 30 |
| Skilled | 12.5 | 152 |
| Semiskilled | 8.7 | 13 |
| Unskilled | 11.4 | 133 |
| Unclassified | 15.5 | 57 |
| Farmer | 14.8 | 739 |

SUMMARY STATISTICS

| Variable | Eta | Beta |
|---|---|---|
| Sex | .04 | .06 |
| Birthplace | .43 | .35 |
| Land | .34 | .20 |
| Age | .28 | .19 |
| Occupation | .29 | .14 |
| Significance main effects    .001 | | |
| $R^2$ = .299 | | |

a. Based on a 10 percent sample of all household heads.

collar workers the Irish in each occupational rank usually had lived in Buffalo longer than the Germans.

Similar relationships existed between birthplace and length of residence in rural Erie County (Table 3.7). Among household heads birth in New England and New York added 3.4 years to average length of residence; English and Irish birth lessened it about equally by 4.2 and 4.1 years, and German birth decreased it by 5.4 years. In other words the average household head born in England or Ireland had been in the same township, town, or village in the county about 8 years less and a German about 9 years less than one born in New England or New York.

Within the city, sex did not alter length of residence among the population as a whole (Table 3.6). However female household heads had lived in Buffalo 3.9 years longer than males—roughly 12 compared to 8 years. Did their prolonged residence reflect choice or a secure economic position, or were they trapped and unable by themselves to move to a more appealing place? We cannot shed very much light at present on this obviously important question. In the county the association of sex and length of residence was exactly the reverse of the situation in the city. There women who headed households had lived in the same town or village 3.5 years less than men. Again we are left with a finding for which there is no ready explanation.

Marriage and the status of household head by themselves had surprisingly little effect on length of residence of males in Buffalo (Table 3.6). In fact by itself marriage added almost nothing to the length of time a person had been in the city. By contrast the men who had been in the city longest lived with their parents. Men 18 to 24 years old living with their parents had been in Buffalo 3.8 and those 25 to 54 years old 5.5 years longer than married men in the same cohorts. Conversely unmarried boarders had dwelled in Buffalo for the shortest time, 2 to 4 years less than married men of the same age.

Inmates of institutions were especially transient. Despite their small numbers all the results do point in the same direction: women aged 16 to 24 in institutions had lived in Buffalo 3.4 years less than the average for women of the same age, a gap that increased to 4.3 and 11.9 years among women in the two older cohorts. Similarly women relatives and boarders had arrived in Buffalo much more recently than either women living with their parents, spouses, or widows. Among women 25 to 54, for example, relatives had been in the city 1.9 and boarders 1.7 years less than wives. It was heading a household and not simply widowhood that increased the length of time a woman had lived in Buffalo: widowed household heads 25 to 54 had been in the city 9 years, compared to 6 for widowed relatives. Over the age of 55 the average length of residence for the two groups was 16 and 9 years. As with men marriage itself had almost no relationship to a woman's length of residence in Buffalo. Similarly employment played virtually no role: hardly any difference existed at any age between those women reporting an occupation and those listing none.

By itself, number of children had no association with a man's length of residence in the city. However when combined with age it became a very significant factor. Generally within each age group a linear relationship existed between number of children living at home and length of residence in the city. Thus household heads 25 to 34 with no children had lived in Buffalo .8 year less than those with one or two children, 2.1 years less than those with three or four, and 3.3 years less than those with five or more children.

Interestingly the relationship between number of children and length of residence became inverse among the oldest household heads; those with the smallest families had been in the city the longest time. However their family size did not reflect fertility, for their children had already begun to leave home. Moreover the range of difference in length of residence varied much less with number of children than it did among younger men, which indicates that family size simply became less important among the elderly. People over the age of 55, as we have seen, did not leave the city very often.

Most students of nineteenth-century cities argue that transiency varied inversely with occupational rank: the unskilled moved most often, professionals and proprietors least. Either the dynamics of population movement differed in Buffalo or other studies have erred, for we discovered little direct association between occupation and length of residence, with other factors controlled.[15]

Men in rank 2 (primarily clerks and other white-collar workers) had been in the city the longest time, but only about six months longer than the average, while men in the highest ranking occupations (mainly merchants, professionals, and other entrepreneurs) had lived there for the shortest period, about one year less than the average (Table 3.6). These differences are trivial. They mean that occupation had virtually no independent relationship to length of residence in Buffalo.

Occupation exerted surprisingly little independent influence upon length of residence in the country too (Table 3.7). Farmers and gentlemen had lived in Erie County longer than others, but among nonfarmers no class-related distinctions existed. Compared to a farmer a laborer had lived 3.4 years less in the same town or village, a professional or proprietor 4.5 years less, and an artisan 2.3 years less.

Why then has occupation been an important factor in other studies? One reason may be that most have relied on descriptive statistics. Simple cross-tabulations may indicate that people in higher occupational ranks had persisted more often than those beneath them, when in reality the distinctions reflected the varied age and ethnic composition of occupational groups. Indeed the contrast of Hamilton with Buffalo demonstrates this effect, for in Hamilton too occupation was only marginally related to persistence.

In Buffalo the interaction between occupation and ethnicity significantly affected length of residence. In each occupational rank New England- and New York-born household heads had lived in Buffalo longer than those born in Ireland and Germany. A native New Yorker in rank 1 had lived in Buffalo 9.1 years, a New Englander also 9.1, an Irishman 8.1, and a German 7.1; in rank 3 the years resident in the city were 12.4, 11.6, 8.6, and 7.8, respectively. Even among laborers the same type of difference held.

Occupation interacted with age as well as with ethnicity. Among 18- to 24-year-olds little difference existed between men in different occupational ranks; in the 25- to-54-year-old cohort some small distinctions began to emerge; and among men over 55 fairly sharp variations in length of residence became evident. Professionals in that age group had lived in Buffalo 1.5 years longer than merchants, 2 years more than clerks, and almost 4 years more than laborers, while patterns among artisans varied with particular trades. Thus until middle age, men with various occupations migrated more or less randomly as both manual and nonmanual workers moved from place to place in search of success. Gradually professionals and entrepreneurs established themselves and settled in one place; unable to do likewise, some artisans and many laborers just kept drifting.

Clear linear relationships existed between economic rank (dwelling value per capita, or DV/C) and length of residence in Buffalo.[16] Household heads in the lowest quarter of the rank order had been in the city about 8 years compared to 10 and 11 years for those in the third and highest quarters. Even though the relationships are linear, however, the differences are not very large, which points to the fact that the association of economic rank with length of residence, though significant, remained slight. Unlike occupation or economic rank property ownership revealed a very strong relationship to length of residence. Employed household heads who rented their homes had been in the city, all factors held constant, 7 years compared to 11.5 for owners. Among men 18 to 24 the difference in length of residence between renters and owners was 6 compared to 9 years; among 25- to 54-year-olds it was 6 and 11 years; and among those 55 or over 11 and 16 years. Property ownership clearly had a greater association with persistence than either economic rank or occupation.

The relationship between economic rank and property ownership makes the importance of property even more striking. Within each economic rank owners had been in the city substantially—about 4 or 5 years—longer than renters. And, controlling for property ownership, economic rank itself had no relationship to length of residence, except near the very top of the rank order. However even the wealthiest renters had been in the city for a shorter time than the poorest owners.

As in the city ownership of land formed the most important correlate of length of residence elsewhere in the county. In fact the actual relationship of property ownership with other factors was quite similar in both areas: the difference in length of residence between owners and nonowners was 5.5 years in the country and 4.4 in the city.

The household heads most likely to have lived in rural Erie County for the longest period of time were men born in New England or New York who owned land, farmed, and were older than 45. By contrast a propertyless German laborer of the same age would have been there for the fewest number of years. Thus the accumulation of differences rather than any one specific factor created the very real distinctions in length of residence among rural household heads. The New Englander cited above would have lived there about 22 and the German about 4 years.

The same point can be made about the city: New England or New York birth combined with a high ranking occupation, middle age, a large family, wealth, and property ownership interacted to prolong length of residence. For instance a man in the highest occupational rank born in New England or New York, aged 45 to 54, with five or more children, who owned his home, and was in the top octile on our measure of economic rank would have lived in Buffalo about 31 years in 1855. By contrast an Irish laborer also 45 to 54 years old, with one or two children, who rented, and ranked in either the first or second octile would have dwelled in the city only about 8 years. (Of course even the knowledge of individual characteristics does not permit the prediction of length of residence with complete accuracy.)

Did the process of residential stability assume a similarly cumulative quality in Hamilton? In particular, what characteristics made it likely that a household head resident in the city in 1871 had lived there ten years earlier? For this purpose we again used multiple classification analysis.[17] Note first of all that the analysis accounts for only a small proportion of the variance—11 percent—which shows that there was a great deal of variation among people with relatively similar characteristics (Table 3.8). Nonetheless the patterns were not random, and some striking trends do emerge.

The factor variables were all significant, and the influence of three

Table 3.8  Persistence since 1861, multiple classification analysis of all household heads: Hamilton, 1871

| Variable | Persistence Percent | N |
|---|---|---|
| *Age* | | |
| Under 25 | 43 | 471 |
| 25–34 | 29 | 1,035 |
| 35–44 | 36 | 1,269 |
| 45–54 | 44 | 877 |
| 55 and over | 51 | 647 |
| *Ethnicity* | | |
| Irish Catholic | 47 | 582 |
| Irish Protestant | 39 | 453 |
| Scottish Presbyterian | 46 | 647 |
| English Anglican | 33 | 681 |
| English Methodist | 39 | 311 |
| Canadian Protestant | 42 | 673 |
| U.S. white | 29 | 172 |
| U.S. nonwhite | 33 | 59 |
| Other | 32 | 721 |
| *Economic rank (percentiles)* | | |
| 0–19 | 36 | 827 |
| 20–39 | 36 | 828 |
| 40–59 | 38 | 952 |
| 60–79 | 39 | 905 |
| 80–89 | 50 | 385 |
| 90–99 | 43 | 402 |
| *Number of houses owned* | | |
| 0 | 35 | 3,122 |
| 1 | 47 | 679 |
| 2 or more | 55 | 498 |
| *Occupational category* | | |
| Professionals/rentiers | 48 | 126 |
| Agents/merchants | 52 | 332 |
| Service/semiprofessionals | 34 | 127 |
| Business employees | 46 | 352 |
| Government employees | 46 | 112 |
| Masters/manufacturers | 46 | 387 |
| Skilled workers | 38 | 1,479 |
| Transport workers | 36 | 195 |
| Other working class | 40 | 99 |
| Laborers | 30 | 628 |
| Female domestics | 49 | 16 |
| Other females | 45 | 44 |
| Agricultural proprietors | 32 | 49 |
| Other | 55 | 31 |
| None | 40 | 332 |

Table 3.8, *continued*

SUMMARY STATISTICS

| Factor | Eta/beta |
|---|---|
| Age | .21/.16** |
| Ethnicity | .13/.12** |
| Occupation | .15/.11** |
| Economic rank | .19/.09** |
| Number of houses owned | .23/.15** |

| Covariates | Beta |
|---|---|
| Number of children | .009 |
| Number of servants | .006 |
| Number of relatives and boarders | .003 |
| $R^2$ = .114 | |

**Significant at .01 level.

of them as indicated by their betas was quite similar: age .16, ethnicity .12, property ownership .15. Occupation and wealth somewhat surprisingly had lower betas, .11 and .09. Economic rank in fact exerted its influence in a less direct fashion than any other variable: its eta was .19, compared to its beta of .09.

Only two personal attributes boosted above 50 percent the probability that a person had lived in the city for at least ten years: the ownership of two or more houses, all factors constant, made the likelihood of a decade's residence 55 percent; and an age of at least 55 made the probability 51 percent.

Significant differences between the categories of each factor variable did exist. For example the youngest household heads were not the least likely to have been in the city for decade. The influence of parents or other kin may have deterred some of them from migrating. In 1871 those least likely to have been in Hamilton ten years earlier were the household heads 25 to 34 years old, whose probability of residence there in 1861 was 14 percentage points lower than that of household heads under the age of 25. The most likely were those 55 or over; they were 22 percent more likely to have lived in the city for at least ten years than the first group and 15 percent more likely than the second.

The differences between ethnic groups remain hard to explain. Irish Catholics scored highest, but their probability was offset by the negative influence of their most common occupation: laborer. Thus

Irish Catholics who were not laborers were particularly likely to have lived in the city for at least a decade. The group least likely was U.S.-born whites, at 4 percentage points lower than U.S.-born nonwhites, whose score was the same as that of the English Anglicans. In short it is difficult to find any meaningful patterns among ethnic groups.

With occupation differences emerge more clearly. First, a line separated the business class from the working-class. With the exception of the proprietors of services and semiprofessionals—a heterogeneous and not entirely satisfactory category—persistence within each of the business class's component groups exceeded the average for the entire linked population of household heads. The probability that a professional or rentier had persisted was 48 percent, compared to 46 percent for business employees, government employees, and masters and manufacturers, and 52 percent for agents and merchants.

In the working-class—skilled workers, transport workers, "other" workers, and laborers—persistence was lower than the average for the population, except in the case of the "other" workers, a broad and very diverse group. The probability that a skilled worker had persisted was 38 percent, a transport worker 36 percent, and at the bottom a laborer at 30 percent. The existence of distinctions between the classes is reinforced by the results of an analysis of variance. The variation between the groups was larger than the variation within them, and the F-score for the difference was significant at a level lower than .01.

Female household heads in all sorts of occupations persisted at rates well above the average: for domestic servants the probability was 49 percent and for women in other occupations 45 percent. Women very likely found it extremely difficult to move by themselves, especially if they had children.

The existence of distinctions among the various occupational designations should not obscure the fact that, with the exception of the small residual category, the spread between the highest and lowest probability was only 22 percentage points. Occupation influenced the odds that a person had remained in Hamilton for a decade, but by itself its influence was not decisive.

Economic rank also influenced the likelihood that a household head had lived in Hamilton since 1861. Despite a general distinction between those low and high on the rank order, relationships were not linear. At the bottom the probability of persistence since 1861 for a person below the twentieth or between the twentieth and fortieth economic ranks was 36 percent in each case. For the top three ranks—60 to 79, 80 to 89, and 90 to 99—the odds were 39 percent, 50 percent, and 43 percent. Thus the range of difference between the highest and lowest persistence probabilities was only 14 percentage points.

The relationship between number of properties owned and persistence was linear. The probability of residence in Hamilton since 1861 rose from 35 percent to 47 percent to 55 percent among those who owned no homes, one home, and two or more homes, respectively. The spread between the highest and lowest probability, 20 percentage points, was exceeded only in the case of age, where the range was 22 points.

Population movement was clearly ubiquitous within the social structure. People with all sorts of social and demographic attributes entered as well as left mid-nineteenth-century Hamilton. Nonetheless patterns did exist. Though no single factor dominated, the accumulation of a variety of characteristics affected the probability that a particular individual had lived in the city for at least a decade. In this respect the process of population movement there resembled the situation in Buffalo.

Consider three cases. First, a 55-year-old Canadian-born Protestant lawyer who owned two houses and was in the top ten economic percentiles had a probability of persistence since 1861 of 83 percent. At the other extreme a 30-year-old Irish-Catholic laborer without property who was in the twentieth to the fortieth economic rank had a probability of persistence of only 21 percent. In between was a 40-year-old Scottish mason, a homeowner, in the fortieth to the sixtieth economic rank; the chance that he had lived in the city for ten years was about even (49 percent).

Interaction effects between variables make precise predictions such as these somewhat hazardous. Nonetheless even if precision is not possible, the probability scores point to large differences between groups. A relatively small group of people—middle-aged, propertied, well-to-do, proprietors or professionals—formed a core of long-term residents. Their persistence and their economic strength gave them a great deal of influence over the life of the city and its people. At the same time a much larger group of poor, younger, unpropertied men entered the city and did not stay there very long. In between floated a group about whom predictions are harder to make. They came and left in ways that elude our capacity to offer systematic explanations.

The study of population movement in nineteenth-century North America has only begun. Case studies show clearly that population turnover in country, town, and city was extraordinarily high. Yet the studies do not use sufficiently similar methods to permit reliable comparisons between their results. Almost none have corrected for mortality, and there has been no systematic attempt to relate rates of population movement to patterns of economic and demographic development.[18]

This analysis shows that the systematic, comparative study of nineteenth-century population movement is possible. It points to reasonable hypotheses about the relationship between rates of population persistence, length of residence, and the economic structure and vitality of individual places. It is unlikely that future research will discover either that rates of population turnover varied in a random fashion or were relatively uniform. Nonetheless differences in rates of in- and out-migration should not mask the underlying structural similarities in the process itself. The odds that any person would live for many years in the same place were the product of the interaction of local circumstances with the accumulation of personal characteristics that for the most part had a similar influence in different towns and cities.

## The Significance of Mobility

A number of principles emerge from our analysis of population movement. First, the rate of population persistence must not be confused with the average length of residence. Neither taken alone expresses the significance of population movement. In Buffalo the short average length of residence did not reflect a population in constant flux, for persistence remained relatively high. Rather it stemmed from large-scale recent in-migration. Second, the variation in rate of persistence between Hamilton and Buffalo shows how population movement varied directly with economic opportunity. Third, a number of factors affected length of residence:

1. Though marriage had little relationship to men's length of residence, the number of children and kin in a household did exert a significant settling effect.

2. The length of time younger men had lived in Buffalo bore no relationship to their occupation. Instead occupation became a more prominent factor in the case of older men: professionals and proprietors successfully established themselves and settled; laborers and some artisans unable to find steady work in one place kept wandering. The relationship of persistence to occupation in Hamilton was somewhat stronger, and its relationship to class was significant though not great.

3. Though quite modest, the association of economic rank with length of residence was direct and linear.

4. Birthplace was related to length of residence in obvious ways: through the recent Irish and German immigration, the fact of birth in New York State, and other patterns of movement, especially the westward migration of New Englanders.

5. Property ownership increased length of residence more than any other factor.

Fourth, the social and demographic structure of length of residence was similar in Buffalo, rural Erie County, and Hamilton, though the same factors operated with varying degrees of strength in different contexts. Fifth, the accumulation of a variety of characteristics—birthplace, age, marital status, family size, occupation, wealth, property ownership—accounted for differences in the length of time that people had lived in the city or county.

One moral of this chapter should be clear: we cannot assume the existence of a relatively uniform rate of population persistence in different towns, cities, and regions. Migration responded to economic opportunity, and the relatively similar rates that historians thus far have uncovered probably reflect the crudity of instruments of measurement rather than a real uniformity in nineteenth-century North America.

Thus our hypothesis is that rates of population persistence and in-migration varied systematically with patterns of economic development. This proposition is testable with the New York State census of 1855. A sample drawn from the entire state would permit the calculation of rates for places as varied as New York City and areas that relied primarily on subsistence farming. What difference, though, would it make to know that rates of population persistence varied systematically from place to place? It matters first because the answer has immense significance for the interpretation of community in North America.

Consider the magnitude and nature of population movement as both index and influence. First, as an index: population movement probably reflected the state of the labor market. A high rate of persistence and an influx of unskilled workers revealed, as in Buffalo, exceptionally attractive job opportunities. High rates of out-migration showed just the opposite, and differential rates may have registered quite sensitively variations in opportunity within particular sectors of the economy.

Patterns of residential stability also showed how the life cycle varied according to social class. In Buffalo we noted that the generally high rate of out-migration among all young men diminished sharply in the case of professionals and proprietors, who settled as they succeeded. Out-migration remained substantially higher among unskilled workers, who much less often had the job stability that permitted them to settle.

Thus migratory patterns reveal one dimension of inequality in nineteenth-century society: the privilege of class was translated into the privilege of stability. Residential stability—like property, a good job, or a reasonable income—became a reward, a tangible benefit spread unevenly among the people. Historians might study the rate of population persistence in nineteenth-century towns and cities as one component in a complex structure of inequality.

Population movement was more than a reflection of economic opportunity and the distribution of privilege. It also affected community cohesion, local political processes, and the permeability of local society. Consider three hypothetical situations. In the first, everyone was on the move. The rate of out-migration remained high and relatively undifferentiated by class, age, or ethnicity. In this situation population movement weakened community cohesion and integration. Local politics were chaotic; little effective civic action or social development could take place. However local society could not exclude people very effectively; social organizations and informal groups were wide open to newcomers.

In the second situation out-migration varied by social class. Though working-class people usually did not stay very long in the city, a prosperous and relatively stable group of community leaders existed. Consequently a small sector of the population shared a highly developed sense of community and controlled local politics. Local political decisions reflected the interests of these community leaders, who vigorously promoted the social and economic development of their town. Working-class social groups remained relatively open to newcomers but all others were relatively closed. We believe that this second pattern characterized nineteenth-century North American cities to varying degrees. For example Hamilton, despite its high rate of population turnover, contained a group of prosperous long-term residents who, relatively unopposed, shaped the development of the city in their own interests. This pattern is the one we should expect to find during the development of industrial capitalism. Poorly paid wage laborers formed a reserve army of the underemployed floating from city to city in response to the variations in a job market controlled by a relatively stable group of businessmen. The amount of working-class population movement, in fact, might have reflected the state of capitalist development. Variations in rates of population movement could reveal not only differences in economic opportunity but the uneven penetration of wage labor as well.

A third hypothetical situation might involve a high degree of stability, contributing to a broadly shared sense of community; effective resistance to the political domination of a faction; a reasonably broad sharing of power; and extensive property ownership, creating along one dimension at any rate a more equal society. General stability and widespread property ownership certainly characterized rural Erie County in contrast to Buffalo. However such stability was not the experience of at least one area in rural Ontario—Peel County. There patterns of migration more closely resembled those in Hamilton.[19] The difference between places with varied rates of stability reflected a good deal more than a simple distinction between city and country. If migration affected the nature of local society, then we should expect marked differences in the cohesion and political processes within these two rural counties roughly fifty miles apart.

The magnitude and composition of migration probably also affected the circulation of information and ideas. People were carriers of news, innovation, and sometimes cultural variety.[20] Though population turnover weakened communal integration, at the same time it enhanced local vitality and introduced a liveliness and cosmopolitanism into places that otherwise would have remained isolated and provincial. Perhaps close study of the nature of migration could provide a substructure for cultural as well as social history.

From a slightly different perspective large-scale migration gave to the forms of culture—especially artisan culture—a significance different from what they originally had in Europe. Old country forms such as societies, riots, festivals, and parades undoubtedly did exist in North America. However here they were rarely based on the face-to-face relationships that grew out of long acquaintance among the members of a stable community. In North America such gatherings brought together strangers, or at least relatively new acquaintances. Thus participation in the same events or societies reflected not long-standing friendship but shared objective characteristics such as birthplace, religion, or occupation. Though the outward form of artisan culture was continuous with the past, it also prefigured the organizational style that emerged in the rationalized bureaucratic order of the modern world.[21] Perhaps high rates of transiency combined with the artisan tradition to facilitate the accommodation of working people to the social relations of industrial capitalism.

Migration surely affected family life and social institutions as well. The effectiveness of local schools, for instance, probably varied directly with the degree of population turnover. Extensive movement limited the potential of even the best of schools and created enormous problems for school boards, which had to attempt to predict the number of children in transient urban populations.[22]

On a more general level the degree to which the population around them swirled and the frequency with which they themselves moved helped shape the way in which people viewed their world. Friendships were difficult to maintain; ties to individual places were tenuous; after a while people were reluctant to invest their emotions heavily in neighbors or places they would soon leave. Rootlessness bred a detachment from community that led people to turn inward toward the one unit that retained its shape: the family of husband, wife, and children. The isolation of the conjugal family, we might speculate, varied directly with the rate of population turnover. Thus the restless movement of nineteenth-century people contributed to the inward concentration, that intensification of domesticity, that became the hallmark of modern families.[23]

We have argued that high rates of population turnover worked against the development of a local sense of community cohesion and integration. Its national effect might have been quite the opposite. The continual circulation of population throughout a continent created continuous human contact, a network of communication, a sense of identification with other places that decreased the strangeness of Boston in Buffalo, diminished the distance between New Hampshire and Wisconsin, and brought Toronto closer to Winnipeg. Whatever its local effects, the restless, driven movement of their people may have helped to create two sprawling and improbable nations on one continent.

To return to the point from which we began this chapter, a massive and continuous flow of population was one side of a coin whose reverse image was a rigid, sharply etched structure of inequality. Many of the restless, searching men and women who crossed the ocean and who drifted from place to place made up the vast reserve army of labor that sustained the development of capitalism in North America.[24]

# 4 Property: Use Value and Exchange Value

"Next to being married to the right woman," asserted the editor of the *Ontario Workman*, "there is nothing so important in one's life as to live under one's own roof," and he commended to his readers the sentiments of a wife:

We have our cosy house; it is thrice dear to us because it is our own. We have bought it with the saving of our earnings. Many were the soda fountains, the confectionery saloons, and the necessities of the market we had to pass; many a time my noble husband denied himself the comfort of tobacco, the refreshing draught of beer, wore his old clothes, and even patched-up boots; and I, O me! I made my old bonnet do, wore the plainest clothes, did the plainest cooking; saving was the order of the hour, and to have "a home of our own" had been our united aim. Now we have it; there is no landlord troubling us with raising the rent, and expecting this and that. There is no fear in our bosom that in sickness or old age we will be thrown out of house and home, and the money saved to pay rent is sufficient to keep us in comfort in the winter days of life.

Commenting on this ode to underconsumption the editor made sure the moral was crystal clear: "What a lesson do the above words teach, and how well it would be if hundreds of families would heed them, and instead of living in rented houses, which take a large share of their capital to furnish, and a quarter of their income to pay the rent, dress and eat accordingly, would bravely curtail expenses, and concentrate their efforts on having 'a home of their own.' Better a cottage of your own than a rented palace."[1]

This disquisition on the virtues of home ownership contains a number of important themes. First, it was offered in a militant working-class newspaper. Homeownership was held out to the workman as the best possible investment, a source of modest capital accumulation open to the humble. Second, it was assumed that home ownership was within the reach of working men. The reason why working men did not own homes stemmed at least as much from their reluctance to save as from their low wages. Third, by implication working-class families were oriented toward consumption. They preferred to spend their money on larger houses than they could afford, new clothes, entertainment, and an immoderate diet. This false sense of values worked against their real interests, represented especially by the acquisition of property. Fourth, property was important because it represented security. Workmen could expect hard times in their old age and little sympathy from rapacious landlords. The only way to beat the system was, in a way, to join it. Fifth, the underconsumption necessary for acquiring property was a joint venture of husband and wife. The family economy required the constant vigilance, foresight, and restraint of both partners. Though the husband might earn the wages, management by the wife was crucial. Sixth, it was assumed that the price of a house was a sum of money that should be saved prior to purchase. The exhortation to home ownership was not an encouragement to acquire a debt in the form of a mortgage.

Indeed mortgages were still frowned on in this period, and not only by representatives of the working class. Carroll Wright, secretary of the Massachusetts Bureau of Statistics of Labor, clearly believed in the importance of home ownership. In his survey of the condition of the wage and salary earning classes in 1875 he asked, "Do you own the home you live in?" Justifying the inclusion of the question he commented, "One is quite likely to judge the general prosperity of a working community by the answers to such a question as this." However homes purchased on mortgages were not an index of prosperity, indeed quite the opposite. Wright observed, "It is evident that when the members of a manufacturing community, to any considerable degree, become burdened with encumbrances upon their homes, then begins the decline of the community itself."[2]

The comments in the *Ontario Workman* and Wright's observations pose important and complex questions: Was property in fact a good investment? Did it have similar returns for both working and business classes? How widespread was ownership and how prevalent were mortgages? Were certain types of people especially likely to purchase property? Did ownership coincide with other dimensions of the social structure? Did early industrialization have any significant impact on the degree of property ownership or its distribution?

## Home Ownership and Social Structure

Carroll Wright's huge survey indicates that home ownership did not conform to the major social structural divisions. In Massachusetts as a whole about 23 percent of manual wage earners owned their own homes, compared to about 20 percent of salaried employees, who earned on the average about twice as much. Though the general averages mask very significant local variations, the problem nonetheless is clear. Class does not seem to have been a powerful influence on the acquisition of a home of one's own.[3]

The situation in Hamilton and Buffalo was equally complex. First, little connection existed between early industrialization and the extent of property ownership in Hamilton. The proportion of home owners varied from 35 percent in 1851 to 30 percent in 1861 to 33 percent in 1871. The only notable aspect of these figures is the slight decline during the depression. The rate of homeownership in Buffalo was somewhat higher—about 37 percent among married household heads in 1855—though very close to the Hamilton figure.

In Hamilton the relationships between individual characteristics and home ownership do not emerge clearly from descriptive statistics. For instance in each year a linear relationship existed between economic rank and property ownership, though the proportion of home owners among the poorest two-fifths of the population dropped from 22 percent to 15 percent and rose among the wealthiest tenth from 63 percent to 77 percent and among those in the eightieth to eighty-ninth economic ranks from 41 percent to 53 percent. Although the nature of the relationship between economic rank and ownership did not alter, the distance between groups did spread somewhat during the first decades of early industrialization, a trend consistent with other aspects of stratification.

Some relationship also existed between age and property ownership. In each year the proportion of owners rose at least to the age of 60, when, except in 1851, it declined slightly. In 1851 and 1861 a small but direct increase existed between number of children and property ownership, but by 1871 this relationship had disappeared.

Occupation was less related to property ownership than one might have expected. Merchants owned comparatively little property throughout the period (34 percent, 37 percent, and 33 percent in each of the three years, respectively), a share not much greater than among laborers, about a quarter of whom owned property in each year. The occupational groups with notably high numbers of property owners were gentlemen (63 percent in 1851 and 76 percent in 1871) and carpenters (57 percent and 54 percent, respectively). Gentlemen were basically rentiers, and carpenters could build their own homes.

To some extent economic rank obscured differences in the relationships between property ownership and occupations. Among men in the lower or middle economic ranks carpenters and laborers were especially likely to own property: for instance 62 percent and 43 percent of laborers in the fortieth to seventy-ninth economic ranks owned houses, compared to 19 percent of the merchants, 18 percent of the gentlemen, and 30 percent of the professionals. In the top ten economic ranks 63 percent of merchants were owners, a figure still rather low in comparison to other groups.

Ethnicity also played a role in property ownership. The Irish were somewhat more likely to own property than were members of other ethnic groups. By contrast the native born often were relatively less likely. Finally, as we observed before, those men who had been in the city for at least ten years were by far more likely to be owners than were newcomers; conversely, owners were far more likely than renters to have remained in Hamilton for at least a decade.

To untangle property ownership we need both multivariate analysis and a better conceptual framework. We need to know the relative influence of various characteristics upon home ownership, with other factors held constant, and we need a better grasp of the significance of home ownership to people situated at different positions on the social hierarchy.

## Use Value and Exchange Value

Making the distinction between use value and exchange value enables us to analyze the significance of property ownership with greater precision. The *use value* of an object is its capacity to satisfy needs. The use value of food rests in its ability to provide nourishment and to satisfy hunger; the use value of an automobile is its capacity to provide transportation; the use value of a work of art is its ability to give aesthetic satisfaction. Thus *use value* refers to the quality of a commodity and is therefore inseparable from the commodity itself. *Exchange value* refers to the quantitative aspects of a commodity—the amount, measured in any unit, for which it may be exchanged. It bears no necessary relationship to the utility of the commodity; hence it is abstract.[4]

Thus it is clear that a commodity possesses both use and exchange value. In the case of a house the use value resides in the satisfaction of the owner's wants: shelter, comfort, and especially in the case of nine-teenth-century working men security against unemployment, sickness, and old age. Indeed the use value of a home to a nineteenth-century working man becomes especially clear when we recall certain aspects of his work. First and foremost was its irregularity, which meant that most workmen would spend at least some time un-employed. Second was the decline of earning power with old age, a factor clearly reflected in the statistics on economic rank and one that working men took for granted. Third is the absence of any sort of insurance to provide compensation for earnings lost as a result of illness or accident and the relative lack of life insurance to protect widows and children. In these circumstances a home for a working man meant not only a modest source of capital accumulation but even more the only realistic protection he could acquire against the common and expected difficulties inherent in working-class life.

To a member of the business class, on the other hand, property could have a different significance, one measured primarily by its exchange value. First of all property was used for investment and speculation. We have already established the pervasiveness of speculation in the early phase of Hamilton's development. Investors would evaluate property in terms of its liquidity and its potential for appreciation and as a source of revenue in the form of rent. All of these qualities, aspects of exchange value, would give to property quite a different significance than it had in the eyes of a working man worried about his security. Of course for members of the business class property would also have use value as a source of shelter and comfort. A home, however, might also have use value as evidence of conspicuous consumption. If members of the business class tried to signal their social rank through their life style, then they would have special concern for the size and appearance of their home.[5]

The suppositions that members of the business class were especially concerned with appearances and that they often approached property in terms of its exchange value help explain actual social patterns in nineteenth-century Hamilton. One reason why many men in high-ranking occupations rented their homes may have been that they lacked the capital with which to buy a house that suited their social standing. Another reason, especially among men of relatively high occupational but more moderate economic rank, could have been that the purchase of a home would have forced them to forgo resident domestic help at a time when the employment of a servant acted as a badge of social rank. Indeed various types of evidence point to an unmistakable inverse relationship between property ownership and employment of servants among business-class men of moderate means. Finally, looking on property primarily as an investment, others may have believed that alternate sources of capital, such as stock for their businesses or a share of a railroad, utility, or manu-facturing concern, offered a prospect of greater or more secure return.

The distinction between use and exchange value certainly could not be made sharply in every case. Working men concerned about their security also might have a lively interest in the resale value of their property. They might even purchase additional property if they had sufficient capital. Indeed some evidence shows that at the turn of the century working men in Hamilton attempted to buy one or two houses other than the one in which they lived in order to provide themselves with an income from rent in lieu of a pension during their old age.[6] At the same time, as we have pointed out, more prosperous men would not be indifferent to the security and comfort provided by a home. What we wish to argue is not an absolute difference but a dis-tinction in emphasis. Among the working class home ownership was viewed more in terms of use than exchange value. Among at least some segments of the business class this emphasis was reversed.

## Characteristics of Property Holders

If this hypothesis is true, distinctions should exist between different types of property holders. Those men who viewed property primarily in terms of its utility for their lives would be more likely to be small-scale owners, to own only one or at the most a few properties. On the other hand those men who used property as a source of investment would be more likely to be multiple owners. Through the separation of property owners according to scale it should be possible to perceive a social structure of ownership more clearly than among all property owners considered together. Fortunately the supplementary schedules to the 1871 census of Canada make possible this discrimination. One of them, indexed back to the population schedule, gives a figure for total number of houses and lots owned. Because of its obvious super-iority to sources that give only the fact and not the extent of owner-ship, we have used the 1871 census as the basis for analyzing this aspect of property ownership in Hamilton.

What were the major characteristics that distinguished multiple property owners? Among all occupational groups only a majority of gentlemen owned more than one property. Next came professionals and farmers (extractive occupations) at 26 percent, followed by mer-chants at 22 percent. By contrast, and in support of the general argu-ment, though the rate of ownership was high among men in the con-struction trades (44 percent), their rate of multiple ownership was much lower (19 percent). Overall 17 percent of household heads owned one house, 7 percent owned two or three, 3 percent had four to six, and nearly 2 percent owned seven or more. Thus multiple owner-ship was highest among occupational rank 1, where 6 percent of household heads owned seven or more houses, and lowest (.3 percent) in rank 5. Similarly 33 percent of those people with two or more servants were multiple property owners, compared to 19 percent of those with one and 11 percent of those with none.

Multiple ownership increased as well with age from 3 percent among the 20- to 29-year-olds to 20 percent among those 50 to 59 and 24 percent among those 60 years old or over. Even within occupational ranks property acquisition had a definite relationship to the life cycle. For instance in rank 1 it increased at a steady rate from 3 percent among 20- to 29-year-olds to 52 percent among those 60 and over. In rank 3 it rose in linear fashion from 3 percent to 12 percent, and even among laborers it increased from 2 percent to 7 percent.

With these relationships in mind we turned to multivariate analysis in order to sort out with more precision the relative influence of various factors on levels of property ownership. First, we examined the results of a discriminant analysis in order to discern whether significant differences in fact separated groups by level of property owner-ship. Dividing the household heads into four groups according to level of property ownership, we were able to predict accurately whether or not an individual was a property owner in 89 percent of the cases. We correctly predicted whether or not an individual owned more than one property in 76 percent of cases. These are impressive results.

There was, however, one exception: the analysis successfully predicted the ownership of just one property only 37 percent of the time. However only 31 percent of the people predicted as owners of one property did not own any. Rather more (32 percent) owned two or more. Thus in 69 percent of the cases these people were correctly identified as property owners even though their assignment to a specific group was often incorrect. In fact, the owners of one and the owners of two to three properties are the most difficult groups to distinguish from one another because their characteristics are very similar. Those property owners incorrectly estimated to own only one property were twice as likely to own two or three as to own four or more.

In order to estimate the relative influence of various characteristics it is necessary to rank standardized scores on the analysis. The scores are expressed in a range from $+1.0$ to $-1.0$ (Table 4.1). A high positive score means that a characteristic contributed to the likelihood that an individual would own property. A high negative score shows that a characteristic detracted from the likelihood of property ownership. Scores are calculated with all other factors held constant.

Table 4.1   Determinants of property ownership, discriminant analysis: Hamilton, 1871.[a]

### A. Relative contribution of selected variables (standardized)

| Variable | Two categories[b] | Four categories[c] |
|---|---|---|
| *Age* | | |
| Under 25 | −.10 | −.03 |
| 25–34 | −.17 | −.08 |
| 35–44 | .00 | .00 |
| 45–54 | .14 | .13 |
| 55 and over | .14 | .15 |
| *Sex* | | |
| Female | −.08 | −.08 |
| Male | .00 | .00 |
| *Ethnicity* | | |
| Irish Catholic | .17 | .14 |
| Irish Protestant | .12 | .13 |
| Scottish Presbyterian | NS[d] | NS |
| English Anglican | −.05 | .00 |
| English Methodist | .12 | .10 |
| Canadian Protestant | NS | NS |
| U.S. white | −.03 | NS |
| Other | .00 | .00 |
| *Number of children* | | |
| 0 | NS | NS |
| 1 | NS | −.04 |
| 2–3 | .00 | .00 |
| 4–5 | NS | NS |
| 6 or more | NS | NS |
| *Number of servants* | | |
| 0 | 0 | 0 |
| 1 | −.05 | −.04 |
| 2 or more | .08 | .03 |
| *Number of relatives and boarders* | | |
| 0 | 0 | 0 |
| 1 | .05 | .06 |
| 2 or more | −.01 | NS |
| *Economic rank (percentiles)* | | |
| 0–19 | −.28 | −.13 |
| 20–39 | −.10 | −.07 |
| 40–59 | 0 | 0 |
| 60–79 | .29 | .23 |
| 80–89 | .34 | .40 |
| 90–99 | .61 | .80 |
| *Occupation* | | |
| Professional | NS | −.01 |
| Gentleman | .05 | .09 |

Table 4.1, *continued*

| Variable | Two categories[b] | Four categories[c] |
|---|---|---|
| *Occupation* (cont.) | | |
| Commerce—high | −.10 | −.10 |
| Commerce—middle | −.10 | −.10 |
| Extractive | .07 | .05 |
| Other white collar | NS | NS |
| Apparel, etc. | NS | 0 |
| Wood products | NS | .02 |
| Metal products | NS | NS |
| Food and beverages | −.09 | −.05 |
| Construction | .30 | .20 |
| Other manufacturing | −.18 | −.02 |
| Labor | 0 | 0 |
| Women | NS | .02 |
| Other | .13 | .13 |

B. SUMMARY STATISTICS

*Variance explained*
| | |
|---|---|
| Two categories[b] | .21 |
| Four categories[c] | .32 |

*Cases predicted correctly*
| | |
|---|---|
| Two categories[b] | 72.1% |
| Four categories[c] | |
| All cases | 55.7% |
| Multiple property owners | 75.7% |
| All property owners | 88.9% |

a. Based on a discriminant analysis of all household heads. Coefficients are derived from the first discriminant function.

b. Property owners and nonowners.

c. Nonowners, owners of one property, owners of two or three properties, and owners of four or more properties.

d. NS, coefficient not significant at .05 level.

By far the most influential characteristic was membership in the ninetieth to ninety-ninth economic rank. Its influence was not only positive but twice that of the next most important feature—membership in the eightieth to eighty-ninth rank (+.80 for the former, +.40 for the latter). The factor that ranked third was also an economic category—membership in the sixtieth to seventy-ninth economic rank, with a score of +.23, roughly half again as important as in the rank above it.

The only occupational category of any real importance ranked fourth: the construction trades (+.20), which is to be expected from the descriptive statistics already presented. Still the size of the score for the construction trades was only one-quarter that of the most important variable. Note, however, that in a separate analysis that used only two groups—owners and nonowners—the relative importance of the construction trades was greater. Wealth became more important when multiple ownership was a question. The men in the construction trades were likely to own their own homes but not more than two properties, a distinction consistent with our general argument.

Age, in fact, was more important in one instance than any occupational category other than construction. The age group 55 and over ranked fifth in importance with a score of +.15. Among ethnic groups, as should be expected, were the Irish Catholics and Irish Protestants, which with scores of +.14 and +.13 ranked sixth and seventh in influence. The only other ethnic group with a significant influence was the English Methodists with a modest +.10.

By contrast two occupational groups had a similar though negative influence on property ownership. The score for both high- and mid-ranking commercial occupations was −.10. Though a commercial occupation actually detracted from the likelihood of property ownership, one other high-ranking occupation, gentleman (+.09), actually promoted it slightly. Still the score for gentlemen, it should be remembered, was less than half that of the construction trades, whose members were substantially less well-to-do. This does not mean that gentlemen were unlikely to be multiple-property owners. Rather it points to the greater influence of their wealth than their occupational title. Carpenters were a special group because the likelihood of their owning homes was independent of their wealth.

The influence of all other factors was slight, below .08. Only one is worth mentioning—the mildly negative influence (−.04) of the employment of one servant in contrast to the employment of two or more, whose influence, though also minor, was positive (+.03). This is the first bit of evidence about the inverse relationship between property ownership and servant employment among men of moderate means.

Though the discriminant analysis gives a relative ranking of influence and demonstrates the overwhelming importance of wealth, it does not permit the estimation of probabilities, or of the likelihood that an individual with any characteristic or set of characteristics would own property. To be able to estimate that at least roughly it is necessary to turn to multiple classification analysis.[7]

Particularly important was the combined influence of occupation and persistence in the city. Masters and manufacturers and government employees who had remained in the city for at least a decade were the people most likely to own property. The probability of ownershp for each was 40 percent compared to 36 percent, 25 percent, and 22 percent among professionals and rentiers, agents and merchants, and business employees who had persisted during the decade. However the odds that men in the same occupations who had arrived during the decade would own property were much lower: professionals and rentiers 25 percent, agents and merchants 21 percent, business employees 18 percent, and masters and manufacturers 23 percent.

Working-class men who had persisted were remarkably likely to own property. Indeed the odds that they would own a home were generally greater than those for most business-class groups. In the case of skilled wage workers the chances were 46 percent, highest of any major group. Even among persistent laborers the chances were 43 percent, higher than among any business-class group. For men in the same occupational categories who had arrived during the decade the odds were much lower: 32 percent for skilled wage workers and 32 percent for laborers. However these figures are still higher than for business-class groups.

The real difference, as our hypothesis should lead us to expect, separated the multiple-property owners by class. The probable number of properties owned by men who had remained in the city for at least a decade varied by occupation in the following way: professionals and rentiers 3.2; agents and merchants 1.1; business employees .3; masters and manufacturers 1.2; skilled wage workers .7; laborers .7. Note that in each of the business-class categories, except for business employees who were much younger, persisters were likely to own more than one property, whereas the persisting working-class men were likely to own less than one. This points to the use of property as a source of investment or speculation among the business class. It underlines the basically different significance of property for each class, for it was unusual for a working-class man to own more than the home in which he lived.

The probable number of properties owned decreased with economic rank in a linear fashion from 2.2 to .1 between the top and the bottom of the scale. The first notable jump in the likelihood of property ownership occurred between the fortieth to fifty-ninth and the sixtieth to seventy-ninth economic ranks, followed by another substantial increase between the eightieth to eighty-ninth and the ninetieth to ninety-ninth ranks. Ranks 80 to 89 marked the first point at which a person was more likely than not to own property.

The propensity of the Irish, both Catholic and Protestant, to own property (.8 for each) appears unmistakable, with that of nonwhites also relatively high (.6). Other ethnic groups had scores in the range of .5 to .6.

At all ages fewer female household heads owned homes than males. The probable number owned by men increased with age from .5 for those less than 25 years old to .8 for those 55 and over. The most notable increase occurred after the age of 35.

The relationship between property and employment of servants is particularly noteworthy. People who employed one servant owned .5 house, compared to .6 among those with no servants and .7 among those with two or more. As we have noted, the relationship between keeping servants and owning property was inverse. That conclusion remains even when persistence in the city for a decade is included in the analysis. In general a close association existed between persistence and property ownership. However even households that had entered the city since 1861 and employed two or more servants were much less likely to own property than those without servants who had been in the city at least a decade. The comparative probabilities were .5 and .8, respectively. Within each category of servant employment the relationships between persistence and property were the same. Interestingly those least likely to own property were household heads with one servant who had arrived during the decade (.4), notably lower than the next group, arriving households with no servants (.5). Indeed even persisters with one servant were slightly less likely to own property (.7) than persisters without domestic help (.8). Thus even with persistence accounted for, those people with one servant were less likely to own property than either those with two or more or those with none. Perhaps the transient businessmen, uncertain about their prospects for success in the city, had been unwilling to encumber themselves with a house, which might hinder their ability to move on.

It is clear that a sector of the population made a choice between the employment of servants and the ownership of property. They were not the wealthiest, who could afford both, but men of moderate means whose ability to save for a house would be seriously reduced by the average servant's wage of $7 per month. Men in these circumstances, earning perhaps $1000 per year, might spend $250 annually on rent. The wages of a servant could easily consume 10 percent of their income. There would be little left to save, even toward a down payment of only $400 or $500. Nevertheless a number of men quite obviously made a symbolic choice and sacrificed the possibility of home ownership to the trappings of social rank.

As we have noted, the Irish had a distinctive pattern of property ownership. Therefore we separated the file into Irish and non-Irish groups and performed multiple classification analyses with each. Those few Irish who entered the ranks of the business class were more likely to own property than their non-Irish counterparts. Among high-ranking commercial occupations the scores were .50 for the Irish and .15 for the non-Irish; among medium-ranking commercial ones they were .52 and .33, respectively. Lower in the occupational rank order scores for Irish and non-Irish were quite similar. The probable number of houses owned by Irish Catholics slightly exceeded that for Irish Protestants. Among the non-Irish the Protestant score was higher.

At every economic rank except the very highest, where they were few in number, the Irish were more likely to own houses than the non-Irish. For instance the probable number of homes owned by those in the bottom twenty percentiles was .2 for Irish compared to .1 for the non-Irish. At the middle of the economic rank order the scores were .6 and .3, respectively, and among the eightieth to eighty-ninth ranks 2.0 and 1.1. Thus those Irish household heads who reached the penultimate economic rank were likely to be multiple-property owners. Irish men over the age of 45 were also more likely to own property.[8]

The Irish drive towards land ownership cannot be doubted. In fact if the argument in a recent essay by Oliver MacDonagh is correct, that drive flowed from the background of Irish immigrants, a disproportionately high number of whom came not from the most destitute, propertyless ranks of Irish society but from the small, struggling land-owners, roughly the second quartile of Irish society in economic standing.[9]

In every analysis a direct relationship exists between age and property ownership. There are good reasons for this. Most homes were purchased with cash, not with mortgages. Even those mortgaged required large down payments, perhaps an average of 30 percent to 40 percent of their selling price, and required repayment in a relatively few years. Men with modest incomes either had to save for long periods of time, perhaps at least a decade, or they had to rely on the extra income provided by working children, who were unlikely to be less than 15 years old. In either case it would be difficult for many people to acquire homes prior to middle age.[10]

Finally, it was possible to predict with reasonable accuracy whether a person would own no property or several (four or more) properties. However it was very difficult to estimate whether any person would own either one, two, or three properties. Just what distinguished petty property owners from others remains unclear. Perhaps the moral is that nothing distinguished them very much. By and large they were men of moderate means who had managed to buy homes, which they approached primarily in terms of use value. Homes were places to live, sources of security. Occasionally these men ventured into modest speculation or purchased houses in order to use the rent to supplement their income or to provide an annuity. They were separated from the men who did not own any property by an income that lifted them above poverty, a bit of good fortune, the ability to save, the willingness to take a risk, or some combination of all of these characteristics. They differed from the men who owned several properties chiefly in wealth. The large owners were primarily men of substantial means, often men who by their very occupational title, gentleman, signified their preoccupation with the conversion of land into profit.

Unfortunately we cannot measure two other extremely important factors that determined the ability of people to purchase homes: security of employment and the ability to obtain credit. In this period mortgage facilities had not become widespread, and this made purchase difficult for families unable to save the entire price of a home. The insecurity of most jobs undoubtedly deterred potential creditors from lending money and potential purchasers, afraid of foreclosure, from buying.

Indeed the relationship of job stability to home ownership emerged as a major theme among Wisconsin workers queried in the late 1880s.[11] In fact the assumption of a relationship between security and ownership was implicit in the question put to them: "Does the town where you live offer any inducements for men of your trade to acquire homes, or is employment so uncertain as to make owning a home undesirable?" A blacksmith in Chippewa Falls answered, "Our town is all right if the state of trade were more regular." One in Elkhorn said, "$1.50 per day to a man who has to work hard is barely enough to live upon, although employment is steady enough to acquire a home in time." A boilermaker from Baraboo, by contrast, complained, "Employment here is very uncertain making it undesirable for men of my trade to invest in a home." Other workmen gave their reasons at more length, stressing in some cases the negative consequences of home ownership for economic and geographic mobility. First, a carpenter from Mineral Point:

> Mineral Point is a very poor place in which to hold or own property. The city is of less importance than it was some years ago, and I fear there is no chance for improvement. We are nearly surrounded by railroads, which fact has taken a great deal of trade from our city . . . A poor man owning a house worth say $500, pays a much larger tax in proportion than those who have large property interests. If you were to buy a piece of property

today for $500, you could not sell it a week later for $450 . . . One of my friends who owns a very nice and comfortable home, has been dissatisfied with the results of his labors for some time. He said that if he could dispose of the property at anything like a reasonable figure, he would not remain at Mineral Point twenty-four hours.

A laborer from Beloit made a more sinister point: "There are good opportunities to acquire a home here; but it is not advisable for common laborers to do so; because as soon as they get a home employers seize the opportunity to cut wages, knowing the men can not get away, selling property here being entirely out of the question. Such was my experience."

There were, of course, always those ready to place the blame on the victims rather than the system, as this carpenter from Marinette:

This is not the worst place under the sun for a carpenter, or any other tradesman, if they have a mind to work and save their money. I have lived here since spring, 1871, and all I have is a home and a very little for a "rainy day." Still, when I look around me, I can't help but see that I am about as well-off as most of them, a great deal better than a good many. There are plenty of men here, as well as in other places, that might be in good circumstances, if they would live within their means; but high living, whisky and women will keep any one down, and we have plenty of all here.

One suspects the actual case is more like that described by a painter from Whitewater: "Employment is so uncertain that a painter here cannot think of paying for a home, as you may readily see by my last year's income. I worked altogether eight months during last year, six months in factory, where I earned $265, and two months at house painting $94, a total of $359. I think I had better look for a job elsewhere, than being idle one-third of the time."

The case was obviously more complex than the writer for the *Ontario Workman*, quoted at the start of this chapter, implied. Home ownership probably was not a realistic aspiration for all thrifty workmen. For many wages were far too close to the level of subsistence to permit any savings. Uncertain work added to low wages and left other workmen with a desire for the freedom to move quickly and without loss or complication when jobs became scarce. For some the ability to move outweighed the security that came from the knowledge that one owned the roof over one's head, regardless of the availability of work. Others made the opposite choice.

To discover whether the configuration of influences apparent in home ownership in Hamilton was unique or whether it reflected forces at work elsewhere we turned to Buffalo. With the Buffalo file it is not possible to estimate the number of properties owned, but it is possible to use precise length of residence in the city as a variable in the analysis.[12]

The most pronounced increase in the impact of length of residence on the chances of property ownership was found to occur between those living in Buffalo from two to five and from six to nine years, a jump in the odds from 25 percent to 42 percent (Table 4.2). The chance that anyone living in Buffalo ten years or more would own exceeded 50 percent, with the highest (58 percent) among those residing there twenty years or more and the lowest (13 percent) among those in the city one year or less.

Though also linear the relationship between economic rank and property was more subtle. The odds were bunched: 25 percent and 26

Table 4.2  Predicted likelihood of property ownership, multiple classification analysis: Buffalo, 1855.[a]

| Length of residence | | | | | |
|---|---|---|---|---|---|
| 0–1 year | 13% | | | | |
| 2–5 years | 25% | | | | |
| 6–9 years | 42% | | | | |
| 10–14 years | 50% | | | | |
| 15–19 years | 55% | | | | |
| 20 or more years | 58% | | | | |

*Dwelling value per capita/birthplace*

| | | Percent born in — | | | |
|---|---|---|---|---|---|
| Dwelling value (octile) | All | New York | New England | Germany | Ireland |
| 1 (low) | 25 | 25 | 41 | 28 | 23 |
| 2 | 26 | 30 | 35 | 31 | 17 |
| 3 | 34 | 29 | 30 | 42 | 26 |
| 4 | 35 | 28 | 38 | 43 | 33 |
| 5 | 42 | 44 | 42 | 50 | 37 |
| 6 | 42 | 43 | 42 | 49 | 35 |
| 7 | 42 | 51 | 52 | 45 | 33 |
| 8 (high) | 48 | 52 | 65 | 47 | 24 |
| All values | — | 32 | 35 | 42 | 31 |

a. Factors include place of birth, length of residence, literacy, occupation, and dwelling value per capita. Age, sex, number of boarders, relatives, and children were entered as covariates. Total N = 11,084.

percent for those in the first two octiles; 34 percent and 35 percent for those in the next pair; an identical 42 percent for the next three; and 48 percent at the top. Thus the spread between the top and bottom of the economic rank order was substantially less than the spread among people who had lived in the city for different lengths of time.

The only birthplace to exert any positive effect was Germany. The chances that an employed German household head would own property were 42 percent, quite high in light of the group's modest economic and occupational standing. The other most common birthplaces had relatively similar odds: New England 35 percent, New York 32 percent, and Ireland 31 percent. The influence of German birth becomes clearer from comparing people in the same economic rank born in different places. Germans of moderate economic rank (ranks 3 to 6) more often owned property than men born in other places. In contrast to Hamilton, in Buffalo the Irish did not buy property more often than other groups. Except for the three highest economic ranks the likelihood that they would own property was quite close to that of other groups—generally slightly lower. What accounts for this difference between the Hamilton and Buffalo Irish is difficult to say. However in other cities the pattern does appear to have been more like that in Hamilton than in Buffalo.[13]

As in Hamilton, occupation had little influence on home ownership. Consider the following odds for ownership among men in different occupations: professionals 43 percent; men in high-ranking commercial occupations 41 percent; those in middle-level commercial occupations 36 percent; apparel, textile, and leather workers 35 percent; wood-product workers 39 percent; metal workers 37 percent; construction workers 43 percent; laborers 31 percent. Between the highest and lowest the spread was only 12 percentage points. Men in high-ranking commercial occupations had a rather higher probability of ownership in Buffalo than in Hamilton (perhaps land was a better investment in Buffalo, given its extraordinary growth), and in both places men in the construction trades did quite well. Otherwise the scores are similar, and the major point is the same: occupation by itself had relatively little impact on the ownership of property.

In Buffalo the greater importance of years in the city probably stems from the precision with which the variable was measured there. It is quite possible that an exact measurement of length of residence would show it to have the strongest relationship to property ownership in Hamilton as well. In both cities length of residence clearly contributed substantially to the odds that a man would own property; and in both places economic rank had a much greater independent impact than occupation, whose influence was surprisingly small.

The very wealthy usually owned their own homes. The poor did not. Beyond these rather obvious conclusions the interesting point is the variability among people of more moderate means. Except for the very wealthy most men approached property more in terms of its use value than its exchange value. They nonetheless remained acutely aware that they were making an investment that they might need to transform into cash quickly, and they consequently worried about the value of their property. Those working-class men who opted for property ownership probably sought security, a hedge against the vagaries of working-class job experiences and old age. Other men saw in their homes a symbol of affluence. Consequently they would choose to rent rather than to purchase a more modest house. Still others particularly concerned about the trappings of class would hire a resident domestic servant rather than buy a home. Finally, some merchants concerned with exchange value considered their capital put to better use through a variety of investments rather than bound up in a house.

### The Returns on Property: Working Men

Can we make some estimation of the rationality of either the working-class belief that a house is the best form of investment or the businessman's perference for investing in land? The question is a tricky one, but some tentative answers may be offered.

Most people, including working men, who bought homes in Hamilton between 1847 and 1881 paid cash. The basis for this conclusion is a study of five large surveys covering every transaction involving houses. In all 924 building lots were included in these surveys, and 898 transactions involved the sale of houses. Only 27 percent of these were bought with a mortgage.[14] Evidence about mortgages in Hamilton proves three important points: first, very few of the mortgages were granted by institutional lenders (banks, insurance companies, building societies). Only about 6 percent of mortgages in Hamilton came from these sources. Another 54 percent were given by the people who sold the property, and most of the rest came from wealthy local residents. Second, the mortgages were short term. Their mean length was 3.9 years and the median 3. Only 8 percent were for periods longer than five years. Third, they were for a relatively small fraction of the purchase price. The median amount was $675, and in this period houses generally sold for between $1,200 and $2,500, although there were wide variations. The mean amount of the mortgages granted to the working men in the sample was lower—about $450. It is reasonable to estimate that mortgages rarely exceeded 75 percent of the purchase price. Throughout the period too interest rates remained relatively stable at around 7 percent. No differences existed in the interest or length of the mortgages granted to working men.

By and large mortgages were not amortized as they are today. People paid a fixed amount of the principal at stated intervals, often each year, and the outstanding interest. For example on April 14, 1871, Alexander R. White, commercial traveler, received a mortgage from John T. Glassco, Esq., for $275 at 7 percent. He was to make two annual payments of $137.50 each and to pay the interest every half year. On June 30 of the same year James Johnson, a laborer, was given a mortgage for $600 at 6 percent by Archibald Kerr, Esq., and required to make four equal payments of $150 plus interest. Another laborer, Arthur Moore, was given a mortgage on May 12, 1873, by William Stark, druggist. He borrowed $700 at 7 percent. The terms were $15.50 monthly for the first year with the remaining $556 to be paid in installments of $100 each on November 9 of the next five years and in a final payment of $56 on May 9, 1877. Interest was payable semiannually.[15]

Were workmen buying homes under these conditions making a wise decision? Would it have been better to rent and try to save money at the approximately 5 percent interest given by most banks? First, consider the majority, those who purchased for cash. (For the sake of simplicity the foregoing rough calculations omit any changes in the market value of property.) A man who rented a six-room house for $10 per month, a common rental, for twenty years would have spent $2,400 on housing. If during the same period he had saved $100 per year (a very high figure), he would have $2,000 plus interest. (Of course if he purchased a house and then rented it, he could potentially save even more, since a rental of $10 per month on a $1,000 home would have yielded an annual return of 12 percent, compared to 5 percent from the bank.) If he saved $100 a year for ten years and purchased a house for $1,000, his housing cost for the next ten years would consist only of the taxes, approximately $60 per year. Potentially he could save the difference between the rent and the taxes, $60. If he continued to save $100 per year for the next ten years, his assets would consist of a $1,000-dollar home (which might have increased in value), $1,600 in savings, and interest, compared to a savings of $2,000 plus interest for the lifelong renter. At the same time his housing cost, excluding maintenance, would have been $1,800, or $600 less.

Few working men could embark on such a program of systematic saving. However all of those who did buy houses, whether by cash or mortgage, were required to make a substantial cash payment, which required some mode of accumulating capital, either through prolonged saving or through the earnings of children, which could boost considerably the family income for a period of several years. To appreciate the magnitude of the savings required, recall that working men would be fortunate to earn $2 per day, or $12 per week. Given periodic seasonal unemployment, most probably did not earn $500 a year. Without income from other family members, to save $100 a year, or even $50, required enormous effort, restraint, and, very likely, rigid underconsumption.

Even those working men who assumed mortgages probably came out ahead in strict financial terms. Considered over a ten-year period a man who had a mortgage for $675 (the median figure) would spend about $1,369.50 on housing. This figure is calculated on the basis of a 7 percent mortgage for three years. In the first year his cost for principal and interest, a very great burden, would be $272.25, falling to $256.50 in the second and $240.75 in the third year. Adding $60 a year for taxes gives the total amount estimated above. In the same ten years a man who paid $12 per month for rent (a figure more likely than the $10 for someone with a mortgage of this size) yields a total cost for housing of $1,440. And the owner would have a home worth perhaps $1,300.

These are very crude figures, but they do indicate that home ownership made economic sense. A working man could not expect a spectacular return on his money, but considering his lack of large amounts of capital and the substantial share of his income (probably about 25 percent) that would have to be spent on rent, in the long run he profited modestly from the purchase of a home. Of course the benefits he received extended beyond those identified by a strict account of profit and loss. Once a house had been paid for, and even for a man with a mortgage this meant a period of only three or four years, his cost for housing dropped dramatically. He had to pay only modest property taxes rather than rent, and even renters frequently paid the taxes on their houses. The home owner was generally assured a place in which to live despite the fluctuations of the economy, seasonal unemployment, sickness, and old age. He was also spared periodic and unpredictable increases in rent, and he certainly gained a sense of independence. Given the stress on independence in the writings of ninteenth-century working men, the satisfaction of even this modest evasion of the dependence inherent in capitalist social relations must not be undervalued.[16]

## Subdivision and Speculation

If the purchase of a home was, on balance, an economically rational decision for a working man, could the same be said for men in the business class? Certainly in many instances the use value of a home would be the same for both groups. The loss represented by the payment of rent, the hedge against the problems of old age, and protection against the vagaries of the business cycle: all these affected men in commerce as well as wage workers. Still the former might adopt a different strategy. A profitable business, for instance, might continue to return a high investment on capital throughout a man's lifetime. The decline of manual skill would not be of as much concern to a merchant as to a machinist. More than that, members of the business class frequently approached property in terms of its exchange value. They bought not only for use but also with the hope of making a profit. How often were they successful?

To answer this question—to explore the rationality of investment in property in terms of its exchange value as contrasted to its use value —it is necessary to unravel the patterns of land speculation and development in nineteenth-century Hamilton. Speculation and development, it is important to observe, are two separable activities. Many of those who traded in land did not develop the properties they acquired, and the object of developers was the sale of the buildings they erected, an outcome that depended on factors in addition to those that raised or depressed the value of undeveloped land.

Two ideas characterize much of the literature about land speculation and development in nineteenth-century cities. One is that an orgy of speculation kept the real estate market in a frenzied state and contributed to the unplanned, sprawling character of urban growth. The other common notion is that speculation almost inevitably was profitable.[17] Urban land was a golden commodity, a source of great riches for those who managed to acquire the sites on which nineteenth-century cities were erected. To some extent, of course, these beliefs are valid, but they reflect a view of city growth rooted in twentieth-century experience and require important modification.

Evidence about nineteenth-century patterns in Hamilton comes from three sources. First, the assessment rolls for 1852 and 1881 show the degree of concentration of vacant lot ownership at two different times. Next, registered plans permit the assessment of changes in the supply of vacant land. Finally, registered instruments from the Hamilton Registry Office reveal the identity of those who bought, sold, and developed property in fourteen selected subdivisions that together contained 1,668 building lots. Between 1847 and 1881, 7,154 instruments were registered for these properties.

Those who arrived first in North American cities often could purchase large areas of land very cheaply. Thus during the early settlement phase the ownership of land was often fairly concentrated.

In Hamilton just after 1800 only nine individuals owned the thirty farm lots that later constituted the entire mid-nineteenth-century city. Although the ownership of vacant land remained concentrated, the number of owners expanded during the next several decades. By 1852 almost three hundred people owned vacant land in Hamilton.

Of course the group of owners contained some people with very large amounts of land. Thirty-five people possessed 73 percent of lots controlled by Hamilton residents, and just nine of them owned 55 percent of these properties. Most of these large owners were long-time residents of the city who had subdivided raw land into building lots during the late 1840s and early 1850s. Not only these large owners but also the nonresidents who owned 40 percent of the city's vacant lots were speculators.

These early subdividers failed to sell their land as quickly as they had anticipated partly because of an oversupply of building lots on the market. In 1852 the lots for sale could house almost 17,000 people at a time when the entire population of the city was about 14,000. Thus one of two conditions was necessary for land speculation to be profitable: tighter control over the supply of lots or an upswing in the economy that would persuade people to invest in the city's land. The economic boom of the mid-1850s provided just the boost that speculators required. The improved economic situation was especially fortunate because no controls on the supply of land existed. New subdivisions came onto the market with a rhythm more closely related to the general economy than to any deliberate attempt to regulate supply to meet demand.

Between 1850 and 1880 almost 4,800 new building lots were surveyed, registered, and offered for sale, and several subdivision plans were registered for areas just beyond the city limits as well. A great many people participated in the subdivision process during these years. Ninety-four different names were associated with the 104 plans that were registered. The sheer number of people involved in the process combined with the continued excess of vacant lots acted to prevent any tight control of the land market.

Between 1852 and 1881 the number of people who owned vacant lots had doubled, and the importance of small-scale owners had increased markedly. At the same time the ownership of lots by nonresidents had declined dramatically from 40 percent to 7 percent. Obviously patterns of ownership had changed during these three decades. To understand the significance of those developments it is necessary to examine activities in selected subdivisions. The fourteen surveys analyzed were of properties placed on the market before 1860, and each contained at least fifty building lots. They had been laid out by the most prominent residents, several of whom promoted the growth and development of the city through services as directors of railways, banks, and other enterprises or through participation in local and provincial politics.[18] More often than not the initial subdividers profited from their forays into the local land market. Subdividers lost money on only two of the ten surveys for which data are available. During the first ten years after registration the annual rate of return for the profitable subdivisions ranged from 7 percent to 54 percent of the original purchase price of the raw land. This profitability is not surprising given the fact that subdividers were converting raw and often unused land into urban building lots, a process that greatly increased the potential intensity at which the land could be utilized.[19]

Few of the subdividers could sell all of their lots quickly. Even ten years after their properties had been first offered for sale most still had some building lots to sell. This reflected the premature nature of many of the surveys, for even the demand for lots by would-be speculators was seldom great enough to ensure the rapid sale of a subdivision, and this reduced profitability since carrying charges, especially taxes and mortgage interest, had to be paid each year.

The properties in the selected surveys changed hands an average of 4.3 times during the period studied. In these years not only the identity but the characteristics of purchasers changed. The first group, the 456 who bought directly from the subdividers, were primarily interested in speculation and not in development. Almost one-quarter of them were nonresidents of the city, though many had close acquaintance with Hamilton in one way or another and many lived within twenty-five miles. Most of this group moreover were members of the business class: 68 percent were either merchants or manufacturers, gentlemen, or servicers of the development industry (lawyers, bankers, agents, and the like).

The distribution of the lots after their initial purchase shows that few of the first owners were interested in anything other than speculation. Fifty-one people had bought at least six properties in these subdivisions. Together they controlled about 63 percent of the building lots. Only one-fifth of the lots were developed—that is, built on—by their original purchasers.

By 1881 78 percent of the properties had been developed, and they had changed hands on the average 3.2 times before development. Nonetheless the frequent turnover of land had not driven land prices up. Given the exodus of many people from the city following the depression of 1857 and the inability of others to retain their properties, which were sold for back taxes, land prices were much lower in the 1860s and 1870s than they had been in the mid 1850s. Added to the dumping of cheap lots on the market at tax sales was the continual increase in the absolute supply of building lots, especially some low-priced subdivisions that came onto the market in the 1870s. Thus investment in land could not always be expected to earn a profit.[20]

We must stress also that not every recorded land transaction represented a real transfer of property ownership. People disposed of land for reasons besides profit. For example many transactions (about 20 percent) were at less than arm's length; that is, vendor and buyer were related to each other. In still other deals ownership switched between people who were friends or business partners. In these cases the change of ownership usually prevented the loss of property to creditors. Under these circumstances profits were not always an important consideration. Nevertheless money was clearly lost in 41 percent of the real transactions involving vacant lots for which we have complete price information. The figure would be considerably higher if we could take all possible carrying charges into account. The conclusion is unmistakable. People who invested in already platted building lots had no better than an even chance to make money. After the initial subdivision speculation was clearly a risky business.

Given the apparently poor odds, why did people continue to invest in land in nineteenth-century cities? The boom mentality undoubtedly influenced many who became caught up in the feverish activity in the local land market. The press played an important role too, for local editors constantly exaggerated the attraction of the real estate market. And land was one of the few genuine avenues for investment in the mid-nineteenth-century city.[21]

The ability to gain capital whenever it was needed was the key to success and expansion for the nineteenth-century businessman, and land served as an important source of collateral in the commerical city. Thus, aside from its attraction as a source of potential profit, land was the key to credit for many businessmen. However land did lose some of its appeal as other more readily liquidated investment possibilities began to emerge.[22]

As the years passed the most wealthy and influential residents became less involved in land ownership in the sample surveys. By the early 1880s property ownership in these subdivisions had spread much more widely. The intermediate transactions, many of which had been made between members of the wealthiest families, had eliminated most of the nonresident owners, but they had not driven land prices beyond the reach of the working class. Workers owned four times more lots and clerks six times more in 1881 than they had after the first round of transactions. Moreover the distribution of lots had also changed, for by the end of the period 54 percent of the properties were in the hands of people who owned no more than two building lots. The speculative phase had come to an end.

Who built the Victorian city? H. J. Dyos and Sam Bass Warner, Jr., both have stressed the small-scale character of the nineteenth-century construction industry, though the former observed a shift toward larger firms by the end of the century.[23] The Hamilton experience basically supports these findings. Few Hamilton builders erected more than six dwellings in any given year. Yet toward the end of the period some new directions had appeared in the city's construction industry. In 1874 several prominent Hamiltonians received a charter from the provincial government for the Hamilton Real Estate Association, which proved to be a forerunner of the modern, vertically integrated development corporation. Nonetheless the importance of the association should not be overemphasized, for it was many years before firms like it dominated the local construction and development scene.

Almost seven hundred people were involved in decisions to develop property in the fourteen surveys during these years. Almost 81 percent of them participated in no more than two development decisions. Thus speculative building took place but did not dominate local construction. By and large houses were built for specific individuals. Certainly some categories of property owners were more likely to develop their land than others. For example only one-fifth of the nonresident landowners decided to develop a lot, compared to one-third of city residents. Those associated with the development industry, on the other hand, were especially likely to build. Small-scale builders purchased a few lots at a time, erected houses, and then used the profits to finance additional projects. Few of them speculated in vacant land. Clerical workers and wage workers were also quite likely to develop property, more so in fact than professionals, merchants, manufacturers, or gentlemen, who often purchased real estate for its exchange value. For these business men land speculation proved an uncertain business. Almost half of those who speculated after the initial sale of subdivided lots lost money. This surely explains why so many men chose to invest their capital elsewhere.

## The Ambiguous Legacy

Dominated by insecurity, working men sought to buy homes whenever they could. Occasionally the fortunate even managed to acquire a second or third house as a source of insurance against unemployment or the hardships of old age. In the business class some men bought property for the same reasons. Others of moderate means, unable either to afford a house that matched their social aspirations or to save for a home and employ a servant, rented. Still others, undoubtedly aware that a large proportion of speculators lost money, chose to put their limited capital into stock for their business or into transportation, utilities, or the development of manufacturing. Nonetheless a substantial group, undaunted by the risks of speculation and lured by the hope of quick profit, bought relatively large amounts of land. For those who viewed property in terms of its use value the decision to purchase property remained relatively straightforward, except in cases where conspicuous consumption had to be balanced against security. However for those to whom property was a source of exchange value the decision was more complex and the outcome more uncertain.

Elements of these early urban attitudes toward property have persisted into contemporary times. Homes remain sources of security, especially for many who cannot both rent and save enough money to invest elsewhere. Many people, too, choose to rent for reasons of life style, and the city has remained an arena in which speculators act out their search for profits. Still important discontinuities exist too. Most of the natural controls on land prices have disappeared, fueling both inflation and speculation. At the same time the proportion of home ownership, especially among the working class, has risen markedly in the twentieth century. In part that increase reflects fundamental shifts in attitudes toward housing as a source of investment and control among those with capital.

Mid-nineteenth-century businessmen showed very little interest in mortgages as a source of investment. Only about a quarter of the houses purchased in Hamilton were mortgaged. In Massachusetts in the mid-1870s the proportion, though higher, was still under half. Moreover the terms of mortgages were relatively short. In the early twentieth century, by contrast, investors began to realize that mortgages amortized over long periods offered very attractive investments, and this, along with other factors, spurred the building of housing for people with relatively low or moderate incomes.

In the urban United States there were 2.9 million owner-occupied dwellings in 1890, compared to 5 million rented ones. By 1930 the figures were 10.5 and 12.4 million, respectively, a very substantial shift. In 1890 only 40 percent of houses were built for sale. By the late 1940s that proportion had risen to nearly 80 percent. Finally, in 1890 only 28 percent of owner-occupied units were mortgaged; this proportion increased to 40 percent by 1920 and to 45 percent in 1930.[24]

Around the time of the First World War industrial employers undertook to alter the migratory habits of the manufacturing population. This reorientation in the attitude of employers toward the residential stability of their work force coincided roughly with the increased provision of working-class housing for sale. As working people themselves knew, and as their employers certainly had observed, the ownership of a house decreased a man's mobility. Whether it was the difficulty of resale or a reluctance to leave a home of one's own, ownership made a man far more likely to remain where he was. A mortgage also gave him an added incentive to work hard and regularly, and it made him less willing to risk the unemployment and loss of income that often resulted from strikes or other early organized labor activity. Thus though a home of one's own brought a workman security and even a little capital accumulation, it served his employers and creditors equally well. In the long run its legacy for the North American working man remains at the least ambiguous.

# 5 Social Mobility

The acquisition of a home provided security and modest assets. Working people saw a home of their own as a signal achievement, a circumscribed though significant form of social mobility. At the same time their purchases increased the wealth of the vendors of property, often already well-to-do, and the mortgages they assumed, particularly after the turn of the century, added significantly to the capital of banks, insurance companies, and other creditors. In short the purchase of homes by working people, especially in the twentieth century, contributed to the accumulation and centralization of the capital whose skewed distribution makes possible the perpetuation of inequality. Owning a home, though often a source of comfort in old age, may have prevented many working people from moving on in search of higher-paying work, engaging in militant action, or resisting reductions in their pay.

Did property ownership contribute to social mobility? There is no straightforward, unequivocal answer to this question. If mobility is defined as movement between classes or the relative improvement in the position of one group relative to others, then home ownership had little impact. However if social mobility is defined as an individual's perceived improvement in his life situation, then home ownership was indeed consequential. The contradictory answers to the question pose a delicate issue for the social analyst. Experience must be evaluated in terms of both its meaning for the individual and its impact on larger social patterns. The two will very often be quite different, and the significance of that disjunction between levels of impact must be examined.[1]

It cannot be assumed that individual people evaluate their own experience in consistent or unambiguous ways. The ability to buy a home, for instance, might have been judged by nineteenth-century working men as a significant improvement in their lives, a fulfillment of their aspirations, even a validation of the promise of democratic capitalism. At the same time in regard to other aspects of their experience these people could have judged their social order harshly. The contradiction may be seen in the pages of a labor newspaper such as the *Ontario Workman*, whose editors simultaneously advanced a labor theory of value to criticize economic organization while arguing that home ownership was within the reach of every working man and should be one of his primary goals. The editors advocated the fundamental reorganization of the social and economic order while teaching young men how to move ahead as individuals within it.[2]

Another example of disjuncture in evaluating personal experience comes from a survey of Wisconsin wage workers in the mid-1880s. Over five hundred of them were asked, "Does your trade afford opportunities for graduation into foremen, superintendents, or business men?" Sixty-five percent answered yes, 24 percent no, and 12 percent did not answer. The same men were asked, "What trade would you choose for a boy?" Only about 9 percent would choose the trade that they themselves practiced.[3] If their prospects were so favorable, why would they not advise a boy to enter their trade? It could be that the prospect of advancement was a myth with which they sustained their lives but that they were too realistic to impose on a young man. Or it could be that they were right. Their prospects were good, but the cost of their modest achievement had been so high and so painful that they would advise a boy to choose an easier and more certain route. Certainly whatever the interpretation these working men simultaneously offered different perceptions of their experience.

That the structure of inequality in Hamilton remained relatively fixed during the transition from commercial to industrial capitalism is one important thesis we have sought to document. The question that remains concerns the experience of the people who lived in the city. Did their lives remain stable and unaltered? In part the answer is already obvious. Most of the people present at any one moment were newcomers, and most would not continue to live in Hamilton very long. However even the knowledge of mass transiency tells us little about the experience of the people who remained in the city. It is possible that they remained relatively fixed in social space, working at the same jobs, earning about the same amount of money. Or it could be that their lives reflected the fluidity of individual experience captured by the statistics of transiency. In that case the image of social structural stability could reflect either the distribution of newcomers into positions vacated by long-term residents or at least in part the reshuffling of the more permanent residents themselves.

The task thus becomes one of tracing social mobility. The evidence we have offered so far concerns the mobility of groups or strata and their relative positions over time. Ultimately this is a more effective measure of social justice than the proportion of individuals who improved their own circumstances.[4] By definition, individual movement on a vertical rank order presupposes inequality. The greater the degree of inequality, the more dramatic the movement that can take place. In stratified societies, of course, varying amounts of individual social movement are possible, and the amount and type that take place define one key aspect of a social system. Moreover they bear directly on one central problem of this book: the reproduction of inequality.

Deep, rigid patterns of inequality define capitalist society. During the period with which we are concerned—and, based on the evidence of other scholars, during later periods as well—relatively little group or stratum mobility occurred.[5] The same sorts of people remained the losers in the process through which power and privilege were distributed. And yet ample evidence exists that by and large they did not seriously question the legitimacy of the social order and their place within it. For the most part people have aspired to improve their own position or that of their children. They have not sought to alter fundamentally the relative position of groups within the social order itself.[6]

The reproduction of inequality is thus both an empirical and an ideological question. It is empirical because it matters very much how various ranks are filled. Whether privilege is passed on through families and retained within individual lifetimes or whether a continual resorting occurs between or even to some extent within generations assumes great and obvious significance for the attempt to understand any one place and time. Ideology matters as well because if a social order is to survive people must not question its fundamental legitimacy. How people learn that they should be losers—or that they are not entitled to the highest rewards and greatest pleasures offered in their time—remains one of the foggiest and most consequential areas of knowledge. They probably learn it in part through the deliberate transmission of ideology and in part through unselfconscious and customary patterns of socialization within the family. It may also be that the socialization of the unconscious happens partly as a consequence of the structural characteristics of one's life experience. This is one question that must be considered as we examine patterns of mobility.[7]

## Occupational Change

Occupation is an imperfect indicator of social position or social mobility. Nonetheless recognition of its ambiguities does not dictate its abandonment but rather calls for its use in a discriminating and careful way. We have tried to extract as much meaning as possible from patterns of occupational movement without overstepping the boundaries inherent in their study.[8] To do so we have used three different types of occupational grouping: specific occupations; occupations grouped according to sector (primary, secondary, tertiary) and subdivision within sector; and the five ranks employed elsewhere in this book that order occupations into a simple hierarchy.

The hierarchical classification is the most ambiguous because the meaning of ranks is not entirely clear. However the significance of some movements between ranks is less obscure than others. Rank 5, which consists almost entirely of laborers, remains unambiguously at the bottom of any hierarchy. Two pieces of evidence reinforce this conclusion: on every measure of economic rank between 1851 and 1881 laborers remain clearly at the bottom. Moreover people by and large did not choose to work as laborers when other options were open. In 1871 there were 1,183 laborers in Hamilton. Only 287 of them had lived in the city for at least ten years. At the same time the proportion of men who worked as laborers among those who persisted declined.[9] If laboring jobs had been as desirable as they were abundant, they would have retained and attracted a greater proportion of the work force.

At the other end of the hierarchy, occupations in rank 1 consistently conferred the greatest economic rewards and undoubtedly the most prestige and power as well. However it is difficult to draw a line between occupations in rank 1 and the clerical and related occupations in rank 2. Indeed they were both part of the same class, although rank 2 positions generally remained less remunerative. However a fair amount of shifting between the two ranks took place, though some of it may reflect changes in occupational title only rather than status. The shared social universe of men in ranks 1 and 2 becomes especially clear from one fact: 78 percent of the sons of merchants traced from 1861 to 1871 worked in rank 2 positions.[10]

Despite these ambiguities ranks 3 and 4 remain the most problematical. Rank 3 consists primarily of men with skilled artisans' titles. About 11 percent were actually self-employed masters or manufacturers who were members of the business class. The rest were wage workers. A movement from rank 5 to rank 3 probably represented an improvement to the people of the time, even if it kept them within the working class. A movement from rank 3 to rank 2 remains much more ambiguous. It probably represented an upward shift, for example, to the sons of skilled wage workers who entered clerical careers. Still, shifts between ranks 2 and 3 must be treated with caution, especially as relatively well-paid positions opened in larger industries.

Finally rank 4 remains the most elusive and least satisfactory of all. It contains semiskilled workers, typified by teamsters, porters, and waiters. The careers of men in rank 4 were very fluid, and the frequency with which they later appeared in rank 2 suggests that the category must be used with caution. For instance many of the men shifting rank may have continued to do the same sort of work but called it something else.

In analyzing occupational change we used three major files: people linked from 1851 to 1861 and 1861 to 1871 and those traced for the twenty-year period from 1851-1871. We wished to show first, that the determinants of occupational rank persisted over time with only minor variation. Second, we attempted to sort out the impact of occupational mobility on the structure of inequality by showing the similarity in the occupational distribution of the linked population at different times and the only slightly modified relationships between occupational success and ethnicity. Third, we examined mobility from the perspective of the individual and attempted to assess its quantity. The amazing amount of change in occupational rank points unmistakably to the fact that occupational mobility—both upward and downward—was a dominant fact of life. Nonetheless the net effect of mobility was the redistribution of the population into already existing categories in about the same proportion as before.

Let us first consider the determinants of mobility. How important were initial occupation, age, ethnicity, and marital status in the promotion of occupational mobility, and how did they exert their influence? To answer these questions we utilized a series of multiple classification analyses with males aged 18 and over linked between 1851 and 1861 and between 1861 and 1871.[11]

The first major pattern is the stability evident in the process of mobility, shown by the strikingly consistent underlying relationships between factors affecting mobility in each decade. This stability is demonstrated by the betas (Table 5.1). For instance in rank 3 the beta for initial occupational rank varied only from .60 to .62 between groups traced from 1851 to 1861 and from 1861 to 1871. At the bottom of the rank order the betas were .49 and .51 and at the top .59 and .53. The only real shift occurred in rank 4, where the beta for initial occupation rose from .30 to .43.

The betas measuring the strength of the relationship between ethnicity and membership in an occupational rank remained very similar and very low: for rank 1, .07 and .09; for rank 3, .10 and .05; for rank 5, .24 and .16. Only in the latter case was the association statistically significant in each group. Similarly age remained insignificant for each group, and the combination of age and ethnicity, though more influ-

Table 5.1 Occupational mobility, controlling for ethnicity, age, and marital status, multiple classification analysis, males 18 and over: Hamilton, 1851–1861, 1861–1871.

A. PROBABILITY OF MEMBERSHIP IN OCCUPATIONAL CATEGORY

| Occupational rank, 1851 | Occupational rank, 1861 | | | | | N |
|---|---|---|---|---|---|---|
| | 1 | 2 | 3 | 4 | 5 | |
| 1 | 71 | 12 | 5 | 2 | 7 | 122 |
| 2 | 15 | 56 | 11 | 1 | 11 | 202 |
| 3 | 4 | 7 | 72 | 2 | 8 | 516 |
| 4 | 5 | 16 | 17 | 32 | 15 | 75 |
| 5 | 4 | 6 | 15 | 8 | 62 | 178 |
| 6 | 7 | 17 | 35 | 8 | 26 | 84 |

| Occupational rank, 1861 | Occupational rank, 1871 | | | | | N |
|---|---|---|---|---|---|---|
| | 1 | 2 | 3 | 4 | 5 | |
| 1 | 63 | 16 | 9 | 1 | 5 | 126 |
| 2 | 17 | 55 | 14 | 4 | 5 | 309 |
| 3 | 1 | 8 | 80 | 3 | 4 | 610 |
| 4 | 1 | 16 | 13 | 52 | 13 | 95 |
| 5 | 5 | 9 | 17 | 8 | 52 | 252 |
| 6 | 13 | 22 | 37 | 14 | 7 | 129 |

B. SUMMARY STATISTICS

| | Occupational rank, 1861 | | | | | Occupational rank, 1871 | | | | |
|---|---|---|---|---|---|---|---|---|---|---|
| | 1 | 2 | 3 | 4 | 5 | 1 | 2 | 3 | 4 | 5 |
| $R^2$ | .41 | .26 | .40 | .14 | .43 | .31 | .24 | .41 | .21 | .37 |
| *1851 occupation* | | | | | | | | | | |
| Eta | .60 | .49 | .61 | .30 | .60 | .53 | .46 | .63 | .43 | .57 |
| Beta | .59** | .48** | .60** | .30** | .49** | .53** | .45** | .62** | .43** | .51** |
| *Age-ethnicity* | | | | | | | | | | |
| Eta | .31 | .20 | .26 | .21 | .49 | .21 | .21 | .22 | .15 | .41 |
| Beta | .19** | .16 | .16 | .21 | .27** | .14 | .16 | .12 | .13 | .22** |
| *Ethnicity*[a] | | | | | | | | | | |
| Eta | .20 | .13 | .19 | .05 | .48 | .15 | .16 | .16 | .06 | .38 |
| Beta | .07 | .07 | .10 | .09 | .24** | .09** | .09 | .05 | .03 | .16** |
| *Marital status* | | | | | | | | | | |
| Eta | .08 | .05 | .11 | .09 | .09 | .07 | .07 | .09 | .08 | .08 |
| Beta | .10** | .09 | .08 | .11 | .07 | .06 | .09 | .08 | .07 | .05 |

a. The betas for ethnicity alone are taken from a multiple classification analysis with age as covariate, ethnicity as factor, and other variables identical to other MCAs.

**Significant at .01 level or better.

ential than either variable alone, had far less importance than occupation.

The associations measured by the betas show not surprisingly that a person's occupation at the start of a decade exerted more influence than any other factor on his occupation at its close. The weight of ethnicity, age, and marital status were negligible. The betas also reveal overall stability in the relationships between occupational rank and other factors. In other words they suggest stability in the processes underlying social structure. Unlike analyses that rest on cross-sectional information the linked files permit the examination of relationships across time. Here too a picture of stability emerges. However some changes did take place, and these point to some loosening at the very top and bottom of the occupational rank order. The probability that a man would retain his membership in an occupational rank declined between 1851 and 1861 from 71 percent to 63 percent for men in rank 1 and from 62 percent to 52 percent among men in rank 5. It increased for those in rank 3 from 72 percent to 80 percent, for men in rank 4 from 32 percent to 52 percent, and remained stable for those in rank 2. The increase in rank 4 probably reflected the growth and diversification of the transportation industry, which may have offered increasingly secure and well-paid employment.

In order to sort out the relationships between occupation, age, ethnicity, and marital status more closely we created two files—men in ranks 1 and 2 together and men in rank 5. A multivariate analysis explored the role of key variables in the retention of occupational rank in each of these categories. Again the amount of occupational stability remained greater at the top than at the bottom of the rank order: 72 percent of men in ranks 1 and 2 combined retained their occupational position in each decade, whereas the proportion remaining laborers dropped from 73 percent to 57 percent during the second decade (Table 5.2).

Except for Irish Catholics, ethnicity exerted very little influence on the degree to which men remained in these occupational ranks. Irish Catholic men had greater difficulty than others retaining positions in ranks 1 and 2, and their precarious hold even decreased during the second decade. The odds that an Irish Catholic in rank 1 or 2 would occupy the same position ten years later dropped from 47 percent between 1851 and 1861 to 37 percent ten years later. At the same time, though Irish Catholics remained more likely than men in any other ethnic group to be laborers, here too the probability that they would retain their occupational rank decreased, in this case from 82 percent to 64 percent. To some extent improvement at the bottom of the rank

Table 5.2 Occupational persistence in occupational ranks 1, 2, and 5, by ethnicity, controlling for age and marital status, multiple classification analysis, males, 18 years and older: Hamilton, 1851–1861, 1861–1871.

| | Rank 1-2 | | | | Rank 5 | | | |
|---|---|---|---|---|---|---|---|---|
| | 1851–1861 | | 1861–1871 | | 1851–1861 | | 1861–1871 | |
| Variable | N | Probability | N | Probability | N | Probability | N | Probability |
| *Ethnicity* | | | | | | | | |
| Irish Catholic | 15 | .47 | 21 | .37 | 109 | .82 | 130 | .64 |
| Irish Protestant | 38 | .79 | 43 | .72 | 28 | .60 | 34 | .65 |
| Scottish Presbyterian | 36 | .69 | 67 | .72 | 10 | .22 | 24 | .40 |
| English Anglican | 27 | .77 | 45 | .65 | 8 | .75 | 29 | .51 |
| English Methodist | 13 | 1.00 | 21 | .72 | 3 | .37 | 8 | .23 |
| Canadian Protestant | 21 | .72 | 49 | .88 | 1 | .42 | 5 | .41 |
| Other | 52 | .67 | 63 | .81 | 19 | .59 | 22 | .47 |
| SUMMARY STATISTICS | | | | | | | | |
| Grand mean | | .72 | | .73 | | .72 | | .57 |
| $R^2$ | | .11 | | .11 | | .16 | | .10 |
| *Ethnicity* | | | | | | | | |
| Eta | | .24 | | .25 | | .38 | | .22 |
| Beta | | .24 | | .27 | | .36 | | .21 |
| *Marital status* | | | | | | | | |
| Eta | | .23 | | .19 | | .17 | | .23 |
| Beta | | .23 | | .20 | | .11 | | .22 |
| *Age (covariate)* | | | | | | | | |
| Beta | | .000 | | .001 | | −.003 | | −.001 |
| *Significance* | | | | | | | | |
| Main effect | | .047 | | .002 | | .008 | | .014 |
| Ethnicity | | .076 | | .003 | | .001 | | .044 |
| Marital status | | .120 | | .065 | | .999 | | .049 |
| Age | | .999 | | .999 | | .999 | | .999 |

order counterbalanced the declining ability of Irish Catholics to retain their hold near the top. In reality, since relatively few Irish Catholics had been in ranks 1 and 2 at the start of each decade, the number improving their position substantially exceeded the number whose rank declined.

Interestingly, among Irish Catholic laborers who remained in Hamilton most improvement in occupational rank took place among men under the age of 45. The likelihood that an Irish Catholic laborer less than 45 years old would remain in rank 5 declined from between 80 and 89 percent during the decade 1851-1861 to between 60 and 65 percent during the next ten years. By contrast the odds that a man between the age of 45 and 54 would remain a laborer actually increased somewhat during the same period. This differential in experience underlines the connection between the life cycle and jobs among the working class to which we pointed earlier. Among the Irish Catholics younger men undoubtedly had a greater ability to seize new opportunities in industry and appeared more attractive to employers.

Despite extensive individual occupational change a similar proportion of the linked population remained in each occupational rank at the end of each decade, and the ethnic composition of each rank remained quite stable as well. In other words, occupational mobility by and large reshuffled the population. Consider the people linked between 1861 and 1871. The proportion increased from 8 percent to 11 percent in rank 1, remained steady at 20 percent in rank 2, rose from 40 percent to 43 percent in rank 3, held at 6 percent in rank 4, and decreased a bit from 16 percent to 14 percent in rank 5. The most notable change occurred among the proportion who moved out of the unclassifiable category—12 percent to 4 percent, a result of their entry into the work force.

In 1861 Irish Catholics represented 52 percent of the linked men in rank 5; in 1871 they were 50 percent.[12] Similarly in 1861 they formed 3 percent of the linked men in rank 1 and ten years later were 4 percent. Of the men in rank 3 in 1861, 27 percent were Scottish and in 1871, 25 percent; the proportion of English Protestants in rank 2 varied only between 29 percent and 28 percent; Canadian Protestants accounted for 21 percent of the men in rank 1 in 1861 and 18 percent a decade later. As these figures show, very little change occurred in the overall relationship between occupation and ethnicity among those men who remained in Hamilton.

The entrance of young men into the labor force reflected the influence of age and persistence on occupation. The men traced for twenty years did distinctly better than those followed for ten years: 11 percent of the ten-year group and 8 percent of the twenty-year group were laborers; 29 percent of the former and 37 percent of the latter entered rank 1. Obviously a combination of age and length of residence contributed to occupational success.

English Protestants were overrepresented among those entering the labor force in wood products and the metal and luxury trades; Scottish men were overrepresented in the same trades and in apparel as well. Conversely, Canadian Protestants were notably underrepresented among the metal trades and slightly overrepresented among men entering clerical jobs and construction. Perhaps English, Scottish, and to some extent Irish immigrant young men fixed their aspirations on the expanding metal trades, while men who grew up in Canada aspired to commercial careers. However Canadian-born Protestants formed a clear plurality of young men entering the labor force in every occupational group except laborers. Among those who entered the work force as laborers Irish Catholic young men were overrepresented by about six times compared to three times among laborers in the entire traced population. Irish Catholic young men also entered the apparel, wood, and transportation trades in disproportionately high numbers. However Irish young men, both Catholic and Protestant, had less access to clerical work than those born elsewhere. In sum the occupational distribution by ethnicity of men entering the labor force generally paralleled the experience of older men who remained in the city.

How much occupational mobility took place? To some extent the answer must be subjective: the definition of *a lot or not very much* depends partly on the observer. However some of the patterns in Hamilton do appear relatively unambiguous, and our point is that a great deal of movement took place between occupational ranks. Among household heads traced from 1851 to 1861 and from 1861 to 1871 about 25 percent of men changed occupational rank during each decade. The most striking changes between decades were the drop in the proportion of men who remained laborers from 75 percent in the first to 60 percent in the second decade and the increase in the proportion who remained in rank 4 from 18 percent to 60 percent (Table 5.3). Both of these shifts reflected the development of industry in the city. The expansion of industrial opportunities decreased the overall proportion of laborers in the population and provided avenues out of unskilled work for men who remained in Hamilton. The expansion of the transport industry and the requirements of other industries improved the prospects of teamsters, carters, and men in similar occupations.

Most striking are the movements of people traced for 20 years (Table 5.4). Between 1851 and 1871 only about half of these men re-

Table 5.3 Occupational persistence, by rank, of all household heads, ranks 1–5: Hamilton, 1851–1861, 1861–1871.

| Occupational rank first year | 1851–1861 | 1861–1871 |
|---|---|---|
| 1 | 72.3 | 73.2 |
| 2 | 69.4 | 63.0 |
| 3 | 77.5 | 83.8 |
| 4 | 17.6 | 59.5 |
| 5 | 75.4 | 60.0 |
| N | 741 | 1,061 |

Table 5.4 Occupational mobility among individuals linked between 1851 and 1871: Hamilton.

| Occupational rank in 1851 | Occupational rank in 1871 | | | | | |
|---|---|---|---|---|---|---|
| | 1 | 2 | 3 | 4 | 5 | N |
| A. ALL LINKED PEOPLE | | | | | | |
| 1 | 69.4 | 22.4 | 4.1 | 2.0 | 2.0 | 49 |
| 2 | 24.7 | 52.7 | 19.4 | 2.2 | 1.1 | 93 |
| 3 | 4.7 | 11.7 | 73.0 | 4.3 | 6.3 | 256 |
| 4 | 2.9 | 29.4 | 17.6 | 32.2 | 17.6 | 34 |
| 5 | 3.5 | 7.0 | 26.3 | 17.5 | 45.6 | 57 |
| B. HOUSEHOLD HEADS (EXCLUDING THOSE NOT IN RANKS 1–5) | | | | | | |
| 1 | 69.8 | 20.9 | 4.7 | 2.3 | 2.3 | 43 |
| 2 | 22.5 | 60.6 | 14.1 | 1.4 | 1.4 | 71 |
| 3 | 4.6 | 8.6 | 78.2 | 4.6 | 4.0 | 174 |
| 4 | 3.7 | 33.3 | 14.8 | 29.6 | 18.5 | 27 |
| 5 | 5.1 | 5.1 | 23.1 | 17.9 | 48.7 | 39 |

tained the same occupational rank at each point. Moreover this figure masks a much greater amount of occupational change, for it notes neither change in occupational rank within a decade nor changes in job but not rank. Thus in a period of twenty years an absolute minimum of half the people changed occupational rank at some point, and the real amount of change was undoubtedly very much higher.

About equal proportions of men moved upward and downward, and about an equal share shifted place in each decade. However very few people rose in occupational rank and then fell, although a drop followed by a recovery was relatively common. A notable drop in occupational persistence occurred, as we have observed, in rank 5, probably as a result of the ability of men who remained in the city to take advantage of new industrial opportunities. Over half (51 percent) of the laborers who were household heads and who stayed in the city for twenty years improved their occupational position.

Although a great deal of movement took place, very little of it was long distance. Only 4 percent of the men in rank 1 ended up in rank 3 and 2 percent in each of ranks 4 and 5; only about 5 percent of the men in rank 3 moved into either rank 1 or 2 and about 6 percent into ranks 4 and 5; and about 11 percent of the men in rank 5 moved into ranks 1 and 2.

A distinction in occupational persistence existed between professionals and men in high-ranking commercial occupations. The former were much more likely to retain their occupational rank. However the latter remained more stable than men in clerical and related jobs, less than half of whom had stayed at the same sort of work at either ten- or twenty-year intervals. Interestingly, persistence within individual trades does not appear to have been affected by technology or general prosperity. For instance no very meaningful variations appeared in occupational persistence in the apparel and metal trades. The least stable occupations not surprisingly were the lowest-ranking commercial jobs such as huckster and peddler and the jobs in various forms of service.

Finally, let us consider some specific patterns of occupational change in order to dispel some of the ambiguity inherent in changes between occupational ranks. First, there is the puzzling case of the men who moved between rank 4 and rank 2—eighteen in number between 1861 and 1871. Of these between seven and ten probably moved upward in occupational rank. Among the ten traced for twenty years seven probably improved their position. In most cases men moved into lower-level commercial positions or petty proprietorship, though some changes are difficult to interpret. For instance between 1861 and 1871 two mariners became sea captains. They might have acquired their own boat or they might have been captains all along. Others probably did not change the nature of their work very much if at all: the barkeeper who became a hotel keeper and the peddler who became a bible agent probably did the same type of work at both ends of the decade.

The case for upward mobility is clearer among laborers. Not much difference exists between those traced for ten or twenty years or, interestingly, for those from different ethnic backgrounds. Laborers moved into three sorts of work: into transport as carters, teamsters, railway workers, and blacksmiths; into metal trades as molders, machinists, and engineers; and sometimes they became petty proprietors—innkeepers or grocers. The kinds of occupations they entered clearly reflected the expansion of work opportunities in the city: the development of the metal trades, transportation, and the service sector. Very few if any laborers actually reached the upper levels of the occupational hierarchy.

Last of all let us consider the case of shoemakers and tailors, men whose occupations were altered by the invention of the sewing machine in the middle of the nineteenth century. Over a ten-year period about 81 percent of the shoemakers remained in the shoe industry, and about 84 percent of tailors stayed in the apparel business. The proportions remaining in the same industry dropped to 65 percent and 68 percent, respectively, over twenty years, proportions quite typical for other trades. Only one of the occupational shifts among shoemakers and perhaps two or three among tailors could conceivably be counted as downward mobility. Technological change did not drive these shoemakers or tailors out of their trades. Rather the impact of technological change registered most heavily on their sons, especially those of shoemakers, who began to avoid their fathers' craft. The proportion of young men among shoemakers dropped sharply. Tailors remained more prosperous than shoemakers as a consequence of the different organization of the two industries. The mechanization of the shoe industry did not entail an increase in the number of women employed; the mechanization of the clothing industry did.[13] Large numbers of poorly paid women performed much of the work, and the male tailors who remained in the trade either employed women or worked as cutters, the aristocracy of both the shoe and clothing industries.

Several important conclusions emerge from this investigation of occupational change:

1. The determinants of occupational mobility remained relatively stable between 1851 and 1861 and between 1861 and 1871.

2. The occupational distribution of the linked population also remained relatively stable. Occupational mobility by and large reshuffled the same people into different ranks.

3. Occupational mobility only marginally altered the relationships between work and ethnicity.

4. The changes that did take place were: the increased ability of laborers to improve their economic standing by moving into expanding sectors of the economy, notably the metal trades, transportation, and petty proprietorship; the increased occupational stability of men in rank 4, a reflection of the improvement of opportunities in trans-

portation; and the slightly increased ability of Irish Catholic men to improve their occupational position.

5. Despite the relative stability in the process of mobility a very great amount of individual rank change took place. Well over half the men who remained in the city for twenty years changed their occupational rank at least once.

6. The rate of upward and downward occupational movement was about equal, and most of it covered a very short distance. By and large people did not leave their class.

Once again the picture that emerges contrasts a rigid structure with individual fluidity. Despite a considerable amount of individual movement between jobs and even between ranks, the occupational structure and the relationships between work and ethnicity remained relatively fixed.

Occupational mobility recruited people into the expanding sectors of the economy and drew them away from those areas in which the demand for labor was decreasing. The rapid interchange of occupational rank may possibly have fostered an illusion of a society more open than it actually was. Recall the Wisconsin working men who believed, by a margin of two to one, that they might rise to the position of foreman, superintendent, or businessman. The combination of limited ladders of mobility—climbed and descended at a dizzying pace —with reasonable chances for home ownership could have distracted people from the larger structural consequences of mobility patterns and property transactions—namely, the perpetuation of the structure of inequality. If this was the case, then one ideological consequence of occupational mobility was the reinforcement of the identification of a high rate of mobility with equality that has marked popular, social, and political thought in North America for at least a century and a half.[14]

## The Dimensions of Mobility

A statistical account of mobility is an abstraction, and despite its complexity a reduction of the varieties of human experience. What those statistical patterns represent becomes clearer from some examples drawn from the experience of household heads traced from 1861 to 1871 in Hamilton. First, there is the occasional dramatic case in which mobility becomes evident in every measurable dimension. In 1861 Henry McDonald, a Scottish Presbyterian clerk, 30 years old, had lived in Hamilton for at least ten years. Already relatively prosperous, McDonald was in the eightieth to eighty-ninth economic ranks and employed three resident domestic servants, though he did not own the house in which he lived. Ten years later he had become a merchant, a homeowner, one of the wealthiest 10 percent of men in the city, and the employer of eight resident domestic servants. Perhaps even more stunning was the fortune of another Scottish Presbyterian, Henry McLaren, in 1861 a 24-year-old storekeeper who had arrived in Hamilton sometime during the previous decade. A relatively poor man (among the bottom forty economic ranks in 1861) and a renter, by the end of the decade McLaren was listed as a merchant in the top tenth of the economic hierarchy and the owner of a home, though still not the employer of any resident servants.

Other men retained roughly the same characteristics at each end of the decade. A 40-year-old Irish Catholic laborer, Patrick Doherty, remained in the bottom forty economic percentiles, renting the house in which he lived with his wife and children. Another Irish Catholic, John O'Shea, also 40 years old, was more comfortable; a carpenter who owned his own home, O'Shea remained throughout the decade in the eightieth to eighty-ninth economic ranks.

It was common for men to change economic rank while remaining in the same occupation. Robert Sullivan, a 38-year-old Irish Protestant merchant, suffered serious financial losses, dropping from the eightieth to eighty-ninth ranks to the bottom forty economic ranks during the decade. Sullivan did own a house, but he no longer employed a servant as he had in 1861. Samuel Higgins, a 38-year-old Irish Protestant tailor, improved his economic standing by moving from the eightieth to eighty-ninth ranks to the top ten economic percentiles. In the course of the decade Higgins also bought a house and managed to retain a resident domestic servant.

Less often men retained the same economic rank but changed their occupation. Harry McCraken, a Scottish Presbyterian plumber, 36 years old in 1861, had become a merchant ten years later. Although in that time he acquired a house and a servant he remained at the middle of the economic rank order, in the fortieth to seventy-ninth percentiles.

Thus changes in home ownership and the employment of servants often accompanied both upward and downward movement in economic rank or occupation. Another example is Peter Davidson, a 46-year-old Scottish Presbyterian jeweler, who dropped from the top ten economic percentiles in 1861 to the fortieth to seventy-ninth percentiles ten years later. At the start of the decade Davidson had employed two servants; at its close he had none. In 1861, to cite another case, Thomas Smith was a 37-year-old English Anglican tavern keeper in the eightieth to eighty-ninth economic ranks. He lived in a rented house and employed one servant. A decade later, though in the same economic rank, Smith had become an importer, purchased a home, and acquired a second servant.

Some people, as we have seen, made choices between servants and home ownership when they could not afford both, and some merchants apparently chose to invest their capital in various forms of enterprises while renting a house. Generally the choice between servants and home ownership split along class lines. A 35-year-old Scottish Presbyterian merchant, Thomas Strachan, managed to climb from the fortieth to seventy-ninth percentile to the eightieth to eighty-ninth during the decade. Despite his economic gain he did not purchase a house, but he did hire two resident domestic servants. Contrast him with Walter Jones, a 22-year-old Canadian-born Protestant, who changed occupation from telegraph operator to railway conductor during the decade. Jones also improved his economic position in exactly the same way as Strachan, yet he purchased a home and did not employ a servant at either end of the decade. Similarly Robert Newman, a 35-year-old English Anglican builder, styled himself a carpenter in 1871 though his economic rank had risen from the fortieth to seventy-ninth economic percentile to the top ten. At each end of the decade he owned a home, though despite his greatly improved economic position he did not hire a resident servant. Unlike him, Harold Harnsworth, a 31-year-old English Anglican bookkeeper who became a merchant, though remaining in the fortieth to seventy-ninth economic ranks and renting a house, acquired a resident domestic.

The histories of other people reveal the problems of old age in a social order without pensions. Dora McDougal, a 59-year-old Scottish Presbyterian dressmaker, dropped from the fortieth to seventy-ninth percentile to the bottom forty and in the process lost both her house and her servant. Lemuel Miller, a 50-year-old shoemaker, became a stevedore, probably displaced in his trade by younger men, and like McDougal slipped from the middle to the bottom of the economic rank order. However during the same years he also acquired a house of his own, which probably cushioned his economic decline. The reason why he was able to purchase a home probably rests in the fact that in 1861 he had seven children living at home, five of whom were still there ten years later. In all likelihood it was their earnings that enabled the Millers to become home owners.

The foregoing examples show that occupation is only one dimension along which change in individual fortune may be charted. The historian of mobility has at least three others to consider: economic rank, the ownership of property, and the employment of servants. In fact, as the examples demonstrate, the fit between dimensions is far from perfect, and a first inspection of their relationships produces an image of an almost random universe. Occupational and economic mobility appear almost unrelated processes, and the relationship of each to the ownership of property and the employment of servants is surprisingly loose. The first moral to which this absence of strong relationships points is cautionary: no automatic assumptions can be made about the movement of a person on one type of scale from his movement on another.[15]

However movement within the dimensions of social space was actually less chaotic than first appearances imply. Relationships did in fact exist between the dimensions of mobility. However they did not take a form that permits precise prediction of movement in one dimension from the knowledge of movement on another. That is why on first inspection they appear almost random. It is important to understand that the paradox is only apparent.[16]

We set out to acquire summary measures of the associations between the major dimensions of mobility in each decade (Table 5.5). In general the measures of association between 1851 and 1861 were remarkably similar to those between 1861 and 1871. Once again the stability in the processes underlying and reproducing the social structure stands out. Only a few moderate changes occurred. The association between economic rank in the first and second years studied increased during the second decade, which shows that economic rank became more stable. Ownership of property and employment of servants also varied less often, in the latter case a reflection of the general decrease in keeping servants.

In some cases an important discrepancy existed between two measures of association. One measure (lambda) estimates the degree to which knowledge of the position of a person on one scale improves the ability to predict his position on another. For instance, to what extent does knowledge of economic mobility improve the ability to predict occupational mobility? The other measure (Somer's D) examines the association between two variables through a consideration of every cell in a table. In essence it measures whether or not an individual's scores on two scales remain close to each other. For instance it shows that economic and occupational rank remain near each other, regardless of whether they are identical or whether one is a bit higher or lower than the other.[17]

In a number of instances a discrepancy existed between the measure of predictability and the measure of association. This means that although the exact direction of the movement of an independent variable (for instance occupation) could not be predicted, the position

Table 5.5   Measures of association, mobility variables: Hamilton, 1851–1861 and 1861–1871.

| Independent variable | Dependent variable | Asymmetric Λ | | Somer's D | |
|---|---|---|---|---|---|
| | | 1851–1861 | 1861–1871 | 1851–1861 | 1861–1871 |
| Occupation, first year | Occupation, second year | .47 | .50 | .62 | .66 |
| Economic rank, first year | Economic rank, second year | .23 | .32 | .51 | .56 |
| Property, first year | Property, second year | .38 | .43 | .41 | .52 |
| Servants, first year | Servants, second year | .18 | .20 | .28 | .41 |
| Occupational mobility | Economic mobility | .12 | .12 | .48 | .51 |
| Economic mobility | Occupational mobility | .08 | .08 | .41 | .45 |
| Occupational mobility | Servant mobility | .14 | .09 | .34 | .31 |
| Servant mobility | Occupational mobility | .08 | .05 | .40 | .50 |
| Occupational mobility | Property mobility | .09 | .05 | .04 | .05 |
| Property mobility | Occupational mobility | .00 | .00 | .05 | .07 |
| Economic mobility | Servant mobility | .22 | .13 | .34 | .31 |
| Servant mobility | Economic mobility | .07 | .08 | .46 | .57 |
| Economic mobility | Property mobility | .15 | .20 | .18 | .21 |
| Property mobility | Economic mobility | .05 | .06 | .23 | .29 |
| Servant mobility | Property mobility | .00 | .00 | .01 | .00 |
| Property mobility | Servant mobility | .00 | .00 | .01 | .00 |

of variables on their respective scales (for instance occupational rank and economic rank) remained close. Knowledge of a person's occupation in nineteenth-century Hamilton does not help us to predict with certainty his economic rank. Nor does economic rank help us very much to predict his occupation. However from a knowledge of occupation we gain a reasonable idea of the range within which an individual's economic standing is likely to have existed, and from his economic rank we learn much the same about his occupational standing. In other words it was uncommon for a person who remained in a relatively high-ranking occupation to fall very far in economic rank. Similarly men who remained low in occupational rank frequently improved their economic position but not by very much. A good deal of short-distance movement took place within a restricted range.

Similar conclusions may be reached about the relationship between the employment of servants, occupational mobility, and economic rank and about the association between economic and property mobility as well. There was, however, a much weaker connection between occupation and property. Indeed change in property ownership had a surprisingly tenuous relationship to change in other mobility variables. Occupational mobility did not affect property at all, and economic mobility affected it only slightly. Conversely property mobility had no impact whatsoever on occupational rank and only a modest effect on economic standing. Nor did employment of servants and property mobility affect each other. Indeed the ownership, rental, acquisition, or loss of property appears the most independent of the four types of mobility.

Thus relationships between the dimensions of mobility were not random. Certainly the fit between them was far from perfect, and each clearly tapped a different aspect of experience. Still associations clearly existed between them, and though most movement could not be predicted precisely, most people retained a relatively similar ranking on each scale.

In general the amount of occupational mobility remained quite similar in each decade, and most movement was over a short distance. Similarly the patterns of economic mobility in each decade resembled each other quite closely, and most economic movement took place across short distances. The retention of rank, however, did increase slightly, except at the top of the economic rank order. The magnitude of economic mobility in each decade not only was quite similar but also considerably exceeded occupational movement in quantity.

When occupational and economic ranks are collapsed from five to three categories, a moderate increase in rank stability appears in both measures (Table 5.6). The proportion remaining in the lowest occupational rank increases from 57 percent to 70 percent, in the middle from 76 percent to 84 percent, and in the highest from 74 percent to 83 percent. Similarly the proportion remaining in the lowest economic rank increases from 49 percent to 57 percent and in the middle from 51 percent to 59 percent, and at the top it remains the same at 75 percent.

Table 5.6 Occupational mobility of people linked four ways: Hamilton, 1861–1871.

| Occupational rank in 1861 | Occupational rank in 1871 | | | | N | Percent |
|---|---|---|---|---|---|---|
| | 1 | 2 | 3 | 4–5 | | |
| 1 | 73.8 | 16.7 | 8.3 | 1.2 | 84 | 10.0 |
| 2 | 17.6 | 62.1 | 11.0 | 9.3 | 182 | 21.6 |
| 3 | 1.6 | 8.3 | 84.4 | 5.6 | 372 | 44.2 |
| 4–5 | 2.9 | 10.3 | 17.2 | 69.6 | 204 | 24.2 |
| N | 106 | 179 | 376 | 181 | 842 | |
| Percent | 12.6 | 21.3 | 44.7 | 21.5 | | 100.0 |

| Economic rank in 1861 | Economic rank in 1871 (percentile) | | | | N | Percent |
|---|---|---|---|---|---|---|
| | 0–39 | 40–79 | 80–89 | 90–99 | | |
| 0–39 | 57.3 | 35.4 | 5.6 | 1.7 | 232 | 27.6 |
| 40–79 | 14.8 | 59.2 | 16.0 | 10.0 | 400 | 47.5 |
| 80–89 | 6.5 | 26.1 | 37.4 | 29.9 | 107 | 12.7 |
| 90–99 | 5.8 | 11.7 | 15.5 | 67.0 | 103 | 12.2 |
| N | 205 | 340 | 133 | 145 | | |
| Percent | 24.3 | 40.4 | 15.8 | 17.2 | | |

| | Direction (1861–1871) | |
|---|---|---|
| | Economic | Occupational |
| Stable | 62.6 | 80.4 |
| Up | 24.1 | 11.8 |
| Down | 13.3 | 7.8 |
| N | 842 | 842 |

In each decade the proportion of people with a high economic rank dropping to a low one remains 6 percent; the proportion moving from one that was low to one that was high decreases slightly from 10 percent to 7 percent.

Using the three-rank scale the proportion of men who did not change economic rank rose from 57 percent to 63 percent between the first and second decades, and the proportion remaining in the same occupational rank increased very slightly as well, from 77 percent to 80 percent. The proportion moving upward in occupational and economic rank remained the same in each decade—12 percent for the former and 24 percent for the latter. However an important shift did occur in the proportion of downward movement, which for economic rank decreased from 19 percent to 13 percent and for occupational rank from 12 percent to 8 percent. In the second decade upward movement among the linked population clearly exceeded downward; and the pattern in Hamilton resembled that in virtually every American city that has been studied—a marked difference from the pattern for the previous decade, when the roughly equal amount of upward and downward movement appeared to set Hamilton apart. The earlier pattern probably reflected two things: greater fluidity among the population of a raw, new city and, perhaps most influential, the hardships of the depression of the late 1850s.[18]

Trends for property mobility and employment of servants parallel those for occupational and economic movement. Property ownership became more stable during the second decade: only the proportion of men who lost property decreased.[19] Thus less downward property mobility also characterized the experience of the people traced during the second decade. Given the relationship between property ownership and persistence already discussed elsewhere in this book, it should be no surprise to learn that property ownership was much higher among the men traced in each decade than among the population as a whole.

Patterns of servant employment reflected the general decrease in the proportion of people with resident domestics. The proportion with at least one servant in each year declined as did the proportion acquiring a servant and, interestingly, the proportion losing one as well. Thus, though fewer people employed servants, those who did were less likely to lose them, again an example of the slightly greater stability among the people traced during the second decade.

The relationship between occupational mobility and economic mobility increased somewhat between 1861 and 1871, though movement in different directions on each scale still remained common (Table 5.7). For example of those moving upward economically 55 percent remained occupationally stable, 32 percent moved up in occupational rank, and 13 percent down in the first decade. However in the second decade the proportion moving upward declined to 24 percent and the proportion moving downward dropped to 9 percent. A distinct shift had occurred. Upward occupational movement more often accompanied upward economic movement in the first than in the second decade. Nonetheless in each decade upward and downward occupational movement remained quite common among men who slipped in economic rank.

The economic movements of those men who remained stable or changed occupational rank were less clear cut. There was, for instance, more downward mobility in economic rank among those moving upward in occupation than among those dropping. Relationships here have a kind of random quality, but the measures of association do point out that though movement on the two scales frequently

Table 5.7 Occupational mobility and economic mobility: Hamilton, 1851–1871.

A. 1851–1861

| Occupational mobility | Economic mobility (percent) | | | N |
| --- | --- | --- | --- | --- |
| | Stable | Up | Down | |
| Stable | 55.4% | 55.1% | 40.0% | 308 |
| Up | 28.9 | 31.6 | 33.3 | 169 |
| Down | 15.7 | 13.3 | 26.6 | 92 |
| N | 426 | 98 | 45 | 569 |

B. 1861–1871

| Occupational mobility | Economic mobility | | | N |
| --- | --- | --- | --- | --- |
| | Stable | Up | Down | |
| Stable | 78.2 | 67.2 | 67.2 | 611 |
| Up | 13.2 | 24.0 | 16.4 | 147 |
| Down | 8.6 | 8.8 | 16.4 | 84 |
| N | 409 | 287 | 146 | 842 |

| Occupational rank | Economic rank[a] | | | | |
| --- | --- | --- | --- | --- | --- |
| | Stable | | | | |
| | 1 to 1 | 2 to 2 | 3 to 3 | 4 to 4 | 5 to 5 |
| Stable | 81.2 | 57.5 | 73.6 | 77.6 | 81.2 |
| Up | 8.7 | 25.0 | 17.6 | 10.5 | 10.5 |
| Down | 11.9 | 17.5 | 8.8 | 11.9 | 8.3 |
| N | 69 | 40 | 91 | 76 | 133 |

| Occupational rank | Upward movement from − | | | | | | | | | |
| --- | --- | --- | --- | --- | --- | --- | --- | --- | --- | --- |
| | 2 to 1 | 3 to 1 | 3 to 2 | 4 to 1 | 4 to 2 | 4 to 3 | 5 to 1 | 5 to 2 | 5 to 3 | 5 to 4 |
| Stable | 75.0 | 69.0 | 64.6 | 63.6 | 68.8 | 67.3 | 25.0 | 53.8 | 68.8 | 70.0 |
| Up | 12.5 | 24.1 | 20.8 | 27.2 | 18.8 | 25.0 | 75.0 | 46.2 | 21.9 | 26.0 |
| Down | 12.5 | 6.9 | 14.6 | 9.2 | 12.4 | 7.7 | 0.0 | 0.0 | 9.3 | 4.0 |
| N | 32 | 29 | 48 | 11 | 16 | 52 | 4 | 13 | 32 | 50 |

| Occupational rank | Downward movement from − | | | | | |
| --- | --- | --- | --- | --- | --- | --- |
| | 1 to 2 | 1 to 3 | 2 to 3 | 3 to 4 | 3 to 5 | 4 to 5 |
| Stable | 75.0 | 54.5 | 85.7 | 77.8 | 66.7 | 63.4 |
| Up | 18.8 | 18.2 | 14.3 | 11.1 | 11.1 | 19.5 |
| Down | 6.2 | 27.3 | 0.0 | 11.1 | 22.2 | 17.1 |
| N | 16 | 11 | 21 | 18 | 18 | 41 |

a. Economic rank: 1, 90–99 percentile; 2, 80–89; 3, 60–79; 4, 40–59; 5, 0–39.

did not go in the same direction, the relative standing of most people on each of them generally remained close.

In fact some patterns can be discerned by examining specific types of moves. All upward movement in economic rank except from ranks 2 to 1 was accompanied by greater upward than downward occupational mobility. Upward movement from the bottom of the economic rank order to rank 2 was especially likely to be accompanied by upward occupational mobility and on no occasion was accompanied by downward mobility. Similarly of those moving from the bottom to the middle of the economic rank order 22 percent moved upward in occupation and only 9 percent downward. By contrast among those who dropped from the top to the middle of the economic rank order downward occupational mobility was more common than upward, as it was among those who slipped from the middle to the lowest economic ranks. In fact it was the numerous, short, one-rank moves that most often went in different directions. Since these were the most frequent types, they obscure the closer association between economic rank and occupation among people whose movement through social space was of a longer distance.

In both sets of people traced across a decade the ownership of property was related much more closely to economic than to occupational mobility, and during the second decade the relationships between economic rank and property sharpened (Table 5.8). There was by contrast less association between employment of servants and economic mobility from 1861 to 1871 than in the earlier decade. No relationship existed between occupational mobility and the employment of servants in either decade.

In order to explore the simultaneous relationships between the four dimensions of mobility, multivariate analyses were necessary. They are presented in detail elsewhere.[20] Here we highlight their most important results; the complex patterns make simple summary statements exceedingly difficult. First, the impact of occupational mobility on economic rank varied at different economic levels. That is, occupational mobility exerted most influence on men at the bottom of the economic scale, undoubtedly because movement upward in occupation, often out of laboring, brought about economic improvement.

Employment of servants, property mobility, ethnicity, and age, however, had no impact on the extent to which people changed economic rank. In general, patterns of association between economic rank and other variables remained quite similar between the 1851-1861 and 1861-1871 groups, again underlining the stability of social processes.

It proved possible to account for a substantial amount of the varia-

Table 5.8   Employment of servants and property status, by economic and occupational mobility: Hamilton, 1861–1871.

A. EMPLOYMENT OF SERVANTS

| | Employed servants, 1861–1871 | Gained servants | Lost servants | Did not employ servants, 1861–1871 | N |
|---|---|---|---|---|---|
| *Economic mobility* | | | | | |
| Stable | 14.2 | 4.9 | 13.0 | 68.0 | 409 |
| Up | 9.8 | 5.2 | 11.5 | 73.5 | 287 |
| Down | 15.1 | 5.5 | 21.9 | 57.5 | 146 |
| *Occupational mobility* | | | | | |
| Stable | 13.1 | 4.4 | 12.4 | 69.6 | 611 |
| Up | 10.2 | 10.9 | 15.6 | 63.3 | 147 |
| Down | 10.7 | 11.9 | 11.9 | 65.5 | 84 |

B. PROPERTY STATUS

| | Owner, 1861–1871 | Gained property | Lost property | Renter, 1861–1871 | N |
|---|---|---|---|---|---|
| *Economic mobility* | | | | | |
| Stable | 32.5 | 19.3 | 2.7 | 45.5 | 409 |
| Up | 38.0 | 30.7 | 2.4 | 28.9 | 287 |
| Down | 11.0 | 13.0 | 15.8 | 60.3 | 146 |
| *Occupational mobility* | | | | | |
| Stable | 33.2 | 19.3 | 4.4 | 43.0 | 64 |
| Up | 22.4 | 32.0 | 10.2 | 49.0 | 147 |
| Down | 26.2 | 25.0 | 8.3 | 40.5 | 84 |

tion in the probability that any person would be at the top or bottom of the economic rank order but not in between. Associations between the measures of mobility were clearly sharpest at the extremes of the social structure.

As with economic rank, the association between each of the major dimensions of mobility and occupational rank were remarkably similar in each decade. In every case occupational rank at the start of each decade exerted more influence on occupational rank at the end than did economic mobility. Thus change in occupational rank exerted a greater effect on economic rank than did change in economic rank on occupation. However in most cases economic mobility ranked second and was statistically significant. Other factors generally had no influence.

These relationships mean that with simultaneous controls for all variables introduced, occupational and economic mobility had complex and significant relationships with each other. However property, servants, and ethnicity exerted almost no influence on either of them. Thus the correlations between them and economic or occupational standing that appear in bivariate statistics result from multicollinearity, that is, from the correlations among the independent variables.

However, occupational and economic mobility, especially the latter, did exert a significant influence on property ownership and servant employment. By itself the relationship between property and servants is especially interesting because, as in our earlier cross-sectional discussion, it was inverse. A person who employed servants was more likely to remain a renter than to own property at each end of either decade. In the decade 1861-1871 the probabilities were 55 percent compared to 13 percent, substantial differences. The likelihood that those men who acquired servants would rent or lose their property exceeded the odds that they would own or acquire property. Furthermore men who rented in each year had a greater chance of employing a servant than those who owned property. The very wealthy were quite likely both to own property and to employ a servant; the poor were likely to rent and unlikely to have a servant. In between the relationships were less clear, and in a significant number of instances people chose one rather than the other, and their choices were related to class.

The relationship between occupational and economic rank varied at different points along each hierarchy. The probability of membership in occupational rank 1 was substantial where economic rank was also 1 or even when it dropped from 1 to 2. However the chances of membership in occupational rank 1 for men who slipped to economic rank 3, 4, or 5 was nil. Similarly if economic rank improved from 2 to 1 or remained at 2 a reasonable probability of membership in the highest occupational rank existed. At the other end of the scale the probability that someone who remained at the bottom of the economic rank order would be in occupational rank 5 was substantial and much higher than the odds for someone who moved from the bottom to the middle of the economic rank order. The probability that anyone starting a decade in either the highest or lowest economic ranks would end in the opposite occupational rank was very low. Finally, as we might expect, little connection existed between any type of economic movement and a middle-ranking occupation. Those who moved from occupational rank 2 to 1 or remained in rank 1 were most likely to be at the top of the economic rank order as well. Those who dropped from occupational rank 1 had a considerably lower probability of membership in the highest economic rank. At the same time upward movement from occupational rank 3 to 2 or 3 to 1 boosted the probability of membership in economic rank 1. This means that those men who traded an artisanal for a mercantile occupational title usually moved upward in economic standing too.

Men who remained laborers were most likely to be at the bottom of the economic rank order. Those who moved from labor to skilled trades did considerably better. Thus the movement from laborer to artisan usually signified an improvement in wealth as well. Conversely the worst possible move in terms of economic rank was from artisan to laborer, for it more often than not meant that a man would end the decade in the lowest economic rank regardless of where he began.

By the second decade relationships had become somewhat more ordered. Men who moved from occupational rank 3 to 1 were much more likely to be in economic rank 1 or 2 at the end of that decade than at the close of the preceding decade. Most people who remained in occupational rank 2 were unlikely to find themselves below economic rank 3 at the end of either decade, a clear indication of the general attractiveness of clerical and related work. By contrast men who remained artisans were far more likely than those in clerical work to end each decade in economic rank 4 or 5.

Men who owned property were much more likely to be in economic rank 1 than renters. Similarly renters were much more likely to be in economic rank 5. In each decade, moreover, those who lost property were more likely to be in the bottom two economic ranks than those who acquired it. However the relationships of servant employment to economic rank were less clear. The men most likely to employ or acquire a servant in the first decade were in economic rank 1. In the second decade those in economic rank 3 were the most likely to acquire domestic help, followed by those in economic rank 2. In each decade the probability that a man who did not employ a servant would be in rank 5 was greater than the likelihood that he would be in any other economic rank.

Occupational and economic mobility worked in somewhat different ways. The chance that someone on the bottom of the economic rank order would improve his position actually decreased. But the odds that a laborer would improve his occupational standing had become more favorable. The odds of remaining in economic rank 5 increased from 34 percent to 42 percent; for remaining a laborer they dropped from 55 percent to 49 percent.

Those on the bottom of the economic rank order stayed there a bit more often; those in the lowest-ranking occupations moved into other types of work somewhat more frequently. About the same proportion of working-class men managed to enter ranks 1 and 2 in each decade, while fewer men made it from the bottom or middle to the top two economic ranks. Men in clerical jobs retained their economic and occupational standing quite well and fared even better during the second than the first decade. By and large the prospects of the men at the top of both the economic and occupational rank orders remained about the same in each period.

Both economic and occupational rank, it is important to stress, were cumulative. With a few exceptions membership in no occupational or economic rank increased the probability of membership in a particular economic or occupational category very much above 50 percent and often far less. Thus it is necessary to consider the cumulative impact of a man's attributes if we are to estimate his economic or occupational rank at the end of any decade. For instance consider the probability that a man with the following characteristics would be at the bottom of the economic rank order in 1871: economic rank 5 in 1861; occupational rank 5 in each year; renter; no servants. For him the odds would be 83 percent. On the other hand the probability was 90 percent that a man with precisely the opposite characteristics would be in economic rank 1 in 1871. If he had dropped from occupational rank 1 to 2 the odds that he would remain in economic rank 1 would still be a substantial, though reduced, 74 percent. If the man in the first example shifted out of laboring into skilled wage work, the odds that he would still be at the bottom of the economic rank order would dip to 64 percent. If he had begun the decade in economic rank 3, the odds that this laborer would slip to the bottom of the economic scale would decrease to 48 percent. In short when the cumulative influence of variables is considered, relationships between the dimensions of mobility do not appear random. Relationships were complex and far from neat, but the attainment of economic and occupational rank was nonetheless an ordered process.

To conclude, the major trends in the relationships between the four dimensions along which mobility can be measured were these:

1.  the stability of the processes determining the acquisition of occupational and economic rank and of property ownership and servant employment
2.  the decrease in downward mobility
3.  the general tightening of the system, reflected in a modest decrease in the amount of economic mobility in the second decade

4. the decreased prospects for those at the bottom of the economic rank order and the unchanged prospects of those at the top
5. the cumulative nature of the processes by which an individual attained a particular occupational or economic rank
6. the partial independence of movement along each dimension
7. the general similarity or closeness of position on economic and occupational rank orders even when movement on each did not go in the same direction
8. the association of long-distance moves on one dimension with moves in the same direction on others
9. the short, intraclass nature of most movement
10. the stronger relationship of property with economic than with occupational rank
11. the inverse relationship between the ownership of property and the employment of servants

The relationships between occupation, economic rank, property, and servants formed a rough pattern that may be described briefly. A major change in occupational position often brought about a corresponding change in economic rank. However men often changed economic rank while remaining in the same occupation. An alteration in economic rank nonetheless often affected property ownership. By contrast, with the exception of major shifts, changes in occupational rank did not affect the ability of men to own property. Property ownership moreover had an inverse relationship to the employment of servants. People who employed or acquired servants were less likely to own property than those without sufficient means both to employ a servant and own a home. That choice was related to class: men in high-ranking occupations more often chose servants; those in skilled trades more frequently chose property. Ethnicity did not much alter these processes; it was occupation and wealth, not birthplace or religion, that did most to fix the life chances of men in nineteenth-century Hamilton.

The fundamental dimensions without doubt were occupation and wealth, from which property ownership and servant employment largely derived. Property and servants had so little impact on occupation and economic rank that they may be excluded quite safely from an analysis of the relationship between these two basic characteristics. Nonetheless the ownership of property and the employment of servants did not simply derive from economic and occupational mobility. To some extent they remained outside the factors we can measure, the product of influences at which we only can guess.

## Fathers and Sons: The Transmission of Inequality

At least half the men who remained in Hamilton during its early industrialization changed occupational rank. However the structure of inequality in the city did not alter. Rather occupational movement generally reshuffled people between ranks close to each other on the occupational hierarchy. However the persistence of inequality within generations does not imply its automatic persistence between them. Fathers might be unable to transmit their advantages systematically to their children; or conversely young men might overcome the handicap of poverty and cross class boundaries. That, at any rate, is the North American dream.

To investigate that possibility of upward mobility we compared the occupations of sons still living at home with those of their fathers. For this purpose we examined patterns in Hamilton in 1851 and 1871 and in Buffalo in 1855.[21] The comparison between the two cities illuminates not only the problem of intergenerational mobility but also the extent to which similar patterns characterized early industrial capitalism in both cities. We also compared the occupations of men traced in Hamilton for ten or twenty years with those of their fathers. We were thus able to study the occupational movement of some older men and discover as well how the simple fact of persistence within the city altered the life chances of working-class children.

The comparison of occupational inheritance in Hamilton and Buffalo reveals: that during early industrialization the association between the characteristics of fathers and the occupations of their sons loosened somewhat, partially through a lessening of occupational inheritance but even more through the decreased influence of ethnicity; that striking similarities existed between patterns of occupational inheritance in Buffalo in 1855 and in Hamilton in 1871; and that the structure of inequality in each city reproduced itself in remarkably similar ways through the process of occupational transmission.

Parallels are strongest between Buffalo in 1855 and Hamilton in 1871, a pattern that makes good sense, because Hamilton developed more slowly than Buffalo. Hamilton in 1871 was only about 38 percent the size of Buffalo in 1855; and though in 1855 Buffalo was still a commercial city, it already possessed an industrial base far more developed than Hamilton's was before the late 1860s.

The direct inheritance of occupation in Hamilton declined from 41 percent to 32 percent among sons living at home. In Buffalo in 1855 inheritance was 35 percent, remarkably close to the rate in Hamilton sixteen years later. The comparative distribution of occupations between fathers and sons was also parallel in the two cities. In each fewer sons than fathers entered high-ranking professional or commercial occupations (a reflection of age: in both places more sons than fathers were clerks). Conversely, more sons than fathers worked as artisans, and fewer sons were laborers: 23 percent of fathers and 19 percent of sons in Hamilton in 1871 and 26 percent and 20 percent, respectively, in Buffalo in 1855.

In both cities fewer sons than fathers entered the declining apparel, textile, and leather trades, but more of them entered the expanding metal trades. With its concentration of foundries Hamilton had relatively more metal workers than Buffalo, while that city, in the midst of an enormous growth spurt, had considerably more construction workers (21 percent of fathers and 22 percent of sons, compared to 14 percent and 10 percent in Hamilton).

In Hamilton in virtually all types of work sons followed their fathers' occupations less frequently in 1871 than in 1851. The proportion of fathers in professional or commercial occupations whose sons entered the same sort of work declined during the twenty years from 72 percent to 66 percent; in Buffalo in 1855 the rate was 67 percent. A striking 90 percent of artisans' sons entered the skilled trades in Hamilton in 1851; twenty years later the proportion was 80 percent, slightly higher than the 74 percent in Buffalo. Conversely in Buffalo a greater proportion of artisans' sons entered semi- or unskilled work than in Hamilton. However in Hamilton the sons of laborers improved most notably on their fathers' position. In 1851 70 percent of unskilled men's sons were in unskilled work; by 1871 that proportion had dropped to 50 percent. Most (42 percent) had entered skilled trades. In Buffalo in 1855 a similar 52 percent of laborers' sons inherited their fathers' occupational position, and 44 percent worked at trades.

Multivariate analysis helped sort out the influence of various factors on the occupation of sons. Our purpose in making the analysis was to estimate the likelihood that a son with a given set of characteristics would enter a particular occupational category. First, we considered the overall strength of the relationship between the occupations of sons and a number of other factors (Table 5.9). Fathers' occupation exerted by far the strongest influence on sons in Hamilton. The strength of the relationship between the two remained virtually unchanged at the top and bottom of the occupational rank order, though it dipped in the middle. (Here we used the five occupational ranks discussed earlier.) The combined influence of birthplace and

Table 5.9 Probability of membership of coresident sons in occupational ranks, by father's characteristics, multiple classification analysis: Hamilton, 1851 and 1871, and Buffalo, 1855.

A. HAMILTON

| Variable | | Son's occupational rank (probability in percent) | | | |
|---|---|---|---|---|---|
| | | 1 or 2 | 3 | 4 | 5 |
| *Father's occupational rank* | | | | | |
| 1 | 1851 | 69 | 21 | 0 | 3 |
| | 1871 | 63 | 21 | 1 | 4 |
| 2 | 1851 | 51 | 23 | 0 | 7 |
| | 1871 | 52 | 36 | 4 | 4 |
| 3 | 1851 | 8 | 86 | 1 | 3 |
| | 1871 | 14 | 78 | 4 | 3 |
| 4 | 1851 | 0 | 53 | 43 | 12 |
| | 1871 | 20 | 51 | 26 | 3 |
| 5 | 1851 | 7 | 26 | 10 | 56 |
| | 1871 | 7 | 36 | 7 | 49 |
| *Father's ethnicity* | | | | | |
| Irish Catholic | 1851 | 16 | 50 | 0 | 30 |
| | 1871 | 22 | 57 | 8 | 12 |
| Irish Protestant | 1851 | 11 | 63 | 2 | 13 |
| | 1871 | 26 | 55 | 6 | 11 |
| Scottish Presbyterian | 1851 | 19 | 63 | 0 | 14 |
| | 1871 | 37 | 34 | 12 | 14 |
| English Anglican | 1851 | 14 | 37 | 16 | 9 |
| | 1871 | 17 | 62 | 7 | 13 |
| English Methodist | 1851 | 14 | 51 | 4 | 13 |
| | 1871 | 21 | 61 | 5 | 12 |
| Canadian Protestant | 1851 | 55 | 56 | 0 | 3 |
| | 1871 | 33 | 48 | 5 | 13 |
| U.S. white | 1851 | 17 | 72 | 5 | 9 |
| | 1871 | 21 | 41 | 5 | 19 |
| Other | 1851 | 15 | 58 | 8 | 4 |
| | 1871 | 23 | 53 | 3 | 14 |

| | | 1 or 2 | Construction | Metal | Apparel | Other trades | 4 | 5 |
|---|---|---|---|---|---|---|---|---|
| *Father's occupation (related trades)* | | | | | | | | |
| Apparel, textiles, leather | 1851 | 20 | 0 | 11 | 45 | 11 | 0 | 10 |
| | 1871 | 18 | 5 | 11 | 38 | 22 | 3 | 1 |
| Wood products | 1851 | 4 | 27 | 0 | 0 | 67 | 0 | 7 |
| | 1871 | 13 | 3 | 11 | 0 | 68 | 1 | 4 |
| Metal products | 1851 | 16 | 14 | 39 | 0 | 31 | 2 | 0 |
| | 1871 | 18 | 4 | 65 | 0 | 7 | 5 | 3 |

Table 5.9, *continued*

| Variable | | 1 or 2 | Construction | Metal | Apparel | Other trades | 4 | 5 |
|---|---|---|---|---|---|---|---|---|
| *Father's occupation* (related trades) (cont.) | | | | | | | | |
| Food and | 1851 | 1 | 0 | 0 | 11 | 79 | 8 | 0 |
| beverage | 1871 | 12 | 5 | 15 | 0 | 34 | 7 | 26 |
| Construction | 1851 | 4 | 65 | 5 | 0 | 24 | 1 | 1 |
| | 1871 | 11 | 47 | 17 | 2 | 14 | 0 | 0 |
| Other trades | 1851 | 3 | 27 | 9 | 8 | 52 | 1 | 1 |
| | 1871 | 10 | 4 | 16 | 2 | 60 | 0 | 6 |
| Laborer | 1851 | 9 | 0 | 7 | 11 | 13 | 10 | 57 |
| | 1871 | 9 | 5 | 10 | 3 | 18 | 6 | 48 |

B. Buffalo

| | Son's occupational rank (probability in percent) | | | | |
|---|---|---|---|---|---|
| | 1 or 2 | 3 | 4 | 5 | N |
| *Father's occupational rank* | | | | | |
| 1 | 74 | 16 | 5 | 4 | 60 |
| 2 | 51 | 35 | 5 | 9 | 103 |
| 3 | 15 | 73 | 6 | 6 | 292 |
| 4 | 12 | 32 | 39 | 17 | 26 |
| 5 | 10 | 42 | 7 | 42 | 123 |
| *Property and years in city* | | | | | |
| Renter, 0–5 years | 28 | 52 | 5 | 15 | 142 |
| Owner, 0–5 years | 24 | 52 | 9 | 15 | 49 |
| Renter, 6–9 years | 25 | 46 | 5 | 23 | 51 |
| Owner, 6–9 years | 22 | 55 | 5 | 18 | 60 |
| Renter, 10 or more years | 30 | 48 | 9 | 13 | 80 |
| Owner, 10 or more years | 25 | 57 | 8 | 10 | 222 |
| *Dwelling value per capita (dollars)* | | | | | |
| 0–296 | 20 | 50 | 15 | 15 | 72 |
| 296–592 | 24 | 50 | 4 | 22 | 111 |
| 593–1,294 | 19 | 58 | 7 | 16 | 205 |
| 1,295 or more | 35 | 51 | 6 | 8 | 216 |
| *Birthplace of father and son* | | | | | |
| New York–New York | 34 | 45 | 10 | 12 | 61 |
| New York–other | 34 | 45 | 11 | 10 | 9 |
| New England–New York | 40 | 38 | 9 | 13 | 44 |
| New England–other | 25 | 43 | 16 | 14 | 23 |
| Germany–New York | 20 | 49 | 0 | 31 | 31 |
| Germany–other | 23 | 61 | 3 | 13 | 248 |
| Ireland–New York | 50 | 20 | 21 | 6 | 7 |
| Ireland–other | 23 | 54 | 16 | 6 | 41 |
| Other–any | 23 | 52 | 8 | 17 | 140 |

religion declined notably. Most dramatically the beta expressing the association between birthplace and religion and son's membership in the lowest occupational rank dropped from .25 to .04.[22] These decreases point to the increasingly independent emergence of class, unmuddied by ethnicity, as the defining characteristic of social structure during early industrialization.

Patterns in Buffalo once again mirrored those in Hamilton. The betas measuring the strength of the relationship between occupation of fathers and sons' membership in occupational ranks 1 or 2 were .49 in Buffalo and .46 in Hamilton in 1871. For rank 3 they were .42 and .45. However in rank 5 the association in Buffalo was weaker (.41, compared to .56 in Hamilton), an indication that father's occupation had slightly less influence on son's membership at the lowest occupational level in the American city.

As in Hamilton neither the birthplace of father or son nor the relation between them made very much difference. Moreover, and quite interestingly, neither the economic rank of fathers, measured by dwelling value per capita, nor property ownership nor years in the city exercised any important influence on the occupational rank of sons. Despite the inclusion of a greater variety of variables in the analysis of sons' occupations in Buffalo the amount of variation accounted for, except for rank 1, remained a bit lower than in Hamilton. Perhaps the growth and prosperity of the city promoted a slightly more flexible and therefore less predictable occupational structure.

Though father's occupation remained a powerful influence in Hamilton, the actual probability that a son would occupy the same rank as his father declined for all major groups between 1851 and 1871. For example the odds that the son of a man in rank 1 would enter ranks 1 or 2 dropped from 69 percent to 63 percent, for the son a laborer from 56 percent to 49 percent. (Remember that these figures express probabilities with all other factors held constant.) At the same time the likelihood that the son of a man in rank 5 would enter rank 3 improved from 26 percent to 36 percent, and the likelihood that the sons of clerks and men in related occupations would enter skilled work rose from 23 percent to 36 percent.

In Hamilton young men were avoiding the declining apparel, textile, and leather trades. The probability that the son of a man who worked in these areas would enter his father's occupation dropped from 45 percent to 38 percent. At the same time there was also a sharp drop in the likelihood that the son of a construction worker would enter the same trade as his father (65 percent to 47 percent). That decrease probably reflected the slower growth of the city after the expansion of the late 1840s and early 1850s. By contrast in the metal trades, the most dynamic sector of the economy, the probability that the son of a metal worker would enter his father's trade rose from 39 percent to 65 percent. Among the major groups of skilled workers only the sons of men in the food and beverage trades had become more likely to work as laborers between 1851 and 1871. Though relatively few sons of laborers had moved into the metal trades, their prospects did improve, and they managed to avoid the apparel trades.

In 1851 ethnicity partially shaped the occupational chances of a young man. The probability that the son of an Irish Catholic father would work as a laborer was 30 percent, compared to 3 percent for the son of a Canadian Protestant. By 1871 the different chances of ethnic groups varied only between 11 percent and 19 percent, a relatively small amount. In a similar way the odds that the son of Canadian Protestant would enter rank 1 or 2 in 1851 were 55 percent, compared to 11 percent for Irish Protestants. By 1871 the range between highest and lowest chances extended only from 37 percent to 17 percent.

The situation in Buffalo resembled that in Hamilton. The probability that the son of a man in rank 1 would be in rank 1 or 2 was 74 percent, that the son of a laborer would follow his father 42 percent. In Buffalo the son of a laborer had a 6 percent greater chance of entering skilled work than in Hamilton, not a very large difference. Indeed the odds confronting young men from parallel social origins in each city were remarkably similar.

In Buffalo the ownership of property did not exert any influence on the occupational rank of sons. Though the analysis shows that the length of time a man had lived in the city also had little impact, that general conclusion masks some significant relationships between persistence and the occupation of sons (to which we turn shortly). Finally, as in Hamilton, father's birthplace had little independent relationship to the probability that a son would enter any occupational rank.

Several important conclusions stand out from this comparative analysis of the occupations of fathers and sons in Hamilton and Buffalo:

1. In Hamilton the influence of the characteristics of fathers on the occupations of their sons loosened somewhat during early industrialization.

2. The reduced influence reflected a decline in the impact of both occupation and ethnicity, but the drop in the role of ethnicity was by far the steepest.

3. Even though the impact of the father's occupation diminished, it still remained powerful and was by far the most influential determinant of a son's occupation.

4. Occupation continued to exert most influence at the top and

middle of the rank order; its impact lessened most as laborers' sons moved into skilled work. At the same time an increasing proportion of the sons of men in lower-ranking white-collar jobs also moved into skilled work.

5. The distribution of fathers and sons according to occupational rank in Hamilton paralleled the situation in Buffalo. In each city sons moved out of laboring jobs into skilled work. The only major difference between the two cities consisted in the greater proportion of sons moving into metal work in Hamilton and into construction in Buffalo, both readily understandable in light of the distinctive economic development of each city.

6. The factors determining a son's occupational rank also showed striking similarities in the two cities. In each place the father's occupation exerted a powerful influence of roughly the same magnitude. In both cities the influence of birthplace remained much lower. In Buffalo neither wealth, property ownership, nor length of residence in the city exerted much impact.

7. Buffalo's occupational structure was somewhat looser at its base than Hamilton's. Relatively more laborers' sons entered skilled trades in the American city, most likely a reflection of the construction boom in Buffalo rather than of any fundamental difference in the degree of openness in its social structure.

8. The relationship between the occupations of fathers and sons reinforced the structure of inequality. Through the powerful influence of parental occupation the class structure reproduced itself.

The strength of the relationship between the class position of fathers and sons is also the message that emerges from a study of the occupations of 308 pairs of fathers and sons followed from 1851 to 1871 in Hamilton (hereafter called the twenty-year group). The analysis shows how persistence in the city qualified the relationships between fathers and sons and helps explain how the characteristics of their family background exercised a cumulative impact on the occupational prospects of young men.[23]

The comparative distribution of occupations between fathers and sons resembled that already discussed in the case of all young men living at home. The general movement of sons out of rank 5, however, was even more pronounced among the sons traced for ten and twenty years. Similarly a higher proportion of these sons entered skilled work. Relatively fewer sons than fathers entered the highest-ranking professional and commercial occupations, but many became clerks. Indeed an extraordinary 78 percent of sons of men in high-ranking commercial occupations entered clerical work. Obviously it was common for young men to start their working lives in a sort of apprenticeship in the lower branches of commerce, or in the case of sons of masters in skilled wage work. Clerical work also drew a substantial share of the sons of professionals (44 percent), sons of other clerical workers (44 percent), and sons of mid-ranking public employees (40 percent). However only about 15 or 20 percent of sons of skilled workers (including masters) and 8 percent of sons of laborers became clerks.

In the trades the dynamic sectors of the economy exerted a strong attraction. Occupational inheritance was strongest, for instance, in metals (43 percent), and reasonably high in construction (36 percent). In other trades it was considerably lower. To some extent the proportion of sons entering metals (9 percent of the sons of men in high-ranking commercial occupations, 3 percent of professionals' sons, 10 percent of clerical workers') was the reverse of those moving into clerical work. In all about 30 or 40 percent of the sons of men in major trades entered either the metal trades or clerical work. By far the greatest proportion of manual workers' sons, at least 80 percent, stayed in the working class.

Those laborers' sons who moved into skilled work more often entered the metal trades (13 percent) than any other. After metals comes the category of miscellaneous trades (12 percent) followed by construction and clerical work (8 percent each). About 4 percent entered factory and furnace work of some sort or became teamsters, drivers, or other transport workers. The rest were scattered throughout various types of jobs. These young men clearly followed the main lines of opportunity in the working class. In this way they were much like the upwardly mobile laborers discussed earlier, except that in contrast to the older men more of them moved out of laboring, more moved into the lower ranks of nonmanual work, and none entered the type of petty proprietorship—innkeeping, storekeeping—undertaken fairly often by older laborers. Thus among older laborers and their sons the paths to nonmanual work appeared quite different.

Multivariate analysis provides a useful way to sort out some of the relationships between the factors that influenced a young man's occupation.[24] There are important differences between the patterns in this analysis and in the one that considered all fathers and sons living together, not solely those traced over the decade. As in the earlier analysis, father's occupation had roughly double the influence of any other factor (Table 5.10). However in this analysis ethnicity was also significant, though school attendance, household status, and with one exception age were not. Strong, significant relationships did exist between a father's occupational mobility and the membership of sons in ranks 1 or 2 and 5.

Table 5.10 Intergenerational occupational mobility, multivariate analysis: Hamilton, 1861–1871.

| Variable | All sons | | | | | Sons remaining at home | | | | |
|---|---|---|---|---|---|---|---|---|---|---|
| | 1 or 2 | 3 | 4 | 5 | N | 1 or 2 | 3 | 4 | 5 | N |
| *Father's occupational rank, 1861* | | | | | | | | | | |
| 1 | .69 | .23 | .02 | .06 | 74 | .76 | .20 | .07 | .01 | 53 |
| 2 | .48 | .36 | .03 | .12 | 147 | .51 | .36 | .03 | .10 | 101 |
| 3 | .21 | .67 | .04 | .07 | 328 | .20 | .22 | .04 | .04 | 240 |
| 4 | .35 | .46 | .10 | .08 | 38 | .35 | .55 | .03 | .07 | 261 |
| 5 | .19 | .43 | .08 | .20 | 154 | .13 | .45 | .07 | .36 | 121 |
| 6 | .27 | .60 | .05 | .07 | 118 | .37 | .53 | .12 | .22 | 52 |
| *Father's occupational mobility, 1861–1871* | | | | | | | | | | |
| Out of work force | | | | | | .22 | .59 | .03 | .15 | 120 |
| Stable | | | | | | .33 | .51 | .05 | .11 | 358 |
| Up | | | | | | .46 | .50 | .09 | .00 | 72 |
| Down | | | | | | .13 | .60 | .04 | .22 | 43 |
| *Father's ethnicity and son's birthplace*[a] | | | | | | | | | | |
| IC – foreign | .20 | .51 | .02 | .27 | 69 | .18 | .63 | .00 | .19 | 45 |
| IC – Canadian | .24 | .49 | .11 | .16 | 93 | .24 | .51 | .11 | .14 | 79 |
| IP – foreign | .25 | .53 | .03 | .18 | 45 | .21 | .51 | .00 | .27 | 24 |
| IP – Canadian | .30 | .53 | .05 | .11 | 99 | .36 | .51 | .06 | .08 | 68 |
| SP – foreign | .33 | .54 | .06 | .07 | 81 | .20 | .68 | .06 | .06 | 42 |
| SP – Canadian | .46 | .47 | .02 | .05 | 96 | .47 | .44 | .02 | .06 | 77 |
| EA – foreign | .27 | .55 | .05 | .13 | 63 | .32 | .58 | .04 | .06 | 36 |
| EA – Canadian | .34 | .44 | .05 | .16 | 57 | .32 | .46 | .02 | .20 | 44 |
| EM – foreign | .38 | .46 | .08 | .08 | 37 | .51 | .27 | .10 | .12 | 21 |
| EM – Canadian | .20 | .70 | .01 | .09 | 41 | .19 | .74 | .01 | .07 | 29 |
| CP – all | .46 | .35 | .06 | .13 | 65 | .47 | .35 | .08 | .10 | 47 |
| Other – foreign | .19 | .69 | .01 | .10 | 39 | .10 | .76 | .01 | .13 | 25 |
| Other – Canadian | .29 | .61 | .05 | .04 | 74 | .30 | .58 | .07 | .05 | 56 |

| | | | | | | | | | |
|---|---|---|---|---|---|---|---|---|---|
| **Son's school attendance, 1861** | | | | | | | | | |
| Yes | .30 | .49 | .06 | .15 | 408 | .29 | .48 | .08 | .15 | 218 |
| No | .32 | .55 | .04 | .09 | 451 | .32 | .56 | .03 | .09 | 375 |
| **Son's household status, 1871** | | | | | | | | | |
| Child | .34 | .51 | .04 | .11 | 593 | | | | | |
| Head | .23 | .55 | .08 | .14 | 184 | | | | | |
| Relative | .09 | .77 | .02 | .13 | 20 | | | | | |
| Boarder | .32 | .44 | .06 | .18 | 62 | | | | | |
| **Son's age, 1861** | | | | | | | | | |
| 0–4 | .11 | .72 | .07 | .09 | 37 | .14 | .71 | .07 | .08 | 33 |
| 5–9 | .27 | .54 | .08 | .15 | 259 | .26 | .53 | .08 | .13 | 236 |
| 10–14 | .33 | .52 | .04 | .14 | 292 | .33 | .52 | .03 | .12 | 233 |
| 15–19 | .38 | .47 | .05 | .09 | 153 | .44 | .46 | .04 | .07 | 73 |
| 20 and over | .38 | .47 | .09 | .06 | 118 | .41 | .57 | .00 | .07 | 18 |

*Summary statistics*

**Betas**

| | | | | | | | | |
|---|---|---|---|---|---|---|---|---|
| Father's occupational rank, 1861 | .34** | .31** | .09 | .27** | .42** | .35** | .10 | .41** |
| Father's occupational mobility | — | — | | | .18** | .08 | | |
| Father's ethnicity | .19** | .17** | .12 | .19** | .25** | .23** | .16 | .19 |
| Son's birthplace | .03 | .06 | .04 | .10 | .03 | .08 | .09 | .10 |
| School attendance | | | | | | | | |
| Son's household status, 1871 | .12 | .09 | .07 | .07 | .15** | .10 | .12 | .07 |
| Son's age, 1861 | .19** | .10 | .10 | .10 | .29 | .19 | .07 | .25 |
| R² | .21 | .14 | .16 | .16 | | | | |

a. Father's ethnicity: IC, Irish Catholic; IP Irish Protestant; SP, Scottish Presbyterian; EA, English Anglican; EM, English Methodist; CP, Canadian Protestant.

**Significant at .01 level or better.

More specifically (again with all factors constant), the odds that a son would be in rank 1 or 2 if his father was in rank 1 were a substantial 69 percent and a lower 48 percent for the sons of men in rank 2. These probabilities dropped to 21 percent for sons of men in rank 3 and 19 percent for those of men in rank 5. The chances that the son of a laborer would retain his father's occupational position were quite low (20 percent), even though still higher than those for the sons of men in any other sort of work. In fact the sons of laborers were more than twice as likely (43 percent) to be in the skilled trades as to be themselves unskilled workers. The ability of the sons traced for ten years to improve on their fathers' occupational position substantially exceeded that of the sons of all laborers living at home. The comparison of the occupations of all sons living at home with those of their fathers showed a smaller proportion of laborers among young men than among their parents but not nearly as large a discrepancy as for men traced across the decade.

The most obvious reason for the difference is that persistence within the city might have enabled even men who remained laborers to assist their sons in finding more rewarding work. The mere fact of prolonged residence should have made them more aware of job opportunities and given them a broader range of contacts with potential employers.[25] The only problem with this argument is that length of residence did not have a statistically significant effect on a son's occupation when combined with property ownership in Buffalo. However closer inspection of the Buffalo results shows a pattern consistent with the trend in Hamilton. The two largest categories of fathers in the Buffalo analysis were the 142 who had lived in the city for a maximum of five years and rented property and the 222 who had lived there at least ten years and owned property. The odds that the sons of the latter—the long-term residents who owned property—would be laborers were 50 percent lower than those for sons of short-term renters. For the son of a long-term renter the odds were 30 percent lower. In fact if a category of very short term residence had been included the differences undoubtedly would have been even more striking.

To some extent ethnicity modified the relationship between the occupations of fathers and sons. Recall from the comparison of the occupations of all fathers and sons living together that ethnicity played an influential role in 1851 but not in 1871. That comparison, however, did not properly test for the interaction between the birthplace of fathers and sons. That is, the ethnicity of fathers and birthplace of sons were separate variables. Here they have been combined into one in order that we may observe the distinctions between the native- and foreign-born sons of men with the same ethnicity. The results show striking differences between foreign- and Canadian-born sons. The likelihood that the foreign-born son of an Irish Catholic man would be a laborer was 27 percent compared to 16 percent for a son born in Canada. Among Irish Protestants the chances were 18 percent and 11 percent. The native-born Scots were 13 percentage points (46 percent compared to 33 percent) more likely to be in ranks 1 and 2 than sons born abroad. The difference among the English Anglicans was 7 percentage points (34 percent to 27 percent). Only among the English Methodists did the differences work in the opposite direction, probably on account of the especially strong odds (70 percent) that their native-born sons would enter the skilled trades. Among the sons of Canadian-born Protestants the probability of membership in ranks 1 or 2 was a substantial 46 percent, a figure matched only by the native-born sons of Scots. Though the foreign-born sons of Irish Catholic men were more likely than any others to be laborers, the odds that their native-born sons could escape the very bottom of the occupational rank order compared favorably to those of English Anglicans and even Canadian Protestants. Thus native birth eliminated a great deal of the initial disadvantage faced by the sons of Irish Catholics.

School attendance played no role in occupational mobility. Young men born in Canada were much more likely to attend school between the ages of 13 and 16 than those born elsewhere. Sons of men who remained in Hamilton for at least ten years also were more likely to attend school than were the children of newcomers. However it was their native birth and their relatively long residence in the city and not their school attendance that boosted the occupational prospects of young men. It is difficult to say exactly what advantages native birth and persistence gave young men. Perhaps the absence of an accent helped. Perhaps a prolonged residence in the city provided their fathers with contacts and a knowledge of local conditions.

In this respect Hamilton differed from Buffalo, where no distinction separated the native- and foreign-born sons of men themselves born in different places. The reason is puzzling. It may result from the effect of interaction between factors that the analysis did not tap. If the combined effect of prolonged residence and native birth made the difference, then a differentiation of the Buffalo group according to the comparative birthplace of father and son and length of residence in the city should produce results similar to those in Hamilton.

In Hamilton one other important variable existed that cannot be measured for Buffalo: namely, the occupational mobility of fathers. The likelihood that the son of an upwardly mobile man could be found in ranks 1 or 2, again with all other factors constant, was 46 percent, compared to 33 percent for sons of men who did not change rank and only 13 percent for sons of men who were downwardly mobile. Even more striking, for upwardly mobile men the probability that their sons would be laborers was nil, compared to 11 percent for men who remained stable and 22 percent for men who dropped in occupational rank. Without doubt the experience of fathers affected the prospects of their sons.

A number of factors clearly influenced the chances that a young man would enter any occupational rank. Not solely his father's occupation but his father's occupational experience, his own birthplace, and his father's ethnic background combined to shape his prospects. The scores for the categories of the factor variables reveal the impact of various characteristics. However a word of caution is in order. This analysis contained too many variables to permit proper testing for interaction effects. The purpose of the combined variables was to reduce interaction where it was known to exist, but some must still be present. This means that the sum of the category scores cannot be taken as an exact reflection of probability in any instance. However the magnitudes of the differences are of the greatest interest, and they are sufficiently large to highlight the major distinctions.

Take as an example a young man born in Scotland to a Scottish father occupationally stable in rank 1, who had attended school in 1861 and was 20 to 24 years old and living with his parents ten years later. The odds that he would be in rank 1 or 2 were 67 percent. If his father had been downwardly mobile, his chances would have slipped to 51 percent. On the other hand if he had been born in Canada and his father had been occupationally stable he almost certainly—with odds of 94 percent—would have been in either rank 1 or rank 2. If he had become a household head, and if we could not determine his father's occupational mobility, his chances of membership in rank 1 or 2 would have been 76 percent if he had been born in Canada, 64 percent if born abroad.

At the other end of the social order consider the son of an Irish Catholic laborer. If he had been born in Ireland, his father had remained occupationally stable, he had attended school ten years earlier, and was 20 to 24 years old in 1871, then the odds that he would be a laborer were 33 percent. If he had been born in Canada that probability would drop to 28 percent. If his father had been upwardly mobile, the likelihood that he would be a laborer would be only 17 percent even if he had been born abroad and a mere 12 percent if he had been born in Canada. Looked at another way the native-born son of an upwardly mobile Irish Catholic laborer had a respectable 23 percent chance of entering ranks 1 or 2. The odds that the son of an Irish Catholic laborer would reach the upper ranks of the occupational order became reasonable only if his father was upwardly mobile and if he himself had been born in Canada. The odds that the son of any Irish Catholic laborer would make a modest gain and enter skilled manual work were quite good. Even if his father remained a laborer and he had been born abroad, his chance of entering skilled work was 47 percent, greater than the likelihood that he would remain a laborer. However his father's mobility and his own birthplace would do little to affect his prospects of entering a trade, because those factors exerted their greatest impact at the extremes of the rank order.

Its cumulative character is the primary feature of the process of intergenerational occupational mobility. No single factor overwhelmingly determined the probability that a young man would enter any occupational rank. Rather his position was the result of the complex interweaving of factors associated with privilege or its opposite.

One aspect of privilege does not enter directly into these equations: persistence within the city. These young men all were privileged at the outset because their fathers had remained in Hamilton for at least a decade. That privilege was reflected in their record of school attendance and in the greater ability of laborers' sons to move into more attractive occupations.

The substantial amount of movement upward from the bottom of the city's occupational rank order should not lull us into accepting a benign image of social structure. In the first place we are dealing with the fortunate, those who managed to acquire the economic stability essential to residential persistence. Second, though sons frequently left laboring, they did not very often enter the ranks of the business class. At best they took advantage of the relatively more attractive openings in the working class. They may have been somewhat more comfortable economically than their fathers, but their prospects never would match those of the young men who inherited the accumulation of privileges available to the fortunate. Their individual mobility was primarily the result of a structural economic change, the convergence of skilled and unskilled labor that Clyde and Sally Griffen have attributed to the rise of factory work.[26]

Whatever movement took place in the working class did not lessen the essential ability of privileged fathers to pass on their advantages to their sons. It did not, in other words, fundamentally alter the structure of inequality in any way. The process of intergenerational mobility created movement within the working class, but the major barriers remained as strong as ever. The structure of inequality was essentially the same in mid-nineteenth-century Buffalo and Hamilton. That structure remained fixed during the transition from commercial to industrial capitalism for good reasons. One was the exercise of power. No shift in the source of civic or economic leadership accompanied the shift from commerce to industry in Hamilton. The control of capital, jobs, and city government emanated from essentially the same source. Second, a steady flow of transient workers through the city provided a reserve army of labor willing to take work of any sort, often at any wage. Despite the modest shifts upward on the part of working-class men who remained in the city, the bottom of the economic order constantly renewed itself. Third, sons usually remained in the class, if not at the exact rank, of their fathers. In the last analysis the inheritance of occupation assured the reproduction of inequality.

# 6 The Criminal Class: Image and Reality

In 1867 the Hamilton police chief connected class, character, and crime in a fashion representative of nineteenth-century social thought. Most crime, he wrote, was "confined to a class of persons of low and depraved habits, some of whom have figured at the Police Court ten and twelve times during the year, and even more." Because of "their inability to pay the fine imposed upon them," most had "undergone the punishment of imprisonment . . ." To the chief, poverty was a condition of character. Many of the offenses, he stressed, were "committed by a hardened and degraded class of persons who frequently commit trivial offenses for the sole purpose of being sent to gaol, they knowing that the kind treatment they receive there, and the light work they have to perform, is preferable to the exposure to hunger and cold, which is their inevitable lot, consequent upon their degraded state." To deter these freeloaders at the public trough the chief proposed a "reformatory prison, where they can be sent for longer periods, and where they will have to undergo a certain amount of labor, that will give them cause to remember the consequences of crime."[1]

Obviously to the Hamilton police chief the concept of a reformatory did not imply, as it originally had to reformers, a model family reworking personality through kindness, love, and the power of good example. It signified rather a workhouse where those committed would be punished for their poverty. Though poverty was the source of many crimes, it did not, according to the chief, lurk behind the behavior of another major group of troublemakers in the city. "There are," he reported, "another class of persons, whom I regret to say are very numerous in this city. I allude to a class of young men who have no visible means of support, and who are to be seen in squads on the streets, well dressed but over whom the police have no control . . . I cannot say how desirable it is that a law be passed placing such persons in the hands of the police." The effect of such a law, he claimed, would be felt in "all the cities of Canada . . . in fact it would be a school in itself, teaching such persons their true position, that honest labor is far more desirable than the disgrace which is sure to follow in the footsteps of crime."[2]

The police chief viewed crime as the product of a separate identifiable class with two strata, one notable for idleness, poverty, and depravity, the other consisting of sharp young men who, though not poor, were also fond of idleness and dissipation. To the chief the reduction of crime would come through education, defined as the harsh use of the law to teach the futility of idleness and lawbreaking, to him the same behavior. The chief had no compassion for the desperately poor men and women who found the city jail preferable to the streets, nor did he inquire whether in fact they could have found work had they tried. Nor did he wonder even momentarily if the flashy young men on the corner lounged idly by choice or if a tight labor market full of low-paying futureless jobs might have had some influence on their behavior.

Like the Hamilton police chief most mid-nineteenth-century observers equated immorality, poverty, and crime.[3] They believed that an increase in crime had accompanied the urban and industrial growth of their time because traditional moral values nurtured in rural communities had broken down in cities. Early social scientists shared these widespread views, which they codified into theories that still permeate popular thought about criminality today. Only recently, in fact, have scholars begun to expose the inadequacies of the assumptions on which most theories have been grounded. For instance historians examining criminal statistics in Britain, Europe, and the United States have concluded that no crime wave accompanied the major social changes of the nineteenth century.[4]

Whatever actually was happening, observers in mid-nineteenth-century Canada shared the international expectation that crime would increase with urban development. As J. M. Beattie writes:

> By the 1820's—in England, the United States and in Canada—crime, especially crime in the cities, was rapidly becoming a more frightening phenomenon. It had come to be seen as arising from a class of men outside the law and untouched by moral influences who were the products of drunken and neglectful parents, of idleness, of ignorance and of the hundreds of taverns and grog-shops that tempted them daily. These were not isolated individuals, but a whole class suffering from a moral disease, a disease that they would surely pass on to others until in time the whole working population would be infected.[5]

Similarly, in her discussion of the ideology of crime in mid-nineteenth-century Ontario, Susan Houston claims: "Crime was almost by definition associated with the city. The congestion and disorder of the urban landscape seemed to attract and breed immorality and violence as the anonymity of a largely migrant population seemed to negate the traditional supports of social order."[6] In 1846 a Judge Mondelet gloomily forecast to a grand jury in Montreal that "no one can doubt" that "crime and disorder are on the increase . . . should immorality (especially drunkenness) continue to increase in the city, sooner or later, its destructive effects will extend far and farther every day, until the land becomes overspread with vice and desolation."[7]

Mr. Justice Sullivan's charge to the grand jury at the Home District Assizes in 1849 exemplifies the anxiety about crime that affected many respectable people: "I find by the calendar that several prisoners are confined on charge of burglary, an offense within my recollection almost unknown in the Province, but from which its exemption cannot be hoped as population increases, and vice and poverty become in consequence more abundant. Burglaries and robberies are usually the crime of a class utterly vicious and abandoned; and where persons of this description are permitted to swarm, it is in vain to expect that the crime that usually accompanies their presence shall not be also found."[8] The next year the chief justice at the Home District Assizes commented on the rise in crime and observed, "I can only attribute this extent of crime to the influence either separate or combined of two causes—indulgence in dissipated habits—especially in intoxications—and the want of early moral and religious training and discipline."[9]

In his report to the House of Assembly Committee on Prisons and Penitentiaries in 1836 Charles Duncombe revealed the way in which poverty, a faulty family life, ignorance, and intemperance merged together to lead children almost inevitably to an adult life of crime:

Every person that frequents the streets of this city must be forcibly struck with the ragged and uncleanly appearance, the vile language, and the idle and miserable habits of numbers of children, most of whom are of an age suitable for schools, or for some useful employment. The parents of these children, are, in all probability, too poor, or too degenerate to provide them with clothing fit for them to be seen in school; and know not where to place them in order that they may find employment, or be better cared for. Accustomed, in many instances, to witness at home nothing in the way of example, but what is degrading; early taught to observe intemperance, and to hear obscene and profane language without disgust; obliged to beg, and even encouraged to acts of dishonesty to satisfy the wants induced by the indolence of their parents—what can be expected, but that such children will in due time, become responsible to the law for crimes, which have thus, in a manner, been forced upon them?[10]

Notice the key assumptions in the foregoing observations: that crime increases with urban growth; that poverty and immorality (especially idleness and drunkenness) cause crime; that most crime is committed by an expanding, depraved group that might be called a criminal class; that little difference exists between different types of offenders—thieves, murderers, prostitutes, common drunkards are all more or less interchangeable. This was the image of the criminal class. The question is: To what extent was it a description of reality?

The test of the prevailing image requires answers to two major questions: Did crime increase with industrial and urban growth? And did a criminal class in fact exist? That is, did the characteristics of the people arrested vary significantly from the rest of the population? And were there important distinctions between the types of people charged with various sorts of crime?

In any society the definition of crime mirrors social values. Crime is created by a social and political act, the translation of particular behaviors into punishable offenses. How those behaviors are punished reflects both the severity with which they are judged and the way in which class and power shape social processes.[11] Few societies punish all offenders equally. Just which crimes were punished most severely and how individual traits such as sex, class, and ethnicity affected the nature and severity of punishment are issues of major importance as they demonstrate the characteristics of justice and offer examples of the structure of inequality in action.

In investigating these questions—concerning the rate of crime, the possible existence of a criminal class, and the nature of justice—in Hamilton we examined the records of the Wentworth County Jail, coded in their entirety for the years 1850-1866 and 1872-1873 (1867-1871 are missing) and the Hamilton police register for 1879-1881, also coded in its entirety. The latter is the most complete source, for it lists the names of all people charged or arrested by the police, even those locked up just overnight and not formally charged. The county jail registers by contrast include only those people actually tried or awaiting trial, a number not much more than half as large as the total of those charged or arrested.[12]

The first important question concerns the crime rate: Did crime increase with the growth and industrialization of the city? Dependent as

they are on statistics of either arrest or conviction, crime rates are no-
toriously difficult to analyze. Changes in either law or practice, for instance a decision to clamp down on prostitution or vagrancy, can
affect the official crime rate even though actual behavior did not alter
at all. Despite the problems with recorded rates most historians dealing with them have concluded that, used with caution, they can
indicate rough trends over time. In Hamilton between the 1850s and
early 1880s the criminal code did not alter in any significant way.
Hence, the legal definition of crime remained relatively constant.

The problem in Hamilton relates more to the estimation of the base
population. The most accurate population figures are available only
at decade intervals. Those available for other years are rough estimates. Moreover there always were significant numbers of transients
passing through the city, many of whom were arrested. Just how
many were present at any given time, and whether their number was
roughly constant, is very difficult if not impossible to estimate. A
further problem here is that only the figures for 1850-1866 and 1872-
1873 are strictly comparable since they are both based on the county
jail registers. Those for 1879-1881, as noted above, include many
more people because they incorporate all charges and arrests. Thus
the crime rate (defined as people charged with a crime per 1,000 population) appears to have doubled between 1873 and 1879. However
about half the people charged during the latter years were simply let
go, never sent to the county jail. Thus the real rate was about the same
each year.

In fact the most striking feature of the rates was their rough similarity throughout the period (Table 6.1). In 1851 the rate per 1,000 population was 30, in 1861, 27, and in 1872, 38. The lowest points occurred
during the prosperous mid-1850s, dropping to 23 in 1858 and rising
two years later to 43. Some of the high rates in the mid-1860s were the
result of arrests for military offenses, a new development reflecting the
stationing of troops in Hamilton for the first time. Overall there
appears to have been no connection between industrialization, population increase, and the crime rate.

Generally the proportion of people arrested for various sorts of
crimes remained relatively steady (Table 6.2). One exception was the
jump in the proportion jailed for riot between 1872 and 1873 from .2
percent to 2 percent of all jailed, a reflection of the great strike of
1873.[13] At all times, the proportion of the population convicted of
crimes of violence remained quite low. The number of people jailed
for murder-related offenses (very few of whom actually had committed murder) varied from a low of 7 in a number of years to a high
of 33 in 1852 and 31 in 1856. The mode was around 14 or 15. Between

Table 6.1  Number of persons jailed per 1,000 inhabitants:
Hamilton, 1850–1873.

| Year | Rate | N |
|------|------|-----|
| 1850 | 37 | 384 |
| 1851 | 30 | 421 |
| 1852 | 28 | 398 |
| 1853 | 29 | 471 |
| 1854 | 30 | 517 |
| 1855 | 27 | 485 |
| 1856 | 28 | 556 |
| 1857 | 29 | 690 |
| 1858 | 23 | 635 |
| 1859 | N.A. | 708 |
| 1860 | 43 | 812 |
| 1861 | 27 | 517 |
| 1862 | 39 | 857 |
| 1863 | 37 | 849 |
| 1864 | 50 | 854 |
| 1865 | 51 | 909 |
| 1866 | 48 | 1,022 |
| . | . | . |
| . | . | . |
| . | . | . |
| 1872 | 38 | 1,065 |
| 1873 | 36 | 1,073 |

1879 and 1881 only one person actually was charged with murder.
Other murder-related offenses included assault with intent to murder,
abduction, and shooting with intent to murder. In these three years
only 14 people were charged with these offenses.

The rate of arrests for common assault reached a high of 5 per 1,000
population in 1865 and a low of 1 per 1,000 in a few years. No connection appears to have existed between any external events in the
city's history and the rate of arrests for assault, which fluctuated from
year to year in an apparently random way. Most assaults were not
muggings or the types of urban crime that worry people today but
rather the kinds of crimes that occur within families or between neighbors. Indeed those arrested for common assault were more likely to be
residents of Hamilton than were those charged with most other
common categories of crime.

Sexual crimes were rarely reported in these sources. At least in part
this is due to the fact that most sexual crimes were contested in civil
court during this period, not criminal court. Most of those sexual
crimes reported in the police and jail registers were for some form of
indecent exposure, not rape or sexual assault.

The comments of the police chief in the late 1870s reinforce the impression that little serious crime existed in Hamilton: "Hamilton in proportion to its size and population, has during the past year suffered less by thieves, and less serious crime . . . than any city in the Dominion."[14] The chief did not intend his comments to be a reflection on the morality of the city's residents but, to the contrary, a testimony to the efficiency of his force. Indeed, perceptions of the danger of crime were routinely manipulated by the police in an attempt to expand the force. Still the chief's observation was correct. Not much serious crime took place in Hamilton.

Some historians have argued that the nature of crime shifted with the growth of cities. Crimes of violence decreased and crimes against property rose. The statistics available here do not permit a proper test of that hypothesis since it is not possible to compare Hamilton with rural areas. However in the city no increase in the rate of direct theft, which fluctuated unsystematically between 5 and 10 per 1,000, occurred during the period. Arrests for other types of urban crime, such as theft by trick (a category defined by Monkkonen in his intriguing study of Ohio) or counterfeiting remained small in number and did not increase.[15]

Arrests for crimes against morality (primarily obscene and profane language or keeping a disorderly house) peaked during the depression years 1860 to 1861, then declined, though still not to their predepression level. Similarly arrests for prostitution were proportionally greatest during the worst years of the depression, 1859 and 1860, perhaps an indication of economic desperation, and lowest in the relatively prosperous years of early industrialization when jobs were plentiful. Not surprisingly the rate of arrests for drunk, disorderly, and vagrant behavior was highest in 1860. (It may have been even higher in 1859, but no figures for base population are available in that year.) Indeed in each year these offenses accounted for the largest proportion by far—between 40 percent and 50 percent—of both arrests and commitments to jail, a share quite similar to that which occurs in cities today.[16]

During its early industrialization Hamilton was neither a violent nor a dangerous city. What stands out from the record is the infrequency of serious crime. Still each year arrests totaled between 30 and 40 per 1,000 residents. That figure is, however, misleading. Many people were recidivists. Others were transients passing through the city and not recorded in its base population. The rate for the stable population was probably more like 10 per 1,000, perhaps even lower. Whatever their proportion of the population, it is important to ask whether those arrested were broadly representative of the people of

Table 6.2  Percentage of each type of crime by year: Hamilton, 1850–1881.

| Year | Riot | Treason | Accessory | Domestic | Murder, related | Sexual violence | Weapons | Common assault | Personal nonviolent crimes | Direct theft | Trick | Other property crimes |
|------|------|---------|-----------|----------|-----------------|-----------------|---------|----------------|----------------------------|--------------|-------|-----------------------|
| 1850 | 0.8 | — | — | — | 3.9 | 0.8 | — | 10.4 | — | 18.8 | 2.1 | 3.4 |
| 1851 | 2.6 | — | — | — | 5.7 | 0.5 | — | 7.1 | — | 17.3 | 0.2 | 3.3 |
| 1852 | 1.5 | — | — | 0.5 | 8.3 | 0.3 | — | 5.5 | 0.5 | 18.1 | 1.3 | 4.5 |
| 1853 | 2.5 | — | — | 0.2 | 4.7 | 0.2 | — | 3.2 | 0.4 | 15.5 | 1.1 | 1.9 |
| 1854 | 0.8 | — | 1.4 | — | 4.1 | — | 0.2 | 6.8 | 0.2 | 14.3 | 1.7 | 2.3 |
| 1855 | 0.2 | — | — | — | 1.6 | 0.8 | — | 7.6 | 0.2 | 23.1 | 0.8 | 2.1 |
| 1856 | 0.4 | — | — | — | 5.6 | 0.2 | — | 4.3 | 0.4 | 19.1 | 0.7 | 2.3 |
| 1857 | — | — | — | — | 1.9 | 0.3 | — | 5.8 | — | 22.2 | 1.2 | 2.3 |
| 1858 | 0.2 | — | 0.2 | — | 1.7 | 0.2 | — | 6.3 | — | 19.4 | 3.0 | 3.6 |
| 1859 | 0.8 | — | — | — | 2.8 | — | 0.1 | 5.5 | 0.3 | 25.7 | 2.1 | 1.7 |
| 1860 | — | — | — | — | 1.8 | — | — | 7.1 | — | 23.5 | 0.6 | 0.6 |
| 1861 | 0.2 | — | — | — | 2.5 | 1.2 | 0.7 | 7.7 | — | 29.2 | 0.6 | 6.6 |
| 1862 | 0.5 | — | — | — | 2.2 | 0.5 | — | 6.5 | — | 20.9 | 0.8 | 1.8 |
| 1863 | — | — | — | — | 1.6 | 0.5 | — | 7.1 | — | 22.5 | 2.5 | 1.8 |
| 1864 | 0.1 | 1.1 | — | 0.4 | 0.8 | 0.4 | 0.1 | 6.9 | — | 16.7 | 0.2 | 1.8 |
| 1865 | 0.1 | 1.5 | — | 0.3 | 0.8 | 0.2 | — | 9.9 | 0.1 | 17.7 | — | 0.8 |
| 1866 | 0.2 | 0.3 | — | 1.4 | 1.4 | 0.4 | — | 7.1 | — | 20.2 | 1.6 | 2.1 |
| · · · | · · · | · · · | · · · | · · · | · · · | · · · | | | | | | |
| 1872 | 0.2 | — | — | 0.1 | 1.3 | 0.8 | 0.1 | 10.5 | — | 8.8 | 1.2 | 3.2 |
| 1873 | 2.1 | — | — | 0.1 | 0.7 | 0.6 | 0.1 | 10.9 | — | 14.8 | 1.7 | 3.8 |
| · · · | · · · | · · · | · · · | · · · | · · · | · · · | | | | | | |
| 1879 | 0.8 | — | — | 0.2 | 1.0 | 0.3 | 0.4 | 12.3 | — | 9.0 | 2.0 | 5.4 |
| 1880 | 0.9 | — | — | 0.2 | 0.7 | 0.2 | 0.2 | 13.5 | — | 9.8 | 0.7 | 7.4 |
| 1881 | 0.3 | — | — | 0.3 | 1.3 | 0.1 | 0.1 | 14.1 | 0.1 | 6.9 | 1.3 | 5.0 |

| Year | Counter-feiting | Liquor | Gambling | Prosti-tution | Miscellaneous statutory | Morality (general) | Court violation | Drunk, disorderly, vagrant | Labor related | Military offense | Other | N |
|---|---|---|---|---|---|---|---|---|---|---|---|---|
| 1850 | 0.3 | 0.3 | — | 4.2 | 0.5 | 1.3 | 1.8 | 44.8 | 0.3 | — | 6.5 | 384 |
| 1851 | — | 1.0 | — | 3.6 | — | 1.4 | — | 44.7 | — | — | 12.4 | 421 |
| 1852 | — | 0.5 | — | 1.0 | — | — | 2.3 | 42.5 | 0.5 | — | 12.8 | 398 |
| 1853 | — | 0.8 | — | 0.2 | 0.6 | — | 1.1 | 55.2 | 0.6 | — | 11.5 | 471 |
| 1854 | — | 0.4 | — | 2.7 | 0.2 | — | 1.5 | 53.6 | 2.1 | — | 7.7 | 517 |
| 1855 | — | 0.6 | — | 2.1 | 0.4 | 0.4 | 1.2 | 47.0 | 0.6 | — | 8.9 | 485 |
| 1856 | 0.2 | — | — | 5.8 | — | — | 2.0 | 48.6 | 0.4 | — | 10.3 | 556 |
| 1857 | 0.3 | 0.4 | — | 1.2 | — | 0.4 | 3.6 | 54.3 | 0.3 | — | 5.7 | 690 |
| 1858 | 0.5 | 1.3 | — | 7.6 | 0.2 | 1.9 | 4.9 | 42.2 | 0.3 | — | 6.8 | 635 |
| 1859 | — | 1.7 | — | 11.2 | 0.8 | 2.4 | 1.8 | 39.0 | — | — | 4.0 | 708 |
| 1860 | — | 1.6 | — | 8.1 | 0.6 | 5.2 | 0.5 | 46.2 | 0.1 | — | 3.8 | 812 |
| 1861 | — | 1.0 | — | 3.1 | — | 7.4 | 0.4 | 38.7 | 0.1 | — | 1.2 | 517 |
| 1862 | — | 1.1 | — | 7.0 | 0.2 | 0.7 | 0.4 | 32.4 | — | 22.2 | 2.9 | 857 |
| 1863 | — | 1.2 | — | 7.4 | 0.4 | 4.7 | 0.7 | 45.9 | 0.1 | 0.1 | 3.5 | 849 |
| 1864 | — | — | — | 7.4 | — | 5.6 | .06 | 48.2 | — | 2.6 | 7.1 | 854 |
| 1865 | 1.7 | 0.1 | 0.4 | 4.2 | 0.6 | 3.6 | 1.4 | 51.5 | 0.2 | 1.3 | 3.5 | 909 |
| 1866 | 0.1 | 0.4 | 0.1 | 3.3 | — | 5.0 | 0.9 | 48.9 | 0.4 | 3.0 | 4.7 | 1,022 |
| • | • | • | • | • | • | • | | | | | | |
| 1872 | — | 0.3 | — | 2.2 | 0.1 | 3.9 | 1.6 | 55.0 | 0.4 | — | 10.2 | 1,065 |
| 1873 | — | 0.3 | — | 0.4 | 0.3 | 3.0 | 1.9 | 52.2 | 0.7 | — | 6.6 | 1,073 |
| • | • | • | • | • | • | • | | | | | | |
| 1879 | 0.4 | 4.9 | 0.6 | 0.6 | 12.8 | 3.3 | — | 42.4 | 1.8 | — | 2.0 | 2,533 |
| 1880 | — | 3.9 | 0.4 | 0.6 | 9.4 | 5.8 | 0.4 | 41.1 | 2.2 | — | 2.3 | 2,542 |
| 1881 | 0.4 | 3.3 | — | 0.9 | 13.3 | 6.5 | 0.2 | 41.5 | 1.9 | — | 2.4 | 2,691 |

Hamilton or whether they formed what might be thought of as a criminal class.[17]

At first it does appear that Hamilton had a criminal class, for the people arrested were not at all representative of the population in any way except age (Table 6.3). The most glaring bias was sex. Only about 35 percent of the people on the Wentworth County Jail registers and 15 percent of those charged with crimes between 1879 and 1881 were women. (The figure is so much lower in the latter period because women charged with crimes were more likely than men to be sent to jail. Hence they formed a greater proportion of the jail population than of those simply arrested.) Criminals also were more likely than other people of the same age to be unmarried. Between 1850 and 1857, for instance, 16 percent of the 21- to 25-year-olds on the jail registers, 14 percent of the 26- to 30-year-olds, and 5 percent of those 31 to 35 were unmarried, compared to 15 percent, 7 percent, and 2 percent of the entire population of the same ages enumerated on the 1851 census.

Birthplace bore no relationship to criminality except in the case of the Irish born who were overrepresented in the criminal population. Between 1858 and 1866 for example 43 percent of all those on the jail registers were Irish born, compared to 24 percent of the 1861 population as a whole. In the period 1879-1881 the comparable figures were 23 percent for the criminals and 9 percent for the entire population. The largest discrepancy existed between the Irish born and the native born. In the period 1872-1873 28 percent of the criminals and 52 percent of the entire population had been born in Canada. Similarly Catholics were overrepresented among criminals. Of those committed to jail in 1872-1873 41 percent were Catholic, compared to the 21 percent representation of Catholics in the city.

The proportion of offenders who could neither read nor write declined from a strikingly high 44 percent in 1850-1857 to 38 percent between 1858 and 1866, 24 percent in 1872 and 1873, and 13 percent between 1879 and 1881. This sharp drop probably reflected increasing standards of education both in the countries from which criminals had emigrated and in Canada, where increasing numbers had been born. Indeed as a result of the coming of age of immigrant children the proportion of native born among the criminals rose from 12 percent to 24 percent, then to 28 percent, and finally to 42 percent by the end of the period. Although the incidence of illiteracy among them was higher than in the population as a whole, the people arrested were by no means a mostly illiterate group, as some contemporary commentaries on crime would have led one to expect. Indeed the trends must have discouraged those who argued that education decreases crime,[18] for the most notable trend was the drop in the proportion of illiterate

Table 6.3 Demographic characteristics of people jailed or arrested: Hamilton, 1850–1881.

| Variable | 1850–1857 | | 1858–1866 | | 1872–1873 | | 1879–1881 | |
|---|---|---|---|---|---|---|---|---|
| | N | Percent | N | Percent | N | Percent | N | Percent |
| Total[a] | 3,926 | 100.0 | 7,168 | 100.0 | 2,138 | 100.0 | 7,766 | 100.0 |
| *Sex* | | | | | | | | |
| Male | 2,642 | 67.3 | 4,490 | 62.7 | 1,489 | 69.6 | 6,616 | 85.2 |
| Female | 1,284 | 32.7 | 2,674 | 37.3 | 648 | 30.4 | 1,146 | 14.8 |
| *Age* | | | | | | | | |
| 0–15 | 160 | 4.0 | 571 | 8.0 | 55 | 5.9 | 625 | 8.0 |
| 16–20 | 545 | 14.6 | 1,361 | 19.0 | 311 | 14.5 | 829 | 10.7 |
| 21–25 | 697 | 17.8 | 1,490 | 20.8 | 353 | 16.5 | 1,180 | 15.2 |
| 26–30 | 800 | 20.4 | 998 | 13.9 | 333 | 15.6 | 1,004 | 12.9 |
| 31–35 | 513 | 13.1 | 725 | 10.1 | 280 | 13.1 | 862 | 11.1 |
| 36–40 | 486 | 12.4 | 684 | 9.5 | 259 | 12.1 | 924 | 11.9 |
| 41–45 | 271 | 6.9 | 425 | 5.9 | 169 | 8.0 | 726 | 9.3 |
| 46–50 | 183 | 4.7 | 329 | 4.6 | 131 | 6.1 | 601 | 7.7 |
| 51–55 | 101 | 2.6 | 198 | 2.8 | 83 | 3.8 | 347 | 4.5 |
| 56–60 | 83 | 2.1 | 151 | 2.1 | 77 | 3.6 | 303 | 3.9 |
| 61–65 | 21 | 0.5 | 127 | 1.8 | 18 | 0.8 | 155 | 2.0 |
| 66–70 | 27 | 0.7 | 39 | 0.5 | 45 | 2.1 | 131 | 1.7 |
| 71 and over | 9 | 0.2 | 66 | 0.9 | 24 | 1.1 | 79 | 1.0 |
| *Literacy* | | | | | | | | |
| Neither read nor write | 1,718 | 44 | 2,749 | 38 | 513 | 24 | 1,010 | 13 |
| *Marital status* | | | | | | | | |
| Single | 1,437 | 45.0 | 2,464 | 47.1 | 821 | 46.3 | — | — |
| Married | 1,745 | 54.7 | 2,761 | 52.8 | 951 | 53.7 | — | — |

a. Subtotals do not always sum to totals because of the exclusion of missing cases.

criminals and the increase in the share with at least an elementary education to 84 percent between 1879 and 1881.

Likewise by no means were all criminals drunkards, as many contemporary commentators would have led one to believe. Between 1879 and 1881, 49 percent of the men and 31 percent of the women arrested for common assault and 35 percent of the men and 38 percent of the women arrested for direct theft were recorded as intemperate (Table 6.4). The proportion of all those arrested who were recorded as intemperate was higher (56 percent of men), but that figure was swelled by the inclusion of the large category of drunk, disorderly, and vagrant persons who by definition were nearly universally con-

Table 6.4  Proportion of people arrested who were intemperate, by sex and type of crime: Hamilton, 1879–1881.

| Crime | Percent intemperate | | Total arrested | |
|---|---|---|---|---|
| | Male | Female | Male | Female |
| Riot | 66.7 | 0.0 | 27 | 1 |
| Domestic | 53.8 | 0.0 | 13 | 1 |
| Murder | 50.0 | 25.0 | 8 | 4 |
| Sexual | 50.0 | — | 12 | 0 |
| Weapon | 41.7 | — | 12 | 0 |
| Common assault | 49.1 | 31.3 | 623 | 83 |
| Personal nonviolent | 51.4 | 12.5 | 37 | 8 |
| Theft | 35.3 | 37.7 | 377 | 77 |
| Trick | 36.1 | 14.3 | 72 | 7 |
| Other property | 32.4 | 35.7 | 299 | 28 |
| Counterfeit | 25.0 | 25.0 | 12 | 4 |
| Liquor | 31.5 | 27.8 | 143 | 36 |
| Gambling | 38.9 | — | 18 | 0 |
| Prostitution | 33.3 | 37.5 | 21 | 32 |
| Statutory | 11.1 | 3.2 | 660 | 62 |
| Morality | 55.7 | 50.8 | 158 | 130 |
| Court related | 61.5 | 0.0 | 13 | 1 |
| Drunk, disorderly, vagrant | 86.5 | 82.2 | 2,019 | 276 |
| Labor | 14.8 | 0.0 | 88 | 17 |
| Other | 31.1 | 22.7 | 103 | 22 |
| Total | 56.1 | 49.6 | 4,715 | 789 |
| Lambda[a] | .42 | .46 | | |
| Contingency coefficient | .52 | .49 | | |

a. Lambda is computed with temperance being the dependent variable.

sidered intemperate. The observations about the connection between drunkenness and crime quoted at the start of this chapter referred to offenses against property or persons, which, it was widely believed, nearly always were committed by the intemperate. This clearly was not the case.

Finally, a strong occupational bias characterized the persons jailed or arrested. Of the entire male working population in 1871 about 27 percent were professionals, proprietors, or business employees compared to 4 percent of the jailed men with classifiable occupations in 1872-1873 (Table 6.5). About 39 percent of the criminals, compared to 50 percent of the population, were skilled workers; 3 percent compared to 8 percent were semiskilled; nearly half, 47 percent of those jailed compared to 15 percent of the male work force, were unskilled laborers. Though exhibiting the same biases the proportions for 1879-1881 were less extreme, since the statistics included all persons charged. Of these about 16 percent were in the business class, a higher figure than in the earlier group for two reasons. First, it included the large

Table 6.5   Occupation of criminals, by sex: Hamilton, 1872–1881.

| Occupation | 1872–1873 | | 1879–1881 | |
|---|---|---|---|---|
|  | N | Percent | N | Percent |
| A. MALES |  |  |  |  |
| Professional | 1 | 0.1 | 32 | 0.5 |
| Proprietor | 18 | 1.2 | 611 | 9.2 |
| Employee/semiprofessional | 43 | 2.9 | 392 | 5.9 |
| Skilled | 581 | 39.0 | 2,016 | 30.5 |
| Semiskilled | 38 | 2.6 | 354 | 5.4 |
| Unskilled | 706 | 47.4 | 2,527 | 38.2 |
| Unclassifiable | 102 | 6.9 | 684 | 10.3 |
| Total[a] | 1,489 | 100.0 | 6,616 | 100.0 |
| B. FEMALES |  |  |  |  |
| Professional | 0 | — | 0 | — |
| Proprietor | 0 | — | 25 | 2.2 |
| Employee/semiprofessional | 0 | — | 6 | 0.5 |
| Skilled | 59 | 9.1 | 12 | 1.0 |
| Semiskilled | 522 | 80.6 | 240 | 20.9 |
| Unskilled | 0 | — | 4 | 0.3 |
| Unclassifiable | 67 | 10.3 | 859 | 75.0 |
| Total[a] | 648 | 100.0 | 1,146 | 100.0 |

a. Subtotals do not sum to totals because of the exclusion of missing cases.

number of people charged with violations of city by-laws and merely fined—for example men who did not shovel the snow in front of their stores, vendors who sold their wares in places made illegal by the city council, cab drivers who violated various licensing laws. Of course these people were disproportionately proprietors. Second, of those charged with crimes the unskilled were most likely to be sent to jail. Hence they were represented even more disproportionately on the registers of the county jail than on the records that listed all people arrested.

At first the notion that a criminal class existed appears to be supported by the statistics of recidivism as well as by the general characteristics of the people arrested or sent to jail. Between 1850 and 1866, 11,089 people were incarcerated in the Wentworth County Jail. In 7,460 of these cases, or 67 percent, the same people had been jailed more than once during these years. Likewise a similar proportion of the commitments to jail in 1872-1873 were of people with prior criminal records.

Nonetheless these figures are misleading. A relatively small proportion of recidivists accounted for a large proportion of commitments to jail or of arrests. Of all the individuals jailed in Hamilton from 1850 to 1866, 30 percent were committed more than once (14 percent twice, 6 percent three times, and 10 percent more than three times). Similarly of all the individuals arrested between 1879 and 1881 only 21 percent were arrested more than once during those three years. Thus in the earlier period about 30 percent of the individual criminals accounted for over two-thirds of all the commitments to jail, and in 1879-1881 about 20 percent of the individuals apprehended accounted for 56 percent of the total arrests. A group of people arrested or jailed repeatedly did indeed exist, but it was not substantial. Still it is important to ask if this group had any special characteristics, if it could be said to form a dangerous class of criminals.

According to nineteenth-century observers, one key characteristic of the criminal class was the engagement of its members in all sorts of illegal activity. If this had been the case, then those people arrested repeatedly should have been charged at various times with a variety of crimes. Only a weak relationship should exist between the type of crime for which they were first arrested and the subsequent offenses with which they were charged.[19]

This was not the case. Rather quite the opposite was true. Among recidivists quite a close association existed between the crimes for which they were arrested on the first and subsequent occasions. This close association appears in 1879-1881 from the statistics summarizing the relationships between the types of crimes for which recidivists had been arrested. The contingency coefficient, showing the general strength of the relationship between the first and the subsequent nine arrests, in each case was at least .80 (Table 6.6). The lambda, expressing the proportional increase in the ability to predict a subsequent offense solely from knowledge of the first, also was substantial in most instances, for example .27 for the second and .26 for the eighth offense.[20]

Not only did strong associations exist between first and subsequent crimes, but those shifts between types of crime that did occur happened in precisely the opposite direction from that which prevailing social thought would have predicted. Drunkenness, for example, did not lead to more serious crime. Between 1850 and 1866 only 22 percent of recidivists jailed for murder-related offenses, 24 percent jailed for common assault, and 21 percent for direct theft had been committed first for drunkenness. The proportions among recidivists jailed for prostitution-related and moral offenses were, as might be expected, somewhat higher—38 percent and 31 percent—though hardly constituting a majority. In fact of the 613 recidivists jailed first for drunkenness the proportion subsequently committed at least once for other crimes was 4 percent for murder-related crimes, 13 percent for common assault, 6 percent for direct theft, 6 percent for other crimes against property, 13 percent for prostitution-related offenses, 8 percent for moral offenses, and 80 percent for drunk, disorderly, or vagrant behavior. Most recidivists first committed for drunkenness, disorderliness, or vagrancy were, when jailed again, convicted of the same offense. Only a relatively small proportion were later arrested for other and more serious crimes. By contrast 37 percent of those first jailed for assault and 31 percent for theft were committed subsequently for drunk, disorderly, and vagrant behavior. Thus, drunkenness led most often to more drunkenness, not to serious crime. If there was any shift in the type of crime committed by recidivists it was in precisely the opposite direction—away from more serious crime to drunk, disorderly, and vagrant conduct—a trend probably more reflective of the problems faced by ex-convicts in particular and the poor in general than of any inherent deficiency of character.

Likewise between 1879 and 1881 the major trend among recidivists was toward increasing charges of drunkenness: 37 percent of second, 52 percent of fifth, and 71 percent of tenth arrests were for drunk, disorderly, or vagrant behavior. Thus those people apprehended first for other crimes were, if arrested on several more occasions, increasingly likely to be picked up for drunkenness or vagrancy. Insofar as there was a criminal class it consisted of petty offenders who drifted into drunk and disorderly behavior or who became vagrants. As in the

Table 6.6 Relationship of first to subsequent crimes, recidivists: Hamilton, 1879–1881[a]

| Subsequent crimes | N | First crime | | | | | |
|---|---|---|---|---|---|---|---|
| | | Murder | Property | Drunk, disorderly, vagrant | Statutory offense | Moral | Other |
| *Second charge* | | | | | | | |
| Assault | 158 | 44.3 | 10.1 | 25.0 | 3.2 | 10.8 | 6.6 |
| Theft | 117 | 9.4 | 60.8 | 19.7 | 0.9 | 2.6 | 6.6 |
| Statutory | 112 | 8.9 | 5.4 | 10.7 | 59.8 | 1.8 | 13.4 |
| Morality | 69 | 21.7 | 18.8 | 26.1 | 4.3 | 11.6 | 17.5 |
| Drunk, disorderly, vagrant | 465 | 11.4 | 13.0 | 62.8 | 2.6 | 3.9 | 6.3 |
| *Third charge* | | | | | | | |
| Assault | 71 | 33.8 | 11.2 | 25.4 | 4.2 | 8.5 | 16.9 |
| Theft | 51 | 19.6 | 51.0 | 21.6 | 3.9 | 2.0 | 1.9 |
| Statutory | 43 | 4.7 | 4.6 | 7.0 | 46.5 | 9.3 | 27.9 |
| Morality | 21 | 28.6 | 14.3 | 28.6 | 4.8 | 19.0 | 4.7 |
| Drunk, disorderly, vagrant | 219 | 9.6 | 10.9 | 64.8 | 3.7 | 6.8 | 4.2 |
| *Fourth charge* | | | | | | | |
| Assault | 29 | 24.1 | 20.7 | 24.1 | 3.4 | 10.3 | 17.4 |
| Theft | 25 | 12.0 | 48.0 | 28.0 | 0.0 | 8.0 | 4.0 |
| Statutory | 12 | 8.3 | 8.3 | 25.0 | 41.7 | 0.0 | 16.7 |

| | n | | | | | | |
|---|---|---|---|---|---|---|---|
| Morality | 11 | 18.2 | 9.1 | 54.5 | 9.1 | 0.0 | 9.1 |
| Drunk, disorderly, vagrant | 125 | 8.8 | 14.4 | 67.2 | 0.8 | 3.2 | 5.6 |
| *Fifth charge* | | | | | | | |
| Assault | 12 | 16.7 | 8.5 | 41.7 | 16.7 | 0.0 | 16.4 |
| Theft | 15 | 20.0 | 26.7 | 33.3 | 6.7 | 13.3 | 0.0 |
| Statutory | 8 | 12.5 | 0.0 | 12.5 | 62.5 | 0.0 | 12.5 |
| Morality | 6 | 16.7 | 0.0 | 50.0 | 0.0 | 33.3 | 0.0 |
| Drunk, disorderly, vagrant | 71 | 8.5 | 8.4 | 73.2 | 5.6 | 1.4 | 2.9 |

SUMMARY STATISTICS

| | Charge numbers | | | | | | | | | |
|---|---|---|---|---|---|---|---|---|---|---|
| | 1 | 2 | 3 | 4 | 5 | 6 | 7 | 8 | 9 | 10 |
| Drunk, disorderly, vagrant as % of all charges | 40.1 | 37.4 | 39.4 | 45.7 | 51.9 | 58.8 | 58.0 | 51.3 | 65.2 | 71.4 |
| Contingency coefficient[b] | — | .84 | .80 | .80 | .82 | .82 | .83 | .82 | .80 | .81 |
| Lambda | — | .27 | .23 | .20 | .20 | .18 | .14 | .26 | .37 | .50 |

a. Entries refer to second crime. Thus, in the first row, 25 percent of all persons whose second crime was assault had first been charged with drunk, disorderly, or vagrant behavior.

b. Association between first and subsequent charge.

earlier period those people arrested for drunk, disorderly, and vagrant behavior between 1879 and 1881 were not likely to be charged with other forms of criminal activity. In fact the odds that they would be picked up for anything else usually decreased with each subsequent arrest. The proportion arrested for the same offense when charged a second time was 63 percent, on a third occasion 65 percent, a fourth 67 percent, and a fifth 73 percent. Conversely the proportion of people charged with theft on a subsequent offense who had first been arrested for drunkenness varied only from 20 percent to 33 percent. Those people whose first arrest was for a murder-related crime were much more likely to be charged with assault than with drunkenness when picked up a second or third time. Finally, those people arrested for statutory offenses, primarily violations of city by-laws, formed a distinct group unlikely to be charged with drunkenness and usually only charged again with the violation of a city statute.

With these trends as background it is not surprising to find that relatively few characteristics differentiated the recidivists from those men and women jailed only once between 1850 and 1866. Summary statistics show relatively strong relationships between number of times jailed and demographic factors only for sex and type of crime. Women more often than men were sent to jail more than once: 72 percent of men and 63 percent of women prisoners were in jail only once during those years. Conversely, 4 percent of men compared to 13 percent of women had been sent to jail six or more times during these years. Intemperate women were also jailed more frequently than men with the same character flaw, a measure of the prevailing anxiety over unacceptable moral conduct on the part of women. Of men recorded as intemperate 30 percent were jailed more than once compared to 42 percent of women, and 5 percent of these men compared to 16 percent of the women were committed six or more times. Likewise 29 percent of the men and 43 percent of the women jailed for prostitution-related offenses were committed more than once, and 11 percent of the men compared to 21 percent of the women were committed six or more times. The same contrasts between the sexes hold for offenses against morality (26 percent of men and 58 percent of women jailed more than once; 8 percent of men and 16 percent of women six or more times) and for drunk, disorderly, and vagrant conduct (30 percent of men, 43 percent of women jailed more than once; 6 percent of men and 18 percent of women six or more times).

Among men no factor—age, birthplace, education, type of crime, or habits—differentiated those jailed only once from those committed more frequently. However those women convicted of victimless or moral crimes (prostitution, immorality, drunkenness, disorderliness, vagrancy) were sent to jail more frequently than either women charged with other crimes or men convicted of the same ones.

Although it accounts for only a fairly small share of the variation, a multivariate analysis of the number of times an individual was arrested between 1879 and 1881 does highlight important differences between sexes. Among men those who were members of the working class or residents of Hamilton and those arrested first for theft, violations of the liquor laws, or for drunk, disorderly, or vagrant conduct were most likely to be charged again. The most notable association— the connection between place of residence and number of charges— is hardly remarkable. Those men who did not live in the city were unlikely to remain there long enough to be arrested again.

Among women the very young (under 20) and the late middle aged and elderly (45 to 49 and 50 or over) were least likely to be arrested more than once. At all other ages women were more likely than men to be arrested more than once. Furthermore Irish Catholic women arrested at least once averaged a much higher total number of arrests than those from any other ethnic group, a pattern different from that for men, among whom ethnicity contributed little to recidivism. As with men those women who lived in Hamilton were more likely than those from outside the city to be arrested more than once, as were those arrested for drunk, disorderly, or vagrant conduct. Indeed the average total number of arrests among women first charged with drunkenness during those years was 20 percent higher than the number among men first arrested for the same offense.

Those men and women arrested more than once between 1879 and 1881 did not form a homogeneous criminal class. They were rather, a varied group, merchants who repeatedly violated the city's by-laws, small-time tavern keepers who did not obey the liquor law, drunks and vagrants, petty thieves who drifted toward drink, impoverished women—not a dangerous class but rather, aside from the many proprietors who violated local by-laws, the casualties of early industrial capitalism in a nineteenth-century city.

According to nineteenth-century definitions offenders against decency, order, property, and persons should not have differed very much from one another. Whether dangerous or not the people arrested for different sorts of crime should have been more alike than different, members of a class apart. However nineteenth-century perceptions were inaccurate, and some quite important distinctions separated the people charged with the major varieties of crime in Hamilton.

Between 1879 and 1881 the people arrested for various types of crime differed first in sex (Table 6.7). Only about 14 percent of all

Table 6.7 Percentage of each type of crime, by age, occupation, and ethnicity: Hamilton, 1879–1881.

| Variable | All crimes | | Assault | | Theft | | Other property | | Drunk, disorderly, vagrant | | Statutory | |
|---|---|---|---|---|---|---|---|---|---|---|---|---|
| | Mᵃ | Fᵃ | M | F | M | F | M | F | M | F | M | F |
| *Age* | | | | | | | | | | | | |
| Under 20 | 19.9 | 18.3 | 25.5 | 18.1 | 46.4 | 40.3 | 53.2 | 28.6 | 14.3 | 15.9 | 8.0 | 1.6 |
| 20–24 | 11.8 | 8.6 | 18.1 | 8.4 | 15.4 | 11.7 | 14.0 | 7.1 | 10.5 | 6.2 | 6.1 | 1.6 |
| 25–29 | 12.8 | 10.0 | 17.2 | 15.7 | 11.1 | 5.2 | 9.7 | 21.4 | 12.9 | 7.2 | 9.5 | 1.6 |
| 30–34 | 11.0 | 12.5 | 10.6 | 13.3 | 8.2 | 7.8 | 8.0 | 10.7 | 10.9 | 14.9 | 11.4 | 11.3 |
| 35–39 | 10.5 | 12.9 | 9.1 | 10.8 | 6.1 | 16.9 | 3.0 | 10.7 | 11.1 | 12.7 | 11.4 | 6.5 |
| 40–44 | 9.6 | 12.3 | 7.5 | 14.5 | 2.9 | 1.3 | 4.0 | 7.1 | 11.0 | 16.7 | 12.7 | 17.7 |
| 45–49 | 8.1 | 7.4 | 4.5 | 9.6 | 2.9 | 3.9 | 3.7 | 3.6 | 10.0 | 6.9 | 13.2 | 9.7 |
| 50 and over | 16.3 | 18.0 | 7.4 | 9.6 | 6.9 | 13.0 | 4.3 | 10.7 | 19.2 | 19.6 | 27.7 | 50.0 |
| *Occupation* | | | | | | | | | | | | |
| Professional | 0.5 | — | 0.0 | — | 0.3 | — | 0.3 | — | 0.4 | — | 1.5 | — |
| Proprietor/merchant | 8.9 | 2.4 | 7.4 | 3.6 | 1.6 | 1.3 | 3.0 | 0.0 | 3.1 | 0.4 | 19.8 | 6.5 |
| Business employee | 6.9 | 0.5 | 7.2 | 1.2 | 8.0 | 1.3 | 5.0 | 6.0 | 4.7 | 0.7 | 9.7 | 0.0 |

|  | M | F | M | F | M | F | M | F | M | F | M | F |
|---|---|---|---|---|---|---|---|---|---|---|---|---|
| Skilled | 31.5 | 2.4 | 33.5 | 6.0 | 32.4 | 1.3 | 30.4 | 3.6 | 34.3 | 1.8 | 24.3 | 3.2 |
| Semiskilled | 4.8 | 19.9 | 5.8 | 13.3 | 5.8 | 39.0 | 4.7 | 17.9 | 3.5 | 31.9 | 7.1 | 0.0 |
| Unskilled | 37.5 | 0.5 | 36.4 | 0.0 | 29.7 | 0.0 | 30.1 | 0.0 | 47.0 | 0.7 | 27.6 | 0.0 |
| Other | 10.0 | 74.3 | 9.6 | 75.9 | 22.3 | 57.1 | 26.4 | 78.6 | 7.0 | 64.5 | 9.8 | 90.3 |
| *Ethnicity* | | | | | | | | | | | | |
| English Anglican | 17.4 | 14.7 | 16.4 | 21.7 | 15.4 | 6.5 | 10.4 | 10.7 | 16.0 | 14.9 | 24.8 | 19.4 |
| Other English | 11.4 | 1.4 | 1.1 | 2.4 | 1.9 | 1.3 | 2.3 | 3.6 | 1.4 | 1.1 | 1.1 | 0.0 |
| Scottish Presbyterian | 7.8 | 5.2 | 4.2 | 8.4 | 3.4 | 7.8 | 5.0 | 0.0 | 10.3 | 4.7 | 9.5 | 8.1 |
| Other Scottish | 0.6 | 0.6 | 0.2 | 0.0 | 0.5 | 0.0 | 0.0 | 0.0 | 0.7 | 0.7 | 0.6 | 1.6 |
| Irish Catholic | 12.6 | 21.2 | 9.8 | 14.5 | 7.4 | 15.6 | 5.7 | 7.1 | 16.9 | 28.3 | 12.3 | 29.0 |
| Other Irish | 7.7 | 10.5 | 4.5 | 6.0 | 4.0 | 9.1 | 1.3 | 7.1 | 10.0 | 16.3 | 8.5 | 9.7 |
| Canadian Protestant | 27.1 | 24.8 | 31.6 | 20.5 | 37.4 | 42.9 | 36.8 | 38.3 | 21.8 | 17.8 | 26.7 | 17.7 |
| Canadian Catholic | 13.8 | 10.5 | 18.8 | 19.3 | 17.2 | 7.8 | 28.4 | 17.9 | 12.9 | 8.3 | 6.1 | 6.5 |
| U.S. Protestant | 6.0 | 6.5 | 7.4 | 3.6 | 8.5 | 5.2 | 6.7 | 7.1 | 4.6 | 4.0 | 6.1 | 3.2 |
| Other U.S. | 2.0 | 1.9 | 2.9 | 1.2 | 2.4 | 2.6 | 1.3 | 3.6 | 2.3 | 1.8 | 0.6 | 0.0 |
| German Catholic | 0.3 | 0.6 | 0.0 | 0.0 | 0.0 | 0.0 | 0.3 | 0.0 | 0.4 | 0.0 | 0.3 | 1.6 |
| Other German | 1.8 | 0.9 | 1.9 | 1.2 | 0.3 | 1.3 | 0.7 | 3.6 | 0.7 | 0.4 | 3.0 | 3.2 |
| Other | 1.5 | 1.1 | 1.3 | 1.2 | 1.6 | 0.0 | 1.0 | 0.0 | 1.9 | 1.8 | 0.5 | 0.0 |
| N | 4,715 | 789 | 623 | 83 | 377 | 77 | 299 | 28 | 2,019 | 276 | 660 | 62 |

a. M = male; F = female.

people arrested were women, compared to 33 percent of those charged with murder-related offenses, 25 percent with counterfeiting, 20 percent with liquor-law violations, 60 percent with prostitution, and 45 percent with crimes against morality. The abundance of women among those charged with violations of the liquor law reflects the large number of women who operated grocery stores (which sold liquor) and small taverns. Crimes against morality and prostitution were closely linked. The largest category of arrests for crimes against morality (101 of 180 among women) was for the use of obscene and profane language, followed by keeping a disorderly house (41), frequenting a disorderly house (37), and attempting to procure an abortion (1). Murder-related offenses and counterfeiting were small categories—only 15 offenses in the former and 12 in the latter during the three years. Murder or attempted murder, as one historian of crime in nineteenth-century Britain and France has argued persuasively, was sometimes the product of the pressures on women caught in the contradictions of prevailing notions of domesticity.[21] Counterfeiting, a crime that takes more skill than strength, is one in which women could have participated in various ways.

Those arrested for the major types of crime differed in age as well as in sex. Men and women charged with property offenses were more likely to be young than those arrested for drunk, disorderly, or vagrant conduct. Of the men 14 percent were under the age of 20, compared to 46 percent charged with theft and 53 percent with other property offenses. Those men charged with assault were somewhat overrepresented among men under 30 and over 40. The men charged with statutory offenses, primarily by-law violations, were overrepresented among those aged 35 or older. Thus in terms of age thieves and drunkards were quite distinct groups, and most serious crime was committed by young men. Though the distinctions were less dramatic, the same patterns prevailed among women. Of all women arrested 18 percent were less than 20 years old, compared to 40 percent of those charged with theft, 29 percent with other property offenses, 18 percent with assault, 16 percent with drunkenness, disorderliness, and vagrancy, and 2 percent with statutory offenses. Only those arrested for drunk, disorderly, and vagrant conduct and for statutory offenses were overrepresented among women aged 50 or older.

No interesting patterns marked the relationship between occupation and crime among women, since almost three-quarters of the women arrested listed no occupation. However some significant distinctions did exist among men. Those arrested for drunk, disorderly, or vagrant behavior were much more often unskilled workers (47 percent) than those arrested for assault (36 percent), theft (30 percent), other property offenses (30 percent), or statutory offenses (28 percent). Only 9 percent of all men arrested were proprietors or merchants, compared to 20 percent of those charged with statutory offenses, 3 percent of those charged with drunk, disorderly, or vagrant conduct, 7 percent with assault, and 2 percent with theft. Very few professionals were charged with any crime. The business employees arrested had committed a variety of crimes, none in proportions far out of line with their 7 percent share of the arrests. Finally, a substantial 32 percent of those arrested were skilled workers; like those of the business employees, their offenses were scattered fairly evenly among the major types of crime.

A few major trends stand out in the relationship between occupation and crime among men. First, relatively few nonworking-class men were arrested. Second, though the proportion of unskilled men among those arrested was high, crime was not committed primarily by men lacking occupational skills. Indeed 49 percent of the men charged with assault, 63 percent with murder, and 75 percent with sexual crimes were either skilled workers, business employees, or proprietors and merchants. Third, the crimes for which unskilled men most often were arrested were not threats to persons or to property but rather, drunkenness, disorderliness, or vagrancy.

Measures of relationships between ethnicity and crime do not sustain stereotypes about the existence of a criminal class any more than do those for occupation. By and large foreigners did not compose a disproportionate share of serious criminals. Of all the men arrested 27 percent were Canadian-born Protestants, rather a low figure in terms of the entire population. However Canadian-born Protestants accounted for 32 percent of the arrests for assault, 37 percent of both theft and nontheft-related property offenses, and 22 percent for drunkenness, disorderliness, and vagrancy. By contrast the Irish Catholics, accounting for 13 percent of all arrests, were only 10 percent of those arrested for assault, 7 percent for theft, and 6 percent for other property offenses. They were, however, 17 percent of those arrested for drunk, disorderly, or vagrant behavior. Similarly Irish Protestants were underrepresented among those arrested for crimes against persons and property and overrepresented among drunks and vagrants. Interestingly the pattern for Canadian-born Catholics, many of Irish background, resembled that of the Canadian-born Protestants more than that of Irish. Native birth, for reasons not entirely clear, had a critical impact on behavior. Nevertheless over half the serious crime in Hamilton was committed by men of native birth, and the most economically depressed and allegedly degraded group, the Irish Catholics, were underrepresented in every category of crime against persons or property.

Relationships between ethnicity and crime among women were similar to those among men. However 21 percent of the women arrested were Irish Catholic, compared to 13 percent of the men. As with men the Irish Catholic women were underrepresented among those arrested for crimes against persons and property and overrepresented among those picked up for drunk, disorderly, and vagrant conduct. Canadian-born Protestant women were heavily overrepresented among women arrested for theft—43 percent compared to 25 percent of all arrested.

It is clear that the loose equation thought to exist between criminal tendencies, drunkenness, immorality, and prostitution was in fact imaginary. Irish Catholic women (21 percent of all arrested) accounted for 28 percent of those charged with drunkenness and 23 percent with immorality, but only 6 percent with prostitution. Likewise Irish Protestant women were 11 percent of those arrested, 16 percent of those charged with drunkenness, 7 percent with moral offenses, and 3 percent with prostitution. In fact those most overrepresented among women arrested for prostitution and moral offenses were Protestants born in the United States. Only 7 percent of the women arrested, they accounted for 36 percent of those charged with prostitution and 9 percent with moral offenses. Indeed even Canadian-born Protestant women were slightly overrepresented among prostitutes. Those women arrested for drunkenness and those charged with prostitution thus appear to have made up two fairly distinct groups. Among the Irish at any rate drink was not the road to ruin.

A simple cross-tabulation of two or three variables does not permit the precise estimation of the relative contribution various individual characteristics made to different types of criminal activity. It is unclear to what extent, for instance, ethnicity was an independent influence and to what degree it merely reflected occupation or class position. To answer that and related questions we used multivariate analysis. The question for analysis was framed this way: What is the probability that an individual arrested between 1879 and 1881 would have been charged with either crimes against the person (assault, murder, sexual offenses), crimes against property, or drunk, disorderly, or vagrant conduct?

Only in the third category was it possible to account for a relatively substantial share of the variation. Both men and women became more likely to be arrested for drunkenness, disorderliness, or vagrancy as they grew older. The probability that a man under 20 would be charged with this offense was 26 percent, compared to 39 percent for a man 25 to 29 years old and 51 percent for one over the age of 50 (Table 6.8). The odds that a skilled worker would be so charged were 49 percent and for an unskilled one 51 percent; probabilities were about 20 percent lower for all other occupational groups except semiskilled workers. Among those arrested the group most likely to be charged with drunk, disorderly, or vagrant conduct, when other variables are controlled, was, surprisingly, the Scottish, but their scores were not much higher than those of other groups. Both widowed and unmarried people were more likely than those who were married to be charged with drunk, disorderly, or vagrant behavior. Strangers to the city, whether married or single, were the most likely of all to be arrested on these grounds. The probability was only 25 percent that a married resident of Hamilton who was arrested would be charged with drunk, disorderly, or vagrant behavior; the probability was 55 percent for a married person who lived elsewhere in Wentworth County and 63 percent for someone from outside the county. For single people the same three probabilities were 50 percent, 64 percent, and 78 percent, respectively.

Place of residence worked in exactly the opposite fashion with crimes against persons. People charged with these offenses were more likely than not to be residents of Hamilton. The odds that an arrested married man who resided in Hamilton would be charged with a crime against persons was 18 percent, compared to 8 percent for one who lived elsewhere in the county and 7 percent for someone from outside it. The odds for single or widowed men were similar. Those arrested and charged with crimes against property were slightly more likely to live outside the city than within it, though the differences were not great. In neither crimes against persons nor crimes against property did marital status make any difference.

The professionals arrested in Hamilton were more than twice as likely as arrested unskilled workers to be charged with crimes against property, though they were very unlikely to be charged with crimes against persons. The odds that a merchant or proprietor who had been arrested would be charged with a crime against persons was 10 percent, compared to 15 percent for both business employees and skilled workers and 14 percent for unskilled workers—not very large differences. Thus only in the case of drunkenness and vagrancy were unskilled workers the most likely to be charged with one of the major categories of crime.

Differences between other groups were mostly small and the role of ethnicity statistically insignificant for either crimes against person or property. However in each group men were much more likely than

Table 6.8 Probability that a person arrested would be charged with a specific crime, multiple classification analysis: Hamilton, 1879–1881.

| Variable | | N | Assault/ murder | Theft/ property | Drunk/ vagrant |
|---|---|---|---|---|---|
| *Age/sex* | | | | | |
| Under 20 | M[a] | 853 | 19% | 33% | 26% |
| | F[a] | 136 | 11 | 11 | 36 |
| 20–24 | M | 547 | 23 | 21 | 30 |
| | F | 68 | 10 | 10 | 35 |
| 25–29 | M | 593 | 19 | 16 | 39 |
| | F | 78 | 17 | 6 | 42 |
| 30–34 | M | 507 | 14 | 14 | 42 |
| | F | 92 | 11 | 1 | 57 |
| 35–39 | M | 482 | 13 | 11 | 48 |
| | F | 101 | 7 | 7 | 51 |
| 40–44 | M | 437 | 11 | 9 | 50 |
| | F | 95 | 12 | 0 | 64 |
| 45–49 | M | 379 | 8 | 9 | 52 |
| | F | 56 | 16 | 2 | 52 |
| 50 and over | M | 756 | 6 | 8 | 51 |
| | F | 141 | 7 | 0 | 50 |
| *Occupation* | | | | | |
| Professional | | 23 | 2 | 26 | 32 |
| Proprietor/merchant | | 436 | 10 | 7 | 23 |
| Business employee | | 310 | 15 | 11 | 31 |
| Skilled | | 1,388 | 15 | 12 | 49 |
| Semiskilled | | 376 | 14 | 21 | 38 |
| Unskilled | | 1,746 | 14 | 11 | 51 |
| Other | | 1,042 | 14 | 25 | 30 |
| *Ethnicity* | | | | | |
| English Anglican | | 930 | 15 | 15 | 39 |
| Other English | | 77 | 12 | 21 | 40 |
| Scottish Presbyterian | | 407 | 11 | 14 | 53 |
| Other Scottish | | 33 | 4 | 8 | 51 |
| Irish Catholic | | 760 | 12 | 13 | 49 |
| Other Irish | | 443 | 12 | 12 | 50 |
| Canadian Protestant | | 1,414 | 14 | 16 | 48 |
| Canadian Catholic | | 712 | 17 | 15 | 41 |
| U.S. Protestant | | 334 | 16 | 18 | 32 |
| Other U.S. | | 103 | 18 | 12 | 45 |
| German Catholic | | 19 | 2 | 10 | 46 |
| Other German | | 89 | 14 | 13 | 24 |
| Other | | 80 | 14 | 14 | 36 |
| *Marital status/residence* | | | | | |
| Married: | Hamilton | 2,163 | 18% | 15% | 25% |
| | Wentworth | 120 | 8 | 11 | 55 |
| | Other | 213 | 7 | 19 | 63 |

Table 6.8, *continued*

| Variable | | N | Assault/ murder | Theft/ property | Drunk/ vagrant |
|---|---|---|---|---|---|
| *Marital status/residence* (cont.) | | | | | |
| Single: | Hamilton | 2,049 | 13 | 14 | 50 |
| | Wentworth | 87 | 4 | 19 | 64 |
| | Other | 364 | 1 | 15 | 78 |
| Widowed: | Hamilton | 260 | 13 | 17 | 38 |
| | Wentworth | 14 | 7 | 14 | 58 |
| | Other | 51 | 11 | 20 | 63 |
| *Literacy and education* | | | | | |
| Unable to read | | 633 | 15 | 18 | 44 |
| Unable to write | | 125 | 19 | 16 | 44 |
| Unable to read or write | | 7 | 18 | 9 | 0 |
| Elementary instruction | | 4,534 | 14 | 15 | 42 |
| Superior instruction | | 22 | 20 | 2 | 37 |
| SUMMARY STATISTICS (ETA / BETA) | | | | | |
| Age/sex | | | .15/.16** | .27/.28** | .15/.20** |
| Occupation | | | .05/.04 | .15/.16** | .25/.21** |
| Ethnicity | | | .11/.06 | .16/.04 | .19/.13** |
| Marital status/residence | | | .14/.14** | .16/.04 | .29/.32** |
| Literacy and education | | | .02/.03 | .04/.04 | .05/.03 |
| Grand mean | | | 14% | 15% | 42% |
| $R^2$ | | | .05 | .10 | .19 |

a. M = male; F = female.
** Significant at .01 level.

women to be charged with crimes against property and young people more likely than older ones. The odds that an arrested 20- to 24-year-old man would be charged with a crime against property were 21 percent, compared to 9 percent for a man 40 to 44 years old. Men were also more likely than women to be charged with crimes against persons, though age made relatively little difference.

In sum the most important influences on the type of crime with which a person was charged were sex, age, and place of residence. Occupation played a lesser role and ethnicity an insignificant one. Those arrested for the major types of crime did not constitute a unified criminal class. The men and women picked up for drunkenness or vagrancy were likely to be older and unskilled, often strangers in the city. People who committed crimes against persons were distinguished primarily by their residence within the city; those whose offenses were against property were marked by their youth. The explanation of these patterns and their meaning become clearer from a description of some actual cases.

Most instances of assault involved relatives, friends, or acquaintances. That is why assault usually was a crime committed by residents of the city. "Ellen Gillesby was charged by her husband, Samuel Gillesby, with assaulting him. The charge was dismissed."[22] "Lawrence Kelly was charged by Mrs. Furlong with striking her boy in his breast with a hoe, while he was looking over Kelly's fence."[23] "Edward Harrington was bound over to keep the peace on the charge of assaulting and threatening Mary Harrington."[24] "John Keating was charged with assaulting Bridget Keating. Settled out of court."[25] "W. Gallagher got drunk and went to Yaldon's hotel yesterday and acted in a disorderly manner; he assaulted the hired girl with whom he had been keeping company. He was fined $2 and bound over to keep the peace."[26] "James Belford, a youth of 16, was charged with assaulting his mother, and using abusive language towards her. When asked by the Magistrate what he had to say for himself, he denied having committed the assault . . . when asked what was his mother's name, he said that he had never heard her called by any other name but Belford ·. . . his mother appeared and appealed for his discharge, which was granted."[27] "Mary Thornton, an elderly woman living on the mountain, charged her daughter-in-law, Mary Spriggs, with assaulting her. Complainant . . . stated that she went to her son's house on Wednesday and when there he asked her for $100 when she would sell her 'little property.' She replied that she would not because . . . he was living in adultery when prisoner struck her with a stick of cordwood . . . Defendant was fined $2 and costs."[28]

To Hamilton's working class the Police Court was not remote. Rather, as the assault cases in particular show, it was used to settle disputes within families or between friends and neighbors and to resolve the tensions that resulted when the strains of everyday life erupted into minor incidents of violence. By and large those people arrested for assault were not criminals nor had they intended to commit a crime; in most cases an unresolved personal quarrel simply ended in blows. The Police Court was used by ordinary people to deal with private, often domestic problems. Very likely, this private usage of the courts had probably not been envisioned by the architects of the legal system; nor was it welcomed, since it burdened the court calendar and added to public expense. Nevertheless ordinary people continued to use public institutions in ways that contradicted or at least fit uneasily with official objectives. Like other aspects of public policy the law was supposed to tame and subdue the uncontrolled, uninhibited aspects of popular behavior. Instead by setting the ground rules and providing an umpire who settled disputes it unwittingly sanctioned, even reinforced, the very behavior it was supposed to stop.

Descriptions of the raucous atmosphere in which justice was dispensed reinforce the popular image of the Police Court: "In consequence of the rumor that several prosecutions under the License Act would take place this morning, a large and promiscuous crowd of people filled the space allotted . . . The crowd this morning was more varied than usual, there being some slight sprinkling of respectability mixed with the well-known loafers who infest the auditorium. The colored element, male and female, were largely represented."[29] Or, "The court room was crowded again this morning with a gang of the most worthless-looking loafers and vagabonds that could possibly be picked from the lowest dens in the city."[30] Finally, consider the setting for justice described in this "journalist's complaint": "A great nuisance invariably occurs in the Police Court, especially if a case of any interest is being investigated, in the shape of numbers of worthless curs being allowed to enter with their owners, and when there generally manage to create a disturbance by fighting and howling when their feet are trod upon."[31] Justice in Hamilton was evidently a popular spectator sport.

From these descriptions the Police Court emerges as a popular institution, its frequenters regarded with scorn by the respectable patrons of the *Spectator*. Its magistrates were mediators of popular life and participants in popular drama. To leave the description of the Police Court at that, however, would be to neglect the contradiction that characterized justice in nineteenth-century Hamilton. Whether the people felt close to the court or not, the justice dispensed there was not equal, nor did it reflect the interests of the working class. Rather justice was differential, an extension of the structure of inequality that shaped social process and social organization in this early industrial capitalist city.

Like most assault larceny usually was petty and the thief often known to the victim. Lawrence Kelly stole a game cock from Michael Bourke; Hugh Scott stole a dog belonging to Edward Armstrong.[32] In both instances the ownership of the animal had been in dispute. Two girls, Lucy and Ellen Fritz, aged 9 and 10, "were charged with entering a garden belonging to Henry Kronsbein and pulling up five gooseberry bushes."[33] The children were found innocent. A servant, Mary

Schal, was arrested for stealing between $17 and $18 from the pockets of her employer's wife.[34] Malcolm Cranberry, a teamster, was arrested for stealing "between two and three pounds of tobacco" from James Turner and Company, for which he received ten days' hard labor in jail.[35] John Grainer charged Mary Fleming with stealing a $5 bill from him when in his house.[36] Fleming contested his claim. Nathaniel Chappel was "charged with stealing three small pigs from the stye of John Harris" but it was proved that he had paid for them before.[37] Mary Askett, "an old woman" who had come to the city from Brantford two weeks before her arrest, drank too much whiskey one Saturday night and "was tempted to steal a pair of pants from Francis McGuire. Prisoner told a very pitiful story . . ."[38] Because it was her first offense, the judge dismissed the case.

Sometimes, of course, people stole because they were in need. William Harvey, sentenced to thirty days at hard labor, said he would not have stolen a watch "had he not been out of work and in need."[39] John Wynn was given six months in the Central Prison for stealing "a coat because he had no employ and no home. Wanted to sell it for food and lodging."[40] Harsh sentences indeed. The courts punished theft, whatever its motive, more severely than assault. Property was more important than people, especially when those people were poor.

A few thieves might be described as semiprofessional, such as one young woman who had apparently attempted to make a minor career out of petty larceny:

> Mary Ann Watt, the sneak thief, hall robber, clothes line stripper and shop-lifter . . . was arrested a few days ago . . . There were five charges against her, and the following were heard: Stealing a hymn book from the John Street W. M. Church. To this she pleaded not guilty. The owner identified the property and the prisoner shed tears. A silver card basket found in her possession was proven to be the property of Dr. Hamilton . . . On the charge of stealing an overcoat the property of Alex Findlay, who is boarding at No. 2 Catherine Street, the prisoner pleaded guilty. Three sponges stolen from M. Magann, the druggist, Market Square, were identified . . . A pair of sheets and two pails belonging to Dennis McCarthy . . . were identified . . . Prisoner was committed for trial.[41]

Finally, professional thieves occasionally passed through Hamilton, especially "all grades of pickpockets and sharpers who always follow race meetings."[42]

The major class of professional lawbreakers in Hamilton were the city's prostitutes and the keepers of bawdy houses. However these people and their clients were rarely punished for their sexual activities, which were well known to the police. Indeed, "George Brand was charged with keeping a house of ill-fame on King William Street, two doors west from the police station," hardly an inconspicuous location. Another brothel was in a well-known "large block of three story brick buildings, which are let into tenements" and located prominently on the corner of King and Queen Streets."[43] Ellen Haggarty was a "notorious street walker"; so was Lizzie Williams.[44] Prostitutes like these, owners of houses of ill fame, and patrons usually were charged only when their activities disturbed their neighbors, when fights erupted, or when complaints were filed against them for some other reason. Thus Brand, whose house was "a nuisance to the neighbors, the inmates thereof being drunk and disorderly," was charged by the police because "a woman came to the station and said that there was a fight going on, and that she was afraid they would kill each other."[45] The police raided the place and arrested the proprietor, the women, and their clients. Similarly the police raided the house at King and Queen after the neighbors' complaints had accumulated and a fight had broken out.[46]

Little distinction existed between cases in which keeping a house of ill fame and keeping a disorderly house were the offenses. In fact on another occasion keeping a disorderly house was the charge levied against George Brand and his wife, Frances. To repeat, their real crime was the nuisance they caused their neighbors through loud, boisterous behavior.[47] In fact little distinction was made between houses in which prostitution took place and ones where loud, uninhibited behavior annoyed the neighbors or attracted the attention of the police. For instance one Mrs. Mapham kept a "boarding house" for "several of the men working at the rolling mills" who were "a very noisy lot" and caused "great annoyance to the neighbors." One Saturday "they sent to the brewery and got an eight gallon keg of beer, which they finished on Sunday morning. On Monday night, they were all the worse for liquor, except Joseph Mapham, who is but a boy, and considerable fighting was going on. It was owing to this that the police were sent for" and Mrs. Mapham, young Joseph, and the men arrested. All but Joseph were convicted and fined.[48]

Aside from keeping a disorderly house the other major crime against morality consisted of indecent and profane language, a charge that arose in a variety of circumstances. James Sullivan, for instance, was so charged "for using bad language toward his wife Mary Ann, and beating his children . . ."[49] Jonathan Barker was "accused by a boy named James Nowlan" and proved himself innocent.[50] Thomas Delany was charged with "using abusive language toward his first cousin, Mrs. Wynne."[51] Occasionally the anger that the use of profane or obscene language provoked in the magistrate revealed more about prevailing social values than about the seriousness of the offense: "This morning a young man was found guilty by Mr. Cahill of using most indecent language, toward a little girl, the daughter of a respectable citizen, only eight years of age. The Magistrate in passing sentence said he regretted very much that he could not inflict the punishment of whipping, but, as it was, he would fine the prisoner $13, including costs, or 60 days in jail. Those young men who are in the habit of insulting young girls would do well to take warning by this case, for there can be no doubt that his Worship will not be so lenient on the next occasion."[52]

The rowdy, abusive young ne'er-do-wells so obviously an irrepressible and problematic element in their city formed part of the criminal class that worried respectable Hamiltonians. Often the unruly spectators at public trials, these young men offended good citizens with their abusive language, drank too much, made too much noise, fought with each other, committed a large proportion of thefts, and caused a disproportionate share of willful damage, the most frequent offense in the category of nontheft-related crimes against property. Often the damage was a broken window resulting from a fight. Hence charges of assault might be laid as well. Thus people arrested for willful damage were often arrested for assault on other occasions, and they were disproportionately young: "Robert Polly, a news-boy, 9 years old, was charged with breaking one of the glass panels in the door of Messrs. Hamilton and Co.'s drug store, corner of King and James Streets. Mr. Hamilton said that he was very much annoyed by news-boys crowding around his door crying out 'SPECTATOR only a penny,' and that they were obstructing customers going into the store. The boy said that one Sullivan, another vendor of evening papers, pushed him through the glass . . ."[53]

On another occasion a group of boys was accused of breaking the windows of the German Catholic Church on Jackson Street, and all of them were fined. John Brown "got on a bender, tumbled against Mr. W. Bradford's windows on Market Street, and broke some panes."[54] In a case that again illustrates the use of the Police Court to solve private disputes John Mulholland was accused by his father of damaging his property, but when his father did not appear in court the case was dismissed. Sometimes willful damage could be serious, and when it was the law zealously protected property, as the case of George Morrow illustrates: a carpenter working on John White's farm, Morrow got drunk and burned the farm down; for his crime he received seven years in the penitentiary.[55]

The Police Court was considered an appropriate place for the working class but not for respectable citizens. That is undoubtedly why its noisy carnival atmosphere was allowed to remain unreformed. An editorial in the *Spectator* made clear the class character of justice when it complained of the treatment received by the substantial number of people who failed to comply with the city's by-law requiring them to shovel snow in front of their property. The police, noted the editor, tried to ignore the violations of the snow removal by-law until complaints were made. Then they issued a summons. The following morning "a congregation" of the city's "most respected citizens" occupied the Police Court. "Now, put the best face on this as we may, it is irritating and unpleasant to most people. The Police Court has far from an inviting appearance to those unaccustomed to visit it, and it is associated in the imagination with things that are far from lovely or of fair repute." Not only were the sensibilities of refined citizens offended by contact with the vulgar lower-class world of the petty criminals, but their dignity also was affronted as they became players in the city's most popular spectator sport. "The grinning audience outside the bar is scarcely of the kind for the benefit of which one would care to make an exhibition of oneself." Even more, the proceedings cast a shadow across the rest of one's life. Intent on their reputation into eternity, these solid citizens now knew that at the very time when their "virtues shall be engraven upon" a "tombstone" their "shortcomings" were "recorded in the police books of the city where . . . fame was won, ready to be dragged to light by some curious enquirer of resurrectionary proclivities."[56]

The maudlin character of the *Spectator's* anxiety about the dignity and reputation of the city's solid citizens contrasted unpleasantly with its lack of compassion toward poor drunks, about whom it wrote with mock humor and sarcasm. If Hamilton had a group of people who committed the same crime over and over again, it consisted of those charged with drunk, disorderly, and vagrant conduct. These repeat offenders were treated with special harshness by both the press and the courts:

The incorigible Peter Kane was again brought into court, he having been arrested . . . last night on John Street, where he was very drunk and boisterous and using bad language. Peter was sent to jail for ten days without the option of a fine. Upon being removed from the dock, Peter cried like a baby, and would not stir until he was forced, pleading piteously to be fined and not to be sent to jail, but His Worship turned a deaf ear to his entreaties, as he had on so many times previously made faithful promises to abstain from liquor.[57]

Then there was the case of James Henry Livingston: "Yesterday afternoon the notorious James Henry Livingston created no little amusement to the public on King William Street. James, who had been discharged from jail the day previously, managed to procure more whiskey than he could comfortably carry, became disorderly and was arrested by detective McMenemy, and not being desirous to return to his old quarters, resisted his captor and laid down on the sidewalk. He had to be carried to the cells among the jeers and jokes of those who witnessed it."[58] One can only applaud James Henry Livingston's spirit of independence, uncrushed after a term in the wretched city jail, and sympathize with Peter Kane's misery at the prospect of incarceration. Though it was February, James Henry Livingston preferred the streets to the jail, a different choice from the one often made by the poor, desperate people committed for vagrancy. "Miles Walker, an elderly man unable to work, and having no place of abode, went to the cells for lodging. His Worship out of compassion for him sent him to jail for 30 days to be taken care of."[59] "John Brown came from Montreal in search of employment and failing to get work he was compelled to seek shelter in the cells for the last four nights. He was sent to jail for 30 days in default of paying a fine of $2."[60]

At a time when the average male wage for unskilled work was about $1 a day, the sentence given John Brown seems harsh; so do the ones meted out to Mary McQuillican and Eliza Brown: "Mary McQuillican, one of the many women who infest the city, void of all shame and decency, was arrested by Constable Holmes on the charge of vagrancy. Ordered to pay $2 and $1 costs, or 30 days in jail. Eliza Brown, another disgrace to her sex, was arrested . . . and fined $1 and $1 in costs or 20 days in jail. Both were sent up."[61] Those people sent to jail for three weeks or a month because they could not afford to pay a fine of $2 were desperately poor. It was their poverty rather than their crime that put most of those found guilty of drunkenness or vagrancy in jail. These were not criminals in any meaningful sense but rather the casualties of an unequal social order.

As everyone in the city knew, the courts existed primarily to keep public order, protect property, and mediate the quarrels that arose in everyday life, especially among the poor. The way in which assumptions about class and sex actually skewed this process of justice emerges from a systematic examination of what happened to those people arrested in nineteenth-century Hamilton.

In Hamilton most jail sentences were short. Of those dispensed between 1879 and 1881 about 37 percent given to men were for no more than ten days, over 75 percent for a maximum of thirty days, and only 2 percent for a year or more. For sentences given to women the corresponding proportions were 23 percent, 57 percent, and 3 percent. Similarly most fines were small: 58 percent of those given to men and 46 percent to women were for $1 or $2 and 88 percent and 81 percent, respectively, for a maximum of $5.

The outcome of cases in 1879 to 1881 reveals the position of women. They were both let go more often than men (38 percent compared to 28 percent) and committed to jail more often (27 percent compared to 23 percent). Indeed, as the figures for length of sentence attest, those women jailed were punished somewhat more severely than men. Predictably those males most likely to be jailed (63 percent) had been arrested for murder-related offenses. By contrast few of those arrested for assault (12 percent) actually were sent to jail, though relatively few (28 percent) were let go. Most (48 percent) paid a fine. Theft must have been difficult to prove, for 51 percent of those charged with larceny were released, as were half of those arrested for counterfeiting. Those least likely to be discharged, and most undeniably guilty of the crime for which they had been apprehended, were those men and women picked up for drunk, disorderly, or vagrant conduct. Only 16 percent of them were let go, and 40 percent were jailed.

The substantial proportion of people arrested for fairly serious crimes who were let go or acquitted is puzzling. It might attest to the fairness of the criminal justice system, an unwillingness to convict without overwhelming evidence. Or it might signify a cavalier attitude on the part of the police, a habit of indiscriminate arrest based on flimsy evidence. Certainly it is difficult to imagine that police magistrates presiding over the raucous people's court had very much patience with legal niceties. A more compelling explanation involves the fragility of the criminal justice system itself—the lack of professional evidence, the difficulty of apprehending criminals in a transient society, and the ability of smart lawyers to exploit the ambiguities of the law.

Class also affected sentencing. Unskilled workers were the occupational group most often jailed and least often discharged. Next came the skilled workers. Of all the unskilled men arrested 34 percent were eventually jailed, as were 23 percent of skilled workers, compared to 8 percent of professionals, 6 percent of merchants and proprietors, and 15 percent of business employees. The proportion of unskilled workers released without punishment was only 21 percent and of skilled workers 28 percent, in contrast to 54 percent, 34 percent, and 40 percent among the other occupational groups.

Given these statistics it is no surprise that people unable to read and write were sent to jail more often and released less often than those with either an elementary or superior education. In some ways the largest distinction of all separated the temperate and intemperate: 10 percent of the former and 36 percent of the latter were sent to jail. Among ethnic groups the proportions of arrested people committed to jail were 34 percent for Irish Catholics, 46 percent for Irish Protestants, 17 percent for Canadian Protestants, and 25 percent for Canadian Catholics, again an illustration of the advantages of native birth. Finally strangers were incarcerated more often than residents of the city: 46 percent of the men and 40 percent of the women who did not live in Hamilton or Wentworth County were jailed, compared to 20 percent and 26 percent of those who resided in the city and 28 percent and 23 percent of those from elsewhere in the county.

Once again the extent to which factors such as occupation, ethnicity, and residence overlapped creates a serious analytic problem. As before it is necessary to turn to multivariate analysis. A particularly important independent influence on whether a person who had been arrested was sent to jail was a combination of marital status and residence (Table 6.9). Married people were less likely to go to jail than single or widowed ones. The odds that a married resident of Hamilton who had been arrested would be committed to jail were 17 percent, compared to 28 percent for a single person and 27 percent for a widow or widower. However within each category of marital status strangers were by far the most likely to be sent to jail. Indeed married strangers who had been charged with crimes were far more apt to find themselves in jail than unmarried residents of the city. The odds that a person from outside the county would be committed to jail were 33 percent, 45 percent, and 36 percent for married, single, and widowed persons, respectively, odds 94 percent, 61 percent, and 33 percent greater than those for city residents of the same marital status.

Also influential on the outcome of a charge was the number of times a person had been arrested previously. The probability that a person who had been arrested ten or more times would be released without a fine or jail term was only 9 percent, compared to 29 percent for someone arrested for the first time, 25 percent for a person with two to five arrests, and 23 percent for one with six to nine arrests. The kind of crime with which a person had been charged influenced the outcome as well. The odds that someone charged with a murder-related offense would be jailed were 45 percent, compared to 16 percent for sexual offenses, 17 percent for common assault, 39 percent for theft, and 37 percent for drunk, disorderly, or vagrant conduct. People charged with the last were especially unlikely to be released with no penalty (19 percent), compared to chances of 27 percent for those arrested for common assault, 48 percent for theft, and 56 percent for murder-related offenses.

These figures reinforce the patterns observed with simple descriptive statistics. The same is true for age. Younger people were the least likely to be jailed. However within each age group women were sent to jail more often than men. Among those under 20, for example, the odds that a man would be jailed were 10 percent but 15 percent for a woman; for those 30 to 34 they were 24 percent and 38 percent, respectively.

Occupation likewise exercised an independent influence. Those with the greatest odds of being jailed (31 percent) and the least of being released (23 percent) were the unskilled wage workers. Compare these to the odds of 10 percent and 54 percent for professionals and 20 percent and 33 percent for merchants and proprietors. A skilled wage worker who had been arrested faced a 24 percent chance of a jail sentence and a 26 percent chance of release, odds still better than those for an unskilled worker.

The one major factor whose importance disappeared in the multivariate analysis was ethnicity. Once class was controlled, ethnic distinctions hardly affected the chances that a person arrested in Hamilton would be sent to jail or discharged without penalty.

The biases of the criminal justice system in Hamilton reflected the larger structure of inequality in which it was embedded. Those with the greatest chance of a jail sentence were women, older people, unskilled workers, and recidivists. Judges were probably unwilling to send young people to jail because they realized that the jails themselves were often the best nurseries of crime. That magistrates were reluctant to release repeat offenders and treated frequent recidivists most harshly should be expected. In those cases judges may have seen no alternative. Some of the repeat offenders even asked for a jail sentence as a respite from the harshness and poverty of their lives on the street.

Women, the elderly, and the unskilled were frequently unable to afford adequate legal assistance. More than that many people went to jail, as they still do today, because they could not afford the modest fines levied. The relative poverty of women and their inability to pay fines is revealed by the following: between 1879 and 1881 of the men given a choice between a fine and a jail sentence 62 percent paid, compared to 43 percent of women. Thus only 38 percent of the men sen-

Table 6.9   Probability that a person arrested would be committed to jail or given no sentence, multiple classification analysis: Hamilton, 1879–1881.

| Variable | | Committed to jail | No sentence |
|---|---|---|---|
| *Age/sex* | | | |
| Under 20 | M[a] | 10% | 35% |
| | F[a] | 15 | 46 |
| 20–24 | M | 17 | 26 |
| | F | 31 | 31 |
| 25–29 | M | 23 | 25 |
| | F | 39 | 22 |
| 30–34 | M | 24 | 27 |
| | F | 38 | 30 |
| 35–39 | M | 28 | 25 |
| | F | 33 | 31 |
| 40–44 | M | 31 | 26 |
| | F | 42 | 22 |
| 45–49 | M | 32 | 25 |
| | F | 34 | 25 |
| 50 and over | M | 33 | 26 |
| | F | 36 | 30 |
| *Occupation* | | | |
| Professional | | 10 | 54 |
| Proprietor/merchant | | 20 | 33 |
| Business employee | | 19 | 39 |
| Skilled | | 24 | 26 |
| Semiskilled | | 24 | 31 |
| Unskilled | | 31 | 23 |
| Other | | 20 | 32 |
| *Ethnicity* | | | |
| English Anglican | | 22 | 28 |
| Other English | | 25 | 33 |
| Scottish Presbyterian | | 26 | 26 |
| Other Scottish | | 29 | 29 |
| Irish Catholic | | 25 | 27 |
| Irish Protestant | | 32 | 27 |
| Canadian Protestant | | 22 | 29 |
| Canadian Catholic | | 23 | 27 |
| U.S. Protestant | | 24 | 27 |
| Other U.S. | | 26 | 21 |
| German Catholic | | 20 | 44 |
| Other German | | 31 | 36 |
| Other | | 26 | 22 |
| *Marital status/residence* | | | |
| Married: | Hamilton | 17 | 31 |
| | Wentworth | 15 | 28 |
| | Other | 33 | 26 |

Table 6.9, *continued*

| Variable | Committed to jail | No sentence |
|---|---|---|
| *Marital status/residence* (cont.) | | |
| Single:    Hamilton | 28 | 26 |
|          Wentworth | 32 | 20 |
|          Other | 45 | 26 |
| Widowed: Hamilton | 27 | 27 |
|          Wentworth | 32 | 22 |
|          Other | 36 | 36 |
| *Number of charges* | | |
| 1 | 23 | 29 |
| 2–5 | 33 | 25 |
| 6–9 | 42 | 23 |
| 10 or more | 39 | 9 |
| *Crime* | | |
| Riot | 21 | 23 |
| Domestic | 2 | 72 |
| Murder | 45 | 56 |
| Sexual | 16 | 51 |
| Weapon | 18 | 23 |
| Common assault | 17 | 27 |
| Nonviolent | 18 | 26 |
| Theft | 39 | 48 |
| Trick | 20 | 50 |
| Other property | 22 | 35 |
| Counterfeit | 15 | 50 |
| Liquor | 9 | 30 |
| Gambling | 24 | 15 |
| Prostitution | 16 | 41 |
| Statutory | 3 | 29 |
| Morality | 20 | 37 |
| Court related | 5 | 57 |
| Drunk, disorderly, vagrant | 37 | 19 |
| Labor | 4 | 37 |
| Other | 4 | 47 |

SUMMARY STATISTICS (ETA / BETA)

| | Committed to jail | No sentence |
|---|---|---|
| Age/sex | .14/.21** | .15/.11** |
| Occupation | .20/.11** | .17/.11** |
| Ethnicity | .17/.07* | .10/.05 |
| Marital status/residence | .26/.19** | .08/.06* |
| Number of charges | .09/.10** | .04/.04* |
| Crime | .39/.31** | .27/.23** |
| Grand mean | 25% | 28% |
| R² | .22 | .10 |
| Total N = 7,766 | | |

a. M = male; F = female.
**Significant at .01 level; * significant at .05 level.

tenced to jail actually were committed, compared to 57 percent of the women.

The harshness with which judges treated offenses against property and morality, especially by women, clearly underlines some of the key values of early industrial capitalism. In their protection of property and propriety the courts revealed the preoccupations of the respectable classes, the primacy of commodities in an acquisitive age, and the investment in an ideal femininity that justified the elimination of women from the marketplace and their confinement within the family. Women, especially those who were poor, were in fact the principal losers in the process of criminal justice. Though arrested less frequently, those women charged with crimes were jailed more often and for longer periods than men who had committed the same offenses. The drunk or riotous behavior or profane language expected if not condoned among impoverished men violated more than aesthetic sensibilities when engaged in by women, for their behavior challenged the restraint, the containment of sexuality and passion, the sublimation through which men of the time channeled their impulses into the service of capitalism.

Somewhat more puzzling than the severe treatment of offenses against property and morals is the special severity with which strangers were treated. Perhaps jail was used as a last resort when family or friends were unavailable to share the task of discipline or custody. And residents of the city who were fined could more easily borrow from friends or relatives if they had no money themselves. Yet the matter is not that simple. Strangers, who after all had committed primarily victimless crimes, could simply have been sent on their way, told never to return to Hamilton. That was an inexpensive solution for which ample historical precedent existed.[62] It was the way in which troublesome strangers had been handled for centuries. Perhaps magistrates felt that sending away strangers who could not pay a fine would be inequitable because the option for residents of the city was not a fine or migration but a fine or jail. It could be too that respectable citizens identified strangers with the disruption and disorder they believed, with considerable exaggeration, to be characteristic of expanding nineteenth-century cities. They may well have projected onto the alien poor their own guilt and anxiety and as a consequence punished them harshly. Whatever concatenation of factors determined the relatively severe way in which the courts treated strangers, the more lenient sentences received by residents clearly underscored the relationship of transiency to inequality. Not only did prolonged residence in a city promote prosperity and advance the prospects of one's children; it often helped to keep one out of jail as well.

Our exploration of inequality makes understandable, even predictable, most of the biases of the process of criminal justice in Hamilton. The people who fared worst in the larger structure of inequality
—the unskilled, the elderly, and women—also fared worst in the
courts. They were arrested for violations of the culture of capitalism
or for crimes that grew out of their unequal and dependent position.
Whatever the charge they were punished mainly for poverty and the
behavior that was assumed to accompany it.

One group that proved a constant source of trouble to respectable
citizens does not appear to fit this definition. That group is youth, the
flashy young men who loitered on corners, sometimes stole, offended
the sensibilities of respectable young women, fought with each other,
broke store windows, destroyed the decorum of the court, and by implication posed a serious threat to the morals of the city. Who in fact
were they? Why did youth pose such a special and serious problem in
the nineteenth-century city?

# 7 Youth and Early Industrialization

With the development of capitalism, wrote Harry Braverman, "whole new strata of the helpless and dependent are created, or familiar old ones enlarged enormously."[1] In this way the development of capitalism stimulates the origins of new institutions. One of the new categories of dependence that had special implications for social institutions was adolescence.

Of course, as S. N. Eisenstadt argues, youth exists everywhere. No society fails to recognize the years between the onset of puberty and the arrival of adulthood as a separate and special phase within the life cycle. Human biology overrides cultural distinction. Though we call it adolescence, others have recognized the same period by other names.[2] In her argument for the recognition of youth in early modern France, Natalie Davis has stressed the same point.[3] She portrays peer groups of young people sanctioned by cultural tradition playing well-defined and important roles, especially in the charivari, through which they enforced community morality and vented political protest. "The problem of adolescence, and the nuisance it causes to society were familiar enough to Europeans since the fifteenth-century," claims Lawrence Stone. "The idea that adolescence, as a distinctive age-group with its distinctive problems was a development of the nineteenth century is entirely without historical foundation."[4] In less sophisticated terms the assumption that something called adolescence exists as a fixed biological and psychological phase underlies much social policy. In educational reform, for instance, it has shaped the attempt to design and redesign secondary schools. However educators have rarely asked if adolescence itself need be taken as a given.

Some historians have nevertheless raised the question, and not all agree with Stone. John and Virginia Demos have argued that Americans invented adolescence in the nineteenth century, and Frank Musgrove has credited Europeans with its invention in roughly the same period.[5] Joseph Kett likewise asserts, "Along with most historians of the family, I believe that the concept of adolescence was conditioned by social forces, that it reflected the demographic and industrial conditions of the late-nineteenth and early-twentieth centuries." Kett also stresses that "moral values which often masqueraded as psychological laws were at the root of the concept" and reflected "distinctive values relating to children and the family that originated in America as early as the 1830's."[6]

To some extent the issue is semantic. Stone, for example, shows that the life cycle of young people in early modern England clearly differed from its counterpart today, and Kett does not deny that the years between puberty and marriage have long been recognized as a distinctive stage in human life. When Kett speaks of the invention of the adolescent what he means is the deliberate creation of "the youth whose social definition—and, indeed, whose whole being—was determined by a biological process of maturation . . . To speak of the 'invention of the adolescent' rather than of the discovery of adolescence underscores a related point: adolescence was essentially a conception of behavior imposed on youth, rather than an empirical assessment of the way in which young people actually behaved."[7]

Kett's definition of adolescence stresses its behavioral and psychological qualities. It is possible, however, to offer a complementary definition rooted in structural factors. In this view adolescence is a phase of prolonged institutionalized dependency, a span of years between puberty and marriage in which young people remain not only dependent on their parents but governed by a historically new social institution, mass public education. The problems created by prolonged institutionalized dependency may in fact have generated the particular forms of behavior that the newly emergent profession of psychology labeled adolescent and elevated to universality.

Given the profound differences in the life cycle of young people that developed during the nineteenth century and the distinctive meaning of the concept of adolescence that emerged in the same period, it is more helpful and accurate to speak of the years between puberty and marriage in earlier times as a phase of youth, which is the term commonly used by contemporaries to describe it. This differentiation between youth and adolescence underscores a very important point which historians of the family have to offer not only to those interested in the past but also to those whose major concern is the present and the future. That point is that the life cycle is malleable. To a very significant extent technology, economic organization, social order, and cultural tradition shape the manner in which the irreducible aspects of human biology find expression during the lives of particular people.

Two examples other than adolescence reinforce the point. All physically normal people mature sexually, but the age of menarche in women has declined steadily during past centuries. Though puberty comes as always, its onset is variable, depending on factors only imperfectly understood; through some mechanism historical forces have affected human biology to alter the timing of stages in the lives of women. Second, increased longevity combined with altered patterns of marital fertility have made common a new phase in the life cycle: the extended period that couples spend alone together after all their children have left home.[8]

An equally important shift in the life cycle is the origin of the transition from youth to adolescence. We have compared the relative timing of key life events in Hamilton prior to and during early industrialization: the age at which young people left home, when they left school, when they began to work, and when they married. We also paid special attention to where they lived when they did not live with their parents.

### Residence

During the early years of industrialization young people changed their patterns of residence. Young people had customarily left their parents' homes when they found work; however in the early industrial city they began to remain at home during the initial years of employment, often until they married. This was a shift of major importance. When young people had moved away from their parents' homes, they had usually moved in with other families, living as boarders, relatives, or servants, thus becoming quasi-members of other households.

This experience formed a distinct stage in the life cycle that virtually disappeared during industrialization. Not only in Hamilton but virtually everywhere that historians have looked membership in one or more households for a prolonged period of time between puberty and marriage was once the common practice. It has been described for seventeenth-century London apprentices by Steven R. Smith, for the family of a seventeenth-century clergyman and men of similar social position by Alan McFarlane, for an eighteenth-century English village by Roger Schofield, for eighteenth-century Germany by John Gillis, for Colonial New England by Edmund Morgan, for late eighteenth-century and early nineteenth-century America by Joseph Kett.[9] Lawrence Stone calls it "fostering out" and writes, "What one sees at . . . middle- and lower middle-class levels is a vast system of exchange by which parents sent their own children away from home—usually not very far—and the richer families took in the children of others as servants and laborers." On the basis of "some very fragmentary census data" Stone estimates "that from just before puberty until they married some ten years later, about two out of every three boys and three out of every four girls were living away from home."[10] Peter Laslett terms the common custom of dwelling as an employee in another household during the years between about 12 and 22 "life-cycle service" and claims for seventeenth- and eighteenth-century England, "At most one in five . . . of all young people escaped the experience of living with servants or of living as servants."[11]

We call this lost phase of the life cycle semiautonomy, because young people had exchanged the complete supervision of their parents for a relatively more autonomous though still subordinate relationship with another household. The London Apprentices, claims Steven Smith, were "almost . . . children of other parents, but not quite."[12] *Autonomy* as used here refers not only to activity but to the psychological tenor of the relationshp, for we assume that the relationship between parents and their children is almost always more complex and intense than the relationship between young people and other adults, even those with whom they live and who supervise their activities.

Two historical works deal systematically with boarding, the form of residence most common among young men who lived away from home in nineteenth-century cities, and both of them argue that it represented an emancipation from the family, fulfilling a desire for independence. Modell and Hareven assert that "the desire for independence from family ties was no doubt a major factor in the decision of boarders to pay rent rather than live with their kin."[13] The need to find work also drove many young people away from home. In the walking city it was necessary to live near one's work. If a young person was unable to find work within walking distance of home—and remember that prior to the development of large work settings the number of jobs within easy reach of any one place was relatively limited—it would be necessary to leave home. The important point is that until relatively recently it was expected that those young people who left home would live with another family rather than by themselves, in groups of single people, or in lodging houses. A family remained the culturally preferred setting in which young people passed the years between puberty and marriage.

Young men who lived as boarders were semiautonomous—less dependent than those who remained at home though not yet masters of their own households. Consider, for example, the experience of the 138 17-year-old men in Hamilton in 1851 (Table 7.1). Most of them (seventy-three) did not live with their parents; of these most were

Table 7.1   Household status, employment, and school attendance of young people: Hamilton, 1851–1871.

| Age (years) | Males | | | Females | | |
|---|---|---|---|---|---|---|
| | 1851 | 1861 | 1871 | 1851 | 1861 | 1871 |
| A. LIVING WITH PARENTS (%) | | | | | | |
| 12 | 77 | 81 | 94 | 74 | 86 | 86 |
| 13 | 86 | 83 | 93 | 75 | 80 | 85 |
| 14 | 75 | 80 | 89 | 56 | 71 | 84 |
| 15 | 64 | 79 | 88 | 56 | 61 | 82 |
| 16 | 56 | 80 | 85 | 55 | 60 | 72 |
| 17 | 49 | 66 | 82 | 48 | 54 | 64 |
| 18 | 38 | 62 | 70 | 37 | 50 | 57 |
| 19 | 37 | 63 | 63 | 30 | 39 | 49 |
| 20 | 24 | 54 | 61 | 21 | 33 | 43 |
| 21 | 22 | 43 | 53 | 27 | 33 | 39 |
| 22 | 28 | 45 | 44 | 17 | 28 | 27 |
| 23 | 14 | 34 | 32 | 18 | 25 | 27 |
| 24 | 25 | 32 | 25 | 16 | 18 | 24 |
| 25 | 14 | 19 | 27 | 10 | 22 | 19 |
| | B. MALE BOARDERS (%) | | | C. FEMALE SERVANTS (%) | | |
| 12 | 15 | 2 | 5 | 15 | 6 | 2 |
| 13 | 10 | 8 | 6 | 16 | 8 | 3 |
| 14 | 18 | 10 | 7 | 31 | 14 | 8 |
| 15 | 23 | 9 | 7 | 29 | 20 | 8 |
| 16 | 34 | 7 | 10 | 28 | 27 | 16 |
| 17 | 43 | 19 | 15 | 39 | 39 | 18 |
| 18 | 49 | 24 | 24 | 35 | 32 | 17 |
| 19 | 51 | 23 | 32 | 41 | 37 | 20 |
| 20 | 62 | 36 | 29 | 40 | 32 | 23 |
| 21 | 61 | 38 | 33 | 31 | 26 | 14 |
| 22 | 53 | 34 | 36 | 28 | 25 | 16 |
| 23 | 50 | 35 | 32 | 21 | 22 | 13 |
| 24 | 42 | 29 | 40 | 19 | 16 | 15 |
| 25 | 41 | 40 | 29 | 20 | 21 | 10 |
| D. MARRIED OR WIDOWED (%) | | | | | | |
| 18 | 2 | 1 | 0 | 0 | 4 | 9 |
| 19 | 1 | 1 | 1 | 12 | 7 | 13 |
| 20 | 5 | 4 | 5 | 24 | 17 | 15 |
| 21 | 9 | 8 | 7 | 28 | 27 | 28 |
| 22 | 11 | 8 | 15 | 40 | 36 | 41 |
| 23 | 25 | 24 | 31 | 39 | 40 | 45 |
| 24 | 26 | 25 | 31 | 29 | 55 | 46 |
| 25 | 45 | 33 | 36 | 60 | 58 | 57 |
| 26 | 46 | 52 | 53 | 71 | 72 | 63 |
| 27 | 55 | 60 | 54 | 76 | 79 | 66 |
| 28 | 64 | 64 | 60 | 79 | 79 | 71 |
| 29 | 63 | 66 | 74 | 80 | 77 | 78 |
| 30 | 60 | 70 | 65 | 83 | 80 | 80 |

Table 7.1, *continued*

| Age (years) | Males | | | Females | | |
|---|---|---|---|---|---|---|
| | 1851 | 1861 | 1871 | 1851 | 1861 | 1871 |

E. INDEX OF MARRIAGE TO INDEPENDENT HOUSEHOLD STATUS

| | | | | | | |
|---|---|---|---|---|---|---|
| 18 | 1.5 | 0.5 | 0.3 | 1.5 | 1.3 | 1.3 |
| 19 | 1.0 | 0.3 | 0.7 | 1.4 | 1.5 | 1.1 |
| 20 | 1.3 | 1.5 | 0.9 | 1.4 | 1.2 | 1.1 |
| 21 | 1.2 | 0.9 | 0.9 | 1.3 | 1.2 | 1.1 |
| 22 | 1.0 | 0.8 | 1.1 | 1.2 | 1.2 | 1.1 |
| 23 | 0.9 | 1.1 | 1.0 | 1.2 | 1.2 | 1.1 |
| 24 | 1.1 | 1.1 | 1.1 | 1.2 | 1.2 | 1.1 |
| 25 | 1.2 | 1.1 | 1.0 | 1.2 | 1.2 | 1.0 |
| 26 | 1.1 | 1.1 | 1.0 | 1.2 | 1.1 | 1.2 |
| 27 | 1.3 | 1.1 | 1.0 | 1.2 | 1.1 | 1.0 |
| 28 | 1.1 | 1.0 | 1.1 | 1.2 | 1.1 | 1.1 |
| 29 | 1.0 | 1.0 | 1.0 | 1.1 | 1.2 | 1.1 |
| 30 | 1.1 | 1.1 | 1.0 | 1.2 | 1.1 | 1.1 |

F. PROPORTION OF SERVANTS AMONG EMPLOYED FEMALES (%)

| | | | | | | |
|---|---|---|---|---|---|---|
| 13–16 | | | | 87 | 92 | 68 |
| 17–20 | | | | 80 | 87 | 54 |
| 21–25 | | | | 73 | 69 | 47 |
| Mean of means, ages 13–25 | | | | 79 | 82 | 56 |

G. PROPORTION EMPLOYED (%)

| | | | | | | |
|---|---|---|---|---|---|---|
| 11 | 2 | 1 | 1 | 15 | 3 | 1 |
| 12 | 12 | 2 | 4 | 15 | 6 | 3 |
| 13 | 15 | 2 | 7 | 18 | 8 | 4 |
| 14 | 21 | 9 | 22 | 35 | 15 | 12 |
| 15 | 41 | 18 | 53 | 34 | 23 | 16 |
| 16 | 51 | 29 | 66 | 34 | 30 | 26 |
| 17 | 67 | 46 | 74 | 48 | 35 | 30 |
| 18 | 76 | 53 | 85 | 49 | 36 | 35 |
| 19 | 77 | 64 | 89 | 51 | 36 | 39 |
| 20 | 76 | 69 | 91 | 48 | 39 | 39 |
| 21 | 81 | 75 | 91 | 43 | 37 | 35 |
| 22 | 85 | 79 | 94 | 37 | 39 | 30 |
| 23 | 88 | 82 | 91 | 31 | 30 | 25 |
| 24 | 88 | 81 | 93 | 25 | 26 | 30 |
| 25 | 89 | 89 | 94 | 30 | 27 | 24 |
| 26 | 93 | 94 | 96 | 21 | 17 | 21 |
| 27 | 89 | 96 | 96 | 22 | 15 | 21 |
| 28 | 93 | 91 | 97 | 19 | 13 | 19 |
| 29 | 96 | 94 | 96 | 11 | 17 | 17 |
| 30 | 92 | 93 | 95 | 15 | 18 | 15 |

Table 7.1, *continued*

| Age (years) | Males | | | Females | | |
|---|---|---|---|---|---|---|
| | 1851 | 1861 | 1871 | 1851 | 1861 | 1871 |
| H. ATTENDING SCHOOL (%) | | | | | | |
| 3 | 1 | 1 | 1 | 0 | 2 | 1 |
| 4 | 4 | 5 | 8 | 4 | 3 | 7 |
| 5 | 22 | 20 | 42 | 11 | 13 | 38 |
| 6 | 30 | 45 | 70 | 29 | 43 | 61 |
| 7 | 49 | 64 | 85 | 40 | 57 | 79 |
| 8 | 52 | 70 | 86 | 41 | 72 | 85 |
| 9 | 57 | 74 | 89 | 46 | 75 | 84 |
| 10 | 45 | 77 | 90 | 47 | 75 | 90 |
| 11 | 55 | 75 | 85 | 42 | 60 | 83 |
| 12 | 42 | 73 | 81 | 31 | 65 | 81 |
| 13 | 37 | 75 | 62 | 33 | 59 | 67 |
| 14 | 29 | 51 | 48 | 20 | 54 | 53 |
| 15 | 17 | 37 | 26 | 15 | 42 | 36 |
| 16 | 11 | 27 | 17 | 8 | 22 | 18 |
| 17 | 7 | 17 | 8 | 5 | 11 | 9 |
| 18 | 3 | 12 | 2 | 0 | 6 | 4 |
| 19 | 4 | 3 | 1 | 2 | 4 | 3 |
| 20 | 3 | 2 | 0 | 0 | 1 | 0 |
| 21 | 1 | 1 | 0 | 0 | 1 | 0 |

boarders and virtually all were employed. Probably not more than five or six of the boarders worked for the head of the household in which they lived. Their situation contrasts sharply with that of the (sixty-five) young men who lived with their parents. Of these nine attended school and (thirty-five) worked. Probably about fourteen of the thirty-five worked for their fathers and the rest worked for other employers. Thus twenty-one were neither at work nor in school, and all of these must have been economically dependent on their parents. Very likely those who worked contributed a large share of their earnings to the family income. By contrast even if boarders sent money to their parents, they could not supply as much as if they had remained at home, because they had to pay their landlord for room and board. Thus it is reasonable to suppose that economic ties between family members weakened when sons left home. If our psychological assumption is correct, emotional bonds lessened as well.

Young men who lived as boarders should have been financially and emotionally closer to independence than men of the same age who remained at home. If this argument is correct they should have married sooner, and this is exactly what happened. Between 1851 and 1861, 29 percent of male children and 33 percent of boarders aged 15 to 19 became household heads. During the next decade the proportions were 36 percent and 74 percent of young men of the same age. Looking only at those who married (as distinct from becoming the head of a household), the proportions were 36 percent for young men living with their parents, 65 percent for those living with relatives, and 68 percent for those who were boarders. These figures do not imply that children who remained at home were less likely ever to marry, for the figures for young men aged 20 to 24 in 1861 are virtually identical for each status.

It is easier to describe the stage of semiautonomy than it is to account for its existence and to explain its consequences. One apparent consequence was that young men who did leave home achieved full independence, defined socially by marriage and heading a household, sooner than those who remained with their parents. One reason that they left undoubtedly was to find work when jobs nearby were unavailable. However that cannot be the whole story, for the practice of fostering out was very ancient and characterized even social classes in which children did not have to begin work early for economic reasons. Indeed the mid-nineteenth-century patterns represent only the last manifestation of a long-standing cultural tradition.

According to Stone fostering out had four major consequences. First, it "greatly reduced . . . oedipal and other tensions" that cause conflict between parents and assertive adolescents, especially pronounced where a long delay exists between puberty and marriage, as in Western society. Second, a point that McFarlane also makes as well as the previous argument, the custom "reduced the danger of incest . . . where housing was poor and there were insufficient bedrooms." Third, as a result of the early age at which their children left home no parents from any social class "saw very much of their children." And fourth, it supported the "strong contemporary consciousness of adolescence (then called 'youth'), as a distinct stage of life between sexual maturity . . . and marriage."[14]

There were two sides to the practice of fostering out. One was the notion that young people should leave home. The other, as noted, was that they should live with a family, not by themselves. Thus the boarding of young people represents an essentially noneconomic tradition: the oversight of a community's youth by the well-to-do. It was a tradition that reflected an older social order in which the boundaries between family and community were indistinct and in which households, places of both residence and work, were the basic units of social organization.

The remnants of this tradition in mid-nineteenth-century Hamilton were swiftly eroded during the early years of industrialization. In 1851 half of the 17-year-old men in Hamilton had left home; by 1861 half the young men were not leaving home until the age of 21; and by 1871 the age had risen to 22. In 1851 24 percent of 20-year-old men lived at home; that proportion rose to 54 percent in 1861 and 61 percent ten years later. By 1871 27 percent of 25-year-old men lived at home, compared to 14 percent and 19 percent in the two earlier decades, respectively. Throughout the period it was unusual for a young man to marry before his mid-twenties.

Those young men not living at home were primarily boarders in other households. In 1851 at least 40 percent of all young men between the ages of 17 and 25 were living as boarders; by 1871 that proportion had dropped substantially from 43 percent to 15 percent of 17-year-olds and from 50 percent to 32 percent of the 23-year-olds, to take but two examples. To what extent were these figures, especially for 1851, an artifact of the heavy immigration of young unmarried men into the city? The question is enormously difficult to answer. Evidence from Buffalo in 1855 does show that young men who were boarders had lived in the city for markedly fewer years than those who lived with their parents. On the other hand demographic estimates based on the population of Hamilton, though still crude, do make it plausible that the shifts in the proportions of young people living at home represent real trends and not merely the processes of population movement. These estimates are supported by the fact that the proportion of young people in the entire population remained almost unchanged between 1851 and 1871. Furthermore, as we observed in the discussion of trends in population persistence in Chapter 2, the proportion of young children remaining in the city increased during the decade 1861-1871, a reflection of the fact that more of them were living longer with their parents. Finally, if the high proportion of young people living away from home had been merely an artifact of immigration, then the proportion should have been at least as high in Buffalo in 1855 as it was in Hamilton in 1851, since the American city was growing at an amazing rate. In fact notably more young people, both native and foreign born, lived with their parents in Buffalo in 1855 than in Hamilton in 1851, and the proportion in Buffalo resembled that in Hamilton in 1871, a fact consistent with the argument we already have advanced about the earlier development of the American city.

One other characteristic of boarders should be stressed: they did not distribute themselves randomly throughout the households of the city, nor did they live most often with those most in need of extra income. To the contrary, with the exception of widows, wealthy families had boarders substantially more often than poor ones. In 1851, for instance, half the wealthiest 10 percent of households contained a boarder, compared to one-fifth of the poorest 20 percent; in 1861 the proportions were 28 percent and 12 percent of the two groups, respectively.

Few boarders (by one estimate 9 percent at most) could have been employees of the household head. Rather their presence signified the persistence of an essentially moral arrangement, and its subsequent association with poverty (by the late-nineteenth century boarding had become almost wholly an economic arrangement associated with the lower classes) marked a significant shift in the relationship between family and community. Once boarding acquired its association with poverty middle-class reformers, increasingly refracting social reality through the new ideal of the private family, began a campaign of denunciation. Boarding emerged in respectable eyes as a cause and symptom of family pathology, a lower-class disease to be cleansed with domesticity.[15]

Although young men exchanged earlier habits of boarding for an increasingly long residence in the home of their parents, they did not start to work later in early industrial Hamilton. In 1851 half of the 16-year-old men were employed; in 1871 half were working by the age of 15. Thus the period between starting work and leaving home had been extended in two decades from at most a year to about seven years, a radical shift.

The trends in the residential experience of young women paralleled those of men. In 1851 half the 17-year-old women did not live at home; by 1871 that age had increased to 19. In 1851 48 percent of 17-year-old women lived at home, a proportion that increased to 54 percent and 64 percent during each of the next two decades. Similarly the share of 23-year-old women living at home rose from 18 percent to 27 percent between 1851 and 1871. (The fact that women married about four years earlier than men meant that fewer of them lived with their parents during their early and mid-twenties.)

A new phase had entered the life cycle: a prolonged period of time spent with parents between puberty and marriage. If we are right, this shift occured wherever industrial capitalism developed. The process took place in two stages. The first was the transition from apprenticeship to boarding. In the Early Modern situations described by Smith, Stone, Schofield, and McFarlane young people worked as servants for the household heads with whom they lived (a status then common to men as well as women) or as apprentices. Apprenticeship, and for men service, declined prior to the erosion of the two key cultural prescriptions that sustained fostering out: the notion that everyone should live in a family or household and the belief that the well-to-do had an obligation to oversee the behavior of the young people in their communities, a responsibility to participate in the upbringing of young people who were not their own. Because these two traditions lingered, young people who left home, even though they were less likely to work as apprentices or servants, went to live as boarders in households rather than on their own, and most often they lived with the well-to-do.

Later on relatively large industries made it easier for young people to find work near home. They may have found it cheaper to live with parents than in lodgings. Certainly this was the case among one group of working girls surveyed in Minnesota in the 1880s. There the Bureau of Labor Statistics estimated that the cost of boarding at home was $4 per week, compared to $6 per week for board with strangers. "It will be seen," concluded the secretary of the Bureau of Labor, "that a large proportion of working girls live at home. This is a great advantage to the girls who are so fortunately situated; but the benefit to this class of girls is counterbalanced by the injury to that class who are not able to earn good wages and must bear the whole expense of their own support . . . They are not able to secure good wages, because girls with homes and merely nominal expenses can work very cheap, and are, therefore, employed in preference."[16]

Parents surely welcomed the additional income provided by working children. More than that the older practice of family or life-cycle boarding had reflected the last flicker of the tradition of paternalistic responsibility, in which the leading members of communities assumed an active role in the socialization of the young. However the boundaries between family and community gradually became more distinct as a result of the process of specialization that accompanied the development of industrial capitalism. The encroachment of the market on the family separated home from work place and prefigured the doom of domestic arrangements that reflected the social relations of an earlier economic order.

## School

The prolonged residence of young people with their parents in part reflected increased school attendance. Between 1851 and 1871 the proportion of young people at school rose within each age group. The figures in Table 7.2 are based only on young people living with their parents; this should eliminate any distorting effects that immigration

Table 7.2   Percentage of children attending school, by age and sex: Hamilton, 1851–1871 (all children living with parents).

| Age | Males | | | Females | | | All | | |
|---|---|---|---|---|---|---|---|---|---|
| | 1851 | 1861 | 1871 | 1851 | 1861 | 1871 | 1851 | 1861 | 1871 |
| 5–6 | 27.0 | 29.6 | 53.8 | 20.4 | 26.5 | 49.3 | 24.0 | 28.0 | 51.6 |
| 7–12 | 54.1 | 72.6 | 85.7 | 46.5 | 70.8 | 84.5 | 50.6 | 71.7 | 85.1 |
| 13–16 | 30.1 | 51.5 | 42.6 | 25.6 | 52.0 | 49.4 | 27.9 | 51.7 | 45.8 |

patterns, orphanage, or other unusual circumstances might exert on the underlying trends. Among the youngest group, ages 5 to 6, school attendance increased from 24 percent to about 52 percent, with the largest increase in the second decade. At the same time attendance became nearly universal for children of ordinary school age (7 to 12), rising from 51 percent to 72 percent to 85 percent in twenty years.[17]

In sharp contrast to the experience of younger children attendance among the 13- to-16-year-olds followed a bell-shaped curve; it rose from 28 percent to 52 percent between 1851 and 1861, a startling leap, but had fallen back to 46 percent ten years later. The reasons for this peculiar pattern relate to the connection between schooling, work, and the state of the job market. The commercial city in 1851 offered people over the age of 12 or 13 little in the way of employment; their labor simply remained unnecessary. At the same time educational provisions, unsystematic and ungraded, were inappropriate for teenagers. During the 1850s the city, conscious of its educational backwardness, modernized its school system, primarily through the introduction of a central school, a remarkably progressive institution for its time. Thus by 1861 young people could attend an age-graded secondary school.

Moreover during the same period there had been virtually no increase in job opportunities. Indeed the depression of the late 1850s made the employment situation for young people bleak, and in these circumstances they turned to the schools. However during the next decade employment opportunities for young people grew quite remarkably, and many left school in order to take up jobs in newly expanded or developed industries.

Boys and girls did not attend school in equal numbers (Table 7.2). In 1851 boys at every age went to school in greater numbers: among 5-to-6-year-olds the relative proportions were 27 percent for males and 20 percent for females, and comparable disparities occurred at each age. By 1861, when the differences had lessened somewhat, young women aged 13 to 16 went to school in the same proportion as young men; and by 1871, though boys under the age of 12 retained the edge, young women aged 13 to 16 had established a notable lead over men: 49 percent of females compared to 43 percent of males the same age attended school.

The reason for the increased attendance of young women over the age of 12 rested, as with men, in the job market. As industrial employment increased young men could leave school and find work without very much difficulty. In fact working-class teenage men actually went to school less often in 1871, after industrialization was under way, than they had twenty years earlier in the commercial city. Young men from affluent homes, who remained more often in school, probably saw in school the route to nonmanual work. Similarly some young women from relatively affluent homes stayed in school because they had nothing else to do; others viewed school as the way to the newest nonindustrial occupation open to women—teaching. And for some schooling may have provided a moderately attractive alternative to domestic service, for there was very little work in industry available to girls under the age of 16. Thus the explanation for trends in school attendance lies in part in the labor market.

## Work

Early industrialization did little to alter the customary age at which young people began to work. Young men entered the work force on the average about one year earlier in 1871 than in 1851. During the depression of the late 1850s teenage employment had dropped, but with the return of prosperity and the expansion of industrial opportunities it had climbed well above its level in the commerical city: the proportion of employed 16-year-olds rose from 51 percent to 66 percent and of 18-year-olds from 76 percent to 85 percent, both between 1851 and 1871. The increase took place not only among all young men but among those living with their parents as well. For instance the proportion of employed 13- to 16-year-olds living at home rose from 15 percent to 32 percent between 1851 and 1871. This rough doubling supports our contention that young men had begun to live with their parents during their early working years.

Among women employment trends were quite different. The proportion of all young working women in the city decreased slightly, though the share of those living with their parents and working did increase a bit, for example from 3 percent to 6 percent of the 13- to 16-year-olds. Nonetheless the proportion of employed 16-year-olds among all women in the city dropped from 34 percent to 26 percent; for 18-year-olds the decrease was from 49 percent to 35 percent and for 20-year-olds from 48 percent to 39 percent, all between 1851 and 1871. Most employed young women worked as resident domestic servants, which is why the proportion of all women at work so greatly exceeds the proportion at work and living with their parents.

Table 7.3 shows the combined effects of increased school attendance and, in the case of men, increased employment opportunities. Together they raised the number of occupied young people quite dramatically. In 1851 a large proportion of idle youth neither in work nor at school, had roamed the streets of Hamilton and similar cities. For instance 55 percent of the 13- to 16-year-old young people living with their parents in 1851 were neither in work nor at school. It is worth dwelling for a moment upon the problem of idle youth.[18] Contrary to popular impression little paid, regular work outside the home existed for young men in cities prior to industrialization. No shortage of labor made it necessary to press boys into unskilled work, and formally structured, long-term apprenticeships had ceased to exist by the mid-nineteenth century. In fact apprenticeship had not operated in anything like its traditional form for many years. In Great Britain, the source of most of Hamilton's population, the Elizabethan Statute of Artificers, which prescribed rules for apprenticeship, had been ignored for a long period prior to its formal repeal in 1814. Thus it was not industrialization that had undermined apprenticeship but capitalism. Apprenticeship was incompatible with a system of wage labor that stressed the manipulation of mobile resources in order to maximize profit.

In earlier days it had been clear how young people should spend their time during each phase of their life cycle. Idleness had been an unimaginable social problem. However the erosion of apprenticeship and the lack of work for young people, which occurred prior to the creation of any institution to contain and control them, created a veritable crisis in early nineteenth-century cities. To some citizens

Table 7.3    Percentage of employment and school attendance among young people 13–16 years old living at home: Hamilton, 1851–1871.

| Status | Males | | | Females | | |
|---|---|---|---|---|---|---|
| | 1851 | 1861 | 1871 | 1851 | 1861 | 1871 |
| In school | 30.1 | 51.5 | 42.6 | 25.6 | 52.0 | 49.4 |
| Employed | 14.9 | 9.4 | 31.7 | 3.1 | 1.8 | 6.3 |
| Neither employed nor in school | 55.0 | 39.1 | 25.7 | 71.3 | 46.2 | 44.3 |

in mid-nineteenth-century Toronto, writes Susan Houston, "the increasingly familiar figure of the street urchin—ill-clad, undisciplined, and, most importantly, unschooled—assumed sinister significance."[19] Similarly in New York the problem of idle and vagrant children, writes Carl Kaestle, was "sizeable enough and ominous enough to play a prominent part in school and police reports from the 1820's to mid-century and beyond . . . A school report of 1856 complained that there were 'between 20,000 and 60,000 children now being educated in our streets in habits of idleness, and a knowledge of vice, where they will graduate enemies to themselves and curses to the community, and enter upon careers of debauchery and crime.' "[20] In 1824 in Philadelphia the president of the Controllers of the Public Schools, Roberts Vaux, warned, "It ought not to be concealed that many children who should have partaken of the benefits of education, have voluntarily denied themselves those advantages. These neglected beings, in addition to the most pernicious domestic example, are allowed to range at large through this populous district, the easy prey of every temptation to vicious conduct."[21] Two years later Vaux asserted, "Some remedy should likewise be provided to rid our streets and wharves, and the immediate vicinity of the town, of the small children, who, either as beggars or petty depredators, wander about to seek a pittance for the support of their indolent and worthless parents—these vicious youths learning and teaching others the way to ruin, should be arrested in their career of iniquity and placed where they may be employed and receive some useful school learning."[22]

With the introduction of expanded educational facilities and then industrial employment the proportion of idle young men in Hamilton dropped sharply to 39 percent in 1861 and 26 percent ten years later. The proportion of idle young women decreased in the same years from 71 percent to 46 percent to 44 percent. Certainly the existence of idle youth not only spurred the creation of a school system but provided as well a source of cheap mobile labor that fueled the rapid industrialization of the city.

Trends within the city as a whole reflected those for young people living with their parents. For instance the proportion of 15-year-old men neither at work nor at school dropped from 41 percent to 21 percent between 1851 and 1871; in the same years the proportion of idle 18-year-olds dipped from 21 percent to 13 percent. Similar patterns marked the experience of younger teenage girls: the proportion of idle 13-year-olds declined from 49 percent to 29 percent and of 14-year-olds from 45 percent to 25 percent, while the share of young women 16 years of age and older neither at work nor at school held relatively constant, a trend reflecting the more limited job opportunities for women even during industrialization.

The rise in the proportion of occupied young men took two stages: between 1851 and 1861 school attendance accounted for virtually all of the increase, and attendance itself reflected both newly expanded educational facilities and the lack of work for young men in the commercial city, a problem exacerbated by the depression but by no means unique to hard times. During the next decade, however, increased employment opportunities fostered by industrialization brought about the continuing rise in the proportion of young men who were occupied.

Industrialization exerted more of an impact in the kind of work young women did than on the proportion employed. That is, its effect was primarily redistributive. The proportion of women employed dipped slightly from 25 percent to 22 percent between 1851 and 1871, and the major shift came in the proportion employed in domestic service, which decreased from 72 percent to 50 percent to 47 percent of all employed women between 1851, 1861, and 1871 (see Chapter 2). At the same time the share of women employed in various sorts of industrial work rose to about one-third of all those employed.

Though young men had a wide variety of occupations in both the commercial and early industrial city, they entered the newer, expanding sectors of the economy in disproportionate numbers. For instance, considering only young men living with their parents, between 1851 and 1871 the proportion of those employed who worked as molders increased from 2 percent to 5 percent; of machinists from less than 1 percent to 10 percent, and of clerks and bookkeepers from 7 percent to 16 percent. (Clerical occupations expanded very rapidly in both the commercial and early industrial city.) Conversely stagnating sectors or sectors of the economy adversely affected by mechanization did not attract very many young men: the proportion of shoemakers, for instance, dropped between 1851 and 1871 from 5 percent to 2 percent of young men working and living at home and among all young men aged 15 to 24 from 35 percent to 3 percent, an enormous decline.

The same patterns emerge from another point of view as well. Consider fathers who had working sons living at home (Table 7.4): 66 of the men were in the metal trades compared to 170 of their sons; 133 of the men and 222 of their sons worked in commerce; 31 fathers and 42 sons were wood workers. At the same time 96 fathers but only 52 sons worked in the apparel industry, and 204 fathers and only 123 sons were laborers. Young men clearly did not enter the work force in a random fashion. They chose expanding sectors of the economy and avoided those that were unattractive. Their ability to choose reflected the relatively favorable job market that confronted young men in the early industrial city. It makes their eagerness to leave school understandable.

Table 7.4  Distribution of occupations by sector among fathers and sons living at home: Hamilton, 1871.

| | N | |
|---|---|---|
| Sector and occupation | Father | Son |
| *Primary* | | |
| Agriculture | 7 | 2 |
| Extractive | 14 | 7 |
| *Secondary* | | |
| Textile and leather | 2 | 2 |
| Apparel | 96 | 52 |
| Wood and wood products | 31 | 42 |
| Metal and metal products | 66 | 170 |
| Food and beverages | 22 | 18 |
| Luxury items | 12 | 18 |
| Other | 51 | 130 |
| Construction | 142 | 97 |
| Labor | 204 | 123 |
| *Tertiary* | | |
| Commerce | 133 | 222 |
| Transport | 58 | 51 |
| Service | 21 | 13 |
| Domestic service | 12 | 5 |
| Professions | 26 | 8 |
| Education and government | 43 | 23 |
| Arts/culture | 7 | 6 |
| Unclassifiable | 42 | 0 |
| Total | 989 | 989 |

## Marriage

Youth, as we define it, ended with marriage. Unlike residence, school, and work, marriage patterns apparently changed very little during the early years of industrialization. More detailed work with parish registers may alter this conclusion somewhat, but on the basis of the information in the census there was little overall relationship between early industrialization and the age of marriage.

Throughout the period marriage retained its European pattern: that is, people married late. A selection of marriage registers from the largest Anglican and Catholic churches in Hamilton between the late 1840s and the late 1860s gives the average age of marriage for men as 27 and for women 23.[23] In 1855 age at marriage in Buffalo, according to the census, was exactly the same. The census for Hamilton lists half of the men as married by the age of 27 in 1851 and by 26 in 1861 and

Table 7.5   Percentage of married males, by occupational rank within age groups: Hamilton, 1851–1871.

| Age and occupational rank | 1851 | 1861 | 1871 |
|---|---|---|---|
| *21–23:* | | | |
| 1 | 13 | 14 | 13 |
| 2 | 9 | 9 | 10 |
| 3 | 17 | 12 | 17 |
| 4 | 28 | 29 | 18 |
| 5 | 17 | 34 | 38 |
| All | 14.8 | 12.6 | 16.0 |
| *24–26:* | | | |
| 1 | 54 | 38 | 33 |
| 2 | 37 | 32 | 32 |
| 3 | 43 | 43 | 42 |
| 4 | 31 | 47 | 56 |
| 5 | 52 | 54 | 56 |
| All | 38.7 | 36.4 | 40.8 |
| *27–29:* | | | |
| 1 | 54 | 53 | 55 |
| 2 | 49 | 52 | 56 |
| 3 | 67 | 71 | 64 |
| 4 | 71 | 74 | 62 |
| 5 | 70 | 75 | 68 |
| All | 60.5 | 61.4 | 61.5 |
| *30–32:* | | | |
| 1 | 64 | 68 | 52 |
| 2 | 79 | 71 | 65 |
| 3 | 74 | 77 | 79 |
| 4 | 57 | 77 | 76 |
| 5 | 68 | 86 | 85 |
| All | 68.4 | 72.7 | 74.0 |

1871. Looked at another way, men appeared to marry a bit later during the depression of the late 1850s and very slightly earlier in 1871 than they had twenty years previously. For example in 1851 15 percent of the 21- to 23-year-olds were married, compared to 13 percent in 1861 and 17 percent in 1871; during the same period the proportion of married 24- to 26-year-olds varied from 39 percent to 36 percent to 41 percent (Table 7.5).

The experience of women differed somewhat. According to the census of 1851 half the women aged 25 were married, compared to half of the 24-year-olds in 1861 and half the 25-year-olds ten years later. However by 1871 fewer women in their late twenties had married than in either of the previous census years. In 1851, 76 percent of the 27-year-old and 79 percent of 28-year-old women were married, compared to 66 percent and 71 percent, respectively, twenty years later. This decline reflects the unbalanced sex ratios in the city, especially severe in the aftermath of the depression of the late 1850s, when young unmarried men often left. In 1871, for example, there were only eighty-two men for every hundred women aged 25 to 29 in the city.

Once married, couples usually established their own households. In sharp contrast to the situation in Preston, England, described by Michael Anderson, very few young married couples in Hamilton did not live in their own homes either prior to or during early industrialization.[24] Between 1851 and 1871 the proportion of young couples not living in independent households remained about 10 percent. This difference between Hamilton and Preston probably reflected housing supply rather than cultural preference. Anderson points out that a severe shortage of housing existed in Preston, whereas in Hamilton almost all families lived in single-family dwellings, and cheap rental housing remained easily available. In this respect families in Hamilton were more like those that Lynn Lees found among Irish and English working-class people in London during the same period.[25] There too young couples generally lived by themselves once they had married. Also in Preston, unlike Hamilton, the textile industry employed a large number of married women who needed the baby-sitting service that a resident grandmother could provide.

The sequence of events in the life cycle of young people in Buffalo resembled that in Hamilton. The data for one year do not permit the analysis of the extent to which patterns changed over time. However they do show that as in the Canadian city young people left home several years prior to marriage and spent that time as members of one or more households. Here the conclusions rest on a multivariate analysis and reflect the probabilities that young people of different ages would occupy various statuses, with other factors controlled. Young men left home between the ages of 17 and 18. The first point at which they were more likely than not to be married was between the ages of 24 and 25. Thus a period of about seven years existed in which they were neither children nor household heads. In those years more of them were boarders than relatives, servants, and so on. Indeed after the age of 20 young men were more likely to be listed as boarders than as children.

Young women left home much earlier, between the ages of 13 and 14. They first became more likely than not to be married between the ages of 19 and 20, making a gap of about six years between leaving home and marrying. Many who left home became servants. Indeed the odds were 22 percent that a young woman in Buffalo aged 18 or 19 would be a resident domestic.

The number of years that a person had lived in the city modified these patterns somewhat. Young men who had lived longest in the city were the most likely to dwell with their parents: the odds were 39 percent for a young man living in Buffalo ten or more years, compared to 22 percent for one there two to four years. Conversely men there for the shortest span of time were the most likely to be boarders. The chances that a young man living in Buffalo less than a year would be a boarder were 25 percent, compared to 11 percent for one who had lived in the city five to nine years. Length of time in the city made a difference with women only in the likelihood of their remaining with their parents. Those living in the city for the longest time were most likely to live at home. However length of residence had no impact on the chance that a young woman would be a servant.

## Class and Ethnic Variation

Young people from all backgrounds were staying at home longer and going to school in greater numbers during the early industrialization of Hamilton. However experiences of young people of varying ethnic and class origins did differ significantly. The census for 1871 was the first to list national origin, which makes it possible to distinguish between the ethnic background of individuals born in Canada.[26] Women of Irish origin born in Canada remained at home longer than Irish-born Catholics. The proportion of each group working as resident domestic servants reflects the difference: 40 percent of 15- to 17-year-old Irish-born Catholic women, compared to 18 percent of Catholic women of Irish origin born in Canada. Conversely among 9- to 11-year-olds only 43 percent of the former compared to 87 percent of the latter attended school. Finally, striking differences between the two age groups of Irish Catholic women existed in marriage statistics. A very low proportion, only half, of Catholic women of Irish origin born in Canada had married by their late twenties, an age higher than that for any other group. Why they remained spinsters so often is obscure. Perhaps it was especially difficult to find suitable marriage partners. The answer must be part of the larger, still unresolved issue of the relative weight of improved economic position and cultural assimilation in the behavior of Irish Catholic women born in Canada.

Little ethnic difference existed among young men in the age of leaving home, though the Scottish stayed longer with their parents and married later. However differentials similar to those among young women did exist in school attendance. Irish-born Catholic young men left school earlier than Catholics of Irish origin born in Canada: of 12- to 14-year-olds 36 percent of the Irish born and 56 percent of the Canadian born had attended school. Nonetheless the rate for native-born Catholics remained low by comparison with other Canadian-born groups. For the most part ethnic differences in school attendance reflected employment trends: Catholics born in Ireland were more likely than Canadian-born Catholics to start work between the ages of 12 and 14. However by ages 15 to 17 little difference remained between Catholic men born on different continents.

Social rank affected the age at which young people left home. Of course we have no direct measure of the occupation or wealth of the fathers of young men living as boarders; consequently our conclusions rest on estimates developed through more indirect methods. One is a comparison of the ethnic and class variation in the proportion of men of a given age (45 and over) who had children of a particular age (over 17) living at home. This measure reveals a linear relationship between the occupational rank of fathers and the length of time their children remained at home (Table 7.6). The proportion of fathers aged 45 or over with a least one 17-year-old son at home was 47 percent for men in rank 1, 39 percent for rank 2, and lowest, 31 percent for rank 5 (generally laborers). The same results exist for daughters and for all children together. Thus it is clear that the children of more affluent fathers remained at home longest. Similarly, 43 percent of Irish Catholic men aged 45 or over compared to 64 percent of Canadian Protestants, the most affluent group, had a child aged 17 or over at home.

One factor cut across both class and ethnic divisions: namely, widowhood. Children of widows remained at home in greater numbers than all others, doubtless to assist their mothers. For instance 65 percent of widows aged 40 or over had a child aged 17 or older at home, compared to 52 percent of male household heads. This distinction held for all ethnic groups.

As in Hamilton ethnicity affected the life cycle of young people in Buffalo. Young men born in New England or New York remained longest at home, on the average about four years more than others. The youngest age group in which fewer than half the members lived with their parents was the 20- to 21-year-olds. Conversely, both Irish and Germans married relatively early, especially the latter. The youngest age group in which more than half the native-born Americans were household heads was the 28- to 29-year-olds. For the Irish it was the 24- to 25-year-olds and for the Germans the 22- to 23-

Table 7.6   Families with adolescent children aged 17 and over at home, by ethnicity, occupation, and marital status: Hamilton, 1871.

| Variable | Sons | Daughters | Sons and/or daughters |
|---|---|---|---|
| **A. Married male household heads aged 45 and over, percent with one or more adolescents at home (N = 1,427)** | | | |
| Total household heads | 36.0 | 32.5 | 51.5 |
| *Occupational rank* | | | |
| 1 | 47.1 | 38.4 | 62.3 |
| 2 | 39.0 | 38.2 | 56.9 |
| 3 | 36.5 | 36.7 | 55.0 |
| 4 | 31.5 | 23.1 | 38.9 |
| 5 | 31.4 | 20.3 | 40.7 |
| Other | 50.0 | 50.0 | 50.0 |
| *Ethnicity of men* | | | |
| Irish Catholic | 31.9 | 26.0 | 42.5 |
| Irish Protestant | 43.5 | 39.5 | 59.3 |
| Scottish Presbyterian | 37.6 | 36.5 | 55.3 |
| Other Scottish | 40.0 | 42.4 | 57.0 |
| English Anglican | 30.6 | 27.8 | 48.2 |
| English Methodist | 45.9 | 49.5 | 67.6 |
| Other English | 36.7 | 25.6 | 51.1 |
| Canadian Protestant | 52.0 | 34.7 | 64.0 |
| Canadian Catholic | 62.5 | 12.5 | 62.5 |
| U.S. nonwhite | 34.8 | 21.7 | 39.1 |
| Other U.S. | 21.7 | 30.0 | 41.7 |
| Other | 30.4 | 21.4 | 40.2 |

**B. Widows aged 40 and over, percent with one or more adolescents at home (N = 454)**

| | | | |
|---|---|---|---|
| *Children* | | | |
| Sons | 44.7 | | |
| Daughters | 42.3 | | |
| Sons and/or daughters | 64.5 | | |
| *Ethnicity of women* | | | |
| Irish Catholic | 45.8 | | |
| Irish Protestant | 34.2 | | |
| Scottish Presbyterian | 41.7 | | |
| English Anglican | 57.1 | | |
| English Methodist | 42.3 | | |
| Canadian Protestant | 57.1 | | |

year-olds. Among 24- to 25-year-olds the chances that a native-born American man would be married were 42 percent, compared to 55 percent for the Irish and 62 percent for the Germans; for 28- to 29-year-olds the same probabilities were 71 percent, 86 percent, and 91 percent. Irish- and German-born young men were most likely to be boarders. The probability that a native-born young man 20 to 21 would board was 19 percent, compared to 26 percent for the Irish and 22 percent for the Germans.

Among young women trends were similar. The youngest age group in which native-born American women were likely to live away from their parents was the 18- to 19-year-olds, compared to the 14- to 15-year-olds for both Irish and Germans. Thus among young women too the age of leaving home differed on the average by about four years between natives and immigrants. The age group of 24- to 25-year-olds was the youngest in which over 50 percent of native-born American women were wives; by contrast the age was 22 to 23 for the Irish and 20 to 21 for the Germans. Indeed the probability that a native-born American woman of 20 to 21 would be married was 48 percent; for an Irish-born woman it was 49 percent and for a German 63 percent. At the ages of 22 to 23 the odds were, respectively, 50 percent, 56 percent, and 63 percent. These differences in marriage age account to some extent for the higher fertility rate among German women noted by Glasco.[27]

The differences among ethnic groups reflect for the most part the variation in prosperity between them. Overwhelmingly working class, Irish and German families were unable to support unemployed children for as long as the more prosperous natives, and they probably hoped that working children would remit some portion of their wages home. The kinds of work that immigrant children entered, moreover, did not require prolonged schooling, and it made economic sense to start work as young as possible. Since wages peaked relatively early, immigrant young men had much less incentive to delay marriage than those aspiring to commercial or professional careers. Thus with the exception of the very early marriage of the Germans these ethnic differences probably reflect class position more than cultural choice.

## Class, Ethnicity, and School Attendance

In Hamilton children from advantaged families stayed home longer than others. They usually went to school in somewhat greater numbers as well. However school attendance is a complex subject. Again we used multiple classification analysis with school attendance as the dependent variable.[28] The proportion of the variation in school attendance accounted for by characteristics entered into the analysis dropped in each year. This decline did not stem simply from the increased proportion of children attending school, for the amount of variation accounted for in the attendance of 13- to 16-year-olds dropped between 1861 and 1871 even though the rate of attendance also declined. It is tempting to argue that attendance simply became increasingly random, freed from its relationship to social structure. Among children 5 to 6 and 7 to 12 that was probably the case. However clear connections between attendance and social-structural characteristics continued to exist in the 13- to 16-year-old group, and the probability that young people from different backgrounds would attend school varied substantially and systematically.

Consider first the general relationships between school attendance and other factors. Among 5- to 6-year-olds in 1851 the relationship between birthplace of father and birthplace of child (hereafter called father/child birthplace) and occupation had roughly equal associations with school attendance for both males and females. Next in importance came wealth and number of children combined with property status (hereafter termed children/property), both substantially lower, followed by religion, which had less association with attendance among females than among males. By 1871 the distinction between the influence of the various factors had dropped to the point that none of them are worth discussing. At the same time the proportion of variance accounted for declined from 28 percent to 15 percent for males and from 23 percent to 12 percent for females. The school attendance of young children had become an increasingly common occurrence not especially related to family background.

The differentiating power of the factor variables also declined for 7- to 12-year-olds. As Table 7.7 shows, in 1851 economic rank (beta = .24) was most influential among males, followed closely by father/child birthplace (.20) and occupation (.21). The other two factors both had relatively low betas (.12). Among young women the variable with the strongest association with attendance was religion (.23), and economic rank scored lower than either occupation or birthplace. Apparently different patterns existed among young men and women, and these merit further exploration. However by 1861 religion no longer influenced attendance very much among women, and by 1871 patterns among both young men and women had become essentially identical and random.

As with younger children the influence of each factor declined among 13- to 16-year-olds between 1851 and 1871. In 1851 occupation scored highest among males, economic rank among females. However

Table 7.7  School attendance of all children: multiple classification analysis, Hamilton, 1851–1871.[a]

| Children | Etas/betas | | | | | Mean (%) | R² | Significance (main effects) |
| | Birthplace (father/child) | Religion | Economic rank | Occupation | Children/ property | | | |
| --- | --- | --- | --- | --- | --- | --- | --- | --- |
| *6-year-olds* | | | | | | | | |
| Male: 1851 | .33/.29 | .16/.16 | .25/.19 | .34/.28 | .22/.18 | 32 | .28 | .02 |
| 1861 | .25/.28 | .14/.08 | .15/.13 | .21/.19 | .12/.18 | 30 | .23 | .07 |
| 1871 | .14/.12 | .15/.15 | .12/.08 | .12/.12 | .12/.10 | 54 | .15 | .18 |
| Female: 1851 | .19/.24 | .06/.08 | .19/.18 | .22/.25 | .23/.19 | 22 | .23 | .99 |
| 1861 | .28/.29 | .14/.11 | .11/.12 | .15/.20 | .15/.16 | 27 | .29 | .06 |
| 1871 | .14/.14 | .13/.13 | .06/.05 | .16/.16 | .10/.08 | 49 | .12 | .40 |
| *7- to 12-year-olds* | | | | | | | | |
| Male: 1851 | .28/.20 | .24/.12 | .33/.24 | .33/.21 | .13/.12 | 62 | .23 | .001 |
| 1861 | .13/.13 | .18/.15 | .25/.30 | .20/.26 | .10/.10 | 73 | .14 | .001 |
| 1871 | .15/.09 | .14/.10 | .17/.09 | .19/.14 | .10/.05 | 86 | .07 | .001 |
| Female: 1851 | .22/.19 | .26/.23 | .20/.15 | .24/.19 | .10/.14 | 51 | .17 | .001 |
| 1861 | .21/.16 | .17/.10 | .20/.16 | .25/.22 | .07/.08 | 71 | .14 | .001 |
| 1871 | .17/.13 | .11/.10 | .11/.04 | .15/.15 | .11/.09 | 85 | .06 | .001 |
| *13- to 16-years olds* | | | | | | | | |
| Male: 1851 | .36/.25 | .32/.26 | .37/.27 | .39/.30 | .16/.16 | 37 | .43 | .001 |
| 1861 | .30/.23 | .19/.16 | .25/.27 | .20/.22 | .16/.19 | 60 | .31 | .01 |
| 1871 | .24/.13 | .17/.09 | .30/.16 | .34/.24 | .16/.03 | 42 | .30 | .001 |
| Female: 1851 | .37/.34 | .24/.27 | .34/.36 | .32/.27 | .18/.17 | 34 | .37 | .002 |
| 1861 | .31/.25 | .20/.25 | .34/.35 | .20/.21 | .26/.13 | 61 | .32 | .005 |
| 1871 | .17/.12 | .13/.13 | .19/.11 | .24/.20 | .12/.06 | 49 | .24 | .001 |

a. Covariates are number of relatives, number of boarders, number of servants, and age.

father/child birthplace, religion, economic rank, and occupation had a very similar association with attendance for each sex. Children/ property was considerably less important. By 1861 the primary change among both young men and women was the diminished importance of religion. At the same time the relative influence of economic rank, especially among young women, increased. Between 1861 and 1871, however, the pattern changed once again: occupation replaced economic rank as the most influential factor. Among young men economic rank came second and among females third, behind father/child birthplace. Among young men the birthplace factor was also close in importance to economic rank.

Thus two important trends emerged: the declining importance of religion (undoubtedly a result of the growth of a separate system of Catholic schools) and the increasingly independent influence of occupation considered apart from economic rank. A third and continuous pattern was the importance of the birthplace of children compared to that of their fathers. In order to understand what these trends actually meant—how, for instance, the specific occupations of their fathers affected the school attendance of children—we considered the categories of each factor variable. We examined first the analyses in which year itself was a variable and then the instances in which the patterns in specific years modify the general conclusions. Our results were expressed as the probability that a young person with a particular characteristic would attend school, with all other factors held constant.

Consider the birthplace of children compared to the birthplace of their fathers. Among 13- to 16-year-olds the native-born children of immigrants were more likely than foreign-born offspring to attend school. For the sons of Irish fathers the probabilities were 31 percent for the foreign born compared to 48 percent for the native born and 39 percent compared to 45 percent for daughters (Table 7.8). For the Scottish, the immigrant group with the highest attendance rate, the scores were 43 percent and 54 percent for males and 48 percent and 53 percent for females. Among the English they were 33 percent compared to 46 percent, and 46 percent compared to 50 percent. The same patterns existed for young (aged 5 to 6) children of Irish parents but not for those of Scottish and English parents.

Among 13- to 16-year-olds Canadian-born children of Canadian parents were most likely to attend school: 59 percent of males and 57 percent of females. However they were rather less likely than others to attend at the ages of 5 to 6. In this age group the Scottish ranked highest. Except for the relatively low probability for Irish-born children of Irish parents very little difference existed among 7- to 12-year-olds born in different places.

Table 7.8  School attendance of children aged 5–6, 7–12, and 13–16, multiple classification analysis: Hamilton, 1851–1871 (composite).

| | Males | | | Females | | |
|---|---|---|---|---|---|---|
| Variable | 5–6 | 7–12 | 13–16 | 5–6 | 7–12 | 13–16 |

A. Probability of school attendance (percent)

| | | | | | | |
|---|---|---|---|---|---|---|
| *Ethnicity of child/parent* | | | | | | |
| Irish/Irish | 23 | 64 | 31 | 38 | 59 | 39 |
| Irish/Canadian | 41 | 77 | 48 | 35 | 73 | 45 |
| Irish/other | 53 | 72 | 48 | 35 | 85 | 46 |
| Scottish/Scottish | 57 | 83 | 43 | 47 | 79 | 48 |
| Scottish/Canadian | 44 | 77 | 54 | 40 | 76 | 53 |
| Scottish/other | 33 | 79 | 44 | 35 | 70 | 42 |
| English/English | 46 | 72 | 33 | 44 | 67 | 46 |
| English/Canadian | 41 | 78 | 46 | 37 | 75 | 50 |
| English/other | 44 | 80 | 39 | 35 | 69 | 44 |
| Canadian/Canadian | 31 | 75 | 59 | 34 | 72 | 57 |
| Other/Canadian | 38 | 71 | 46 | 24 | 68 | 42 |
| Other/other | 38 | 70 | 39 | 23 | 70 | 51 |
| *Religion* | | | | | | |
| Church of England | 41 | 75 | 45 | 38 | 69 | 44 |
| Church of Scotland | 36 | 77 | 44 | 39 | 77 | 53 |
| Catholic | 34 | 71 | 41 | 30 | 70 | 46 |
| Free Church Presbyterian | 42 | 81 | 48 | 32 | 75 | 46 |
| Other Presbyterian | 33 | 82 | 51 | 36 | 76 | 54 |
| Wesleyan and other Methodist | 46 | 77 | 46 | 39 | 73 | 50 |
| Episcopal and New Connection Methodist | 32 | 65 | 41 | 40 | 68 | 62 |
| Baptist | 44 | 73 | 43 | 39 | 73 | 50 |
| Other | 45 | 77 | 49 | 34 | 75 | 51 |
| *Economic rank (percentile)* | | | | | | |
| 0–19 | 39 | 71 | 40 | 36 | 71 | 47 |
| 20–39 | 38 | 70 | 39 | 34 | 68 | 37 |
| 40–59 | 45 | 79 | 42 | 40 | 74 | 44 |
| 60–79 | 37 | 79 | 50 | 35 | 74 | 47 |
| 80–89 | 47 | 82 | 58 | 37 | 79 | 59 |
| 90–99 | 39 | 82 | 59 | 35 | 71 | 63 |
| *Occupation* | | | | | | |
| Professional | 37 | 74 | 67 | 25 | 67 | 52 |
| Gentleman | 22 | 73 | 50 | 42 | 85 | 56 |
| Commerce – high | 38 | 77 | 64 | 26 | 69 | 60 |
| Commerce – middle | 44 | 79 | 52 | 34 | 26 | 57 |
| Extractive | 59 | 85 | 64 | 53 | 68 | 21 |
| Other white collar | 46 | 75 | 53 | 37 | 79 | 52 |
| Apparel, textile, leather | 39 | 76 | 44 | 42 | 71 | 48 |
| Wood products | 39 | 79 | 59 | 24 | 79 | 58 |
| Metal products | 42 | 80 | 44 | 35 | 77 | 55 |

Table 7.8, *continued*

| Variable | Males | | | Females | | |
|---|---|---|---|---|---|---|
| | 5–6 | 7–12 | 13–16 | 5–6 | 7–12 | 13–16 |
| *Occupation* (cont.) | | | | | | |
| Food, beverages | 35 | 68 | 38 | 31 | 84 | 43 |
| Construction | 44 | 78 | 50 | 39 | 78 | 47 |
| Other manufacturing | 41 | 77 | 38 | 42 | 73 | 42 |
| Semiskilled | 37 | 77 | 42 | 40 | 69 | 45 |
| Labor | 37 | 68 | 37 | 34 | 64 | 42 |
| Widow | 58 | 86 | 30 | 24 | 64 | 40 |
| Other | 35 | 73 | 40 | 36 | 68 | 44 |
| *Property ownership and year* | | | | | | |
| Renter: 1851 | 26 | 54 | 32 | 16 | 48 | 26 |
| 1861 | 28 | 73 | 61 | 25 | 71 | 52 |
| 1871 | 51 | 85 | 42 | 50 | 82 | 51 |
| Owner: 1851 | 41 | 64 | 32 | 29 | 49 | 28 |
| 1861 | 37 | 69 | 52 | 31 | 69 | 35 |
| 1871 | 56 | 84 | 44 | 49 | 86 | 53 |

B. SUMMARY STATISTICS

*Main effects (etas/betas)*

| Variable | Males | | | Females | | |
|---|---|---|---|---|---|---|
| | 5–6 | 7–12 | 13–16 | 5–6 | 7–12 | 13–16 |
| Ethnicity of child/parent | .18/.13* | .26/.10*** | .24/.16*** | .15/.10 | .25/.11*** | .19/.09 |
| Religion | .17/.10 | .18/.08* | .18/.06 | .11/.07 | .14/.06 | .15/.08 |
| Economic rank | .12/.07 | .19/.11*** | .26/.14*** | .06/.04 | .12/.06* | .21/.14*** |
| Occupation of parent | .16/.09 | .21/.10*** | .28/.17*** | .12/.10 | .20/.13*** | .22/.12 |
| Property ownership and year | .28/.24*** | .30/.26*** | .22/19*** | .28/.27*** | .33/.30*** | .22/.20*** |

*Covariates (betas)*

| Variable | Males | | | Females | | |
|---|---|---|---|---|---|---|
| | 5–6 | 7–12 | 13–16 | 5–6 | 7–12 | 13–16 |
| Number of relatives | −.009 | −.000 | −.002 | −.038 | −.003 | .010 |
| Number of boarders | .021 | .002 | −.005 | .016 | −.005 | −.015* |
| Number of servants | .012 | .018 | .015 | .038* | .026** | .033 |
| Age of child | .228*** | .005 | −.0158*** | .248*** | .011** | −.153 |
| Number of children | .005 | .001 | −.001 | .002 | −.000 | .007*** |
| R² | .18 | .16 | .26 | .17 | .17 | .21 |
| Number | 1,497 | 3,937 | 1,824 | 1,460 | 3,728 | 1,677 |
| Grand mean | 40% | 75% | 45% | 36% | 72% | 48% |

*Significance at least .05; ** Significance at least .01; *** Significance at least .001.

The association between school attendance and native birth has two probable sources. First, the fathers of young people born in Canada had lived there substantially longer than the fathers of young people born abroad. For a young person aged 14 or 15 the difference was at least a decade and a half. These men had had longer to establish themselves and to acquire the modest amount of financial security necessary to permit their children to remain longer at school. Indeed the few pieces of evidence available show a relationship between modest prosperity and length of residence in North America. The second reason relates to the structure of the life experience of young people. Those who had been born abroad would have been out of phase with the Canadian school system. They may well have received less schooling than Canadian young people of the same age. Therefore in the local schools they would have been placed with younger pupils, subject to regulations that chafed, assigned juvenile material to read. We should expect this lack of fit between the educational level of young immigrants and North American schools to become progressively more marked throughout the late nineteenth and early twentieth centuries, for as school systems became more bureaucratic, grading by attainment became more rigid.

Religion made little difference in any group. Catholics were not especially unlikely to attend school, when other factors were controlled. The critical factors affecting the school attendance of Catholics were the existence of Catholic schools and class. The concentration of Catholics in jobs at the lowest ranks of the working class can obscure the separate influence of religion and occupation. Once Catholic schools existed, and with the influence of occupation controlled, Catholic children were as likely as any others to attend school.

Economic rank, as might be expected, clearly influenced school attendance, especially among 13- to 16-year-olds. Two basic groups existed: those above and those below the sixtieth economic percentile. Above that rank all boys aged 13 to 16 had a probability of attendance of at least 50 percent, a level not reached by girls whose fathers were below the eightieth economic percentile. However the likelihood that young women from families in the top ten economic ranks would attend school exceeded that of young men (63 percent compared to 59 percent). Similarly, at the bottom of the economic rank order the probability of attendance among young women was higher (47 percent) than among young men (40 percent).

Economic rank did not much affect the school attendance of children 5 to 6 or 7 to 12. Among 7- to 12-year-old males the probability of attendance was slightly higher above the middle of the economic rank order, but no pattern existed for girls. Among the younger children attendance was highest at the middle of the rank order for females and at the middle and in the eightieth to eighty-ninth ranks for males, though differences between categories were quite small.

Occupational as well as economic rank affected the school attendance of 13- to 16-year-olds. Professionals were most likely to send sons of this age to school (67 percent) but not as likely to send their daughters (52 percent) as men in other occupations. Those young men who were least likely to attend (30 percent) were the sons of widows, who probably depended on the income earned by their children. The probability that widows' daughters would attend was also low (40 percent).

The likelihood that children of laborers would attend school was relatively small (37 percent for males and 42 percent for females), though others had scores nearly as low, for example people in the food and beverage trades and in the "other manufacturing" category. The teenage daughters of farmers not surprisingly were the least likely (21 percent) to attend school. Conversely the probability of attendance was high among both the sons and daughters of men in high-ranking commercial occupations (64 percent and 60 percent) as well as among the children of men in middle-ranking commercial positions (primarily clerks), at 52 percent and 57 percent.

Masters and manufacturers sent a greater proportion of children to school than skilled wage workers. Their behavior in this respect resembled that of other members of the business class more closely than that of the working class. The difference is especially evident among the 15- to 19-year-olds: the probable proportion of males attending schools was 19 percent for fathers who were masters and manufacturers, compared to 7 percent for skilled wage workers. Among young women the same proportions were 24 percent and 14 percent. However, unlike professionals and merchants, masters and manufacturers sent more of their daughters than sons to school, as did business employees. Although clerks may have been unable to keep their sons in school, they did encourage their daughters to attend (and a high 33 percent did) as a preparation for the genteel occupation of teaching.

The masters and manufacturers were a divided group: one stratum consisted of well-off, secure men and the other of men who moved back and forth between proprietorship and wage work. The latter, of course, were considerably less prosperous and may have needed the income of their working sons. The more prosperous masters may have been able to offer their sons work and on-the-job training that was more valuable than schooling.

Thus two patterns emerge: first, among 13- to 16-year-olds the children of the business class (professionals, men in commercial occupations, masters and manufacturers) were more likely to attend school than children of the working class. Second, men in professions and commerce more often sent their sons than their daughters to school. With the exception of the construction trades, the pattern among children of masters, skilled wage workers, and laborers was reversed: their daughters attended more often. These patterns underline the increased connection between schooling and employment perceived by parents of the business class and the attractiveness to the children of masters and to the working class of jobs that did not require prolonged schooling. Professionals and merchants encouraged their sons to stay longer at school than their daughters probably because they felt that schooling had become increasingly important for male occupations. Conversely young working-class men left school earlier than their sisters because they could find work more easily.

Patterns differed among young children. With the exception of men in the apparel trades artisans were more likely to send their 5- to 6-year-old sons to school than their daughters. For instance the likelihood of attendance for males and females, respectively, was 39 percent and 24 percent for children of men in the wood-product trades; 42 percent and 35 percent in the metal trades; 44 percent and 39 percent in the construction trades; and 37 percent and 34 percent among laborers. Professionals, merchants, and clerks appeared even more reluctant than working-class men to send their young daughters to school; the probability of attendance for sons and daughters, respectively, was among professionals 37 percent and 25 percent and among men in high-ranking commercial occupations 38 percent and 26 percent. Thus professionals and merchants sent fewer sons or daughters to school than working-class men. Perhaps this points to the business class's lingering distrust of the socially mixed common school and their fear of committing their children at a young age. In fact the working class began to send more of its young sons to school as the business class sent fewer. Nonetheless no distinctions of significance existed among 7- to 12-year-olds. Thus business-class parents apparently hesitated to commit only their very young children to the company of the working class.

Between 1851 and 1871 the relationship between property ownership and school attendance generally disappeared for young children. In 1851 property owners were much more likely than renters to send their 5- to 6-year-olds to school (41 percent compared to 26 percent for males and 29 percent to 16 percent for females). By 1871 that distinction had vanished. By and large none of the other relationships between property and attendance were significant.

A year-by-year analysis changes the general pattern very little. The one additional factor included in the year-by-year analysis is number of children, which in general appeared to be of little influence. The greatest proportional increase in the attendance of 13- to 16-year-olds occurred among the children of the poorest parents. Between 1851 and 1871 the probability that a young man below the twentieth economic rank would attend school increased from 18 percent to 37 percent and in the twentieth to thirty-ninth ranks from 15 percent to 40 percent, compared to 52 percent and 54 percent in the eightieth to eighty-ninth ranks and 45 percent to 61 percent in the top ten percentiles. Thus in terms of percentage points the increase in the proportion of poorest and wealthiest was quite similar, and the disparity between them remained almost unaltered. By 1871 the 13- to 16-year-old daughters of the poor were about 11 percentage points more likely to attend than sons. Otherwise the patterns of increase were similar for each sex.

In general the influence of persistence on attendance was surprisingly small. The probable proportion of 15- to 19-year-old sons of male persisters attending school was 18 percent, compared to 14 percent for sons of men who had arrived during the decade. Among young women of the same age the proportions were 22 percent and 26 percent. The factor producing the largest difference was clearly sex of the head of household. The children of women who headed households and had arrived in the city during the decade were unlikely to go to school beyond the age of 14. The estimated proportion attending school was for young men and women 6 percent and 5 percent, respectively. These low proportions parallel the low attendance of the children of widows. With little paid work available widows depended on the earnings of their teenage children.

It is apparent that the probability of school attendance did not result from any single factor; the likelihood that a young person would attend school at the ages at which attendance had not become virtually universal resulted from the accumulation of a series of characteristics. Birth in Canada and a father with a high-ranking occupation and a good income boosted the likelihood that a young man would attend school. By contrast the combination of foreign birth and a father in a professional or commercial occupation decreased the probability that a girl aged 5 to 6 would go to school in any year.

We should like to offer precise predictions of the probability that a person with any set of characteristics would attend school. However the possibility of interaction between variables makes that type of prediction hazardous. Nonetheless the large differences that result from adding together the effect of certain factors cannot arise from unexamined interactions. That is, the probabilities may not be exact, but the magnitude of the distinction is certainly real.

Here are some examples. The probability of school attendance for the 13- to 16-year-old native-born son of a Scottish Presbyterian merchant in the ninetieth to ninety-ninth economic ranks who rented his home and had three or four children was 60 percent in 1851, 100 percent in 1861, and 96 percent in 1871. The probability of attendance for the 13- to 16-year-old Irish-born son of an Irish Catholic laborer in the twentieth to thirty-ninth economic ranks who rented his home and had three to four children altered from 0 in 1851 to 43 percent in 1861 to 16 percent ten years later. This is a graphic illustration of the way in which the depression of the late 1850s boosted working-class school attendance and the manner in which the expansion of job opportunities during the next decade lowered it again. The probability of school attendance among 5- to 6-year-old sons of men with characteristics identical to those already described confirms the diminished importance of class distinctions. The likelihood that the young son of a merchant would attend school altered from 24 percent to 6 percent to 54 percent during the two decades, compared to 7 percent to 26 percent to 38 percent for the son of a laborer.

It is clear that school attendance had a much closer relationship to social structure among teenagers than among very young children. However the likelihood of school attendance did not arise from class in a simple or straightforward way. For one thing it was influenced by birthplace as well. Native-born children were much more likely than the foreign born to attend, regardless of the birthplace of their parents. Sex also affected attendance. In part the relationships between sex and attendance mirrored a changing labor market: it made sense for men in the business class to keep their sons at school. Sons of the working class, on the other hand, with much more abundant job opportunities than their sisters, left school earlier. Religion affected attendance only prior to the development of Catholic schools. Though wealth promoted the attendance of older children, it had the opposite effect on young children, for the business class appeared reluctant to entrust its 5- to 6-year-olds to the common schools.

## School and Work

The nature of the labor market explains the bifurcation in the school experience of young men from different social classes that occurred during early industrialization. Vertical social mobility between the occupations of fathers and their teenage sons remained quite limited (see Chapter 5). In 1871 nearly two-thirds of sons of fathers in entrepreneurial occupations had entered nonmanual jobs. Most of the rest were skilled artisans. At the same time over three-quarters of the sons of skilled artisans and about half of the laborers' sons remained in the same occupational rank as their parents. Significantly industrialization increased the opportunity for sons of laborers to enter skilled trades, for the proportion jumped from a quarter to a third. Across all occupational levels those young men not following their fathers' occupations most often entered skilled trades: over a fourth of the sons of lower-level white-collar workers, over half the sons of semiskilled workers, and about a third of the sons of laborers.

Only a few working-class sons—at most 5 percent of laborers', 15 percent of semiskilled workers', and 12 percent of artisans'—managed to enter nonmanual work while still living at home. Thus most sons continued to inhabit the occupational world of their fathers. Those who did move into a different occupational rank, and most of the sons of skilled workers, entered the manufacturing sector of the economy, for which extended formal education was not necessary. Indeed this conclusion reinforces the general pattern of youthful employment described earlier: young men more frequently moved not only into trades but into the newer, expanding industrial opportunities. Their ability to find work in these industries in their early and mid-teens reveals the irrelevance of prolonged schooling to the type of employment to which they aspired. By contrast sons of men in higher-ranking occupations may well have prolonged their schooling to take advantage of the expanded commercial opportunities available to young men of their class.

Class of origin continued to count heavily in the early job history of young men. However ethnicity lost much of its association with class during early industrialization. In the commercial city ethnicity and class operated in a related though often independent fashion to shape the lives of young people; in the early industrial city the independent influence of ethnicity had become muted while the influence of class origins remained virtually as strong as, and perhaps more visible than, ever. Thus the combination of two factors—the expansion of industrial jobs and the customary association between the occupation of fathers and sons—explains the bifurcation in school attendance of males during early industrialization.

School attendance itself, it is important to stress, did virtually nothing to promote occupational mobility. With other factors held constant, school attendance exerted no influence on the occupation of young men traced from one decade to another.

Ethnic and class differences affected the kind of work young women as well as young men entered. Generally Catholic women born in Ireland worked most often and overall more foreign- than Canadian-born women were employed. However 57 percent of the 24-

to 26-year-old Canadian-born women of Irish Catholic origin worked in 1871, a very high proportion that reflected their low marriage rate.

Though the proportion of women working as servants declined, the decrease was not uniform. First, age played an important role: older women more often found alternatives to domestic service. Among Irish-born Catholic women, for instance, the proportion of working women who were servants in 1871 decreased from 100 percent of the 15- to 17-year-olds to 75 percent of the 18- to 20-year-olds to 70 percent of the 21- to 23-year-olds and 57 percent of the 24- to 26-year-olds. Among Canadian-born women of Scottish origin, to take another example, the proportion diminished from 61 percent for working women 15 to 17 to 31 percent of 24- to 26-year-old women.

Age aside, Irish-born Catholics were by far the most likely to be servants—roughly twice as likely as Canadian-born women of Irish Catholic origin. Foreign-born young women were in general more likely than Canadian young women to live as resident domestics. Thus at least in part Irish Catholic and other foreign-born young women probably left school earlier than others because they were either willing or forced by economic necessity to take jobs as servants.

Similar ethnic differences in the probability of working as a resident domestic servant marked the experience of Buffalo's young women. There the odds that a native-born American woman would be a domestic were nil before the age of 20 and only 2 percent at the ages of 20 to 21. By contrast the probability of working as a servant was 38 percent for Irish and 35 percent for German women aged 16 to 17 and 37 percent and 42 percent for the 18- to 19-year-olds. For Irish and German women the likelihood of becoming a servant declined after the age of 19 to 20 as they began to marry. However the odds for native-born women continued to climb, reflecting the need for work and the limitations of the job market for unmarried women. In fact native-born American women were the least likely to be married at any age. Thus the gap between them and the immigrants in the likelihood of working as a servant decreased substantially among women 26 to 27 and 28 to 29. For the latter the odds were 12 percent for an American, 18 percent for an Irish, and 14 percent for a German woman.

The nature of work affected school attendance in part through shifts in the labor market and through the connection between occupation, class, and ethnicity. At the same time it affected attendance through its irregularity. In a very real sense the rhythm of school and the rhythm of work reflected each other. No problem troubled late and mid-nineteenth-century schoolmen more than irregular attendance. Despite compulsory education laws children simply did not go to school regularly, and the actual daily attendance always remained well below the number formally enrolled. In Hamilton, for instance, in 1872 barely half the enrolled students attended each day.[29] In part attendance varied with the seasons for obvious causes: it peaked in the fall, fell away during the winter, increased in the spring to about its fall level, and finally, dropped off again during the summer. Though apparent in the attendance of children from all classes this seasonal rhythm especially marked the behavior of working-class children. Thus the statistics that show the children of both business- and working-class parents in school mask the probability that the more affluent child had attended for a longer period of time.

Obviously the effects of irregular attendance modified the impact of school attendance. Although most children attended at some point during the year, it is doubtful that many went often enough to learn very much. Thus though schooling appeared nearly universal, few children spent most of their time in school. Working-class children left school earlier and attended less regularly. In addition, as our one piece of evidence shows, they remained disproportionately concentrated in the lower grades, doubtless a consequence in part of their irregular attendance. The introduction of grading by age had been a key nineteenth-century innovation, designed, according to its sponsors, to regulate and systematize the educational process. It served another purpose too, whether intentional or not: it kept apart the social classes. The evidence comes from the Hess Street School in Hamilton for the years 1889-1891 (Table 7.9). Of the 2,632 students on the registers, 32 percent were in grade seven or above and 44 percent in the kindergarten and first three grades. Most of the students came from either lower-business-class (18 percent), skilled (45 percent), or semiskilled (12 percent) families. Only 8 percent were children of laborers and 6 percent children of professionals or proprietors; the parents of 4 percent were widows. The distribution of children throughout the grades did not reflect the social composition of the school, for the children of laborers were greatly underrepresented among students in the higher grades: 13 percent compared to 39 percent of children of professionals and proprietors. Conversely 29 percent of the latter's children compared to 44 percent of the former's were in the first three grades. Given these disproportions the age range of children in various grades differed according to their social class. The ages of skilled manual workers' children in grades one to three, for instance, varied from 5 to 12, in contrast to 6 to 10 for those whose fathers were professionals and proprietors. It was unusual, in fact, for a working-class child to progress beyond grade six.

Schoolmen often attributed the poor achievement of working-class

Table 7.9   Students of Hess Street Public School, Hamilton, by occupational rank of parents, 1889–1891.

| | Occupational rank | | | | | | |
|---|---|---|---|---|---|---|---|
| Grade | 1 | 2 | 3 | 4 | 5 | Other (widow) | Total |
| Kindergarten | 8.8% | 21.3% | 13.8% | 12.9% | 13.6% | 11.8% | 14.7% |
| 1–3 | 28.8 | 22.9 | 28.0 | 36.0 | 43.6 | 14.7 | 28.9 |
| 4–6 | 23.1 | 20.0 | 24.7 | 25.6 | 29.5 | 24.5 | 24.2 |
| 7 and over | 39.4 | 35.8 | 33.5 | 25.6 | 13.2 | 49.0 | 32.1 |
| Total | 5.6 | 17.8 | 44.6 | 12.4 | 7.7 | 3.5 | 100.0 |
| AGE RANGE | | | | | | | |
| Kindergarten | 5–6 | 4–7 | 4–7 | 4–7 | 5–7 | 5–7 | 4–7 |
| 1–3 | 6–10 | 5–14 | 5–12 | 5–12 | 5–14 | 5–12 | 5–14 |
| 4–6 | 8–14 | 7–14 | 7–14 | 7–14 | 7–15 | 8–14 | 7–15 |
| 7 and over | 9–17 | 10–16 | 10–16 | 10–16 | 9–15 | 10–16 | 9–17 |
| N =2,632 | | | | | | | |

SOURCE: Compiled from daily attendance registers, Hess Street Public School, 1889–1891.

children to their irregular attendance, which they blamed on the neglect, indifference, and carelessness of their parents. However these moralistic explanations missed the point: the connection between the rhythm of work and the rhythm of school. Those factors that contributed to poverty and economic insecurity—trade depressions, crop failure, transient work patterns, and seasonal employment—largely determined the irregularity of attendance in Hamilton and indeed throughout the province.

One of these factors deserves special mention: the transiency that characterized nineteenth-century society. Time and again, as we noted in Chapter 3, not only young men but families were on the move, and the poor moved most often. Inability to find work, seasonal unemployment, and economic depression all promoted the continual movement of working people from one place to another. Of course transiency militated against regular school attendance. Many young people simply lived too short a time in any one place to attend school very often or very long.

## Marriage and Class

Marriage as well as school attendance increasingly reflected the diverging social class responses to the creation of an industrial capitalist society. In 1851 not much difference existed in the marital patterns of men with different occupations, with the exception of clerks below the age of 30, who were least likely to be married. However by 1871 new distinctions had emerged. Men in professional, commercial, and clerical occupations were beginning to postpone marriage, while laborers were beginning to marry earlier. For instance among 21- to 23-year-olds between 13 percent and 10 percent of men in the two nonmanual occupational categories had married, compared to 37 percent of laborers; by the age of 30 to 32, 52 percent and 65 percent of the two nonmanual groups and 85 percent of the laborers had married. The marriage practices of skilled and semiskilled workers resembled those of the laborers more than the clerks, merchants, and professionals.

It is possible, of course, that occupational differences in marriage reflected cultural rather than class distinctions. The divergent ethnic structure of various occupations rather than social stratification may have created these patterns. Multivariate analysis, however, enables us to discount this possibility. The association of occupation with marriage remained consistently higher than that of any other variable, including birthplace, religion, and in 1871 ethnic origin (Table 7.10).

More striking, all other factors held constant, the likelihood that a laborer would marry early more than doubled, a sharp difference from patterns among any other group. In 1871 the probability that a 21- to 23-year-old clerk would be married was 11 percent, compared to 37 percent for a laborer; at the ages of 24 to 26 the likelihood of marriage was 30 percent for clerks and 58 percent for laborers. By contrast if a man had been born in Ireland his likelihood of marriage would have been reduced by five percentage points and if born in Ontario by two percentage points, effects less important than those associated with occupation.

From 1851 to 1871 clerks remained less likely to marry early than men with most other occupations: among 27- to 29-year-olds, for instance, a clerical occupation reduced the probability of marriage for a man, compared to the average, by 47 percent in 1851 and 1861 and 24 percent in 1871. In 1871 in fact professionals married latest: the probability of marriage for professionals aged 27 to 29 was a striking 34 percent less than the average, compared to only 5 percent less twenty years earlier. Thus the increasing influence of class on marriage showed in the pronouncedly earlier marriage of laborers and a few other manual workers and the progressively later marriage of clerks and especially professionals. At the same time no religion made any significant difference in marriage age, and only Scottish birth acted consistently and independently to retard the age of marriage.

One other factor exerted a significant influence on marriage age in 1871: illiteracy. In three out of four age groups illiterates married

Table 7.10  Probability of marriage among men in selected occupational and literacy groups, all factors constant: Hamilton, 1851 and 1871.[a]

| Group | Age 21–23 | | Age 24–26 | | Age 27–29 | | Age 30–32 | |
|---|---|---|---|---|---|---|---|---|
| | 1851 | 1871 | 1851 | 1871 | 1851 | 1871 | 1851 | 1871 |
| *Occupation* | | | | | | | | |
| High commercial | .05 | .13 | .60 | .27 | .63 | .67 | .70 | .62 |
| Clerical | .08 | .11 | .38 | .30 | .48 | .59 | .75 | .65 |
| Apparel, textile, leather | .27 | .21 | .48 | .44 | .60 | .44 | .73 | .66 |
| Metal trades | .19 | .16 | .39 | .41 | .75 | .66 | .95 | .78 |
| Construction | .20 | .20 | .50 | .46 | .67 | .63 | .75 | .86 |
| Labor | .16 | .37 | .50 | .58 | .66 | .68 | .70 | .83 |
| *Literacy* | | | | | | | | |
| Literate | NA | .17 | NA | .41 | NA | .61 | NA | .74 |
| Illiterate or semiliterate | NA | .35 | NA | .29 | NA | .95 | NA | .89 |
| Grand mean | .15 | .17 | .39 | .41 | .60 | .62 | .68 | .74 |

a. Derived from multiple classification analysis, with marriage divided into age groups as dependent variable. In 1851 factor variables were occupational group, religion, and birthplace; in 1871 they were occupational group, religion, birthplace, origin, and literacy. In each year age was covariate. All main effects were significant at better than .05. NA = not available.

earlier. The few illiterate 21- to 23-year-olds were more than twice as likely as those who could read and write to have married. The difference persisted in older groups too. The 27- to 29-and 30- to 32-year-old illiterates were, respectively, 34 percent and 15 percent more likely to be married than the literates of the same ages.

Increasingly cut off from traditional communal restraints and rural practices, young laborers could enter the job market earlier than before, earn a living wage, and marry sooner than they could have in a rural or nonindustrial urban setting. By contrast aspiring clerks and professionals adopted a rational, calculated mode of behavior appropriate to their later age of entry into the job market, initial low wages, and precarious early careers. The difference in marriage patterns underscores the distinction between men who saw in their future careers rewards that made the postponement of marriage necessary and worthwhile and men who quite rightly believed that they would never increase their earnings substantially. Though forced to accept the discipline of industrial work habits and public education workers nonetheless managed to evade some of the culture of capitalism. No amount of rhetoric could turn a job into a career or mask the fact that the man of 23 earned as much as or more than a man two score years his senior. If saving and postponing pleasure made sense to the clerk or the professional, it did not to the early industrial laborer. Each man responded appropriately and realistically to his place in a shifting social and economic order.

## Conclusion

In Hamilton from 1851 to 1871 young people remained increasingly longer at home, went more often to school, and married at about the same age as before or very slightly earlier. At the same time ethnicity and class cut across these general trends: working-class young men and women welcomed the expansion of industrial opportunity; the former left school to work while the latter left domestic service whenever possible. The emerging industrial proletariat married earlier than had laborers in the commercial city.

In the commercial city gross educational inequalities existed: many poor children received almost no exposure to schooling. By contrast, during industrialization this situation changed dramatically: by 1871 schooling for children between the ages of 7 and 12 had become nearly universal, and many more young people over the age of 12 attended school. Did this development represent an increase in equality of opportunity? The answer is clearly no.

First, the economic benefits of school attendance accrue from the differential advantage it bestows. That is, two levels of educational attainment always coexist: that reached by most people and that reached by a fortunate minority. It is the distance between the two rather than their intrinsic qualities that counts. If only 5 percent of the population graduates from high school, then a high school diploma confers the first and greatest advantage in the search for employment. When everyone has graduated from high school, it is a B.A. degree that counts, and so on. Although children of manual workers began to go to school in greater numbers and for longer periods of time in mid-nineteenth-century Hamilton, the children of more affluent parents stayed at school even longer. They preserved their lead and reaped the differential advantage of longer school attendance. Thus the sheer increment in the number of years a working-class child attended school did nothing to increase the tangible occupational benefit that he or she received from school.

More than that the pattern and structure of school attendance undercut some of the potential benefits of formal education, for working-class children attended school less regularly and were more likely than affluent young people of the same age to be found in the lower grades. Thus they not only left school earlier but during the years they did attend working-class children received less exposure to school and generally did not reach the highest educational levels.

In these circumstances schooling could not be expected to do very much to promote social mobility. Indeed both the analysis of the influence of school attendance on occupation and our comparison of the occupations of fathers and children support this contention. Children of professionals, merchants, and clerks generally entered commercial or clerical occupations. If schooling had become increasingly necessary for entrance into clerical or commercial jobs, then affluent parents used the expanded educational facilities to prepare their sons to retain their customary occupational advantage. Similarly they used the schools to prepare their daughters for the one genteel occupation open to women: teaching.

Young men from working-class families, on the other hand, generally entered manual occupations. In many instances their jobs probably were better than those of their fathers, especially those of young men who managed to enter the newer, more dynamic sectors of the economy or of the substantial proportion of laborers' sons who became skilled manual workers. However education had not contributed to their occupational improvement. Its unimportance is reflected in the fact that working-class boys began to leave school earlier in order to work; employers clearly did not require prolonged schooling. Thus any improvement in the prospects of young men compared to those of their fathers should be credited to the expansion and industrialization of the economy rather than to the extension and modernization of schooling.

Industrialization increased the job opportunities for young men. More than ever they had the financial ability to leave home and fend for themselves. If industrialization worked as many of its interpreters would lead one to expect, that is what should have happened. Ties between parents and children should have diminished; children should have lived at home for shorter periods and experienced increased friction in their relationships with their parents. It is difficult to measure the quality of relationships but easier to estimate their duration. A sizable increase in the length of time children lived with their parents accompanied early industrialization. Instead of leaving home when they found work young people increasingly lived with their families for years, in many instances as much as a decade. Young people, we suspect, began to live at home longer than at any previous time in Western history.

This development is especially remarkable because, as Michael Anderson has pointed out, an increasing variety of alternatives existed within the city.[30] Boarding had been a customary practice, and it would be no more difficult than before to arrange. And the development of lodging houses meant that a young person could live alone with far less supervision than under more traditional arrangements. Added to this were the relatively high wages paid to young people, which would allow men at any rate to support themselves. Given these circumstances the prolonged residence of young people in the home of their parents reflects a conscious choice, not an adaptation to necessity. Young people apparently lived at home at least in part because they wanted to. Thus it is reasonable to suppose that during early industrialization ties between parents and their teenage children actually grew stronger.

The presence of working children affected the economic condition of the family as a whole. The impact of industrialization on the standard of living remains a fiercely contested issue, and there is even less evidence assembled in Canada than elsewhere on which to base a conclusion. From one point of view workers testified that wages and security of employment decreased during the early stages of industrialization. On the other hand working-class home ownership increased a bit, and the proportion of the work force in unskilled laboring jobs decreased. Whatever the experience of individual workers no answer to the question of what happened to the standard of living is adequate if it does not account for the income of the entire family unit. It is reasonable to suppose that the income from employed, resident children increased the prosperity of working-class families for a substantial portion of their existence.

The prolonged residence of children within the homes of their parents brings us, finally, to a third general point: the alteration in the life stages through which a young person passed. Earlier practices in Hamilton reflected the last gasp of a long-standing custom that cut across social classes. For centuries parents had customarily sent their children to live between puberty and marriage as a member of another household. During early industrialization this practice became less common. By contemporary standards the years between puberty and marriage gradually assumed a more familiar cast. Young people spent most of their lives before marriage in the home of their parents. Whether this new stage can be called adolescence hinges partly on a question of definition. The characteristic feature of adolescence as a concept is not its recognition of the years between puberty and marriage as a special stage but, as Kett has pointed out, its definition of youths as creatures whose "whole being" is "determined by a biological process of maturation."[31] This concept became current in the late nineteenth and early twentieth centuries, when social commentators found it necessary to coin a new phase to correspond to a new stage in the lives of young people. The prolonged dependency of young people on their parents and their increased education in specialized age-segregated institutions formed the basis for recognizing adolescence. *Adolescence*, we would argue, may be defined as a phase of institutionalized dependency that came to characterize the experience of youth in the nineteenth century. It proceeded, as do many social changes, in an uneven fashion. It was first evident among the affluent, spreading, sometimes over fierce opposition, downward through the social ranks as working-class children began to attend high school and eventually college. Thus the origins of behavior we have come to associate with adolescence may lie not in puberty but in the reaction to dependency, in the curious new conflict between biological maturity and cultural childhood that nineteenth-century society inflicted on its youth. Adolescence, as we know it, is a product of culture and of history.

# 8 Families: Cycle, Structure, and Economy

Three attributes characterize all families: a cycle, a structure, and an economy. Families all pass through a sequence of stages from formation through dissolution; all are formed by a set of relationships between people with different roles and statuses; and all must acquire and allocate the means for their subsistence. The similarities do not imply the lack of historical change in domestic organization. Rather these three attributes have assumed different forms and related in various ways to one another. According to Peter Laslett the Western family, for as far in the past as historians have been able to determine, has been defined by "the simultaneous presence during the period of primary socialization of . . . four . . . separable but interdependent characteristics." These are, first, the "shape and membership of the familial group," in the West "confined for the most part to the parents and children themselves, what is called the nuclear family form." Second, mothers have had children "rather late, both in the life experience of the mother and also in the period of fecundity." Third, the age gap between husbands and wives has consisted of a "relatively few" years "with a relatively high proportion of wives older than their husbands, and marriage tending towards the companionate." Fourth has been "the presence as fully recognized members in a significant proportion of households of persons not belonging to the immediate family or even to the kin," primarily servants, whose prevalence points to a Western "peculiarity in the individual life cycle of those who went out to service as well as a characteristic of the domestic groups."[1] It is the simultaneous presence of these characteristics, Laslett stresses, not any one of them individually, that has marked the Western family. Laslett is unclear about when this configuration arose or why, but he does believe that it began to erode with industrialism in the nineteenth century.[2]

Insofar as we can tell the characteristics that Laslett outlines existed in modified form in North America. Marriage age appears to have been a few years younger for women, and fewer women were older than their husbands. As we have seen, a modified form of life-cycle service existed in the commercial capitalist city, and its more traditional form does appear to have existed in at least some places in Colonial America. The nuclearity of the family is a point of contention, a question of definition as much as it is an empirical question.

We prefer to argue that the development of the nuclear household (a word we use deliberately as distinct from *family*) was one of five major changes that took place in the organization of family life during the development of industrial capitalism. The other four were the separation of home and work (also emphasized by Laslett), the prolonged period during which children lived in the home of their parents, the decline in marital fertility, and the prolonged period during which husbands and wives lived together after their youngest child left home. The first four of these changes had begun to happen in Hamilton by the early years of industrialization.[3]

### The Family Cycle

The family cycle begins with the formation of the family through marriage. Throughout the years between 1851 and 1871 the average age at marriage for men in Hamilton was 27 and for women 23. These figures were identical in Buffalo and throughout Erie County.[4] By contrast in the English cases reported by Laslett women married between the ages of 25 and 27 and men a few years later.[5] In this respect the North American pattern diverged quite sharply, though marriage still came several years after the onset of puberty and can by no means be called early. Very likely scarcity of land, inheritance practices, and the consequent problem of acquiring the means of a livelihood delayed marriage in England. All of these factors operated with relatively less intensity in the more abundant setting of the New World. Indeed evidence from Colonial New England points to an earlier marriage age from the very beginning of settlement.[6]

Because marriage came earlier, women bore their first child at a younger age than in seventeenth- or eighteenth-century England. Again the figures for Hamilton in each year and for Buffalo and the rest of Erie County—estimated crudely by subtracting the age of the eldest child from the age of mothers under 30—was identical—22. This finding is, of course, different from that in England, where marriage took place later. Although class differences in marriage age were emerging in Hamilton, they had not yet begun to affect the estimates for age at the birth of the first child, although the proportion of women in Hamilton who had given birth to their first child before they were 20 years old rose from 16 percent in 1851 to 20 percent two decades later, and the proportion bearing a child before the age of 22 rose from 42 percent to 49 percent during the same period.[7]

The trend toward earlier marriage may have been even more pronounced than the figures show. The reason is that the trends in the residential experience of young people should have militated against early marriage. As we have seen, young men who lived as boarders married earlier than men of the same age who remained in the home of their parents. Since the proportion of young men living as boarders declined notably between 1851 and 1871, it might be thought that marriage age would rise. Thus the modest trend toward earlier marriage assumes greater significance in view of the prolonged coresidence of parents and children.

"The substantial proportion of female spouses older than male spouses," writes Laslett, "ranging from one-fifth to one-quarter, I believe, must establish itself as the most consistent indicator of 'Westerness' in familial matters."[8] In Hamilton the proportion was considerably lower (about 14 percent to 16 percent), though still a noteworthy minority. The reason for the differences may rest in sex ratios. Laslett does not give the sex ratios for the villages on which he bases his conclusion, but it is reasonable to imagine that they might be relatively balanced or show an excess of young men.[9] There is no reason to suppose that young women would have in-migrated in large numbers, though there is indication that they sometimes moved to cities more often than men. Indeed in Hamilton there was a large excess of young women over young men in the most marriageable age groups. The implication of this fact is that in English villages men would have a restricted number of younger women from whom to choose a marriage partner and often might have to turn to a widow in order to find a mate. Widows who had property might have been sought by young men, and as Michael Drake has shown in his study of Norway, men wishing to limit the size of their families might choose to marry widows, who had fewer fecund years remaining.[10] In Hamilton, by contrast, young men wishing to marry had more than a sufficient number of young women from whom to choose.

The choice of categories with which to describe the experience of families is partially arbitrary, and as with occupational classification the scheme selected obviously affects the results. Our classification is based on the age of women, since the cycle is connected so closely with the age of children. Three stages immediately come to mind: young families who do not yet have children, families with children, and families whose children all have left home. Another obvious category consists of those women who have passed their child-bearing years; the conventionally employed age of 45 marks the start of this period.

Given the analytical purposes the categories should serve, we felt that it was important to distinguish between phases of the cycle in which families would be under the greatest and the least financial strain. The greatest strain would occur when all children were young. The periods of least strain should be those when no children lived at home or when at least one child was old enough to contribute to the family income. Another significant division separated families all of whose working-age children were female. We suspected that the expectations placed on young women in these families would be different from those placed on girls who had working-age brothers living at home; and this indeed proved to be the case. The application of these principles yielded twelve family-cycle categories.

The proportion of families in each category was relatively stable throughout the period, with the exception of shifts owing to the general aging of the population.[11] The most notable discovery was that the proportion of late-cycle families without children (by and large, we assume, families whose children had left home) more than doubled, from 3 percent to 7 percent of the total, and the proportion of late-cycle families as a whole rose from 18 percent to 28 percent. Similarly the proportion of young families with children aged 1 to 6 declined from 8 percent to 6 percent. A plurality of families (33 percent in 1851, 30 percent in 1861, and 25 percent in 1871) were in the early midcycle, with all children under the age of 15. A substantial fraction of families—about 17 percent—had at least one male or female child of working age. The proportion of families without children remained quite constant, with the exception of late-cycle families noted above, and thus probably resulted from infertility rather than family planning (Table 8.1).

In Buffalo the proportion of families in which the wife was over 45 was 16 percent, quite close to that in Hamilton in 1851. However it was higher in the villages (23 percent) and on the farms (33 percent). The higher figures in the latter two areas undoubtedly reflect the longer average residence of households compared to Buffalo and also to Hamilton, which in 1851 had a young and newly recruited population. In Buffalo 16 percent of households had been in the city a year or less, compared to 10 percent of the farmers; 33 percent had been in the city ten years or more, compared to 53 percent of the farmers. The category in which the most pronounced difference existed between country and city was late-cycle families (wife aged 45 or more) with at least one son aged 15 or over at home. In Hamilton between 10 percent and 14 percent of families were in this category, in Buffalo 9

Table 8.1  Characteristics of households, by family cycle: Hamilton, 1851–1871.

| Family characteristics | Year | N | Percent |
|---|---|---|---|
| *Young (wife under 25)* | | | |
| (1) No children | 1851 | 98 | 5.0 |
| | 1861 | 111 | 3.6 |
| | 1871 | 187 | 4.3 |
| (2) All children aged 1-6 | 1851 | 160 | 8.2 |
| | 1861 | 188 | 5.9 |
| | 1871 | 252 | 5.7 |
| *Early midcycle (wife 25–34)* | | | |
| (3) No children | 1851 | 115 | 5.9 |
| | 1861 | 185 | 6.0 |
| | 1871 | 246 | 5.6 |
| (4) All children aged 1–14 | 1851 | 636 | 32.5 |
| | 1861 | 927 | 30.2 |
| | 1871 | 1,079 | 24.5 |
| *Late midcycle (wife 35–44)* | | | |
| (5) No children | 1851 | 64 | 3.3 |
| | 1861 | 102 | 3.3 |
| | 1871 | 168 | 3.8 |
| (6) All children aged 1–14 | 1851 | 250 | 12.8 |
| | 1861 | 396 | 12.9 |
| | 1871 | 596 | 13.6 |
| (7) At least one male child 15 or over | 1851 | 133 | 6.8 |
| | 1861 | 230 | 7.5 |
| | 1871 | 371 | 8.4 |
| (8) All children 15 or over female | 1851 | 87 | 4.4 |
| | 1861 | 109 | 3.6 |
| | 1871 | 191 | 4.3 |
| *Late cycle (wife 45 or over)* | | | |
| (9) At least one male child 15 or over | 1851 | 202 | 10.3 |
| | 1861 | 409 | 13.3 |
| | 1871 | 639 | 14.5 |
| (10) All children 15 or over female | 1851 | 96 | 4.9 |
| | 1861 | 176 | 5.7 |
| | 1871 | 254 | 5.8 |
| (11) No children | 1851 | 67 | 3.4 |
| | 1861 | 153 | 5.0 |
| | 1871 | 316 | 7.2 |
| (12) Other | 1851 | 48 | 2.5 |
| | 1861 | 86 | 2.8 |
| | 1871 | 97 | 2.2 |

percent, and on Erie County farms 20 percent. This reflects the larger number of older families rather than a greater propensity for farmers' sons to stay at home, because the mean number of male children aged 15 or over living with families in this cycle category was identical (1.5) in city, village, and farm.

The family cycle ended with dissolution, most often the result of death. In fact widowhood formed a significant part of the life cycle of many women. In Hamilton 72 percent of all the people who lost a spouse between 1861 and 1871 were women. A third of all women over the age of 50 traced throughout the decade lost a spouse, compared to 16 percent of the men. The differences were also quite large at other ages: less than 1 percent of men and 7 percent of women aged 20 to 29, 3 percent of men and 11 percent of women aged 30 to 39, and 9 percent of men and 21 percent of women aged 40 to 49. The experience of widowers and widows also differed. Men were often able to remarry: all three men in their twenties who were widowed during the decade remarried, compared to four of the eight women; half the men in their forties who had been widowed remarried, compared to 6 percent of the women. Thus women were much more likely to be widowed than men and much less likely to remarry, patterns that provide a demographic basis for the concern with widows evident in nineteenth-century philanthropy, as in the case of the Hamilton Ladies' Benevolent Society, the city's major charitable organization.[12]

In families traced for a decade the actual changes in the number of children living at home reinforce the patterns to which cross-sectional life-cycle categories point. In 1851, for instance, 40 percent of the families in which the household head was less than 30 years old had no children, compared to 11 percent of the same families a decade later; for the next decade the comparable proportions were 29 percent and 13 percent. At the other end of the family cycle 12 percent of household heads aged 50 or over in 1851 had no children, compared to 26 percent in 1861; between 1861 and 1871 the proportion among people of the same age rose from 16 percent to 37 percent. In fact, as should be expected, the proportion of childless household heads began to increase among those in their forties at the start of each decade.

Thus the family cycle changed very little in Hamilton between 1851 and 1871. Marriage may have begun to occur somewhat earlier, but the major shifts in the proportion of families at different points in their cycles reflected the aging of the population, which had been unusually young in 1851, rather than any shift in habits. Similarly, differences in age combined with length of residence account for distinctions between Buffalo and Erie County towns and villages. The situation in Buffalo, moreover, resembled that in Hamilton quite closely. Most married couples had children living with them throughout the greater portion of their married life.

Because women commonly bore children until the close of their fecund years, and because death came earlier than it does today, an extraordinarily high proportion of children could expect to be orphaned before they reached adulthood, and very few people knew their grandparents. For example consider a couple married when the wife was 23 and the husband 27, the mean ages throughout this period. Assuming a birth interval of about thirty months, the woman bore six children, of whom four survived infancy and early childhood. The last child was born when she was 40, the penultimate one when she was 37. If both children lived and their parents died at the age of 60, then one of the living children would be orphaned before the age of 21 and the other would lose his or her father before that age. That is, half of the couple's living offspring could expect to lose at least one parent before adulthood. Furthermore if two of the four children were female, married at the age of 23, and had four surviving children, the couple's first grandchild—assuming their eldest child to be a daughter —would be born when its grandmother was 48 and its grandfather 52. If two or more of the surviving children were born in the next eight years, then three out of four would know both grandparents, and possibly all four would know their grandmother. Assuming the next eldest child to be a son born after the death of one child and married at the age of 27, his first child would be born after his father had died and when his mother was in her mid-fifties. Thus of their sixteen grandchildren the husband of the original couple could expect to know perhaps three and the wife five.

In addition these assumptions do not take into account the possible geographical mobility of any of the family members; it is unlikely that all of the surviving children would remain in the same place as their parents. Together demographic constraints and geographic mobility severely limited the number of married couples who might take a living parent into their household. Of course the proportions derived from this example should not be taken as accurate statistical probabilities applicable to the entire population. Nonetheless none of the features of the example are improbable, and all reflect the averages derived from the population as a whole. They show why we should expect to find few three-generation families, why few couples could expect to live together alone after their children had left home, why very many children would be orphans, and why only a small proportion of people could expect to know their grandparents.

Orphanage is a subject about which little is known.[13] How many orphans went to live with kin or relatives, how many became the wards of public or private orphan asylums are questions whose answers remain obscure. Certainly the establishment of orphanages in nineteenth-century cities hints that an increased number, if not a majority of young children had nowhere to turn after the death of their parents. In Hamilton the Ladies' Committee of the Hamilton Orphan Asylum attempted to apprentice orphans to families for the duration of their minority.[14] The families were supposed to care for the children and to deposit a sum each year into a bank account on their behalf. The records of the asylum make it difficult to estimate just how well the children were treated. Some ran away, a very few complained of harsh treatment, but in most cases the books show the payment of the annual deposit year after year. And in a number of cases the arrangements obviously worked well. Indeed some families actually adopted the child they had apprenticed.

Consider the following case, which speaks eloquently of the affection within a working-class family at this time, the anxieties of parents, and the particular problems of women. When only a little over 2 years old in 1881 Minnie Nichol was apprenticed to John L. Tomlinson, a molder who lived at 107 McNab Street and later moved to Toronto, living at three different addresses there during the next eight years. The Tomlinsons almost immediately adopted Minnie, whom they baptized Edna May Tomlinson. On August 23, 1889, Mrs. Mary Tomlinson wrote to the head of the Ladies' Committee of the orphanage:

Dear Madam

I am sending you $4.00 on my little Daughter's account and would like to have sent more but could not on account of my Husband being sick for nearly 2 weeks which leaves us rather short of funds, however, I hope to get it settled as soon as possible then on the new year pay in advance you will hear from me again on the 23 of Septbr.

We are paying for a . . . piano for Edna and giving her a good Musical education so that if anything should happen to her Papa or I she will be able to earn a living for herself and be independent of the world of course she knows no different but that we are her own parents we love her dearly and could not part with her unless called away to another world . . .

Mary Tomlinson[15]

## Family Structure and the Family Cycle

The major reinterpretation of family structure in recent years did not account for the family cycle. Peter Laslett's assertion that most

Western families were at all times nuclear rested on aggregate figures that did not break down family structure by age.[16] As his critics have pointed out, most families could have incorporated extensions at certain points in their cycles. This was the case with the Austrian peasant families studied by Lutz Berkner and with the working-class families in nineteenth-century Lancashire reconstructed by Michael Anderson.[17]

Laslett himself in a recent book notes the force of the objection that he has ignored the family cycle in his discussions of family structure. "A household has a higher probability of containing the parents or a parent of the spouses at the stage of family formation than it has in later years, when these parents are likely to be dead, and this possibility is higher again at the stage when offspring are themselves getting married. It follows that the proportion of simple family households at any one time, in any one list of inhabitants, is not a direct measure of the propensity for any household in that community to be extended or multiple at some point in its domestic cycle." The problem with estimating that probability is that lists are drawn up at "isolated points in time" and do not permit one to follow individual households throughout their histories.[18]

Why might it be expected that the composition of the domestic group has altered with the family cycle? A variety of answers are possible. One is that in some places, such as mid-nineteenth-century Lancashire, it was obviously common for young people to live with their parents for a short time after marriage.[19] This pattern probably characterized areas with a shortage of housing.[20] Certainly in other places it was common for elderly or infirm parents to live with their married children. Because parents had more than one child and because death came relatively early, only a small minority of married couples would have a parent living with them at any one point.[21]

From a different perspective, changes in domestic organization could reflect the economic requirements of the family. At certain points of strain—for example when children were young—a female relative, often a mother, might live with a family in order to permit the wife to work outside the home. Or on peasant farms the labor requirements of families with young children could require the incorporation into the household of individuals who could participate in the operation of the farm.[22] Extending this line of argument, and assuming, as most studies have shown to be the case, that one working-class income was not sufficient to support a family, working-class families with young children might have supplemented the family income through the incorporation of boarders or kin who could contribute in some way.[23] Similarly we should expect to find the fewest kin or the smallest proportion of boarders among those families with the least economic need, namely either those with no children or with children of working age. Finally, given the paucity of job opportunities for women and the underdevelopment of life insurance, we should expect to find women who headed households especially likely to have people other than children dwelling with them.

As it happens only the last of these expectations is met fully by the situation in Hamilton. Some relationships between life cycle and domestic organization (defined as the number and identity of people living together) did exist, but they were by and large minor and sometimes contrary to expectation.

The first aspect of family structure that stands out is the reduction in the proportion of families with either a relative or a boarder (Table 8.2). Between 1851 and 1871 this reduction primarily affected families in the young, early mid-, and late midcycles and was most pronounced among the first two. Younger families, it would appear, had begun to alter their behavior during this period. (One might expect the reduction in coresident relatives and boarders to appear among families in later stages of the life cycle as these young families, among whom the change began, aged). The proportion of young families with small children who had boarders dropped from 35 percent to 15 percent between 1851 and 1871; the proportion with relatives declined from 17 percent to 7 percent; and the proportion with either a boarder or relative dipped from 46 percent to 21 percent. By contrast the proportion of late-cycle families with at least one male 15 years old or over who had a boarder shifted from 23 percent to 22 percent; the proportion with a relative dipped from 13 percent to 7 percent and with either a boarder or relative, from 34 percent to 26 percent.[24]

The proportion with an elderly relative coresiding was quite small in each year. However two patterns are evident. Three or four times as many families included elderly females as males, and families in the young or early midcycle stages without children were the most likely to contain an elderly female relative. In 1851 9 percent of the young families with no children had a coresiding female relative aged 40 or over, as did 7 percent of childless families in the early midcycle. By 1871 these proportions had dropped to 4 percent and 2 percent. The 4 percent was still the highest for any category of family.

Even fewer families at any point in the family cycle had a very young coresiding relative (aged 1 to 4), either male or female. The only point at which the proportion rose above 1 percent or 2 percent with any consistency was among the late-cycle families with children of working age in 1861, where it reached about 5 percent. Perhaps this was a reflection of family problems caused by the depression. Coresident relatives aged 15 to 19 and 20 to 29, both male and female, were

Table 8.2  Proportion of households with relatives or boarders, by life-cycle categories: Hamilton, 1851–1871.

| Life-cycle category | Percent with boarders | | | Percent with relatives | | | Percent with either boarders or relatives | | |
|---|---|---|---|---|---|---|---|---|---|
| | 1851 | 1861 | 1871 | 1851 | 1861 | 1871 | 1851 | 1861 | 1871 |
| *Young (wife under 25)* | | | | | | | | | |
| (1) No children | 30 | 19 | 18 | 30 | 24 | 9 | 49 | 38 | 25 |
| (2) All children aged 1–6 | 35 | 18 | 15 | 17 | 19 | 7 | 46 | 39 | 21 |
| *Early midcycle (wife 25–34)* | | | | | | | | | |
| (3) No children | 44 | 22 | 29 | 23 | 24 | 9 | 55 | 39 | 36 |
| (4) All children aged 1–14 | 32 | 19 | 19 | 15 | 14 | 5 | 41 | 30 | 23 |
| *Late midcycle (wife 35–44)* | | | | | | | | | |
| (5) No children | 39 | 23 | 34 | 12 | 16 | 9 | 47 | 35 | 40 |
| (6) All children aged 1–14 | 24 | 20 | 18 | 12 | 11 | 4 | 33 | 28 | 20 |
| (7) At least one male child 15 or over | 22 | 17 | 17 | 9 | 10 | 5 | 29 | 26 | 22 |
| (8) All children 15 or over female | 26 | 19 | 18 | 6 | 12 | 2 | 32 | 30 | 20 |
| *Late cycle (wife 45 or over)* | | | | | | | | | |
| (9) At least one male child 15 or over | 23 | 18 | 22 | 13 | 15 | 7 | 34 | 30 | 26 |
| (10) All children 15 or over female | 24 | 23 | 28 | 15 | 22 | 6 | 36 | 40 | 33 |
| (11) No children | 36 | 25 | 35 | 4 | 16 | 6 | 39 | 35 | 39 |
| (12) Other | 25 | 29 | 24 | 2 | 7 | 4 | 27 | 35 | 26 |

somewhat more common, especially in 1851 and 1861 (4 percent to 7 percent of families in most of the young and early-cycle categories). By 1871 the numbers had dropped quite dramatically, in only a couple instances going as high as 3 percent.

By and large few families contained married children. Among families in the late midcycle with children aged 15 or over at most 2 percent in any category in one year had a married child living with them. Late-cycle families had somewhat more, though the rate had declined by 1871. In 1851, 7 percent of late-cycle families with at least one son aged 15 or over had a married son at home, and 8 percent had a married daughter. By 1871 those proportions had dropped to 5 percent and nil, respectively. For families with only females aged 15 or over at home (6 percent in 1851) a quite high 16 percent in 1861 and 2 percent ten years later had a married daughter at home. Probably a slight squeeze on housing supply had boosted the proportion in 1851; the depression raised the number in 1861 in spite of a housing surplus; by 1871 the combination of prosperity and plentiful housing allowed virtually all married children to live away from their parents, which was clearly the preferred pattern.

The relationships between boarders and the family cycle were similar to those for relatives, although boarders lived with a greater proportion of families, and families more frequently had male than female boarders. (An interesting exception occurred in 1851 among late-cycle families with only daugters aged 15 or over. These families had twice as many female as male boarders aged 15 to 19 and 20 to 29. Perhaps this reflected sexual fears. At any rate by 1871 the sex ratio for 15- to 19-year-olds was reversed, and among the older cohort the proportions were nearly equal.) Families in all categories more often had boarders aged 15 to 19 or 20 to 29 than any other age. There was in any year only a sprinkling of very young boarders and a somewhat greater number over the age of 40. In 1851 elderly boarders were particularly common among families with no children. In that year 16 percent of late-cycle families without children at home had a male boarder aged 40 or over, and 7 percent had a female boarder. In 1871 the proportions were 3 percent and 7 percent, respectively. A larger proportion of families contained elderly male boarders than elderly male relatives. It is unlikely that men had fewer kin in the city than women. Thus it was apparently more common for elderly men to live with nonfamily members than with relatives. Evidence from New York State in the 1870s and 1880s, moreover, shows that elderly men more often than women lived in poorhouses. Children, it would seem, were more willing to take in their mothers than their fathers, a pattern that deserves much more attention from historians of the family.

The size of the household over time expressed both the characteristics of each stage of the family cycle and the changes that occurred during the decades. The mean household size rose throughout each stage, and households at their peak were in fact quite large. In 1851 the late midcycle households with at least one male child aged 15 or over contained on the average 8.4 members, a number that had dropped only to 7.5 two decades later. Interestingly, on the average households with no children usually contained at least three and sometimes nearly four members. This is a clear indication that these households were especially likely to contain extensions.

The influence of various factors on the likelihood that any household would contain a relative or boarder is summarized by the multiple classification analysis reported in Table 8.3. In this analysis the dependent variable is the total number of relatives and boarders living with a family. The files for all three census years—1851, 1861, 1871 —were combined.

The analysis, though holding no surprises, neatly summarizes the trends already noted. Observe first that the number decreased sharply over time in virtually all family-cycle categories. Among early midcycle families with no children the predicted number of boarders and relatives dropped from 1.5 to .8 between 1851 and 1871; in the same years it declined from 1.2 to .6 in early midcycle families with children aged 1 to 14 and from 1.2 to .5 among late midcycle families all of whose children over the age of 15 were daughters. In most instances, moreover, the decline was progressive—that is, the number dropped during each of the two decades. In general there was more variation between than within years. Nonetheless some differences between families in different phases of their cycles did exist. For the most part in each phase of the cycle families with no children had the largest number of relatives and boarders.

Families in the periods of greatest strain generally contained relatively few relatives and boarders, certainly in numbers not greatly different from those in households with a son of working age, which were in their most prosperous phase. In 1851 among late midcycle families the predicted number for families in which all children were aged 1 to 14 was 1.02 compared to .7 for those with a son of working age. Twenty years later the relationship was reversed, and the predicted numbers were .5 and .6. Again it is clear that families usually did not compensate for the pressures exerted by young children through the addition of boarders and kin.

The differences between occupational categories reflect the distinctions pointed out earlier: all occupations in the business class had scores that exceeded those in the working class. Thus, with all other

Table 8.3   Determinants of number of relatives and boarders in households, multiple classification analysis: Hamilton, 1851–1871.

| Variable | | Predicted number of boarders and relatives |
|---|---|---|
| *Family-cycle category* | | |
| Young (wife under 25) | | |
| No children: | 1851 | 1.14 |
| | 1861 | .76 |
| | 1871 | .63 |
| All children aged 1–6: | 1851 | 1.26 |
| | 1861 | .73 |
| | 1871 | .61 |
| Early mid-cycle (wife 25–34) | | |
| No children: | 1851 | 1.49 |
| | 1861 | .96 |
| | 1871 | .81 |
| All children aged 1–14: | 1851 | 1.23 |
| | 1861 | .69 |
| | 1871 | .55 |
| Late mid-cycle (wife 35–44) | | |
| No children | 1851 | 1.73 |
| | 1861 | .79 |
| | 1871 | 1.91 |
| All children aged 1–14: | 1851 | 1.02 |
| | 1861 | .68 |
| | 1871 | .47 |
| At least one male child 15 or over: | 1851 | .70 |
| | 1861 | .56 |
| | 1871 | .57 |
| All children 15 or over female: | 1851 | 1.15 |
| | 1861 | .62 |
| | 1871 | .45 |
| Late cycle (wife 45 or over) | | |
| At least one male child 15 or over: | 1851 | .75 |
| | 1861 | .59 |
| | 1871 | .50 |
| All children 15 or over female: | 1851 | .95 |
| | 1861 | .79 |
| | 1871 | .61 |
| No children: | 1851 | 1.04 |
| | 1861 | .69 |
| | 1871 | .71 |
| Other: | 1851 | .46 |
| | 1861 | .56 |
| | 1871 | .96 |

Table 8.3, *continued*

| Variable | Predicted number of boarders and relatives |
|---|---|
| *Occupation* | |
| Professionals and rentiers | .71 |
| Agents and merchants | .90 |
| Service and semiprofessionals | 3.19 |
| Business employees | .68 |
| Government employees | .79 |
| Masters/manufacturers | 1.13 |
| Skilled workers | .66 |
| Transport workers | .63 |
| Other workers | .43 |
| Laborers | .60 |
| Female domestics | .00 |
| Female other | 1.19 |
| Agricultural proprietors | .55 |
| Other | .66 |
| None | .29 |
| *Number of children employed* | |
| 0 | .75 |
| 1 | .68 |
| More than 1 | .74 |
| *Sex of household head* | |
| Male | .59 |
| Female | 1.63 |
| *Ethnicity* | |
| Irish Catholic | .84 |
| Irish Protestant | .68 |
| Scottish Presbyterian | .73 |
| English Anglican | .66 |
| English Methodist | .73 |
| Canadian Protestant | .81 |
| U.S. white | .74 |
| Other | |

SUMMARY STATISTICS

| Variable | Eta/beta |
|---|---|
| Family cycle and year | .15/.13 |
| Occupational category | .23/.22 |
| Number of employed children | .02/.01 |
| Sex | .09/.16 |
| Ethnicity | .03/.03 |

| Covariates | Significance |
|---|---|
| Age of wife | .136 |
| Age of husband | .999 |
| Total number of children | .026 |

$R^2 = .077$

Grand mean    .74 (relatives plus boarders in household)

factors controlled, those families in more rewarding occupations had a greater number of boarders and relatives than those who were poor. The most striking score is the 3.2 for proprietors of services and semi-professionals, which results from the inclusion of innkeepers and hotel keepers in this group. The score for masters and manufacturers, 1.1, is also notably high and quite different from the .7 for the skilled wage workers who were their employees. Women who worked as domestics and headed households, a very poor group, were especially unlikely to house boarders and relatives. By contrast other females often did. In fact female household heads, as we observed earlier, had more boarders and relatives (1.6) than did males (.6).

Boarders and relatives did not substitute for employed children, nor did the existence of employed children have any effect on their number in a household, and ethnicity was of negligible importance. Some types of families were much more likely than others to contain them. However, with a few outstanding exceptions, the presence of boarders or relatives in individual households was more a matter of circumstance or chance than of systematic relationships between family cycle and structure.

Thus one more point about family structure must be stressed: its volatility. Some examples make the fluidity of household structure clear. In 1851 Charles Rivers, an Irish grocer 45 years old, lived with his wife, Jane, 25 years old, who had been born in Scotland, and three daughters aged 2, 5, and 10, all born in Canada West. Ten years later Rivers' household included his wife, his older daughters, and three more daughters, all born during the decade and aged 2, 6, and 7. In addition he now had a servant, Maureen McDougall, 20 years old, unmarried, and born in Scotland. Between 1861 and 1871 Jane Rivers died, perhaps in giving birth to their seventh child, Warren, a son born in 1862. In 1871 Charles lived at home with three of his daughters, aged 25, 16, and 17, and his young son. The family no longer had a servant.[25]

In 1851 Jacob Nelson, an English Anglican innkeeper aged 48, lived with his wife, Mary Amelia, born in the United States and aged 30; three children, a daughter 2 years old and sons aged 4 and 8, all born in Canada West; an unmarried boarder, John Hutchinson, also an English Anglican, 26 years old; and one servant, Cathleen Parnel, an Irish Presbyterian, 21 years old and unmarried. A decade later Nelson had four children at home, all but one born since 1851. His elder son, by then 18, probably had left home, his daughter may have died. (That the latter was probably the case is suggested by the fact that a child born during the decade had the same initial as the daughter no longer in his household.) Of his four children the two youngest, aged 1 and 3, were sons, and the two eldest, aged 5 and 7, daughters. He no longer had a boarder, and his servant now was Mary Williams, a 20-year-old single Anglican born in England. By 1871 the Nelsons had another son, now 7 years old, and the four children listed in 1861 still lived with their parents. The eldest, Nathan, was 24 years old. The family by that time had no boarders or servants in their household.

In 1851 William Brewer, a 42-year-old carriage maker born in England, lived with his wife, Margaret, 44 years old and also born in England; five sons, all born in England, aged 6, 8, 10, 12, and 17; and four boarders, all unmarried males—Tom Duncomb, a tanner aged 24, born in Canada West; William Bourne, a carriage maker aged 40; and two brothers born in Ireland, Tom David, an upholsterer aged 21, and Michael David, a carriage maker aged 25. Brewer's eldest son was also a carriage maker. By 1861 Brewer was styling himself a cabinet maker, and he lived with his four younger sons, his wife, and two boarders—James Marvell, a railroad clerk, single, aged 27, born in England, and Franklin Jones, a stationer also born in England, aged 31. By 1871 Brewer's household had shrunk to himself, his wife, and their sons, 30-year-old Frank, a bookbinder, and 26-year-old William, Jr., a machinist.

In 1851 John Mallory, a 30-year-old Irish Catholic carpenter, lived with his 25-year-old wife, Mary, also born in Ireland; one child, Peter, only a year old, and born in Canada West; one boarder, Tom Conners, a Canadian-born Catholic printer, unmarried and 17 years old; and Mallory's widowed mother, Ann, aged 54. A decade later the Mallorys had two children at home, a son aged 6 and a daughter 3. Peter had probably died. Living with them also was Mrs. Mallory's mother, Amelia Harnness, an Irish Catholic widow 62 years old. By 1871 Mrs. Harnness had probably died, and the Mallory household contained only John, Mary, and two children, a daughter now 13 and a son aged 16, who, like his father, was a carpenter.

Jason Armstrong, an English Anglican mason aged 28, lived in 1851 with his 23-year-old wife, Maude, also born in England. With them lived two sons, both born in England, aged 1 and 3 (the Armstrongs apparently arrived in Canada in 1850 or 1851), and two boarders, Roger Blackmoor, also an English Anglican mason, aged 26, and his 22-year-old wife, Elizabeth. By 1861 the Armstrongs had added two more sons, aged 2 and 6, and two daughters, aged 4 and 8, to their family. They no longer had any boarders. A decade later Jason called himself a stonecutter; aside from himself and his wife his household included five children and Anna Smith, a widowed English boarder aged 67.

Finally there was H. B. Turnbull, in 1851 an English Anglican printer 28 years old, who lived with his wife, Margaret, also an English Anglican, 32 years old; their two sons, both born in Canada, aged 1 and 3; Turnbull's 57-year-old widowed mother; a boarder, Samuel Aiken, a Canadian-born Anglican who was an unmarried printer 17 years old; and one servant, 17-year-old Mary Baker from England. In 1861 Turnbull called himself a coroner. During the decade his wife had died and he had married a 37-year-old Irish Anglican named Catherine. They lived with his two children by his first marriage; two visitors, George Gardner, a 26-year-old Canadian-born farmer, and his 24-year-old wife, Sadie, born in Ireland; four boarders, none of whom listed occupations; two unmarried Canadian-born Anglican men aged 15 and 17, Charles Hatch and Frederick Morgan; two unmarried Irish Anglican women aged 30 and 39, Ann Wyley and Elizabeth Rigley; and one servant, Bridgit Burns, a Canadian-born Catholic aged 19. A decade later Turnbull had declined in occupational rank, calling himself a laborer. Both of his sons still lived at home and were clerks, as was one of his two boarders, Thomas Jenkins, a 24-year-old English Anglican, the husband of the other boarder, Ester, also born in England and 26 years old. Though Turnbull had dropped in occupation, his household, perhaps sustained by the income of his sons and boarder, still contained a servant, Ann Foley, a 33-year-old unmarried Irish Catholic.

As these examples make clear, a high degree of compositional change characterized families followed from 1851 to 1861 and 1861 to 1871. Between 1851 and 1861, 72 percent of households lost all the boarders they had contained, and 71 percent lost all relatives. For the next decade the proportions were 65 percent and 90 percent, respectively. Only 12 percent of families acquired a boarder and 20 percent a relative in the first decade and 16 percent and a low 5 percent in the second. Similarly in the first decade 30 percent and in the second 55 percent of households lost all of their servants, while 16 percent and later 7 percent of families acquired at least one. Looked at another way, 56 percent of these families included either a relative or boarder between 1851 and 1861, and 46 percent had one at some point during the next decade. These are, of course, minimum estimates since they catch families only at two points in time. In actuality boarders and relatives probably moved in and out of households fairly often. Again the conclusion is unmistakable that in the mid-nineteenth century it was common for families to have other people living with them at various points in their histories.

However two qualifying points need to be stressed. First, the relationship between the presence of boarders and relatives and the family cycle was tenuous. There was little pattern to their distribution.

Boarders and relatives did not compensate for the strain undergone by young working-class families; grandmothers did not live in enough homes to assist with child care; very few children lived with their parents after marriage; most families did not contain an elderly relative. To some extent families without children were more likely to have boarders than others. Undoubtedly they had more room and might have felt more responsibility; but the differences by and large were not great.

This does not mean that boarding or living as kin was random. Life-cycle boarding, to use Peter Laslett's apt phrase, was common.[26] Boarders and relatives were most often young unmarried people between the ages of 15 and 29, though a substantial fraction were elderly. Of the latter men lived more often with nonkin than with relatives. However with the exception of female household heads who took in boarders as a source of income, there was not very much relationship between the individual life cycle and the characteristics of the family at different points in its cycle. The needs of a widowed mother or an orphaned nephew, an extra room, the desire to house an employee, the arrival in town of a kinsman or friend: these circumstances rather than the phase of the cycle probably determined the presence or absence of a boarder or relative in a home.

The second general point is this: the proportion of families that housed a boarder or relative declined. The decline, moreover, was quite steep. It is reflected, among the linked families, in the substantially greater proportion losing than acquiring a boarder or relative. At the same time, though perhaps for different reasons, the proportion of families employing a resident servant also dropped drastically. There can be no doubt that the composition of the household had begun to change: it was becoming much less common for persons other than married couples and their children to live together. Whether that trend was permanent or the product of a shift in immigration and housing supply to be reversed later in the century remains to be seen. For the moment, though, it does appear that households in Hamilton became increasingly nuclear during early industrialization.

In this way the experience of families in Hamilton differed from the pattern described in Britain by Laslett and Anderson. Laslett asserts that the "shape and membership of the family group" in the West "has been confined for the most part to the parents and children themselves, what is called the nuclear family form or simple family formation."[27] If industrialization had any impact on this pattern it was to increase the proportion of families with resident kin, an argument made convincingly for British textile centers by Michael Anderson.[28] Laslett's assertion of the primacy of the nuclear family must be put alongside his contention that a high proportion of families contained nonkin members—prior to industrialization usually some sort of servant or employee (and in commercial cities, we would argue, frequently boarders). In one way these two assertions—the primacy of the nuclear family and the large proportion of households with nonkin members—appear to conflict with each other. We do not share Laslett's exclusion of resident nonkin from the definition of *household.* If the argument advanced in the preceding chapter is correct, these people did have a quasifamilial relationship with other members, and indeed the distinction between family and household had little meaning for people at the time. Thus Laslett's stress on the predominance of the nuclear family while statistically correct obscures two important trends. The first is the progressive reduction in the number of people who lived together, the stripping away of the nonkin members of households and, at least in Hamilton, relatives as well. The second point obscured is the dynamic nature of the household, which continually expanded and contracted its membership around a nuclear core. That expansion and contraction bore little relationship to the family cycle, but it did mean that many, perhaps the great majority of people lived at some point in their lives, often during their youth, with people other than their parents, spouses, and children.

## Hamilton, Buffalo, and Erie County: A Comparison

Again comparative questions become critical: Was the lack of systematic relationship between the family cycle and domestic organization peculiar to Hamilton or a more general feature of North American cities? Was it in fact an urban phenomenon? Were rural families organized differently?

One clear difference between Buffalo in 1855 and Hamilton in 1851 is that households in Erie County, even on farms and in county towns, were smaller. For instance in Hamilton the mean household size of young families with children was 5.3 in 1851, compared to 4.2 in Buffalo, 4.0 in Erie County towns, and 3.9 on farms. In late midcycle families with only young children it was 6.4 in Hamilton in 1851 and still 6 in 1871, compared to 5.6 in Buffalo, 5.5 in the towns, and 6.1 on the farms. Thus the first question is: Why were households generally smaller in Buffalo than in Hamilton?

The distinction did not result from any difference in the average number of children in a family. In both cities, in the towns, and on the farms the number of children living with families at different cycle stages was quite similar. A distinct difference, though, did exist in the number of boarders. Throughout the period many more boarders lived with families in Hamilton than in either Buffalo or rural Erie County. For instance the proportion of boarders living with young families with young children in Hamilton dropped from 35 percent to 15 percent between 1851 and 1871. In Buffalo it was 11 percent, in Erie County villages and on farms 3 percent. Among early midcycle families with young children the proportion dropped from 32 percent to 19 percent, still above the 11 percent in Buffalo, 7 percent in towns, and 6 percent on farms. Among those aged 45 or older all of whose children had left home the proportion with boarders was 36 percent and 25 percent in Hamilton at the start and close of the two decades, compared to 11 percent in Buffalo, 3 percent in Erie County towns, and 11 percent on farms.

Thus three patterns emerge. Hamilton households had more boarders than those in Buffalo, and Buffalo households had more boarders than those in the surrounding towns or on farms. Third, Buffalo in 1855 did not differ as much from Hamilton in 1871 as in 1851. One factor that caused the large difference in the earlier years was housing supply. Recall that about 43 percent of families in Buffalo lived in multifamily dwellings, compared to a negligible proportion in Hamilton. Families in the American city must have been more cramped and lacked the space in which to house boarders. Also, because Buffalo was more economically advanced than Hamilton family boarding probably had declined there somewhat sooner than in the Canadian city, an argument consistent with our other observations that Buffalo in 1855 resembled Hamilton in 1871 more than in 1851. Finally young people did not live as boarders in the countryside, for by and large young people did not move to the country in search of work.

As in Hamilton the families most likely to contain boarders (with the exception of the youngest ones) were those within each age group who did not have children. In some instances boarders probably contributed to the family income. In other cases these families simply had more room.

By and large the proportion of families containing relatives was similar in Buffalo and Hamilton. The differences do not appear to have been systematic. The real differences separated city and farm families: many more of the latter contained kin. Consider the comparative proportion of families with at least one coresident relative in Buffalo and on the farms: young families with children, 20 percent and 25 percent; late midcycle families with only young children, 12 percent and 25 percent; late midcycle families with only female children aged 15 or over, 11 percent and 25 percent; late-cycle families with male children aged 15 or over, 14 percent and 24 percent.

Why did people on farms generally share their homes with more relatives? The answer cannot be found within the family cycle, for the proportion did not vary much between stages. Certainly there is no indication that families with young children took in either relatives or boarders to help with their work. In fact the higher proportion on the farm may simply reflect greater population stability. Because people had remained in the same place longer, it is more likely that children lived near their siblings or that parents had a married child nearby. Thus kin networks were probably more cohesive, and people in need could find a relative with whom to live more easily than in the city. The practice of housing kin might also have been sustained by community traditions, which could be enforced more easily in a rural than in an urban setting.

Parallels between Buffalo in 1855 and Hamilton in 1871 once again exist in a comparison of the proportion of households with servants. In 1851 Hamilton households had notably more servants than those in Buffalo. For example in Hamilton 38 percent of young families with children had servants compared to 17 percent in Buffalo. Similarly, 24 percent of late midcycle families with young children had servants in Hamilton compared to 17 percent in Buffalo. For late-cycle families with no children the proportions were, respectively, 30 percent and 11 percent. However in Hamilton by 1871 in the same categories the proportions with servants had dropped close to the Buffalo figures: 11 percent, 12 percent, and 11 percent. Overall in 1855 16 percent of Buffalo households had servants, compared to 30 percent in Hamilton in 1851, 21 percent in 1861, and 12 percent ten years later.

In Buffalo the families least likely to have servants were those with no children. Among those who had children the distinctions were not very great. The same is true for Hamilton. Farm families without children, however, were considerably more likely to contain servants or other employees than similar families in the city. There was little difference in the proportions of families with children that employed servants in city, village, or on the farms. It would appear that the one case in which families clearly needed to augment their labor supply was when no children lived at home, a pattern that points to the importance even of young children in the family economy of the farm.

More married children apparently lived with their parents in Erie County towns and on farms than in either of the two cities. The proportion of couples aged 45 or over with married sons at home varied in Hamilton between 7 percent and 5 percent. The figure was 7 percent in Buffalo and 9 percent in country towns and on farms. The proportion of families in the same category with a married daughter at home dropped in Hamilton from 8 percent to 5 percent to nil across two decades. In Buffalo it was 4 percent, in country towns 3 percent, and on farms 7 percent. Among all whose only coresiding children over the age of 15 were daughters the proportion with a married daughter at home shifted from 6 percent to 16 percent (a reflection of the depression) to 2 percent. In Buffalo that proportion was 10 percent, in country towns an inexplicably high 19 percent, and on farms 7 percent. About all that can be said with relative certainty from these patterns is that it was somewhat more common for newly married children to live with parents in rural than in urban areas, except when a depression or shortage of housing modified the preferred pattern in cities.

In both Hamilton and Buffalo quite similar proportions of households contained elderly relatives (defined here as relatives at least 40 years old). In Hamilton the proportion, not large at the start of the period, declined during the two decades. The highest proportion with a male relative over the age of 40 in any year was 3 percent, and the highest proportion with a female relative, 9 percent, was reached among young families without children in 1851 and young families with young children in 1861. By 1871 the largest proportion of families with an elderly female relative was only 4 percent (young families without children). In Buffalo the proportion with an elderly female relative varied between 2 percent and 6 percent, and the proportion with an elderly male kinsman fluctuated only between 1 percent and 3 percent.

Real differences marked rural areas. Substantially more families on farms had elderly relatives living with them: for example the proportion with a female relative aged 40 or more was 16 percent of young childless families, 7 percent of young families with children, 12 percent of early midcycle families both with and without children; and 13 percent of late midcycle families in which the only children over 15 were female. The proportion with elderly relatives declined, of course, among older families. For some reason, probably a combination of greater residential stability and custom, farm families more often than urban ones housed their elderly kin.

One instance of a striking difference between Buffalo and Hamilton was in the proportion of coresident children who were employed, which was much higher in the Canadian city. Among late midcycle families with at least one male child over 15 the proportion with a male child at work varied from 41 percent to 30 percent (an effect of the depression) to 72 percent (as industrial jobs opened). In Buffalo in 1855 the proportion was only 28 percent. Among late-cycle families in Hamilton the equivalent proportions were 67 percent, 59 percent, and 85 percent, compared to 44 percent in Buffalo. Though fewer young women worked, the differences assumed the same pattern. Consider families in which the only children of working age were female; in Hamilton these were the families most likely to contain working daughters. Among the late midcycle families in Hamilton the proportion with a daughter at work varied from 7 percent to 5 percent to 16 percent, compared to 4 percent in Buffalo. In the late-cycle families the Hamilton proportions were 20 percent, 13 percent, and 25 percent and in Buffalo 8 percent.

Why did young people work more often in Hamilton than in Buffalo? The answer is not at all clear. In part the distinction may reflect differences in the job market. In Hamilton in 1871 the largest employer of relatively young men was the newly developed metal industry. In Buffalo the metal industry employed a substantially smaller proportion of the work force than in Hamilton, and there may not yet have developed suitable industrial work for young people in the American city. The distinction between the cities may also reflect different patterns of school attendance. In both 1851 and 1871 school attendance for teenagers was higher in Buffalo than in Hamilton. Although the 1855 census includes no information on school attendance, samples drawn from the federal censuses of 1850 and 1870 suggest that school attendance was much more common in Buffalo than in Hamilton in those years. The school attendance rates for males and females who were 11 years old were 55 percent and 42 percent in Hamilton in 1851 and 86 percent and 96 percent in Buffalo in 1850, while among 15-year-olds the figures were 17 percent and 15 percent in Hamilton and 30 percent and 42 percent in Buffalo. By the years 1870-1871 the differences had been reduced, but Buffalo retained a substantial lead over Hamilton.[29] Finally, the reason that young people started work earlier in Hamilton may have reflected, at least in part, the relative prosperity of the two cities. Wages do appear to have been higher in Buffalo and living costs about the same. Thus more families there may have been able to forgo the earnings of their children for another year or two.

Hamilton, Buffalo, and the countryside also contained different proportions of female heads of household (Table 8.4). In most though not all family-cycle categories there were fewer female-headed households in Buffalo than in Hamilton. For instance of early midcycle families with young children 8 percent were headed by a female in Hamilton in 1851, 13 percent in 1861, and 14 percent in 1871, compared to only 4 percent in Buffalo. Of those late-cycle families with at least one male over 15 at home the proportion in Hamilton headed by a female varied from 31 percent to 32 percent to 45 percent, compared to a much lower 24 percent in Buffalo. These differences once again are

Table 8.4  Percent of households female-headed, by family-cycle category: Buffalo and Erie County, 1855.

| Family-cycle category number[a] | Buffalo | Erie County nonfarmers | Erie County farmers |
|---|---|---|---|
| (1) | 2.2 | 0.0 | 0.0 |
| (2) | 1.2 | 1.6 | 0.0 |
| (3) | 4.3 | 6.3 | 0.0 |
| (4) | 3.9 | 7.6 | 0.3 |
| (5) | 10.2 | 4.5 | 0.0 |
| (6) | 7.1 | 10.4 | 1.5 |
| (7) | 15.8 | 11.1 | 1.1 |
| (8) | 13.0 | 8.3 | 3.0 |
| (9) | 23.7 | 38.5 | 1.7 |
| (10) | 24.3 | 45.9 | 0.0 |
| (11) | 21.5 | 27.5 | 2.7 |
| (12) | 16.5 | 10.7 | 0.0 |
| N | 12, 090 | 530 | 1,187 |

a. See Table 8.1 for definitions of categories.

very difficult to explain. It could be that in a significant number of instances the reason for the absence of a male household head was not death but departure in search of work, which would be more necessary in the limited and less dynamic economy of Hamilton.

The lowest proportions of female-headed households occurred on the farms. There were none at all in the first five stages of the family cycle, only 2 percent in stage 6, 1 percent in stage 7, and 3 percent in stage 8. Even among the elderly there were practically none. This difference sets the farms apart from the cities and from the country towns as well, for there the proportions were similar to those in the cities. Four possible reasons account for the difference: one is that farmers lived longer and left fewer widows. Second, in rural areas widows more often had children to whom they could turn and did not need to maintain their own household. Third, women alone, finding it difficult to operate farms, might have sold their property (86 percent of farmers owned their farms) and either moved in with kin or moved to the city. Fourth, widows with farms were attractive as spouses and may have remarried quickly. Very likely some combination of these factors worked to keep the proportion of female-headed households very low.

The propensity of female-headed households to contain more relatives and boarders was not as striking in Buffalo as in Hamilton. However in both cities masters and manufacturers did have more than the average number of boarders and kin in their households. Some of these undoubtedly were employees. And in both cities the working class, especially laborers, least often had people other than parents and children living in their households.

The similarity in household structure between Hamilton and Buffalo points to the generality of the major patterns we identified in the Canadian city. The variations in the proportions of families in the different stages of the family cycle reflect distinctions in age structure. In neither city did families take in boarders or relatives to offset a labor shortage when their children were very young. In neither place did the structure of the household vary in any very systematic way with the family cycle.

There were, however, three principal differences between the two cities. In Buffalo there were a smaller proportion of households with boarders, households headed by women, and employed children. These distinctions can be accounted for by housing supply, economic development, the nature of the job market, differing patterns of school attendance, and possible variations in prosperity. They do not reflect any fundamental structural differences or any distinctions in the basic relationships between family, class, and economy.

Striking distinctions, though, did exist between farm and city. The most notable of these was the much greater proportion of farm families with coresiding relatives; the larger share with married coresident children; the virtual absence of female-headed households; and the relatively substantial proportion in the later stages of the life cycle. Most of these differences probably reflected greater residential stability and the persistence of social customs and obligations that could not be sustained as easily in cities.

## Family Cycle and Family Economy

The economy of the family is a product of its class, its cycle, and its cultural context. Class determines the rewards that the family receives, the life chances of its members, the necessity for more than one income. Family cycle determines whether or not there are members of the family other than the household head who can earn wages to supplement the family income. The cultural context affects a variety of issues: the acceptability of wage work by women outside the home, attitudes toward education, the age at which children legitimately may work, the role of family members in the allocation of family income, the proportion of children's wages turned over to the family, and the requirements of an adequate standard of living.

The theme of most accounts of the relationship between the family and the economy, of course, is the separation between the two. In this interpretation the functions of the family split apart as work came to be carried on outside the home, which was no longer the setting of both production and residence. As Peter Laslett has written: "The most important of all the effects on the family group of the process of modernization has undoubtedly been the physical removal of the father and other earners for all of every working day. The perpetual presence of the father, the paterfamilias, the household head, must have had an enormous effect on the pre-industrial family and household. It follows that the influence of the shape of the family on the formation of the personality of the child must have been greater in the past than it is today."[30] Deprived of its economic role, the home became a retreat, a "haven in a heartless world," and a specialized agency for the nurture of the young.[31]

There are serious flaws in this interpretation. One is that it sometimes neglects to emphasize that families always have an economy, whether or not all members are engaged in the production of food, commodities, or wages. The nature of that economy and its internal relationships vary greatly, but all families must meet their needs for subsistence, and all must establish patterns for the allocation of resources. Moreover the separation of home and work is usually considered a middle-class or bourgeois practice. Indeed it is sometimes simply assumed that the bourgeoisie was the first class to manifest all modern family traits. That assumption, however, has no foundation whatsoever.[32]

There is no reason to assume that the relationship between home and work in Hamilton was especially different from that in other cities prior to the advent of mass transportation. There the working class, virtually to a person, worked away from home. With a few exceptions the working class consisted of wage workers hired to work in a shop, on the streets, on the docks, on the railway, but not at home. The working class were clearly the first urban people for whom home and work became separate. (An analogous process, of course, happened in the countryside, where the first people to live away from their work were probably agricultural laborers, who did not own land.)

By contrast during its early industrialization a substantial proportion of Hamilton's business class continued to combine their place of work with their place of residence. Figures for members of the business class and a few others have been derived from the city directories of 1853 and 1871, which usually specified the address of a man's place of employment if it differed from his home. We have taken all people listed in the business section of the directory and wherever possible compared home and work addresses. People have been placed in one of three categories for a variety of specific occupations in 1853 and

1871. The categories are home and work place identical; home and work place different; and unknown (that is, we were unable to judge whether they were the same or different). The later directory was compiled much more precisely; consequently it was possible to make a decision in a much greater proportion of cases. Therefore conclusions should not be drawn simply from comparing 1853 and 1871.[33]

There was less noticeable change during the two decades of early industrialization than prevailing theories would predict (Table 8.5). In 1871, 50 percent of professionals, 29 percent of agents and merchants, 75 percent of grocers, 86 percent of proprietors of services and semi-professionals, and 51 percent of masters and manufacturers still lived at their place of work. In the last group the distinction was not solely between the more modern and traditional crafts, for though none of the owners of sewing machine factories lived at his place of work, the owners of the two agricultural implements establishments did. Despite the technological developments in the shoe industry in 1871, 30 master/manufacturer shoemakers worked at home and 11 at shops or manufactories elsewhere; the numbers among master/merchant tailors were 15 and 10, respectively. Indeed little pattern can be discerned within the trades other than the persistence of a mixture that included about half of the master/manufacturers living away from their place of work.

Among other groups physicians predominantly worked at home, in contrast to lawyers for whom the ratio between those working at home and elsewhere was around 1 to 3, a figure common to a number of the more important commercial occupations as well in both 1853 and 1871. Thus far more than its workers Hamilton's business class managed to combine work and residence.

Between 1851 and 1871 young people began to live at home more often during their early working years. Although their place of work and residence remained separate, the existence of larger work places enabled them to find employment relatively close to their parents' homes and to continue to live with their families. This coresidence meant that working-class families had a greater number of incomes at particular points in their cycle. This is one way in which the family cycle and the family economy intersected.

The economic strain placed on families varied with their stage of development. Young families with children faced the greatest economic burdens; families with working children had a potentially greater household income. The variation affected wage-earning families, because the income of adult male workers was both irregular and low. Men with higher incomes could more easily absorb the strain that existed when they were the sole income earners in their families.

Table 8.5 Relationship between home and workplace for selected self-employed workers and employers: Hamilton, 1853 and 1871.

| | 1853 | | | | 1871 | | | |
| | Home and workplace are— | | | | Home and workplace are— | | | |
| Occupational category | N | Same | Different | Unknown | N | Same | Different | Unknown |
|---|---|---|---|---|---|---|---|---|
| Professionals | 54 | 29.6% | 42.6% | 27.8% | 70 | 50.0% | 48.6% | 1.4% |
| Agents and merchants | 139 | 19.4 | 55.4 | 25.2 | 256 | 29.3 | 65.6 | 5.1 |
| Grocers | 31 | 51.6 | 29.0 | 19.4 | 145 | 74.7 | 22.6 | 2.1 |
| Service and semi-professionals | 51 | 56.8 | 27.5 | 15.7 | 138 | 86.2 | 12.3 | 1.4 |
| Public employees | 30 | 23.3 | 30.0 | 46.7 | N/A[a] | — | — | — |
| Masters and manufacturers | 167 | 41.3 | 38.9 | 19.8 | 456 | 50.7 | 46.0 | 3.3 |
| Female manufacturers | 6 | 33.3 | 16.7 | 50.0 | 10 | 90.0 | 0.0 | 10.0 |
| Other | 22 | 40.9 | 18.2 | 40.9 | 34 | 61.8 | 32.4 | 5.9 |

a. NA, not available.

In Hamilton, moreover, very few married women worked outside their homes.

We have advanced the hypothesis that working-class families compensated for the economic pressures of young children through the incorporation into the household of other wage earners who contributed part of their wages to the family directly or in the form of rent. Although none of the evidence has sustained that possibility, before we dismiss the relationship between the family cycle, structure, and economy, a more precise or standardized measure should be used to investigate possible interconnections.

The measures used here are a work/consumption index and a wage/consumption index. The work/consumption index attempts to provide a crude measure of the work potential of a family compared to its consumption needs.[34] A problem with the index immediately became apparent. It applies to family members only. How should boarders, relatives, and servants be treated? Boarders and relatives were scored according to their age and sex. That is, we assumed that a boarder or relative would both consume and contribute in the same amount as a family member of the same age and sex. Servants posed a more intricate problem: they earned their wages from the household head. Thus they consumed food and shelter as well as income. On the other hand servants contributed to the work of the household: they added labor rather than cash. Occasionally they might have freed other family members to engage in the wage economy. In the end we compromised: servants would be given identical scores (.6) for both consumption and work, but the scores would be lower than those of adult male family workers. With these weights two index scores are possible: one is the *family* work/consumption index, a measure based simply on parents and children. The other is the *household* work/consumption index, a measure based on all individuals living together. (In interpreting these indexes the closer to 1 the score, the less strain exists, because work and consumption are more nearly balanced.)

The distinction between the family and household indexes actually is crucial to our hypothesis. If families compensated for the strain imposed by young children by incorporating other wage earners, then their *household* index should be higher than their *family* index. In effect the family index should vary with the family cycle; the household index should remain relatively constant. That is, the balance between the work and consumption needs of households should not vary very much, but the actual balance within individual families should vary considerably with their stage of development.

Before we consider the actual index scores, however, another issue must be raised. The index as defined here is based on potential rather than actual work contribution. Individuals were given weights according to their age and sex regardless of whether or not they were employed. Thus if the 15- to 19-year-old sons of professionals ordinarily did not work because their fathers did not require the additional income whereas coresident shoemakers' sons of the same age invariably did enter the work force, the index scores for families with similar numbers of children would nonetheless be identical. In an urban as opposed to a rural setting this identity of index scores would mask critical differences. Therefore we utilized a *wage*/consumption index. In this index the denominator for consumption remained the same as in the other index but the numerator changed: everyone who worked, with the exception of domestic servants, received a 1. All of those with no occupation listed were scored 0 and resident domestics .6. Of course the wage/consumption index does not make any adjustment for actual wages. Its purpose is simply to identify the number of income-producing individuals in a family or household. Once again separate indexes for families and households were developed, and the two were compared.

Note first some summary statistics that show the mean score on each index for families headed by individuals in each occupational category and in several ethnic groups and the mean household size and mean number of children for the same groups (Table 8.6). These figures are averages across the family cycle and hence are very crude indicators.

As should be expected the mean household work/consumption indexes exceeded the mean family indexes. However the difference between the two decreased during the twenty-year period. That decrease resulted from the progressive decline in the number of extensions (relatives, boarders, servants) living with families. The decline is reflected too in the drop in mean household size from 5.96 to 5.47 to 5.24. The drop of nearly one person occurred at a time when the proportion of late-cycle families and the age of the population increased and when the mean number of children rose very slightly (from 2.51 to 2.49 to 2.61), an indication that the drop in household size did not reflect a decline in the size of families.

Both the family and household wage/consumption indexes were, of course, lower than comparable work/consumption indexes, since not all members of working age actually were employed. The same decrease in the difference between family and household scores occurred in the wage/ as in the work/consumption indexes.

Throughout the period the indexes remained relatively stable, except for changes that reflected the increased number of family

Table 8.6  Summary statistics on occupational and ethnic designations by work/consumption and wage/consumption indexes, mean household size, and mean number of children: Hamilton, 1851–1871.

| | | | | Mean work/consumption index | | | | | |
| | N | | | Family | | | Household | | |
| Variable | '51 | '61 | '71 | '51 | '61 | '71 | '51 | '61 | '71 |
|---|---|---|---|---|---|---|---|---|---|
| *Occupational category* | | | | | | | | | |
| Professionals and rentiers | 90 | 144 | 110 | .63 | .61 | .62 | .68 | .67 | .67 |
| Agents and merchants | 133 | 232 | 297 | .58 | .57 | .60 | .66 | .63 | .62 |
| Services and semiprofessionals | 69 | 104 | 127 | .58 | .59 | .61 | .72 | .69 | .71 |
| Business employees | 69 | 118 | 213 | .58 | .59 | .59 | .62 | .62 | .62 |
| Government employees | 48 | 76 | 111 | .60 | .57 | .60 | .64 | .61 | .61 |
| Masters/manufacturers | 120 | 229 | 339 | .57 | .59 | .58 | .65 | .62 | .60 |
| Skilled workers | 670 | 834 | 1,447 | .59 | .59 | .59 | .61 | .60 | .59 |
| Transport workers | 78 | 140 | 187 | .60 | .57 | .57 | .63 | .59 | .57 |
| Other working class | 31 | 63 | 102 | .60 | .60 | .58 | .63 | .61 | .59 |
| Laborers | 357 | 553 | 694 | .58 | .58 | .59 | .60 | .58 | .59 |
| Female domestics | 13 | 20 | 39 | .45 | .50 | .50 | .48 | .53 | .53 |
| Other females | 43 | 85 | 89 | .53 | .53 | .54 | .56 | .55 | .55 |
| Agricultural proprietors | 36 | 32 | 54 | .59 | .62 | .65 | .62 | .65 | .65 |
| Other | 20 | 33 | 20 | .66 | .67 | .56 | .68 | .68 | .58 |
| None | 179 | 402 | 567 | .55 | .58 | .61 | .59 | .60 | .63 |
| F-ratio | | | | 3.17 | 2.54 | 3.82 | 8.23 | 8.49 | 10.71 |
| *Ethnic group* | | | | | | | | | |
| Irish Catholic | 412 | 645 | 695 | .57 | .56 | .58 | .59 | .58 | .59 |
| Irish Protestant | 343 | 401 | 474 | .58 | .58 | .59 | .61 | .60 | .61 |
| Scottish Presbyterian | 223 | 505 | 629 | .57 | .59 | .58 | .63 | .61 | .60 |
| English Anglican | 250 | 439 | 734 | .58 | .60 | .60 | .63 | .62 | .61 |
| English Methodist | 116 | 195 | 366 | .59 | .59 | .59 | .63 | .61 | .60 |
| Canadian Protestant | 130 | 232 | 465 | .58 | .60 | .60 | .63 | .63 | .62 |
| U.S. white | 103 | 127 | 164 | .60 | .62 | .63 | .66 | .64 | .64 |
| Other | 379 | 52 | 869 | .59 | .69 | .58 | .63 | .62 | .60 |
| All families | 1,956 | 3,065 | 4,396 | .58 | .58 | .59 | .62 | .61 | .60 |
| F-ratio | | | | 1.35 | 3.12 | 2.21 | 4.84 | 6.21 | 3.61 |

| Mean wage/consumption index | | | | | | Mean household size | | | Mean number of children | | |
|---|---|---|---|---|---|---|---|---|---|---|---|
| Family | | | Household | | | | | | | | |
| '51 | '61 | '71 | '51 | '61 | '71 | '51 | '61 | '71 | '51 | '61 | '71 |
| .38 | .31 | .34 | .45 | .40 | .41 | 7.14 | 6.82 | 6.34 | 2.73 | 2.97 | 2.97 |
| .36 | .36 | .39 | .46 | .39 | .41 | 6.48 | 6.07 | 6.03 | 2.17 | 2.54 | 2.78 |
| .36 | .44 | .56 | .52 | .48 | .58 | 9.34 | 8.35 | 8.13 | 2.46 | 2.62 | 2.35 |
| .34 | .35 | .37 | .39 | .39 | .40 | 5.88 | 5.70 | 5.19 | 2.32 | 2.48 | 2.42 |
| .35 | .34 | .39 | .41 | .33 | .38 | 6.69 | 8.83 | 6.60 | 2.96 | 2.90 | 3.11 |
| .33 | .33 | .35 | .45 | .37 | .38 | 7.68 | 6.03 | 5.97 | 3.00 | 2.69 | 3.15 |
| .35 | .34 | .38 | .39 | .35 | .38 | 5.61 | 5.17 | 5.14 | 2.49 | 2.50 | 2.69 |
| .35 | .35 | .36 | .40 | .35 | .37 | 5.21 | 5.09 | 5.13 | 2.01 | 2.33 | 2.84 |
| .40 | .51 | .48 | .41 | .50 | .46 | 4.65 | 4.73 | 4.92 | 2.16 | 2.05 | 2.62 |
| .33 | .34 | .38 | .35 | .34 | .37 | 5.72 | 5.09 | 4.96 | 2.56 | 2.53 | 2.64 |
| .93 | 1.00 | 1.28 | .86 | .91 | 1.19 | 4.15 | 3.65 | 3.54 | 2.62 | 2.00 | 1.72 |
| 1.14 | 1.29 | 1.35 | .96 | .97 | 1.10 | 4.81 | 4.53 | 5.40 | 1.91 | 1.45 | 1.51 |
| .31 | .33 | .43 | .34 | .37 | .45 | 6.31 | 5.22 | 4.61 | 3.36 | 2.75 | 2.04 |
| .23 | .32 | .52 | .30 | .34 | .40 | 5.45 | 4.94 | 5.70 | 2.10 | 2.33 | 2.60 |
| .15 | .13 | .18 | .22 | .18 | .23 | 5.12 | 4.64 | 4.13 | 2.55 | 2.37 | 2.13 |
| 81.0 | 158.7 | 181.3 | 50.7 | 97.7 | 137.02 | 13.82 | 16.92 | 16.08 | 2.21 | 3.24 | 7.03 |
| .34 | .35 | .40 | .36 | .35 | .39 | 6.00 | 5.05 | 5.24 | 2.53 | 2.50 | 2.85 |
| .36 | .34 | .39 | .39 | .35 | .40 | 5.86 | 5.79 | 5.63 | 2.62 | 2.80 | 2.88 |
| .34 | .35 | .39 | .42 | .37 | .40 | 6.24 | 5.39 | 5.47 | 2.69 | 2.56 | 2.78 |
| .37 | .36 | .37 | .42 | .38 | .38 | 5.98 | 5.63 | 5.14 | 2.51 | 2.58 | 2.49 |
| .36 | .35 | .37 | .43 | .36 | .39 | 5.83 | 5.78 | 5.41 | 2.95 | 2.52 | 2.92 |
| .32 | .35 | .41 | .39 | .39 | .42 | 6.09 | 6.00 | 4.93 | 2.48 | 2.33 | 2.08 |
| .35 | .32 | .37 | .44 | .33 | .38 | 6.26 | 4.89 | 4.81 | 2.29 | 1.85 | 2.04 |
| .34 | .36 | .38 | .40 | .37 | .38 | 5.76 | 5.48 | 5.13 | 2.35 | 2.33 | 2.51 |
| .35 | .35 | .38 | .40 | .36 | .39 | 5.96 | 5.47 | 5.24 | 2.51 | 2.49 | 2.61 |
| 0.81 | .28 | 1.16 | 3.07 | 1.93 | 1.56 | 0.72 | 3.40 | 2.41 | 0.91 | 4.18 | 9.80 |

members in the labor force. Thus throughout the period the mean family work/consumption index rose only from .58 to .59, which points to the absence of any very marked shift in the wage-earning potential of families. However in the same two decades the mean family wage/consumption index increased 9 percent from .35 to .38, since more family members actually were employed. These shifts in mean figures are very small since they include all families. The trends become more striking when we consider families by occupational and family-cycle category. The mean household work/consumption index declined from .62 to .60 and the mean household wage/consumption index from .40 to .39, the latter sustained by the increased employment of family members, which offset the drop in the number of boarders, relatives, and servants.

Variations according to occupational category not only were significant but they increased. They far exceeded variations according to ethnicity. The differences between occupational categories were greater in the household than the family work/consumption indexes. There was thus more difference in the number of boarders, relatives, and servants living with families of different occupational backgrounds than in the number of their children. However there was a greater difference in the family than in the household wage/consumption index, which points to a distinction among actual family members employed that was somewhat muted when the employment of additional household members entered into the composition of the index. However in each year and in each instance differences in wage/consumption far exceeded those in work/consumption indexes. For instance the F-ratio for occupation in 1871 for the family work/consumption index was 3.82 and for wage/consumption 181.3. The F-ratios for household indexes for the same groups were 10.71 and 137.02. It is quite clear that families of different occupational background varied much more in the proportion of their members actually employed than in the proportion of potential wage workers that they contained.

The variations by occupation are most evident when the index scores are broken down by family-cycle stage, for the indexes varied more with family cycle than with any other characteristic. In 1851, for example, the family work/consumption index (the index that showed least variation between groups) varied among young families between .79 for those with no children and .57 for those with children aged 1 to 6. Among late midcycle families the index scores were .78 for families with no children, .47 for families with all children under the age of 15, .58 for those with at least one male aged 15 or more, and .51 for those with only females among children aged 15 or more.

Families experiencing the greatest strain did not compensate through the addition of extensions to the household. By 1871 in fact there existed little distinction between mean family and household indexes at any point in the family cycle.

Within occupational groups two patterns were evident. Among those families in the period of greatest strain household indexes were greater for those in more prosperous occupations. However among those with children of working age, wage indexes were highest in the working class. In other words the working-class families were least able to compensate for the burden of young children through the incorporation of another wage earner into the household. They were, however, most likely to have more than one wage earner in the family when children reached the age at which they could be employed. For example consider first the case of families in which wives were aged 25 to 34 and all children were under the age of 14. Almost no difference existed in the family work/consumption index of the major occupational groups. In 1871 the scores varied between .44 and .48, with no apparent pattern. However in the case of household indexes the scores for three of the four business-class groups exceeded those of the working-class groups. The figures for masters and manufacturers were identical to those for the skilled workers and laborers. The differences were small to be sure, but they indicated that men with more rewarding occupations were more able than workers to supplement their potential household income in periods of economic strain. To take one other instance in 1851 among families in the same stage the household index for professionals and rentiers was .68 and for laborers .60. Each of the four business class groups had a household score that exceeded that of the two working-class groups despite a near identity in family indexes.

Among families of all occupational backgrounds the family wage/consumption index rose between 1851 and 1871 on account of the entrance of more adolescent children into the work force. In a number of instances too that rise had been preceded by a decline during the depression of the late 1850s. By 1871, however, clear differences existed. In families with at least one working-age son the index score was higher among the working class. For late-cycle families the scores for the major occupational groups were: professional and rentier .47; agent and merchant .48; business employee .41; master and manufacturer .47; skilled worker .51; laborer .52. These distinctions, with the exception of the low score for the professionals and rentiers, had not been evident twenty years earlier. They developed as work opportunities opened and children began to remain longer in the home of their parents.

The work/consumption indexes in Buffalo and the rest of Erie County closely resembled their counterparts in Hamilton (Table 8.7). Especially striking is the similarity of indexes on farms and in the cities. It might have been thought that farm families with young children would more often supplement their labor supply with resident relatives or employees, but this definitely was not the case.

Some differences did exist between the wage/consumption indexes in Buffalo and Hamilton. Boosted by the greater proportion of working children the Hamilton indexes, particularly in 1871, were higher

Table 8.7  Family and household work/consumption and wage/consumption indexes, by family-cycle category: Hamilton, 1851–1871, and Erie County, 1855.

| Family-cycle category number a | Hamilton | | | Erie County, 1855 | | |
|---|---|---|---|---|---|---|
| | 1851 | 1861 | 1871 | Buffalo | Towns | Farms |
| A. WORK / CONSUMPTION INDEX (FAMILY / HOUSEHOLD) | | | | | | |
| (1) | .79/.79 | .77/.76 | .78/.78 | .79/.79 | .80/.80 | .80/.80 |
| (2) | .57/.63 | .57/.60 | .57/.59 | .58/.61 | .57/.59 | .58/.60 |
| (3) | .78/.79 | .77/.76 | .77/.76 | .79/.79 | .79/.78 | .80/.81 |
| (4) | .49/.56 | .47/.52 | .47/.49 | .52/.54 | .49/.52 | .50/.53 |
| (5) | .78/.78 | .77/.77 | .76/.76 | .77/.77 | .79/.75 | .80/.79 |
| (6) | .47/.52 | .46/.50 | .46/.48 | .49/.52 | .47/.49 | .47/.50 |
| (7) | .58/.60 | .59/.61 | .58/.59 | .60/.62 | .57/.58 | .58/.59 |
| (8) | .51/.55 | .54/.57 | .51/.53 | .54/.58 | .52/.53 | .55/.55 |
| (9) | .71/.72 | .71/.71 | .72/.71 | .71/.72 | .72/.72 | .73/.73 |
| (10) | .61/.63 | .62/.63 | .62/.64 | .62/.64 | .63/.64 | .64/.64 |
| (11) | .76/.78 | .74/.75 | .73/.72 | .75/.76 | .75/.74 | .80/.78 |
| (12) | .58/.61 | .56/.69 | .55/.59 | .55/.57 | .54/.55 | .58/.58 |
| B. WAGE / CONSUMPTION INDEX (FAMILY / HOUSEHOLD) | | | | | | |
| (1) | .53/.55 | .58/.54 | .56/.54 | .53/.50 | .45/.43 | .50/.57 |
| (2) | .53/.43 | .36/.38 | .37/.38 | .37/.38 | .28/.31 | .36/.38 |
| (3) | .59/.57 | .58/.53 | .63/.57 | .52/.49 | .53/.52 | .50/.52 |
| (4) | .29/.37 | .29/.32 | .30/.32 | .31/.33 | .28/.30 | .30/.32 |
| (5) | .48/.57 | .64/.55 | .66/.56 | .50/.47 | .36/.34 | .50/.48 |
| (6) | .28/.32 | .26/.30 | .26/.28 | .27/.29 | .27/.29 | .24/.24 |
| (7) | .28/.32 | .26/.29 | .37/.39 | .25/.27 | .28/.29 | .31/.32 |
| (8) | .21/.27 | .24/.26 | .24/.26 | .20/.23 | .13/.14 | .21/.23 |
| (9) | .39/.41 | .37/.38 | .47/.48 | .31/.33 | .37/.37 | .41/.41 |
| (10) | .37/.39 | .56/.51 | .34/.37 | .24/.27 | .13/.15 | .27/.28 |
| (11) | .51/.54 | .28/.34 | .48/.49 | .46/.47 | .38/.35 | .55/.55 |
| (12) | .31/.36 | .31/.33 | .32/.35 | .28/.29 | .21/.25 | .30/.29 |

a. See Table 8.1 for definitions of categories.

than those in Buffalo. For example the family wage/consumption index for families with at least one male child over the age of 14 in which the mother was 35 to 44 years old was .37 in Hamilton in 1871, compared to .25 in Buffalo in 1855. For families in which the wife was at least 45 and in which again at least one son of working age lived at home the comparative indexes were .47 and .31.

The occupational differentials in work/ and wage/consumption indexes generally were the same in Hamilton as in Buffalo. The very small numbers in some categories make drawing conclusions difficult in a few instances, but the parallels nonetheless are striking. For the most part the indexes of families in various occupations varied little when family-cycle stage was held constant. The differences that did exist showed that, as in Hamilton, those in the least rewarding occupations—laborers and to some extent skilled wage workers—had lower index scores. The scores for professionals, merchants, and masters and manufacturers were generally higher. Again extra resources were most common among the more affluent families, and the poor by and large were unable to compensate for their low, unequal incomes through the incorporation of additional working people into their households.

The similarity in urban and farm work/ and wage/consumption indexes is the most puzzling conclusion that emerges from this comparative analysis. Farms in Erie County were not small. The average number of cultivated acres was forty. Yet the average household was no larger or more complex on these farms than in the city, where the entire income was earned by the head of the household when children were young or by the father and working children among older families. One possibility is that farmers supplemented their labor supply at seasonal intervals with wage laborers who did not live with their households. Certainly there was a large number of laborers living in country towns, and underemployed laborers in the city might have been drawn to work on the farms at various times during the year. This pattern, impressionistic evidence indicates, was common elsewhere. In fact most of the farmers interviewed in the 1880s in a Minnesota inquiry into the farm economy said that they employed hired laborers who lived in neighboring towns.[35] More than that the similarity in scores points to the inadequacy of the index itself as a measure of labor potential in both farm and city, for it gives to persons of the same sex and age the identical score in both settings. In the city very likely the contribution of 6- , 7- , or 8-year-old children to the family economy was minimal, but on the farm children undoubtedly began to do useful work at an early age. Thus a true index of the labor potential of a farm family would have to use quite a different set of scores than one adapted to an urban setting. The most that can be said from the use of the same index for both places is that farm families were able to meet most of their labor requirements without the assistance of resident help, a fact that points to the active role that virtually all members had to play in the family economy.

The work and wage indexes were among the most regular and predictable patterns in nineteenth-century social organization. Consider for instance the amount of variance for which we can account in each of them in Hamilton (Table 8.8).[36] This analysis accounted for 85 percent of the variation in the family work/ and wage/consumption index; 72 percent in the household work/ and wage/consumption index; 62 percent in the family and 51 percent in the household wage/consumption index. The major influence on work/consumption indexes was family cycle. However the major influence on wage/consumption indexes was the variable occupation and year. The beta for ethnicity was significant though low.

The family cycle influenced indexes in predictable ways: scores for families with young children were in every instance negative. For each of the indexes they were by far the highest among late-cycle families with at least one male child 15 years old or over. Differences, with a couple of exceptions, were less pronounced among families with no children or with only daughters among their children of working age. Again, this time with other factors controlled, the general inability of families with young children to add to their income through the incorporation of boarders or relatives becomes apparent, for there existed very little difference between family and household scores.

The primary distinction among occupational groups was the extraordinarily high scores on wage indexes for women who headed households. This is because these women worked far more often than married women with husbands present; they had far more boarders; and their children lived longer at home, presumably to assist their mothers. The other large deviation from the majority of scores occurred for the proprietors of services and semiprofessionals, who had high family and household wage indexes. This is because their ranks included innkeepers and hotel keepers, in whose households frequently lived employees as well as customers.

With these exceptions differences are not very marked for either year or occupational group. In fact the only other trend evident is the decreasing difference in household indexes between groups. In 1851 the household indexes of occupational groups in the business class generally exceeded those in the working class, again a reflection of the disproportionate share of boarders and relatives living in the homes of the well-to-do. By 1871, with the general withdrawal of boarders,

Table 8.8 Determinants of family and household work/consumption and wage/consumption indexes: Hamilton, 1851–1871.

| Variable | Work/consumption index | | Wage/consumption index | |
|---|---|---|---|---|
| | Family | Household | Family | Household |
| *Ethnicity* | | | | |
| Irish Catholic | −.01 | −.01 | .01 | −.00 |
| Irish Protestant | .00 | .00 | −.00 | −.01 |
| Scottish Presbyterian | .00 | .01 | .01 | .01 |
| English Anglican | .00 | .00 | −.00 | .00 |
| English Methodist | .00 | .01 | −.00 | .00 |
| Canadian Protestant | .01 | .01 | −.01 | .00 |
| U.S. white | .00 | .01 | −.02 | −.01 |
| Other | −.00 | −.00 | −.00 | .00 |
| *Family cycle* | | | | |
| Wife over 25 | | | | |
| No children | .09 | .06 | −.00 | −.01 |
| All children 1–6 | −.05 | −.04 | −.12 | −.09 |
| Wife 25–34 | | | | |
| No children | .09 | .06 | .06 | .01 |
| All children 1–14 | −.10 | −.08 | −.10 | −.08 |
| Wife 35–44 | | | | |
| No children | .06 | .04 | .12 | .04 |
| All children 1–14 | −.09 | −.08 | −.07 | −.06 |
| At least one male 15 or over | .10 | .09 | .06 | .06 |
| All 15 or over female | .02 | .02 | −.06 | −.05 |
| Wife 45 and over | | | | |
| At least one male 15 or over | .17 | .16 | .21 | .18 |
| All 15 or over female | .02 | .02 | .02 | .02 |
| No children | .01 | .01 | .13 | .09 |
| Other | −.07 | −.05 | −.01 | −.01 |

Table 8.8, continued

| Variable | Work/consumption index | | Wage/consumption index | |
|---|---|---|---|---|
| | Family | Household | Family | Household |
| *Occupation and year* | | | | |
| Professionals and rentiers: | | | | |
| 1851 | -.05 | -.03 | .03 | .08 |
| 1861 | .00 | .04 | -.00 | .05 |
| 1871 | .00 | .03 | .02 | .06 |
| Agents and merchants: | | | | |
| 1851 | .02 | .06 | .03 | .10 |
| 1861 | .00 | .03 | .03 | .04 |
| 1871 | .00 | .01 | .04 | .04 |
| Service and semiprofessionals: | | | | |
| 1851 | .00 | .10 | .01 | .16 |
| 1861 | .00 | .07 | .05 | .08 |
| 1871 | .00 | .06 | .14 | .15 |
| Business employees: | | | | |
| 1851 | .01 | .02 | .01 | .03 |
| 1861 | .02 | .03 | .03 | .05 |
| 1871 | .01 | .01 | .05 | .04 |
| Government employees: | | | | |
| 1851 | .02 | .04 | .03 | .06 |
| 1861 | .00 | .00 | .04 | -.01 |
| 1871 | .00 | -.01 | .07 | .03 |
| Masters and manufacturers: | | | | |
| 1851 | .01 | .06 | .03 | .13 |
| 1861 | .00 | .01 | .01 | .02 |
| 1871 | .00 | .00 | .06 | .05 |
| Skilled workers: | | | | |
| 1851 | .01 | .01 | .03 | .03 |
| 1861 | .01 | -.00 | .02 | .00 |
| 1871 | .01 | -.01 | .06 | .03 |
| Transport workers: | | | | |
| 1851 | .02 | .02 | .02 | .04 |
| 1861 | .00 | -.01 | .02 | -.01 |

|  |  |  |  |  |  |
|---|---|---|---|---|---|
| Other workers: | 1851 | .02 | .02 | .09 | .06 |
|  | 1861 | −.01 | −.01 | .13 | .10 |
|  | 1871 | −.01 | −.02 | .06 | .09 |
| Laborers: | 1851 | .02 | .02 | .02 | .02 |
|  | 1861 | .00 | −.01 | .02 | −.01 |
|  | 1871 | .01 | −.01 | .06 | .03 |
| Female domestics: | 1851 | −.07 | −.07 | .39 | .35 |
|  | 1861 | −.06 | −.05 | .42 | .36 |
|  | 1871 | −.08 | −.08 | .66 | .61 |
| Other females: | 1851 | −.06 | −.06 | .55 | .40 |
|  | 1861 | −.08 | −.09 | .66 | .39 |
|  | 1871 | −.08 | −.10 | .73 | .52 |
| Agricultural proprietors: | 1851 | −.01 | −.01 | .01 | .00 |
|  | 1861 | .00 | .01 | −.01 | −.01 |
|  | 1871 | .01 | −.00 | .08 | .08 |
| Other: | 1851 | .01 | .02 | −.16 | −.10 |
|  | 1861 | .01 | .02 | −.04 | −.05 |
|  | 1871 | −.00 | −.01 | .17 | .03 |
| None: | 1851 | −.03 | −.03 | −.44 | −.33 |
|  | 1861 | −.02 | −.03 | −.46 | −.37 |
|  | 1871 | −.02 | −.03 | −.44 | −.35 |
| *Eta/beta* |  |  |  |  |  |
| Ethnicity |  | .07/.03** | .10/.15** | .02/.03** | .05/.03** |
| Family cycle |  | .77/.64** | .68/.57** | .40/.40** | .35/.37** |
| Occupation and year |  | .12/.12** | .20/.19** | .64/.70** | .55/63** |
| *Beta covariates* |  |  |  |  |  |
| Age of household head |  | .001** | .000** | .001** | .001 |
| Total number of children |  | .002** | .001** | −.006** | −.005** |
| Total household size |  | −.047** | −.049** | −.043** | −.039** |
|  |  | .000 | .005** | .004** | .002** |
| Grand mean |  | .59 | .61 | .37 | .38 |
| R² |  | .85 | .72 | .62 | .51 |

**Significant at .01 level; N = 9,417.

relatives, and servants from households, almost no difference existed between occupational groups. Finally, no difference of consequence existed between ethnic groups on any of the four indexes.

Very little difference existed as well between Hamilton, Buffalo, and rural Erie County. In fact it is the similarity between the places that emerges as the most striking conclusion from a series of separate multivariate analyses of each of the four indexes for Buffalo, Erie County towns, and Erie County farms (Table 8.9). The mean scores on the indexes for each place are very similar and the ranking of those variables used in each analysis virtually identical. In both the Canadian and American settings the family-cycle stage exerted most impact on the indexes, and that influence was not offset by any other factors. To some extent in Buffalo and the towns as well as in Hamilton female-headed households had higher indexes because women without husbands present frequently worked. Other than that occupation had little influence in any location and in the American cities and towns birthplace had as minimal an influence as ethnicity had in Hamilton.

With the Buffalo and Erie County material it was possible to test some factors not included in the analyses of the indexes for Hamilton. One of these was property ownership and number of years in the city combined into one variable. In none of the settings did it exert any influence at all. In Buffalo economic rank, as approximated by per capita dwelling value, had no influence on family indexes, though the highest octile had a slightly higher score on household measures. This means that the wealthiest people in the city were the only ones a bit more likely than most families to have added a potential or actual worker to their household.

The most surprising result of the analysis is that the number of acres cultivated by farmers exerted no influence on the balance of workers and consumers within their households. Even farmers with more than one hundred cultivated acres were no more likely than the average to supplement their families with additional help. Indeed there was no statistically significant interaction between farm size and any of the four indexes. In order to check the possibility that in some cases an interaction undetected by the multivariate analyses might exist, we examined the mean index score for each farm size at every phase of the family cycle. Overwhelmingly the indexes varied in a similar way with the family cycle whatever the size of the farm. The household indexes for families with only young children on large farms (seventy to ninety-nine and over one hundred cultivated acres) often were about 10 percent larger than the family indexes, which indicates that some of these families augmented their labor supply with resident help. But they did not do so consistently or usually.

Thus this fine-grained analysis also reinforces the argument that most hired agricultural laborers did not reside on the farms on which they worked.

One other factor exerted a very important influence on the balance of workers to consumers in Buffalo households. This was the age of marriage, estimated in a special series of multivariate analyses using only families in which the wife was under 35 and all children were under the age of 15. These families were chosen because the children were unlikely to have left home. Consequently, by subtracting the age of the eldest child from the age of the mother and then subtracting another year, it was possible to estimate very roughly the age of the mother at the time of her marriage.[37]

The timing of life events, in this instance age at marriage, clearly affected the household economy greatly. A direct, linear relationship existed between age at marriage and the family or household score on every index. The earlier the wife had married, the lower the score, which meant the greater the imbalance between workers and consumers within households and the greater the strain on the family economy. The family work/consumption index, for instance, rose from .47 for women who had had their first child at 18 or 19 to .62 for those who first gave birth between the ages of 28 and 34. The reason for this, of course, is that women who married earlier had more children before the age of 34. The addition of young children to the family lowered the work/ and wage/consumption indexes.

For women in each age group the household index was slightly higher than the family index, an indication that some families added a potential worker. However the relationships between age at birth of first child and the indexes remained perfectly linear, and the distinctions between the scores for women of different ages narrowed only very slightly. Thus larger families with young mothers did not offset the economic strain they experienced through the incorporation of other workers any more often than did those families with fewer children.

Occupation appears to be an especially important variable for the wage/consumption indexes, but the result is an artifact of the inclusion in the analysis of those families (about 20 percent of the total) whose occupation the census taker did not record. The demographic and economic characteristics of those families did not differ in any way from those whose occupation was listed, and among those with listed occupations none of the major groups showed any differences in index scores.

In each of the analyses, moreover, the beta for age at birth of first child exceeded the eta very substantially. This is because the age of the

Table 8.9   Family and household work/consumption and wage/consumption indexes, multiple classification analysis: Erie County, 1855.

| Variable | Index for — | | | N | | |
|---|---|---|---|---|---|---|
| | Buffalo | Towns | Farmers | Buffalo | Towns | Farmers |
| A. FAMILY WORK / CONSUMPTION INDEX | | | | | | |
| *Family cycle category number* [a] | | | | | | |
| (1) | .22 | .25 | .26 | 710 | 53 | 43 |
| (2) | .00 | .02 | .04 | 1,078 | 62 | 90 |
| (3) | .20 | .21 | .25 | 828 | 32 | 43 |
| (4) | −.08 | −.08 | −.07 | 3,974 | 197 | 289 |
| (5) | .17 | .18 | .19 | 361 | 22 | 17 |
| (6) | −.12 | −.14 | −.13 | 1,589 | 96 | 133 |
| (7) | .00 | −.05 | −.04 | 808 | 45 | 93 |
| (8) | −.06 | −.10 | −.08 | 412 | 24 | 55 |
| (9) | .09 | .08 | .05 | 1,113 | 96 | 242 |
| (10) | .00 | −.01 | −.04 | 407 | 37 | 88 |
| (11) | .12 | .09 | .10 | 487 | 40 | 73 |
| (12) | −.07 | −.11 | −.09 | 266 | 28 | 21 |
| *Birthplace* | | | | | | |
| New England | .03 | .00 | .02 | 707 | 92 | 212 |
| New York | .02 | .00 | .01 | 1,457 | 222 | 507 |
| Other U.S. | .01 | .01 | .02 | 339 | 62 | 53 |
| Ireland | −.01 | .00 | −.01 | 2,038 | 33 | 29 |
| Germany | .00 | .00 | −.03 | 4,846 | 245 | 273 |
| Other | .00 | .00 | −.01 | 2,646 | 78 | 113 |
| *Property and years in city* | | | | | | |
| Renter, 0–1 years | .01 | .01 | .01 | 1,229 | 114 | 37 |
| Owner, 0–1 years | .00 | .03 | −.01 | 167 | 39 | 80 |
| Renter, 2–4 years | .02 | .00 | .00 | 2,253 | 120 | 44 |
| Owner, 2–4 years | .01 | .01 | .01 | 544 | 80 | 207 |
| Renter, 5–9 years | .00 | .00 | .00 | 2,063 | 32 | 27 |
| Owner, 5–9 years | −.01 | .00 | −.02 | 1,269 | 75 | 161 |
| Renter, 10 years or more | −.01 | −.02 | .02 | 1,816 | 60 | 62 |
| Owner, 10 years or more | −.02 | −0.01 | .00 | 2,192 | 212 | 569 |
| *Occupation* | | | | | | |
| Professionals/rentiers | .01 | .01 | — | 254 | 29 | — |
| Agents/merchants | .01 | .01 | — | 606 | 34 | — |
| Service/semiprofessionals | .00 | .03 | — | 156 | 10 | — |
| Business employees | .00 | .13 | — | 266 | 1 | — |
| Government employees | −.01 | .00 | — | 85 | 4 | — |
| Masters/manufacturers | .00 | −.04 | — | 432 | 13 | — |
| Skilled workers | .00 | .00 | — | 4,233 | 272 | — |
| Transport workers | .01 | −.11 | — | 384 | 5 | — |
| Other working class | .00 | .01 | — | 216 | 10 | — |
| Laborers | .00 | .01 | — | 1,799 | 165 | — |
| Female domestics | −.12 | −.02 | — | 6 | 1 | — |
| Other females | −.06 | −.11 | — | 86 | 12 | — |
| Other | .00 | — | — | 45 | — | — |
| None | .00 | .00 | — | 3,176 | 175 | — |

Table 8.9, *continued*

| Variable | Index for — | | | N | | |
|---|---|---|---|---|---|---|
| | Buffalo | Towns | Farmers | Buffalo | Towns | Farmers |
| A. FAMILY WORK / CONSUMPTION INDEX (cont.) | | | | | | |
| *Dwelling value per capita (octiles)* | | | | | | |
| 1 (low) | .02 | — | — | 1,460 | — | — |
| 2 | .01 | — | — | 1,365 | — | — |
| 3 | .00 | — | — | 1,714 | — | — |
| 4 | .00 | — | — | 1,247 | — | — |
| 5 | .00 | — | — | 1,829 | — | — |
| 6 | −.01 | — | — | 1,465 | — | — |
| 7 | −.01 | — | — | 1,489 | — | — |
| 8 (high) | −.01 | — | — | 1,464 | — | — |
| *Acres cultivated* | | | | | | |
| 0 | — | — | −.01 | — | — | 212 |
| 1–9 | — | — | .00 | — | — | 90 |
| 10–24 | — | — | .01 | — | — | 174 |
| 25–39 | — | — | .01 | — | — | 195 |
| 40–69 | — | — | .00 | — | — | 260 |
| 70–99 | — | — | .00 | — | — | 129 |
| 100 or more | — | — | −.01 | — | — | 127 |
| Grand mean | .60 | .60 | .61 | | | |
| $R^2$ | .65 | .69 | .67 | | | |

| Variable | Index for — | | |
|---|---|---|---|
| | Buffalo | Towns | Farmers |
| B. HOUSEHOLD WORK / CONSUMPTION INDEX | | | |
| *Family-cycle category number* [a] | | | |
| (1) | .19 | .23 | .24 |
| (2) | .01 | .02 | .04 |
| (3) | .18 | .19 | .23 |
| (4) | −.07 | −.06 | −.06 |
| (5) | .15 | .12 | .17 |
| (6) | −.11 | −.13 | −.11 |
| (7) | −.01 | −.05 | −.04 |
| (8) | −.06 | −.10 | −.08 |
| (9) | .08 | .07 | .04 |
| (10) | .00 | −.02 | −.05 |
| (11) | .12 | .09 | .09 |
| (12) | −.06 | .09 | −.09 |
| *Birthplace* | | | |
| New England | .03 | .00 | .02 |
| New York | .02 | .00 | .01 |
| Other U.S. | .01 | .00 | .01 |
| Ireland | −.01 | .02 | −.01 |
| Germany | .00 | .00 | −.03 |
| Other | .00 | −.01 | −.01 |

Table 8.9, *continued*

| Variable | Index for — | | |
|---|---|---|---|
| | Buffalo | Towns | Farmers |
| B. HOUSEHOLD WORK / CONSUMPTION INDEX (cont.) | | | |
| *Property and years in city* | | | |
| Renters, 0–1 years | .01 | −.01 | .00 |
| Owners, 0–1 years | −.01 | .03 | .00 |
| Renters, 2–4 years | .01 | −.01 | −.01 |
| Owners, 2–4 years | .00 | .01 | .01 |
| Renters, 5–9 years | .00 | .00 | .01 |
| Owners, 5–9 years | .00 | .01 | −.02 |
| Renters, 10 years or more | −.01 | −.01 | .00 |
| Owners, 10 years or more | −.02 | .00 | .00 |
| *Occupation* | | | |
| Professionals/rentiers | .02 | .00 | — |
| Agents/merchants | .02 | .03 | — |
| Service/semiprofessionals | .05 | .15 | — |
| Business employees | .00 | .19 | — |
| Government employees | −.03 | −.01 | — |
| Masters/manufacturers | .01 | −.03 | — |
| Skilled workers | .00 | .00 | — |
| Transport workers | .00 | −.05 | — |
| Other working class | .01 | .01 | — |
| Laborers | .00 | .00 | — |
| Female domestics | −.11 | .03 | — |
| Other females | −.06 | −.12 | — |
| Other | .00 | — | — |
| None | .00 | .00 | — |
| *Dwelling value per capita (octiles)* | | | |
| 1 (low) | .00 | — | — |
| 2 | .00 | — | — |
| 3 | −.01 | — | — |
| 4 | −.01 | — | — |
| 5 | −.01 | — | — |
| 6 | −.01 | — | — |
| 7 | .01 | — | — |
| 8 (high) | .04 | — | — |
| *Acres cultivated* | | | |
| 0 | — | — | −.01 |
| 1–9 | — | — | .00 |
| 10–24 | — | — | .00 |
| 25–39 | — | — | .00 |
| 40–69 | — | — | .00 |
| 70–99 | — | — | .01 |
| 100 or more | — | — | .01 |
| Grand mean | .62 | .61 | .62 |
| $R^2$ | .53 | .59 | .58 |

Table 8.9, *continued*

| Variable | Index for — | | |
|---|---|---|---|
| | Buffalo | Towns | Farmers |
| C. FAMILY WAGE / CONSUMPTION INDEX | | | |
| *Family cycle category number*[a] | | | |
| (1) | .13 | .18 | .20 |
| (2) | .02 | .04 | .07 |
| (3) | .13 | .20 | .18 |
| (4) | −.03 | .03 | −.01 |
| (5) | .12 | .09 | .17 |
| (6) | −.06 | −.09 | −.08 |
| (7) | −.05 | −.02 | −.03 |
| (8) | −.10 | −.13 | −.13 |
| (9) | .02 | .06 | .01 |
| (10) | −.06 | −.16 | −.13 |
| (11) | .10 | .05 | .13 |
| (12) | −.04 | −.10 | −.08 |
| *Birthplace* | | | |
| New England | .02 | .02 | .02 |
| New York | .01 | .01 | .00 |
| Other U.S. | .01 | −.01 | .03 |
| Ireland | −.01 | −.02 | −.05 |
| Germany | .00 | −.01 | −.02 |
| Other | .00 | .00 | −.02 |
| *Property and years in city* | | | |
| Renters, 0–1 years | .00 | .00 | .00 |
| Owners, 0–1 years | .00 | −.01 | .02 |
| Renters, 2–4 years | .01 | .02 | .00 |
| Owners, 2–4 years | .00 | −.01 | .00 |
| Renters, 5–9 years | .01 | −.01 | .00 |
| Owners, 5–9 years | .00 | .00 | −.03 |
| Renters, 10 years or more | .00 | −.02 | .04 |
| Owners, 10 years or more | −.02 | .00 | .00 |
| *Occupation* | | | |
| Professionals/rentiers | .10 | .12 | — |
| Agents/merchants | .09 | .07 | — |
| Service/semiprofessionals | .19 | .05 | — |
| Business employees | .08 | .20 | — |
| Government employees | .09 | −.02 | — |
| Masters/manufacturers | .08 | .08 | — |
| Skilled workers | .09 | .07 | — |
| Transport workers | .09 | −.02 | — |
| Other working class | .10 | .13 | — |
| Laborers | .09 | .07 | — |
| Female domestics | −.37 | .96 | — |
| Other females | .81 | .68 | — |
| Other | .08 | — | — |
| None | −.27 | −.28 | — |

Table 8.9, *continued*

| Variable | Index for — | | |
| --- | --- | --- | --- |
| | Buffalo | Towns | Farmers |
| C. WAGE / CONSUMPTION INDEX (cont.) | | | |
| *Dwelling value per capita (octiles)* | | | |
| 1 (low) | .00 | — | — |
| 2 | .01 | — | — |
| 3 | .00 | — | — |
| 4 | .00 | — | — |
| 5 | .00 | — | — |
| 6 | −.01 | — | — |
| 7 | −.01 | — | — |
| 8 (high) | .00 | — | — |
| *Acres cultivated* | | | |
| 0 | — | — | −.01 |
| 1–9 | — | — | −.01 |
| 10–24 | — | — | .01 |
| 25–39 | — | — | .01 |
| 40–69 | — | — | .00 |
| 70–99 | — | — | −.01 |
| 100 or more | — | — | .00 |
| Grand mean | .27 | .30 | .35 |
| $R^2$ | .66 | .69 | .46 |
| D. HOUSEHOLD WAGE / CONSUMPTION INDEX | | | |
| *Family cycle category number* [a] | | | |
| (1) | .11 | .13 | .18 |
| (2) | .03 | .03 | .07 |
| (3) | .10 | .18 | .17 |
| (4) | −.02 | −.02 | −.01 |
| (5) | .09 | .05 | .14 |
| (6) | −.05 | −.09 | −.08 |
| (7) | −.06 | −.03 | −.04 |
| (8) | .09 | −.14 | −.13 |
| (9) | .01 | .06 | .01 |
| (10) | −.05 | −.14 | .12 |
| (11) | .08 | .05 | .14 |
| (12) | −.04 | −.06 | .10 |
| *Birthplace* | | | |
| New England | .04 | .03 | .02 |
| New York | .03 | .01 | .01 |
| Other U.S. | .00 | −.02 | .03 |
| Ireland | −.02 | −.04 | −.05 |
| Germany | .00 | −.01 | −.03 |
| Other | .00 | .00 | −.02 |

Table 8.9, *continued*

| Variable | Index for — | | |
|---|---|---|---|
| | Buffalo | Towns | Farmers |
| **D. HOUSEHOLD WAGE / CONSUMPTION INDEX** (cont.) | | | |
| *Property and years in city* | | | |
| Renters, 0–1 years | .00 | −.01 | −.01 |
| Owners, 0–1 years | .00 | −.01 | .01 |
| Renters, 2–4 years | .00 | .01 | −.01 |
| Owners, 2–4 years | .01 | −.03 | .00 |
| Renters, 5–9 years | .00 | −.02 | .00 |
| Owners, 5–9 years | .00 | .01 | −.03 |
| Renters, 10 years or more | .00 | −.01 | .02 |
| Owners, 10 years or more | −.01 | .01 | .01 |
| *Occupation* | | | |
| Professionals/rentiers | .10 | .11 | — |
| Agents/merchants | .10 | .10 | — |
| Service/semiprofessionals | .14 | .27 | — |
| Business employees | .07 | .31 | — |
| Government employees | .07 | −.01 | — |
| Masters/manufacturers | .08 | .07 | — |
| Skilled workers | .08 | .07 | — |
| Transport workers | .08 | .06 | — |
| Other working class | .09 | .13 | — |
| Laborers | .07 | .06 | — |
| Female domestics | .31 | .45 | — |
| Other females | .59 | .56 | — |
| Other | .07 | — | — |
| None | −.24 | −.27 | — |
| *Dwelling value per capita* (octiles) | | | |
| 1 (low) | .00 | — | — |
| 2 | .00 | — | — |
| 3 | −.01 | — | — |
| 4 | −.01 | — | — |
| 5 | −.02 | — | — |
| 6 | −.01 | — | — |
| 7 | .01 | — | — |
| 8 (high) | .05 | — | — |
| *Acres cultivated* | | | |
| 0 | — | — | −.01 |
| 1–9 | — | — | −.01 |
| 10–24 | — | — | .01 |
| 25–39 | — | — | .00 |
| 40–69 | — | — | −.01 |
| 70–99 | — | — | .01 |
| 100 or more | — | — | .02 |
| Grand mean | .29 | .31 | .36 |
| $R^2$ | .57 | .62 | .38 |

a. See Table 8.1 for definitions of categories.

mother was entered as a covariate. When her age at the time of the census was held constant in the final stage of the analysis, the effect of the age at which she bore her first child, and by implication the age at which she married, became notable and important. What these indexes show, aside from the increased strain on families with young wives, is the importance of marriage age as a regulator of fertility and the clear link between fertility and economic strain within the family economy.

The only relationships that existed between the work/ or wage/ consumption indexes and the social and demographic characteristics of families were their position on the family cycle and the age of the wife at the time of her marriage. Families with only young children, even those in rural areas, did not compensate for the strain on their resources by incorporating additional resident help into their households. What little relationship did exist between the composition of the household and other factors increased the resources of the very wealthiest families in Buffalo through the occasional addition of extra workers to their households.

Although no relationship existed between ethnicity and household composition in either Hamilton or Buffalo, one important ethnic distinction in family patterns in the Canadian city must be stressed: namely, the proportion of families at different points in their cycle who in 1871 contained at least one employed child. A greater proportion of late midcycle Irish Catholic homes generally contained a working child aged 15 or over. In 1871 87 percent of these Irish Catholic families in which there was a son of working age contained at least one male aged 15 or over who was employed, compared to 69 percent of Irish Protestants, 76 percent of Scottish Presbyterians, 66 percent of the English Methodists, 70 percent of the Canadian Protestants, and 50 percent of American whites. Similar differences existed for female employment among families with only daughters of working age.

In fact one of the most interesting observations that can be made from this analysis is that working daughters were found far more frequently in families that did not contain sons of working age. This pattern occurred in most ethnic groups and in late-cycle families across class lines as well. To take some examples: in 1871 the proportion of late midcycle families with a son of working age in which a daughter was employed was 7 percent, compared to 27 percent when no sons of working age were present. Among late-cycle families headed by masters and manufacturers in 1871 the proportions were 4 percent and 18 percent, respectively. In the business class very few late midcycle families had employed daughters. However among the working class the distinction existed: in 1871 the comparative proportions with a working daughter were 4 percent and 27 percent among laborers' families with and without sons aged 15 or over. Most families clearly expected a contribution from their children. Sons most often worked. When there were no sons at home, daughters had to enter the labor market. Thus one of the circumstances that determined whether or not a young woman would enter wage labor was the presence of a working-age brother in her home.

The proportion of families with employed sons followed the familiar pattern: it generally dropped in 1861 on account of the depression and by 1871, when job opportunities had become relatively abundant rose above its 1851 level. Furthermore by 1871 clear class differences had emerged in the proportion of families with employed sons over the age of 15. In 1851 for instance fewer families of laborers had an employed son than did some categories of the business class. Indeed one of the most severe problems confronting working-class families in the early 1850s was the lack of jobs for their sons. By 1871 however the situation had altered. In late midcycle families the proportion with at least one employed son differed sharply between occupational groups: professionals and rentiers 29 percent; agents and merchants 47 percent; business employees 59 percent; masters and manufacturers 68 percent; skilled workers 73 percent; laborers 95 percent. Among late-cycle families the proportion in each occupational category had increased (for instance to 63 percent among professionals and rentiers), but the distinctions remained. Laborers' children went to work earliest and most often.

## Fertility and the Family Economy

The number of children born to married couples has declined in virtually all modern industrial societies. From the work of demographers, who have traced the timing and rate of decline in different countries or regions, a clear connection emerges between fertility and economic history.[38] Still it is unclear exactly how and when the transition to smaller families began in different places—how, for instance, occupation, ethnicity, and economic development intersected with the way in which ordinary people sought to order their reproductive lives. At least one issue is clear, though, and that is the role of conscious behavior. The history of fertility decline is not simply the tale of a growing discovery of better modes of contraception. Contraceptive techniques have been available and fairly widely understood for centuries, and demographic history has made it clear that peasant populations customarily regulated fertility through late marriages.[39]

The acceptability of family limitation is not, of course, a story of calm, rational decisions reached mutually by husbands and wives and reinforced by medical advice and changed cultural standards. Its history is one of conflict between accepted values and new problems, between the shrill prophets of race suicide and the dilemmas of men and women struggling to raise and educate children. It is especially noteworthy that the decline in marital fertility occurred in the face of determined disapproval from most medical, cultural, religious, and political authorities.[40]

The limiting of family size was, in a very real sense, a movement that began despite, not because of, ideology or policy. It originated in the adaptations of ordinary people to the changed circumstances of their lives. A satisfactory theory relating fertility to economic and social change remains to be developed. What we offer is first, some data that show precisely the origins of the fertility transition in one industrializing city and that point to the complex interaction between fertility, class, and ethnicity, and second, a speculation on the significance of those trends for understanding the family economy in this period.

It has been known for some time, of course, that fertility in Ontario declined during the 1851-1871 period. According to Jacques Henripin, the general fertility rate dropped from 329 per 1,000 in 1842 to 212 in 1851 to 204 in 1861 and to 191 in 1871. But those aggregate figures obscure the rates for different places and subpopulations. In fact at least in Hamilton they mask important distinctions in the behavior of classes and ethnic groups.[41]

The measure of fertility used here is the age-specific fertility ratio.[42] The analysis draws on the censuses of 1851, 1861, and 1871 and on the tax roll of 1871 as well. It shows that during early industrialization in Hamilton ethnicity became an increasingly important factor in fertility. The reason, however, rested not in culture but in the dominant class position of different ethnic groups.

Specifically, the fertility ratios show that the distinctions between the various occupational groups were not great (Table 8.10). In each year the lowest fertility ratio was about 75 percent of the highest. Because of the closeness of scores the rank order of different groups, especially the smaller ones, fluctuated eratically. Nonetheless the fertility ratios of the business class and the working class altered position dramatically during the two decades. In 1851 the fertility ratio of the former exceeded that of the latter by about 5 percent. Twenty years later the working-class ratio was about 6 percent greater than that of the business class.

These shifts resulted from absolute changes in numbers (Table

Table 8.10   Fertility: Hamilton, 1851–1871.

A. ANALYSIS OF VARIANCE OF FERTILITY RATIO BY SEVERAL VARIABLES: (F-SCORES)

| Variable | 1851 | 1871 |
|---|---|---|
| Occupational group | 1.55 | 1.47 |
| Class | 1.29 | 2.00 |
| Ethnicity | 1.33 | 2.44 |
| Persistence | — | 2.47 |
| Wealth | — | 4.30 |
| Property ownership | — | 2.93 |

B. FERTILITY RATIO BY SOCIAL CLASS AND AGE

| Class and year | N | 20–49 | | 20–24 | 25–29 | 30–34 | 35–39 | 40–44 | 45–49 |
| | | Unadj. | Std. | | | | | | |
|---|---|---|---|---|---|---|---|---|---|
| *Business class* | | | | | | | | | |
| 1851 | 502 | 1,181 | 1,112 | 1,057 | 1,470 | 1,487 | 1,200 | 926 | 178 |
| 1861 | 795 | 1,122 | 1,108 | 919 | 1,475 | 1,413 | 1,276 | 882 | 287 |
| 1871 | 1,005 | 1,093 | 1,064 | 832 | 1,427 | 1,521 | 1,066 | 818 | 349 |
| *Working class* | | | | | | | | | |
| 1851 | 970 | 1,120 | 1,062 | 1,107 | 1,367 | 1,423 | 1,050 | 887 | 295 |
| 1861 | 1,393 | 1,175 | 1,138 | 1,068 | 1,614 | 1,484 | 1,329 | 730 | 220 |
| 1871 | 2,182 | 1,149 | 1,126 | 958 | 1,450 | 1,474 | 1,227 | 947 | 320 |

8.11). During the period the business-class ratio dropped 4 percent and the working-class ratio grew 6 percent. Thus during the early industrialization of Hamilton the city's fertility pattern shifted from a typical preindustrial one, in which the wealthiest families had the most children, to the common industrial pattern marked by larger families among the working class.[43] In its early phase it is important to emphasize, this shift did not come about solely because of a decline in the number of children born to business-class families but because of an increase among the numbers of the working class as well.

Within occupational groups the fertility of four of the six business-class groups declined. The most notable drop, 12 percent, occurred among business employees. By contrast the fertility ratio of three of the four working-class groups rose. The groups that deviated from the common pattern, particularly the government employees and other working class, are the two least satisfactory and least homogeneous in the classification.

Changes between 1851 and 1861 reveal the impact of the depression on fertility and show the different reaction of each class to economic

Table 8.11   Percentage change in standardized child/woman ratio, by occupation and ethnicity: Hamilton, 1851–1871.

| Variable | Change from — | | |
|---|---|---|---|
| | 1851–1861 | 1861–1871 | 1851–1871 |
| *Occupation* | | | |
| Professionals and rentiers | +18.0 | −9.7 | +6.7 |
| Agents and merchants | +0.9 | −9.4 | −8.6 |
| Service/semiprofessionals | −2.2 | +0.5 | −1.7 |
| Business employees | −7.5 | −4.5 | −11.7 |
| Government employees | +45.0 | −25.5 | +8.1 |
| Masters and manufacturers | −6.5 | +3.4 | +3.3 |
| Skilled workers | +4.5 | +1.0 | +3.5 |
| Transport workers | +35.6 | −3.3 | +31.0 |
| Other working class | +2.5 | −11.7 | −9.5 |
| Laborers | +9.7 | −1.6 | +7.9 |
| Business class | −0.4 | −4.0 | −4.3 |
| Working class | +7.2 | −1.1 | +6.0 |
| *Ethnicity* | | | |
| Irish Catholics | +18.3 | +6.9 | +26.5 |
| Irish Protestants | +11.6 | −4.5 | +6.6 |
| Scottish Presbyterians | −10.9 | −4.8 | −15.2 |
| Other Scottish | +3.9 | −3.1 | +0.8 |
| English Anglicans | +4.5 | −0.2 | +4.3 |
| English Methodists | −5.8 | +2.4 | −3.6 |
| Other English | +3.7 | −13.4 | −10.3 |
| Canadian Protestants | −10.2 | −4.3 | −14.1 |
| Canadian Catholics | +48.2 | −27.9 | +6.8 |
| U.S. nonwhites | −47.3 | +7.7 | −43.2 |
| U.S. whites | +9.9 | −4.7 | +4.7 |
| Other | −6.9 | +9.3 | +1.7 |

hardship. The business-class rate changed very little, but the working class's fertility ratio rose over 7 percent during the decade, an increase shared by all four occupational groups within it. This rise slowed during the 1860s, indicating its clear relationship to the depression. Though this behavior at first might seem irrational given the strain that the depression put on family resources, it made good sense from the perspective of working-class families in Hamilton. The depression reinforced the haunting spectre of an impoverished old age, always present to some extent in a society lacking in any form of social security. Children had always been viewed as a long-term asset to the family economy, a potential source of support in old age; given this viewpoint, the increase in working-class fertility had a reasonable foundation.[44]

The relationship of fertility to ethnicity as well as to class also altered during the depression. The fertility ratio of the poorest ethnic group, the Irish Catholics, increased a striking 18 percent from 1851 to 1861. The rate of the Canadian Catholics, another poor group, climbed as well. By contrast, the fertility ratio among more affluent groups—Scottish Presbyterians, English Methodists, and Canadian Protestants—declined markedly. During the prosperous second decade the Canadian Catholic and English Methodist fertility ratios changed direction, perhaps a reflection of the immigration of working-class Englishmen and the increased prosperity of Catholics who had lived longer in the country. In the course of the two decades the most striking changes in fertility ratios were the 27 percent increase among Irish Catholics and the decline of 15 percent among the Scottish Presbyterians, 10 percent among the other English (non-Anglican or Methodist), and 14 percent among the Canadian Protestants.

It is also clear that first-generation immigrants had a higher fertility ratio than members of the same ethnic groups born in Canada (Table 8.12). The reason remains obscure, though it does complement the other differences between native and foreign-born members of the same ethnic groups, particularly in school attendance and social mobility.[45]

The two groups whose fertility altered most markedly, the business employees and Irish Catholics, merit special attention. Among busi-

Table 8.12  Fertility ratio, by ethnic group: first generation versus Canadian-born, 1871.

| | Standard fertility ratio for women 20–49 | 20–24 | 25–29 | 30–34 | 35–39 | 40–44 | 45–49 |
|---|---|---|---|---|---|---|---|
| Canadian Protestant— England, Wales | 976 | 889 | 1,196 | 1,286 | 929 | 1,105 | 167 |
| English Anglican | 1,115 | 1,046 | 1,439 | 1,576 | 1,154 | 775 | 375 |
| Canadian Protestant— Scotland | 984 | 952 | 1,048 | 1,474 | 909 | 722 | 600 |
| Scottish Presbyterians | 1,146 | 744 | 1,494 | 1,598 | 1,171 | 1,110 | 271 |
| Canadian Protestant— Ireland | 1,061 | 682 | 1,407 | 1,652 | 1,000 | 1,100 | — |
| Irish Protestant | 1,127 | 1,129 | 1,738 | 1,431 | 1,159 | 682 | 362 |
| Canadian Catholic— Ireland | 794 | 571 | 1,333 | 1,714 | 750 | 500 | — |
| Irish Catholic | 1,303 | 973 | 1,594 | 1,821 | 1,543 | 1,020 | 300 |

ness employees the age structure of fertility as well as the overall rate altered between 1851 and 1871. In both 1851 and 1861 the rate among younger couples, those aged 25 to 29 and 30 to 34, was singularly low. By contrast these were the most fertile ages for other occupational groups. Business employees had an especially high rate among people 40 to 44 years old—in fact the highest rate of any occupational group. Apparently during the 1850s business employees and their wives, though not yet limiting their total fertility, planned their families by delaying childbirth until relatively late. To some extent this may have resulted from late marriage, but it was nonetheless a strategy that made family growth contingent upon the prior accumulation of economic resources.

By 1871 this pattern had altered completely. The fertility of business employees was higher in the 25- to 34-year-old cohort and distinctly lower among those 40 to 44 years old. Indeed the fertility ratio of the latter cohort was less than a third of what it had been two decades earlier. The business employees had thus adopted a much more contemporary pattern, limiting the total number of children and concentrating their birth in the early years of married life.

In the category of business employees the decline in fertility was lowest among the clerks and highest among the other commercial occupations: bookkeepers, accountants, salesmen. These were the newly emergent occupations in the more general category of commercial employees, the most attuned to the specialization of tasks within increasingly large and complex enterprises. It is interesting to speculate that they may also have been the most aggressive and ambitious aspirants to upward mobility in the business class.[45]

The increase in Irish Catholic fertility was very large and, at first glance, might be thought attributable to some factor other than a genuine increase in the number of children born to married couples. Two possibilities are a decline in marriage age and infant mortality. However marriage age did not drop, and the greatest increase in fertility took place among couples 30 to 44 years old. As for infant mortality, a detailed analysis of the parish registers of St. Mary's Church (the largest and oldest Roman Catholic Church in Hamilton) shows that the infant death rate actually rose slightly during the period.[46] Thus the leap in Irish Catholic marital fertility was genuine, not an artifact of either changing marriage age or infant mortality.

The demographic behavior of the Irish Catholic population changed outside of marriage as well as within it, for the proportion of illegitimate births (again as derived from the St. Mary's parish register) increased dramatically after 1855 (Table 8.13). Before 1855 there had rarely been more than one illegitimate birth for every hundred

Table 8.13    Illegitimate births per 1,000 live births, St. Mary's and Christ's Church parishes: Hamilton, 1840–1870.

| Year | St. Mary's | Christ's Church |
|------|------------|-----------------|
| 1840 | 17 | 12 |
| 1841 | 4 | 15 |
| 1842 | 12 | 18 |
| 1843 | 7 | 21 |
| 1844 | 6 | 21 |
| 1845 | 6 | 20 |
| 1846 | 5 | 17 |
| 1847 | 5 | 26 |
| 1848 | 5 | 21 |
| 1849 | 10 | 30 |
| 1850 | 9 | 15 |
| 1851 | 5 | 24 |
| 1852 | 4 | 16 |
| 1853 | 6 | 16 |
| 1854 | 5 | 9 |
| 1855 | 16 | 8 |
| 1856 | 19 | 13 |
| 1857 | 28 | 11 |
| 1858 | 31 | 9 |
| 1859 | 45 | 16 |
| 1860 | 52 | 40 |
| 1861 | 52 | 55 |
| 1862 | 50 | 49 |
| 1863 | 51 | 42 |
| 1864 | 46 | 27 |
| 1865 | 44 | 19 |
| 1866 | 36 | 31 |
| 1867 | 36 | 31 |
| 1868 | 30 | 34 |
| 1869 | 31 | 9 |
| 1870 | 32 | 11 |

total births. Beginning in 1855 the proportion climbed to a peak of more than 5 percent between 1860 and 1864. Though the depression of the late 1850s undoubtedly did boost the rate, it is important to note that the increase began in prosperous times and remained above its earlier level even after the depression had ended. In this way Catholic behavior contrasted with Anglican: Anglican illegitimacy also increased during the depression, but its rise did not begin until 1856, it peaked between 1861 and 1864, and then began a rapid decline to its predepression level.[47]

The cause of the distinctive Catholic pattern remains elusive. It certainly fits the pattern of a rise in illegitimacy among the popular classes during the growth of industrial capitalism, as identified by Edward Shorter.[48] Shorter attributes the increase to a breakdown of the mechanisms used by peasants to control fertility and to the simultaneous growth of a desire for erotic self-fulfillment on the part of young women. There is no evidence for Hamilton that either confirms or disproves Shorter's thesis. However it is possible that the increase in illegitimacy was related as much to unbalanced sex ratios as to the erosion of customary behavior, for as we have seen there were many more young Irish Catholic women than men in precisely those age groups among which illegitimacy was most common. Perhaps this discrepancy heightened the competition for husbands among young women and encouraged them to abandon usual restraints on premarital sexual behavior.[49]

Aside from the special case of business employees and Irish Catholics, the two large groups that underwent the most dramatic change in fertility, the experience of shoemakers and tailors also points to the clear connection between economic factors and family size. Shoemakers and tailors were the craftsmen most adversely affected by technological change during these years, and among both groups marked increases in fertility took place. The fertility ratio of tailors rose from 903 to 1,135, or 26 percent, and of shoemakers from 1,003 to 1,269, or 27 percent. This rise contrasts with the decline or stability in fertility among more prosperous wage workers such as carpenters, blacksmiths, and tinsmiths. Once again a rise in fertility appears to have been a working-class response to economic hardship.

For 1871 it is possible to examine the effect of wealth, home ownership, and property on fertility. The relationship between wealth and fertility is the most interesting because it was curvilinear: fertility was highest among the very wealthiest and very poorest groups. The fertility ratio for those in the ninetieth to ninety-ninth economic percentiles was 1,180, compared to 1,186 for the poorest group. Significantly, the lowest fertility occurred among the eightieth to eighty-ninth economic ranks, a group that included a substantial share of the business employees. The very wealthy had clearly not yet departed from traditional fertility patterns. Rather change was occurring among relatively affluent families and the poor.

Persistence within Hamilton boosted fertility. Those who had arrived in the city between 1861 and 1871 had a fertility ratio 9 percent lower than those who had been there for ten years and 7 percent lower than those there for twenty years. Unlike persistence home ownership had very little relationship to fertility in 1871.

We used a series of multivariate analyses to estimate the extent to which the relationships of fertility to occupation, class, ethnicity, wealth, home ownership, and persistence, apparent with simple descriptive statistics, held with simultaneous controls on all factors. In general the multivariate analyses support the conclusions already presented.[50] It does appear that, with corrections for occupational status, the Irish Protestant fertility ratio increased as much as the Irish Catholic, an indication that it was not religion that shaped the high rate among the latter. Moreover the distinction between first- and second-generation immigrants actually grows stronger in the multivariate analysis, clear support for the conclusion that native birth began to dissolve the distinctive paterns of fertility exhibited by various ethnic groups.

The increasing differences between the fertility of ethnic groups arose from the group occupational or ethnic standing. The great rise in Irish Catholic fertility was at least in part a function of its working-class character, and the decline among the Scottish Presbyterians, English Methodists, and Canadian Protestants related to the prominence of business-class occupations among them. Ethnicity, in short, served as a mediator between class and fertility.

Like all social behavior, fertility is learned through socialization; it is not the result of mechanical forces. The milieu in which socialization occurs is thus of critical importance. Attitudes toward fertility are probably acquired relatively early in adulthood or in adolescence and may not change very dramatically later in life. Thus it would be the dominant attitudes within the milieu in which young men and women grew up and not so much their adult occupations that contributed most to their attitudes toward fertility.[51]

The most homogeneous settings for socialization in nineteenth-century Hamilton were the subcommunities in which ethnicity and class overlapped. Thus the son of an Irish Catholic laborer who managed to become a clerk or grocer may well have retained the approach to fertility more common among Irish Catholic laborers than among the members of the class he had entered. Similarly a downwardly mobile Scottish Presbyterian might have spent his youth and young adulthood in a higher class than the one in which he eventually found himself. This hypothesis about the importance of the setting in which socialization takes place makes understandable the lower fertility of the native-born children of immigrants. More likely than their foreign-born contemporaries to attend school, they came of age in a more ethnically and socially diverse setting. Never having lived in Ireland, England, or Scotland, they would have felt less direct impact of ethnicity on their lives. The agencies that mediated between class and fertility in their case extended beyond their ethnic group and embraced the school, peers, and culture of urban North America, which interacted in ways that we are unable to trace.

Speculative though the reasoning may be about the mediating effect of ethnicity on the relationship between class and fertility, it is clear that class trends in fertility were consistent with the forces influencing the family economy described elsewhere in this book. Those families most actively limiting their fertility were the commercial employees in the upper-middle sectors of the economic rank order. Recall that their adolescent children lived longer at home and remained longer in school, not contributing by and large to the family's income. The aspirations that many of these families held and the economic pressures upon them are evident in the inverse relationship between property ownership and servant employment. It was precisely the business-class families of moderate means unable to both purchase a home and employ a servant who more often chose to have a resident domestic, the conventional sign of affluence and gentility. Caught thus in a squeeze between their aspirations for their children—a realistic assessment of the relationship of prolonged schooling to jobs in commerce and the professions—and their aspirations for themselves, these families began to limit their fertility.[52]

Working-class families of similar economic standing more often chose to purchase a home. For them the prolonged residence of their children at home was not a drain but a source of prosperity, because teenage sons and sometimes daughters worked and contributed to the family income. During the early years of industrialization jobs near home for young men became more widely available, and industrial work opened to young women as well. With no pressure to keep their children at school beyond the age at which they could enter industrial work, working-class families could view an additional child as another potential source of support. Thus it is important to remember that in Hamilton the prolongation of adolescent residence at home, the increase in the proportion of working-class adolescents employed, and the rise in working-class fertility all happened at about the same time.

## The Family and Social Change

Families in Hamilton followed a cycle that altered only a little during the course of the two decades of early industrialization. Some people began to marry a bit earlier and others to have fewer children. However the proportion of families in different phases of the cycle remained relatively constant, altered only by a slight aging of the population. Households, however, did alter notably. Far fewer of them included relatives, boarders, and servants in 1871 than in 1851. Thus the balance of potential workers to consumers within families remained constant, while within households the proportion of potential workers declined. To some extent the prolonged residence at home and increased employment of adolescent children compensated for the decline in numbers of other household members.

By and large only minimal relationships existed between the structure of households and their cycle, and this was true in Buffalo and in Erie County towns and villages as well. The major exceptions occurred among families with no children and families headed by women, both of which were more likely to contain relatives or boarders. Families experiencing the phase of greatest strain—when all children were too young to work—usually were unable to compensate for their difficulties through the incorporation of other people into the household. Throughout the various phases of the family cycle affluent households more often contained members other than parents and children. The distinction was greater in 1851 than in 1871, when the general decline in the proportion of households with nonconjugal family members had lessened the degree of difference between groups. The distinction was almost entirely one of class. In virtually no instance did ethnicity appear to be a significant variable differentiating the family cycle, structure, or economy.

Households, it must be stressed, were fluid. The composition of most of them changed during a decade and probably much more often. Throughout the period a sizable though diminishing portion occasionally housed a relative or boarder.

Class also affected the likelihood that children would work. Before jobs for adolescents had become widely available little class distinction existed in rates of adolescent employment. Working-class families probably experienced enormous strain during these years, and the unavailability of local jobs undoubtedly influenced the frequent early departure of young men and women from home. When employment opportunities became more widely available, working-class children entered the labor force earlier. By contrast more affluent young people remained more often in school. Families, especially those in the working-class, clearly expected a contribution from their adolescent sons. Families apparently preferred to have their sons rather than their daughters employed, and only when no son of employable age lived at home did a sizable fraction, though still a minority, of families send their daughters to work.

Few couples could expect to live very long together after their children had left home. In fact a very high proportion of women over the age of 45 were widows, and at all ages women were widowed more often than men. Men who had been widowed found it much easier than women to remarry. Thus women could realistically expect a phase in their lives when they would have to support children who remained at home or find a way of earning their own livelihood. Few of them left home to work, for in Hamilton there were few jobs to which they could turn. Rather they often took in boarders to supplement their income or were supported by a working child. Those in dire need were given charity by the Ladies' Benevolent Society, and some elderly women moved in with relatives or other families, a practice much more common on farms than in the city and probably a result of the presence of more kin in rural than in urban areas. However very few elderly widowed men lived with their kin. When unable to maintain their own households, they more often lived as boarders with another family.

Few simple statements can summarize the relationships between families and industrialization. One reason is that industrialization itself is an imprecise concept, too often confused with capitalism. At least one major contrast, though, must be made: namely, between industrialization in the textile industries and industrialization in metals and machinery. In textile producing areas whole families sometimes worked in mills, and the rate of employment among women and young children was quite high. In towns such as Hamilton, which industrialized without a significant textile industry, almost no married women worked for wages, and little employment existed for young children. Whether differences in total family wages also existed remains unknown. However the two employment patterns had very different effects on the organization of family life.[53]

Another reason why simple summary statements about the relationship of families to social change are difficult to make is that they obscure the intimate relationship between families and class. For centuries the timing, direction, and causes of changes in family organization have differed by class. In his history of the family in England between 1500 and 1800 Lawrence Stone makes this point forcefully: "Generalizations about family change have always to be qualified by a careful definition of the class or status group, the literate or the illiterate sector, the zealously godly or the casually conformist, which is under discussion."[54] On a more general level William Goode has argued that the relationship between industrialization and the family is mediated by class. He claims, "When industrialization begins, it is the lower-class family that loses least by participating in it and lower-class family patterns are the first to change in the society . . . in an industrializing process both the peasants and primitives are forced to adjust their family patterns to the demands of industrial enterprise more swiftly, and see less to lose in the adjustment. By contrast, the middle and upper strata are better able to utilize the new opportunities of industrialization by relinquishing their kin ties more slowly, so that these changes will occur in a later phase of industrialization."[55]

Only a model that examines the family by class can explain the contrast between its contemporary and its pre- and early capitalist predecessor. That mode, moreover, cannot be based on a diffusion of innovation from higher to lower classes, for as Goode observes, different types of changes begin at various points in the class structure. The five great changes in family organization that have occurred are: the separation of home and work place; the increased nuclearity of household structure; the decline in marital fertility; the prolonged residence of children in the home of their parents; and the lengthened period in which husbands and wives live together after their children have left home. The first two began among the working class and among the wage-earning segment of the business class (clerks and kindred workers). The third started among the business class, particularly among its least affluent, most specialized, and most mobile sectors. The fourth began at about the same time in both the working and business class, though the children of the former usually went to work and the latter to school. The date at which the fifth commenced and its relationship to class remains unknown; certainly it began well beyond the early industrial era. It is clearly not possible to argue that the bourgeoisie pioneered a modern family form later imitated by the working class.

To some extent the adoption of new patterns of domestic organization has reflected shifts in values, but by itself value change contributes very little to any understanding of why the great alterations in family organization took place. The key lies rather in the family economy, in the strains, opportunities, and anxieties induced by the differential social impact of capitalist development upon domestic life. Individual people have never been automatons, and deterministic models do not adequately explain human experience. Yet people are not completely free either, and it is the reasons why they chose as they did among limited possibilities that historians must discover. In that choice the values that justified traditional cultural patterns or those that challenged them mediated the great forces of social change and family behavior.

The process of family change is not evolutionary but dialectical, for family forms generate in part the contradictions that lead to their supercession. Within the family formations characteristic of industrial capitalist society in North America, for instance, the emergence of newly dependent and exploited strata among women and young people has unleashed the profound social change that public policy lamely tried to tame, moderate, or modify. However, though they contain an inherent dynamic, families never drift free of their anchor in a class structure and economic system, now increasingly secured by the intrusive authority of the state either directly through the schools, the courts, and the welfare system or indirectly as in the sanctioned impetus to consumption and debt carefully cultivated by the media from childhood through old age. For a brief historical moment as it firmed up the boundaries between itself and its community the bourgeois family was very private. By contrast, consistently scrutinized and regulated by newly emergent state and charitable authority, the working-class family never secured similar autonomy, not even fleetingly. It is the myth of the private family that has been diffused, not its reality. In truth we have returned to a point at which the boundaries between families in all classes and their surrounding social, economic, and political context have become tenuous and indistinct. Whether this should be counted a gain or a loss is not an objective question.[56]

# 9 Early Industrial Capitalism: The Institutional Legacy

Institutions touched families most intimately and universally through the agency of public schools. The widespread belief in the pathological domestic life of the poor that helped spur the early development of public education revealed the willingness of early nineteenth-century school promoters to intervene directly and without invitation in the lives of the working class. The scrutiny of impoverished families in order to test their worthiness to receive charity underlined the same point: namely, the relative nuclearity of the poor household, its progressive confinement during early industrialization to husband, wife, and children, does not provide evidence for either privacy or isolation.

Those scholars who have utilized evidence of kin networks to counter arguments for either isolation or nuclearity have pointed only to part of the problem with the viewpoint they criticize.[1] From another perspective the presence or absence of kin is nearly irrelevant to the issue, because since early in the nineteenth century the state and quasi-official agencies have invaded the family life of the poor, intruding on the relationships between parents and children, assessing degrees of poverty and moral worth, and exposing their conclusions to the widest possible audience. In the end what an affluent class anxious about the domestic life of the poor failed to gain through persuasion it won through compulsion. Interpreted as a moral condition, poverty became a blight to be cured through the formation of working-class character in public schools.

No one articulated the perceived relationship between the family life of the poor and the necessity of public schools more clearly than Henry Barnard, one of the great figures in the early history of public education. In 1851 Barnard wrote: "No one at all familiar with the deficient household arrangements and deranged machinery of domestic life, of the extreme poor and ignorant, to say nothing of the intemperate—of the examples of rude manners, impure and profane language, and all the vicious habits of low-bred idleness, which abound in certain sections of all populous districts, can doubt that it is better for children to be removed as early and as long as possible from such scenes and such examples and placed in an infant or primary school, under the care and instruction of a kind, affectionate, and skillful female teacher." The object of that early education, Barnard made clear, had little to do with cognitive skills. "The primary object in securing the early school attendance of children," he observed, "is not so much their intellectual culture as the regulation of the feelings and dispositions, the extirpation of vicious propensities, the pre-occupation of the wilderness of the young heart with the seeds and germs of moral beauty, and the formation of a lovely and virtuous character by the habitual practice of cleanliness, delicacy, refinement, good temper, gentleness, kindness, justice, and truth."[2]

Barnard's argument would not have startled any nineteenth-century educational promoters, for they echoed its essential themes over and over again as they sold public education to North America. In Canada in 1862, for instance, the inspector of asylums and prisons asserted, "In our large cities, particularly, a great proportion of the children of the lower classes are utterly destitute and neglected, and grow up in our midst without receiving any education or training to act their part in life as honest and useful citizens."[3] Contrary to popular mythology public education did not represent the institutional culmination of a humane, democratic, egalitarian impulse. Rather it reflected a horror at the consequences of urban poverty: crime, disorder, and immorality. Public schools embodied the attempt to alleviate the casualties of an urban capitalist social order through the reformation of character rather than the redistribution of wealth or power. Public school systems were a conservative attempt to shore up a social structure under stress, one element in a new institutional configuration designed to retain a structure of inequality endangered by profound social change.

In the eighteenth century conservatives opposed mass education because they believed it to be dangerous: once educated the poor would revolt. Southern slaveholders in the United States used precisely the same justification to keep their slaves illiterate by law. Thomas Jefferson, who supported mass education, argued in exactly the same way: education would prevent the accumulation of political power and keep alive the capacity for revolt among a people jealous of their liberty.[4]

The achievement of the first generation of public school promoters, led most visibly by Horace Mann and Henry Barnard in the United States and Egerton Ryerson in Canada, was to reverse radically the classic connection between education and political radicalism. They succeeded in creating public school systems because they argued that education would exert a conservative influence. In order to make their case school promoters had to redefine the nature of schooling. To eighteenth-century conservatives schools were dangerous places because they dealt with the mind; they became safe in the nineteenth century when they turned their attention to morality. Staunchly committed to the primacy of the moral, schools have remained safe ever since.

## The Context of Public Education

In the discussion of public educational systems the word *systems* is crucial, for in neither Canada nor the United States were schools unusual or novel creations in the nineteenth century, and in neither place was it unusual for them to receive some sort of public support, though in most places the line between public and private was not drawn with precision until well into the nineteenth century. Indeed in New York and Massachusetts in the last century the proportion of young people attending school achieved its greatest increase in the two or three decades prior to the development of public school systems. Though schools existed and frequently received some public support, the haphazard arrangements of the seventeenth, eighteenth, and early nineteenth centuries cannot be considered true progenitors of the school systems we know today. By the latter part of the nineteenth century the organization, scope, and role of schooling had been fundamentally transformed. In place of a few casual schools dotted about town and country there existed in most cities true educational systems: carefully articulated, age-graded, hierarchically structured groupings of schools, primarily free and often compulsory, administered by full-time experts and progressively taught by specially trained staff. No longer casual adjuncts to the home or apprenticeship, schools were highly formal institutions designed to play a critical role in the socialization of the young, the maintenance of social order, and the promotion of economic development. Within the space of forty or fifty years a new social institution had been invented, and it is this startling and momentous development that we must seek to understand.[5]

The origins of public educational systems cannot be understood apart from their context, for they formed part of four critical developments that reshaped North American society during the first three-quarters of the nineteenth century. They were the spread of capitalist social and economic relations, the assumption by the state of direct responsibility for some aspects of social welfare, the invention of institutionalization as a solution to social problems, and the redefinition of the family.

During the early and mid-nineteenth century massive immigration, urbanization, and profound changes in the organization of work reshaped the economic and social order of North America. The pace and timing of social development varied of course from region to region. However everywhere a close temporal connection existed between social development and the creation of public educational systems. In the United States, for example, the date at which the first high school opened provides a rough but convenient index of educational development, which, across the country, retained a strong association with social and economic complexity.[6] Our understanding of the relationships between the introduction of industrial capitalism, the transformation of technology, the redistribution of the population into cities, and the creation of systems of public education remains far from precise. However it is important to observe and remember the temporal connection between the economy, the social order, and the schools. In fact educational promoters of the time made explicit connections between economic development and the introduction of public educational systems. Very much in the way of contemporary theorists of human capital nineteenth-century school promoters argued that an investment in education would stimulate economic growth and yield a high and immediate return.

The development of systems of public education did not account for the sole thrust of governments into the area of social welfare during the early and mid-nineteenth century. In England, the United States, and Canada it was in this period that governments generally began to exchange their haphazard and minimal concern with social problems for a systematic approach to questions of welfare. At the start of the period problems of poverty, public health, crime, insanity, disease, and the condition of labor remained more or less untended, subject to ancient legislation, custom, sporadic regulation, and public and private charity. By the end of the third quarter of the nineteenth century each had become the subject of public debate, legislative activity, and the supervision of newly created state administrative bodies with full-time expert staffs.[7]

The state did not enter into the area of public welfare without serious opposition. Its activity commenced at a time when the very distinction between public and private had not emerged with any sort of clarity, and in this situation the definition of public responsibility became an especially elusive task. In most cases voluntary activity preceded state action. Philanthropic associations, often composed primarily of women and usually associated with the spread of evangelical religion, first undertook the alleviation of social distress. In part their activity reflected the lack of any public apparatus to cope with the increased misery that people discovered in the growing cities of the late eighteenth and early nineteenth centuries; in part too it reflected the belief that social distress represented a temporary if recurring problem which charitable activity could alleviate. The activities of voluntary associations, however, usually convinced their members that problems were both far more widespread and intractable than they had believed, and consequently they turned to the public for assistance, first usually in the form of money and later in the assumption of formal and permanent responsibility.[8]

However no very clear models for action existed, and people concerned with social policy at the time debated not only the legitimacy of public activity but its organizational form. Concerning education their disagreements over the nature of public organizations reflected fundamental value conflicts and alternative visions of social development. If the shape modern society eventually assumed appears inevitable to us today, it did not appear at all clear to the people of the time, which is an observation we must remember if we are to understand the passion aroused by debates about social institutions and policies in the nineteenth century.

In fact in the United States four distinct models for the organization of formal education coexisted and competed in the early and mid-nineteenth century, and at the time the outcome of their conflict did not appear at all self-evident to many sane and responsible people. The form that triumphed might be called incipient bureaucracy. Though its advocates generally supported the extension of the competitive and laissez-faire approach to economic issues, they encouraged a strong regulatory role for the state in the area of social welfare and morality. Their model organizations were controlled by bodies responsible to legislatures, financed directly through taxation, administered by experts, and relatively large in size. They were, in short, public institutions in a novel and dramatic sense.[9]

Thus the victory of incipient bureaucracy reflected the new faith in the power of formal institutions to alleviate social and individual distress. The novelty of this commitment to institutions must be recalled, for it represented a radical departure in social policy. By the last quarter of the nineteenth century shapers of social policy had embodied in concrete form the notion that rehabilitation, therapy, medical treatment, and education should take place within large, formal, and often residential institutions. This momentous development—the birth of the institutional state—requires special comment.

## The Institutional State

We live in an institutional state. Our lives spin outward from the hospitals where we are born to the school systems that dominate our youth through the bureaucracies for which we work and back again to the hospitals in which we die. If we stray, falter, or lose our grip, we are led or coerced toward the institutions of mental health, justice, or public welfare. Specialists in obstetrics, pediatrics, education, crime, mental illness, unemployment, recreation, to name only some of the most obvious, wait in the yellow pages to offer their expertise in the service of our well-being. Characteristically we respond to a widespread problem through the creation of an institution, the training of specialists, and the certification of their monopoly over a part of our lives.

Institutions and experts often appear inevitable, almost eternal. That, after all, is the way the world works. It is hard—almost impossible—for us to recall that they are a modern invention. In North America prior to the nineteenth century few experts or specialized institutions existed. The sick, the insane, and the poor mixed indiscriminately within almshouses. Criminals of all ages and varieties remained in prison for fairly short periods awaiting trial. If guilty they were punished not by long incarceration but by fine, whipping, or execution. Dependent or troublesome strangers did not receive much charity; they were simply warned out of town. Children learned to read in a variety of ways and attended schools irregularly. In short, families and communities coped with social and personal problems in customary and informal ways.

Everything changed within fifty to seventy-five years. By the last quarter of the nineteenth century specialized institutions were dealing with crime, poverty, disease, mental illness, juvenile delinquency, the blind, the deaf and dumb, and the ignorant. Institutions proliferated so rapidly that by the 1860s some states began to create boards of state charities to coordinate and rationalize public welfare.[10]

The treatment of crime, poverty, ignorance, and disease repeated the same story with different details. Institutions suddenly came to dominate public life in a radical departure in social policy. Aside from their sudden creation most new public institutions experienced a similar cycle of development during their early histories: a shift in official purpose from reform to custody. Mental hospitals, school systems, reformatories, and penitentiaries began optimistically with assumptions about the tractability of problems and the malleability of human nature. Early promoters expected them to transform society through their effect on individual personalities. In some instances, as in the case of early mental hospitals or the first reformatory for young women, the optimism appeared justified for a few years. However institutions, as even their supporters soon came to admit, could not work miracles. Rates of recovery remained low and recidivism high; school systems did not eliminate poverty and vice; on occasion ungrateful inmates even set their institutions on fire.[11]

The public had invested heavily in new institutions that a reasonable person might conclude were failures. Nonetheless the newly created institutional managers did not intend either to admit failure or to abandon the intricate hierarchical professional worlds they had created. Instead they altered their justification, declaring that mental illness and crime frequently arose from heredity and were incurable, lower-class children were incorrigible, and paupers were genetically unable and unwilling to work. Institutions existed to keep deviants off the streets, to prevent a glut on the labor market, to contain rather than cure the ills of society. This shift from reform to custody characterized the history of reformatories, mental hospitals, prisons, and school systems in the first two or three decades of their existence.

Social historians disagree about the impulse underlying institutional development. Why did the institutional state emerge at the time and in the manner it did? The question is straightforward, the answer complex and elusive. Actually two sets of events must be explained: the origins and founding of institutions and the shift from reform to custody.

First, consider the pattern and timing of institutional development. The new institutions of the early nineteenth century divide into various groups. Those on which historians have focused most sharply treated deviance: mental hospitals, poorhouses, reformatories, penitentiaries. The first mental hospital, the private McLean's, opened in Massachusetts in 1818, followed in 1835 by the first state hospital, in Worcester, Massachusetts. The first reformatory, also a private corporation, the New York House of Refuge, opened in 1825; the first state reform school incarcerated its first boys in 1848. Both Massachusetts and New York established a network of poorhouses in the 1820s as a result of the famous Quincy and Yates reports, which urged the virtual abolition of outdoor relief. In Ontario the Provincial Penitentiary opened in 1835 and the Lunatic Asylum in 1850.

New institutions were not solely residential, nor did they serve only those whom we today label deviant. Indeed people became increasingly willing to put their relatives and friends into institutions. Private mental hospitals served the affluent; parents of moderate wealth used early high schools for their children; poor parents committed their own children to reformatories. The most notable of the nonresidential institutions designed to serve a clearly defined sector of more ordinary people was the public school. Nineteenth-century educational promoters equated ignorance with deviance and both with poverty, but they intended public schools to serve a broader portion of the population than the children of the slums. Public schooling became especially popular among the middle classes. Tax-supported schools of sorts had existed for centuries. The novelty during the nineteenth century rested in the creation of systems of public education—age-graded, finely articulated, nominally universal institutions presided over by specially trained experts and administrators. In New York City the system of public schools began with the organization of the Free School Society in 1805. The first state board of education was established in Massachusetts in 1837 and the Superintendency of Public Instruction in the Provinces of Canada in 1841. By 1880 elaborate hierarchical educational systems existed in most urban centers.[12]

New or novel institutions served other groups as well. Private boarding schools for the children of the rich developed in the antebellum period in the United States. The most influential of them, according to their historian, was St. Paul's, started in Concord, New Hampshire, in 1855. Indeed it is fascinating to observe the parallels between private academies and other institutions. In their educational philosophy, organizational ideal, and theory of human nature early reform schools resembled nothing so much as academies for the poor.[13]

In New York City, as Alan Horlick has shown, merchants developed a series of institutions to control and socialize the incoming hordes of young, aggressive, and undeferential clerks. This effort gave rise during the early nineteenth century to the YMCA, the Mercantile Library Association, and similar organizations.[14]

The first general hospitals opened in 1752 in Philadelphia, in 1792 in New York City, and in 1821 in Boston. Construed primarily as charities, early hospitals were supposed to cure both the physical and moral afflictions of the poor, who composed their patient populations. As with schools, prisons, or reformatories, the purposes of early hospitals included the reformation of character; like the sponsors of other institutions hospital supporters compounded poverty, crime, ignorance, and disease into a single amalgam. Hospitals proved no more able than schools, prisons, or reformatories to uplift social character, and by the 1870s their purpose narrowed to the

treatment of specific diseases. At the same time the internal development of hospitals traced a path similar to that followed in other institutions: a growth in size and complexity accompanied by an emphasis
on professional management increasingly divorced from lay influence.[15]

At the most intimate level even the family reflected the thrust of
institutional development in more public spheres. Decreasingly the
place of both work and residence, with boundaries more tightly
drawn between itself and the community, and decreasingly the cus-
todian of the deviant and deficient, the family—the working-class as
well as the middle-class family—became a sharply delimited haven, a
specialized agency for the nurture of the young. Within families sex
roles became more clearly defined, and by the mid-nineteenth century
Catherine Beecher among others was attempting to certify the institutionalization of the home through the conversion of domesticity
into a science.[16]

In sum the institutional explosion did not issue directly or solely
from state sponsorship; neither were institutions directed only toward
deviance, nor were they solely asylums. More accurately institutional
development during the early and mid-nineteenth century should be
described as the creation of formal organizations with specialized
clienteles and a reformist or character-building purpose.

Institutions were not in themselves novel. Poorhouses had existed
in Colonial New England, and the role of religion, institutionalized
through churches, was pervasive and disciplinary. Indeed Michel
Foucault labels the seventeenth century the age of the great confinement. Nonetheless the use of secular institutions as deliberate agencies
of social policy, their specialization, and their emphasis on the formation or reformation of character represented a new departure in
modern history.[17]

Most major social institutions originated in a two-stage process.
They commenced as private corporations to serve public purposes but
within a few decades were imitated, superseded, augmented, or expanded by the state. The transition from voluntarism to the state did
not represent a simple evolution. Certainly the magnitude of the problems undertaken by early voluntary corporations—the alleviation of
poverty, mental illness, delinquency, ignorance—strained private resources. Financially, voluntary corporations did not rely solely, or in
many cases at all, on private contributions. Rather they commonly received public funds. The assumption of primary responsibility for the
operation as well as the funding of institutions consequently represented a shift in generally acceptable models for public organization.
Elsewhere this shift has been called the transition from paternalistic

and corporate voluntarism to incipient bureaucracy. Voluntarism upheld an ideal of organizations controlled by self-perpetuating corporations of wealthy, enlightened, and public-spirited citizens, essentially limited in size, staffed by talented generalists. The shift to the state reflected a belief that public funding required public control, a commitment to expansion of scale, and an emphasis on the importance of specialized, expert administration.[18]

The shift from voluntarism to the state appears in the New York House of Refuge, the New York Free School Society, and another interesting variant, the Boston Primary School Committee. When these voluntary corporations went public, they often altered their purpose as well as their form. In the case of mental hospitals the entrance of the state meant the extension of service from the well-to-do served by McLean's to the poor treated at Worcester; in the case of public schools the opposite occurred, as school promoters sought to incorporate the children of the affluent into the free schools, which in their early years had suffered from their association with pauperism and charity. Both the mental hospitals and the public schools illustrate an attempt to broaden the social composition of public institutions.

The early history of hospitals formed an instructive if partial exception to the shift away from corporate voluntarism. The great early hospitals in Philadelphia, New York, and Boston remained under the control of private nonprofit corporations. When public representatives wanted hospitals to expand their size, role, or scope, they could not bring them under state control. Rather they sometimes had to establish parallel institutions. In Boston in the 1860s the board and staff of the Massachusetts General Hospital fought against the creation of Boston City Hospital, which they explicitly viewed as an institution more democratic and more accessible to public influence in such important ways as admission procedures and internal routines such as visiting hours. The social group that wanted Boston City was not the very poor served by Massachusetts General but the skilled workers, petty proprietors, and clerks who were less welcome at the older hospital yet unable to afford easily the cost of medical care at home. The reason why hospitals remained under private control probably rests in their relationship to the medical profession. Often physicians instigated the founding of hospitals and played the principal roles not only in a strictly professional capacity but also in institutional design and administration. Hospitals differed from other major social institutions in that a prestigious, prosperous, and generally cohesive corps of professionals preceded their establishment. By contrast mental hospitals and schools, to take two examples, created two new professions. The founding of mental hospitals and school systems, therefore, depended more on lay support, and they consequently remained much more susceptible to public influence during their early years.[19]

Although private hospitals did not go public, they still reflected one process that characterized other institutions: the shift in the social origin of their clientele. For years hospital supporters had tried to broaden the social composition of the patient population, but as in the case of early public education the aura of charity clung to hospitals. In sharp contrast to public schools, however, hospitals were unable to shed the aura until a series of demographic changes and medical advances coalesced during the late nineteenth and early twentieth centuries. The transition from home to hospital care by the affluent was symbolized dramatically by the construction of the expensive and luxurious Phillips House as a branch of Massachusetts General in 1917.

The supersession of corporate voluntarism reflected the increasingly sharp distinction between public and private, which formed part of a larger theme in social development: the drawing of sharp boundaries between the elements of social organization; the separation of family and community; the division of community into discrete and specialized functions.

The connection that exists between the emergence of modern society and the expansive specialization of both public and private institutions remains open to interpretation. How are we to account in this case for the origins of public institutions? What precisely did they signify? Historians currently offer two principal competing interpretations, which, put crudely, can be called the fear of social disorder versus the humanitarian impulse. The most notable exponent of the former is David Rothman and of the latter Gerald Grob. Here we must risk some violence to their complex and subtle work in order to highlight the central point in contention and the problems left unresolved. Although Grob has attacked Rothman, the two share much common ground. Both tell a similar story and even stress many of the same factors, but they differ in the interpretation they give to events and ultimately in the meaning they assign to American history in the formative years between the Revolution and the Civil War.

Rothman argues that the fear of disorder arising from the breakdown of traditional communal controls spurred the discovery of the asylum. He writes, "The response in the Jacksonian period to the deviant and the dependent was first and foremost a vigorous attempt to promote the stability of the society at a moment when traditional ideas and practices appeared outmoded, constricted, and ineffective . . . all represented an effort to insure the cohesion of the community in new and changing circumstances." Elsewhere he asserts, "Under the influence of demographic, economic and intellectual developments, they [Americans] perceived that the traditional mechanisms of social control were obsolete."[20]

Grob emphasizes the individualist philosophy and humanitarian impulses that arose from the Second Great Awakening in the early nineteenth century. Although he cannot deny the pervasive fear of social disorder or the manifest influence of class in the social origins of reformers, he argues:

> Since the absence of broad theoretical models relating to public policy made it difficult to gather or to use empirical data in a meaningful way, policy often reflected external factors such as unconscious class interests or similar social assumptions that were never questioned. This is not to imply that mid-nineteenth-century legislators and administrators were deficient in intelligence or malevolent in character. It is only to say that lack of theory and methodology often led to the adoption of policies that in the long run had results which were quite at variance with the intentions of those involved in their formulation.[21]

Grob's arresting and partly true statement rests on the assumption that knowledge—hard data—scientific in character and free from bias does in fact exist and awaits discovery by students of deviance and dependence. It assumes further that the acquisition of scientific knowledge automatically leads to rational, humanitarian solutions framed in the best interests of the people to whom they are directed. The history of social and behavioral science should make us skeptical.

Five problems, which appear in varying degrees in different accounts, underlie most formulations of both the social disorder and humanitarian interpretations, the very problems that appear in most attempts to explain early nineteenth-century social reforms and institutional creation. First, most interpretations do not provide a link between institutions created for deviants and the other institutional developments of the time. An adequate interpretation must encompass not only the asylum, not only prisons, mental hospitals, and poorhouses, but also public schools, academies, the YMCA, and ultimately the family. Striking parallels exist between the timing, theory, and shape of those developments that affect deviants, dependents, children, adolescents, and families. An understanding of any of them depends on the exploration of their interconnection.

Second, definitions of disorder usually remain loose. Scholars invoke industrialization and urbanization, but these broad concepts mask as much as they reveal. What was it exactly about the development of cities that created social disorder? What type of mechanisms broke down, when, and why? The arrival of hundreds of thousands of impoverished immigrants might explain a heightened concern with poverty or account for some of the nervousness on the part of genteel natives, but it assists little with an attempt to comprehend the origins of academies or even the special attention paid to the mentally ill.

Third, the way in which historical context intersects with the perception of people differentially situated in the social order usually remains unclear. The exact relationship between the periodization of socioeconomic change and the identity of institutional sponsors and opponents—and opposition did exist—remains unclear in most accounts. We are left with David Rothman's "Americans," surely a category within which significant differences of opinion existed. Which Americans wanted the asylum? How did their perceptions influence public policy?

There are few if any historical subjects more treacherous than human motivation. Thus the fourth problem with existing interpretations: they use simplistic models of individual behavior. That is they confuse the analysis of individual motivation with the analysis of class. Class analysis does not deny that individuals believe they do good works. It regards individual sincerity as irrelevant. Class analysis concerns the actions of groups and the relationship between activity and class position. It does not deny the role of religion or tradition in the formulation and expression of class action. The theory of class is neither crudely reductionist nor contradicted by the existence of deeply felt humanitarian conviction. To argue that institutional promoters believed they were acting in the best interests of the poor, the criminal, the mentally ill, or the ignorant, and to leave the argument there, is not to refute a class analysis but merely to finesse it.

The reluctance to probe the interconnections between social context, social position, ideology, and policy underlies the fifth problem. Most accounts of institutional development and social reform uncritically accept the interpretation of problems offered by institutional promoters and social reformers. They fail to question the description of crime, poverty, mental illness, or illiteracy offered in official sources. Thus Grob simply accepts the proposition that immigrants were more prone than others to insanity and does not probe the social characteristics shaping definitions of mental illness. Other historians similarly accept the proposition that crime increased disproportionately in early nineteenth-century cities, that industrialization eroded the stability of the lower-class family, or that, as Oscar Handlin has written, the Irish were degraded.

The acceptance of official descriptions of reality ignores important factors. First, deviance is at least in part a social or political category and cannot be defined as a universal. It is the product of prevailing laws, customs, and views. Second, institutional promoters sometimes gauged popular sentiments inaccurately. The poor occasionally used new institutions in ways that violated the purposes and perceptions of their sponsors. For example parents themselves provided the largest source of commitments to reform schools. Poor parents turned to reform schools, which had not yet acquired their present stigma, precisely as other and more affluent parents turned to academies as places that would remove their refractory children from trouble and educate them at the same time. Other poor parents used reform schools in difficult periods as places in which children could stay safely during episodes of family crisis. Indeed wherever historians have looked with care severe disjunctions emerge between official perception of client populations and their actual behavior.[22] Thus a new interpretation of the origin of the institutional state should be set within a revised framework for North American social development between the late eighteenth and mid-nineteenth century, a framework that encompasses the experience and activities of ordinary people and supersedes the usual recourse to industrialization and urbanization with more precise concepts.

Before turning to this task however it is important both to point out that the introduction of the institutional state did not reflect a universal consensus about the direction of social development and to highlight the relationship of institutional development to perceptions of change within families.

Lest it seem inevitable that modern society should have become an institutional state, it is worth pointing out that responsible people did see other choices. In New York for instance Charles Loring Brace proposed the shipment of city urchins to the West as an alternative to their institutionalization, and elsewhere opponents and skeptics critically, perceptively, and, in retrospect, with an eerily modern ring pointed to the dangers and limitations of institutions.[23]

One of their common arguments centered on the family. Both proponents and critics of institutions agreed that the ideal family provides a paradigm for social policy. To their supporters institutions would not supply an alternative to the family but would become quite literally surrogate families for the mentally ill, the criminal, the delinquent, and the schoolchild. In fact it was precisely through their embodiment of a family environment that new institutions, according to their sponsors, would perform their rehabilitative, therapeutic, or educational work. The difficulty, as critics astutely pointed out, was that no institution could imitate a real family.[24]

Nonetheless in the early and mid-nineteenth century both critics and supporters of institutions shared a widespread sense that the family was in some sort of trouble, though about the exact nature of that difficulty they remained somewhat vague. In fact they probably mistook change for deterioration, for the fragments of historical evidence about the family in this period indicate not breakdown but an important shift in domestic structure and relationships (see Chapter 8).

Popular ideas about domesticity and the role of women reflected the redefinition of the family. The cult of true womanhood, as it has been called, urged women to create within the home a haven against the harsh world of commerce and a nest in which children could be reared with attention and affection. From one perspective the ideal of domesticity has justified a not especially subtle attempt to keep women in the home and subservient to their husbands. However it also elevated the importance of women as the moral guardians and spiritual saviors of an increasingly corrupt and irreligious society. Despite this tension in its meaning, popular ideology reinforced the structural changes within the family.[25]

One aspect of the history of women illustrates especially clearly the complex interconnections between educational change and the ideological, demographic, institutional, and technological factors that we have observed. That is the feminization of teaching, which occurred with remarkable swiftness around the middle of the nineteenth century in the eastern United States and a bit later in Canada. In both places, by and large, women took over from men the education of young children in primary schools. As the ideology of domesticity would lead one to expect, the moral and spiritual role assigned to women not only justified but made imperative their entrance into classrooms as surrogate mothers. If the school, like other mid-nineteenth-century institutions, was to resemble a home, it should be presided over by a wise and loving mother. In this sense the shift from men to women in the schoolroom paralleled the shift in primary responsibility from husbands to wives in the ideal middle-class home. As men increasingly left home to work, they left the schoolroom as well.[26]

However cultural imperatives were not the only forces at work in the feminization of teaching. As the state assumed increasing responsibility for the public provision of schools, it became necessary for communities to expand the proportion of school places available. At the same time urbanization and, especially, large-scale immigration greatly enlarged the number of eligible schoolchildren. Obviously the combination of a desire to expand schooling and a substantial population increase placed a severe strain on local financial resources. In this situation women provided a ready solution to a potential problem, for they were paid but half as much as men, who, in an era of expanding commercial and industrial opportunity, increasingly had before them job prospects more attractive than teaching. Thus through the feminization of its teaching force a town could find a sufficient number of teachers to double its school places while holding its expenditures for salary roughly constant.

Although paying women a wage half that given to men was exploitative, it obviously did not deter women from entering teaching. Accounts of hiring usually show that several women applicants competed for every job. The reason is not hard to understand. In the period when teaching opened to women there were essentially only four other occupations available to them: domestic service, dressmaking, work in a mill, or prostitution. To many young women, teaching, despite low wages, probably appeared a welcome and genteel opportunity.[27] Thus the feminization of teaching provides a striking illustration of the way in which the contextual elements we have highlighted intertwined with the origins of systems of public education in the nineteenth century.

## The Origins of the Institutional State and the History of Capitalism

Explanations of the origins of the institutional state should rest on a substitution of a three-stage for a more familiar two-stage paradigm that underlies much of North American history. The focus of the revised framework is the spread of wage labor and the values associated with capitalism rather than urbanization and industrialization.

Most North American history rests on a simple two-stage paradigm —a shift from the preindustrial to an industrial society or from rural to urban life—which obscures the relationship between institutions and social change. Though the transformation of economic structures and the creation of institutions did take place at roughly the same period, attempts to construct causal models or to develop tight and coherent explanations usually appear mechanistic or vague.[28]

When a three-stage paradigm replaces the two-stage one, the connection between social change and institutional creation becomes tighter. In the three-stage paradigm North America shifted from a peculiar variety of mercantile-peasant economy to an economy dominated by commerical capitalism to one dominated by industrial capitalism. Though the pace of change varied from region to region and stages overlapped each other, the most important aspect of the late eighteenth and early nineteenth centuries was not industrialization or urbanization but rather the spread of capitalism, defined in

Maurcie Dobb's words as "not simply a system of production for the market . . . but a system under which labour-power had itself become a commodity and was bought and sold on the market like any other object of exchange."[29] Capitalism was the antecedent of industrialization.

Consider the following as reflections of the spread of capitalist relations prior to industrialization. Between 1796 and 1855, prior to industrialization, the most striking change in New York City's occupational structure, according to Carl Kaestle's figures, was the increase in the proportion of men who listed themselves simply as laborers—an increase from 6 to 27 percent. Moreover apprenticeship, whose emphasis on bound labor is incompatible with capitalism, had ceased to function with anything like its traditional character well before industrialization. In both Buffalo and Hamilton prior to their industrialization there were about eleven skilled wage workers and several semiskilled and unskilled ones for every independent master or manufacturer. From a different point of view, one historian has recently pointed to an unmistakable increase in the wandering of the poor from place to place in late eighteenth-century Massachusetts. The expansion of commerce in this period has been documented extensively, and it was in this era that state governments exchanged their essentially mercantilist policies for a reliance on competition and private initiative to regulate the economy.[30] The problem thus becomes one of formulating the connection between the development of capitalism and the spread of institutions. The drive toward institutional development preceded the industrial takeoff in the Northeast. Any interpretation based on industrialization must fall simply on considerations of time. A much clearer temporal connection exists between institutional origins and the spread of capitalist relations of production.

The most profound statement of the relationship between capitalism and the institutional state occurs in the remarkable book by the late Harry Braverman, *Labor and Monopoly Capital:*

> The ebbing of family facilities, and of family, community, and neighborly feelings upon which the performance of many social functions formerly depended, leaves a void. As the family members, more of them now at work away from home, become less and less able to care for each other in time of need, and as the ties of neighborhood, community and friendship are reinterpreted on a narrower scale to exclude onerous responsibilities, the care of humans for each other becomes increasingly institutionalized. At the same time, the human detritus of the urban civilization increases, not just because the aged population, its

life prolonged by the progress of medicine, grows ever larger; those who need care include children—not only those who cannot "function" smoothly but even the "normal" ones whose only defect is their tender age. Whole new strata of the helpless and dependent are created, or familiar old ones enlarged enormously: the proportion of "mentally ill" or "deficient," the "criminals," the pauperized layers of the bottom of society, all representing varieties of crumbling under the pressures of capitalist urbanism and the conditions of capitalist employment or unemployment. In addition, the pressures of urban life grow more intense and it becomes harder to care for any who need care in the conditions of the jungle of the cities. Since no care is forthcoming from an atomized community, and since the family cannot bear all such encumbrances if it is to strip for action in order to survive and "succeed" in the market society, the care of all these layers becomes institutionalized, often in the most barbarous and oppressive forms. Thus understood, the massive growth of institutions stretching all the way from schools and hospitals on the one side to prisons and madhouses on the other represents not just the progress of medicine, education, or crime prevention, but the clearing of the marketplace of all but the "economically active" and "functioning" members of society.[31]

Note that Braverman isolates three processes that link capitalism and institutions: the absolute growth of a dependent population through changes in the character of work, accidents, and other means; the end of customary ways of caring for dependents; and the creation of new types of dependents—not just the sick, poor, or criminal, but all who are economically unproductive and are as a consequence put out of the way and out of sight. In fact all three processes were clearly at work in late eighteenth and early nineteenth-century North America. One example was the rise in transiency. By the early nineteenth century a highly mobile class of wage laborers cut off from close ties with any communities drifted about and between cities. Living for the most part in nuclear families with no personal or communal resources for the periods of recurrent poverty or frequent disaster that disfigured their lives, they swelled the dependent class.[32]

The recognition that transiency had become a widespread way of life impelled the reform of the poor laws called for by the Quincy and Yates reports in Massachusetts and New York during the second decade of the nineteenth century. Previously towns or counties had retained legal responsibility for their own poor almost wherever they wandered. Poor strangers were warned out of town or shipped back to the communities from which they had come. But after a point who could claim that any particular community could be considered home for the poor who wandered through it? The upsurge in population movement made obsolete the concept of a community of origin, and the very size of the problem meant that the customary practice would produce an endless stream of poor people shipped back and forth between counties. The sensible solution appeared to be to end the traditional practice and to require each county to support the poor within its boundaries, whatever their place of origin, in a new network of poorhouses strung out across the state.[33]

The problem of the poor illustrates both the growth of dependency and breakdown of customary ways of coping with poverty. Other developments underscore the third process: the creation of new categories of dependency. One of these categories was youth. As we have seen in earlier times the life cycle of young people had followed a clear and well-defined sequence. At no point in their lives were they uncertain how they should spend their time or in what setting they should live. But the erosion of apprenticeship and, contrary to popular belief, the lack of wage work for young men in the early phase of capitalist development occurred before the creation of any set of institutions to contain or instruct them. In consequence young people in the nineteenth-century city faced a crisis that cut across class lines. In the 1820s, for instance, a group of Boston merchants gathered at the home of William Ellery Channing to discuss their anxieties about their sons, no longer needed in the counting house or on shipboard at the age of 14. The result of that meeting was Boston English High School. In Hamilton the rapid creation of a public school system with special provisions for adolescent students followed the period in which the crisis of idle youth became most acute. Similarly the disruption of traditional career patterns and living arrangements for young men in New York City provoked worried merchants to create new institutions to guide their behavior and refine their manners.[34]

The nineteenth century's institutionalized population represented the casualties of a new social order: landless workers exposed without buffers to poverty and job-related accidents; men broken by the strain of achievement in a competitive, insecure world; women driven to desperation by the enforced repression inherent in contemporary ideals of domesticity; even children, who were casualties on account of their age. But how did institutions assume the shape they did? Why did the response to problems take the form not simply of institutions but of ones specialized in organization and reformist in intent?

Peter Dobkin Hall offers an answer applicable to the early voluntarist stage of institutional development. After the Revolution, he argues, merchants sought to expand the scope of their activities. To do so they had to increase specialization, pool risks, create joint stock corporations, and accumulate capital outside family firms:

> The disengagement of capital from family firms was achieved through two fundamental innovations in the means of wealth transmission: the testamentary trusts and the charitable endowment. Under testamentary trusts it became possible for testators to entirely avoid the partible division of their estates . . . The charitable endowment was also a kind of trust. Through it moneys could be left in perpetuity to trustees or to a corporate body for the accomplishment of a variety of social welfare purposes—most of which had, in Massachusetts, been traditionally carried out through families. Once the merchants began to search for means of disengaging capital from familial concerns, they quickly recognized the usefulness of charitable endowments both for the accumulation of capital and for relieving their families from the burdens of welfare activity.[35]

The specialization in mercantile life between institutions for credit, insurance, wholesaling, retailing, warehousing, and other activities reflected the division of labor that characterizes capitalist development. That division, as Marx observed, takes opposite forms in social life and in industry. In manufacturing the division of labor results from the combination of previously distinct operations into one process. By contrast the social division of labor requires the decomposition of tasks—all originally performed by the family—into separate organization. "In one case," wrote Marx, "it is the making dependent what was before independent; in the other case, the making independent what was before dependent." Equally with cotton mills, foundries, or shoe factories, new social institutions—schools, penitentiaries, mental hospitals, reformatories—exemplified in their own way the division of labor as the dynamic organizational principle of their age.[36]

The spread of what Christopher Lasch called the "single standard of honor" accompanied the early history of capitalism in North America.[37] By that standard the unproductive became more than a nuisance; they became unworthy. In an attempt to raise their usefulness the unproductive were swept into massive brick structures that looked distressingly like factories and there were taught lessons in social and economic behavior that, it was hoped, would facilitate their reentry into real workplaces. The depressing sameness about the look of schools, prisons, mental hospitals, and factories belied the sentimentality of the age. The romantic proclamation of the child's innocence, purity, and potential masked the disdain and exasperation that designed urban schools or reformatories. As in the case of children a transmutation of disdain into purity justified the confinement of women in the institution called home. Indeed the unwillingness to acknowledge confinement as nasty proved a remarkable feature of early nineteenth-century institutional promotion. But promoters protested too much: their love for, or at least neutrality toward, those they would incarcerate sounds hollow when echoing through the halls of a nineteenth-century mental hospital, prison, or school. We do no better today, though our particular speciality is the elderly. We construct ghettoes for them ostensibly because they want them. In fact we want to have them out of the way. The single standard of honor remains our legacy and our trademark.

Early capitalist development was experienced by the immediate heirs of the Enlightenment and the Revolution, by people swept simultaneously by optimistic theories of human nature and evangelical religion. Their intellectual and religious heritage created complex lenses through which people filtered their perceptions of social and economic change. The refraction undoubtedly contributed to their interpretation of crime, poverty, mental illness, ignorance, and youth as conditions of character. Imbued with a belief in progress and committed to either a secular or spiritual millenium institutional promoters approached their work optimistically, defining their task as the shaping of souls. Nonetheless characters were to be shaped to a standard with clear components: sensual restraint, dependability, willingness to work, acquiescence in the legitimacy of the social order, and acceptance of one's place within it—all serviceable traits in early capitalist America.

One example sums up the problem of character—its relationship to social institutions, to cultural definitions of deviance, and to the personal strain exacted by early capitalism: the trouble with the first patient admitted to the New York State Lunatic Asylum when it opened on January 14, 1843—he thought he was Tom Paine.

## Public Education and Social Problems

Although educational development must be viewed as part of a larger series of changes in North American society, particularly the development of the institutional state, it should become the focus of attention in its own right. School promoters argued that the introduction of public educational systems would alleviate a number of specific and substantial problems in contemporary society. In the most general sense school promoters shared a profound ambivalence about the emerging economic and social order in which they lived. Cities, railroads, and factories were exciting harbingers of progress, symbols of civility, guarantors of prosperity. At the same time they were profoundly frightening. The example of poverty and social disorder in English industrial cities haunted American midwives to industrial capitalism. The material exuberance of the nineteenth century elevated ambition, greed, and sensuality at the expense of traditional values, which by exercising restraint on men's passions had guaranteed the perpetuation of civilized social life. The new social and economic order could become a new barbarism in which the bonds that connected men and women dissolved to be replaced by the competitive savagery of class warfare, in which the confrontation between indolent luxury and destitution could ignite a conflagration that would destroy the New World as surely as it had the great empires of the past.[38]

For influential people ambivalent about the world they were industriously creating education became a mechanism for simultaneously promoting and regulating social change. School systems would promote economic growth and stave off social chaos. They would foster both economic development and social harmony. Early and mid-nineteenth-century school promoters argued that public educational systems could attack five major problems, which, with hindsight, appear products of early capitalist development. If these problems appear familiar, it should not be surprising. For a century and a half they have continued to haunt North American society, which has repeatedly turned unsuccessfully to public schooling for their solution. Although observers at the time were more definite about symptoms than causes, they surely would have agreed with the identity and urgency of this list: urban crime and poverty; increased cultural heterogeneity; the necessity to train and discipline an urban and industrial work force; the crisis of youth in the nineteenth-century city; and the anxiety among the so-called respectable classes about their adolescent children.

According to nineteenth-century social commentators a great increase in both crime and poverty accompanied the growth of cities and the development of modern industry. Though the actual dimensions of the problem remain unclear—that is, whether crime and poverty increased disproportionately or merely kept pace with population growth (see Chapter 6)—what matters here is the widespread belief among the respectable classes in an epidemic of lawlessness and pauperism threatening the foundations of morality and the maintenance of social order. Like "a weltering flood," wrote Horace Mann, the secretary of the Massachusetts Board of Education, in 1848, "do immoralities and crimes break over all moral barriers, destroying and profaning the securities and sanctities of life . . . the great ocean of vice and crime overleaps every embankment, pours down upon our heads, saps the foundations under our feet, and sweeps away the securities of social order, of property, liberty, and life."[39] In the formulation of the time, it is important to observe, crime and poverty were not two distinct problems. Rather the terms *criminal* and *pauper* overlapped and merged into synonyms for deviant and antisocial behavior that stemmed from individual moral failure. According to Egerton Ryerson, the dominant spokesman for public education in mid-nineteenth-century Canada West, "ignorance is the fruitful source of idleness, intemperance and improvidence, and these the fosterparents of pauperism and crime . . . pauperism and crime prevail in proportion to the absence of education amongst the laboring classes."[40]

The process or causal mechanism through which urbanization worked its mischief remained vague in mid-nineteenth-century social commentaries. Nonetheless neither crime nor poverty appeared to be as they once had been the accidental results of misfortune or deviance among an otherwise stable and reliable population. To the contrary the emergence of fundamentally new classes of people, it was argued, had accompanied social transformation. Criminals and paupers were not merely individuals but representatives of the criminal and pauper class, and it was the emergence of a new and undeferential class that particularly frightened respectable people.

Although people concerned with the explanation of crime and poverty often relied on environmental rather than genetic explanations, their arguments still reflected the lack of any very deep understanding of the relationship between social structure and social deviance. In the last analysis blame fell on the lower classes. Crime and poverty became moral problems, which arose because the lower-class urban family failed to implant earnestness and restraint in the character of its children. A Massachusetts judge observed in 1846, "There is seldom a case of a juvenile offender in which I am not well satisfied that the parents or person having the child in charge, is most blamable; they take no pains to make him attend school; they suffer him to be out nights without knowing or caring where; and, in many instances, they are incapable of taking care of themselves, much less the children; they have no home fit for a child; their residence is a grog shop; their companions drunkards and gamblers or worse; they bestow no thought upon their child." Raised in an atmosphere of intemperance, indulgence, and neglect, the lower-class urban child began life predisposed to criminality and unprepared for honest work. By definition, in this argument, the lower-class family became the breeding place of paupers and criminals.[41]

Given these premises schooling held an obvious attraction. Exposure to public education, it was widely believed, would provide the lower-class child with an alternative environment and a superior set of adult models. Through its effect on the still pliable and emergent personalities of its clientele a school system would prove a cheap and superior substitute for the jail and the poorhouse. As some of the more acute commentators at the time observed, the school was to become a form of police. Thus though expenditures on public schooling might seem high, they would in fact ultimately lessen the burden imposed on society by adult crime and poverty. Orestes Brownson commented caustically in 1839, "In the view of this respectable board [the Massachusetts State Board of Education], education is merely a branch of general police, and schoolmasters are only a better sort of constable. The board would promote education, they would even make it universal, because they esteem it the most effectual means possible of checking pauperism and crime and making the rich secure in their possessions. Education has, therefore, a certain utility which may be told in solid cash saved to the commonwealth."[42]

Mid-nineteenth-century social policy blurred more than the distinction between poverty and criminality; it equated cultural diversity with immorality and deviance as well. Thus the ethnic composition of expanding cities became a source of special anxiety. At first it was the large-scale immigration into North America of the famine-stricken Irish that made the problem acute. In 1851 for instance a writer in the *Massachusetts Teacher* noted that, "the constantly increasing influx of foreigners during the last ten years has been, and continues to be, a cause of serious alarm to the most intelligent of our own people." Would it "like the muddy Missouri, as it pours its waters into the clear Mississippi and contaminates the whole united mass, spread ignorance and vice, crime and disease through our native population?" The "chief difficulty," said the author, was "with the Irish . . . down-trodden, priest-ridden of centuries." Seven years later the Boston School Committee summarized its task as "taking children at random from a great city, undisciplined, uninstructed, often with inveterate forwardness and obstinacy, and with the inherited stupidity of centuries of ignorant ancestors; forming them from animals into intelligent beings; giving to many their first appreciation of what is wise, what is true, what is lovely, and what is pure—and not merely their first impressions, but what may possibly be their only impressions."[43]

To the respectable classes of North America poor Irish Catholics appeared alien, uncouth, and menacing. Once again we must confront the relationship between reality and the perception of the people at the time because most contemporary research indicates that the Irish were not intemperate, shiftless, and ignorant, as the nativists portrayed them. To the contrary the immigrants, it now is reasonable to suppose, probably represented a select, especially highly motivated, and unusually literate portion of Irish society. Whatever instability their lives in North America might have revealed probably stemmed—as in the case of former slaves—from the harsh and discriminatory urban social structure they encountered rather than from any moral slackness within their culture.[44]

Nonetheless social commentators proved unable or unwilling to connect the problem they thought they saw around them with its structural basis, and consequently they once again retreated to an explanation that traced the source of a social problem to a moral weakness, in this case embedded in a set of foreign and inferior cultural traditions. As with most cases of nativist behavior the shrill exaggeration with which observers dwelled on the subversive potential of the immigrants' alleged sensual indulgence reveals more about the critics themselves than about the objects of their attack. It is tempting to argue that nativists projected onto the Irish the sensuality that they consciously repressed within their own lives and hated them for acting out the fantasies they denied themselves. Certainly the key phrases in contemporary prescriptions of the good life were restraint and the substitution of higher for lower pleasures, attributes precisely the opposite of those that many thought they saw in the lives of the Irish immigrant poor.[45] Whatever the truth of this speculation, it is quite clear that the brittle and hostile response to Irish immigrants revealed an underlying fear and distrust of cultural diversity.

Once more the implications of a widespread social problem for the role of schooling are transparent. Although the cultural predispositions of adult immigrants might prove intractable, the impending rot of Anglo-American civilization could be averted through a concerted effort to shape the still pliable character of their children into a native mold. This huge task of assimilation required weakening the connection between the immigrant child and its family, which in turn required the capture of the child by an outpost of native culture. In short the anxiety about cultural heterogeneity propelled the establishment of systems of public education; from the very beginning schools became agents of cultural standardization.

The need to discipline an urban work force interacted with the fear of crime and poverty and the anxiety about cultural diversity to hasten the establishment of public educational systems. Although the problem still persists in developing societies today, it perhaps first arose in its modern form during the early industrialization of Britain, as E. P. Thompson has described eloquently. The difficulty emerged from the incongruity between customary rhythms of life and the requirements of urban and industrial work settings. In contrast to the punctuality, regularity, docility, and deferral of gratification demanded in a modern work force, populations both peasant and urban usually had governed their activities more by the sun than by the clock, more by the season and customary festivities than by an externally set production schedule, more by the relationships established within small work groups than by the regimentation of the factory.[46]

At the same time rewards had been distributed more on the basis of ascribed than achieved qualities. Social position devolved on successive generations mainly as a result of heredity, and it would be considered not corrupt but correct to favor a kinsman over a more qualified stranger in the award of jobs or favors. The contrast in this respect between earlier and modern custom certainly remains less than absolute in practice. Nonetheless the ideal that governs behavior has nearly reversed itself, for democratic ideology, with its emphasis on merit and concepts such as equality of educational opportunity, advocates the substitution of achievement for ascription as the ideal basis for the distribution of rewards in contemporary society.

Their promoters expected public school systems to bring about precisely this substitution of achievement for ascription combined with the inculcation of modern habits of punctuality, regularity, docility, and the postponement of gratification. It is not an accident that the mass production of clocks and watches began at about the same time as the mass production of public schools.[47]

A writer in the *Massachusetts Teacher* made explicit the connection between time, modern civilization, and schooling:

> The habit of prompt action in the performance of the duty required of the boy, by the teacher at school, becomes in the man of business confirmed; thus system and order characterize the employment of the day laborer. He must begin each half day with as much promptness as he drops his tools at the close of it; and he must meet every appointment and order during the hours of the day with no less precision. It is in this way that regularity and economy of time have become characteristic of our community, as appears in the running "on time" of long trains on our great network of railways; the strict regulations of all large manufacturing establishments; as well as the daily arrangements of our school duties . . . Thus, what has been instilled in the

mind of the pupil, as a principle, becomes thoroughly recognized by the man as the first importance in the transaction of business.[48]

Disciplinary goals became especially obvious in the reports of local school committees across the continent. Everywhere the major obsessions—and difficulties—were punctuality and regularity of attendance, while the villains were parents uneducated to the importance of schooling who allowed or encouraged their children to remain at home for what to school promoters appeared whimsical reasons or who took the side of their child against the teacher. In 1858 the superintendent of schools in Toronto referred to the "chilling indifference shown even by the parents of the children attending the Schools, as proved by the great want of regularity and punctuality on the part of . . . their children—for a large proportion of them really seem to come to, or stay away from school, just as they please—and the most trifling matters of domestic life are considered to be sufficient excuse for being late or absent."[49]

At a higher level state and provincial authorities continually complained about the refusal of local school committees to introduce universal criteria into the hiring of teachers, who too often were simply kin or friends. In this way the school system as a whole became an object lesson on the organization of modern society, a force as its promoters were fond of pointing out that would radiate its influence outward through entire communities. Through the establishment, organization, and correct operation of school systems the habits of a population would be transformed to match the emerging and radically new social and economic order.[50]

Among their litany of complaints about urban populations social commentators repeatedly included a denunciation of the masses of idle and vagrant youth roaming city streets. The school committee of the town of Roxbury, Massachusetts, for instance, worried about "a class of large boys, numerous and we fear increasing, who seldom or never go to school and have little or no visible occupation." The town's selectmen complained, "We have been called upon frequently to take charge of boys and give them a place in our Alms House, who have been in the habit of lodging in barns and sheds, and exposed to everything which is bad, and dangerous to society, who have no friends to direct them and if they have cannot control them. We have noticed the most profligate and profane, who are strolling about the streets, who never go to school because they have no one to make them."[51] It is tempting to treat observations about idleness and vagrancy as middle-class moralizing. Although they are moralistic to be sure, the evidence points to their firm anchor in social reality, for school promoters saw about them a very real crisis of youth in the nineteenth-century city. Young people who once would have worked as apprentices or servants now had literally nothing to do, for in a preindustrial urban economy, contrary to what often is believed, there existed little work for young men. Their labor in fact was scarcely more necessary than that of adolescents today. Without schools or jobs, large numbers of youths undoubtedly remained in an unwilling state of idleness until, in the case of young men, they became old enough to find work, or, in the case of young women, until they married. The existence of these idle young people is the situation we have called the crisis of youth in the nineteenth-century city, and which propelled the establishment of school systems with special provisions for adolescents (see Chapter 7).

Affluent parents also promoted the establishment of school systems partly on account of their own family anxieties. The point is not that the working class cared less about its families but simply that many of its members could not share one of the two fundamental concerns that made more affluent parents anxious. One of those worries was downward social mobility, and the lower segment of the working class had already hit the bottom. The anxiety about slipping down the social ladder that permeates both nineteenth-century social commentary and fiction relates in a complex manner to actual experience. Nineteenth-century cities revealed at once a curious combination of rigidity and fluidity. Within them sharply entrenched patterns of inequality persisted, while the experience of individual people and the very identity of the population itself changed with dazzling rapidity.

Studies of individual social mobility also reveal this combination of stability and transience in nineteenth-century cities. On the one hand they show a high rate of status transmission from father to son. The popular image of a continent of opportunity wide open to talent simply cannot be sustained, although many men made modest gains, especially within their class of origin, that undoubtedly appeared critical to their lives. Though few laborers replicated the rags-to-riches version of success, many eventually managed to buy a small house. At the same time entrepreneurs failed in business with extraordinary frequency. Indeed entrepreneurial activity entailed risks that made the threat of catastrophe ever present (see Chapter 5).

For different reasons the position of master craftsmen became increasingly insecure as technological development eroded the association of skill and reward that had been the hallmark of many crafts. In the 1850s for instance the introduction of the sewing machine suddenly brought about a deterioration in the position of shoemakers and tailors, as manufacturers flooded the market with cheap goods. Master artisans no longer could assure the comfort and prosperity of their sons through passing their skills on to them. Indeed it is poignant to observe the extent to which in the course of one decade the sons of artisans, especially those affected by technological innovation, ceased to enter their fathers' crafts. In practical terms, in order for the master artisan to assure his son a position commensurate to his own he had to help him enter into different occupations, particularly commerce or the expanding public bureaucracies.[52] Commenting on the implications of economic change for social mobility, Egerton Ryerson wrote:

> Men must now not only work, but compete, to live; and the successful competitor of twenty years ago would be distanced by the ordinary competitor of now-a-days . . . And how is the uneducated and unskillful man to succeed in these times of sharp and skillful competition and sleepless activity? And these times are but the commencement of a spirit of competition and enterprise in the country. The rising generation should, therefore, be educated not for Canada as it has been, or even now is, but for Canada as it is likely to be half a generation hence. No man can hope to succeed who does not keep pace with the age and country in intelligence, skill, and industry.[53]

The establishment of public schools for adolescents—high schools —was not promoted solely in terms of the interests of the well-to-do. Though high school sponsors did point out to affluent parents the advantages of local tax-supported secondary education, their arguments focused on the prosperity of the community and the prospects of working-class children. High schools, they argued, would raise land values through attracting to communities affluent families concerned about the education of their children. At the same time they would provide working-class children with an avenue for social mobility. High schools would make accessible to children of the poor the educational qualifications previously reserved for the wealthy, thereby equipping them for careers in commerce and the professions.[54]

"Shall we," asked one town school committee trying to persuade local citizens to establish a high school, "stand still, and see our children outstripped in the race of life, by the children of those who are willing to pursue a liberal and far-sighted policy?" In Beverly, Massachusetts, a local high school promoter argued that "the best educated community will *always* be the most prosperous community . . . nothing so directly tends to promote the increase of *wealth* of a community as the thorough mental training of its youth." Emphasizing the relationship between the high school and social mobility another promoter in the same town contended, "The state had an interest in the education of the best talent of the community. And this talent was as often found among the middling and lower classes as among the rich." The high school would make available "preparation for college and the higher branches of learning . . . to distinguished industry and talent, in whatever condition and circumstances it might be found."[55]

Working-class parents sometimes were skeptical of the arguments advanced by high school promoters. They realized that high schools formed part of a package of economic and social development of which they were not the prime beneficiaries. More interested in jobs than in schools for their adolescent children, they viewed high schools as a way of siphoning their taxes to the more affluent members of the community. In various places in fact working-class parents opposed and delayed the introduction of high schools. Thus despite a good deal of egalitarian rhetoric to the contrary, the anxiety of the affluent about their children formed the driving force behind the establishment of public secondary schools and solidified (and sustained until the present) their commitment to public education itself.[56]

Observe that this discussion of the purposes of public schooling has omitted one area of concern: the transmission of cognitive skills. Put very simply, the cultivation of skills and intellectual abilities as ends in themselves did not have nearly as much importance in the view of early school promoters as the problems already described. "It is obvious," asserted one urban superintendent, "that heart-culture should be paramount to brain-culture, moral-culture to intellectual-culture." Public school systems existed to shape behavior and attitudes, alleviate social problems, and reinforce a social structure under stress. In this context the character of pupils remained of far greater concern than their minds.[57]

The goals of public schooling were too important to be left to chance. The belief that schooling should be universal and compulsory followed inexorably from assumptions about its importance. "Compulsory education," wrote one Ontario supporter in 1875, "is the necessary sequence of free public schools, and may be regarded as the crowning act in the great educational drama we have been permitted to witness during the past thirty years." From one direction abridgment of the freedom of property owners by compulsory taxation for school support forecast the elimination of the freedom to be unschooled. "The power which compels the citizen to pay his annual tax for the support of schools," reasoned the state superintendent in Maine, "should, in like manner, fill the schools with all of those for whose benefit a contribution was made." Taxation represented a "solemn compact between the citizen and the state." The citizen contributed in order to protect his person and secure his property. The "State compelling such contributions, is under reciprocal obligation" to compel attendance at schools, and compulsory education became "a duty to the taxpayer."[58]

School promoters had tried a number of expedients to promote the universal attendance of the poor, but it became evident to them that only compulsion would bring the hard core of recalcitrant youngsters into school. "For those who will avail themselves of our schools, open to every child, provision is already made," wrote a Massachusetts legislative commission in 1847. "But for those who blind to their own interests, choose the school of vicious associates only, the State has yet to provide a compulsory school as a substitute for the prison—it may be for the gallows." The Massachusetts Reform School at West-borough, opened the following year, represented the first form of compulsory schooling in the United States.[59]

Soon it became apparent that the reform school was too small to accomodate all those who were reluctant to attend the common schools. Nor did the various truant schools in individual towns and cities solve the problem. So in 1851 Massachusetts passed the first general compulsory education law. A serious confrontation with the realities of nonattendance in that state and others had forced school promoters to recognize the logic of their long-standing position. The Pennsylvania Board of State Charities, for instance, came to the advocacy of compulsion by uniting the traditional relationship between ignorance and crime with equally familiar arguments about the nature of cities and city children: "The character of great cities exerts a powerful, and often a sadly controlling influence in the country, near and remote. They may be fountains of blessing to a State, or they may be sources of wide-spread corruption, nests of iniquity, festering sores upon the body politic. The children that grow up neglected in the city do not always remain there. They may carry the pestilential influence of their vices all over the State." It was, furthermore, "precisely those children whose parents or guardians are unable or indisposed to provide them with an education . . . for whom the State is most interested to provide and secure it." Those youngsters who preferred "the pleasures and license of vagabondage and truancy" most required education. "Clearly," reasoned the board, "it is the duty, that is, it is the highest interest of the state, to secure the education of the 'neglected children,' " and the only way to accomplish this was through compulsion.[60]

## Bureaucracy and the Results of Public Education

By 1880 in larger urban settings school promoters had successfully established public school systems, sometimes won compulsion, and reorganized teaching into a hierarchical occupation complete with its own source of training, entrance requirements, and active national organizations. The process had taken less than half a century, a truly remarkable and swift accomplishment.[61] How did it come about? Some characteristics of the process emerge from a close look at the development of bureaucracy in the Boston public schools.

Between 1850 and 1875 the Boston school system became a full-scale bureaucracy. Control over the system was shifted from diffuse supervision by more than a hundred lay officials to a small school board and full-time central administrators (a superintendent and board of supervisors). Administrative duties became fixed and defined by regulation, and departments, specialist teachers, specialized schools, and age grading were introduced. A whole corps of specialist teachers, most of whom traveled between two or more schools, developed, and as the system expanded the salary gap between the highest and lowest positions widened.[62]

Appointment and promotion were increasingly based on objective qualifications, the substitution for the loose earlier teacher examinations of predetermined, professionally derived and administered standards. By the mid-1870s, moreover, a sizable proportion of teachers had been trained in normal schools, especially the one operated by the city. Objectivity and expertise were supposed to be advanced as well by the increasing delegation of decisions to career administrators who exerted more and more influence on elected school board members.

The meager statistics gathered in 1850 and the lax administrative routine had been supplanted by the gathering of elaborate statistical information and the promulgation of detailed rules governing policy. However despite the complaints of schoolmen and their supporters, no tenure system assured a continuity of personnel, and both administrators and teachers remained insecure, the most glaring weakness in their new bureaucratic armor.

Bureaucracy, finally, meant an increase in secrecy at the core of the system, a gathering of power at the center through the withholding of information. No secret or private information was collected in Boston in 1850; by 1876, however, the supervisors had introduced a "black book," in which they recorded judgments on individual teachers open only to school board members and the superintendent.

That Boston was not the only urban school system to become a bureaucracy in this period was emphasized by various commentators in the 1870s and 1880s. One of them was B. A. Hinsdale, then president of Hiram College in Ohio:

> Our common schools constitute a highly complex and differentiated, a vast and powerful system. The machinery of this system is tens of thousands of school houses, thousands of libraries, vast illustrative apparatus, boards of directors and boards of examiners, normal schools and institutes, reports and bureaus, commissioners and superintendents, and more than a quarter of a million of teachers. In the towns and cities, the system has taken on a form especially complex and costly. There are the primary, grammar and high schools, with their grades, A, B, C, and D, not to mention the minor divisions which a layman can hardly keep in his head while hearing them; each one of which is supposed to represent some definable stage in the training of a man. There are the teachers of the various grades, from the primary teachers up by way of the principal to the Superintendent of Public Instruction and his staff of assistants. Behind these come trooping in the kindergarten teachers, the normal and training teachers, followed by the music and drawing masters—each one having his bundle of reports under his arm and his sheet of percentages in his hand. The whole body of public school teachers constitute an intelligent, active and powerful profession; presenting in some respects the appearance of an hierarchy of education.[63]

It is one thing to observe that school systems became bureaucracies; it is another to say why. From the timing of the various developments in Boston one important fact about the nature of bureaucratization becomes clear: it did not emerge full-blown. Although the structural features of the system were clearly interrelated, they had developed singly and at different times. It must be remembered that bureaucratization encompassed a number of distinct innovations and alterations such as age grading, the introduction of a superintendent, and the centralization of the school board. It was in short a piecemeal process.

Although an account of the reasons for each structural change is necessary in order to explain the particular evolution of the system, a more general approach is still possible, because underlying the different innovations were certain pressures, predicaments, and values that forced educational development in the direction of bureaucracy. Bureaucracy, it must be stressed, did not thereby represent an inevitable development. It is not the setting that determined the structure but the values and goals with which particular problems were confronted or defined. It has been the particular way in which industrial capitalist societies have viewed social tasks, the priorities they have brought to their solution, that has made bureaucracy the dominant organizational form of our time.

Boston school administrators faced an increasingly complex situation. In 1855 the city had only a superintendent and a school committee of seventy-six part-time lay members to supervise and coordinate more than 160 primary schools, which fed nearly fifty grammar schools that led in turn to the two high schools. As the part-time pursuit of busy people the school committee could not oversee the work of individual schools with any care. Under the recently abolished primary school committee someone had at least been responsible for each school. In some cases this undoubtedly led to close if paternalistic supervision. Now however the schools, taught by largely untrained young women chosen by haphazard methods, were left without guidance. For all his remarkable energy the superintendent could not regularly visit and advise more than two hundred schools. Thus with little coordination or direction the school system staggered under an increasingly crowded and heterogeneous population. Grammar school masters had no assurance that the children coming to them from the primary schools had received a reasonably systematic, competently taught primary education. Nor could the high schools be certain that their students had a reasonably common educational background. No reliable or systematic process existed for weeding out ineffectual teachers or for preventing their entry into the system at the primary level. It was thus reasonable to argue that in order to function with any degree of efficiency and effectiveness the school system desperately needed more coordination and increased supervision. In 1851 that line of argument had been effective in persuading the school committee to hire the first superintendent; it was convincing in 1876 in spurring the appointment of a board of supervisors, streamlining the school committee, making the grammar school masters principals of the primary schools in their districts.

The complexity of administration formed an implicit assumption in the educational ideal of urban superintendents throughout the country, who argued that all large organizations, from industry to the army, depended for coordination on centralized professional direction by a superintending officer. The success of professional supervision, especially in the various branches of industry, indicated the need for the same type of direction in education. Supervision they deemed necessary because organizations had to be based on a division of labor, which to these superintendents as much as to Adam Smith or to Marx was the process underlying social development.

Schoolmen pointed out that a professionally supervised school system based on the division of labor ideally should contain certain structural features and that its participants should have certain attitudes. An elaborate hierarchical structure and an explicit chain of command would keep each member working at his or her particular task in a responsible and coordinated fashion. At the head of the hierarchy should be one "vested with sufficient authority" to "devise plans in general and detail" and to "keep all subordinates in their proper places and at their assigned tasks." Within the hierarchy roles and duties should be defined clearly to avoid conflict, and all members should give unquestioning, prompt obedience to the orders of their superiors. The great danger in a complex organization, wrote a professor of pedagogy, was "disintegration," caused chiefly by "nonconformity," something not to be tolerated in either pupils or teachers.

To perfect their hierarchies schoolmen argued that career lines within school systems should be developed further. If education was to become a profession attractive to men, promotion from the ranks was an absolute requisite. The introduction of tenure and pensions were also important, for subject to annual election by a school board, superintendents and teachers were thoroughly insecure, forced into timidity for the sake of survival.

Hardly anyone at the time would have quarreled with the position that teachers should be chosen for their qualifications and not for reasons of personal favoritism or nepotism; but diffuse, lay-controlled school systems made objectivity a scarce commodity. Politics exacerbated the situation, for to anchor school boards to city wards was to put them in the midst of the most intense political pressures with often predictable results. Features of bureaucracy designed to provide impartial standards and centralize control were defenses against favoritism. The introduction of supervisors in Boston, for instance, was considered a means of lifting the appointment of teachers above the personal, amateur, and political level, since the supervisors conducted examinations for teaching positions.

Bureaucracy offered specific advantages to schoolmen in their quest for professionalism. It therefore, enlisted their wholehearted and vigorous support. The first of these advantages, as we have already noted, was the development of career lines within education. The other advantage was the way in which bureaucratization mitigated an emerging problem: the regulation of behavior within the occupation itself. In a presidential address to the National Council of Education, Thomas Bicknell disclosed the concern of schoolmen with this issue. He noted that the alluring prospect of a rapidly ascending career was tempting ambitious individuals and often introducing into school systems destructive careerist competition that generated hostility and tension among an entire staff. The division of educational opinion in the country offered "perpetual temptation" to "undignified intrigue" and "violent excitement." The newly formed council, composed of the elite of practicing American educators, would serve as a "warning to ambitious young teachers" by offering authoritative pronouncements on the bewildering array of innovations being peddled around the country. Most likely schoolmen hoped that the council would reinforce on a national level the sort of regulation of behavior that bureaucracies were trying to enforce on a local level. Bureaucracy places a premium on acquiescence and rule following. In this type of organization the individualist, the aggressively ambitious person, is not only uncomfortable but unacceptable. The instruments that educational bureaucrats had for regulating behavior were uniform rules and prescribed patterns of action (such as centrally defined courses of study) coupled with the sanctions of colleagueship and promotion obtainable only for faithful service and quiet good behavior.

Thus in the third quarter of the nineteenth century increasingly complex administrative problems, reinforced by the nepotism and politics that afflicted school practice, made rationalization and coordination seem necessary for urban school systems. Faced with this situation schoolmen, and some laymen as well, justified their organizing principles by loose analogies from industry, which they believed had successfully solved the same basic problem: the management of large numbers of people performing different tasks. The process of bureaucratic growth within education was so thorough and so rapid because of the enthusiasm of the schoolmen themselves, who saw in the new organizational forms the opening up of careers and a partial solution to the problem of regulating behavior within the occupation.

The schoolmen's ability to foster the development of hierarchical, differentiated systems as rapidly as they did was due to another important factor: they met little opposition. One reason was that in the beginning influential laymen agreed with their goals. Bureaucracy represented a crystallization of capitalist social values: efficiency, order, rationality. It seemed a way to help schools solve the problems of early industrial capitalism that had spurred their creation. Besides particular innovations often gave differential advantages to the children of the affluent. Complementing these facts, the years of the rapid spread of bureaucracy were precisely the years of withdrawal of lay interest in education. By the mid-1850s the first enthusiastic phase of the educational revival had begun to decline, and the lay interest that had sustained the movement dwindled. The earlier reformers, however, had started the development of bureaucracy by fostering an increase in the number of common schools and teachers, by urging grading, and by sponsoring the development of high schools. Moreover they had called into being the first professional administrators, the superintendents, to help them with the management of these rather sprawling and uncoordinated systems. As lay interest lessened, the new class of professional educators consolidated the systems they had inherited. For roughly two decades schoolmen were able to carry on the task of consolidation with a minimum of lay interference. In the process they introduced into their new school systems the features of bureaucracy examined above. The withdrawal of lay zeal had left school systems open to capture by professionals who, quickly perceiving the advantages of bureaucracy, had acted with dispatch to build large hierarchical, differentiated, uniform, and rigid organizations.

The same story with different details could be told about other major social institutions. Gerald Grob, most notably, has outlined for mental hospitals how a combination of unrealistic ideals, overcrowding, inadequate staff, a largely lower-class and foreign patient population, and the ambitions of the newly developing profession of asylum superintendence coalesced to bring about a shift from reform to custody, a development of internal bureaucracy at the expense of therapy. Much the same process happened in prisons and reform schools as well. Everywhere new social institutions begun with a flush of optimism rather quickly turned into custodial bureaucracies presided over and defended by the members of the new professions that their founding had called into existence.[64]

In every case the story can be interpreted as one of men and women of good will struggling with intractable problems and inadequate resources eventually overwhelmed despite their best intentions. That story is true. To some extent the history of institutions subsequent to their founding must be sought in the processes internal to their development, in a dialectic of institutional growth that fuels itself.

Still the story is not quite so straightforward. It is not inevitable that education, mental illness, or criminality be treated in any particular way. In fact the issue of whether or not bureaucracy is an unavoidable, if lamentable, aspect of a complex industrial society, according to Anthony Giddens is one of the central points of contention between Marx and Weber. For Weber, "The application of scientific innovation to technology is combined, in the modern economy, with the introduction of methods of rational calculation, exemplified in bookkeeping, which promote that methodical conduct of entrepreneurial activity which is so distinctive of contemporary capitalism. The conduct of rational capitalism in turn entails unavoidable consequences in the sphere of social organization, and inevitably fosters the spread of bureaucracy."[65]

Weber, according to Giddens, viewed the "rationalization of activity" and not wage labor as the principal "characteristic of modern capitalist production." Thus "bureaucratic specialization of tasks is treated by Weber as the most integral feature of capitalism." For Weber the "expropriation of the worker from his means of production" has not been confined to industry but "instead applies . . . to other institutional contexts . . . any form of organization which has a hierarchy of authority can become subject to a process of 'expropriation': for the Marxian notion of the 'means of production' Weber substitutes the 'means of administration.' " To Weber therefore bureaucracy is an inevitable component not only of capitalism but of any complex modern social order. "Since the trend toward bureacratization is irreversible in capitalism, it follows that the growth of functional specialization is a necessary concommittant of the modern social order." Though Weber could not foresee any way in which to overcome the domination of bureaucracy, he did not accept his conclusion without regret. He was, according to Giddens, more the reluctant realist than the champion of modern society. He recognized the contradiction between democratic values and bureaucracy, between egalitarian ideals and organizations built upon elaborate hierarchies. The "great question," wrote Weber, "thus is . . . what we can set against this mechanization to preserve a certain section of humanity from the fragmentation of the soul, this complete ascendancy of the bureaucratic ideal of life?"[66]

Marx took a different view of bureaucracy, observes Giddens. He agreed with Weber that "the bureaucratic state in Europe arose as an instrument serving the monarchy in its attempts to reduce the feudal dispersal of powers: the centralization of the state in the hands of the monarch was a major condition allowing the rise of bourgeois interests, which then appropriated power to themselves. But in Marx's view this is not, as it is for Weber, an irreversible general trend towards bureaucratic specialization of the division of labor in all spheres of social life. To Marx, bureaucratic centralization is rather one particular manifestation of the bourgeois state, and consequently is as transitory a social form as is capitalism itself."[67]

Marx argued that in a socialist society the state no longer would need to be a "political power independent of civil society," and he predicted that it would be possible to simplify administration since there no longer would exist the need for a class with special and particular interests to seize, defend, and crystallize in law the means for the perpetuation of its own power. Within industry, according to Giddens, Marx thought that the "authority system of the modern factory . . . is intrinsically linked to the necessities engendered by the capitalist economy. But the various forms of co-operative factory which had been set up show that a quite different type of authority structure can be created, which will break down the bureaucratic hierarchy. In the cooperative factories, there is no longer a unilateral distribution of authority."[68]

Although nearly always justified in terms of efficiency and increased output, hierarchical authority and the division of labor have been crucial to the successful attempt by management to strip wage workers of control over the work process. The winning of control by management resulted from a struggle waged by and large after the ownership of the means of production had already been centralized, for in early factories skilled wage workers frequently retained considerable control over the actual organization of their tasks. As workers well knew, as long as their control lasted the domination of management remained incomplete. Consequently they bitterly resisted the eventually successful effort to subdivide their jobs into decreasingly skilled operations coordinated by a central administration.[69]

Thus the unspoken purpose implicit in the division of labor—and in bureaucracy—has been the control and domination of the work process. That is why the division of labor has always formed an integral feature of capitalist social organization in factories, offices, and services. In education, for example, a revealing analogy may be made between the early nineteenth-century private schoolmaster and the skilled craftsman of the same period. Both were forced out of business, though not at first through the introduction of new technology but through the reorganization of work, the expropriation of the means of production, and the centralization of work in large settings. Like early craftsmen entering factories schoolmasters who entered the new public systems at first retained a great deal of autonomy in the organization and conduct of their work.

However neither the control exerted by skilled workers or by schoolmasters satisfied the managers of their respective work settings. After all part of the purpose of forcing schoolmasters into public systems had been to insure that education play its allotted role in a newly crystallizing configuration of social institutions. Thus as in the factory a struggle for control between formerly autonomous schoolmen and newly centralized authorities marked the early history of large school systems. The outcome of the struggle in both the factory and the school was similar: the reduction of control over work through a process of dilution of skills justified as the division of labor and the co-ordination of activities by central administrators. In schools skill dilution was manifested by the replacement of relatively well educated schoolmasters with young, much less well educated women.[70]

Finally, just as skilled wage workers eventually exchanged autonomy for the rewards within the system assured by trade unions, schoolmasters exchanged control for the promise of advancement and modest power within educational bureaucracies. As principals they became the labor aristocrats of schools. Through advancement to superintendencies a few even entered the ranks of management itself.

For Weber bureaucracy, though a product of history and at the very core of capitalism, could not be overcome by the advent of socialism. By contrast for Marx wage labor remained the essence of capitalism and bureaucracy its organizational expression. Both would be superseded by the advent of socialism. Historical development has proved neither of these great theorists correct. The will to alter bureaucratic organizational forms never has been very strong in either the advanced capitalist or socialist societies. Despite Weber's pessimism, though, visible alternative models of organization have been proposed and tried on varying scales at different times. As for Marx's optimism, most industrial socialist societies have not shed bureaucracy, but then they have not fully abolished wage labor either. Weber's forecast undoubtedly has been a more accurate predictor for state capitalism as practiced, for example, in the Soviet Union. A modern social order modeled on lines that Marx might approve remains an evanescent vision.

The great service of both Weber and Marx to modern students of bureaucracy is to anchor social organization within social values. Whether inevitable or capable of transcendence, bureaucracy must be understood clearly as an artifact of capitalism. More than that, as Weber, despite his prediction of its permanence, quite clearly argued, bureaucracy contradicts the egalitarian and democratic values in whose name it so frequently has been erected and defended. It is a form of organization that both produces and reproduces the alienation of men and women from their work and from themselves.

Bureaucracy is not a rational, value-free organizational response to complexity. Nor is it merely reflective, a structural expression of social values. Rather it is in its own right a dynamic factor that reproduces itself and the values on which it rests. Bureaucracy reproduces itself, first, through the distribution of power. The alienation of the means of administration removes any effective control over the internal character of work or larger institutional purposes from the great mass of organizational workers. The fragmentation of skills, the intricate division of labor, the elaboration of hierarchy: all of these combine to make the ordinary bureaucrat as dependent on the coordinating effort through which management perpetuates its power as the ordinary worker on an assembly line.

More subtly bureaucracy shapes personality. Early critics of school systems argued that educational hierarchies bred martinets, rigid personalities obsessed with rules and unable to respond to the variety of human personalities. Their perceptions were strikingly similar to those presented more systematically and forcefully almost a century later by Robert Merton in his famous essay on the impact of bureaucracy on personality. The effect of prolonged work in a bureaucratic structure, wrote Merton, was the recasting of personality into a new and more rigid mold.[71]

The structural components of any setting transmit powerful lessons about the basis on which rewards are distributed, the nature of acceptable behavior, and the criteria by which actions should be evaluated. Indeed as Robert Dreeben has argued, it is the structure of the school setting and experience rather than deliberate pedagogy that has the greatest impact on young people.[72] For example age grading, a key component of plans for educational systematization since the 1840s when it first entered the Boston schools, has taught children that they are members of categories. It has enforced the lesson that people should be treated according to characteristics that they share as members of a group, that they are not entitled to special treatment on account of their individual qualities. As another instance consider the fact that it is in school that youngsters learn that helping their friends is called cheating. The utility of popular commitment to these propositions for a society that stresses individual competition and that shuffles its citizens between mass settings is self-evident.

Schoolmen in the mid-nineteenth century worried that what David Riesman later would label other-direction had begun to dominate social life. Common educational practices such as the awarding of medals for achievement were reinforcing other-directedness by their stressing external incentives rather than an internal sense of purpose.[73] They thought that a society of students weaned on the current motivational techniques would require a continued reliance on external police and artificial incentives. Though acceptable in an authoritarian state external incentives were inappropriate and insufficient in an open, democratic society. For a democratic society to function, for its work to be done, for the aspirations of its populace to remain decently restrained, for harmony rather than envy to govern social relations, a massive internalization of the will to achieve and the work ethic had to be learned in the schools. Those qualities, moreover, could never be taught didactically. They would emerge from the students' identification with role models and from the lessons transmitted through the organizational aspects of a carefully designed educational structure. Thus no issue was trivial; for instance whether or not to continue to award medals in the Boston schools emerged as a major controversy.

Ultimately the moral mission of the schools—as educators would refer to the teaching of attitudes and behavior—was political, for its goal was to legitimize inequality. The extent to which ordinary people have not protested the legitimacy of a social and economic order in which they have been the losers remains the most effective evidence that the panoply of devices securing the hegemony of industrial capitalism—among which education has been prominent—has achieved its goal.

Make no mistake: there has been no golden age in modern North American history. As we have shown, a sharply etched structure of inequality crystallized early and has remained intact with only minor modifications throughout the last century and a half. Despite occasional protest at moments when, as Herbert Gutman has shown, new populations had to be incorporated into the industrial capitalist order, the most remarkable aspect of the history of inequality has been the degree to which it has been accepted or acquiesced in not only by its beneficiaries but by its casualties as well.

The question is why. The answer is enormously complex and involves a variety of agencies and practices, some of which we have noted earlier, such as the high rate of short-distance occupational movement, the creation of limited ladders of success within the working class, and the widespread distribution of home ownership. Schools have also been one of the important mechanisms through which capitalism has achieved its hegemony, for within schools children learn to blame themselves for failure. That lesson is as old as the creation of public school systems. Early schoolmen waged a campaign to introduce promotion based on achievement. Over the complaints of parents and students they emphasized that promotion from one grade or educational level to another had to be earned. The system owed them nothing; children who did not pass examinations were entirely responsible for their own failures. Thus schoolchildren of the last 150 years have received their first lesson in political economy: the unequal distribution of rewards mirrors the unequal distribution of ability. Those who achieve deserve their success; those who fail are, very simply, less worthy.

The lesson coincides with the ideology of social mobility in America. The virtue of North American society, according to both popular thought and political rhetoric, has resided in equality of opportunity, not in equality of condition. The measure of the good society has not been the extent to which the disparities between groups have lessened; rather that measure has been the degree to which the individual has remained free to rise as far as his talents could take him. (The masculine pronoun is used deliberately here because occupational mobility has primarily been a game restricted to men.) In this view the measure of the good society is the extent to which it permits individual achievement, not the degree of equity. That definition is harmful because it creates a sense of worthlessness among the majority of people. To some extent mobility is a zero-sum game: most people must always lose. If they believe that the inequity they suffer on account of their loss reflects their own inherent unworthiness, they are doomed to a life that systematically robs them of self-esteem.

Bureaucratic organizational structures contribute to this definition of equality in terms of individual achievement. Thereby they sustain and reproduce capitalist relations not only through the distribution of power, the reworking of personality, and the distribution of values but in one other way in which education is central. As the marketplace has become less effective, as the allocation of rewards no longer appears to follow simply from effort and virtue, as the possibility of a rise from rags to riches or from dependence to independence cannot be sustained even on the level of myth, it has fallen to bureaucracy to administer the illusion of opportunity in which industrial capitalist societies vest their claim to moral worth.

# Afterword

The description of social organization in this book appears almost obsolete when applied to North America at the start of the twentieth century. By then early industrial capitalism had been transformed into corporate capitalism, a social formation with features radically different from any ever known before. Class structure had grown more complex. An army of specialized office workers, scientists, academics, professional social reformers, and public officials composed what some commentators have called the new middle class. The assessment of the adequacy of that label requires a more extensive and subtle interplay between empirical research and social theory than has yet been attempted. Still the production of services did enter economic life in an expansive new fashion, grafting onto social structure control of the means of administration within large organizations as a novel axis in the distribution of power.

The emergence of huge, powerful firms dominating national and international markets, the vastly expanded utilization of technology, and the increasingly minute division of labor have all been documented often. Together they created an industrial and political landscape that would have seemed unfamiliar to most workers or businessmen of the third quarter of the nineteenth century. The size and power of the national labor movement would also have appeared a new element in industrial organization. Nor would the ethnic composition of North America have been any more familiar, altered as it was by the waves of immigrants arriving annually from eastern and southern Europe.

The texture of everyday life had altered too with the advent of cheap mass transportation, the disappearance of the walking city, the segregation of residential neighborhoods by social class, and the growth of suburbs. In the cities the vast expansion of public bureaucracies, the professionalization of welfare, and the new corps of social specialists transformed the nature of the transactions that confronted ordinary people in the course of their daily lives.

Remarkable changes had also occurred within families. Life-cycle boarding and service had dwindled in significance. By the turn of the century it was the poorest families, not the most affluent, who took in boarders, and they did so not because of civic duty but out of economic necessity. Moreover most couples had far fewer children than families of similar class or ethnic composition a few decades earlier, and the children that they did have spent increasingly longer periods in schools differentiated more noticeably by the class backgrounds of pupils. Finally a network of public policies affecting families, including juvenile courts and child-labor laws, had been put into place.

If the world that emerged in the early twentieth century was so different from its immediate predecessor, of what importance is it to know about the social organization of early industrial capitalism? Why, in short, should anyone care about the issues discussed in this book? The history described here is important, first, because corporate capitalism did not emerge suddenly or by chance from a simple Arcadian society of small towns and farms. It resulted from a historical process at work for centuries and, most immediately, from the driving forces within early industrial capitalism.

The continual need for cheap labor created by industrial expansion lay behind the altered ethnic composition of North America, as opportunities for work at high wages attracted the poor, dispossessed, and ambitious in southern and eastern Europe after the great pools of surplus labor in Britain and Germany had been largely exhausted. The massing of workers in large plants where great numbers were subject to similar patterns of authority fostered the shared consciousness that erupted in the labor movement. The expansive specialization of social institutions evident as early as the mid-nineteenth century created a stratum of white-collar workers and fostered the connection between schooling and genteel work that encouraged many families to limit their fertility in order to afford the education children now required. The increasingly universal, age-graded character of public schooling even defined the life cycle of young people itself, as key life events acquired a close association with the rhythm of maturity imposed by education. From these examples it should be apparent that the social formation that had emerged by the onset of the twentieth century can be understood only in terms of a historical process, a dynamic set of arrangements that issued from the impulses and contradictions within early industrial capitalism.

Therefore early industrial capitalism is important because of its role in creating a more modern social order. Nonetheless the social formation characteristic of early twentieth-century North America did not differ as sharply from early industrial capitalism as might at first appear. Indeed early industrial capitalism is relevant not only because it preceded the social formation immediately prior to our own but because it was the era in which key elements of contemporary social organization first crystallized. Studies of income distribution, for example, show remarkable continuities for at least a century. Not only has a sharply unequal distribution of rewards remained characteristic of capitalist society, but the structure of that inequality has endured with remarkable tenacity as well. The relationship between occupation and income, for example, has remained quite stable, and the processes by which inequality is transmitted or reproduced have not altered in any fundamental way during the last century or more. Nor have the two great classes described in this book disappeared. Indeed the source of their relationship remains relatively unchanged. Although the working class has used labor unions to increase its power and probably its real income as well, it has not acquired the capacity to guide the economy in its own interests, as any analysis of the differential loss through inflation or the energy crisis would show.

The novel element in social structure—the layers of sales clerks, office workers, social bureaucrats, and managers—has been superimposed on an older structure; it has not superceded it. Indeed the debate over whether white-collar workers and the intelligentsia should be considered a new class has been short on historical perspective. Early in the century these groups appeared to make up a new class when in reality they occupied a transitional role. The growth of white-collar unions shows that the members of this supposedly new class have come to realize their affinity with other wage workers. As a result class structure may become increasingly polarized. If that happens, the basic antagonisms of capitalism will become more clearly etched, as they were a century ago.

Although it may be hard to recognize the school systems of 1880 in the elaborate, specialized, enormous bureaucracies of modern cities, most of their basic elements already existed. Indeed the framework of the institutional state was intact by 1880. The principles that social tasks should be performed by specialized institutions, organized hierarchically, operated by specialists, and ever more remote from the community they served had all become axioms of the conventional wisdom among those with the power to put their policies into action.

Even the family had assumed the primary structural characteristics that it has retained. By 1870 or 1880 extensions to households in the form of servants or life-cycle boarders reflected increasingly archaic and unusual arrangements. The nuclear household had clearly become the norm within each class. The well-to-do household already was, in Christopher Lasch's phrase, "a haven in a heartless world," at least in popular ideology. In reality it served not only as a haven but as the place in which the values appropriate to an emergent social order were first instilled. Moreover family life complemented industrial life by using women to maintain the homes in which the active members of the labor force were raised and sustained. By and large industrial capitalism did not require the labor of women and children, and the division of responsibilities between the sexes and between home and work served its interests well. Nonetheless the prolongation of social childhood far past the time that biological childhood had ended nurtured the tensions that exploded with greatest force about a decade ago, giving rise to the movements that, depending upon one's evaluation, are tearing apart, liberating, or simply reshaping families.

Despite these general trends, class distinctions in family life remain strong. As in the era of early industrial capitalism, working-class children leave school earlier and enter the work force younger than do children from more affluent families, and they benefit relatively less than affluent children from public investment in higher education. The lower aspirations and expectations transmitted by working-class families, which social scientists observe today, have undoubtedly not become more prominent during the last century. Indeed there is every reason to believe that they were features of working-class life then as now. Thus despite the proponents of embourgeoisement or the celebrants of a camper in every back yard, the tensions between family and class repeatedly have created within the working class what Lillian Rubin has termed in her book of the same name, "worlds of pain." As the literature of introspection has made clear, real pain exists in affluent families too, but it is of a different order—the frustrations addressed by *Passages* rather than the anxiety and frustration of an inadequate income and meaningless work.

Since early in the nineteenth century processes of social mobility have been central to the stability and progress of industrial capitalism, shifting skills upward as required but until recently not producing a serious, long-term overabundance of educated, unemployable aspirants. Stability has been fostered too by the distribution and application of power, the retention by the same class of the control of the state.

Nonetheless social orders do not last very long when based on force alone. An acceptance of their legitimacy is required as well. In the case of industrial capitalism all the major factors that have fostered acceptance of the legitimacy of its structure of inequality even among those who have fared least well were in place by the end of the third quarter of the nineteenth century. These factors included limited ladders of success that provided illusions of opportunity and mobility; the ways in which schools taught people to blame themselves for failure; an ideology in which merit and regard became synonymous and in which the good society was defined by opportunity for individual talent rather than the promotion of collective well-being; and finally patterns of socialization within families that shaped aspirations and expectations in ways that reinforced class relations.

Psychological testing, counseling, and the mass media have refined the instruments through which the ideology of legitimation is transmitted, but its core remains the same. However it may be that the objective basis of that ideology, always tenuous, has been eroded even further and that public acceptance has reached an unprecedented low marked by cynicism and a widespread challenge to authority evident throughout society everywhere from the rise in medical malpractice suits to the discipline problems in schools. Whether the forces sustaining institutions can be regrouped and social consciousness rechanneled through various reforms and ideological reformulations remains one of the most interesting and consequential questions of our time. A number of developments will probably work toward that end. They are the commercialization of leisure; the illusion of freedom promoted by open classrooms, longer vacations, and wider consumer choice; and repressive desublimation in the form of greater tolerance of sexuality and soft drugs. Whether these aspects of cultural policy can obscure the fundamental inequities of late corporate capitalism or provide adequate substitutes for security, community, and meaningful work remains unknown. This is one key issue that will determine the level of social and political tension in the years to come.

Social commentators in the age of early industrial capitalism were not very precise about the cause of social problems. They lumped together the poor, ignorant, unemployed, and criminal in an unflattering and unsympathetic image of a degraded class, and they imagined their cities to be ravaged by a criminal class when in fact no such class existed. In part the image of a criminal class enabled respectable citizens to avoid an accurate diagnosis of social problems, which would lead to more radical surgery than most of them were willing to contemplate. The early reliance on education to cure social disease was another manifestation of the same evasive strategy. Both of these responses became reflexes, which are still activated by issues of crime, poverty, or unemployment today. The moral condemnation of the poor and the translation of social problems into deficiencies of character make up one of our most useful legacies from the nineteenth century, a way of avoiding both social justice and guilt.

Thus early industrial capitalism is not a world we have lost, nor was it merely a world that was a predecessor to one more familiar today. To the contrary, in its underlying structure, contradictions, and motive power it is the world in which we still live. To understand it is to begin to understand ourselves.

# Notes

## Introduction

1. The importance of international migration in shaping the American class and economic structure has been restated forcefully by Gabriel Kolko, *Main Currents in Modern American History* (New York, 1976), ch. 3. See also Imre Ferenczi, ed., *International Migrations* (New York, 1929), vol. 1; Walter F. Wilcox, ed., *International Migrations* (New York, 1931), vol. 2.

2. Don D. Lescohier, *Labor Market* (New York, 1923).

3. H. J. Habakkuk, *American and British Technology in the Nineteenth Century: The Search for Labour-Saving Inventions* (Cambridge, 1954). For another view of international migration and the American labor market see Brinley Thomas, *Migration and Economic Growth: A Study of Great Britain and the Atlantic Economy* (Cambridge, 1954).

4. On reformers' concern with the problems of labor turnover see Kolko, *Main Currents*, pp. 165-167, and Lescohier, *Labor Market*.

5. Karl Marx, *Capital*, 3 vols. (Moscow, 1954), vol. 1, pp. 598-599.

6. For a brief history of Hamilton during this period see Michael B. Katz, *The People of Hamilton, Canada West: Family and Class in a Mid-Nineteenth-Century City* (Cambridge, Mass., 1975), pp. 1-7; Michael J. Doucet, "Building the Victorian City: The Process of Land Development in Hamilton, Ontario, 1847-1881" (Ph.D. diss., University of Toronto, 1977), p. 61.

7. Michael B. Katz, "Early Industrialization," Working Paper 3, in York Social History Project, "First Research Report" (Downsview, Ontario, 1975), pp. 41-64.

8. On the textile model of industrialization see Bruce Laurie, "Beyond the Textile Paradigm: Philadelphia Manufacturing Sector, 1850-1880," n.d., Philadelphia Social History Project.

9. Leo A. Johnson, *History of the County of Ontario, 1615-1875* (Whitby, Ontario, 1973); Steven Langdon, *The Emergence of the Canadian Working Class Movement, 1845-1875* (Toronto, 1975).

10. Gregory S. Kealey, ed., *Canada Investigates Industrialism* (Toronto, 1973).

11. J. J. Henderson, *Annual Statement of the Trade and Commerce of Buffalo* (Buffalo, 1855), p. 31.

12. Erie County Medical Society, *Buffalo Medical Journal* 4 (1849). On the history of mid-nineteenth-century Buffalo see Laurence Admiral Glasco, "Ethnicity and Social Structure: Irish, Germans, and Native-Born of Buffalo, New York, 1850-1860" (Ph.D. diss., SUNY-Buffalo, 1973). On the development of the region see Richard L. Erlich, "The Development of Manufacturing in Selected Counties in the Erie Canal Corridor, 1815-1860" (Ph.D. diss., SUNY-Buffalo, 1972). Our population figures for Buffalo include the village of Black Rock, which was annexed to the city in 1853.

13. The authors would like to thank Robert Kilduff for allowing us to read a draft of his uncompleted thesis on the Charity Organization Society of Buffalo.

14. J. H. French, *Gazetteer of the State of New York* (Syracuse, 1860), pp. 279-294.

15. All figures cited in the text have been rounded off to the nearest percent. In the tables, figures are given to the tenth of a percent.

16. Business directories have been used to identify individuals' class position by Clyde and Sally Griffen, *Natives and Newcomers: The Ordering of Opportunity in Mid-Nineteenth Century Poughkeepsie* (Cambridge, Mass., 1978); Susan E. Hirsch, *Roots of the American Working Class: The Industrialization of Crafts in Newark, 1800-1860* (Philadelphia, 1978).

17. The five-group occupational ranking used here is discussed in Theodore Hershberg, Michael Katz, Stuart Blumin, Laurence Glasco, and Clyde Griffen, "Occupation and Ethnicity in Five Nineteenth-Century Cities: A Collaborative Inquiry," *Historical Methods Newsletter* 7 (1974).

## 1. A Two-Class Model

1. *First Annual Report of the Children's Aid Society*, (New York, 1854), p. 3.

2. Ibid., pp. 3-4.

3. Ibid., p. 4.

4. *Second Annual Report of the Children's Aid Society*, (New York, 1855), p. 3.

5. Ibid., p. 3.

6. Carl F. Kaestle, *The Evolution of an Urban School System: New York City, 1750-1850* (Cambridge, Mass., 1973), pp. 126-129; Susan E. Houston, "Victorian Origins of Juvenile Delinquency: A Canadian Experience," in Michael B. Katz and Paul H. Mattingly, eds., *Education and Social Change: Themes from Ontario's Past* (New York, 1976), pp. 84-85; Michael B. Katz, *The Irony of Early School Reform: Educational Innovation in Mid-Nineteenth-Century Massachusetts* (Cambridge, Mass., 1968), part 3.

7. Mary O. Furner, *Advocacy and Objectivity: A Crisis in the Professionalization of American Social Science, 1865-1905* (Lexington, Ky., 1975), p. 22.

8. Edward Young, *Labor in Europe and America: A Special Report* (Philadelphia, 1875).

9. Ibid., p. 176.

10. Ibid., pp. 176-178.

11. Ibid., p. 178.

12. Ibid.

13. Ibid., pp. 178-179.

14. Ibid., p. 179.

15. Anthony Giddens, *The Class Structure of the Advanced Societies* (London, 1973), p. 141. For a powerful statement about the distinction between capitalism and industrialization and the process of mechanization see Raphael Samuels, "The Workshop of the World: Steam Power and Hand Technology in Mid-Victorian Britain," *History Workshop* 3 (Spring 1977), 6-72.

16. Gabriel Kolko, *Main Currents in Modern American History* (New York, 1976), p. 68.

17. The literature on social mobility will be dealt with in Chapter 5.

18. The literature on transiency will be considered in Chapter 4.

19. Furner, *Advocacy and Objectivity*.

20. Giddens, *Class Structure*, p. 114; Stanislow Ossowski, *Class Structure in the Social Consciousness* (London, 1963), p. 114.

21. On the ideological perspective of the American working class in antebellum America see Bruce Laurie, *The Working People of Philadelphia, 1850-1880* (Philadelphia, 1980); Alan Dawley, *Class and Community: The Industrial Revolution in Lynn* (Cambridge, Mass., 1976); David Montgomery, *Beyond Equality: Labor and the Radical Republicans, 1862-1872* (New York, 1967).

22. The role of the moneylender in precapitalist society is discussed in Maurice Dobb, *Studies in the Development of Capitalism* (New York, 1947), chs. 1-2.

23. As Montgomery has noted: "The peculiar relationship of manufacturers to the leaders of finance and commerce was reflected in the ambivalent rhetoric of the period. At times the new elite spoke of themselves as 'capitalists' and described disputes with their employees as conflicts between labor and capital. More frequently they referred to themselves as part of the 'producing classes,' or as 'labor,' or even as 'workingmen,' as distinct from the 'capitalists' (i.e., the old elite). A generation later conventional American symbolism would term employers 'middle class,' and William Jennings Bryan would seek to ennoble the worker, farmer, and corner grocer by calling each of them, like the industrialist, 'a business man.' But in the 1860s the phrase 'middle class' was such a novelty that, when it appeared at all, it was enclosed in quotation marks. The speaker who valued precision might term the wage earners the 'mechanical interests' or 'industrial classes' or even 'working classes' (always plural), but common practice indiscriminately spoke of labor as a group of which employers at times were a part and at times were not" (Montgomery, *Beyond Equality*, p. 14).

24. On the Canadian nine-hour movement see Steven Langdon, *The Emergence of the Canadian Working Class Movement* (Toronto, 1975); Robert H. Storey, "Industrialization in Canada: The Emergence of the Hamilton Working Class, 1850-1870's" (M.A. thesis, Dalhousie University,

1975); Bryan D. Palmer, *A Culture in Conflict: Skilled Workers and Industrial Capitalism in Hamilton, Ontario 1860-1914* (Montreal, 1979), ch. 5. Palmer attributes the failure of the nine-hour movement to a lack of solidarity among the various segments of the working class.

25. *Hamilton Spectator*, January 26, 1872.

26. Ibid., February 2, 1872.

27. H. J. Habakkuk, in *American and British Technology in the Nineteenth Century: The Search for Labour-Saving Inventions* (Cambridge, 1962), argues that this shortage of skilled labor and the abundance of unskilled labor was the impetus for the rapid technological advancement of American industry.

28. *Hamilton Spectator*, April 19, 1872, p. 2.

29. *Ontario Workman*, April 18, 1872.

30. Ibid.

31. Ibid., July 4, 1872.

32. Ibid., October 10, 1872.

33. *Montreal Northern Journal*, quoted in *Ontario Workman*, July 25, 1872.

34. *Ontario Workman*, April 25, 1873, p. 3.

35. *Ontario Workman*, May 2, 1872, p. 3.

36. R. Q. Gray, in *The Labour Aristocracy in Victorian Edinburgh* (London, 1976), argues that the cultural position of the labor aristocracy in Edinburgh was ambiguous. On the one hand it demonstrated the hegemonic position of middle-class respectability among this stratum of the working class. Yet on the other hand the labor aristocracy shaped this system of values to its own purposes. Thus the same temperance that appeared as a surrender to middle-class notions of behavior also served as a means of maintaining an industrial discipline in opposition to employers. For a brilliant discussion of the various influences on the temperance movement and its cultural meaning see Brian Harrison, *Drink and the Victorians: The Temperance Question in England, 1815-1872* (London, 1971).

37. Michael B. Katz, *The People of Hamilton, Canada West: Family and Class in a Mid-Nineteenth-Century City* (Cambridge, Mass., 1975), ch. 4.

38. *Hamilton Spectator and Journal of Commerce*, August 18, 1849, pp. 2-3.

39. Eric Ricker, "Consensus and Conflict: City Politics at Mid-Century" (unpublished, Toronto, 1973).

40. The R. G. Dunn records are part of the Dunn and Bradstreet Collection at the Baker Library, Harvard Business School, Cambridge, Mass. Robert W. Lovett of the Baker Library made these records available to us. For a description of these records and examples of their contents see Katz, *People of Hamilton*, ch. 4, and Clyde and Sally Griffen, *Natives and Newcomers: The Ordering of Opportunity in Mid-Nineteenth Century Poughkeepsie* (Cambridge, Mass., 1978), chs. 4-6.

41. On credit markets in nineteenth-century America see John A. James, *Money and Capital in Postbellum America* (Princeton, 1978).

42. *Hamilton Spectator*, August 18, 1871.

43. J. A. Bryce, "Patterns of Profit and Power: Business, Community, and Industrialization in a Nineteenth-Century City," Working Paper 28, in York Social History Project, "Third Report," (Downsview, Ontario, 1978), pp. 369-412. The authors are indebted to Bryce for the use of his excellent research.

44. Bryce, "Patterns of Profit," p. 401. For the debate over the origins of the Canadian elite see Wallace Clement, *The Canadian Corporate Elite: An Analysis of Economic Power* (Toronto, 1975); L. R. MacDonald, "Merchants against Industry: An Idea and Its Origins," *Canadian Historical Review* 56, no. 3 (September 1975), 276-277; Alfred Dubuc, "Problems in the Study of the Stratification of the Canadian Society from 1760 to 1840," in Michael Horn and Ronald Sabourin, eds., *Studies of Canadian Social History* (Toronto, 1974), pp. 123-139.

45. Bryce, "Patterns of Profit," p. 407, describes the methods used to code and manipulate the data from the Dunn records.

46. MacDonald, "Merchants against Industry," pp. 276-277.

47. Griffen and Griffen, *Natives and Newcomers*, ch. 4.

48. Bryce, "Patterns of Profit"; Griffen and Griffen, *Natives and Newcomers*.

49. Bernard Farber, *Guardians of Virtue: Salem Families in 1800* (New York, 1972), ch. 3.

50. On the role of land speculation in Hamilton's economy see Michael J. Doucet, "Building the Victorian City: The Process of Land Development in Hamilton, Ontario, 1847-1881" (Ph.D. diss., University of Toronto, 1977).

51. Bryce, "Patterns of Profit," pp. 399-400.

52. Ibid.

53. *Hamilton Spectator*, June 3, 1872, quoted in Bryce, "Patterns of Profit," p. 404.

54. Young, *Labor in Europe and America*, p. 829.

55. Griffen and Griffen, in *Natives and Newcomers*, ch. 9, argue that industrialization brought about a convergence of the conditions of skilled, semiskilled, and unskilled workers in Poughkeepsie.

56. Dominion of Canada, *Census of Industry*, 1871 ms.

57. On the struggle for control of the work process see Harry Braverman, *Labor and Monopoly Capital: The Degradation of Work in the Twentieth Century* (New York, 1974); Richard Edwards, *Contested Terrain: The Transformation of the Workplace in the Twentieth Century* (New York, 1979); David Montgomery, *Workers' Control in America* (Cambridge, 1980); and Palmer, *Culture in Conflict*, ch. 3.

58. Bruce Laurie, Theodore Hershberg, and George Alter, "Immigrants and Industry: The Philadelphia Experience, 1850-1880," and Bruce Laurie and Mark Schmitz, "Manufacture and Productivity: The Making of an Industrial Base, Philadelphia, 1850-1880," in Theodore Hershberg, ed., *Philadelphia: Work, Space, Family, and Group Experience in the Nineteenth Century* (New York, 1981).

59. Young, *Labor in Europe and America*, p. 798.

60. John Foster, "Nineteenth-Century Towns: A Class Dimension," in H.

J. Dyos, ed., *The Study of Urban History* (London, 1968), pp. 281-300.

61. Katz has dealt with this problem in "Occupational Classification in History," *Journal of Interdisciplinary History* 3, no. 1 (Summer 1972), 63-88.

62. The first book in the revival of social mobility history was Stephan Thernstrom, *Poverty and Progress: Social Mobility in a Nineteenth-Century City* (Cambridge, Mass., 1974). Many of the same issues underlie Thernstrom's, *The Other Bostonians: Poverty and Progress in the American Metropolis, 1880-1970* (Cambridge, Mass., 1973).

63. Theodore Hershberg, Alan Burstein, and Robert Dockhorn, "Record Linkage," *Historical Methods Newsletter* 9, nos. 2 and 3 (March-June 1976), 137-163. This article cites the other important work in the area of historical record linkage.

64. Giddens, *Class Structure of the Advanced Societies*, p. 106.

65. David Harvey, *Social Justice and the City* (Baltimore, 1973), pp. 202-203.

66. Ossowski, *Class Structure*, pp. 135-136; Giddens, *Class Structure of the Advanced Societies*, p. 111.

67. Nicos Poulantzas, *Classes in Contemporary Capitalism* (London, 1975), makes the distinction between a mode of production, which is an analytical category for describing a set of social relationships, and the social formation, which is an actual historical situation representing a merging of a number of modes of production.

68. The analysis of class is of course integrally connected with the nature of the social formation. We contend that the early nineteenth century saw the rise of capitalism as the dominant mode of production. Then in the late nineteenth century commercial capitalism was superseded by industrial capitalism. This three-stage paradigm is discussed in Chapter 9.

69. Giddens, *Class Structure of the Advanced Societies*, p. 142; Dobb, *Studies in the Development of Capitalism*, p. 6.

70. The way in which class is to be defined in late capitalist society is a subject of much debate. Among the essential works to consult are C. Wright Mills, *White Collar: The American Middle Classes* (New York, 1951); Poulantzas, *Classes*; Eric Olin Wright, "Class Boundaries in Advanced Capitalist Society," *New Left Review* 98 (1976), 3-41; G. Carchedi, "Reproduction of Social Classes at the Level of Production Relations," *Economy and Society* 4 (1975), 361-417.

71. The notion that North American cities were typified by a three-class social structure in the mid-nineteenth century with artisans representing the middle class has been advanced in Katz, *People of Hamilton*, pp. 27, 311.

72. Massachusetts Bureau of Statistics of Labor, *Seventh Annual Report*, Public Document No. 31 (Boston, 1876), pp. 2-3.

73. Braverman, *Labor and Monopoly Capital*, pp. 294-295.

74. Records of the Great Western Railway (1863), Hamilton Public Library.

75. On the class position of women see Katz, *People of Hamilton*, pp 56-60, 310.

76. On the class structure of the countryside see David E. Schob, *Hired*

*Hands and Plowboys: Farm Labor in the Midwest, 1815-1860* (Urbana, Ill., 1975).

77. Harold Rock, *Artisans of the New Repubic: The Tradesmen of New York City in the Age of Jefferson* (New York, 1979), p. 266; Kaestle, *Evolution*, p. 102.

78. In each of these analyses a dummy variable representing class membership was the dependent variable. The factors were age, ethnicity, marital status, and persistence since 1851 and since 1861. The analysis was performed for the 1871 data only. For a detailed presentation of this and subsequent statistical analyses see Michael B. Katz, Michael J. Doucet, and Mark J. Stern, "Occupation and Class," Working Paper 24, in York Social History Project, "Third Report" (Downsview, Ontario, 1978), pp. 199-253.

79. Extreme caution must be used in adding deviations and the grand mean in order to derive an adjusted score. Such an operation assumes that there is no interaction between the various factors in the analysis. Wherever we utilize such a procedure, we have examined the character of the interactions and found them to be of minor importance.

80. Griffen and Griffen, *Natives and Newcomers*, ch. 7, make the same point concerning the composition of stagnant and growing trades.

81. The index of representativeness used here measures the degree to which a group is over- or underrepresented on a given characteristic—in this case assessed wealth. A score of 100 suggests that the group's share of the total is equal to its representation in the population.

82. Gray, *Labour Aristocracy*, ch. 6.

83. On the differences between the linked and unlinked populations see Chapter 4.

84. These figures differ from those cited above because the base for these indices is the linked population, not the total population.

85. See note 80.

86. The stratification of the business class is discussed in greater detail in Chapter 2.

87. Griffen and Griffen, *Natives and Newcomers*, p. 63, note that "during the fifties 22 percent and during the sixties 23 percent of the journeymen at the start of each decade had become self-employed by its end, but during the seventies that proportion almost halved to 13 percent, largely wiping out the great advantage which artisans previously had over the semi-skilled and the unskilled in becoming shopowners."

88. Daniel T. Rodgers, *The Work Ethic in Industrial America, 1850-1920* (Chicago, 1978), p. 30.

## 2. Social Stratification

1. These figures are based on our use of the proportion of Canadian-born children of a given age of parents of a given ethnicity as a rough equivalent of length of time lived in Canada. For example of the 443 children aged 10 to 14 of Irish parents in 1851 seventy-eight (18 percent) were Canadian born. From this we estimate that 18 percent of the Irish parents had been here at least ten

years. This calculation clearly does not take into consideration differential fertility and mortality among individuals in Ireland and Canada. Still it provides a conservative estimate of the proportion of long-term residents. These and other data are presented in more detail in Michael B. Katz, "Age, Ethnicity, and Sex," Working Paper 6, in York Social History Project, "First Research Report" (Downsview, Ontario, 1975), pp. 147-228.

2. On the trends and character of the Irish migration to North America see Oliver MacDonagh, "The Irish Famine Emigration to the United States," *Perspectives on American History*, 10 (1976), 357-448.

3. *Gentleman* was apparently a title adopted by land speculators and developers in Canada. Interestingly this title was quite common in Hamilton but virtually nonexistent in Buffalo. On the role of gentlemen in Hamilton's economy see Michael J. Doucet, "Building the Victorian City: The Process of Land Development in Hamilton, Ontario, 1847-1881" (Ph.D. diss., University of Toronto, 1977), chapter 6. On the declining importance of land dealings in the economy see Chapter 1 and J. A. Bryce, "Patterns of Profit and Power: Business, Community, and Industrialization in a Nineteenth-Century City," Working Paper 28, in York Social History Project, "Third Report" (Downsview, Ontario, 1978), pp. 369-412.

4. On changes in the production of shoes at midcentury see Alan Dawley, *Class and Community: The Industrial Revolution in Lynn* (Cambridge, Mass., 1976), and Clyde and Sally Griffen, *Natives and Newcomers: The Ordering of Opportunity in Mid-Nineteenth-Century Poughkeepsie* (Cambridge, Mass., 1978), pp. 157-167.

5. On trends in social and geographic mobility see Chapters 3 and 5.

6. Edward Young, *Labor in Europe and America* (Philadelphia, 1875).

7. On the cost of living in Canada see J. G. Snell, "The Cost of Living in Canada in 1870," *Histoire Sociale/Social History* 12, no. 23 (1979), 186-191; Young, *Labor in Europe and America*.

8. For a detailed discussion on changes in the distribution of wealth see Michael B. Katz, "The Structure of Inequality and Early Industrialization," Working Paper 18, in York Social History Project, "Third Report" (Downsview, Ontario, 1978), pp. 1-47, especially table 1.

9. Michael B. Katz, "The Structure of Inequality and Early Industrialization," Working Paper 4, in York Social History Project, "First Research Report" (Downsview, Ontario, 1975), table 4.6.

10. Multiple classification analyses were carried out with identical factors for the 1851, 1861, and 1871 data with economic rank as the dependent variable. The independent variables included a composite variable of occupation and age, ethnicity and property ownership, sex and number of children, number of servants, and the number of relatives and boarders.

11. On the relationship of earnings to the life cycle see Michael R. Haines, "Industrial Work and the Family Life Cycle, 1889/90," *Research in Economic History* 4 (1979), and "Poverty, Economic Stress, and the Family in a Late-Nineteenth-Century American City: Whites in Philadelphia, 1880," in Theodore Hershberg, ed., *Philadelphia: Work, Space, Family, and Group Experience in the Nineteenth-Century* (New York, 1981).

12. Wisconsin Bureau of Labor and Industrial Statistics, *Third Biennial Report* (Madison, 1888), table 5, pp. 190-213.

13. E. J. Hobsbawm, *Industry and Empire* (London, 1969), p. 157; Michael B. Katz, *The People of Hamilton, Canada West: Family and Class in a Mid-Nineteenth-Century City* (Cambridge, Mass., 1975), p. 27.

14. Katz, "The Structure of Inequality," p. 36 provides a more detailed presentation of this analysis.

15. On servants in the nineteenth century see Patricia Branca, "A New Perspective on Women's Work: A Comparative Typology," *Journal of Social History* 9 (1975), 129-153; Teresa McBride, *The Domestic Revolution, The Modernization of Household Service in England and France, 1820-1920* (London, 1976).

16. The figure of $7 per month is based on Young, *Labor in Europe and America.*

17. Other studies of social mobility in nineteenth-century America include Stephan Thernstrom, *The Other Bostonians: Poverty and Progress in the American Metropolis, 1880-1970* (Cambridge, Mass., 1974); S. Thernstrom, *Poverty and Progress: Social Mobility in a Nineteenth-Century City* (Cambridge, Mass., 1964); Howard P. Chudacoff, *Mobile Americans: Residential and Social Mobility in Omaha, 1880-1920* (New York, 1972); Peter R. Knights, *The Plain People of Boston, 1830-1860: A Study in City Growth* (New York, 1971); Katz, *People of Hamilton;* Griffen and Griffen, *Natives and Newcomers.*

18. No direct measure of wealth or economic rank appears in the New York State census of 1855. The only economic figure is the value of the dwelling in which each person resided. At first this appeared an unhelpful statistic until we discovered that our problems with interpreting it arose from the fact that when more than one family lived in the same dwelling, each had been assigned the total dwelling value. Twenty-four percent of the dwellings housed more than one household; or put another way 46 percent of households lived in multifamily dwellings, probably a reflection of the city's rapid growth. Furthermore dwellings were often not divided between families of equal size. Houses built for one family were subdivided, sometimes into a space for a family and a small apartment for one person or a couple. Thus we determined the most discriminating figure to be the per capita dwelling value (DV/C) of the space occupied by each family, calculated by the following formula:

DV/C = Dwelling Value X (number in household per number in dwelling)

This figure is analogous to the total assessed value used as a surrogate for economic rank in our work in Hamilton. In fact the cross-tabulation of per capita dwelling value with other variables indicates that it serves as a rough proxy for economic rank.

19. Michael B. Katz, "The Structure of Inequality and Length of Residence in Buffalo, New York, 1855," Working Paper 13, in York Social History Project, "Second Report" (Downsview, Ontario, 1976), table 13.3.

20. In this analysis all males 18 years and older were divided into five

groups according to occupational rank, and a separate MCA was carried out to estimate the role of major demographic factors in influencing the likelihood that an individual would be a member of a particular rank. The variables included were birthplace, length of residence, literacy, and age. Perhaps the most important variable, father's occupation, was not available. For a more detailed presentation of these results see Katz, "Structure of Inequality," table 13.9.

21. See Chapter 5.

22. Our conclusions stem from another series of MCAs with the population partitioned by birthplace with economic rank as the dependent variable. See Katz, "Structure of Inequality," table 13.10.

23. On the stability of income shares in twentieth-century America see Gabriel Kolko, *Wealth and Power in America* (New York, 1962), and G. Kolko, *Main Currents in Modern American History* (New York, 1976), pp. 339-347.

24. These results are a summary of the findings of Michael B. Katz, in "Women and Early Industrialization," Working Paper 2, in York Social History Project, "First Research Report" (Downsview, Ontario, 1975), pp. 26-40.

25. Our argument concerning the impact of industrialization on women's social position draws on Louise A. Tilly and Joan W. Scott, *Women, Work, and Family* (New York, 1978) and their various articles, especially Joan W. Scott and Louise A. Tilly, "Women's Work and the Family in Nineteenth-Century Europe," *Comparative Studies in Society and History* 17 (1975), 36-64.

26. Norman MacDonald, *Canada: Immigration and Colonization, 1841-1903* (Aberdeen, 1966), pp. 136-137.

27. Minnesota Bureau of Labor Statistics, *First Biennial Report* (Minneapolis, 1888), p. 142.

28. Ibid., p. 149. The interpretation of domestic service offered here is supported by an excellent work that appeared after this section was written, David Katzman, *Seven Days a Week* (New York, 1978). See also Mark Ebery and Brian Preston, "Domestic Service in Late-Victorian and Edwardian England, 1871-1914," Geographical Papers, Department of Geography, University of Reading (Reading, England, 1976).

29. Minnesota Bureau of Labor Statistics, *First Biennial Report*, p. 149.

30. Ibid., pp. 164-173. One must keep in mind that the balancing of expectations and reality for both employers and employees varied with the labor market and that these were not identical in Minnesota and Hamilton. Nevertheless the decline in the employment of servants and the increase in other forms of women's employment suggest that the situation in Minnesota is applicable to Hamilton.

31. See Katz, *People of Hamilton*, pp. 56-57, for an example of the opportunities that this form of entrepreneurship offered to one woman in Hamilton.

## 3. Transiency

1. New York Board of State Charities, *Fourteenth Annual Report* (Albany, 1881), p. 35.

2. Ibid., p. 35.

3. Ibid., p. 31.

4. Quoted in New York Board of State Charities, *Twenty-Sixth Annual Report* (Albany, 1893), pp. 69-70.

5. Ibid., p. 70.

6. For the story of Dr. Brigham see *Buffalo Medical Journal and Monthly Review of Medical and Surgical Science* 5 (1850), 397-403.

7. Stephan Thernstrom and Peter R. Knights, "Men in Motion: Some Data and Speculations about Urban Population Mobility in Nineteenth-Century America," *Journal of Interdisciplinary History* 1 (1970), 18-19. For other studies that reveal the same phenomenon see James C. Malin, "The Turnover of Farm Population in Kansas," *Kansas Historical Quarterly* 4 (1935), 339-372; Howard Chudacoff, *Mobile Americans: Residential and Social Mobility in Omaha, 1880-1920* (New York, 1972); David Gagan and Herbert Mays, "Historical Demography and Canadian Social History: Families and Land in Peel County, Ontario," *The Canadian Historical Review* 54 (1973), 35-45; Michael B. Katz, *The People of Hamilton, Canada West: Family and Class in a Mid-Nineteenth-Century City* (Cambridge, Mass., 1975), pp. 111-134. Two useful reviews of relevant contemporary literature are T. H. Hollingworth, "Historical Studies of Migration," *Annales de Demographie Historique 1970* (Paris, 1970), pp. 87-96, and James W. Simmons, "Changing Residence in the City: A Review of Intraurban Mobility," *The Geographical Review* 58 (1968), 622-651.

8. Stephan Thernstrom, *The Other Bostonians: Poverty and Progress in the American Metropolis, 1880-1970* (Cambridge, Mass., 1973), p. 225.

9. On record linkage see Ian Winchester, "On Referring to Ordinary Historical Persons," and "A Brief Survey of the Algorithmic, Mathematical, and Philosophical Literature Relevant to Historical Record Linkage," in E. A. Wrigley, ed., *Identifying People in the Past* (London, 1973), pp. 17-40, 128-150.

10. We should note that we lack an independent check on the accuracy of the most important variable in this chapter, the number of years people reported they had lived in Buffalo or rural Erie County. However the information should be more accurate than that derived from record linkage. There was no reason why people should have lied, and even if their memories had become a bit hazy, they should have remembered the approximate year of their arrival. The likelihood of very great error is much less than in record linkage. Also the distribution of years lived in the city or town is encouraging: virtually no heaping exists prior to twenty years. Thus most people apparently gave an exact rather than an estimated answer when asked how long they had lived in Buffalo or rural Erie County.

11. In our attempts to make estimates of persistence in this manner we encountered two problems. First, the 1845 census for New York State did not break down the population by age groups. Therefore we have to assume a similarity in the age structure between 1845 and 1855. This undoubtedly introduced some bias into the estimates. We also had to assume in estimating the number of household heads that household size remained the same, which also probably introduced a minor degree of error into the calculations. The

other problem is mortality. Most studies of persistence do not account for death: rates usually reflect the assumption that all residents at one time remain alive at the next census. This of course cannot be true. The real question is: How much difference would mortality make in the calculations of persistence? In Buffalo correcting for mortality increased the estimate of total male persistence by 12 percent and of the persistence of household heads who had been 30 to 59 years old in 1845 by 10 percent.

We derived estimates of persistence for survivors in Buffalo between 1845 and 1855 from the Coale and Demeny model life table, Model West, level 12, with a life expectancy from birth of 47.5 years for women and 44.5 years for men. For the model life tables see Ansley J. Coale and Paul Demeny, *Regional Model Life Tables and Stable Populations* (Princeton, N.J., 1966). Although this schedule is less severe than the model we used for Hamilton its use is justified, because by underestimating death we also underestimate persistence. Since we argue that persistence was higher in Buffalo than Hamilton, our assumption in this respect works against our hypothesis. Using these tables we computed the probability of survival for each age cohort and compared the actual number within the cohort who had reported living in Buffalo at least ten years with the predicted number of survivors.

A more detailed discussion of these data may be found in our "Migration and the Social Order in Erie County, New York, 1855," *Journal of Interdisciplinary History* 8, no. 4 (Spring 1978), 669-701, and "Population Persistence and Early Industrialization in a Canadian City: Hamilton, Ontario, 1851-1871," *Social Science History* 2, no. 2 (Winter 1978), 208-229. 1978), 208-229.

12. Using mortality estimates calculated by Michael Haines for the native- and foreign-born urban populations of seven New York counties between 1850 and 1865 we computed a set of age- and sex-specific decennial survival ratios that expressed the proportion of a population that would be alive a decade later. The ratios were then applied to the population as a whole and to various occupational and ethnic subpopulations. For a description of Haines's methodology see Michael R. Haines, "Mortality in Nineteenth-Century America: Estimates from New York and Pennsylvania Census Data, 1865 and 1900," *Demography* 14, no. 3 (1977), 311-331. We would like to thank Dr. Haines for providing us with unpublished life tables based on his research.

13. Economic rank is derived, as in Chapter 2, from the total value of each individual's assessed property and taxable income within the city as listed on the city's assessment rolls. Renters were assessed according to the value of the property they inhabited.

14. The data cited in this section are based on an MCA carried out on data from Buffalo in 1855. The dependent variable is length of residence in the city, and the factors are age, marital status, sex, household status, dwelling value per capita, number of children, property ownership, and occupational rank. Where appropriate, age and sex were combined to account for interaction effects, as were household and marital status, occupation and birthplace and property ownership and dwelling value per capita. Separate analyses were carried out for the entire population and for household heads. All figures reported are predicted means, with other factors held constant.

15. The occupational ranking used here consists of five ranks: the group consisting mainly of professionals and proprietors; clerks, white-collar workers, small proprietors; skilled workers; semiskilled workers; and unskilled workers, primarily laborers.

16. For the definition of dwelling value per capita see Chapter 2, note 18.

17. The dependent variable is persistence in the city since 1861. The factor (or independent) variables are age, ethnicity, occupation (sixteen categories), economic rank, and number of houses owned (0, 1, 2 or more). The covariates are number of children, number of resident servants, and the number of relatives and boarders.

18. On the relationship between mobility and economic context see Anthony E. Boardman and Michael P. Weber, "Economic Growth and Occupational Mobility in Nineteenth-Century Urban America: A Reappraisal," *Journal of Social History* 11, no. 1 (Fall 1977), 52-74.

19. Gagan and Mays, "Historical Demography." For data on another rural area see Ingrid Erikson and John Rodgers, "Mobility in an Agrarian Community: Practical and Methodological Considerations," in Kurt Agren, et al., eds., *Aristocrats, Farmers, Proletarians: Essays in Swedish Demographic History* (Uppsala, Sweden, 1973), p. 60.

20. See Allan R. Pred, *Urban Growth and the Circulation of Information: The United States System of Cities, 1790-1840* (Cambridge, Mass., 1973).

21. The role of artisan culture in the shaping of the American working class has been treated by Herbert G. Gutman, "Work, Culture, and Society in Industrializing America, 1815-1919," *American Historical Review* 78 (1973), 531-589; Bruce Laurie, *The Working People of Philadelphia, 1800-1850* (Philadelphia, 1980). For Canada see Gregory S. Kealey, "The Orange Order in Toronto: Religious Riot and the Working Class," and Bryan D. Palmer, "Give us the Road and We Will Run It: The Social and Cultural Matrix of an Emerging Labour Movement," in Gregory S. Kealey and Peter Warrian, eds., *Essays in Canadian Working Class History* (Toronto, 1976), pp. 13-34, 106-124; Bryan D. Palmer, *A Culture in Conflict: Skilled Workers and Industrial Capitalism in Hamilton, Ontario, 1860-1914* (Montreal, 1979). The rise of rational bureaucratic social structure in late nineteenth-century America is discussed in Robert H. Wiebe, *The Search for Order, 1877-1920* (New York, 1967), and Samuel P. Hays, *The Response to Industrialism, 1855-1914* (Chicago, 1957). Gabriel Kolko, in *Main Currents in Modern American History* (New York, 1976), pp. 67-99, argues that the immigrants' high rate of transiency and shallowness of cultural ties were key elements in the development of the American working class.

22. Haley P. Bamman, "Patterns of School Attendance in Toronto, 1844-1878: Some Spatial Considerations," in Michael B. Katz and Paul H. Mattingly, eds., *Education and Social Change: Themes from Ontario's Past* (New York, 1975), pp. 217-245.

23. See for example Edward Shorter, *The Making of the Modern Family* (New York, 1976), pp. 205-254.

24. Gabriel Kolko, *Main Currents*, pp. 68-72, emphasizes the role of immigrants as a reserve army of labor. American immigration has also been treated in international perspective in Philip Taylor, *The Distant Magnet: European*

*Emigration to the USA* (New York, 1971), and Michael J. Piore, *Birds of Passage: Migrant Labor and Industrial Societies* (Cambridge, 1979).

## 4. Property: Use Value and Exchange Value

1. *Ontario Workman*, June 27, 1872, p. 6.

2. Massachusetts Bureau of Labor Statistics, *Seventh Annual Report*, Public Document no. 31 (Boston, 1876), p. xii.

3. Ibid., p. xii.

4. For a discussion of the difference between use and exchange value see Karl Marx, *Capital*, 3 vols. (Moscow, 1954), vol. 1, p. 43. This distinction is also discussed in contemporary society by David Harvey, in "Labor, Capital, and Class Struggle around the Built Environment in Advanced Capitalist Societies," *Politics and Society* 6 (1977), 265-295.

5. Thorstein Veblen, *The Theory of the Leisure Class* (New York, 1899).

6. Jane Synge, "The Transition from School to Work: Working Class Adolescence in Early Twentieth Century Hamilton" (unpublished, Hamilton, Ontario, n.d.).

7. The multivariate analysis of property ownership is presented in full in Michael B. Katz, "The Structure of Inequality and Early Industrialization," Working Paper 18, in York Social History Project, "Third Report" (Downsview, Ontario, 1978), tables 11-14.

8. Among both the Irish and non-Irish, persisters were more likely to own property than newcomers to the city. See Katz, "The Structure of Inequality," table 14.

9. Oliver MacDonagh, "The Irish Famine Emigration to the United States," *Perspectives in American History* 10 (1976), 357-448.

10. On the means of financing home ownership see Stephan Thernstrom, *Poverty and Progress: Social Mobility in a Nineteenth-Century City* (Cambridge, Mass., 1964), pp. 115-137.

11. The comments cited are from Wisconsin Bureau of Labor and Industrial Statistics, *Third Biennial Report, 1887-1888* (Madison, 1888) pp. 15-36.

12. Length of residence was the single most influential factor affecting property ownership in Buffalo (beta = .32). Next in influence came economic rank, substantially lower (.17), followed by birthplace (.13), occupation (.09), and literacy, which had virtually no influence. Age, household structure, and family size, which were entered as covariates, had no statistically significant influence on home ownership. See Michael B. Katz, "The Structure of Inequality and Length of Residence in Buffalo, New York, 1855," Working Paper 13, in York Social History Project, "Second Report" (Downsview, Ontario, 1976), table 13.7.

13. Theodore Hershberg, Michael Katz, Stuart Blumin, Laurence Glasco, and Clyde Griffen, "Occupation and Ethnicity in Five Nineteenth-Century Cities: A Collaborative Inquiry," *Historical Methods Newsletter* 7 (1974).

14. Our data on the financing of home purchases in Hamilton come from a systematic examination of the five largest land surveys, examined by Michael J. Doucet, in "Building the Victorian City: The Process of Land Development

in Hamilton, Ontario, 1847-1881" (Ph.D. diss., University of Toronto, 1977). These were the surveys of V. H. Tisdale, P. H. Hamilton, and H. B. Wilson (both his north and south survey), and of Kerr, McLaren, and Street. Taken together these plans include a total of 924 building lots. The abstracts of land transactions on these lots were searched to determine the total number of transactions between 1847 and 1881 on those lots that contained a structure (898 total transactions). Then through a search of the deed abstracts we determined that 240 of these transactions (27 percent) involved mortgages. Of these mortgages thirty-seven, or approximately 15 percent, were traced to the actual deeds in order to determine the terms of the mortgages as summarized in the text. All of the land records examined are available at the Ontario Provincial Archives in Toronto. For a description of the data see Doucet, "Building the Victorian City," ch. 4.

15. It is possible that families borrowed money without taking out mortgages. Still our results suggest the extent to which the means of financing property ownership have changed in the past century.

16. The failure to understand the role of property ownership in working-class life in the nineteenth century is particularly evident in Daniel D. Luria's "Wealth, Capital, and Power: The Social Meaning of Homeownership," *Journal of Interdisciplinary History* 7 (1976), 261-282. According to Luria, "In the context of capitalist society during the 1890 to 1910 period, homeownership did not impart to working class families any advantage over renters." This conclusion is based on the fact that, according to Luria, "returns to investment in real estate are seldom competitive with returns to alternative investment."

In drawing these conclusions Luria substitutes narrow economic abstractions for the concrete reasons why actual working people decided to purchase homes in the nineteenth century. Such narrow economic conclusions, which attempt to portray working-class actions as irrational, do not take into consideration the important reasons why home ownership was rational, particularly the use value of a home in a period of frequent unemployment and no old age pensions.

Luria's mistaken conclusions are based on a number of important methodological flaws. Luria attempts to prove that home ownership had no value through an examination of data on assessed wealth of families in the Boston area. He divided these data into home wealth and "non-home" wealth, or value of personal wealth and additional property holdings. His methods and evidence cannot support his argument. First, the data cover only 124 families between 1890 and 1910. Second, his equation of "social power" and "non-home wealth" is indefensible; it ignores the fact that in the right hands, real estate can be a form of power and that other types of social power, including political power and influence, exist. Third, the data analysis does not take into consideration the effect of life-cycle or persistence on property acquisition. Finally, he is guilty of making what in statistics is called a type-II error: Using his sketchy data, he cannot establish a relationship between property ownership, the acquisition of other wealth, and social mobility. From this he concludes that there is no relationship among the variables. Yet even if these relationships existed, it is doubtful that Luria could find them in his data.

These methodological errors are compounded by Luria's theoretical fuzziness. Although Luria has an appreciation of the nature of capitalist social relations, he fails to understand that, given these constraints, working-class families pursued economic strategies that were a rational adaptation to circumstances. To Luria the working class was simply duped: they had been sold on the virtues of home ownership, even though it was not in their self-interest. This patronizing attitude toward the intelligence of the decisions of working-class men and women is no more defensible when it comes from those on the left than it is when it comes from those on the right.

17. Doucet, "Building the Victorian City," pp. 28-52; Michael Doucet, "Speculation and the Physical Expansion of Mid-Nineteenth-Century Hamilton" (Paper presented at the Canadian Urban History Conference, University of Guelph, Guelph, Ontario, May, 13, 1977).

18. Doucet, "Building the Victorian City," pp. 213-216, 243-346.

19. Ibid., pp. 254-258.

20. Ibid., pp. 277-283.

21. Ibid., pp. 136-164.

22. Ibid., pp. 183-190; see Chapter 1.

23. H. J. Dyos, "The Speculative Builders and Developers of Victorian London," *Victorian Studies* 11 (1968), 641-690; Sam Bass Warner, Jr., *Streetcar Suburbs: The Process of Growth in Boston, 1870-1900* (Cambridge, Mass., 1972).

24. U.S. Bureau of the Census, Eleventh Census (1890), volume 13, *Report on Farms and Homes: Proprietorship and Indebtedness in the United States* (Washington, D.C., 1896).

## 5. Social Mobility

1. On the importance of examining both the structural and interpretive aspects of social experience see Anthony Giddens, *New Rules of Sociological Method: A Positive Critique of Interpretive Sociologies* (London, 1976). On the tension between actual and perceived mobility in nineteenth-century America the best discussion is to be found in Stephan Thernstrom, *Poverty and Progress: Social Mobility in a Nineteenth-Century City* (Cambridge, Mass., 1964).

2. See Chapters 1 and 4.

3. Wisconsin Bureau of Labor and Industrial Statistics, *Third Biennial Report, 1887-1888* (Madison, 1888), pp. 165-213.

4. American scholars have shown a marked willingness to accept a high rate of individual mobility as prima facie evidence of a just society. Yet as Michael Katz has noted in *The People of Hamilton, Canada West: Family and Class in a Mid-Nineteenth-Century City* (Cambridge, Mass., 1975), ch. 2, the high degree of mobility in Hamilton was complemented by a low degree of structural change.

5. Thernstrom, *Poverty and Progress;* Stephan Thernstrom, *The Other Bostonians: Poverty and Progress in the American Metropolis, 1880-1970*

(Cambridge, Mass., 1973); Clyde and Sally Griffen, *Natives and Newcomers: The Ordering of Opportunity in Mid-Nineteenth Century Poughkeepsie* (Cambridge, Mass., 1978). Edward Pessen, ed., *Three Centuries of Social Mobility in America* (Lexington, Mass., 1974), presents a review of a wide range of studies of social mobility from the Colonial period to the present.

6. John Foster, in "Nineteenth-Century Towns—A Class Dimension," in H. J. Dyos, ed., *The Study of Urban History* (London, 1968), pp. 281-300, suggests that when faced with a situation in which major social transformation seems impossible individuals will focus on more particularistic social hierarchies. Thus the very permanence of American society may have encouraged Americans to focus more on individual advancement. Gabriel Kolko, in *Main Currents in Modern American History* (New York, 1976), pp. 157-194, in his discussion of the structure of the American working class agrees with this assessment.

7. The concept of the "socialization of the unconscious" is taken from Christopher Lasch, *Haven in a Heartless World: The Family Besieged* (New York, 1977), pp. 3-4.

8. The problems of using occupational mobility as a measure of social mobility have been discussed by Michael Katz, *The People of Hamilton*, pp. 139-140, and Griffen and Griffen, *Natives and Newcomers*, ch. 3.

9. On the position of laborers see Griffen and Griffen, *Natives and Newcomers*, ch. 10.

10. Griffen and Griffen, *Natives and Newcomers*, pp. 66-68.

11. This and the following analyses of the linked census data on social mobility are discussed thoroughly in Michael B. Katz, "Occupational Mobility and the Illusion of Change," Working Paper 19, and "A Comparison of Occupational, Economic, Property, and Servant Mobility in Hamilton, Ontario, 1851-1861 and 1861-1871," Working Paper 21, both in York Social History Project, "Third Report" (Downsview, Ontario, 1978), pp. 48-87, 111-161.

12. Michael B. Katz, "Occupational Mobility and the Illusion of Change," table 4.

13. On the history of the shoemaking industry during this period see Alan Dawley, *Class and Community: The Industrial Revolution in Lynn* (New York, 1976), and Griffen and Griffen, *Natives and Newcomers*, pp. 151-157. On tailors see Griffen and Griffen, *Natives and Newcomers*, pp. 170-174.

14. On the ideology of mobility see Thernstrom, *Poverty and Progress*, pp. 57-79.

15. Katz, in *People of Hamilton*, ch. 3, demonstrates the distinctness of the four dimensions of mobility—occupation, wealth, property, and servant employment—between 1851 and 1861. Here we wish to emphasize the interrelationships among these dimensions.

16. See Katz, "A Comparison," for a systematic methodological discussion.

17. Katz, "A Comparison," pp. 112-116, provides a more detailed presentation of these statistics. For a discussion of the computation of lambda and Somer's D see Hubert M. Blalock, *Social Statistics* (New York, 1972), pp. 302-303, and Norman H. Nie, et al., *Statistical Package for the Social*

*Sciences,* 2nd ed. (New York, 1975), pp. 222-230. Mobility figures for 1851-1861 can be found in Katz, *People of Hamilton,* ch. 3.

18. Katz, "A Comparison," pp. 117-118, table 2.

19. Ibid., table 4.

20. Ibid., pp. 124-144, tables 6-15. In this analysis the following economic ranks were used: 1 (90-99 percentile), 2 (80-89 percentile), 3 (60-79 percentile), 4 (40-59 percentile), 5 (0-39 percentile).

21. Michael B. Katz, "Fathers and Sons: A Comparison of Occupations, Hamilton, Ontario, 1851 and 1871, Buffalo, New York, 1855," Working Paper 15, in York Social History Project, "Second Report" (Downsview, Ontario, 1976).

22. Ibid., pp. 148-153. The Hamilton data are based on a series of multiple classification analyses with father's occupation, birthplace, and religion and son's birthplace and age as factors and age of father, number of children, number of relatives and boarders, and number of servants as covariates. The Buffalo analysis includes as factors father's occupational rank, property ownership, length of residence in the city, dwelling value per capita, and the birthplace of father and son.

23. Michael B. Katz, "Inter-Generational Mobility and the Transmission of Inequality" Working Paper 20, in York Social History Project, "Third Report" (Downsview, Ontario, 1978).

24. This analysis is based on two multivariate analyses. The data in the first analysis include all sons living with their fathers in 1871. The analysis includes the following factors: father's occupation, father's ethnicity, son's birthplace, son's age, son's school attendance, and household status. The second analysis is of all sons who lived with their fathers in both 1861 and 1871. In addition to the other variables it includes father's occupational mobility. See Michael B. Katz, "Inter-generational Occupational Mobility and the Transmission of Inequality," tables 4, 5.

25. Before the managerial revolution of the late nineteenth and early twentieth century much industrial hiring was done by foremen and in other ways not under the direct control of management. These arrangements would emphasize the advantage of residential stability on work experience. See Alfred D. Chandler, *The Visible Hand: The Managerial Revolution in American Business* (Cambridge, Mass., 1977), p. 69.

26. Griffen and Griffen, *Natives and Newcomers,* pp. 193-206.

## 6. The Criminal Class: Image and Reality

1. Police Report, Hamilton *Spectator,* January 11, 1867.

2. Ibid.

3. On the nineteenth-century view of immorality, poverty, and crime in Canada see Susan E. Houston, "The Impetus to Reform: Urban Crime, Poverty, and Ignorance in Ontario, 1850-1875" (Ph.D. diss., University of Toronto, 1974).

4. On crime rates in nineteenth-century Britain, Europe, and the United States see Louis Chevalier, *Laboring Classes and Dangerous Classes* (New

York, 1973); Eric H. Monkkonen, *The Dangerous Class: Crime and Poverty in Columbus, Ohio, 1860-1885* (Cambridge, Mass., 1973); J. J. Tobias, *Crime and Industrial Society in the Nineteenth Century* (Harmondsworth, England, 1972); J. M. Beattie, "The Pattern of Crime in England, 1660-1800," *Past and Present* 62 (1974), 47-95; V. A. C. Gattrell and T. B. Hadden, "Criminal Statistics and Their Interpretation," in E. A. Wrigley, ed., *Nineteenth-Century Society* (Cambridge, England, 1972), pp. 336-386; Roger Lane, "Crime and Criminal Statistics in Nineteenth Century Massachusetts," *Journal of Social History* 2 (1968), 157-163; Howard J. Zehr, Jr., "The Modernization of Crime in Germany and France, 1830-1913," *Journal of Social History* 8 (1975), 117-133. An imaginative approach to urban crime written after this chapter was completed is in Roger Lane, *Violent Death in the City: Suicide, Accident, and Murder in Nineteenth-Century Philadelphia* (Cambridge, Mass., 1979).

5. J. M. Beattie, *Attitudes towards Crime and Punishment in Upper Canada, 1830-1850* (Toronto, 1977), p. 34.

6. Houston, "Impetus to Reform," p. 19.

7. Quoted in Beattie, *Attitudes towards Crime*, p. 44.

8. Ibid., p. 54.

9. Ibid., p. 55.

10. Ibid., p. 109.

11. On the relationship of crime and social values see David Rothman, *The Discovery of the Asylum: Social Order and Disorder in the Early Republic* (Boston, 1971), and Michael Foucault, *Discipline and Punish: The Discovery of the Prison* (New York, 1978).

12. The items on each set of registers are somewhat different. Most notably the 1850-1866 set did not include occupation. All of them, however, did record important demographic data and information about the nature of the charge and the sentence. In our analysis the actual number of commitments to jails or arrests was used to estimate rates over time. For other purposes the recidivists in the records were located and we created new files containing only one entry for each individual no matter how many times arrested or committed. We used these files to analyze recidivism and to examine the characteristics of individual offenders. A recidivist file was not made for the 1872-1873 group. However their records did list the number of previous arrests, which though not entirely accurate does permit the identification of most people jailed more than once.

We would like to thank John C. Weaver of the Department of History, McMaster University, for his comments on this chapter and especially for his suggestions for correcting several technical flaws.

13. On the nine-hour movement see Chapter 1, n. 24.

14. Hamilton *Spectator*, January 4, 1872.

15. Monkkonen, *Dangerous Class*.

16. James P. Spradley, *You Owe Yourself a Drunk: An Ethnography of Urban Nomads* (Boston, 1970), pp. 9-10.

17. On the concept of the criminal class see Monkkonen, *Dangerous Class*, and Chevalier, *Laboring Classes*.

18. On the relationship of illiteracy and crime from the standpoint of

Hamilton's school promoters see Harvey Graff, *The Literacy Myth: Literacy and Social Structure in the Nineteenth Century City* (New York, 1979).

19. Beattie, *Attitudes towards Crime*, pp. 7, 34.

20. For a discussion of these statistics see Hubert M. Blalock, *Social Statistics* (New York, 1972), ch. 15.

21. Mary S. Hartmann, *Victorian Murderesses* (New York, 1977).

22. Hamilton *Spectator*, February 21, 1872, p. 3.

23. Ibid., June 5, 1872, p. 3.

24. Ibid., August 26, 1872, p. 2.

25. Ibid.

26. Ibid., June 10, 1872, p. 3.

27. Ibid., January 23, 1872, p. 3.

28. Ibid., February 16, 1872, p. 3.

29. Ibid., February 16, 1872, p. 3.

30. Ibid., March 12, 1872, p. 3.

31. Ibid., January 17, 1872, p. 3.

32. Ibid., February 28, 1872, p. 3; May 20, 1872, p. 3.

33. Ibid., May 4, 1872, p. 3.

34. Ibid., March 15, 1872, p. 3.

35. Ibid., June 17, 1872, p. 3.

36. Ibid., June 12, 1872, p. 3.

37. Ibid., February 16, 1872, p. 3.

38. Ibid., January 17, 1871.

39. Ibid., March 7, 1879.

40. Ibid., March 14, 1879.

41. Ibid., February 15, 1872, p. 2.

42. Ibid., June 28, 1872, p. 3.

43. Ibid., March 9, 1872, p. 3; May 6, 1872, p. 3.

44. Ibid., June 24, 1872, p. 3.

45. Ibid., March 9, 1872.

46. Ibid., May 6, 1872.

47. Ibid., February 26, 1872, p. 3.

48. Ibid., January 21, 1880.

49. Ibid., April 1, 1879.

50. Ibid., April 5, 1879.

51. Ibid., April 8, 1879.

52. Ibid., April 8, 1879.

53. Ibid., February 9, 1872.

54. Ibid., April 10, 1879.

55. Ibid., March 28, 1879.

56. Ibid., January 7, 1870.

57. Ibid., June 14, 1872, p. 3.

58. Ibid., February 10, 1872, p. 3.

59. Ibid., February 26, 1872, p. 3.

60. Ibid., January 29, 1872, p. 3.

61. Ibid., January 17, 1871, p. 3.

62. On warning out see, for example, Rothman, *Discovery of the Asylum*, pp. 20-25.

## 7. Youth and Early Industrialization

1. Braverman, *Labor and Monopoly Capitalism: The Degradation of Work in the Twentieth Century* (New York, 1974), p. 280.

2. S. N. Eisenstadt, "Archetypal Patterns of Youth," in Erik H. Erikson, ed., *The Challenge of Youth* (New York, 1965), pp. 29-50.

3. Natalie Z. Davis, *Society and Culture in Early Modern France* (Stanford, 1975), pp. 108-109.

4. Lawrence Stone, *The Family, Sex, and Marriage in England, 1500-1880* (New York, 1977), p. 377.

5. John and Virginia Demos, "Adolescence in Historical Perspective," *Journal of Marriage and the Family* 31 (November, 1969), 632-38; Frank Musgrove, *Youth and the Social Order* (Bloomington, Ind., 1965), chs. 3 and 4.

6. Joseph Kett, *Rites of Passage: Adolescence in America, 1790 to the Present* (New York, 1977), pp. 6-7.

7. Kett, *Rites of Passage*, p. 243.

8. Peter Laslett, "Age of Menarche in Europe Since the Eighteenth Century," and Robert V. Wells, "Demographic Change and the Life Cycle of American Families," in Theodore K. Rabb and Robert I. Rotberg, eds., *The Family in History* (New York, 1973), pp. 28-47, 85-94; Mary Jo Bayne, *Here to Stay: American Families in the Twentieth Century* (New York, 1976), pp. 24-26.

9. Steven R. Smith, "The London Apprentices as Seventeenth-Century Adolescents," *Past and Present* 61 (November 1973), 149-161; John R. Gillis, *Youth and History: Tradition and Change in European Age Relations* (New York, 1974), pp. 16-18; Alan Macfarlane, *The Family Life of Ralph Josselin, A Seventeenth-Century Clergyman: An Essay in Historical Anthropology* (Cambridge, 1970); Edmund Morgan, *The Puritan Family: Religion and Domestic Relations in Seventeenth-Century New England*, rev. ed. (New York, 1966); Kett, *Rites of Passage*, pp. 14-36; R. S. Schofield, "Age-Specific Mobility in an Eighteenth Century Rural English Parish," *Annals de Demographie Historique 1970* (Paris, 1971), pp. 261-274.

10. Stone, *Family, Sex, and Marriage*, pp. 106-108.

11. Peter Laslett, *Family Life and Illicit Love in Earlier Generations* (London, 1977), pp. 34-35.

12. Smith, "London Apprentices."

13. John Modell and Tamara K. Hareven, "Urbanization and the Malleable Household: An Examination of Boarding and Lodging in American Families," *Journal of Marriage and the Family* 35 (August 1973), 467-478.

14. Stone, *Family, Sex, and Marriage*, pp. 108-109; Macfarlane, *Family Life*, pp. 205-210.

15. On the perception of boarding as pathological see Modell and Hareven, "Urbanization and the Malleable Household." The Buffalo data came from a multiple classification analysis of the New York census of 1855 for Buffalo. The results of this analysis of length of residence in the city are discussed in Chapter 3.

16. Minnesota Bureau of Labor Statistics, *First Biennial Report* (St. Paul, 1888), p. 178-196.

17. Ian E. Davey, "Educational Reform and the Working Class: School Attendance in Hamilton, Ontario, 1851-1891" (Ph.D. diss. University of Toronto, 1975); Ian E. Davey, "School Reform and School Attendance: The Hamilton Central School, 1853-1861," in Michael B. Katz and Paul Mattingly, eds., *Education and Social Change: Themes from Ontario's Past* (New York, 1975), pp. 294-314.

18. Michael B. Katz, *The People of Hamilton, Canada West: Family and Class in a Mid-Nineteenth-Century City* (Cambridge, Mass., 1975), pp. 241-292; Susan E. Houston, "The Impetus to Reform: Crime, Poverty, and Ignorance in Ontario, 1850-1875" (Ph.D. diss., University of Toronto, 1974).

19. Susan E. Houston, "Victorian Origins of Juvenile Delinquency: A Canadian Experience," *History of Education Quarterly* 12 (Fall, 1972), 255-275.

20. Carl Kaestle, *The Evolution of an Urban School System: New York City, 1750-1850* (Cambridge, Mass., 1974), pp. 113-115.

21. Controllers of the Public Schools of the First School District of the State of Pennsylvania, *Sixth Annual Report* (Philadelphia, 1824), p. 4.

22. Controllers of the Public Schools of the First School District of the State of Pennsylvania, *Eighth Annual Report* (Philadelphia, 1826), p. 7.

23. J. Hajnal, "European Marriage Patterns in Perspective," in D. V. Glass and D. E. C. Eversley, eds., *Population in History: Essays in Historical Demography* (London, 1965), pp. 101-146; Mark J. Stern, "Birth, Marriage, and Death: Aggregate Analysis of an Anglican Parish," Working Paper 7, in York Social History Project, "First Research Report" (Downsview, Ontario, 1975).

24. Michael Anderson, *Family Structure in Nineteenth-Century Lancashire* (New York, 1971), pp. 48-56. During the postwar housing shortage young couples' inability to establish their own households was a cause of friction in London's East End; see Michael Young and Peter Wilmott, *Family and Kinship in East London* (Harmondsworth, England, 1957).

25. Lynn Lees, "Patterns of Lower-Class Life: Irish Slum Communities in Nineteenth-Century London," in Stephan Thernstrom and Richard Sennett, eds., *Nineteenth-Century Cities* (New Haven, 1969), pp. 359-385.

26. Full tables showing the relationships between life-cycle variables, sex, and ethnicity may be found in Michael B. Katz, "Early Industrialization and the Life-Cycle," Working Paper 1, in York Social History Project, "First Research Report" (Downsview, Ontario, 1975).

27. Elsewhere Laurence Glasco, using descriptive statistics, has argued that marked ethnic differences characterized the timing of key events in the lives of young people in Buffalo. Here we use multivariate analysis to gain a more precise indication of the extent to which ethnicity affected the age at which people born in different countries left home, the age at which they married, and the likelihood that they would be boarders or servants. This inquiry generally confirms Glasco's conclusions, though it permits comparisons to be expressed in more exact terms. Again the figures here represent probabilities with other factors held constant. See Laurence Admiral Glasco, "Ethnicity and Social Structure: Irish, Germans, and Native-Born of Buffalo,

New York, 1850-1860" (Ph.D. diss., SUNY-Buffalo, 1973), pp. 181-201.

28. Earlier work showed clearly that patterns of attendance varied by age and sex. Therefore we subdivided the file into six subfiles (males and females aged 5 to 6, 7 to 12, 13 to 16) and performed a separate analysis for each of these in each of the three census years. One problem with this procedure was that the number of cases was very small. Therefore for one analysis all three years were combined into one file and year itself was entered as a variable in the analysis. The purpose of the MCA was to provide a figure that would express the relative contribution of each one of a set of independent or factor variables to school attendance and second, to show the effect that each category of each factor (for instance type of occupation) had on attendance. The actual choice of variables used in the analysis as factors and as covariates (essentially held constant in the last phase of the analysis) resulted from systematic experimentation with a variety of combinations. For a more detailed discussion of these data see Michael B. Katz, "School Attendance and Social Structure: A Multivariate Analysis," Working Paper 23, in York Social History Project, "Third Report" (Downsview, Ontario, 1978), pp. 183-198.

29. Davey, "Educational Reform"; see also, Davey, "School Reform and School Attendance," and Michael B. Katz, "Who Went to School?" in Michael B. Katz and Paul H. Mattingly, eds., *Education and Social Change*; pp. 271-293, 294-314.

30. Anderson, *Family Structure*, pp. 139-144.

31. Kett, *Rites of Passage*, p. 243.

## 8. Family Cycle, Structure, and Economy

1. Peter Laslett, *Family Life and Illicit Love in Earlier Generations* (London, 1977), p. 13.

2. Ibid.

3. The history of the family has become a topic of immense interest in the past decade. Among the most important recent studies in the field are Laslett, *Family Life*; Peter Laslett, ed., *Household and Family in Past Times* (London, 1972); Edward Shorter, *The Making of the Modern Family* (New York, 1976); Michael Anderson, *Family Structure in Nineteenth-Century Lancashire* (London, 1971); Lawrence Stone, *The Family, Sex, and Marriage in England, 1500-1800* (New York, 1977). For a discussion of families in North America see Michael B. Katz, *The People of Hamilton, Canada West: Family and Class in a Mid-Nineteenth-Century City* (Cambridge, Mass., 1975), ch. 5. For a useful collection of recent scholarship see Michael Gordon, ed., *The American Family in Socio-Historical Perspective*, 2nd ed. (New York, 1978). For a dissenting view of family history see Christopher Lasch, *Haven in a Heartless World* (New York, 1977).

4. These figures were derived from the Wentworth County register of marriage for these years.

5. Laslett, *Family Life*, p. 42.

6. On marriage age in Colonial New England see John Demos, *A Little Commonwealth; Family Life in Plymouth Colony* (New York, 1970), p. 151;

Daniel Scott Smith, "The Demographic History of Colonial New England," *Journal of Economic History* 32 (1972), 165-183.

7. The reason why class-related differences do not show here is that they probably had begun to develop only a few years prior to the census of 1871, and the average age at birth of the first child in 1871 reflects the experience of women who had been married in the early and mid-1860s. A similar measure in 1881 should show distinct class differences unless the poor had a rate of infant mortality sufficiently high to offset their earlier marriage.

8. Laslett, *Family Life*, p. 42.

9. On the role of sex ratios on marriage patterns in Ireland see Robert E. Kennedy, Jr., *The Irish Emigration, Marriage, and Fertility* (Berkeley, 1973), p. 215.

10. Michael Drake, *Population and Society in Norway, 1735-1865* (Cambridge, 1969), pp. 136, 140.

11. For a more detailed treatment of these data see Michael B. Katz, "The Family and Early Industrialization in Hamilton, Ontario: Cycle, Structure, and Economy," Working Paper 25, in York Social History Project, "Third Report" (Downsview, Ontario, 1978), pp. 254-313.

12. Haley Bamman, "The Ladies' Benevolent Society of Hamilton, Ontario: Form and Function in Mid-Nineteenth-Century Urban Philanthropy," in Michael B. Katz, ed., "The Canadian Social History Project, Interim Report" no. 4 (Toronto, 1972), pp. 161-217.

13. On orphans see Laslett, *Family Life*, pp. 160-173.

14. Ladies' Committee of Orphan Asylum, Hamilton Orphan Asylum, 1872-1898 manuscripts, Hamilton Public Library.

15. Mary Tomlinson to Hamilton Orphan Asylum, August 23, 1889, Hamilton Orphan Asylum manuscripts.

16. Laslett, *Family Life*, p. 38.

17. Lutz K. Berkner, "The Stem Family and the Developmental Cycle of the Peasant Household: An Eighteenth-Century Austrian Example," *American Historical Review* 77 (1972), 398-418; Anderson, *Family Structure in Nineteenth-Century Lancashire*.

18. Laslett, *Family Life*, p. 38; see also pp. 174-213.

19. Anderson, *Family Structure in Nineteenth-Century Lancashire*, pp. 139-144.

20. See Michael Young and Peter Wilmott, *Family and Kinship in East London* (Harmondsworth, England, 1957) for a similar phenomenon in post-war England.

21. E. A. Wrigley, in *Population in History* (New York, 1969), calculated that taking early modern rates of mortality into consideration, no more than 15 percent of households would ever have three generations present at any time.

22. The historiography of Eastern Europe in particular is filled with examples of cases in which farm labor requirements were met through extending the household; see Edward Shorter, *The Making of the Modern Family* (New York, 1976), ch. 1, for examples and a bibliography. The relationship of family structure to labor requirements was the focus of the work of A. V.

Chayanov, *On the Theory of Peasant Economy*, David Thorner, Basile Kerbby, and R. E. F. Smith, eds., (Homewood, Ill., 1966).

23. Steven Dubnoff, in "The Life Cycle and Economic Welfare: Historical Change in the Economic Constraints on Working Class Family Life, 1860-1974" (paper, Ann Arbor, 1978), has estimated that not until the 1940s could the average working-class family expect to maintain an adequate standard of living on one income throughout the family life cycle.

24. By and large the decline in the proportion of boarders and relatives took place in two stages: the proportion of boarders dropped most notably between 1851 and 1861; the proportion of relatives dipped during the following decade. The assertion cannot be thoroughly tested because of our lack of direct information on whether individuals were boarders or relatives in 1871. For a discussion of how this determination was made see Michael J. Doucet, "Discriminant Analysis and the Delineation of Household Structure: Towards a Solution of the Boarder/Relative Problem in the 1871 Canadian Census," Working Paper 14, in York Social History Project, "Second Report" (Downsview, Ontario, 1976), pp. 123-136.

25. This and the following examples come from the linked census files.

26. Laslett, *Family Life*, pp. 45-46.

27. Ibid., p. 13.

28. Anderson, *Family Structure in Nineteenth-Century Lancashire*, pp. 139-144.

29. The Buffalo data reported here came from two 10 percent samples of the youth population (11 to 19 years old) of Erie County drawn from the census manuscripts of 1850 and 1870. In addition to the census record of the youth, information concerning the household head and the head's spouse was also coded.

30. Laslett, *Family Life*, p. 37.

31. Lasch, *Haven in a Heartless World*.

32. Stone, in *Family, Sex, and Marriage in England*, makes the case for the leadership of the middle or upper classes in the modernization of the family.

33. These data were gathered by hand. The city business directories of Hamilton for 1853 and 1871 were searched to determine the business address of each individual. He was then traced back to the residential address, and his address was noted. The authors would like to thank Carol Seifert for performing this aspect of the research.

34. Individuals are assigned weights for both work and consumption according to their age and sex. The highest score for both work and consumption (1) goes to an adult male. Given the paucity of hard information about actual consumption patterns and our inability to measure contribution other than wage earning to the household economy, the weights must remain more or less arbitrary. Here we used weights similar to those employed by Kaestle and Vinovskis in order to facilitate comparative analysis. See Carl F. Kaestle and Maris A. Vinovskis, *Education and Social Change in Nineteenth-Century Massachusetts* (Cambridge, Mass., 1980).

35. Minnesota Bureau of Labor Statistics, *First Biennial Report* (Minneapolis, 1888).

36. Each of the four indexes has been used in turn as a dependent variable in an MCA in which all three years were combined and year (1851, 1861, and 1871) used as a factor variable in combination with occupation; see Katz, "The Family and Early Industrialization," table 13.

37. The authors would like to thank Glen Elder of Cornell University for his suggestion concerning the use of the age of the eldest child as a rough measure for determining duration of marriage.

38. For a discussion of the literature concerning the fertility decline in Europe and America see Michael B. Katz and Mark J. Stern, "Differential Fertility and Industrial Development" (research report, University of Pennsylvania, 1979), ch. 2. For a review of recent trends in European research see Michael R. Haines, "Recent Developments in Historical Demography: A Review of the European Fertility Project with some Comparisons from Japan," *Historical Methods* 11 (1979), 162-173.

39. For a discussion of the traditional methods of regulating fertility see Ansley Coale, *The Demographic Transition Reconsidered* (Liege, 1973).

40. For a discussion of the politics of birth control see Linda Gordon, *Woman's Body, Woman's Right: A Social History of Birth Control* (New York, 1976); David M. Kennedy, *Birth Control in America: The Career of Margaret Sanger* (New Haven, 1970); James Reed, *From Private Vice to Public Virtue: The Birth Control Movement and American Society since 1830* (New York, 1978). The related topic of public policy and abortion is examined in James Mohr, *Abortion in America* (New York, 1979).

41. Canadian fertility rates are discussed in Jacques Henripin, *Trends and Factors of Fertility in Canada* (Ottawa, 1972). The data on fertility in Hamilton are examined in more detail in Mark J. Stern, "Differential Fertility and Early Industrialization in Hamilton," Working Paper 26, in York Social History Project, "Third Report" (Downsview, Ontario, 1978), pp. 314-340.

42. Fertility ratio or the ratio of children to women is here defined as the number of children under age 5 per 1,000 married women aged 20 to 49. We have standardized all fertility ratios by multiplying the set of six age-specific fertility ratios (20-4, 25-9, and so on to 45-9) by the set fractions .10, .17, .21, .22, .17, .13 and then summing the products. This method was suggested by Tamara K. Hareven and Maris A. Vinovskis, "Marital Fertility, Ethnicity, and Occupation in Urban Families: An Analysis of South Boston and the South End in 1880," *Journal of Social History* 8 (1975), 69-93.

43. For the European data on the preindustrial pattern see Shorter, *Making of the Modern Family*, pp. 38, 329-331.

44. Mark J. Stern, "The Demography of Capitalism: Industry, Class, and Fertility in Erie County, New York, 1855-1915" (Ph.D. diss., York University, 1979), ch. 1.

45. See Chapters 5 and 7.

46. See Stern, "Differential Fertility and Early Industrialization," p. 321.

47. Illegitimacy in Christ's Church parish is discussed in Mark J. Stern, "Birth, Marriage, and Death: Aggregate Analysis of an Anglican Parish," Working Paper 7, in York Social History Project, "First Research Report" (Downsview, Ontario, 1975), pp. 229-260; Stern, "Differential Fertility and Early Industrialization," table 7.

48. Shorter, *Making of the Modern Family*, pp. 80-98.

49. Other explanations of illegitimacy have been proposed by Louise A. Tilly, Joan W. Scott, and Miriam Cohen, in "Women's Work and European Fertility Patterns," *Journal of Interdisciplinary History* 6, no. 3 (1976), 447-476, and David Levine, *Family Formation in an Age of Nascent Capitalism* (New York, 1977).

50. Here as elsewhere one must exercise caution in examining multivariate results because of the high degree of correlation between ethnicity and occupation. Since the two are not simply correlated but theoretically intertwined the attempt to separate their influences statistically is to some extent impossible.

51. This same point has recently been made by Peter H. Lindert, in *Fertility and Scarcity in America* (Princeton, N.J., 1978), p. 18.

52. This thesis concerning the squeeze on middle-class income leading to fertility restriction was first proposed by J. A. Banks, *Prosperity and Parenthood: A Study of Family Planning Among the Victorian Middle Classes* (London, 1954).

53. On the relationship of work and family in textile towns see Anderson, *Family Structure*; Tamara K. Hareven, "Family Time and Industrial Time: Family and Work in a Planned Corporation Town, 1900-1924," in T. Hareven, ed., *Family and Kin in Urban Communities, 1700-1930* (New York, 1977), pp. 187-206.

54. Stone, *Family, Sex, and Marriage*, p. 10.

55. William Goode, *World Revolution and Family Patterns* (New York, 1963), p. 13.

56. Lasch, *Haven in a Heartless World*, see Chapter 9.

## 9. Early Industrial Capitalism: The Institutional Legacy

1. Lutz K. Berkner, "The Stem Family and the Developmental Cycle of the Peasant Household: An Eighteeenth-Century Austrian Example," *American Historical Review* 77 (1972), 398-418; Bernard Farber, *Guardians of Virtue: Salem Families in 1880* (New York, 1972), pp. 191-205; M. B. Sussman and L. G. Burchinal, "Kin Family Network in Urban-Industrial America," and E. Litwack and I. Szelengi, "Kinship and Other Primary Groups," in Michael Anderson, ed., *Sociology of the Family* (Harmondsworth, England, 1971), pp. 99-119, 149-164; Elizabeth Bott, *Family and Social Network* (New York, 1957).

2. Henry Barnard, "Sixth Annual Report of the Superintendent of Common Schools to the General Assembly of Connecticut for 1851," *American Journal of Education* 5 (1865), 293-310.

3. Separate report of E. A. Meredith. *Annual Report of the Board of Inspectors of Asylums, Prisons, etc.*, Province of Canada, Sessional Papers 19 (1862), reprinted in Alison L. Prentice and Susan E. Houston, eds., *Family, School, and Society in Nineteenth-Century Canada* (Toronto, 1975), pp. 270-271.

4. For a collection of Jefferson's thoughts on education see Gordon C. Lee, ed., *Crusade Against Ignorance: Thomas Jefferson on Education* (New

York, 1961); William R. Taylor, "Toward a Definition of Orthodoxy: The Patrician South and the Common Schools," *Harvard Educational Review* 36, no. 4 (Fall 1966), 412-426; Carl F. Kaestle, "Between the Scylla of Brutal Ignorance and the Charybdis of a Literary Education: Elite Attitudes Toward Mass Schooling in Early Industrial England and America," in Lawrence Stone, ed., *Schooling and Society* (Baltimore, 1977), pp. 177-191.

5. David Tyack, *The One Best System* (Cambridge, Mass., 1974); Carl F. Kaestle, *The Evolution of an Urban School System: New York City, 1750-1850* (Cambridge, Mass., 1974); Stanley K. Schultz, *The Culture Factory: Boston Public School, 1789-1860* (New York, 1973); Selwyn Troen, *The Public and the Schools: Shaping the St. Louis System, 1838-1920* (Columbia, Mo. 1975).

6. Michael B. Katz, "Secondary Education to 1870," *The Encyclopedia of Education* 9 vols. (New York, 1971), vol. 8, pp. 159-165.

7. David Roberts, *Victorian Origins of the British Welfare State* (New Haven, 1960); Oscar Handlin and Mary Flug Handlin, *Commonwealth: A Study of the Role of Government in the American Economy: Massachusetts, 1774-1861* (New York, 1947); Karl Polanyi, *The Great Transformation: The Political and Economic Origins of Our Time* (1944; reprint ed. Boston, 1957).

8. Carroll Smith-Rosenberg, *Religion and the Rise of the American City* (Ithaca, N.Y., 1971); Raymond Mohl, *Poverty in New York, 1783-1825* (New York, 1974); Susan E. Houston, "The Impetus to Reform: Urban Crime, Poverty, and Ignorance in Ontario, 1850-1875" (Ph.D. diss., University of Toronto, 1974).

9. Michael B. Katz, *Class, Bureaucracy, and Schools: The Illusion of Educational Change in America*, expanded ed. (New York, 1973), ch. 1.

10. For general discussion and interpretations of the rise of institutions see David Rothman, *The Discovery of the Asylum: Social Order and Disorder in the New Republic* (Boston, 1971); Gerald N. Grob, *The State and the Mentally Ill: A History of Worcester State Hospital in Massachusetts, 1830-1920* (Chapel Hill, N.C., 1966); Gerald N. Grob, *Mental Institutions in America: Social Policy to 1875* (New York, 1973); W. David Lewis, *From Newgate to Dannemora: The Rise of the Penitentiary in New York, 1796-1848* (Ithaca, N.Y., 1965); Robert M. Mennel, *Thorns and Thistles: Juvenile Delinquents in the United States, 1825-1940* (Hanover, N.H., 1973); Houston, "The Impetus to Reform"; Richard B. Spane, *Social Welfare in Canada, 1791-1893* (Toronto, 1965); Michael Hindus, "Prison and Plantation: Criminal Justice in Nineteenth-Century Massachusetts and South Carolina" (Ph.D. diss., University of California, Berkeley, 1975), pp. 6-48.

11. Michael B. Katz, *The Irony of Early School Reform: Educational Innovation in Mid-Nineteenth Century Massachusetts* (Cambridge, Mass., 1968), part 3; Grob, *Mental Institutions*, pp. 257-258; Rothman, *Discovery of the Asylum*, pp. 265-295.

12. Susan E. Houston, "Politics, Schools and Social Change in Upper Canada," in Michael B. Katz and Paul H. Mattingly, eds., *Education and Social Change: Themes from Ontario's Past* (New York, 1975), pp. 26-57; Alison Prentice, *The School Promoters: Education and Social Class in Mid-*

*Nineteenth-Century Upper Canada* (Toronto, 1977); M. B. Katz, *Class, Bureaucracy, and Schools.*

13. James McLachlan, *American Boarding Schools: A Historical Study* (New York, 1970).

14. Alan S. Horlick, *Country Boys and Merchant Princes: The Social Control of Young Men in New York* (Cranbury, N.J., 1975).

15. Morris J. Vogel, "Boston's Hospitals, 1870-1930: A Social History" (Ph.D. diss., University of Chicago, 1974), pp. 6-48.

16. On the ideology of domesticity see Barbara Welter, "The Cult of True Womanhood: 1820-1860," *American Quarterly* 18 (1966), 151-174; Kathryn Kish Sklar, *Catharine Beecher: A Study in American Domesticity* (New Haven, 1973); Ann Douglas, *The Feminization of American Culture* (New York, 1977); Nancy F. Cott, *The Bonds of Womanhood: "Women's Sphere" in New England, 1780-1835* (New Haven, 1977).

17. Michel Foucault, *Madness and Civilization: A History of Insanity in the Age of Reason* (New York, 1965); Richard Fox, "Beyond 'Social Control': Institutions and Disorder in Bourgeois Society," *History of Education Quarterly* 16 (1976), 203-207.

18. Katz, *Class, Bureaucracy, and Schools,* 1; Carroll Smith-Rosenberg, *Religion and the Rise of the American City;* Mohl, *Poverty in New York.*

19. Vogel, "Boston's Hospitals," pp. 49-107, 188-244. See also Charles Rosenberg, "And Heal the Sick: The Hospital and the Patient in Nineteenth-Century America," *Journal of Social History* 10 (1977), 428-477.

20. Rothman, *Discovery of the Asylum,* pp. xviii, 58.

21. Grob, *Mental Institutions,* pp. 48, 86-87.

22. Barbara Brenzel, "Lancaster Industrial School for Girls: A Social Portrait of a Nineteenth-Century Reform School for Girls," *Feminist Studies* 3 (1975), 40-53; Katz, *Irony of Early School Reform,* part 3; Herbert Gutman, *The Black Family in Slavery and Freedom, 1750-1825* (New York, 1976). On the contrast between common ideas about the Irish poor and actual patterns see Oliver MacDonagh, "The Irish Famine Emigration to the United States," *Perspectives in American History* 10 (1976), 357-488; Michael Anderson, *Family Structure in Nineteenth-Century Lancashire* (Cambridge, 1971); Lynn H. Lees, "Patterns of Lower Class Life: Irish Slum Communities in Nineteenth-Century London," in Stephan Thernstrom and Richard Sennett, eds., *Nineteenth-Century Cities: Essays in the New Urban History* (New Haven, 1969), pp. 359-387; Virginia Yans-McLaughlin, *Family and Community: Italian Immigrants in Buffalo, 1880-1930* (Ithaca, N.Y., 1977); Michael B. Katz, *The People of Hamilton, Canada West: Family and Class in a Mid-Nineteenth-Century City* (Cambridge, Mass., 1975), ch. 5; Erik H. Monkkonen, *The Dangerous Class: Crime and Poverty in Columbus, Ohio, 1860-1885* (Cambridge, Mass., 1975); Gareth Stedman Jones, *Outcast London* (Oxford, 1971).

23. Charles Loring-Brace, *The Dangerous Class of New York and Twenty Years' Work Among Them* (New York, 1872); Katz, *Irony of Early School Reform,* part 3.

24. Houston, "Impetus"; Alison Prentice, "Education and the Metaphor of

the Family: The Upper Canadian Example," *History of Education Quarterly* 12 (Fall 1972); 281-303.

25. Welter, "The Cult of True Womanhood," 151-174; Sklar, *Catharine Beecher*; Gwendolyn Wright, *Moralism and the Model Home: Domestic Architecture and Cultural Conflict in Chicago, 1873-1913* (Chicago, 1980).

26. Katz, *Irony of Early School Reform*, pp. 56-58; Alison Prentice, "The Feminization of Teaching in British North America and Canada, 1845-1875," *Histoire Sociale/Social History* 8 (May 1975); 5-20; Dee Garrison, "The Tender Technicians: The Feminization of Public Librarianship, 1876-1905," *Journal of Social History* 6 (Winter 1972-73); 131-159.

27. Joan W. Scott and Louise Tilly, "Women's Work and the Family in Nineteenth-Century Europe," in Charles E. Rosenberg, ed., *The Family in History* (Philadelphia, 1975), pp. 145-178; Patricia Branca, "A New Perspective on Women's Work: A Comparative Typology," *Journal of Social History* 9 (Winter 1975), 129-153; Theresa McBride, *The Domestic Revolution: The Modernization of Household Service in England and France, 1820-1920* (New York, 1976).

28. As an example see Herbert G. Gutman, "Work, Culture, and Society in Industrializing America," *American Historical Review* 78 (1973), 540.

29. Maurice Dobb, *Studies in the Development of Capitalism*, rev. ed. (New York, 1974), p. 7; Karl Marx, *Capital*, 3 vols. (Moscow, 1954), vol. 1, pp. 318-347.

30. Carl F. Kaestle, *The Evolution of an Urban School System: New York City, 1750-1850* (Cambridge, Mass., 1974), p. 102; Douglas Lamar Jones, "The Strolling Poor: Transiency in Eighteenth-Century Massachusetts," *Journal of Social History* 8 (1975), 28-55; Oscar Handlin and Mary Flug Handlin, *Commonwealth: A Study of the Role of Government in the American Economy: Massachusetts, 1774-1861* (New York, 1974). The material on Buffalo and Hamilton is in the York Social History Project, "Third Annual Report" (Downsview, Ontario, 1978).

31. Harry Braverman, *Labor and Monopoly Capital: The Degradation of Work in the Twentieth Century* (New York, 1974), pp. 279-280.

32. Stephan Thernstrom and Peter R. Knights, "Men in Motion: Some Data and Speculations about Urban Population Mobility in Nineteenth-Century America," in Tamara K. Hareven, ed., *Anonymous Americans: Explorations in Nineteenth-Century Social History* (Englewood Cliffs, N.J., 1971), pp. 17-47. See Chapter 3.

33. Martha Branscombe, *The Courts and the Poor Laws in New York State, 1784-1929* (Chicago, 1943); David M. Schneider, *The History of Public Welfare in New York State, 1609-1866* (Chicago, 1938); Walter I. Trattner, *From Poor Law to Welfare State: A History of Social Welfare in America* (New York, 1974), pp. 44-74.

34. Katz, *People of Hamilton*, ch. 5; Michael B. Katz and Ian E. Davey, "Youth and Early Industrialization in a Canadian City," *American Journal of Sociology* 84 (1978 Supplement), 81-119.

35. Peter Dobkin Hall, "Family Structure and Economic Organization: Massachusetts Merchants, 1700-1850," in Tamara K. Hareven, ed., *Family*

*and Kin in Urban Communities, 1700-1930* (New York, 1977), pp. 38-61.

36. Marx, *Capital*, vol. 1, p. 333.

37. Christopher Lasch, "Origins of the Asylum," in C. Lasch, *The World of Nations: Reflections on American History, Politics, and Culture* (New York, 1973).

38. Katz, *Irony of Early School Reform*, part 1; Prentice, *School Promoters*, p. 25.

39. Houston, "Impetus"; Harold Schwartz, *Samuel Gridley Howe: Social Reformer, 1801-1876* (Cambridge, Mass., 1956); Katz, *Irony of Early School Reform*; Raymond Mohl, *Poverty in New York*; Twelfth Annual Report of the Secretary of the Massachusetts Board of Education (1848), excerpted in Lawrence A. Cremin, ed., *The Republic and the School: Horace Mann on the Education of Free Men* (New York, 1957), pp. 99-100.

40. Egerton Ryerson, "Report on a System of Elementary Public Instruction for Upper Canada" (Montreal, 1847), reprinted in Prentice and Houston, eds., *Family, School, and Society*, p. 69.

41. Commonwealth of Massachusetts, Senate Document No. 86 (1846), pp. 2-16.

42. Orestes Brownson, "Second Annual Report of the Board of Education, together with the Second Annual Report of the Secretary of the Board" (Boston, 1839); reviewed in *The Boston Quarterly Review* 2 (October 1839), 393-418.

43. "Immigration," *The Massachusetts Teacher* 4 (October 1851), 289-291; Boston School Committee, *Annual Report*, 1858, pp. 10-11.

44. Kaestle, *Evolution*; Harvey J. Graff, *The Literacy Myth: Literacy and Social Structure in the Nineteenth-Century City* (New York, 1979); Frank F. Furstenberg, Jr., Theodore Hershberg, and John Modell, "The Origins of the Female-Headed Black Family: The Impact of the Urban Experience," *Journal of Interdisciplinary History* 6 (Autumn 1975), 211-234; Oliver MacDonagh, "The Irish Famine Emigration," pp. 357-448.

45. Katz, *Irony of Early School Reform*, pp. 120-121.

46. E. P. Thompson, "Time, Work, Discipline, and Industrial Capitalism," *Past and Present* 38 (December 1967), 56-97; Gutman, "Work, Culture and Society."

47. Leo Marx, *The Machine in the Garden: Technology and the Pastoral Ideal in America* (New York, 1964), p. 248.

48. *The Massachusetts Teacher* 14 (September 1861), 329.

49. *Copies of Documents Relating to the Common Schools of the City, Forwarded by the Board of School Trustees to the City Council and Ordered to be Printed* (Toronto, 1858); reprinted in Prentice and Houston, eds., *Family, School, and Society*, p. 99.

50. Katz, *Class, Bureaucracy and Schools*, pp. 32-37; Katz, *Irony of Early School Reform*, pp. 45-46.

51. From the manuscript, Massachusetts State Archives, Boston, Mass.

52. Alan Dawley, *Class and Community: The Industrial Revolution in Lynn* (Cambridge, Mass., 1976), ch. 3. See Chapter 5.

53. Egerton Ryerson, "The Importance of Education to a Manufacturing

and a Free People," *Journal of Education* 1, no. 10 (October 1848), 199.

54. Katz, *Irony of Early School Reform*, part 1.

55. Winchendon School Committee, *Annual Report, 1852-1853*, p. 15; Report of Rufus Putnam as superintendent of schools in Beverly School Committee, *Annual Report, 1853-1854*, pp. 24-26; Albert Boyden, *Here and There in the Family Tree* (Salem, Mass., 1949), pp. 117-120.

56. Katz, *Irony of Early School Reform*, part 1.

57. Lawrence School Committee, *Annual Report, 1857-1858*, p. 48.

58. Archibald Macullum, "Compulsory Education," *Annual Report of the Ontario Teachers' Association, 1875* (Toronto, 1875); reprinted in Prentice and Houston, eds., *Family, School, and Society*, p. 176. Maine State Superintendent quoted in "Compulsory Education," from the Report of the Board of Public Charities of the State of Pennsylvania (1871); reprinted in Michael B. Katz, ed., *School Reform: Past and Present* (Boston, 1971), p. 66.

59. Massachusetts Legislature, Senate Document 10 (January 1847).

60. Reprinted in Katz, ed., *School Reform*, pp. 65-66.

61. Rothman, *Discovery*.

62. The description is based on the more lengthy discussion of the process of bureaucratization in Katz, *Class, Bureaucracy, and the Schools*, ch. 2.

63. B. A. Hinsdale, quoted in Katz, ed., *School Reform*, p. 259.

64. Grob, *State and the Mentally Ill*.

65. Anthony Giddens, *Capitalism and Modern Social Theory: An Analysis of the Writings of Marx, Durkheim, and Max Weber* (London, 1971), p. 235.

66. Ibid., p. 236.

67. Ibid., p. 237.

68. Ibid., p. 238.

69. See for example Richard Edwards, *Contested Terrain: The Transformation of the Workplace in the Twentieth Century* (New York, 1979); Braverman, *Labor and Monopoly Capital*.

70. On the struggles of schoolmasters see the Mann-Masters controversy in Katz, *Irony of Early School Reform*, part 2.

71. Robert Merton, "Bureaucratic Structure and Personality," in R. Merton et al., *Reader in Bureaucracy* (New York, 1952), pp. 361-371.

72. Robert Dreeben, *On What Is Learned in Schools* (Reading, Mass., 1968).

73. David Riesman, in collaboration with R. Denney and N. Glazer, *The Lonely Crowd: A Study of the Changing American Character* (New York, 1950).

# Index